ACCA

PRACTICE & REVISION KIT

PAPER P2

CORPORATE REPORTING (INTERNATIONAL AND UNITED KINGDOM)

BPP Learning Media is an **ACCA Approved Content Provider** for the ACCA qualification. This means we work closely with ACCA to ensure our products fully prepare you for your ACCA exams.

In this Practice and Revision Kit, which has been reviewed by the **ACCA examination team,** we:

- Discuss the **best strategies** for revising and taking your ACCA exams
- Ensure you are well **prepared** for your exam
- Provide you with **lots of great guidance** on tackling questions
- Provide you with **three** mock exams
- Provide **ACCA exam answers** as well as our own for selected questions

Our **Passcards** also support this paper.

FOR EXAMS IN SEPTEMBER 2017, DECEMBER 2017, MARCH 2018 AND JUNE 2018

First edition 2007
Eleventh edition February 2017

ISBN 9781 5097 0862 8
(previous ISBN 9781 4727 4443 2)
e-ISBN 9781 5097 1000 3

British Library Cataloguing-in-Publication Data
A catalogue record for this book
is available from the British Library

Published by

BPP Learning Media Ltd
BPP House, Aldine Place
London W12 8AA

www.bpp.com/learningmedia

Printed and bound by CPI Group (UK) Ltd
Croydon
CR0 4YY

Your learning materials, published by BPP Learning Media Ltd, are printed on paper obtained from traceable, sustainable sources.

We are grateful to the Association of Chartered Certified Accountants for permission to reproduce past examination questions. The suggested solutions in the practice answer bank have been prepared by BPP Learning Media Ltd, unless otherwise stated.

BPP Learning Media is grateful to the IASB for permission to reproduce extracts from the International Financial Reporting Standards including all International Accounting Standards, SIC and IFRIC Interpretations (the Standards). The Standards together with their accompanying documents are issued by:

The International Accounting Standards Board (IASB) 30 Cannon Street, London, EC4M 6XH, United Kingdom. Email: info@ifrs.org Web: www.ifrs.org

Contents

Question index

The headings in this checklist/index indicate the main topics of questions, but questions often cover several different topics.

Questions set under the previous syllabus *Advanced Corporate Reporting* paper are included because their style and content are similar to those which appear in the P2 exam. The questions have been amended to reflect the current exam format.

BPP
LEARNING MEDIA

Mock exam 3 (ACCA September/December 2016 Exam)

Topic index

Listed below are the key Paper P2 syllabus topics and the numbers of the questions in this Kit covering those topics.

If you need to concentrate your practice and revision on certain topics or if you want to attempt all available questions that refer to a particular subject, you will find this index useful.

Syllabus topic	Question numbers
Associates	35
Complex groups	36 – 39
Consolidated statement of financial position	46
Consolidated statement of profit or loss and other comprehensive income	39
Consolidated statement of cash flows	52 – 55, 73
Disposals	40 – 48
Employee benefits	10, 11
Environmental issues	56
Ethics	Qu 47 c, Mock Exam 1 Qu 1 c, Mock Exam 2 Qu 1 c,
Financial instruments	18 – 21
Foreign currency	49 – 51
IAS 1 (revised)	Throughout
Impairment	6 - 8
International issues	65
IFRS 2	25
IFRS 3	33 – 55
IFRS 9	18 – 21
IFRS 10 to 12	33 – 55
IFRS 13	7, 58, throughout
IFRS 15	3, 4
IFRS 16	22 - 24, 57 75(c)
Joint ventures	63
Leasing	22 - 24, 57 75(c)
Measurement of performance	26 – 31
Non-current assets	6 – 8
Provisions	12 – 14
Related party transactions	7, 32,
Reporting performance	31
Revenue recognition	3, 4
Share-based payment	25
Small and medium-sized entities	71, 72
Taxation	15 – 17

Helping you with your revision

BPP Learning Media – ACCA Approved Content Provider

As an ACCA **Approved Content Provider**, BPP Learning Media gives you the **opportunity** to use revision materials reviewed by the ACCA examination team. By incorporating the ACCA examination team's comments and suggestions regarding the depth and breadth of syllabus coverage, the BPP Learning Media Practice & Revision Kit provides excellent, **ACCA-approved** support for your revision.

Tackling revision and the exam

Using feedback obtained from the ACCA examination team review:

- We look at the dos and don'ts of revising for, and taking, ACCA exams
- We focus on Paper 2, we discuss revising the syllabus, what to do (and what not to do) in the exam, how to approach different types of question and ways of obtaining easy marks

Selecting questions

We provide signposts to help you plan your revision.

- A full **question index**
- A **topic index** listing all the questions that cover key topics, so that you can locate the questions that provide practice on these topics, and see the different ways in which they might be examined

Making the most of question practice

At BPP Learning Media we realise that you need more than just questions and model answers to get the most from your question practice.

- Our **Top tips** included for certain questions provide essential advice on tackling questions, presenting answers and the key points that answers need to include
- We show you how you can pick up **Easy marks** on some questions, as we know that picking up all readily available marks often can make the difference between passing and failing
- We include **marking guides** to show you what the examining team rewards
- We include **comments from the examining team** to show you where students struggled or performed well in the actual exam
- We refer to the **BPP Study Text** for exams in **September 2017, December 2017, March 2018 and June 2018** for detailed coverage of the topics covered in questions

Attempting mock exams

There are three mock exams that provide practice at coping with the pressures of the exam day. We strongly recommend that you attempt them under exam conditions. **Mock exams 1 and 2** reflect the question styles and syllabus coverage of the exam.

Mock exam 3 is the ACCA September/December 2016 exam paper. This exam is compiled from questions selected by the examination team from the September 2016 and December 2016 exams. They do not reflect the entire September or December exams but contain questions most appropriate for students to practise.

Revising P2

Topics to revise

P2 has the reputation of being a difficult paper. However its pass rate is usually quite high. Although the ACCA examining team sets challenging questions, the styles of question used are now familiar. The ACCA examining team has also provided a great deal of feedback via examiner's reports and in the very detailed published marking schemes, many of which are included in this Kit.

The ACCA examining team has warned very strongly against question-spotting and trying to predict the topics that will be included in the exam. On occasions the same topic has been examined in two successive sittings. The ACCA examining team regards few areas as off-limits for questions, and nearly all of the major areas of the syllabus can and have been tested.

That said, exams over the years have shown that the following areas of the syllabus are very important, and your revision therefore needs to cover them particularly well.

- **Group accounts.** You should not omit any aspect of group accounts, as they come up every sitting. We would advise against question spotting, but if a statement of cash flows, say, has not come up for a few sittings, it might be a good bet. Group accounts will always be examined as part of the 50-mark case study question, in which you may also expect a question on some aspect of **ethics**.
- **Emerging issues.** The impact of a change in accounting standards on the financial statements is often examined. Look on the IASB website for details: www.iasb.org
- **Share based payment** usually comes up as part of a question.
- **Financial instruments** was the subject of regular *Student Accountant* articles, and it is regularly tested. IFRS 9 (July 2014) is now fully examinable.
- **Developments in financial reporting**, for example, the recent standard on leasing and the exposure draft on the *Conceptual Framework*.

Question practice

Question practice under timed conditions is essential, so that you can get used to the pressures of answering exam questions in **limited time** and practise not only the key techniques but allocating your time between different requirements in each question. Our list of recommended questions includes compulsory Section A and optional Section B questions; it's particularly important to do all the Section A case-study-style questions in full as a case study involving group accounts will always come up.

Passing the P2 exam

Avoiding weaknesses

Our experience of, and examination team feedback from, other higher level exams enables us to predict a number of weaknesses that are likely to occur in many students' answers. You will enhance your chances significantly if you ensure you avoid these mistakes:

- **Failing to provide what the question verbs require** (discussion, evaluation, recommendation) or to write about the topics specified in the question requirements
- **Repeating the same material** in different parts of answers
- **Stating theories and concepts** rather than applying them
- **Quoting chunks of detail** from the question that don't add any value
- **Forcing irrelevancies into answers**, for example irrelevant definitions or theories, or examples that don't relate to the scenario
- **Giving long lists or writing down all that's known** about a broad subject area, and not caring whether it's relevant or not
- **Focusing too narrowly on one area** – for example only covering financial risks when other risks are also important
- **Letting your personal views prevent you from answering the question** – the question may require you to construct an argument with which you personally don't agree
- **Unrealistic or impractical recommendations**
- **Vague recommendations** - instead of just saying improve risk management procedures, you should discuss precisely **how** you would improve them
- **Failing to answer sufficient questions**, or all parts of a question, because of poor time management

What to expect on the paper

Of course you cannot know in advance what questions are going to come up, but you can have a fair idea of what kind of questions.

Question 1

This will always be a case study, with half or a little more than half on group accounts. It will often involve high speed number crunching. Easy marks, it cannot be said too often, will always be available for basic consolidation techniques. You cannot pass the groups part on these alone, but it can give you a foothold. Question 1 usually has a bit of a twist, for example financial instruments or pensions. This question will also contain an element of written explanation and a question on ethics or corporate social accounting. For example, the June 2014 paper had two disposals; then you were asked to discuss an ethical dilemma for a new financial controller arising from the finance director 's wish to avoid treating a lease as a finance lease.

The ACCA examining team has stressed the importance of answering the written parts of Question 1. Many students ignore parts (b) and (c), but marks can be gained for common sense.

Question 1 will always have more than half the marks allocated to the computational part. Generally, it will be in the order of 35 marks.

Questions 2 and 3

These each cover several IFRSs and are very often – although not always – mini-case-studies, involving you in giving advice to the directors on accounting treatment, possibly where the directors have followed the wrong treatment. Being multi-standard, you may be able to answer parts, but not all of a question, so it makes sense to look through the paper to select a question where you can answer most of it. If Part (a) is on an area you are not confident about, do not dismiss the question out of hand.

The ACCA examining team is testing whether you can identify the issues. Even if you don't get the accounting treatment exactly right, you will still gain some credit for showing that you have seen what the problem is about. So do not be afraid to have a stab at something, even if you are not sure of the details.

These questions can be on a single standard or theme. Question 3 will usually be the specialised industry question.

Question 4

This question is generally on developments in financial reporting. It may cover an aspect of reporting financial performance – for example Integrated Reporting but it can also be set on just one standard if this standard is undergoing revision. This question can feature criticism of existing standards, as well as aspects of new or proposed standards.

While you certainly cannot bluff your way through Question 4, if you know your material it is a good way of earning marks without high speed number crunching.

Question 4 may now include a computational aspect illustrating the topic you have just discussed. Usually these are fairly straightforward.

Important advice from the examining team!

The examining team stress that it is important to learn principles rather than rote-learning techniques. He has also said on a number of occasions that candidates should use the information in the scenario. For example, in June 2012:

'Often the content of the scenario will help students answer the question as the scenario gives candidates direction in terms of their answers.'

The examining team have stated that students need to have a basic/good understanding of all standards and the capability of applying them. They should always give an explanation of the IFRSs which underpin their answer.

The examining team have also emphasised that students should use their experience in answering the questions. 'What may seem irrelevant may be relevant.'

Students are also advised to look at articles in *the online resources at accaglobal.com.*

Exam technique for P2

Do not be needlessly intimidated

There is no shortcut to passing this exam. It looks very difficult indeed, and many students wonder if they will ever pass. But most students generally do. Why is this?

Gaining easy marks

All the questions are demanding, but there are many easy marks to be gained. Suppose, for example, you had a consolidated statement of cash flows with a disposal, a pension complication and a financial instruments calculation. There will be easy marks available simply for the basic cash flow aspects, setting out the proforma, setting up your workings, presenting your work neatly. If you recognise, as you should, that the disposal needs to be taken into account, of course you will get marks for that, even if you make a mistake in the arithmetic. If you get the pension bit right, so much the better, but you could pass the question comfortably while omitting this altogether. If you're short of time, this is what you should do.

Be ruthless in ignoring the complications

Look at the question. Within reason, if there are complications – often only worth a few marks – that you know you will not have time or knowledge to do, cross them out. It will make you feel better. Then tackle the bits you can do. This is how people pass a seemingly impossible paper.

Be ruthless in allocating your time

At BPP, we have seen how very intelligent students do two almost perfect questions, one averagely good and one sketchy. The first eight to ten marks are the easiest to get. Then you have to push it up to what you think is 15 (30 for the case study question), to get yourself a pass.

Do your best question either first or second, and the compulsory question either first or second. The compulsory question, being on groups, will always have some easy marks available for consolidation techniques.

Choosing which questions to answer first

We recommend that you spend time at the beginning of your exam carefully reading through all of the questions in the paper, and each of their requirements. Once you feel familiar with your exam paper we then recommend that you attempt the compulsory Section A question first, ensuring that you spend adequate time reading and planning before you begin to write up your answer. Comments from examination teams of other syllabuses that have similar exam formats suggest that students appear less time-pressured if they do the big compulsory questions first.

During the second half of the exam, you can put Section A aside and concentrate on the two Section B questions you've chosen.

However our recommendations are not inflexible. If you really think the Section A question looks a lot harder than the Section B questions you've chosen, then do those first, but **DON'T run over time on them**. You must leave yourself at least one hour and 38 minutes to tackle the Section A question. When you come back to it, once you have had time to reflect, you should be able to generate more ideas and find the question is not as bad as it looks.

Remember also that small overruns of time during the first half of the exam can add up to leave you very short of time towards the end.

Exam information

Format of the exam

		Number of marks
Section A:	1 compulsory case study	50
Section B:	Choice of 2 from 3 questions (25 marks each)	50
		100

Section A will consist of one scenario based question worth 50 marks. It will deal with the preparation of consolidated financial statements including group statements of cash flow and with issues in financial reporting.

Students will be required to answer two out of three questions in Section B, which will normally comprise two questions which will be scenario or case-study based and one question which will be an essay. Section B could deal with any aspects of the syllabus.

Time allowed: 3 hours and 15 minutes. The **pass mark** remains at 50%.

Additional information

The Study Guide provides more detailed guidance on the syllabus.

Analysis of past papers (by syllabus topic)

The table below provides details of when each element of the syllabus has been examined and the question number and section in which each element appeared.

With the introduction of the four exam sessions, ACCA will continue to publish the same number of exams, two per year, and at the same times, after the December and June exam sessions. These exams will be compiled from questions selected from the two preceding sessions. The first of this kind was published in December 2015, compiled from September 2015 and December 2015 exams, and this, together with the March/June 2016 and September/December 2016 hybrids has been included in the analysis below.

Covered in Text chapter		June 2014	Dec 2014	June 2015	ACCA Sep/Dec 2015	ACCA Mar/Jun 2016	ACCA Sep/Dec 2016
A	**THE PROFESSIONAL AND ETHICAL DUTY OF THE ACCOUNTANT**						
2	Professional behaviour and compliance with accounting standards	Q1(c)	Q1(c)	Q1(c)		Q1(c)	
2	Ethical requirements of corporate reporting and the consequences of unethical behaviour	Q1(c)	Q1(c)		Q1(c)	Q1(c)	
18	Social responsibility						
B	**THE FINANCIAL REPORTING FRAMEWORK**						
1	The applications, strengths and weaknesses of an accounting framework						
1	Critical evaluation of principles and practices						
	– Revenue recognition	Q3			Q4		
	– Substance over form issues						
C	**REPORTING THE FINANCIAL PERFORMANCE OF ENTITIES**						
10	Performance reporting			Q4	Q2	Q1(b) Q4	
42	Non-current assets						
	– Property, plant and equipment	Q1(a)	Q3, Q6				
	– Intangible assets			Q3		Q3	
	– Impairment					Q4	
	– Investment properties						
	– Government grants						
	– Borrowing costs					Q3	
	– Fair value			Q2		Q2, Q3	
7	Financial instruments	Q1, Q2, Q4	Q1, Q2, Q4		Q1(a), Q3	Q2	
8	Leases						
10	Segment reporting			Q3			
4	Employee benefits	Q1(a)				Q1(a)	
6	Income taxes	Q2				Q2	
5	Provisions, contingencies and events after the reporting period						
	– Provisions, contingency liabilities and contingent assets	Q3				Q3	

Covered in Text chapter		June 2014	Dec 2014	June 2015	ACCA Sep/Dec 2015	ACCA Mar/Jun 2016	ACCA Sep/Dec 2016
	– Events after the reporting period						
11	Related parties		Q2				
9	Share-based payment	Q1(a)				Q1(a)	Q1(c)
21	Reporting requirements of small and medium-sized entities						
D	**FINANCIAL STATEMENTS OF GROUPS OF ENTITIES**						
12-17	Group accounting including statements of cash flow – Complex groups – Associates – Joint ventures – Group statements of cash flows	Q3 Q1(a)	Q3		Q2 Q3	 Q1(a)	
15	Continuing and discontinued interests – Discontinued operations – Non-current assets held for sale	 Q3				 Q3	 Q3(c)
14	Changes in group structure – Mid year acquisitions – Disposals – Business combinations achieved in stages	 Q1(a)	 Q1(a)	 Q1(a) Q1(a) Q1(a)	 Q1(a)	 Q1(a)	
	– Group reorganisations						
16	Foreign transactions and entities – Foreign currency transactions – Foreign subsidiaries	 Q2 Q2			 Q1(a) Q1(b)	 Q2 Q2	 Q3(a)
E	**SPECIALISED ENTITIES**						
20	Financial reporting in specialised, not-for-profit and public sector entities	Q3			Q3	Q3	Q1(b),(c)
E2	Entity reconstructions						
F	**IMPLICATIONS OF CHANGES IN ACCOUNTING REGULATION ON FINANCIAL REPORTING**						
Throughout	The effect of changes in accounting standards on accounting systems						
18	Proposed changes to accounting standards					Q4	
G	**THE APPRAISAL OF FINANCIAL PERFORMANCE AND POSITION ENTITIES**						Q2(c)
10	The creation of suitable accounting policies				Q1(c)		
10	Analysis and interpretation of financial information and measurement of performance						
H	**CURRENT DEVELOPMENTS**						
18	Environmental and social reporting						
19	Convergence between national and international reporting standards						

Covered in Text chapter		June 2014	Dec 2014	June 2015	ACCA Sep/Dec 2015	ACCA Mar/Jun 2016	ACCA Sep/Dec 2016
H3	Current reporting issues						
	– Conceptual Framework						
	– Disclosures in financial statements						Q4(b)
	– Fair value measurement			Q2		Q2, Q3	
	– Financial instruments	Q4				Q2	
	– Revenue recognition				Q4		Q3(b)
	– Provisions and measurement of financial liabilities						
	– Integrated reporting			Q4		Q1(b)	

IMPORTANT!

The table above gives a broad idea of how frequently major topics in the syllabus are examined. It should not be used to question spot and predict for example that Topic X will not be examined because it came up two sittings ago. The examination team's reports indicate that the examination team is well aware some students try to question spot. The examination team avoid predictable patterns and may, for example, examine the same topic two sittings in a row.

Analysis of past papers (by sitting)

Section A

Consolidated statement of cash flows; usefulness of SOCF; ethics and intragroup loan

Section B

Scenario question, mainly on IFRS 13 and also IFRS 9
Specialised industry question set in the context of a sports organisation, covering borrowing costs, intangibles and fair value measurement
Move to a new IFRS; IAS 8; IAS 36; IAS 38

ACCA September/December 2016 exam

Section A

1 Consolidated SPLOCI with disposal; employee benefits

Section B

2 Functional currency; trademark; related parties
3 Bonus issue to be settled as liability or equity; classification as held for sale; 'bargain purchase' not part of a business combination
4 Materiality and IR framework; ED on statement of cash flows

The ACCA September/December 2016 Exam is Mock Exam 3 in this Kit.

ACCA March/June 2016 exam

	Question in this Kit
1 Consolidated statement of cash flows; usefulness of SOCF; ethics and intragroup loan	53
Section B	
2 Scenario question, mainly on IFRS 13 and also IFRS 9	7
3 Specialised industry question set in the context of a sports organisation, covering borrowing costs, intangibles and fair value measurement	
4 Move to a new IFRS; IAS 8; IAS 36; IAS 38	59 60

Examiner's comments

The ACCA examining team reiterated the importance of the *Conceptual Framework for Financial Reporting*. The objective of financial reporting and the other main concepts set out in the *Conceptual Framework*. Must be considered, together with the economics of the particular transaction or event.

IFRS financial statements are based on estimates, judgements and models. Candidates need to have awareness of IFRS judgements and estimates, and develop competence in making IFRS judgements and estimates. In order to facilitate this approach, there are several video/web clips issued by firms of accountants, which may be helpful.

ACCA September/December 2015 exam

Section A	
1 Consolidated statement of financial position with foreign subsidiary; IAS 21 explanation; ethics	51
Section B	
2 Scenario question covering IAS 38, IAS 1 and IAS 12	17
3 Specialised industry question set in the natural gas industry, covering IFRS 9, IFRS 11 and IAS 10.	61
4 IFRS 15: discussion and application	3

Examiner's comments. The ACCA examining team stressed that application and thought, rather than rote learning is the key to knowledge and understanding. The examination contains a significant amount of technical material but at the same time, many questions are based around the application of the fundamental principles within IFRS. Finally, there is often confusion over what constitutes 'current issues'. Current issues are not simply the Exposure Drafts set out in the examinable documents. They also include problems with current accounting standards, recent IFRSs and practice and regulatory issues. However, if a new accounting standard is issued and is included in the examinable documents, it is likely to be dealt with as a current issue topic. A surprising aspect of this examination was the lack of detailed knowledge of IFRS 15 in question 4.It is important for tutors and candidates to always review the examinable documents for recent additions such as IFRS 15.

June 2015

		Question in this Kit
Section A		
1	Consolidated statement of financial position with two acquisitions and a disposal; debt/equity distinction; ethics	46
Section B		
2	Fair value measurement in the context of various scenarios	29
3	Specialised industry question set in the pharmaceutical industry, covering segment reporting, purchase of intangible in exchange for shares and research and development	70
4	Recognition in profit or loss versus other comprehensive income (discussion and application); integrated reporting	30

Examiner's comments

The ACCA examining team was concerned to see that many candidates do not have a basic understanding of the standards. This causes a problem, as most questions require this knowledge. Section B of the paper requires candidates to discuss various issues but many candidates simply deal with the numerical aspect of a question without the necessary explanations. The problem that arises in these circumstances is that if the calculations are incorrect then candidates will lose most of the marks for the question.

Many of the questions are based on real life scenarios, and the marks are allocated for knowledge of the standard and its applications to that scenario. An accountant would not advise a client by quoting a standard to that client. An accountant would give advice that appertains to the specific circumstances of that client and this paper attempts to replicate that scenario. Many of the real issues in practice revolve around some of the core standards .So it is important that candidates understand, for example, the difference between debt and equity, the nature of an intangible asset, how assets 'held for sale' are dealt with .

December 2014

Section A		
1	Business combination in stages with adjustments for non-current asset held for sale and joint venture; share-based payment; ethical issue	-
Section B		
2	Related parties; financial guarantee contracts; interest rate swap; credit risk	19
3	IFRS 3 and control; IAS 16 application to a scenario	64
4	Impairment: factors to consider and application to a scenario	9

Examiner's comments

The performance of candidates in this paper was good. Question 1 often determines whether a candidate is successful in the examination because of the detailed and complex nature of the question. Therefore, it is important for candidates to answer all parts of the question. It is often the case in question 1c, which is based around ethical knowledge and application, that candidates do not attempt the question even though marks can readily be gained for a well-argued answer to this part of the question.

The normal problems of providing irrelevant answers, poor time management and lack of application of knowledge to the scenario are generally evident in every examination from an increasingly smaller number of candidates. A candidate is required to apply their knowledge to scenarios affecting issuers of financial statements in an international context and therefore the scenarios are not necessarily going to be typical of a particular region of the world. Further, the questions are not designed as purely an academic exercise.

June 2014

Section A		*Question in this Kit*
1	Consolidated statement of profit or loss and other comprehensive income with two disposals and various adjustments; fair value in IFRS; ethical issue	-
Section B		
2	Foreign transactions (functional currency, goodwill, deferred tax and a loan)	50
3	Specialised industry question set in the property industry, covering revenue, interim reporting, asset held for sale, provisions and intangibles	27
4	Distinction between debt and equity: discussion and scenario	20

Examiner's comments

The ACCA examining team was concerned to see that many candidates do not have a basic understanding of the standards. This causes a problem, as most questions require this knowledge. Section B of the paper requires candidates to discuss various issues but many candidates simply deal with the numerical aspect of a question without the necessary explanations. The problem that arises in these circumstances is that if the calculations are incorrect then candidates will lose most of the marks for the question.

Many of the questions are based on real life scenarios, and the marks are allocated for knowledge of the standard and its applications to that scenario. An accountant would not advise a client by quoting a standard to that client. An accountant would give advice that appertains to the specific circumstances of that client and this paper attempts to replicate that scenario. Many of the real issues in practice revolve around some of the core standards .So it is important that candidates understand, for example, the difference between debt and equity, the nature of an intangible asset, how assets 'held for sale' are dealt with.

December 2013

Section A		*Question in this Kit*
1	Consolidated statement of cash flows with acquisition of subsidiary and adjustments for deferred tax, a government grant and a pension plan; classification of cash flows; ethics	55
Section B		
2	Revenue recognition; impairment loss; sale and leaseback	23
3	Specialised industry question set in a bank, covering debt versus equity, hedging and the application of IFRS 10 in determining which party is the acquirer	
4	IAS 8: use of judgement in selecting accounting policies; prior period errors (three scenarios)	27

Examiner's comments

Encouragingly, candidates' performance was similar to previous diets. This indicates that the difficulty of question paper was consistent with past examinations, although student feedback suggested that it was perceived as more difficult.

Candidates are required to demonstrate knowledge and application. The knowledge level was that expected of a candidate at this level of a professional qualification. Many marks are lost if candidates do not demonstrate the application of this knowledge. A question on cash flows brings with it benefits and problems for candidates. There are marks for relatively simple adjustments but fewer marks for 'method' and therefore candidates need to ensure accuracy in their calculations. Candidates should always think that the marks are allocated for knowledge and application, and draft their answers accordingly.

A surprising number of candidates fail because they do not answer all parts of all questions. Other problems include failing to read the question clearly and therefore providing irrelevant answers, poor time management where candidates spend too much time on one aspect of a question and too little on others but more particularly, poor application of knowledge to the scenario. Many of the questions are based around real life scenarios, which mean that rote learning of topics will simply not work.

June 2013

Section A		*Question in this Kit*
1	Consolidated statement of financial position with a 'D'-shaped group; comparison of methods for valuing non-controlling interest; ethics	-
Section B		
2	Segment reporting, revenue recognition, provisions and property-related matters	78
3	In-depth analysis of whether a lease was a finance lease, a discontinued operation and fair value of an investment property	79
4	Importance of and barriers to disclosures in annual reports and application to a scenario	2

Examiner's comments

The ACCA examining team stressed again the importance of answering all questions and all parts of questions, and also of exam technique: exam technique consists of a few simple procedures that can help the candidate immeasurably. Answers should have a structure and cover points in an organised way. It may be best to write less on each point, leave out some of the background knowledge but focus on the facts/scenario in the question. The ACCA examining team does not need to know, for example, the role of the IASB in standard setting unless specifically asked in the question but often candidates may outline this as an introduction to an answer.

There is always a model solution to the question but in practice there are always opposing viewpoints, and candidates should not be afraid of expressing these viewpoints as they will not be penalised if the rationale is acceptable. The questions are not written to trick candidates but it is important to read the question carefully. Always ask yourself, is what I am including relevant to the question? Successful candidates demonstrate relevant knowledge by using ideas and concepts from recommended accounting practice. Practical examples from reading current articles are important ways of supporting the points made. Many candidates simply set out everything they know, hoping that some of the material is relevant. There is a need for a broader understanding rather than rote-learnt facts.

Candidates should try and use proper sentences and paragraphs rather than bullet points, as this will contribute to the awarding of professional marks. Candidates should never use abbreviations of words such as text language.

December 2012

Section A		Question in this Kit
1	Consolidated statement of financial position with sub-subsidiary, associate and disposal group; discussion on IFRS 5; ethical considerations of accounting treatment	
Section B		
2	Government grant; foreign exchange and cash flows; IFRS 10 and control; taxation and prior period adjustment	74
3	Investment property; leasing (substance of transaction); provision; impairment	75
4	IFRS 13 *Fair value measurement:* principles, three-level hierarchy; IFRS 13 fair valuing of asset and liability with computations	76

Examiner's comments

Candidates performed quite well in this session. As usual the paper dealt with a wide range of issues and accounting standards. There are several key principles in each standard, which are the basis of most of the examination questions, and candidates should concentrate on understanding and interpreting these principles. Candidates need to understand the standards, and not just learn their content. Understanding will lead to better application in the examination.

Candidates should practice divergent thinking, which is the ability to think of several possible answers to a question before providing the solution. This is the ability to see potentially different outcomes for a given set of circumstances. This will lead to candidates having the ability to apply the standards to different scenarios. Every examination session produces scenarios, which candidates will not necessarily have met before, and thus there is a need for this type of reasoning.

Candidates often simply recite the standard leaving the marker with the task of determining how applicable the answer actually is to the question. Candidates should adopt a model of learning which suits them and by doing this; candidates will be better prepared for the examination.

June 2012

Section A		Question in this Kit
1	Consolidated statement of financial position with business combination achieved in stages and joint operation; de-recognition of financial asset; ethics	48
Section B		
2	Sale and leaseback, defined benefit pension plan, cash-settled share-based payment and contingent liability in the context of a business combination	24
3	Measuring fair value, impairment of goodwill, deferred tax liabilities and the fair value option for an accounting mismatch; shares as financial liability or equity	64
4	Provisions (discussion and calculation)	13

Examiner's comments

Generally candidates performed well on this paper, with Questions 1 and 2 being answered better than Questions 3 and 4.

Candidates approached the examination well and did not appear too time-pressured, but some failed to produce answers of sufficient length and appear to be spending too much time on Question 1. Question 1(a) is designed to test candidates' computational skills and very brief explanations may be useful to the marker but many candidates entered into detailed discussion of the relevant standard, which costs time in the examination, and it is important for candidates to use their time effectively. Very few marks are allocated in Question 1(a) for detailed discussion.

Candidates often wasted time discussing a standard in detail when an application of the standard was required.

Candidates should read the question and formulate an answer in their mind. The answer should be based upon the detail of the question. Simply reading the requirement without application to the scenario does not gain marks.

This examination focussed on application of knowledge and it was application, which often let candidates down. Candidates often do not use the information in the scenario in order to develop their answers. Often the content of the scenario will help students answer the question as the scenario gives candidates direction in terms of their answers. This was particularly true of Question 4.

December 2011

Section A		*Question in this Kit*
1	Consolidated statement of financial position with business combination achieved in stages; segment reporting; ethics	45
Section B		
2	Internal reconstruction	68
3	Specialised industry question: intangible assets and impairment testing rules	7
4	Revenue recognition: current problems and proposed changes	3

Examiner's comments

The standard of answers varied. Many candidates passed the examination because of strong performance on Q1.

Question 1 and the questions answered best by candidates were Question 1a, Questions 3(a/c), and Question 4(a)(i).

Answers to Section B questions are often very general in nature with no relationship to the facts given in the scenario. This can involve just repeating information given in the question without explaining how it impacts on the financial statements or just quoting facts from standards without reference to the question. This can result in long answers that often don't address the issues in a scenario and may leave candidates bemused as to why they have failed when they have written so much. Often these scripts bordered on illegibility, which makes marking difficult. It is often better to explain a few points well than trying to regurgitate all the knowledge that the candidate possesses.

There were however many excellent scripts, particularly in answering the technical aspects of group accounting and the issues surrounding intangible assets.

Too many candidates let themselves down by failing to attempt all parts of the questions chosen, or in some cases by answering all four questions.

June 2011

Section A	*Question in this Kit*
1 Groups with a foreign subsidiary, other adjustments and the remainder on ethical issues	53
Section B	
2 Specialised industry question with IFRS 1, IFRS 3 intangible assets and restructuring plans and provisions	-
3 Specialised industry question with reclassification of long-term debt, correction of an error	29
4 Change to IFRS 9 rules for financial assets; change to expected loss model for impairment of financial assets	-

Exam update

Examinable documents

The following documents are examinable for sittings up from September 2017 to June 2018.

Knowledge of new examinable regulations issued by 31 August will be required in examination sessions being held in the following exam year. Documents may be examinable even if the effective date is in the future.

The documents listed as being examinable are the latest that were issued prior to 31 August 2016 and will be examinable in examination sessions in September 2017, December 2017, March 2018 and June 2018.

The study guide offers more detailed guidance on the depth and level at which the examinable documents will be examined. The study guide should be read in conjunction with the examinable documents list.

	Title
	International Accounting Standards (IASs)/International Financial Reporting Standards (IFRSs)
IAS 1	Presentation of financial statements (amended December 2014 per Disclosure Initiative)
IAS 2	Inventories
IAS 7	Statement of cash flows
IAS 8	Accounting policies, changes in accounting estimates and errors
IAS 10	Events after the reporting period
IAS 12	Income taxes
IAS 16	Property, plant and equipment
IAS 19	Employee benefits
IAS 20	Accounting for government grants and disclosure of government assistance
IAS 21	The effects of changes in foreign exchange rates
IAS 23	Borrowing costs
IAS 24	Related party disclosures
IAS 27	Separate financial statements
IAS 28	Investments in associates and joint ventures
IAS 32	Financial Instruments: presentation
IAS 33	Earnings per share
IAS 34	Interim financial reporting
IAS 36	Impairment of assets
IAS 37	Provisions, contingent liabilities and contingent assets
IAS 38	Intangible assets
IAS 40	Investment property
IAS 41	Agriculture
IFRS 1	First-time adoption of international financial reporting standards
IFRS 2	Share-based payment
IFRS 3	Business combinations
IFRS 5	Non-current assets held for sale and discontinued operations
IFRS 7	Financial instruments: disclosures
IFRS 8	Operating segments
IFRS 9	Financial instruments (revised July 2014)
IFRS 10	Consolidated financial statements
IFRS 11	Joint arrangements
IFRS 12	Disclosure of interests in other entities
IFRS 13	Fair value measurement
IFRS 15	Revenue from contracts with customers
IFRS 16	Leases
IFRS	For Small and Medium-sized Entities (revised 2015)

	Other Statements
	Conceptual Framework for Financial reporting
	Management Commentary
	The International <IR> Framework
	EDs, Discussion Papers and Other Documents
ED	Measuring quoted investments in subsidiaries, joint ventures and associates at fair value
ED	Classification of liabilities – proposed amendments to IAS 1
ED	Conceptual Framework for Financial Reporting
ED	IFRS Practice Statement Application of Materiality in Financial Statements

Important note for UK students

If you are sitting the UK P2 paper you will be studying under International standards and up to 20 marks will be for comparisons between International and UK GAAP. The ACCA UK Syllabus and Study Guide gives the following advice:

> International Financial Reporting Standards (IFRS) are the main accounting standards examined in the preparation of financial information. The key differences between UK GAAP and International Financial Reporting Standards are looked at on a subject by subject basis. The comparison between IFRS and UK GAAP will be based on the new UK GAAP as set out in FRSs 100–102, so the standard by standard comparisons that appeared in previous editions of this study guide are now combined in outcome C11 (c): *Discuss the key differences between the IFRS for SMEs and UK GAAP.*

This Kit is based on International Financial Reporting Standards. An online supplement will be available at www.bpp.com/learning-media, covering the additional UK issues and providing additional question practice.

Useful websites

The websites below provide additional sources of information of relevance to your studies for *Corporate Reporting.*

- www.accaglobal.com

  ACCA's website. The students' section of the website is invaluable for detailed information about the qualification, past issues of *Student Accountant* (including technical articles) and a free downloadable Student Planner App.

- www.bpp.com

  Our website provides information about BPP products and services, with a link to ACCA's website.

- www.ifrs.org
- www.IASPlus.com
- www.ft.com

  This website provides information about current international business. You can search for information and articles on specific industry groups as well as individual companies.

- www.economist.com

  Here you can search for business information on a week-by-week basis, search articles by business subject and use the resources of the Economist Intelligence Unit to research sectors, companies or countries.

- www.investmentweek.co.uk

  This site carries business news and articles on markets from *Investment Week* and *International Investment.*

- www.pwc.com

  The PricewaterhouseCoopers website includes UK Economic Outlook.

- www.cfo.com

  Good website for financial officers.

- www.bankofengland.co.uk

  This website is useful for sourcing Bank of England publications.

- www.accountancyfoundation.com
- www.ifac.org

Questions

PART A: REGULATORY AND ETHICAL FRAMEWORK

Questions 1 to 4 cover Regulatory and Ethical Framework, the subject of Part A of the BPP Study Text for Paper P2.

1 Conceptual framework **49 mins**

12/07, amended

The International Accounting Standards Board (IASB) is working on a joint project with the FASB to revisit its conceptual framework for financial accounting and reporting. The goals of the project are to build on the existing frameworks and converge them into a common framework. The first phase has now been published as the *Conceptual Framework for Financial Reporting.*

Required

(a) Discuss why there is a need to develop an agreed international conceptual framework and the extent to which an agreed international conceptual framework can be used to resolve practical accounting issues. **(14 marks)**

(b) In 2015, the IASB issued an exposure draft: *The Conceptual Framework for Financial Reporting,* which addresses areas found to be deficient in the existing *Conceptual Framework.*

Discuss the changes proposed in the ED in respect of the following matters:

(i) Derecognition of assets and liabilities
(ii) The reintroduction of prudence **(5 marks)**

(c) What criticisms could be made of the proposed changes? **(4 marks)**

Appropriateness and quality of discussion. **(2 marks)**

(Total = 25 marks)

2 Lizzer **49 mins**

6/13

(a) Developing a framework for disclosure is at the forefront of current debate and there are many bodies around the world attempting to establish an overarching framework to make financial statement disclosures more effective, coordinated and less redundant. It has been argued that instead of focusing on raising the quality of disclosures, these efforts have placed their emphasis almost exclusively on reducing the quantity of information. The belief is that excessive disclosure is burdensome and can overwhelm users. However, it could be argued that there is no such thing as too much 'useful' information for users.

Required

(i) Discuss why it is important to ensure the optimal level of disclosure in annual reports, describing the reasons why users of annual reports may have found disclosure to be excessive in recent years. **(9 marks)**

(ii) Describe the barriers, which may exist, to reducing excessive disclosure in annual reports. **(6 marks)**

(b) The directors of Lizzer, a public limited company, have read various reports on excessive disclosure in the annual report. They have decided to take action and do not wish to disclose any further detail concerning the two instances below.

(i) Lizzer is a debt issuer whose business is the securitisation of a portfolio of underlying investments and financing their purchase through the issuing of listed, limited recourse debt. The repayment of the debt is dependent upon the performance of the underlying investments. Debt-holders bear the ultimate risks and rewards of ownership of the underlying investments. Given the debt specific nature of the underlying investments, the risk profile of individual debt may differ.

Lizzer does not consider its debt-holders as being amongst the primary users of the financial statements and, accordingly, does not wish to provide disclosure of the debt-holders' exposure to risks in the financial statements, as distinct from the risks faced by the company's shareholders, in accordance with IFRS 7 *Financial instruments: disclosures.* **(4 marks)**

(ii) At the date of the financial statements, 31 January 20X3, Lizzer's liquidity position was quite poor, such that the directors described it as 'unsatisfactory' in the management report. During the first quarter of 20X3, the situation worsened with the result that Lizzer was in breach of certain loan covenants at 31 March 20X3. The financial statements were authorised for issue at the end of April 20X3. The directors' and auditor's reports both emphasised the considerable risk of not being able to continue as a going concern.

The notes to the financial statements indicated that there was 'ample' compliance with all loan covenants as at the date of the financial statements. No additional information about the loan covenants was included in the financial statements. Lizzer had been close to breaching the loan covenants in respect of free cash flows and equity ratio requirements at 31 January 20X3.

The directors of Lizzer felt that, given the existing information in the financial statements, any further disclosure would be excessive and confusing to users. **(4 marks)**

Required

Discuss the directors' view that no further information regarding the two instances above should be disclosed in the financial statements because it would be 'excessive'.

Note. The mark allocation is shown against each of the two instances above.

Professional marks will be awarded in this question for clarity and quality of presentation. **(2 marks)**

(Total = 25 marks)

3 Tang **49 mins**

Sep/Dec 15

There has been significant divergence in practice over recognition of revenue mainly because International Financial Reporting Standards (IFRS) have contained limited guidance in certain areas. The International Accounting Standards Board (IASB) as a result of the joint project with the US Financial Accounting Standards Board (FASB) has issued IFRS 15 *Revenue from contracts with customers.* IFRS 15 sets out a five-step model, which applies to revenue earned from a contract with a customer with limited exceptions, regardless of the type of revenue transaction or the industry. Step one in the five-step model requires the identification of the contract with the customer and is critical for the purpose of applying the standard. The remaining four steps in the standard's revenue recognition model are irrelevant if the contract does not fall within the scope of IFRS 15.

Required

(a) (i) Discuss the criteria which must be met for a contract with a customer to fall within the scope of IFRS 15. **(5 marks)**

(ii) Discuss the four remaining steps which lead to revenue recognition after a contract has been identified as falling within the scope of IFRS 15. **(8 marks)**

(b) (i) Tang enters into a contract with a customer to sell an existing printing machine such that control of the printing machine vests with the customer in two years' time. The contract has two payment options. The customer can pay $240,000 when the contract is signed or $300,000 in two years' time when the customer gains control of the printing machine. The interest rate implicit in the contract is 11.8% in order to adjust for the risk involved in the delay in payment. However, Tang's incremental borrowing rate is 5%. The customer paid $240,000 on 1 December 20X4 when the contract was signed. **(4 marks)**

(ii) Tang enters into a contract on 1 December 20X4 to construct a printing machine on a customer's premises for a promised consideration of $1,500,000 with a bonus of $100,000 if the machine is completed within 24 months. At the inception of the contract, Tang correctly accounts for the promised bundle of goods and services as a single performance obligation in accordance with IFRS 15. At the inception of the contract, Tang expects the costs to be $800,000 and concludes that it is highly probable that a significant reversal in the amount of cumulative revenue recognised will occur. Completion of the printing machine is highly susceptible to factors outside of Tang's influence, mainly issues with the supply of components.

At 30 November 20X5, Tang has satisfied 65% of its performance obligation on the basis of costs incurred to date and concludes that the variable consideration is still constrained in accordance with IFRS 15. However, on 4 December 20X5, the contract is modified with the result that the fixed consideration and expected costs increase by $110,000 and $60,000 respectively. The time allowable for achieving the bonus is extended by six months with the result that Tang concludes that it is highly probable that the bonus will be achieved and that the contract still remains a single performance obligation. Tang has an accounting year end of 30 November. **(6 marks)**

Required

Discuss how the above two contracts should be accounted for under IFRS 15. (In the case of (b)(i), the discussion should include the accounting treatment up to 30 November 20X6 and in the case of (b)(ii), the accounting treatment up to 4 December 20X5.)

Note. The mark allocation is shown against each of the items above.

Professional marks will be awarded in this question for clarity and quality of presentation. **(2 marks)**

(Total = 25 marks)

4 Venue

49 mins

12/11, amended

The introduction of IFRS 15 *Revenue from contracts with customers* will have a significant impact on the financial statements of many companies. IFRS 15 significantly reduces an entity's discretion to apply judgement when recognising revenue. This represents an improvement on the old revenue standards, which provided limited revenue recognition guidance and led to divergence in practice.

Required

(a) (i) Discuss the main weaknesses in the old revenue standards which led to the introduction of IFRS 15 *Revenue from contracts with customers.* **(8 marks)**

(ii) Discuss the ways in which IFRS 15 attempts to remedy the disadvantages of the previous standards on revenue. **(11 marks)**

Professional marks will be awarded in part (a) for clarity and expression of your discussion. **(2 marks)**

(b) On 1 July 20X6, Venue entered into a contract with Reven for the sale of plant for $500,000. The contract included a call option that gave Venue the right to repurchase the plant for $550,000 on or before 30 June 20X7.

Required

Discuss how the above transaction would be treated in subsequent financial statements of Venue for the year ended 31 July 20X7. **(4 marks)**

(Total = 25 marks)

5 Preparation question: Sundry standards

(a) Penn Co has a defined benefit pension plan and wishes to recognise the full deficit in its statement of financial position.

Required

Using the information below, prepare extracts from the statement of financial position and the statement of comprehensive income, together with a reconciliation of plan movements for the year ended 31 January 20X8. Ignore taxation.

(i) The opening plan assets were $3.6m on 1 February 20X7 and plan liabilities at this date were $4.3m.

(ii) Company contributions to the plan during the year amounted to $550,000.

(iii) Pensions paid to former employees amounted to $330,000 in the year.

(iv) The yield on high quality corporate bonds was 8% and the actual return on plan assets was $295,000.

(v) During the year, five staff were made redundant, and an extra $58,000 in total was added to the value of their pensions.

(vi) Current service costs as provided by the actuary are $275,000.

(vii) The actuary valued the plan liabilities at 31 January 20X8 as $4.54m.

(b) Sion Co operates a defined benefit pension plan for its employees. The following details relate to the plan.

Present value of obligation at start of 20X8 ($'000)	40,000
Market value of plan assets at start of 20X8 ($'000)	40,000

	20X8	*20X9*
	$'000	$'000
Current service cost	2,500	2,860
Benefits paid out	1,974	2,200
Contributions paid by entity	2,000	2,200
Present value of obligation at end of the year	46,000	40,800
Market value of plan assets at end of the year	43,000	35,680
Yield on corporate bonds at end of year	8%	9%

During 20X8, the benefits available under the plan were improved. The resulting increase in the present value of the defined benefit obligation was $2 million.

On the final day of 20X9, Sion Co. divested of part of its business, and as part of the sale agreement, transferred the relevant part of its pension fund to the buyer. The present value of the defined benefit obligation transferred was $11.4 million and the fair value of plan assets transferred was $10.8million. Sion also made a cash payment of $400,000 to the buyer in respect of the plan.

Assume that all transactions occur at the end of the year.

Required

(i) Calculate the net defined benefit liability as at the start and end of 20X8 and 20X9 showing clearly any remeasurement gain or loss on the plan each year.

(ii) Show amounts to be recognised in the financial statements in each of the years 20X8 and 20X9 in respect of the plan.

(c) Bed Investment Co entered into a contract on 1 July 20X7 with Em Bank. The contract consisted of a deposit of a principal amount of $10 million, carrying an interest rate of 2.5% per annum and with a maturity date of 30 June 20X9. Interest will be receivable at maturity together with the principal. In addition, a further 3% interest per annum will be payable by Em Bank if the exchange rate of the dollar against the Ruritanian Kroner (RKR) exceeds or is equal to $1.15 to RKR 1.

Bed's functional currency is the dollar.

Required

Explain how Bed should account for the above investment in the financial statements for the year ended 31 December 20X7.

6 Key

49 mins

12/09

(a) Key, a public limited company, is concerned about the reduction in the general availability of credit and the sudden tightening of the conditions required to obtain a loan from banks. There has been a reduction in credit availability and a rise in interest rates. It seems as though there has ceased to be a clear relationship between interest rates and credit availability, and lenders and investors are seeking less risky investments. The directors are trying to determine the practical implications for the financial statements particularly because of large write downs of assets in the banking sector, tightening of credit conditions, and falling sales and asset prices. They are particularly concerned about the impairment of assets and the market inputs to be used in impairment testing. They are afraid that they may experience significant impairment charges in the coming financial year. They are unsure as to how they should test for impairment and any considerations which should be taken into account.

Required

Discuss the main considerations that the company should take into account when impairment testing non-current assets in the above economic climate. **(8 marks)**

Professional marks will be awarded in part (a) for clarity and expression. **(2 marks)**

(b) There are specific assets on which the company wishes to seek advice. The company holds certain non-current assets, which are in a development area and carried at cost less depreciation. These assets cost \$3 million on 1 June 20X3 and are depreciated on the straight-line basis over their useful life of five years. An impairment review was carried out on 31 May 20X4 and the projected cash flows relating to these assets were as follows:

Year to	*31 May 20X5*	*31 May 20X6*	*31 May 20X7*	*31 May 20X8*
Cash flows (\$'000)	280	450	500	550

The company used a discount rate of 5%. At 30 November 20X4, the directors used the same cash flow projections and noticed that the resultant value in use was above the carrying amount of the assets and wished to reverse any impairment loss calculated at 31 May 20X4. The government has indicated that it may compensate the company for any loss in value of the assets up to 20% of the impairment loss.

Key holds a non-current asset, which was purchased for \$10 million on 1 December 20X1 with an expected useful life of ten years. On 1 December 20X3, it was revalued to \$8.8 million. At 30 November 20X4, the asset was reviewed for impairment and written down to its recoverable amount of \$5.5 million.

Key committed itself at the beginning of the financial year to selling a property that is being under-utilised following the economic downturn. As a result of the economic downturn, the property was not sold by the end of the year. The asset was actively marketed but there were no reasonable offers to purchase the asset. Key is hoping that the economic downturn will change in the future and therefore has not reduced the price of the asset.

Required

Discuss with suitable computations, how to account for any potential impairment of the above non-current assets in the financial statements for the year ended 30 November 20X4. **(15 marks)**

Note. The following 5% discount factors may be relevant.

Year 1	0.9524
Year 2	0.9070
Year 3	0.8638
Year 4	0.8227

(Total = 25 marks)

7 Emcee

49 mins

Mar/Jun 16

Emcee, a public limited company, is a sports organisation which owns several football and basketball teams. It has a financial year end of 31 May 20X6.

(a) Emcee needs a new stadium to host sporting events which will be included as part of Emcee's property, plant and equipment. Emcee therefore commenced construction on a new stadium on 1 February 20X6, and this continued until its completion which was after the year end of 31 May 20X6. The direct costs were $20m in February 20X6 and then $50m in each month until the year end. Emcee has not taken out any specific borrowings to finance the construction of the stadium, but it has incurred finance costs on its general borrowings during the period, which could have been avoided if the stadium had not been constructed. Emcee has calculated that the weighted average cost of borrowings for the period 1 February–31 May 20X6 on an annualised basis amounted to 9% per annum. Emcee needs advice on how to treat the borrowing costs in its financial statements for the year ending 31 May 20X6. **(6 marks)**

(b) Emcee purchases and sells players' registrations on a regular basis. Emcee must purchase registrations for that player to play for the club. Player registrations are contractual obligations between the player and Emcee. The costs of acquiring player registrations include transfer fees, league levy fees, and player agents' fees incurred by the club. Often players' former clubs are paid amounts which are contingent upon the performance of the player whilst they play for Emcee. For example, if a contracted basketball player scores an average of more than 20 points per game in a season, then an additional $5m may become payable to his former club. Also, players' contracts can be extended and this incurs additional costs for Emcee.

At the end of every season, which also is the financial year end of Emcee, the club reviews its playing staff and makes decisions as to whether they wish to sell any players' registrations. These registrations are actively marketed by circulating other clubs with a list of players' registrations and their estimated selling price. Players' registrations are also sold during the season, often with performance conditions attached. Occasionally, it becomes clear that a player will not play for the club again because of, for example, a player sustaining a career threatening injury or being permanently removed from the playing squad for another reason. The playing registrations of certain players were sold after the year end, for total proceeds, net of associated costs, of $25m. These registrations had a net book value of $7m.

Emcee would like to know the financial reporting treatment of the acquisition, extension, review and sale of players' registrations in the circumstances outlined above. **(10 marks)**

(c) Emcee uses the revaluation model to measure its stadiums. The directors have been offered $100m from an airline for the property naming rights of all the stadiums for three years. There are two directors who are on the management boards of Emcee and the airline. Additionally, there are regulations in place by both the football and basketball leagues which regulate the financing of the clubs. These regulations prevent capital contributions from a related party which 'increases equity without repayment in return'. The aim of these regulations is to promote sustainable business models. Sanctions imposed by the regulator include fines and withholding of prize monies. Emcee wishes to know how to take account of the naming rights in the valuation of the stadium and the potential implications of the financial regulations imposed by the leagues. **(7 marks)**

Required

Discuss how the above events would be shown in the financial statements of Emcee under International Financial Reporting Standards.

Note. The split of the mark allocation is shown against each of the three issues above.

Professional marks will be awarded in this question for the clarity and quality of presentation. **(2 marks)**

(Total = 25 marks)

8 Scramble

49 mins

12/11

Scramble, a public limited company, is a developer of online computer games.

(a) At 30 November 20X1, 65% of Scramble's total assets were mainly represented by internally developed intangible assets comprising the capitalised costs of the development and production of online computer games. These games generate all of Scramble's revenue. The costs incurred in relation to maintaining the games at the same standard of performance are expensed to profit or loss for the year. The accounting policy note states that intangible assets are valued at historical cost. Scramble considers the games to have an indefinite useful life, which is reconsidered annually when the intangible assets are tested for impairment. Scramble determines value in use using the estimated future cash flows which include maintenance expenses, capital expenses incurred in developing different versions of the games and the expected increase in turnover resulting from the above mentioned cash outflows. Scramble does not conduct an analysis or investigation of differences between expected and actual cash flows. Tax effects were also taken into account. **(7 marks)**

(b) Scramble has two cash generating units (CGU) which hold 90% of the internally developed intangible assets. Scramble reported a consolidated net loss for the period and an impairment charge in respect of the two CGUs representing 63% of the consolidated profit before tax and 29% of the total costs in the period. The recoverable amount of the CGUs is defined, in this case, as value in use. Specific discount rates are not directly available from the market, and Scramble estimates the discount rates, using its weighted average cost of capital. In calculating the cost of debt as an input to the determination of the discount rate, Scramble used the risk-free rate adjusted by the company specific average credit spread of its outstanding debt, which had been raised two years previously. As Scramble did not have any need for additional financing and did not need to repay any of the existing loans before 20X4, Scramble did not see any reason for using a different discount rate. Scramble did not disclose either the events and circumstances that led to the recognition of the impairment loss or the amount of the loss recognised in respect of each cash-generating unit. Scramble felt that the events and circumstances that led to the recognition of a loss in respect of the first CGU were common knowledge in the market and the events and the circumstances that led to the recognition loss of the second CGU were not needed to be disclosed. **(7 marks)**

(c) Scramble wished to diversify its operations and purchased a professional football club, Rashing. In Rashing's financial statements for the year ended 30 November 20X1, it was proposed to include significant intangible assets which related to acquired players' registration rights comprising registration and agents' fees. The agents' fees were paid by the club to players' agents either when a player is transferred to the club or when the contract of a player is extended. Scramble believes that the registration rights of the players are intangible assets but that the agents fees do not meet the criteria to be recognised as intangible assets as they are not directly attributable to the costs of players' contracts. Additionally, Rashing has purchased the rights to 25% of the revenue from ticket sales generated by another football club, Santash, in a different league. Rashing does not sell these tickets nor has any discretion over the pricing of the tickets. Rashing wishes to show these rights as intangible assets in its financial statements. **(9 marks)**

Required

Discuss the validity of the accounting treatments proposed by Scramble in its financial statements for the year ended 30 November 20X1.

The mark allocation is shown against each of the three accounting treatments above.

Professional marks will be awarded for clarity and expression of your discussion. **(2 marks)**

(Total = 25 marks)

9 Estoil

49 mins

12/14

(a) An assessment of accounting practices for asset impairments is especially important in the context of financial reporting quality in that it requires the exercise of considerable management judgement and reporting discretion. The importance of this issue is heightened during periods of ongoing economic uncertainty as a result of the need for companies to reflect the loss of economic value in a timely fashion through the mechanism of asset write-downs. There are many factors which can affect the quality of impairment accounting and disclosures. These factors include changes in circumstance in the reporting period, the market capitalisation of the entity, the allocation of goodwill to cash generating units, valuation issues and the nature of the disclosures.

Required

Discuss the importance and significance of the above factors when conducting an impairment test under IAS 36 *Impairment of assets.* **(13 marks)**

(b) (i) Estoil is an international company providing parts for the automotive industry. It operates in many different jurisdictions with different currencies. During 20X4, Estoil experienced financial difficulties marked by a decline in revenue, a reorganisation and restructuring of the business and it reported a loss for the year. An impairment test of goodwill was performed but no impairment was recognised. Estoil applied one discount rate for all cash flows for all cash generating units (CGUs), irrespective of the currency in which the cash flows would be generated. The discount rate used was the weighted average cost of capital (WACC) and Estoil used the 10-year government bond rate for its jurisdiction as the risk free rate in this calculation. Additionally, Estoil built its model using a forecast denominated in the functional currency of the parent company. Estoil felt that any other approach would require a level of detail which was unrealistic and impracticable. Estoil argued that the different CGUs represented different risk profiles in the short term, but over a longer business cycle, there was no basis for claiming that their risk profiles were different.

(ii) Fariole specialises in the communications sector with three main CGUs. Goodwill was a significant component of total assets. Fariole performed an impairment test of the CGUs. The cash flow projections were based on the most recent financial budgets approved by management. The realised cash flows for the CGUs were negative in 20X4 and far below budgeted cash flows for that period. The directors had significantly raised cash flow forecasts for 20X5 with little justification. The projected cash flows were calculated by adding back depreciation charges to the budgeted result for the period with expected changes in working capital and capital expenditure not taken into account.

Required

Discuss the acceptability of the above accounting practices under IAS 36 *Impairment of assets.*

(10 marks)

Professional marks will be awarded in this question for clarity and quality of presentation. **(2 marks)**

(Total = 25 marks)

10 Preparation question: Defined benefit plan

> **BPP Note**. In this question, proformas are given to you to help you get used to setting out your answer. You may wish to transfer them to a separate sheet, or alternatively to use a separate sheet for your workings.

Brutus Co operates a defined benefit pension plan for its employees conditional on a minimum employment period of six years. The present value of the future benefit obligations and the fair value of its plan assets on 1 January 20X1 were $110 million and $150 million respectively.

The pension plan received contributions of $7m and paid pensions to former employees of $10m during the year.

Extracts from the most recent actuary's report show the following:

Present value of pension plan obligation at 31 December 20X1	$116m
Fair value of plan assets at 31 December 20X1	$140m
Present cost of pensions earned in the period	$11m
Yield on high quality corporate bonds at 1 January 20X1	10%

On 1 January 20X1, the rules of the pension plan were changed to improve benefits for plan members. The actuary has advised that this will cost $10 million.

Required

Produce the extracts for the financial statements for the year ended 31 December 20X1.

Assume contributions and benefits were paid on 31 December.

Statement of profit or loss and other comprehensive income notes

Defined benefit expense recognised in profit or loss

	$m
Current service cost	
Past service cost	
Net interest on the net defined benefit asset	

Other comprehensive income (items that will not be reclassified to profit or loss)
Remeasurement of defined benefit plans

	$m
Actuarial gain on defined benefit obligation	
Return on plan assets (excluding amounts in net interest)	

Statement of financial position notes

Net defined benefit asset recognised in the statement of financial position

	31 December 20X1 $m	*31 December 20X0* $m
Present value of pension obligation		
Fair value of plan assets		
Net asset		

Changes in the present value of the defined benefit obligation

	$m
Opening defined benefit obligation	
Interest on obligation	
Current service cost	
Past service cost	
Benefits paid	
Gain on remeasurement of obligation(balancing figure)	
Closing defined benefit obligation	

Changes in the fair value of plan assets

	$m
Opening fair value of plan assets	
Interest on plan assets	
Contributions	
Benefits paid	
Loss on remeasurement of assets (balancing figure)	
Closing fair value of plan assets	

11 Macaljoy **49 mins**

12/07, amended

Macaljoy, a public limited company, is a leading support services company which focuses on the building industry. The company would like advice on how to treat certain items under IAS 19 *Employee benefits* and IAS 37 *Provisions, contingent liabilities and contingent assets*. The company operates the Macaljoy Pension Plan B which commenced on 1 November 20X6 and the Macaljoy Pension Plan A, which was closed to new entrants from 31 October 20X6, but which was open to future service accrual for the employees already in the scheme. The assets of the schemes are held separately from those of the company in funds under the control of trustees. The following information relates to the two schemes.

Macaljoy Pension Plan A

The terms of the plan are as follows.

(i) Employees contribute 6% of their salaries to the plan.

(ii) Macaljoy contributes, currently, the same amount to the plan for the benefit of the employees.

(iii) On retirement, employees are guaranteed a pension which is based upon the number of years service with the company and their final salary.

The following details relate to the plan in the year to 31 October 20X7:

	$m
Present value of obligation at 1 November 20X6	200
Present value of obligation at 31 October 20X7	240
Fair value of plan assets at 1 November 20X6	190
Fair value of plan assets at 31 October 20X7	225
Current service cost	20
Pension benefits paid	19
Total contributions paid to the scheme for year to 31 October 20X7	17

Remeasurement gains and losses are recognised in accordance with IAS 19 as revised in 2011.

Macaljoy Pension Plan B

Under the terms of the plan, Macaljoy does not guarantee any return on the contributions paid into the fund. The company's legal and constructive obligation is limited to the amount that is contributed to the fund. The following details relate to this scheme:

	$m
Fair value of plan assets at 31 October 20X7	21
Contributions paid by company for year to 31 October 20X7	10
Contributions paid by employees for year to 31 October 20X7	10

The interest rate on high quality corporate bonds for the two plans are:

1 November 20X6	*31 October 20X7*
5%	6%

The company would like advice on how to treat the two pension plans, for the year ended 31 October 20X7, together with an explanation of the differences between a defined contribution plan and a defined benefit plan.

Warranties

Additionally the company manufactures and sells building equipment on which it gives a standard one year warranty to all customers. The company has extended the warranty to two years for certain major customers and has insured against the cost of the second year of the warranty. The warranty has been extended at nil cost to the customer. The claims made under the extended warranty are made in the first instance against Macaljoy and then Macaljoy in turn makes a counter claim against the insurance company. Past experience has shown that 80% of the building equipment will not be subject to warranty claims in the first year, 15% will have minor defects and 5% will require major repair. Macaljoy estimates that in the second year of the warranty, 20% of the items sold will have minor defects and 10% will require major repair.

In the year to 31 October 20X7, the following information is relevant.

	Standard warranty (units)	*Extended warranty* (units)	*Selling price per unit* (both)($)
Sales	2,000	5,000	1,000
		Major repair $	*Minor defect* $
Cost of repair (average)		500	100

Assume that sales of equipment are on 31 October 20X7 and any warranty claims are made on 31 October in the year of the claim. Assume a risk adjusted discount rate of 4%.

Required

Draft a report suitable for presentation to the directors of Macaljoy which:

(a) (i) Discusses the nature of and differences between a defined contribution plan and a defined benefit plan with specific reference to the company's two schemes. **(7 marks)**

(ii) Shows the accounting treatment for the two Macaljoy pension plans for the year ended 31 October 20X7 under IAS 19 *Employee benefits* (revised 2011). **(7 marks)**

(b) (i) Discusses the principles involved in accounting for claims made under the above warranty provision. **(6 marks)**

(ii) Shows the accounting treatment for the above warranty provision under IAS 37 *Provisions, contingent liabilities and contingent assets* for the year ended 31 October 20X7. **(3 marks)**

Appropriateness of the format and presentation of the report and communication of advice. **(2 marks)**

(Total = 25 marks)

12 Ryder **49 mins**

ACR, 12/05

Ryder, a public limited company, is reviewing certain events which have occurred since its year end of 31 October 20X5. The financial statements were authorised on 12 December 20X5. The following events are relevant to the financial statements for the year ended 31 October 20X5:

(a) Ryder disposed of a wholly owned subsidiary, Krup, a public limited company, on 10 December 20X5 and made a loss of $9 million on the transaction in the group financial statements. As at 31 October 20X5, Ryder had no intention of selling the subsidiary which was material to the group. The directors of Ryder have stated that there were no significant events which have occurred since 31 October 20X5 which could have resulted in a reduction in the value of Krup. The carrying value of the net assets and purchased goodwill of Krup at 31 October 20X5 were $20 million and $12 million respectively. Krup had made a loss of $2 million in the period 1 November 20X5 to 10 December 20X5. **(6 marks)**

(b) Ryder acquired a wholly owned subsidiary, Metalic, a public limited company, on 21 January 20X4. The consideration payable in respect of the acquisition of Metalic was 2 million ordinary shares of $1 of Ryder plus a further 300,000 ordinary shares if the profit of Metalic exceeded $6 million for the year ended 31 October 20X5. The profit for the year of Metalic was $7 million and the ordinary shares were issued on 12 November 20X5. The annual profits of Metalic had averaged $7 million over the last few years and, therefore, Ryder had included an estimate of the contingent consideration in the cost of the acquisition at 21 January 20X4. The fair value used for the ordinary shares of Ryder at this date including the contingent consideration was $10 per share. The fair value of the ordinary shares on 12 November 20X5 was $11 per share. Ryder also made a one for four bonus issue on 13 November 20X5 which was applicable to the contingent shares issued. The directors are unsure of the impact of the above on the accounting for the acquisition. **(8 marks)**

(c) The company acquired a property on 1 November 20X4 which it intended to sell. The property was obtained as a result of a default on a loan agreement by a third party and was valued at $20 million on that date for accounting purposes which exactly offset the defaulted loan. The property is in a state of disrepair and Ryder intends to complete the repairs before it sells the property. The repairs were completed on 30 November 20X5. The property was sold after costs for $27 million on 9 December 20X5. The property was classified as 'held for sale' at the year end under IFRS 5 *Non-current assets held for sale and discontinued operations* but shown at the net sale proceeds of $27 million. Property is depreciated at 5% per annum on the straight-line basis and no depreciation has been charged in the year. **(6 marks)**

(d) The company granted share appreciation rights (SARs) to its employees on 1 November 20X3 based on ten million shares. The SARs provide employees at the date the rights are exercised with the right to receive cash equal to the appreciation in the company's share price since the grant date. The rights vested on 31 October 20X5 and payment was made on schedule on 1 December 20X5. The fair value of the SARs per share at 31 October 20X4 was $6, at 31 October 2005 was $8 and at 1 December 20X5 was $9. The company has recognised a liability for the SARs as at 31 October 20X4 based upon IFRS 2 *Share-based payment* but the liability was stated at the same amount at 31 October 20X5. **(5 marks)**

Required

Discuss the accounting treatment of the above events in the financial statements of the Ryder Group for the year ended 31 October 20X5, taking into account the implications of events occurring after the end of the reporting period.

(The mark allocations are set out after each paragraph above.) **(Total = 25 marks)**

13 Royan — 29 mins

6/12, amended

(a) Discuss the guidance in IAS 37 *Provisions, contingent liabilities and contingent assets* as regards the recognition and measurement of provisions and why it might be felt necessary to replace this guidance. **(10 marks)**

(b) Royan, a public limited company, extracts oil and has a present obligation to dismantle an oil platform at the end of the platform's life, which is ten years. Royan cannot cancel this obligation or transfer it. Royan intends to carry out the dismantling work itself and estimates the cost of the work to be $150 million in ten years' time. The present value of the work is $105 million.

A market exists for the dismantling of an oil platform and Royan could hire a third party contractor to carry out the work. The entity feels that if no risk or probability adjustment were needed then the cost of the external contractor would be $180 million in ten years' time. The present value of this cost is $129 million. If risk and probability are taken into account, then there is a probability of 40% that the present value will be $129 million and 60% probability that it would be $140 million, and there is a risk that the costs may increase by $5 million.

Required

Describe the accounting treatment of the above events under IAS 37. **(3 marks)**

Professional marks will be awarded for the quality of the discussion. **(2 marks)**

(Total = 15 marks)

14 Electron

49 mins

Pilot paper

Electron, a public limited company, operates in the energy sector. The company has grown significantly over the last few years and is currently preparing its financial statements for the year ended 30 June 20X6.

Electron buys and sells oil and currently has a number of oil trading contracts. The contracts to purchase oil are treated as non-current assets and amortised over the contracts' durations. On acceptance of a contract to sell oil, fifty per cent of the contract price is recognised immediately with the balance being recognised over the remaining life of the contract. The contracts always result in the delivery of the commodity. **(4 marks)**

Electron has recently constructed an ecologically efficient power station. A condition of being granted the operating licence by the government is that the power station be dismantled at the end of its life which is estimated to be 20 years. The power station cost $100 million and began production on 1 July 20X5. Depreciation is charged on the power station using the straight line method. Electron has estimated at 30 June 20X6 that it will cost $15 million (net present value) to restore the site to its original condition using a discount rate of five per cent. Ninety-five per cent of these costs relate to the removal of the power station and five per cent relates to the damage caused through generating energy. **(7 marks)**

Electron has leased another power station, which was relatively inefficient, to a rival company on 30 June 20X6. The beneficial and legal ownership remains with Electron and in the event of one of Electron's power stations being unable to produce energy, Electron can terminate the agreement. The leased power station is being treated as an operating lease with the net present value of the income of $40 million being recognised in profit or loss. The fair value of the power station is $70 million at 30 June 20X6. A deposit of $10 million was received on 30 June 20X6 and it is included in the net present value calculation. **(5 marks)**

The company has a good relationship with its shareholders and employees. It has adopted a strategy of gradually increasing its dividend payments over the years. On 1 August 20X6, the board proposed a dividend of 5c per share for the year ended 30 June 20X6. The shareholders will approve the dividend along with the financial statements at the general meeting on 1 September 20X6 and the dividend will be paid on 14 September 20X6. The directors feel that the dividend should be accrued in the financial statements for the year ended 30 June 20X6 as a 'valid expectation' has been created. **(3 marks)**

The company granted share options to its employees on 1 July 20X5. The fair value of the options at that date was $3 million. The options vest on 30 June 20X8. The employees have to be employed at the end of the three year period for the options to vest and the following estimates have been made:

Estimated percentage of employees leaving during vesting period at:

Grant date 1 July 20X5	5%	
30 June 20X6	6%	**(4 marks)**
Effective communication to the directors		**(2 marks)**

Required

Draft a report suitable for presentation to the directors of Electron which discusses the accounting treatment of the above transactions in the financial statements for the year ended 30 June 20X6, including relevant calculations.

(Total = 25 marks)

15 Panel

49 mins

ACR, 12/05

The directors of Panel, a public limited company, are reviewing the procedures for the calculation of the deferred tax liability for their company. They are quite surprised at the impact on the liability caused by changes in accounting standards such as IFRS 1 *First time adoption of International Financial Reporting Standards* and IFRS 2 *Share-based payment.* Panel is adopting International Financial Reporting Standards for the first time as at 31 October 20X5 and the directors are unsure how the deferred tax provision will be calculated in its financial statements ended on that date including the opening provision at 1 November 20X3.

Required

(a) (i) Explain how changes in accounting standards are likely to have an impact on the deferred tax liability under IAS 12 *Income taxes.* **(5 marks)**

(ii) Describe the basis for the calculation of the deferred taxation liability on first time adoption of IFRS including the provision in the opening IFRS statement of financial position. **(4 marks)**

Additionally the directors wish to know how the provision for deferred taxation would be calculated in the following situations under IAS 12 *Income taxes*:

(i) On 1 November 20X3, the company had granted ten million share options worth $40 million subject to a two year vesting period. Local tax law allows a tax deduction at the exercise date of the intrinsic value of the options. The intrinsic value of the ten million share options at 31 October 20X4 was $16 million and at 31 October 20X5 was $46 million. The increase in the share price in the year to 31 October 20X5 could not be foreseen at 31 October 20X4. The options were exercised at 31 October 20X5. The directors are unsure how to account for deferred taxation on this transaction for the years ended 31 October 20X4 and 31 October 20X5.

(ii) Panel is leasing plant over a five year period. A right-of-use asset was recorded at the present value of the lease payments of $12 million at the inception of the lease which was 1 November 20X4. The right-of-use asset is depreciated on a straight line basis over the five years. The annual lease payments are $3 million payable in arrears on 31 October and the effective interest rate is 8% per annum. The directors have not leased an asset before and are unsure as to its treatment for deferred taxation. The company can claim a tax deduction for the annual rental payment as the lease does not qualify for tax relief.

(iii) A wholly owned overseas subsidiary, Pins, a limited liability company, sold goods costing $7 million to Panel on 1 September 20X5, and these goods had not been sold by Panel before the year end. Panel had paid $9 million for these goods. The directors do not understand how this transaction should be dealt with in the financial statements of the subsidiary and the group for taxation purposes. Pins pays tax locally at 30%.

(iv) Nails, a limited liability company, is a wholly owned subsidiary of Panel, and is a cash generating unit in its own right. The value of the property, plant and equipment of Nails at 31 October 20X5 was $6 million and purchased goodwill was $1 million before any impairment loss. The company had no other assets or liabilities. An impairment loss of $1.8 million had occurred at 31 October 20X5. The tax base of the property, plant and equipment of Nails was $4 million as at 31 October 20X5. The directors wish to know how the impairment loss will affect the deferred tax liability for the year. Impairment losses are not an allowable expense for taxation purposes.

Assume a tax rate of 30%.

Required

(b) Discuss, with suitable computations, how the situations (i) to (iv) above will impact on the accounting for deferred tax under IAS 12 *Income taxes* in the group financial statements of Panel. **(16 marks)**

(The situations in (i) to (iv) above carry equal marks.) **(Total = 25 marks)**

16 Kesare

49 mins

Pilot paper

The following statement of financial position relates to Kesare Group, a public limited company, at 30 June 20X6.

	$'000
Assets	
Non current assets:	
Property, plant and equipment	10,000
Goodwill	6,000
Other intangible assets	5,000
Financial assets (cost)	9,000
	30,000
Current assets	
Trade receivables	7,000
Other receivables	4,600
Cash and cash equivalents	6,700
	18,300
Total assets	48,300
Equity and liabilities	
Equity	
Share capital	9,000
Other reserves	4,500
Retained earnings	9,130
Total equity	22,630
Non-current liabilities	
Long term borrowings	10,000
Deferred tax liability	3,600
Employee benefit liability	4,000
Total non-current liabilities	17,600
Current liabilities	
Current tax liability	3,070
Trade and other payables	5,000
Total current liabilities	8,070
Total liabilities	25,670
Total equity and liabilities	48,300

The following information is relevant to the above statement of financial position:

(i) The financial assets are classified as 'investments in equity instruments' but are shown in the above statement of financial position at their cost on 1 July 20X5. The market value of the assets is $10.5 million on 30 June 20X6. Taxation is payable on the sale of the assets. As allowed by IFRS 9, an irrevocable election was made for changes in fair value to go through other comprehensive income (not reclassified to profit or loss).

(ii) The stated interest rate for the long term borrowing is 8%. The loan of $10 million represents a convertible bond which has a liability component of $9.6 million and an equity component of $0.4 million. The bond was issued on 30 June 20X6.

(iii) The defined benefit plan had a rule change on 1 July 20X5, giving rise to past service costs of $520,000. The past service costs have not been accounted for.

(iv) The tax bases of the assets and liabilities are the same as their carrying amounts in the draft statement of financial position above as at 30 June 20X6 except for the following:

(1)

	$'000
Property, plant and equipment	2,400
Trade receivables	7,500
Other receivables	5,000
Employee benefits	5,000

(2) Other intangible assets were development costs which were all allowed for tax purposes when the cost was incurred in 20X5.

(3) Trade and other payables includes an accrual for compensation to be paid to employees. This amounts to $1 million and is allowed for taxation when paid.

(v) Goodwill is not allowable for tax purposes in this jurisdiction.

(vi) Assume taxation is payable at 30%.

Required

(a) Discuss the conceptual basis for the recognition of deferred taxation using the temporary difference approach to deferred taxation. **(7 marks)**

(b) Calculate the deferred tax liability at 30 June 20X6 after any necessary adjustments to the financial statements showing how the deferred tax liability would be dealt with in the financial statements. (Assume that any adjustments do not affect current tax. Candidates should briefly discuss the adjustments required to calculate deferred tax liability.) **(18 marks)**

(Total = 25 marks)

Two marks will be awarded for the quality of the discussion of the conceptual basis of deferred taxation in (a).

17 Chemclean **49 mins**

Sep/Dec 15, amended

(a) Chemclean trades in the chemical industry. The entity has development and production operations in various countries. It has entered into an agreement with Jomaster under which Chemclean will licence Jomaster's know-how and technology to manufacture a chemical compound, Volut. The know-how and technology has a fair value of $4m. Chemclean cannot use the know-how and technology for manufacturing any other compound than Volut. Chemclean has not concluded that economic benefits are likely to flow from this compound but will use Jomaster's technology for a period of three years. Chemclean will have to keep updating the technology in accordance with Jomaster's requirements. The agreement stipulates that Chemclean will make a non-refundable payment of $4m to Jomaster for access to the technology. Additionally, Jomaster will also receive a 10% royalty from sales of the chemical compound.

Additionally, Chemclean is interested in another compound, Yacton, which is being developed by Jomaster. The compound is in the second phase of development. The intellectual property of compound Yacton has been put into a newly formed shell company, Conew, which has no employees. The compound is the only asset of Conew. Chemclean is intending to acquire a 65% interest in Conew, which will give it control over the entity and the compound. Chemclean will provide the necessary resources to develop the compound. **(8 marks)**

(b) In the year to 30 June 20X4, Chemclean acquired a major subsidiary. The inventory acquired in this business combination was valued at its fair value at the acquisition date in accordance with IFRS 3 *Business combinations.* The inventory increased in value as a result of the fair value exercise. A significant part of the acquired inventory was sold in the post-acquisition period but before 30 June 20X4, the year end.

In the consolidated statement of profit or loss and other comprehensive income, the cost of inventories acquired in the business combination and sold by the acquirer after the business combination was disclosed on two different lines. The inventory was partly shown as cost of goods sold and partly as a 'non-recurring item' within operating income. The part presented under cost of goods sold corresponded to the inventory's carrying amount in the subsidiary's financial statements. The part presented as a 'non-recurring item' corresponded to the fair value increase recognised on the business combination. The 'non-recurring item' amounted to 25% of Chemclean's earnings before interest and tax (EBIT). Chemclean disclosed the accounting policy and explained in the notes to the financial statements that showing the inventory at fair value would result in a fall in the gross margin due to the fair value increase. Further, Chemclean argued that isolating this part of the margin in the'non-recurring items', whose nature is transparently presented in the notes, enabled the user to evaluate the structural evolution of its gross margin. **(6 marks)**

(c) (i) In the consolidated financial statements for 20X4, Chemclean recognised a net deferred tax asset of $16m, which represented 18% of its total equity. This asset was made up of $3m taxable temporary differences and $19m relating to the carry-forward of unused tax losses. The local tax regulation allows unused tax losses to be carried forward indefinitely. Chemclean expects that within five years, future taxable profits before tax would be available against which the unused tax losses could be offset. This view was based on the budgets for the years 20X4-20X9. The budgets were primarily based on general assumptions about the development of key products and economic improvement indicators. Additionally, the entity expected a substantial reduction in the future impairment of trade receivables and property which the entity had recently suffered and this would result in a substantial increase in future taxable profit.

Chemclean had recognised material losses during the previous five years, with an average annual loss of $19m. A comparison of Chemclean's budgeted results for the previous two years to its actual results indicated material differences relating principally to impairment losses. In the interim financial statements for the first half of the year to 30 June 20X4, Chemclean recognised impairment losses equal to budgeted impairment losses for the whole year. In its financial statements for the year ended 30 June 20X4, Chemclean disclosed a material uncertainty about its ability to continue as a going concern. The current tax rate in the jurisdiction is 30%. **(7 marks)**

(ii) Briefly summarise the IASB's recent amendment to IAS 12 concerning deferred tax assets and unrealised losses. **(2 marks)**

Required

Discuss how the above items should be dealt with in the financial statements of Chemclean under International Financial Reporting Standards.

Note. The mark allocation is shown against each of the three issues above.

Professional marks will be awarded in this question for clarity and quality of the presentation. **(2 marks)**

(Total = 25 marks)

18 Preparation question: Financial instruments

(a) Graben Co purchases a bond for $441,014 on 1 January 20X1. It will be redeemed on 31 December 20X4 for $600,000. The bond is held at amortised cost and carries no coupon.

Required

Calculate the valuation of the bond for the statement of financial position as at 31 December 20X1 and the finance income for 20X1 shown in profit or loss.

Compound sum of $1: $(1 + r)^n$

Year	*2%*	*4%*	*6%*	*8%*	*10%*	*12%*	*14%*
1	1.0200	1.0400	1.0600	1.0800	1.1000	1.1200	1.1400
2	1.0404	1.0816	1.1236	1.1664	1.2100	1.2544	1.2996
3	1.0612	1.1249	1.1910	1.2597	1.3310	1.4049	1.4815
4	1.0824	1.1699	1.2625	1.3605	1.4641	1.5735	1.6890
5	1.1041	1.2167	1.3382	1.4693	1.6105	1.7623	1.9254

(b) Baldie Co issues 4,000 convertible bonds on 1 January 20X2 at par. The bond is redeemable three years later at its par value of $500 per bond, which is its nominal value.

The bonds pay interest annually in arrears at an interest rate (based on nominal value) of 5%. Each bond can be converted at the maturity date into 30 $1 shares.

The prevailing market interest rate for three year bonds that have no right of conversion is 9%.

Required

Show the statement of financial position valuation at 1 January 20X2.

Cumulative three year annuity factors:

5% 2.723
9% 2.531

19 Coatmin **49 mins**

12/14

(a) Coatmin is a government-controlled bank. Coatmin was taken over by the government during the recent financial crisis. Coatmin does not directly trade with other government-controlled banks but has underwritten the development of the nationally owned railway and postal service. The directors of Coatmin are concerned about the volume and cost of disclosing its related party interests because they extend theoretically to all other government-controlled enterprises and banks. They wish general advice on the nature and importance of the disclosure of related party relationships and specific advice on the disclosure of the above relationships in the financial statements.. **(5 marks)**

(b) At the start of the financial year to 30 November 20X3, Coatmin gave a financial guarantee contract on behalf of one of its subsidiaries, a charitable organisation, committing it to repay the principal amount of $60 million if the subsidiary defaulted on any payments due under a loan. The loan related to the financing of the construction of new office premises and has a term of three years. It is being repaid by equal annual instalments of principal with the first payment having been paid. Coatmin has not secured any compensation in return for giving the guarantee, but assessed that it had a fair value of $1·2 million. The guarantee is measured at fair value through profit or loss. The guarantee was given on the basis that it was probable that it would not be called upon. At 30 November 20X4, Coatmin became aware of the fact that the subsidiary was having financial difficulties with the result that it has not paid the second instalment of principal. It is assessed that it is probable that the guarantee will now be called. However, just before the signing of the financial statements for the year ended 30 November 20X4, the subsidiary secured a donation which enabled it to make the second repayment before the guarantee was called upon. It is now anticipated that the subsidiary will be able to meet the final payment. Discounting is immaterial and the fair value of the guarantee is higher than amount of the loss allowance determined in accordance with the IFRS 9 (revised July 2014) rules on expected credit losses. Coatmin wishes to know the principles behind accounting for the above guarantee under IFRS and how the transaction would be accounted for in the financial records. **(7 marks)**

(c) Coatmin's creditworthiness has been worsening but it has entered into an interest rate swap agreement which acts as a hedge against a $2 million 2% bond issue which matures on 31 May 20X6. Coatmin wishes to know the circumstances in which it can use hedge accounting. In particular, it needs advice on hedge effectiveness and whether this can be calculated. **(7 marks)**

(d) Coatmin provides loans to customers and funds the loans by selling bonds in the market. The liability is designated as at fair value through profit or loss. The bonds have a fair value decrease of $50 million in the year to 30 November 20X4 of which $5 million relates to the reduction in Coatmin's creditworthiness. The directors of Coatmin would like advice on how to account for this movement. **(4 marks)**

Required

Discuss, with suitable calculations where necessary, the accounting treatment of the above transactions in the financial statements of Coatmin.

Note. The mark allocation is shown against each of the questions above.

Professional marks will be awarded in this question for clarity and quality of the presentation. **(2 marks)**

(Total = 25 marks)

20 Avco **49 mins**

6/14 amended

(a) The difference between debt and equity in an entity's statement of financial position is not easily distinguishable for preparers of financial statements. Some financial instruments may have both features, which can lead to inconsistency of reporting. The International Accounting Standards Board (IASB) has agreed that greater clarity may be required in its definitions of assets and liabilities for debt instruments. It is thought that defining the nature of liabilities would help the IASB's thinking on the difference between financial instruments classified as equity and liabilities.

Required

(i) Discuss the key classification differences between debt and equity under International Financial Reporting Standards.

Note. Examples should be given to illustrate your answer. **(9 marks)**

(ii) Explain why it is important for entities to understand the impact of the classification of a financial instrument as debt or equity in the financial statements. **(5 marks)**

(b) The directors of Avco, a public limited company, are reviewing the financial statements of two entities which are acquisition targets, Cavor and Lidan.They have asked for clarification on the treatment of the following financial instruments within the financial statements of the entities.

Cavor has two classes of shares: A and B shares. A shares are Cavor's ordinary shares and are correctly classed as equity. B shares are not mandatorily redeemable shares but contain a call option allowing Cavor to repurchase them. Dividends are payable on the B shares if, and only if, dividends have been paid on the A ordinary shares. The terms of the B shares are such that dividends are payable at a rate equal to that of the A ordinary shares. Additionally, Cavor has also issued share options which give the counterparty rights to buy a fixed number of its B shares for a fixed amount of $10 million. The contract can be settled only by the issuance of shares for cash by Cavor.

Lidan has in issue two classes of shares: A shares and B shares. A shares are correctly classified as equity. Two million B shares of nominal value of $1 each are in issue. The B shares are redeemable in two years' time. Lidan has a choice as to the method of redemption of the B shares. It may either redeem the B shares for cash at their nominal value or it may issue one million A shares in settlement. A shares are currently valued at $10 per share. The lowest price for Lidan's A shares since its formation has been $5 per share.

Required

Discuss whether the above arrangements regarding the B shares of each of Cavor and Lidan should be treated as liabilities or equity in the financial statements of the respective issuing companies. **(9 marks)**

Professional marks will be awarded in this question for clarity and quality of presentation. **(2 marks)**

(Total = 25 marks)

21 Complexity

49 mins

12/09

The definition of a financial instrument captures a wide variety of assets and liabilities including cash, evidence of an ownership interest in an entity, or a contractual right to receive or deliver cash or another financial instrument. Preparers, auditors and users of financial statements have found the requirements for reporting financial assets and liabilities to be very complex, problematical and sometimes subjective. The result is that there is a need to develop new standards of reporting for financial instruments that are principle-based and significantly less complex than current requirements. It is important that a standard in this area should allow users to understand the economic substance of the transaction and preparers to properly apply generally accepted accounting principles.

Required

(a) (i) Discuss how the measurement of financial instruments under International Financial Reporting Standards can create confusion and complexity for preparers and users of financial statements. **(9 marks)**

(ii) Set out the reasons why using fair value to measure all financial instruments may result in less complexity in accounting for financial instruments, but may lead to uncertainty in financial statements. **(9 marks)**

Professional marks will be awarded in part (a) for clarity and expression. **(2 marks)**

(b) A company borrowed $47 million on 1 December 20X4 when the market and effective interest rate was 5%. On 30 November 20X5, the company borrowed an additional $45 million when the current market and effective interest rate was 7.4%. Both financial liabilities are repayable on 30 November 20X9 and are single payment notes, whereby interest and capital are repaid on that date.

Required

Discuss the accounting for the above financial liabilities under current accounting standards using amortised cost, and additionally using fair value as at 30 November 20X5. **(5 marks)**

(Total = 25 marks)

22 Preparation question: Leases

Sugar Co leased a machine from Spice Co. The terms of the lease are as follows:

Inception of lease	1 January 20X1
Lease term	4 years at $78,864 per annum payable in arrears
Present value of future lease payments	$250,000
Useful life of asset	4 years

Required

(a) Calculate the interest rate implicit in the lease, using the table below.

This table shows the cumulative present value of $1 per annum, receivable or payable at the end of each year for n years.

Years (n)		*Interest rates*	
	6%	*8%*	*10%*
1	0.943	0.926	0.909
2	1.833	1.783	1.736
3	2.673	2.577	2.487
4	3.465	3.312	3.170
5	4.212	3.993	3.791

(b) Prepare the extracts from the financial statements of Sugar Co for the year ended 31 December 20X1. Notes to the accounts are not required.

23 Havanna

49 mins

12/13, amended

(a) Havanna owns a chain of health clubs and has entered into binding contracts with sports organisations, which earn income over given periods. The services rendered in return for such income include access to Havanna's database of members, and admission to health clubs, including the provision of coaching and other benefits. These contracts are for periods of between nine and 18 months. Havanna feels that because it only assumes limited obligations under the contract mainly relating to the provision of coaching, this could not be seen as the rendering of services for accounting purposes. As a result, Havanna's accounting policy for revenue recognition is to recognise the contract income in full at the date when the contract was signed. **(6 marks)**

(b) In May 20X3, Havanna decided to sell one of its regional business divisions through a mixed asset and share deal. The decision to sell the division at a price of $40 million was made public in November 20X3 and gained shareholder approval in December 20X3. It was decided that the payment of any agreed sale price could be deferred until 30 November 20X5. The business division was presented as a disposal group in the statement of financial position as at 30 November 20X3. At the initial classification of the division as held for sale, its net carrying amount was $90 million. In writing down the disposal group's carrying amount, Havanna accounted for an impairment loss of $30 million which represented the difference between the carrying amount and value of the assets measured in accordance with applicable International Financial Reporting Standards (IFRS).

In the financial statements at 30 November 20X3, Havanna showed the following costs as provisions relating to the continuing operations. These costs were related to the business division being sold and were as follows.

(i) A loss relating to a potential write-off of a trade receivable owed by Cuba Sport, which had gone into liquidation. Cuba Sport had sold the goods to a third party and the division had guaranteed the receipt of the sale proceeds to the Head Office of Havanna

(ii) An expense relating to the discounting of the long-term receivable on the fixed amount of the sale price of the disposal group

(iii) A provision was charged which related to the expected transaction costs of the sale including legal advice and lawyer fees

The directors wish to know how to treat the above transactions. **(9 marks)**

(c) (i) Havanna has decided to sell its main office building to a third party for $5 million and lease it back on a ten-year lease. The current fair value of the property is $5 million and the carrying value of the asset is $4.2 million. The present value of the lease payments has been calculated as $3.85 million. The remaining useful life of the building is fifteen years. The transaction constitutes a sale in accordance with IFRS 15 *Revenue from contracts with customers.*

Havanna would like advice on how to account for this sale at the start of the lease, including any gain on the sale. **(5 marks)**

(ii) The market for property is uncertain in the jurisdiction, and Havanna therefore requires guidance on the consequences of selling the office building at prices other than the $5 million fair value. Havanna would like a brief statement of the difference it would make if the sale price were:

(1) $6 million
(2) $4 million **(3 marks)**

Required

Advise Havanna on how the above transactions should be dealt with in its financial statements with reference to International Financial Reporting Standards where appropriate.

Note. The mark allocation is shown against each of the three issues above.

Professional marks will be awarded in this question for clarity and quality of the presentation. **(2 marks)**

(Total = 25 marks)

24 William

49 mins

6/12, amended

William is a public limited company and would like advice in relation to the following transactions.

(a) William owned a building on which it raised finance. William sold the building for $6 million, its fair value, to a finance company on 1 June 20X2 when the carrying amount was $3.6 million. The same building was leased back from the finance company for a period of 20 years. The remaining useful life of the building is 25 years. The lease rentals for the period are $441,000 payable annually in arrears. The interest rate implicit in the lease is 7%. The present value of the lease payments is $5 million. The transaction constitutes a sale in accordance with IFRS 15 *Revenue from contracts with customers.*

William wishes to know how to account for the above transaction for the year ended 31 May 20X3.

(7 marks)

(b) William operates a defined benefit pension plan for its employees. Shortly before the year end of 31 May 20X3, William decided to relocate a division from one country to another, where labour and raw material costs are cheaper. The relocation is due to take place in December 20X3. On 13 May 20X3, a detailed formal plan was approved by the board of directors. Half of the affected division's employees will be made redundant in July 20X3, and will accrue no further benefits under William's defined benefit pension plan. The affected employees were informed of this decision on 14 May 20X3. The resulting reduction in the net pension liability due the relocation is estimated to have a present value of $15 million as at 31 May 20X3. Total relocation costs (excluding the impact on the pension plan) are estimated at $50 million.

William requires advice on how to account for the relocation costs and the reduction in the net pension liability for the year ended 31 May 20X3. **(7 marks)**

(c) On 1 June 20X0, William granted 500 share appreciation rights to each of its twenty managers. All of the rights vest after two years' service and they can be exercised during the following two years up to 31 May 20X4. The fair value of the right at the grant date was $20. It was thought that three managers would leave over the initial two-year period and they did so. The fair value of each right was as follows.

Year	*Fair value at the year-end ($)*
31 May 20X1	23
31 May 20X2	14
31 May 20X3	24

On 31 May 20X3, seven managers exercised their rights when the intrinsic value of the right was $21.

William wishes to know what the liability and expense will be at 31 May 20X3. **(5 marks)**

(d) William acquired another entity, Chrissy, on 1 May 20X3. At the time of the acquisition, Chrissy was being sued as there is an alleged mis-selling case potentially implicating the entity. The claimants are suing for damages of $10 million. William estimates that the fair value of any contingent liability is $4 million and feels that it is more likely than not that no outflow of funds will occur.

William wishes to know how to account for this potential liability in Chrissy's entity financial statements and whether the treatment would be the same in the consolidated financial statements. **(4 marks)**

Required

Discuss, with suitable computations, the advice that should be given to William in accounting for the above events.

Note. The mark allocation is shown against each of the four events above.

Professional marks will be awarded for the quality of the discussion. **(2 marks)**

(Total = 25 marks)

25 Leigh

49 mins

ACR, 6/07

(a) Leigh, a public limited company, purchased the whole of the share capital of Hash, a limited company, on 1 June 20X6. The whole of the share capital of Hash was formerly owned by the five directors of Hash and under the terms of the purchase agreement, the five directors were to receive a total of three million ordinary shares of $1 of Leigh on 1 June 20X6 (market value $6 million) and a further 5,000 shares per director on 31 May 20X7, if they were still employed by Leigh on that date. All of the directors were still employed by Leigh at 31 May 20X7.

Leigh granted and issued fully paid shares to its own employees on 31 May 20X7. Normally share options issued to employees would vest over a three year period, but these shares were given as a bonus because of the company's exceptional performance over the period. The shares in Leigh had a market value of $3 million (one million ordinary shares of $1 at $3 per share) on 31 May 20X7 and an average fair value of $2.5 million (one million ordinary shares of $1 at $2.50 per share) for the year ended 31 May 20X7. It is expected that Leigh's share price will rise to $6 per share over the next three years. **(10 marks)**

(b) On 31 May 20X7, Leigh purchased property, plant and equipment for $4 million. The supplier has agreed to accept payment for the property, plant and equipment either in cash or in shares. The supplier can either choose 1.5 million shares of the company to be issued in six months time or to receive a cash payment in three months time equivalent to the market value of 1.3 million shares. It is estimated that the share price will be $3.50 in three months time and $4 in six months time.

Additionally, at 31 May 20X7, one of the directors recently appointed to the board has been granted the right to choose either 50,000 shares of Leigh or receive a cash payment equal to the current value of 40,000 shares at the settlement date. This right has been granted because of the performance of the director during the year and is unconditional at 31 May 20X7. The settlement date is 1 July 20X8 and the company estimates the fair value of the share alternative is $2.50 per share at 31 May 20X7. The share price of Leigh at 31 May 20X7 is $3 per share, and if the director chooses the share alternative, they must be kept for a period of four years. **(9 marks)**

(c) Leigh acquired 30% of the ordinary share capital of Handy, a public limited company, on 1 April 20X6. The purchase consideration was one million ordinary shares of Leigh which had a market value of $2.50 per share at that date and the fair value of the net assets of Handy was $9 million. The retained earnings of Handy were $4 million and other reserves of Handy were $3 million at that date. Leigh appointed two directors to the Board of Handy, and it intends to hold the investment for a significant period of time. Leigh exerts significant influence over Handy. The summarised statement of financial position of Handy at 31 May 20X7 is as follows.

	$m
Share capital of $1	2
Other reserves	3
Retained earnings	5
	10
Net assets	10

There had been no new issues of shares by Handy since the acquisition by Leigh and the estimated recoverable amount of the net assets of Handy at 31 May 20X7 was $11 million. **(6 marks)**

Required

Discuss with suitable computations how the above share-based transactions should be accounted for in the financial statements of Leigh for the year ended 31 May 20X7.

(Total = 25 marks)

26 Zack **49 mins**

12/13

(a) Due to the complexity of International Financial Reporting Standards (IFRS), often judgements used at the time of transition to IFRS have resulted in prior period adjustments and changes in estimates being disclosed in financial statements. The selection of accounting policy and estimation techniques is intended to aid comparability and consistency in financial statements. However, IFRS also place particular emphasis on the need to take into account qualitative characteristics and the use of professional judgement when preparing the financial statements. Although IFRS may appear prescriptive, the achievement of all the objectives for a set of financial statements will rely on the skills of the preparer. Entities should follow the requirements of IAS 8 *Accounting policies, changes in accounting estimates and errors* when selecting or changing accounting policies, changing estimation techniques, and correcting errors.

However, the application of IAS 8 is additionally often dependent upon the application of materiality analysis to identify issues and guide reporting. Entities also often consider the acceptability of the use of hindsight in their reporting.

Required

(i) Discuss how judgement and materiality play a significant part in the selection of an entity's accounting policies.

(ii) Discuss the circumstances where an entity may change its accounting policies, setting out how a change of accounting policy is applied and the difficulties faced by entities where a change in accounting policy is made.

(iii) Discuss why the current treatment of prior period errors could lead to earnings management by companies, together with any further arguments against the current treatment.

Credit will be given for relevant examples.

Note. The total marks will be split equally between each part. **(15 marks)**

(b) In 20X3, Zack, a public limited company, commenced construction of a shopping centre. It considers that in order to fairly recognise the costs of its property, plant and equipment, it needs to enhance its accounting policies by capitalising borrowing costs incurred whilst the shopping centre is under construction. A review of past transactions suggests that there has been one other project involving assets with substantial construction periods where there would be a material misstatement of the asset balance if borrowing costs were not capitalised. This project was completed in the year ended 30 November 20X2. Previously, Zack had expensed the borrowing costs as they were incurred. The borrowing costs which could be capitalised are $2 million for the 20X2 asset and $3 million for the 20X3 asset.

A review of the depreciation schedules of the larger plant and equipment not affected by the above has resulted in Zack concluding that the basis on which these assets are depreciated would better reflect the resources consumed if calculations were on a reducing balance basis, rather than a straight-line basis. The revision would result in an increase in depreciation for the year to 30 November 20X2 of $5 million, an increase for the year end 30 November 20X3 of $6 million and an estimated increase for the year ending 30 November 20X4 of $8 million.

Additionally, Zack has discovered that its accruals systems for year-end creditors for the financial year

30 November 20X2 processed certain accruals twice in the ledger. This meant that expenditure services were overstated in the financial statements by $2 million. However, Zack has since reviewed its final accounts systems and processes and has made appropriate changes and introduced additional internal controls to ensure that such estimation problems are unlikely to recur.

All of the above transactions are material to Zack.

Required

Discuss how the above events should be shown in the financial statements of Zack for the year ended 30 November 20X3. **(8 marks)**

Professional marks will be awarded in this question for clarity and quality of presentation. **(2 marks)**

(Total = 25 marks)

27 Minco

49 mins

6/14, amended

(a) Minco is a major property developer. On 1 June 20X3, Minco entered into a contract with Holistic Healthco for the sale of a building for $3 million. Holistic Healthco intends to use the building as a fitness and leisure centre. The building is located in a busy city, where there are many gyms and leisure centres. Holistic Healthco's experience to date has been in stores selling health foods and aromatherapy oils, and it has no experience of the fitness industry.

Holistic Healthco paid Minco a non-refundable deposit of $150,000 on 1 June 20X3 and entered into a long-term financing agreement with Minco for the remaining 95 per cent of the promised consideration. The terms of the financing arrangement are that if Holistic Healthco defaults, Minco can repossess the building, but cannot seek further compensation from Holistic Healthco, even if the collateral does not cover the full value of the amount owed. The building cost Minco $1.8m to construct. Holistic Healthco obtained control of the building on 1 June 20X3.

Minco argues that this contract falls within the scope of IFRS 15 *Revenue from contracts with customers,* and that the non-refundable deposit should be recognised as revenue. **(7 marks)**

(b) Minco often sponsors professional tennis players in an attempt to improve its brand image. At the moment, it has a three-year agreement with a tennis player who is currently ranked in the world's top ten players. The agreement is that the player receives a signing bonus of $20,000 and earns an annual amount of $50,000, paid at the end of each year for three years, provided that the player has competed in all the specified tournaments for each year. If the player wins a major tournament, she receives a bonus of 20% of the prize money won at the tournament. In return, the player is required to wear advertising logos on tennis apparel, play a specified number of tournaments and attend photo/film sessions for advertising purposes. The different payments are not interrelated. **(5 marks)**

(c) Minco leased its head office during the current accounting period and the agreement terminates in six years' time.

There is a clause in the lease relating to the internal condition of the property at the termination of the lease. The clause states that the internal condition of the property should be identical to that at the outset of the lease. Minco has improved the building by adding another floor to part of the building during the current accounting period. There is also a clause which enables the landlord to recharge Minco for costs relating to the general disrepair of the building at the end of the lease. In addition, the landlord can recharge any costs of repairing the roof immediately. The landlord intends to replace part of the roof of the building during the current period. **(5 marks)**

(d) On 1 June 20X1, Minco acquired a property for $5 million and annual depreciation of $500,000 is charged on the straight line basis with no residual value. At the end of the previous financial year of 31 May 20X3, when accumulated depreciation was $1 million, a further amount relating to an impairment loss of $350,000 was recognised, which resulted in the property being valued at its estimated value in use. On 1 October 20X3, as a consequence of a proposed move to new premises, the property was classified as held for sale. At the time of classification as held for sale, the fair value less costs to sell was $3·4 million. At the date of the published interim financial statements, 1 December 20X3, the property market had improved and the fair value less costs to sell was reassessed at $3·52 million and at the year-end on 31 May 20X4 it had improved even further, so that the fair value less costs to sell was $3·95 million. The property was sold on 5 June 20X4 for $4 million. **(6 marks)**

Required

Discuss how the above items should be dealt with in the financial statements of Minco.

Note. The mark allocation is shown against each of the four issues above.

Professional marks will be awarded in this question for clarity and quality of presentation. **(2 marks)**

(Total = 25 marks)

28 Alexandra

49 mins

6/11

Alexandra, a public limited company, designs and manages business solutions and infrastructures.

(a) In November 20X0, Alexandra defaulted on an interest payment on an issued bond loan of $100 million repayable in 20X5. The loan agreement stipulates that such default leads to an obligation to repay the whole of the loan immediately, including accrued interest and expenses. The bondholders, however, issued a waiver postponing the interest payment until 31 May 20X1. On 17 May 20X1, Alexandra felt that a further waiver was required, so requested a meeting of the bondholders and agreed a further waiver of the interest payment to 5 July 20X1, when Alexandra was confident it could make the payments. Alexandra classified the loan as long-term debt in its statement of financial position at 30 April 20X1 on the basis that the loan was not in default at the end of the reporting period as the bondholders had issued waivers and had not sought redemption. **(6 marks)**

(b) Alexandra enters into contracts with both customers and suppliers. The supplier solves system problems and provides new releases and updates for software. Alexandra provides maintenance services for its customers. In previous years, Alexandra recognised revenue and related costs on software maintenance contracts when the customer was invoiced, which was at the beginning of the contract period. Contracts typically run for two years.

During 20X0, Alexandra had acquired Xavier Co, which recognised revenue, derived from a similar type of maintenance contract as Alexandra, on a straight-line basis over the term of the contract. Alexandra considered both its own and the policy of Xavier Co to comply with the requirements of IFRS 15 *Revenue from contracts with customers* but it decided to adopt the practice of Xavier Co for itself and the group. Alexandra concluded that the two recognition methods did not, in substance, represent two different accounting policies and did not, therefore, consider adoption of the new practice to be a change in policy.

In the year to 30 April 20X1, Alexandra recognised revenue (and the related costs) on a straight-line basis over the contract term, treating this as a change in an accounting estimate. As a result, revenue and cost of sales were adjusted, reducing the year's profits by some $6 million. **(5 marks)**

(c) Alexandra has a two-tier board structure consisting of a management and a supervisory board. Alexandra remunerates its board members as follows:

- Annual base salary
- Variable annual compensation (bonus)
- Share options

In the group financial statements, within the related parties note under IAS 24 *Related party disclosures*, Alexandra disclosed the total remuneration paid to directors and non-executive directors and a total for each of these boards. No further breakdown of the remuneration was provided.

The management board comprises both the executive and non-executive directors. The remuneration of the non-executive directors, however, was not included in the key management disclosures. Some members of the supervisory and management boards are of a particular nationality. Alexandra was of the opinion that in that jurisdiction, it is not acceptable to provide information about remuneration that could be traced back to individuals. Consequently, Alexandra explained that it had provided the related party information in the annual accounts in an ambiguous way to prevent users of the financial statements from tracing remuneration information back to specific individuals. **(5 marks)**

(d) Alexandra's pension plan was accounted for as a defined benefit plan in 20X0. In the year ended 30 April 20X1, Alexandra changed the accounting method used for the scheme and accounted for it as a defined contribution plan, restating the comparative 20X0 financial information. The effect of the restatement was significant. In the 20X1 financial statements, Alexandra explained that, during the year, the arrangements underlying the retirement benefit plan had been subject to detailed review. Since the pension liabilities are fully insured and indexation of future liabilities can be limited up to and including the funds available in a special trust account set up for the plan, which is not at the disposal of Alexandra, the plan qualifies as a defined contribution plan under IAS 19 *Employee benefits* rather than a defined benefit plan. Furthermore, the trust account is built up by the insurance company from the surplus yield on investments. The pension plan is an average pay plan in respect of which the entity pays insurance premiums to a third party insurance company to fund the plan. Every year 1% of the pension fund is built up and employees pay a contribution of 4% of their salary, with the employer paying the balance of the contribution. If an employee leaves Alexandra and transfers the pension to another fund, Alexandra is liable for, or is refunded the difference between the benefits the employee is entitled to and the insurance premiums paid. **(7 marks)**

Professional marks will be awarded in this question for clarity and quality of discussion. **(2 marks)**

Required

Discuss how the above transactions should be dealt with in the financial statements of Alexandra for the year ended 30 April 20X1. **(Total = 25 marks)**

29 Klancet **49 mins**

6/15

Klancet, a public limited company, is a pharmaceutical company and is seeking advice on several financial reporting issues.

(a) Klancet produces and sells its range of drugs through three separate divisions. In addition, there are two laboratories which carry out research and development activities.

In the first of these laboratories, the research and development activity is funded internally and centrally for each of the three sales divisions. It does not carry out research and development activities for other entities. Each of the three divisions is given a budget allocation which it uses to purchase research and development activities from the laboratory. The laboratory is directly accountable to the division heads for this expenditure.

The second laboratory performs contract investigation activities for other laboratories and pharmaceutical companies. This laboratory earns 75% of its revenues from external customers and these external revenues represent 18% of the organisation's total revenues.

The performance of the second laboratory's activities and of the three separate divisions is regularly reviewed by the chief operating decision maker (CODM). In addition to the heads of divisions, there is a head of the second laboratory. The head of the second laboratory is directly accountable to the CODM and they discuss the operating activities, allocation of resources and financial results of the laboratory.

Klancet is uncertain as to whether the research and development laboratories should be reported as two separate segments under IFRS 8 *Operating segments*, and would like advice on this issue. **(8 marks)**

(b) Klancet has agreed to sell a patent right to another pharmaceutical group, Jancy. Jancy would like to use the patent to develop a more complex drug. Klancet will receive publicly listed shares of the Jancy group in exchange for the right. The value of the listed shares represents the fair value of the patent. If Jancy is successful in developing a drug and bringing it to the market, Klancet will also receive a 5% royalty on all sales.

Additionally, Klancet won a competitive bidding arrangement to acquire a patent. The purchase price was settled by Klancet issuing new publicly listed shares of its own.

Klancet's management would like advice on how to account for the above transactions. **(7 marks)**

(c) Klancet is collaborating with Retto Laboratories (Retto), a third party, to develop two existing drugs owned by Klancet.

In the case of the first drug, Retto is simply developing the drug for Klancet without taking any risks during the development phase and will have no further involvement if regulatory approval is given. Regulatory approval has been refused for this drug in the past. Klancet will retain ownership of patent rights attached to the drug. Retto is not involved in the marketing and production of the drug. Klancet has agreed to make two non-refundable payments to Retto of $4 million on the signing of the agreement and $6 million on successful completion of the development.

Klancet and Retto have entered into a second collaboration agreement in which Klancet will pay Retto for developing and manufacturing an existing drug. The existing drug already has regulatory approval. The new drug being developed by Retto for Klancet will not differ substantially from the existing drug. Klancet will have exclusive marketing rights to the drug if the regulatory authorities approve it. Historically, in this jurisdiction, new drugs receive approval if they do not differ substantially from an existing approved drug.

The contract terms require Klancet to pay an upfront payment on signing of the contract, a payment on securing final regulatory approval, and a unit payment of $10 per unit, which equals the estimated cost plus a profit margin, once commercial production begins. The cost-plus profit margin is consistent with Klancet's other recently negotiated supply arrangements for similar drugs.

Klancet would like to know how to deal with the above contracts with Retto. **(8 marks)**

Required

Advise Klancet on how the above transactions should be dealt with in its financial statements with reference to relevant International Financial Reporting Standards.

Note. The mark allocation is shown against each of the three issues above.

Professional marks will be awarded in this question for clarity and quality of presentation **(2 marks)**

(Total = 25 marks)

30 Cloud **49 mins**

6/15

(a) IAS 1 *Presentation of financial statements* defines profit or loss and other comprehensive income. The purpose of the statement of profit or loss and other comprehensive income is to show an entity's financial performance in a way which is useful to a wide range of users so that they may attempt to assess the future net cash inflows of an entity. The statement should be classified and aggregated in a manner which makes it understandable and comparable. However, the International Integrated Reporting Council (IIRC) is calling for a shift in thinking more to the long term, to think beyond what can be measured in quantitative terms and to think about how the entity creates value for its owners. Historical financial statements are essential in corporate reporting, particularly for compliance purposes, but it can be argued that they do not provide meaningful information. Preparers of financial statements seem to be unclear about the interaction between profit or loss and other comprehensive income (OCI) especially regarding the notion of reclassification, but are equally uncertain about whether the IIRC's *Framework* constitutes suitable criteria for report preparation. The International Accounting Standards Board (IASB) has tried to clarify what distinguishes recognised items of income and expense which are presented in profit or loss from items of income and expense presented in OCI.

Required

(i) Describe the current presentation requirements relating to the statement of profit or loss and other comprehensive income. **(4 marks)**

(ii) Discuss, with examples, the nature of a reclassification adjustment and the arguments for and against allowing reclassification of items to profit or loss.

Note. A brief reference should be made in your answer to the IASB's Exposure Draft on the *Conceptual Framework.* **(5 marks)**

(iii) Discuss the principles and key components of the IIRC's *Framework,* and any concerns which could question the Framework's suitability for assessing the prospects of an entity. **(8 marks)**

(b) Cloud, a public limited company, regularly purchases steel from a foreign supplier and designates a future purchase of steel as a hedged item in a cash flow hedge. The steel was purchased on 1 May 20X4 and at that date, a cumulative gain on the hedging instrument of $3 million had been credited to other comprehensive income. At the year end of 30 April 20X5, the carrying amount of the steel was $8 million and its net realisable value was $6 million. The steel was finally sold on 3 June 20X5 for $6·2 million. On a separate issue, Cloud purchased an item of property, plant and equipment for $10 million on 1 May 20X3. The asset is depreciated over five years on the straight line basis with no residual value. At 30 April 20X4, the asset

was revalued to $12 million. At 30 April 20X5, the asset's value has fallen to $4 million. The entity makes a transfer from revaluation surplus to retained earnings for excess depreciation, as the asset is used.

Required

Show how the above transactions would be dealt with in the financial statements of Cloud from the date of the purchase of the assets.

Note. Candidates should ignore any deferred taxation effects. **(6 marks)**

Professional marks will be awarded in the question for clarity and quality of presentation. **(2 marks)**

(Total = 25 marks)

31 Calcula — 49 mins

Asha Alexander has recently been appointed as the CEO of Calcula plc. The company develops specialist software for use by accountancy professionals. The specialist software market is particularly dynamic and fast changing. It is common for competitors to drop out of the market place. The most successful companies have been particularly focused on enhancing their offering to customers through creating innovative products and investing heavily in training and development for their employees.

Turbulent times

Calcula has been through a turbulent time over the last three years. During this time there have been significant senior management changes which resulted in confusion among shareholders and employees as to the strategic direction of the company. One investor complained that the annual accounts made it hard to know where the company was headed.

The last CEO introduced an aggressive cost-cutting programme aimed at improving profitability. At the beginning of the financial year the annual staff training and development budget was significantly reduced and has not been reviewed since the change in management.

Future direction

In response to the confusion surrounding the company's strategic direction, Asha and the board published a new mission, the primary focus of which centres on making Calcula the market leader of specialist accountancy software. Asha was appointed as the CEO having undertaken a similar role at a competitor. The board were keen on her appointment as she is renowned in the industry for her creativity and willingness to introduce 'fresh ideas'. In her previous role Asha oversaw the introduction of an integrated approach to reporting performance. This is something she is particularly keen to introduce at Calcula.

During the company's last board meeting, Asha was dismayed by the finance director's reaction when she proposed introducing integrated reporting at Calcula. The finance director made it clear that he was not convinced of the need for such a change, arguing that 'all this talk of integrated reporting in the business press is just a fad, requiring a lot more work, simply to report on things people do not care about. Shareholders are only interested in the bottom line'.

Required

(a) Discuss what is meant by 'integrated reporting', highlighting how it differs from traditional performance reporting. **(10 marks)**

(b) How may integrated reporting help Calcula to communicate its strategy and improve the company's strategic performance? Your answer should make reference to the concerns raised by the finance director. **(10 marks)**

(c) Advise on the likely implications of introducing 'integrated reporting' which Calcula should consider before deciding to proceed with its adoption. **(5 marks)**

(Total = 25 marks)

32 Egin Group

49 mins

ACR, 6/06

On 1 June 20X5, Egin, a public limited company, was formed out of the reorganisation of a group of companies with foreign operations. The directors require advice on the disclosure of related party information but are reluctant to disclose information as they feel that such transactions are a normal feature of business and need not be disclosed.

Under the new group structure, Egin owns 80% of Briars, 60% of Doye, and 30% of Eye. Egin exercises significant influence over Eye. The directors of Egin are also directors of Briars and Doye but only one director of Egin sits on the management board of Eye. The management board of Eye comprises five directors. Originally the group comprised five companies but the fifth company, Tang, which was a 70% subsidiary of Egin, was sold on 31 January 20X6. There were no transactions between Tang and the Egin Group during the year to 31 May 20X6. 30% of the shares of Egin are owned by another company, Atomic, which exerts significant influence over Egin. The remaining 40% of the shares of Doye are owned by Spade, which exerts significant influence over Doye.

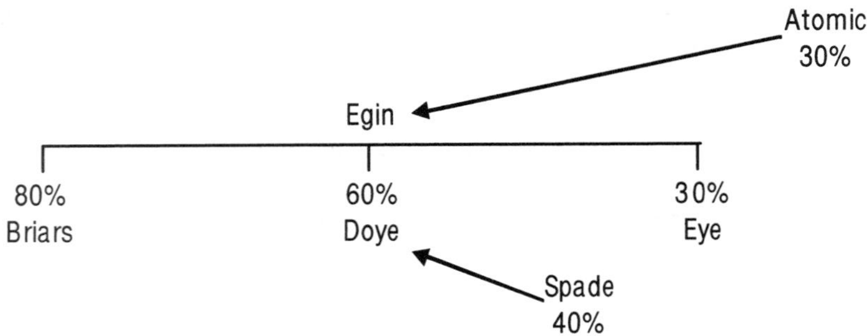

During the current financial year to 31 May 20X6, Doye has sold a significant amount of plant and equipment to Spade at the normal selling price for such items. The directors of Egin have proposed that where related party relationships are determined and sales are at normal selling price, any disclosures will state that prices charged to related parties are made on an arm's length basis.

The directors are unsure how to treat certain transactions relating to their foreign subsidiary, Briars. Egin purchased 80% of the ordinary share capital of Briars on 1 June 20X5 for 50 million euros when its net assets were fair valued at 45 million euros. At 31 May 20X6, it is established that goodwill is impaired by 3 million euros. Additionally, at the date of acquisition, Egin had made an interest free loan to Briars of $10 million. The loan is to be repaid on 31 May 20X7. An equivalent loan would normally carry an interest rate of 6% taking into account Briars' credit rating.

The exchange rates were as follows:

	Euros to $
1 June 20X5	2
31 May 20X6	2.5
Average rate for year	2.3

Financial liabilities of the group are normally measured at amortised cost.

One of the directors of Briars who is not on the management board of Egin owns the whole of the share capital of a company, Blue, that sells goods at market price to Briars. The director is in charge of the production at Briars and also acts as a consultant to the management board of the group.

Required

(a) (i) Discuss why it is important to disclose related party transactions, explaining the criteria which determine a related party relationship. **(5 marks)**

(ii) Describe the nature of any related party relationships and transactions which exists:

(1) Within the Egin Group including Tang **(5 marks)**

(2) Between Spade and the Egin Group **(3 marks)**

(3) Between Atomic and the Egin Group **(3 marks)**

commenting on whether transactions should be described as being at 'arm's length'.

(b) Describe with suitable calculations how the goodwill arising on the acquisition of Briars will be dealt with in the group financial statements and how the loan to Briars should be treated in the financial statements of Briars for the year ended 31 May 20X6. **(9 marks)**

(Total = 25 marks)

33 Preparation question: Control

(a) IFRS 10 *Consolidated financial statements* was published in 2011. It retained control from its predecessor IAS 27 as the key concept underlying the parent/subsidiary relationship but it broadened the definition and clarified its application.

Explain the circumstances in which an investor controls an investee according to IFRS 10

(b) Twist holds 40% of the voting rights of Oliver and twelve other investors each hold 5% of the voting rights of Oliver. A shareholder agreement grants Twist the right to appoint, remove and set the remuneration of management responsible for directing the relevant activities. To change the agreement, a two-thirds majority vote of the shareholders is required. To date, Twist has not exercised its rights with regard to the management or activities of Oliver.

Required

Explain whether Twist should consolidate Oliver in accordance with IFRS 10.

(c) Copperfield holds 45% of the voting rights of Spenlow. Murdstone and Steerforth each hold 26% of the voting rights of Spenlow. The remaining voting rights are held by three other shareholders, each holding 1%. There are no other arrangements that affect decision-making.

Required

Explain whether Copperfield should consolidate Spenlow in accordance with IFRS 10.

(d) Scrooge holds 70% of the voting rights of Cratchett. Marley has 30% of the voting rights of Cratchett. Marley also has an option to acquire half of Scrooge's voting rights, which is exercisable for the next two years, but at a fixed price that is deeply out of the money (and is expected to remain so for that two-year period).

Required

Explain whether either of Scrooge or Marley should consolidate Cratchett in accordance with IFRS 10.

34 Marrgrett

49 mins

12/08

Marrgrett, a public limited company, is currently planning to acquire and sell interests in other entities and has asked for advice on the impact of IFRS 3 (Revised) *Business combinations*. The company is particularly concerned about the impact on earnings, net assets and goodwill at the acquisition date and any ongoing earnings impact that the revised standards may have.

The company is considering purchasing additional shares in an associate, Josey, a public limited company. The holding will increase from 30% stake to 70% stake by offering the shareholders of Josey cash and shares in Marrgrett. Marrgrett anticipates that it will pay $5 million in transaction costs to lawyers and bankers. Josey had previously been the subject of a management buyout. In order that the current management shareholders may remain in the business, Marrgrett is going to offer them share options in Josey subject to them remaining in employment for two years after the acquisition. Additionally, Marrgrett will offer the same shareholders, shares in the holding company which are contingent upon a certain level of profitability being achieved by Josey. Each shareholder will receive shares of the holding company up to a value of $50,000, if Josey achieves a pre-determined rate of return on capital employed for the next two years.

Josey has several marketing-related intangible assets that are used primarily in marketing or promotion of its products. These include trade names, internet domain names and non-competition agreements. These are not currently recognised in Josey's financial statements.

Marrgrett does not wish to measure the non-controlling interest in subsidiaries on the basis of the proportionate interest in the identifiable net assets, but wishes to use the 'full goodwill' method on the transaction. Marrgrett is unsure as to whether this method is mandatory, or what the effects are of recognising 'full goodwill'. Additionally the company is unsure as to whether the nature of the consideration would affect the calculation of goodwill.

To finance the acquisition of Josey, Marrgrett intends to dispose of a partial interest in two subsidiaries. Marrgrett will retain control of the first subsidiary but will sell the controlling interest in the second subsidiary which will become an associate. Because of its plans to change the overall structure of the business, Marrgrett wishes to recognise a re-organisation provision at the date of the business combination.

Required

Discuss the principles and the nature of the accounting treatment of the above plans under International Financial Reporting Standards setting out any impact that IFRS 3 (Revised) *Business combinations* might have on the earnings and net assets of the group.

Note. this requirement includes 2 professional marks for the quality of the discussion. **(25 marks)**

35 Preparation question: Associate

The statements of financial position of J Co and its investee companies, P Co and S Co, at 31 December 20X5 are shown below.

STATEMENTS OF FINANCIAL POSITION AS AT 31 DECEMBER 20X5

	J Co	*P Co*	*S Co*
	$'000	$'000	$'000
Assets			
Non-current assets			
Freehold property	1,950	1,250	500
Plant and equipment	795	375	285
Investments	1,500	–	–
	4,245	1,625	785
Current assets			
Inventories	575	300	265
Trade receivables	330	290	370
Cash	50	120	20
	955	710	655
	5,200	2,335	1,440
Equity and liabilities			
Equity			
Share capital ($1 ordinary shares)	2,000	1,000	750
Retained earnings	1,460	885	390
	3,460	1,885	1,140
Non-current liabilities			
12% debentures	500	100	–
Current liabilities			
Bank overdraft	560		
Trade payables	680	350	300
	1,240	350	300
	5,200	2,335	1,440

Additional information

(a) J Co acquired 600,000 ordinary shares in P Co on 1 January 20X0 for $1,000,000 when the accumulated retained earnings of P Co were $200,000.

(b) At the date of acquisition of P Co, the fair value of its freehold property was considered to be $400,000 greater than its value in P Co's statement of financial position. P Co had acquired the property ten years earlier and the buildings element (comprising 50% of the total value) is depreciated on cost over 50 years.

(c) J Co acquired 225,000 ordinary shares in S Co on 1 January 20X4 for $500,000 when the retained profits of S Co were $150,000.

(d) P Co manufactures a component used by J Co only. Transfers are made by P Co at cost plus 25%. J Co held $100,000 of these components in inventories at 31 December 20X5.

(e) It is the policy of J Co to review goodwill for impairment annually. The goodwill in P Co was written off in full some years ago. An impairment test conducted at the year end revealed impairment losses on the investment in S Co of $92,000.

(f) It is the group's policy to value the non-controlling interest at acquisition at fair value. The market price of the shares of the non-controlling shareholders just before the acquisition was $1.65.

Required

Prepare, in a format suitable for inclusion in the annual report of the J Group, the consolidated statement of financial position at 31 December 20X5.

36 Preparation question: 'D'-shaped group

BPP note. In this question, a proforma is given to you for Part (a) to help you get used to setting out your answer. You may wish to transfer it to a separate sheet or to use a separate sheet for workings.

Below are the statements of financial position of three companies as at 31 December 20X9.

	Bauble Co	*Jewel Co*	*Gem Co*
	$'000	$'000	$'000
Non-current assets			
Property, plant and equipment	720	60	70
Investments in group companies	185	100	–
	905	160	70
Current assets	175	95	90
	1,080	255	160
Equity			
Share capital – $1 ordinary shares	400	100	50
Retained earnings	560	90	65
	960	190	115
Current liabilities	120	65	45
	1,080	255	160

You are also given the following information:

(a) Bauble Co acquired 60% of the share capital of Jewel Co on 1 January 20X2 and 10% of Gem on 1 January 20X3. The cost of the combinations were $142,000 and $43,000 respectively. Jewel Co acquired 70% of the share capital of Gem Co on 1 January 20X3.

(b) The retained earnings balances of Jewel Co and Gem Co were:

	1 January 20X2	*1 January 20X3*
	$'000	$'000
Jewel Co	45	60
Gem Co	30	40

(c) No impairment loss adjustments have been necessary to date.

(d) It is the group's policy to value the non-controlling interest at acquisition at its proportionate share of the fair value of the subsidiary's identifiable net assets.

Required

(a) Prepare the consolidated statement of financial position for Bauble Co and its subsidiaries as at 31 December 20X9.

(b) Calculate the total goodwill arising on acquisition if Bauble Co had acquired its investments in Jewel and Gem on 1 January 20X3 at a cost of $142,000 and $43,000 respectively and Jewel Co had acquired its investment in Gem Co on 1 January 20X2.

(a) BAUBLE – CONSOLIDATED STATEMENT OF FINANCIAL POSITION AS AT 31 DECEMBER 20X9

	$'000
Non-current assets	
Property, plant and equipment	
Goodwill	
Current assets	
Equity attributable to owners of the parent	
Share capital – $1 ordinary shares	
Retained earnings	
Non-controlling interest	
Current liabilities	

37 Preparation question: Sub-subsidiary

The Exotic Group carries on business as a distributor of warehouse equipment and importer of fruit into the country. Exotic was incorporated in 20X1 to distribute warehouse equipment. It diversified its activities during 20X3 to include the import and distribution of fruit, and expanded its operations by the acquisition of shares in Melon in 20X5 and in Kiwi in 20X7.

Accounts for all companies are made up to 31 December.

The draft statements of profit or loss and other comprehensive income for Exotic, Melon and Kiwi for the year ended 31 December 20X9 are as follows.

	Exotic	*Melon*	*Kiwi*
	$'000	$'000	$'000
Revenue	45,600	24,700	22,800
Cost of sales	18,050	5,463	5,320
Gross profit	27,550	19,237	17,480
Distribution costs	(3,325)	(2,137)	(1,900)
Administrative expenses	(3,475)	(950)	(1,900)
Finance costs	(325)	–	–
Profit before tax	20,425	16,150	13,680
Income tax expense	8,300	5,390	4,241
Profit for the year	12,125	10,760	9,439
Other comprehensive income for the year			
Items that will not be reclassified to profit or loss			
Revaluation of property	200	100	–
Total comprehensive income for the year	12,325	10,860	9,439
Dividends paid and declared for the period	9,500	–	–

The draft statements of financial position as at 31 December 20X9 are as follows.

	Exotic	*Melon*	*Kiwi*
	$'000	$'000	$'000
Non-current assets			
Property, plant and equipment (at carrying value)	35,483	24,273	13,063
Investments			
Shares in Melon	6,650		
Shares in Kiwi		3,800	
	42,133	28,073	13,063
Current assets	1,568	9,025	8,883
	43,701	37,098	21,946
Equity			
$1 ordinary shares	8,000	3,000	2,000
Reserves (retained earnings and reval'n surplus)	22,638	24,075	19,898
	30,638	27,075	21,898
Current liabilities	13,063	10,023	48
	43,701	37,098	21,946

The following information is available relating to Exotic, Melon and Kiwi.

(a) On 1 January 20X5 Exotic acquired 2,700,000 $1 ordinary shares in Melon for $6,650,000 at which date there was a credit balance on the retained earnings of Melon of $1,425,000. No shares have been issued by Melon since Exotic acquired its interest.

(b) At the date of acquisition, the fair value of the identifiable net assets of Melon was $5m. The excess of the fair value of net assets is due to an increase in the value of non-depreciable land.

(c) On 1 January 20X7 Melon acquired 1,600,000 $1 ordinary shares in Kiwi for $3,800,000 at which date there was a credit balance on the retained earnings of Kiwi of $950,000. No shares have been issued by Kiwi since Melon acquired its interest.

(d) During 20X9, Kiwi had made intragroup sales to Melon of $480,000 making a profit of 25% on cost and $75,000 of these goods were in inventories at 31 December 20X9.

(e) During 20X9, Melon had made intragroup sales to Exotic of $260,000 making a profit of 25% on sales and $60,000 of these goods were in inventories at 31 December 20X9.

(f) An impairment test conducted at the year end did not reveal any impairment losses.

(g) It is the group's policy to value the non-controlling interest at fair value at the date of acquisition. The fair value of the non-controlling interests in Melon on 1 January 20X5 was $500,000. The fair value of the 28% non-controlling interest in Kiwi on 1 January 20X7 was $900,000.

Required

Prepare for the Exotic Group:

(a) A consolidated statement of profit or loss and other comprehensive income for the year ended 31 December 20X9

(b) A consolidated statement of financial position as at that date

38 Glove

49 mins

ACR, 6/07, amended

The following draft statements of financial position relate to Glove, Body and Fit, all public limited companies, as at 31 May 20X7.

	Glove	*Body*	*Fit*
	$m	$m	$m
Assets			
Non-current assets			
Property, plant and equipment	260	20	26
Investment in Body	60		
Investment in Fit		30	
Investments in equity instruments	10		
Current assets	65	29	20
Total assets	395	79	46
Ordinary shares	150	40	20
Other reserves	30	5	8
Retained earnings	135	25	10
Total equity	315	70	38
Non-current liabilities	45	2	3
Current liabilities	35	7	5
Total liabilities	80	9	8
Total equity and liabilities	395	79	46

The following information is relevant to the preparation of the group financial statements.

(a) Glove acquired 80% of the ordinary shares of Body on 1 June 20X5 when Body's other reserves were $4 million and retained earnings were $10 million. The fair value of the net assets of Body was $60 million at 1 June 20X5. Body acquired 70% of the ordinary shares of Fit on 1 June 20X5 when the other reserves of Fit were $8 million and retained earnings were $6 million. The fair value of the net assets of Fit at that date was $39 million. The excess of the fair value over the net assets of Body and Fit is due to an increase in the value of non-depreciable land of the companies. There have been no issues of ordinary shares in the group since 1 June 20X5.

(b) Body owns several trade names which are highly regarded in the market place. Body has invested a significant amount in marketing these trade names and has expensed the costs. None of the trade names has been acquired externally and, therefore, the costs have not been capitalised in the statement of financial position of Body. On the acquisition of Body by Glove, a firm of valuation experts valued the trade names at $5 million and this valuation had been taken into account by Glove when offering $60 million for the investment in Body. The valuation of the trade names is not included in the fair value of the net assets of Body above. Group policy is to amortise intangible assets over ten years.

(c) On 1 June 20X5, Glove introduced a defined benefit retirement plan. During the year to 31 May 20X7, loss on remeasurement on the defined benefit obligation was $1m, and gain on remeasurement on the plan assets were $900,000. These have not yet been accounted for and need to be treated in accordance with IAS 19, as revised in 2011. The net defined benefit liability is included in non-current liabilities.

(d) Glove has issued 30,000 convertible bonds with a three year term repayable at par. The bonds were issued at par with a face value of $1,000 per bond. Interest is payable annually in arrears at a nominal interest rate of 6%. Each bond can be converted at any time up to maturity into 300 shares of Glove. The bonds were issued on 1 June 20X6 when the market interest rate for similar debt without the conversion option was 8% per annum. Glove does not wish to account for the bonds at fair value through profit or loss. The interest has been paid and accounted for in the financial statements. The bonds have been included in non-current liabilities at their face value of $30 million and no bonds were converted in the current financial year.

(e) On 31 May 20X7, Glove acquired plant with a fair value of $6 million. In exchange for the plant, the supplier received land, which was currently not in use, from Glove. The land had a carrying value of $4 million and an open market value of $7 million. In the financial statements at 31 May 20X7, Glove had made a transfer of $4 million from land to plant in respect of this transaction.

(f) Goodwill has been tested for impairment at 31 May 20X6 and 31 May 20X7 and no impairment loss occurred.

(g) It is the group's policy to value the non-controlling interest at acquisition at its proportionate share of the fair value of the subsidiary's identifiable net assets.

(h) Ignore any taxation effects.

Required

Prepare the consolidated statement of financial position of the Glove Group at 31 May 20X7 in accordance with International Financial Reporting Standards (IFRS). **(25 marks)**

39 Case study question: Jarvis **98 mins**

The following draft statements of profit or loss and other comprehensive income relate to Jarvis, Whitehill and Crow, all public limited companies, for the year ended 31 December 20X8.

	Jarvis	*Whitehill*	*Crow*
	$m	$m	$m
Revenue	4,500	2,800	1,800
Cost of sales	(3,200)	(2,000)	(1,200)
Gross profit	1,300	800	600
Other income	80	20	–
Distribution costs	(220)	(140)	(80)
Administrative expenses	(180)	(110)	(60)
Finance costs	(40)	(20)	(12)
Profit before tax	940	550	448
Income tax expense	(280)	(160)	(120)
Profit for the year	660	390	328
Other comprehensive income (items that will not be reclassified to profit or loss)			
Gains on revaluations of property, net of tax	140	90	80
Total comprehensive income for the year	800	480	408
Total comprehensive income for the year ended 31 December 20X7	600	380	260

The following information is relevant to the preparation of the group financial statements:

(i) Jarvis acquired 80% of the ordinary shares of Whitehill on 1 January 20X7 for $1,400m when the fair value of Whitehill's net assets was $1,500m. Whitehill acquired 60% of the ordinary share capital of Crow on 1 April 20X8 for $800m when the fair value of Crow's net assets was $1,100m.

Jarvis elected to measure the non-controlling interests in Whitehill and Crow at the date of each acquisition at the proportionate share of the net fair value of the identifiable assets acquired and liabilities assumed.

(ii) Whitehill had sold $400m of goods to Jarvis on 31 October 20X8. There was no opening inventories of intragroup goods but the closing inventories of these goods in Jarvis's financial statements was $100m. The profit on these goods was 20% of selling price. The tax rate applicable to both Jarvis and Whitehill is 30%.

(iii) Jarvis have a defined benefit pension plan and the directors have included the following amounts in the figure for cost of sales:

	$m
Current service cost	12
Loss on remeasurement of defined benefit obligation	9
Net interest cost on the net defined benefit obligation	8
Gain on remeasurement of plan assets	(6)
Charged to cost of sales	23

The company's accounting policy is to recognise net interest cost on the net defined benefit obligation as a finance cost.

(iv) During 20X8 Jarvis paid a dividend of $150m and Whitehill paid a dividend of $60m. Neither company paid a dividend in 20X7. Jarvis recorded the dividend received from Whitehall in 'other income'.

(v) There had been no impairment losses recorded relating to the investments in either Whitehill or Crow as at 1 January 20X8. Whitehill and Crow are considered separate cash-generating units. The recoverable amount of Whitehill was $2,500m as at 31 December 20X8. There was no impairment of the investment in Crow. Impairment losses are charged to cost of sales.

(vi) During 20X8 Jarvis sold an investment in an equity instrument which had a carrying value of $50m at 31 December 20X7 for $70m. As at 31 December 20X7 $10m of cumulative revaluation gains had been recognised in profit or loss, on which deferred tax had been provided at 30%. The only accounting entries to have been made for this disposal to date have been to record the proceeds in the bank account. Current tax payable on sale of the investment on the selling price less cost at 30% is included in the current tax charge in income tax expense.

(vii) On 1 January 20X7, Jarvis purchased land and buildings abroad for 1,500m corona (including 400m corona for the land element). The buildings are being depreciated over 50 years to a 100m corona residual value. The depreciation has been correctly accounted for. Jarvis' policy is to revalue land and buildings and a professional valuation has been obtained of 1,760m corona (including 480m corona for the land) as at 31 December 20X8. The valuation has not yet been adjusted for. No previous revaluations had been necessary.

Exchange rates were:

- 1 January 20X7 $1:20 corona
- 31 December 20X7 $1: 21 corona
- Average for 20X8 $1: 21.5 corona
- 31 December 20X8 $1: 22 corona

Revaluations on land and buildings are taxed on disposal in the tax regime in which Jarvis operates.

(viii) In the wake of rising fuel costs, on 1 December 20X8, Jarvis entered into a derivative contract with a financial institution to purchase fuel to cover estimated fuel requirements for the second half of 20X9 for delivery on 1 July 20X9. Jarvis intends to purchase the actual fuel required on the open market and settle the derivative net in cash. All relevant paperwork to allow the derivative to be accounted for as a hedge was set up on 1 December 20X8.

The value of the derivative was a $12m gain on 31 December 20X8 in the wake of an increase in fuel prices which was expected to continue. At year end market prices, the additional amount Jarvis would have to pay for the agreed amount of fuel versus the amount in the contract was $10m. The difference between this and the value of the derivative is due to ineffectiveness of the hedge.

This hedge has not yet been accounted for.

(ix) The current and deferred income tax charges have been correctly calculated for each individual company based on the draft financial statements above. Ignore the deferred tax effects of the derivative and gains and losses on remeasurement of the pension plan asset and obligation.

Required:

(a) Prepare a consolidated statement of profit or loss and other comprehensive income for the Jarvis group for the year ended 31 December 20X8. **(35 marks)**

(b) Discuss what is meant by corporate responsibility and in particular the factors which should encourage companies to disclose social and environmental information. **(10 marks)**

Note: 2 marks will be awarded for the quality of discussion of the ideas and information.

(c) A recent survey has indicated that there has been a vast increase in narrative reporting by FTSE 350 companies on the subject of corporate responsibility however only a very small proportion of companies identify corporate responsibilities as strategic issues or provide key performance indicators in this area.

Discuss the ethical issues of narrative reporting without reference to strategy and the lack of key performance indicators to support the narrative disclosures. **(5 marks)**

(Total = 50 marks)

40 Preparation question: Part disposal

> **BPP note**. In this question, proformas are given to you to help you get used to setting out your answer. You may wish to transfer them to a separate sheet or to use a separate sheet for your workings.

Angel Co bought 70% of the share capital of Shane Co for $120,000 on 1 January 20X6. At that date Shane Co's retained earnings stood at $10,000.

The statements of financial position at 31 December 20X8, summarised statements of profit or loss and other comprehensive income to that date and movement on retained earnings are given below.

	Angel Co	*Shane Co*
	$'000	$'000
STATEMENTS OF FINANCIAL POSITION		
Non-current assets		
Property, plant and equipment	200	80
Investment in Shane Co	120	–
	320	80
Current assets	890	140
	1,210	220
Equity		
Share capital – $1 ordinary shares	500	100
Retained reserves	400	90
	900	190
Current liabilities	310	30
	1,210	220
SUMMARISED STATEMENTS OF PROFIT OR LOSS AND OTHER COMPREHENSIVE INCOME		
Profit before interest and tax	100	20
Income tax expense	(40)	(8)
Profit for the year	60	12
Other comprehensive income (not reclassified to P/L), net of tax	10	6
Total comprehensive income for the year	70	18
MOVEMENT IN RETAINED RESERVES		
Balance at 31 December 20X7	330	72
Total comprehensive income for the year	70	18
Balance at 31 December 20X8	400	90

Angel Co sells one half of its holding in Shane Co for $120,000 on 30 June 20X8. At that date, the fair value of the 35% holding in Shane was slightly more at $130,000 due to a share price rise. The remaining holding is to be dealt with as an associate. This does not represent a discontinued operation.

No entries have been made in the accounts for the above transaction.

Assume that profits accrue evenly throughout the year.

It is the group's policy to value the non-controlling interest at acquisition fair value. The fair value of the non-controlling interest on 1 January 20X6 was $51.4m.

Required

(a) Prepare the consolidated statement of financial position, statement of profit or loss and other comprehensive income and a reconciliation of movement in retained reserves for the year ended 31 December 20X8.

Ignore income taxes on the disposal. No impairment losses have been necessary to date.

PART DISPOSAL PROFORMA

ANGEL GROUP
CONSOLIDATED STATEMENT OF FINANCIAL POSITION
AS AT 31 DECEMBER 20X8

	$'000
Non-current assets	
Property, plant and equipment	
Investment in Shane	
Current assets	
Equity attributable to owners of the parent	
Share capital	
Retained reserves	
Current liabilities	

CONSOLIDATED STATEMENT OF PROFIT OR LOSS AND OTHER COMPREHENSIVE INCOME
FOR THE YEAR ENDED 31 DECEMBER 20X8

	$'000
Profit before interest and tax	
Profit on disposal of shares in subsidiary	
Share of profit of associate	
Profit before tax	
Income tax expense	
Profit for the year	
Other comprehensive income (not reclassified to P/L) net of tax:	
Share of other comprehensive income of associate	
Other comprehensive income for the year	
Total comprehensive income for the year	
Profit attributable to:	
Owners of the parent	
Non-controlling interests	
Total comprehensive income attributable to	
Owners of the parent	
Non-controlling interests	

CONSOLIDATED RECONCILIATION OF MOVEMENT IN RETAINED RESERVES

	$'000
Balance at 31 December 20X7	
Total comprehensive income for the year	
Balance at 31 December 20X8	

(b) Explain the accounting treatment that would be required if Angel had disposed of 10% of its holding in Shane.

41 Preparation question: Purchase of further interest

RBE owns 70% of the ordinary share capital of DCA. The total group equity as at 31 December 20X1 was $4,000,000, which included $650,000 attributable to non-controlling interest.

RBE purchased a further 20% of the ordinary share capital of DCA on 1 October 20X2 for $540,000.

During the year to 31 December 20X2, RBE issued 2 million $1 ordinary shares, fully paid, at $1.30 per share.

Dividends were paid by both group entities in April 20X2. The dividends paid by RBE and DCA were $200,000 and $100,000, respectively.

Total comprehensive income for the year ended 31 December 20X2 for RBE was $900,000 and for DCA was $600,000. Income is assumed to accrue evenly throughout the year.

Required

(a) Explain the impact of the additional 20% purchase of DCA's ordinary share capital by RBE on the equity of the RBE Group.

(b) Prepare the consolidated statement of changes in equity for the year ended 31 December 20X2 for the RBE Group, showing the total equity attributable to the parent and to the non-controlling interest.

42 Case study question: Marchant — 98 mins

6/14

The following financial statements relate to Marchant, a public limited company.

MARCHANT GROUP: STATEMENTS OF PROFIT OR LOSS AND OTHER COMPREHENSIVE INCOME
FOR THE YEAR ENDED 30 APRIL 20X4

	Marchant	*Nathan*	*Option*
	$m	$m	$m
Revenue	400	115	70
Cost of sales	(312)	(65)	(36)
Gross profit	88	50	34
Other income	21	7	2
Administrative costs	(15)	(9)	(12)
Other expenses	(35)	(19)	(8)
Operating profit	59	29	16
Finance costs	(5)	(6)	(4)
Finance income	6	5	8
Profit before tax	60	28	20
Income tax expense	(19)	(9)	(5)
Profit for the year	41	19	15
Other comprehensive income for the year, net of tax – Items that will not be reclassified to profit or loss:			
Revaluation surplus	10	–	–
Total comprehensive income and expense for year	51	19	15

The following information is relevant to the preparation of the group statement of profit or loss and other comprehensive income:

(i) On 1 May 20X2, Marchant acquired 60% of the equity interests of Nathan, a public limited company. The purchase consideration comprised cash of $80 million and the fair value of the identifiable net assets acquired was $110 million at that date. The fair value of the non-controlling interest (NCI) in Nathan was $45 million on 1 May 20X2. Marchant wishes to use the 'full goodwill' method for all acquisitions. The share capital and retained earnings of Nathan were $25 million and $65 million respectively and other components of equity were $6 million at the date of acquisition. The excess of the fair value of the identifiable net assets at acquisition is due to non-depreciable land.

Goodwill has been impairment tested annually and as at 30 April 20X3 had reduced in value by 20%. However, at 30 April 20X4, the impairment of goodwill had reversed and goodwill was valued at $2 million above its original value. This upward change in value has already been included in above draft financial statements of Marchant prior to the preparation of the group accounts.

(ii) Marchant disposed of an 8% equity interest in Nathan on 30 April 20X4 for a cash consideration of $18 million and had accounted for the gain or loss in other income. The carrying value of the net assets of Nathan at 30 April 20X4 was $120 million before any adjustments on consolidation. Marchant accounts for investments in subsidiaries using IFRS 9 *Financial Instruments,* and has made an election to show gains and losses in other comprehensive income. The carrying value of the investment in Nathan was $90 million at 30 April 20X3 and $95 million at 30 April 20X4 before the disposal of the equity interest.

(iii) Marchant acquired 60% of the equity interests of Option, a public limited company, on 30 April 20X2. The purchase consideration was cash of $70 million. Option's identifiable net assets were fair valued at $86 million and the NCI had a fair value of $28 million at that date. On 1 November 20X3, Marchant disposed of a 40% equity interest in Option for a consideration of $50 million. Option's identifiable net assets were $90 million and the value of the NCI was $34 million at the date of disposal. The remaining equity interest was fair valued at $40 million. After the disposal, Marchant exerts significant influence. Any increase in net assets since acquisition has been reported in profit or loss and the carrying value of the investment in Option had not changed since acquisition. Goodwill had been impairment tested and no impairment was required. No entries had been made in the financial statements of Marchant for this transaction other than for cash received.

(iv) Marchant sold inventory to Nathan for $12 million at fair value. Marchant made a loss on the transaction of $2 million and Nathan still holds $8 million in inventory at the year end.

(v) The following information relates to Marchant's pension scheme:

	$m
Plan assets at 1 May 20X3	48
Defined benefit obligation at 1 May 20X3	50
Service cost for year ended 30 April 20X4	4
Discount rate at 1 May 20X3	10%
Re-measurement loss in year ended 30 April 20X4	2
Past service cost 1 May 20X3	3

The pension costs have not been accounted for in total comprehensive income.

Note. The past service costs of $3m are included in the defined benefit obligation at 1 May 20X3.

(vi) On 1 May 20X2, Marchant purchased an item of property, plant and equipment for $12 million and this is being depreciated using the straight line basis over 10 years with a zero residual value. At 30 April 20X3, the asset was revalued to $13 million but at 30 April 20X4, the value of the asset had fallen to $7 million. Marchant uses the revaluation model to value its non-current assets. The effect of the revaluation at 30 April 20X4 had not been taken into account in total comprehensive income but depreciation for the year had been charged.

(vii) On 1 May 20X2, Marchant made an award of 8,000 share options to each of its seven directors. The condition attached to the award is that the directors must remain employed by Marchant for three years. The fair value of each option at the grant date was $100 and the fair value of each option at 30 April 20X4 was $110. At 30 April 20X3, it was estimated that three directors would leave before the end of three years. Due to an economic downturn, the estimate of directors who were going to leave was revised to one director at 30 April 20X4. The expense for the year as regards the share options had not been included in profit or loss for the current year and no directors had left by 30 April 20X4.

(viii) A loss on an effective cash flow hedge of Nathan of $3 million has been included in the subsidiary's finance costs.

(ix) Ignore the taxation effects of the above adjustments unless specified. Any expense adjustments should be amended in other expenses.

Required

(a) (i) Prepare a consolidated statement of profit or loss and other comprehensive income for the year ended 30 April 20X4 for the Marchant Group. **(30 marks)**

(ii) Explain, with suitable calculations, how the sale of the 8% interest in Nathan should be dealt with in the group statement of financial position at 30 April 20X4. **(5 marks)**

(b) The directors of Marchant have strong views on the usefulness of the financial statements after their move to International Financial Reporting Standards (IFRSs). They feel that IFRSs implement a fair value model. Nevertheless, they are of the opinion that IFRSs are failing users of financial statements as they do not reflect the financial value of an entity.

Required

Discuss the directors' views above as regards the use of fair value in IFRSs and the fact that IFRSs do not reflect the financial value of an entity. **(9 marks)**

(c) Marchant plans to update its production process and the directors feel that technology-led production is the only feasible way in which the company can remain competitive. Marchant operates from a leased property and the leasing arrangement was established in order to maximise taxation benefits. However, the financial statements have not shown a lease asset or liability to date.

A new financial controller joined Marchant just after the financial year end of 30 April 20X4 and is presently reviewing the financial statements to prepare for the upcoming audit and to begin making a loan application to finance the new technology. The financial controller feels that the lease relating to both the land and buildings should be recognised in the statement of financial position, but the managing director, who did a brief accountancy course ten years ago, disagrees. The managing director wishes to charge the rental payments to profit or loss. The managing director feels that the arrangement does not meet the criteria for recognition in the statement of financial position, and has made it clear that showing the lease in the statement of financial position could jeopardise the loan application.

Required

Discuss the ethical and professional issues which face the financial controller in the above situation. **(6 marks)**

(Total = 50 marks)

43 Ejoy — 59 mins

ACR, 6/06, amended

Ejoy, a public limited company, has acquired two subsidiaries. The details of the acquisitions are as follows:

Company	*Date of acquisition*	*Ordinary share capital of $1*	*Reserves at acquisition*	*Fair value of net assets at acquisition*	*Cost of investment*	*Ordinary share capital of $1 acquired*
		$m	$m	$m	$m	$m
Zbay	1 June 20X4	200	170	600	520	160
Tbay	1 December 20X5	120	80	310	192	72

Any fair value adjustments relate to non-depreciable land. The draft statements of profit or loss and other comprehensive income for the year ended 31 May 20X6 are:

	Ejoy	*Zbay*	*Tbay*
	$m	$m	$m
Revenue	2,500	1,500	800
Cost of sales	(1,800)	(1,200)	(600)
Gross profit	700	300	200
Other income	70	10	–
Distribution costs	(130)	(120)	(70)
Administrative expenses	(100)	(90)	(60)
Finance costs	(50)	(40)	(20)
Profit before tax	490	60	50
Income tax expense	(200)	(26)	(20)
Profit for the year	290	34	30
Other comprehensive for the year (not reclassified to profit or loss):			
Gain on property revaluation net of tax	80	10	8
Total comprehensive income for the year	370	44	38
Total comprehensive income for year 31 May 20X5	190	20	15

The following information is relevant to the preparation of the group financial statements.

(a) Tbay was acquired exclusively with a view to sale and at 31 May 20X6 meets the criteria of being a disposal group. The fair value of Tbay at 31 May 20X6 is $344 million and the estimated selling costs of the shareholding in Tbay are $5 million.

(b) Ejoy entered into a joint arrangement with another company on 31 May 20X6, which met the IFRS 11 definition of a joint venture. The joint venture is a limited company and Ejoy has contributed assets at fair value of $20 million (carrying value $14 million). Each party will hold five million ordinary shares of $1 in the joint venture. The gain on the disposal of the assets ($6 million) to the joint venture has been included in 'other income'.

(c) On 31 May 20X5, Zbay made a loan of $100m to a customer with a similar credit risk to Zbay. Interest payable on this loan was 4.5% per annum. On 31 May 20X5 the initial present value of expected credit losses over the life of the loan, using a discount factor of 4%, was $25m. At that date, the probability of default over the next twelve months was 10%. An allowance of twelve months' expected credit losses had been recognised at 31 May 20X5 in accordance with IFRS 9 *Financial instruments.*

By 31 May 20X6 it became clear that the customer was in serious financial difficulties, and the directors of Zbay believed that there was objective evidence of impairment. The present value of expected credit losses was revised to $48.1m.

No entries have been made in respect of the loan in the year ending 31 May 20X6.

(d) On 1 June 20X5, Ejoy purchased a five year bond with a principal amount of $50 million and a fixed interest rate of 5% which was the current market rate. The bond is classified as at fair value through profit or loss. Because of the size of the investment, Ejoy has entered into a floating interest rate swap. Ejoy has designated the swap as a fair value hedge of the bond. At 31 May 20X6, market interest rates were 6%. As a result, the fair value of the bond has decreased to $48.3 million. Ejoy has received $0.5 million in net interest payments on the swap at 31 May 20X6 and the fair value hedge has been 100% effective in the period, and you should assume any gain/loss on the hedge is the same as the loss/gain on the bond. No entries have been made in the statement of profit or loss and other comprehensive income to account for the bond or the hedge.

(e) No impairment of the goodwill arising on the acquisition of Zbay had occurred at 1 June 20X5. The recoverable amount of Zbay was $630 million and the value in use of Tbay was $334 million at 31 May 20X6. Impairment losses on goodwill are charged to cost of sales.

(f) Assume that profits accrue evenly throughout the year and ignore any taxation effects.

(g) It is the group's policy to value the non-controlling interest at its proportionate share of the fair value of the subsidiary's identifiable net assets.

Required

Prepare a consolidated statement of profit or loss and other comprehensive income for the Ejoy Group for the year ended 31 May 20X6 in accordance with International Financial Reporting Standards. **(30 marks)**

44 Case study question: Traveler **98 mins**

12/11

Traveler, a public limited company, operates in the manufacturing sector. The draft statements of financial position of the group companies are as follows at 30 November 20X1.

	Traveler	*Data*	*Captive*
	$m	$m	$m
Assets			
Non-current assets			
Property, plant and equipment	439	810	620
Investment in subsidiaries:			
Data	820		
Captive	541		
Financial assets	108	10	20
	1,908	820	640
Net defined benefit asset	72		
Current assets	995	781	350
Total assets	2,975	1,601	990

	Traveler	*Data*	*Captive*
	$m	$m	$m
Equity and liabilities			
Share capital	1,120	600	390
Retained earnings	1,066	442	169
Other components of equity	60	37	45
Total equity	2,246	1,079	604
Non-current liabilities	455	323	73
Current liabilities	274	199	313
Total liabilities	729	522	386
Total equity and liabilities	2,975	1,601	990

The following information is relevant to the preparation of the group financial statements.

(i) On 1 December 20X0, Traveler acquired 60% of the equity interests of Data, a public limited company. The purchase consideration comprised cash of $600 million. At acquisition, the fair value of the non-controlling interest in Data was $395 million. Traveler wishes to use the 'full goodwill' method. On 1 December 20X0, the fair value of the identifiable net assets acquired was $935 million and retained earnings of Data were $299 million and other components of equity were $26 million. The excess in fair value is due to non-depreciable land.

On 30 November 20X1, Traveler acquired a further 20% interest in Data for a cash consideration of $220 million.

(ii) On 1 December 20X0, Traveler acquired 80% of the equity interests of Captive for a consideration of $541 million. The consideration comprised cash of $477 million and the transfer of non-depreciable land with a fair value of $64 million. The carrying amount of the land at the acquisition date was $56 million. At the year end, this asset was still included in the non-current assets of Traveler and the sale proceeds had been credited to profit or loss.

At the date of acquisition, the identifiable net assets of Captive had a fair value of $526 million, retained earnings were $90 million and other components of equity were $24 million. The excess in fair value is due to non-depreciable land. This acquisition was accounted for using the partial goodwill method in accordance with IFRS 3 (Revised) *Business combinations*.

(iii) Goodwill was impairment tested after the additional acquisition in Data on 30 November 20X1. The recoverable amount of Data was $1,099 million and that of Captive was $700 million.

(iv) Included in the financial assets of Traveler is a ten-year 7% loan. Traveler has adopted IFRS 9 Financial instruments and the loan asset is currently held at amortised cost of $31 million. This is net of an allowance, including interest, at 30 November 20X0 of twelve months' expected credit losses of $2m. At 30 November 20X1, the borrower was in financial difficulties and its credit rating had been downgraded, such that the loan may be considered to be in Stage 2 according to the IFRS 9 expected credit loss model. Lifetime expected credit losses are $9.9m. This reflects the difference between the carrying amount and revised expected receipts of three annual amounts of $8 million starting in one year's time discounted at the original effective interest rate of 6.7%. Rather than recognise lifetime expected credit losses, Traveler now wishes to value the loan at fair value using current market interest rates. Current market interest rates are 8%.

(v) Traveler acquired a new factory on 1 December 20X0. The cost of the factory was $50 million and it has a residual value of $2 million. The factory has a flat roof, which needs replacing every five years. The cost of the roof was $5 million. The useful economic life of the factory is 25 years. No depreciation has been charged for the year. Traveler wishes to account for the factory and roof as a single asset and depreciate the whole factory over its economic life. Traveler uses straight-line depreciation.

(vi) The actuarial value of Traveler's pension plan showed a surplus at 1 December 20X0 of $72 million. Losses of $25 million on remeasurement of the net defined benefit asset are to be recognised in other comprehensive income in accordance with IAS 19). The aggregate of the current service cost and the net interest cost amounted to a cost of $55 million for the year. After consulting with the actuaries, the company decided to reduce its contributions for the year to $45 million. The contributions were paid on 7 December 20X1. No entries had been made in the financial statements for the above amounts. The present value of available future refunds and reductions in future contributions was $18 million.

Required

(a) Prepare a consolidated statement of financial position for the Traveler Group as at 30 November 20X1. **(35 marks)**

(b) Traveler has three distinct business segments. The management has calculated the net assets, turnover and profit before common costs, which are to be allocated to these segments. However, they are unsure as to how they should allocate certain common costs and whether they can exercise judgement in the allocation process. They wish to allocate head office management expenses; pension expense; the cost of managing properties and interest and related interest bearing assets. They also are uncertain as to whether the allocation of costs has to be in conformity with the accounting policies used in the financial statements.

Required

Advise the management of Traveler on the points raised in the above paragraph. **(8 marks)**

(c) Segmental information reported externally is more useful if it conforms to information used by management in making decisions. The information can differ from that reported in the financial statements. Although reconciliations are required, these can be complex and difficult to understand. Additionally, there are other standards where subjectivity is involved and often the profit motive determines which accounting practice to follow. The directors have a responsibility to shareholders in disclosing information to enhance corporate value but this may conflict with their corporate social responsibility.

Required

Discuss how the ethics of corporate social responsibility disclosure are difficult to reconcile with shareholder expectations. **(7 marks)**

(Total = 50 marks)

45 Case study question: Joey

98 mins

12/14

(a) Joey, a public limited company operates in the media sector. Joey has investments in two companies. The draft statements of financial position at 30 November 20X4 are as follows.

	Joey $m	*Margy* $m	*Hulty* $m
Assets			
Non-current assets			
Property, plant and equipment	3,295	2,000	1,200
Investments in subsidiaries and other investments			
Margy	1,675		
Hulty	700		
	5,670	2,000	1,200
Current assets	985	861	150
Total assets	6,655	2,861	1,350
Equity and liabilities			
Share capital	850	1,020	600
Retained earnings	3,340	980	350
Other components of equity	250	80	40
Total equity	4,440	2,080	990
Non-current liabilities	1,895	675	200
Current liabilities	320	106	160
Total liabilities	2,215	781	360
Total equity and liabilities	6,655	2,861	1,350

The following information is relevant to the preparation of the group financial statements.

(i) On 1 December 20X1, Joey acquired 30% of the ordinary shares of Margy for a cash consideration of $600 million when the fair value of Margy's identifiable net assets was $1,840 million. Joey treated Margy as an associate and has equity accounted for Margy up to 1 December 20X3. Joey's share of Margy's undistributed profit amounted to $90 million and its share of a revaluation gain amounted to $10 million. On 1 December 20X3, Joey acquired a further 40% of the ordinary shares of Margy for a cash consideration of $975 million and gained control of the company. The cash consideration has been added to the equity accounted balance for Margy at 1 December 20X3 to give the carrying amount at 30 November 20X4.

At 1 December 20X3, the fair value of Margy's identifiable net assets was $2,250 million. At 1 December 20X3, the fair value of the equity interest in Margy held by Joey before the business combination was $705 million and the fair value of the non-controlling interest of 30% was assessed as $620 million. The retained earnings and other components of equity of Margy at 1 December 20X3 were $900 million and $70 million respectively. It is group policy to measure the non-controlling interest at fair value.

(ii) At the time of the business combination with Margy, Joey has included in the fair value of Margy's identifiable net assets, an unrecognised contingent liability of $6 million in respect of a warranty claim in progress against Margy. In March 20X4, there was a revision of the estimate of the liability to $5 million. The amount has met the criteria to be recognised as a provision in current liabilities in the financial statements of Margy and the revision of the estimate is deemed to be a measurement period adjustment.

(iii) Additionally, buildings with a carrying amount of $200 million had been included in the fair valuation of Margy at 1 December 20X3. The buildings have a remaining useful life of 20 years at 1 December 20X3. However, Joey had commissioned an independent valuation of the buildings of Margy which was not complete at 1 December 20X3 and therefore not considered in the fair value of the identifiable net assets at the acquisition date. The valuations were received on 1 April 20X4 and resulted in a decrease of $40 million in the fair value of property, plant and equipment at the date of acquisition. This decrease does not affect the fair value of the non-controlling interest at acquisition and has not been entered into the financial statements of Margy. Buildings are depreciated on the straight-line basis and it is group policy to leave revaluation gains on disposal in equity. The excess of the fair value of the net assets over their carrying value, at 1 December 20X3, is due to an increase in the value of non-depreciable land and the contingent liability.

(iv) On 1 December 20X3, Joey acquired 80% of the equity interests of Hulty, a private entity, in exchange for cash of $700 million. Because the former owners of Hulty needed to dispose of the investment quickly, they did not have sufficient time to market the investment to many potential buyers. The fair value of the identifiable net assets was $960 million. Joey determined that the fair value of the 20% non-controlling interest in Hulty at that date was $250 million. Joey reviewed the procedures used to identify and measure the assets acquired and liabilities assumed and to measure the fair value of both the non-controlling interest and the consideration transferred. After that review, Hulty determined that the procedures and resulting measures were appropriate. The retained earnings and other components of equity of Hulty at 1 December 20X3 were $300 million and $40 million respectively. The excess in fair value is due to an unrecognised franchise right, which Joey had granted to Hulty on 1 December 20X2 for five years. At the time of the acquisition, the franchise right could be sold for its market price. It is group policy to measure the non-controlling interest at fair value.

All goodwill arising on acquisitions has been impairment tested with no impairment being required.

(v) Joey is looking to expand into publishing and entered into an arrangement with Content Publishing (CP), a public limited company, on 1 December 20X3. CP will provide content for a range of books and online publications.

CP is entitled to a royalty calculated as 10% of sales and 30% of gross profit of the publications. Joey has sole responsibility for all printing, binding, and platform maintenance of the online website. The agreement states that key strategic sales and marketing decisions must be agreed jointly. Joey selects the content to be covered in the publications but CP has the right of veto over this content. However on 1 June 20X4, Joey and CP decided to set up a legal entity, JCP, with equal shares and voting rights. CP continues to contribute content into JCP but does not receive royalties. Joey continues the printing, binding and platform maintenance. The sales and cost of sales in the period were $5 million and $2 million respectively. The whole of the sale proceeds and the costs of sales were recorded in Joey's financial statements with no accounting entries being made for JCP or amounts due to CP. Joey currently funds the operations. Assume that the sales and costs accrue evenly throughout the year and that all of the transactions relating to JCP have been in cash.

(vi) At 30 November 20X3, Joey carried a property in its statement of financial position at its revalued amount of $14 million in accordance with IAS 16 *Property, plant and equipment.* Depreciation is charged at $300,000 per year on the straight line basis. In March 20X4, the management decided to sell the property and it was advertised for sale. By 31 March 20X4, the sale was considered to be highly probable and the criteria for IFRS 5 *Non-current assets held for sale and discontinued operations* were met at this date. At that date, the asset's fair value was $15·4 million and its value in use was $15·8 million. Costs to sell the asset were estimated at $300,000. On 30 November 20X4, the property was sold for $15·6 million. The transactions regarding the property are deemed to be material and no entries have been made in the financial statements regarding this property since 30 November 20X3 as the cash receipts from the sale were not received until December 20X4.

Required

Prepare the group consolidated statement of financial position of Joey as at 30 November 20X4.

(35 marks)

(b) The Joey Group wishes to expand its operations. As part of this expansion, it has granted options to the employees of Margy and Hulty over its own shares as at 7 December 20X4. The awards vest immediately. Joey is not proposing to make a charge to the subsidiaries for these options.

Joey does not know how to account for this transaction in its own, the subsidiaries, and the group financial statements.

Required

Explain to Joey how the above transaction should be dealt with in its own, the subsidiaries', and the group financial statements. **(8 marks)**

(c) Joey's directors feel that they need a significant injection of capital in order to modernise plant and equipment as the company has been promised new orders if it can produce goods to an international quality. The bank's current lending policies require borrowers to demonstrate good projected cash flow, as well as a level of profitability which would indicate that repayments would be made. However, the current projected cash flow statement would not satisfy the bank's criteria for lending. The directors have told the bank that the company is in an excellent financial position, that the financial results and cash flow projections will meet the criteria and that the chief accountant will forward a report to this effect shortly. The chief accountant has only recently joined Joey and has openly stated that he cannot afford to lose his job because of his financial commitments.

Required

Discuss the potential ethical conflicts which may arise in the above scenario and the ethical principles which would guide how a professional accountant should respond in this situation. **(7 marks)**

(Total = 50 marks)

46 Case study question: Kutchen — 98 mins

6/15

Kutchen, a public limited company, operates in the technology sector and has investments in other entities operating in the sector. The draft statements of financial position at 31 March 20X5 are as follows.

	Kutchen	*House*	*Mach*
	$m	$m	$m
Assets			
Non-current assets:			
Property, plant and equipment	216	41	38
Investment in subsidiaries			
Mach	52		
Finance lease receivables	50	14	8
	318	55	46
Current assets	44	25	64
Total assets	362	80	110
Equity and liabilities			
Share capital of $1 each	43	13	26
Retained earnings	41	24	15
Other components of equity	12	5	4
Total equity	96	42	45
Non-current liabilities	67	12	28
Current liabilities			
Trade and other payables	199	26	37
Total current liabilities	199	26	37
Total liabilities	266	38	65
Total equity and liabilities	362	80	110

The following information is relevant to the preparation of the group financial statements.

(a) On 1 October 20X4, Kutchen acquired 70% of the equity interests of House, a public limited company. The purchase consideration comprised 20 million shares of $1 of Kutchen at the acquisition date and 5 million shares on 31 March 20X6 if House's net profit after taxation was at least $4 million for the year ending on that date. The market price of Kutchen's shares on 1 October 20X4 was $2 per share and that of House was $4·20 per share. It is felt that there is a 20% chance of the profit target being met.

Kutchen wishes to measure the non-controlling interest at fair value at the date of acquisition. At acquisition, the fair value of the non-controlling interest (NCI) in House was based upon quoted market prices. On 1 October 20X4, the fair value of the identifiable net assets acquired was $48 million and retained earnings of House were $18 million and other components of equity were $3 million. The excess in fair value is due to non-depreciable land. No entries had been made in the financial statements of Kutchen for the acquisition of House.

(b) On 1 April 20X4, Kutchen acquired 80% of the equity interests of Mach, a privately owned entity, for a consideration of $57 million. The consideration comprised cash of $52 million and the transfer of non-depreciable land with a fair value of $5 million. The carrying amount of the land at the acquisition date was $3 million and the land has only recently been transferred to the seller of the shares in Mach and is still carried at $3 million in the financial records of Kutchen at 31 March 20X5. The only consideration shown in the financial records of Kutchen is the cash paid for the shares of Mach.

At the date of acquisition, the identifiable net assets of Mach had a fair value of $55 million, retained earnings were $12 million and other components of equity were $4 million. The excess in fair value is due to non-depreciable land. Mach had made a net profit attributable to ordinary shareholders of $3·6 million for the year to 31 March 20X4.

Kutchen wishes to measure the non-controlling interest at fair value at the date of acquisition. The NCI is to be fair valued using a public entity market multiple method. Kutchen has identified two companies who are comparable to Mach and who are trading at an average price to earnings ratio (P/E ratio) of 21. Kutchen has adjusted the P/E ratio to 19 for differences between the entities and Mach, for the purpose of fair valuing the NCI.

(c) Kutchen had purchased an 80% interest in Niche for $40 million on 1 April 20X4 when the fair value of the identifiable net assets was $44 million. The partial goodwill method had been used to calculate goodwill and an impairment of $2 million had arisen in the year ended 31 March 20X5. There were no other impairment charges or items requiring reclassification. The holding in Niche was sold for $50 million on 31 March 20X5 and the gain on sale in Kutchen's financial statements is currently recorded in other components of equity. The carrying value of Niche's identifiable net assets other than goodwill was $60 million at the date of sale. Kutchen had carried the investment in Niche at cost.

(d) Kutchen has decided to restructure one of its business segments. The plan was agreed by the board of directors on 1 January 20X5 and affects employees in two locations. In the first location, half of the factory units have been closed by 31 March 20X5 and the affected employees' pension benefits have been frozen. Any new employees will not be eligible to join the defined benefit plan. After the restructuring, the present value of the defined benefit obligation in this location is $8 million. The following table relates to location 1.

Value before restructuring	*Location 1*
	$m
Present value of defined benefit obligation	(10)
Fair value of plan assets	7
Net pension liability	(3)

In the second location, all activities have been discontinued. It has been agreed that employees will receive a payment of $4 million in exchange for the pension liability of $2·4 million in the unfunded pension scheme. Kutchen estimates that the costs of the above restructuring excluding pension costs will be $6 million. Kutchen has not accounted for the effects of the restructuring in its financial statements because it is planning a rights issue and does not wish to depress the share price. Therefore there has been no formal announcement of the restructuring. The pension liability is shown in non-current liabilities.

(e) Kutchen manufactures equipment for lease or sale. On 31 March 20X5, Kutchen leased out equipment under a ten year finance lease. The selling price of the leased item was $50 million and the net present value of the lease payments was $47 million. The carrying value of the leased asset was $40 million and the present value of the residual value of the product when it reverts back to Kutchen at the end of the lease term is $2.8 million. Kutchen has shown sales of $50 million and cost of sales of $40 million in its financial statements in respect of this transaction.

(f) Kutchen has impairment tested its non-current assets. It was decided that a building located overseas was impaired because of major subsidence. The building was acquired on 1 April 20X4 at a cost of 25 million dinars when the exchange was 2 dinars to the dollar. The building is carried at cost. At 31 March 20X5, the recoverable amount of the building was deemed to be 17.5 million dinars. The exchange rate at 31 March 20X5 is 2·5 dinars to the dollar. Buildings are depreciated over 25 years.

The tax base and carrying amounts of the non-current assets before the impairment write down were identical. The impairment of the non-current assets is not allowable for tax purposes. Kutchen has not made any impairment or deferred tax adjustment for the above. Kutchen expects to make profits for the foreseeable future and assume the tax rate is 25%.

No other deferred tax effects are required to be taken into account other than on the above non-current assets.

Required

(a) Prepare the consolidated statement of financial position for the Kutchen Group as at 31 March 20X5. **(35 marks)**

(b) When Kutchen acquired the majority shareholding in Mach, there was an option on the remaining non-controlling interest (NCI), which could be exercised at any time up to 31 December 20X5. On 30 April 20X5, Kutchen acquired the remaining NCI which related to the purchase of Mach. The payment for the NCI was structured so that it contained a fixed initial payment and a series of contingent amounts payable over the following two years. The contingent payments were to be based on the future profits of Mach up to a maximum amount. Kutchen felt that the fixed initial payment was an equity transaction. Additionally, Kutchen was unsure as to whether the contingent payments were either equity, financial liabilities or contingent liabilities.

After a board discussion which contained disagreement as to the accounting treatment, Kutchen is preparing to disclose the contingent payments in accordance with IAS 37 *Provisions, contingent liabilities and contingent assets.* The disclosure will include the estimated timing of the payments and the directors' estimate of the amounts to be settled.

Required

Advise Kutchen on the difference between equity and liabilities, and on the proposed accounting treatment of the contingent payments on acquisition of the NCI of Mach. **(8 marks)**

(c) The directors of Kutchen are considering the purchase of a company in the USA. They have heard that the accounting standards in the USA are 'rules based' and that there are significant differences of opinion as to whether 'rules based' standards are superior to 'principles based' standards. It is said that this is due to established national approaches and contrasting regulatory philosophies. The directors feel that 'principles based' standards are a greater ethical challenge to an accountant than 'rules based' standards.

Required

Discuss the philosophy behind 'rules based' and 'principles based' accounting standards, setting out the ethical challenges which may be faced by accountants if there were a switch in a jurisdiction from 'rules based' to 'principles based' accounting standards. **(7 marks)**

(Total = 50 marks)

47 Case study question: Robby

98 mins

6/12

The following draft statements of financial position relate to Robby, Hail and Zinc, all public limited companies, as at 31 May 20X3

	Robby $m	*Hail* $m	*Zinc* $m
Assets			
Non-current assets			
Property, plant and equipment	112	60	26
Investments in subsidiaries:			
Hail	55		
Zinc	19		
Financial assets	9	6	14
Joint operation	6		
Current assets	5	7	12
Total assets	206	73	52
Equity and liabilities			
Ordinary shares	25	20	10
Other components of equity	11	–	–
Retained earnings	70	27	19
Total equity	106	47	29
Non-current liabilities:	53	20	21
Current liabilities	47	6	2
Total equity and liabilities	206	73	52

The following information is relevant to the preparation of the group financial statements of Robby.

(a) On 1 June 20X1, Robby acquired 80% of the equity interests of Hail. The purchase consideration comprised cash of $50 million. Robby has treated the investment in Hail at fair value through other comprehensive income (OCI).

A dividend received from Hail on 1 January 20X3 of $2 million has similarly been credited to OCI.

It is Robby's policy to measure the non-controlling interest at fair value and this was $15 million on 1 June 20X1.

On 1 June 20X1, the fair value of the identifiable net assets of Hail was $60 million and the retained earnings of Hail were $16 million. The excess of the fair value of the net assets is due to an increase in the value of non-depreciable land.

(b) On 1 June 20X0, Robby acquired 5% of the ordinary shares of Zinc. Robby had treated this investment at fair value through profit or loss in the financial statements to 31 May 20X2.

On 1 December 20X2, Robby acquired a further 55% of the ordinary shares of Zinc and gained control of the company.

The consideration for the acquisitions was as follows.

	Shareholding	*Consideration* $m
1 June 20X0	5%	2
1 December 20X2	55%	16
	60%	18

At 1 December 20X2, the fair value of the equity interest in Zinc held by Robby before the business combination was $5 million.

It is Robby's policy to measure the non-controlling interest at fair value and this was $9 million on 1 December 20X2.

The fair value of the identifiable net assets at 1 December 20X2 of Zinc was $26 million, and the retained earnings were $15 million. The excess of the fair value of the net assets is due to an increase in the value of property, plant and equipment (PPE), which was provisional pending receipt of the final valuations. These valuations were received on 1 March 20X3 and resulted in an additional increase of $3 million in the fair value of PPE at the date of acquisition. This increase does not affect the fair value of the non-controlling interest at acquisition. PPE is to be depreciated on the straight-line basis over a remaining period of five years.

(c) Robby has a 40% share of a joint operation, a natural gas station. Assets, liabilities, revenue and costs are apportioned on the basis of shareholding. The following information relates to the joint arrangement activities.

   (i) The natural gas station cost $15 million to construct and was completed on 1 June 20X2 and is to be dismantled at the end of its life of ten years. The present value of this dismantling cost to the joint arrangement at 1 June 20X2, using a discount rate of 5%, was $2 million.

   (ii) In the year, gas with a direct cost of $16 million was sold for $20 million. Additionally, the joint arrangement incurred operating costs of $0.5 million during the year.

   Robby has only contributed and accounted for its share of the construction cost, paying $6 million. The revenue and costs are receivable and payable by the other joint operator who settles amounts outstanding with Robby after the year end.

(d) Robby purchased PPE for $10 million on 1 June 20X0. It has an expected useful life of twenty years and is depreciated on the straight-line method. On 31 May 20X2, the PPE was revalued to $11 million. At 31 May 20X3, impairment indicators triggered an impairment review of the PPE. The recoverable amount of the PPE was $7.8 million. The only accounting entry posted for the year to 31 May 20X3 was to account for the depreciation based on the revalued amount as at 31 May 20X2. Robby's accounting policy is to make a transfer of the excess depreciation arising on the revaluation of PPE.

(e) Robby held a portfolio of trade receivables with a carrying amount of $4 million at 31 May 20X3. At that date, the entity entered into a factoring agreement with a bank, whereby it transfers the receivables in exchange for $3.6 million in cash. Robby has agreed to reimburse the factor for any shortfall between the amount collected and $3.6 million. Once the receivables have been collected, any amounts above $3.6 million, less interest on this amount, will be repaid to Robby. Robby has derecognised the receivables and charged $0.4 million as a loss to profit or loss.

(f) Immediately prior to the year end, Robby sold land to a third party at a price of $16 million with an option to purchase the land back on 1 July 20X3 for $16 million plus a premium of 3%. The market value of the land is $25 million on 31 May 20X3 and the carrying amount was $12 million. Robby accounted for the sale, consequently eliminating the bank overdraft at 31 May 20X3.

Required

(a) Prepare a consolidated statement of financial position of the Robby Group at 31 May 20X3 in accordance with International Financial Reporting Standards. **(35 marks)**

(b) (i) In the above scenario (information point (e)), Robby holds a portfolio of trade receivables and enters into a factoring agreement with a bank, whereby it transfers the receivables in exchange for cash. Robby additionally agreed to other terms with the bank as regards any collection shortfall and repayment of any monies to Robby. Robby derecognised the receivables. This is an example of the type of complex transaction that can arise out of normal terms of trade. The rules regarding derecognition are quite complex and are often not understood by entities.

   Describe the rules of IFRS 9 *Financial Instruments* relating to the derecognition of a financial asset and how these rules affect the treatment of the portfolio of trade receivables in Robby's financial statements. **(9 marks)**

   (ii) Discuss the legitimacy of Robby selling land just prior to the year end in order to show a better liquidity position for the group and whether this transaction is consistent with an accountant's responsibilities to users of financial statements. **(6 marks)**

   Note. Your answer should include reference to the above scenario.

(Total = 50 marks)

48 Case study question: Ashanti

98 mins

6/10, amended

The following financial statements relate to Ashanti, a public limited company.

ASHANTI GROUP: STATEMENTS OF PROFIT OR LOSS AND OTHER COMPREHENSIVE INCOME
FOR THE YEAR ENDED 30 APRIL 20X5

	Ashanti	*Bochem*	*Ceram*
	$m	$m	$m
Revenue	810	235	142
Cost of sales	(686)	(137)	(84)
Gross profit	124	98	58
Other income	31	17	12
Distribution costs	(30)	(21)	(26)
Administrative costs	(55)	(29)	(12)
Finance costs	(8)	(6)	(8)
Profit before tax	62	59	24
Income tax expense	(21)	(23)	(10)
Profit for the year	41	36	14
Other comprehensive income for the year, net of tax –			
Items that will not be reclassified to profit or loss:			
Investment in equity instruments	20	9	6
Gains (net) on PPE revaluation	12	6	–
Actuarial losses on defined benefit plan	(14)	–	–
Other comprehensive income for the year, net of tax	18	15	6
Total comprehensive income and expense for year	59	51	20

The following information is relevant to the preparation of the group statement of profit or loss and other comprehensive income:

(i) On 1 May 20X3, Ashanti acquired 70% of the equity interests of Bochem, a public limited company. The purchase consideration comprised cash of $150 million and the fair value of the identifiable net assets was $160 million at that date. The fair value of the non-controlling interest in Bochem was $54 million on 1 May 20X3. Ashanti wishes to use the 'full goodwill' method for all acquisitions. The share capital and retained earnings of Bochem were $55 million and $85 million respectively and other components of equity were $10 million at the date of acquisition. The excess of the fair value of the identifiable net assets at acquisition is due to an increase in the value of plant, which is depreciated on the straight-line method and has a five year remaining life at the date of acquisition. Ashanti disposed of a 10% equity interest to the non-controlling interests (NCI) of Bochem on 30 April 20X5 for a cash consideration of $34 million. The carrying value of the net assets of Bochem at 30 April 20X5 was $210 million before any adjustments on consolidation. Goodwill has been impairment tested annually and as at 30 April 20X4 had reduced in value by 15% and at 30 April 20X5 had lost a further 5% of its original value before the sale of the equity interest to the NCI. The goodwill impairment should be allocated between group and NCI on the basis of equity shareholding.

(ii) Bochem acquired 80% of the equity interests of Ceram, a public limited company, on 1 May 20X3. The purchase consideration was cash of $136 million. Ceram's identifiable net assets were fair valued at $115 million and the NCI of Ceram attributable to Ashanti had a fair value of $26 million at that date. On 1 November 20X4, Bochem disposed of 50% of the equity of Ceram for a consideration of $90 million. Ceram's identifiable net assets were $160 million and the consolidated value of the NCI of Ceram attributable to Bochem was $35 million at the date of disposal. The remaining equity interest of Ceram held by Bochem was fair valued at $45 million. After the disposal, Bochem can still exert significant influence. Goodwill had been impairment tested and no impairment had occurred. Ceram's profits are deemed to accrue evenly over the year.

(iii) Ashanti has sold inventory to both Bochem and Ceram in October 20X4. The sale price of the inventory was $10 million and $5 million respectively. Ashanti sells goods at a gross profit margin of 20% to group companies and third parties. At the year-end, half of the inventory sold to Bochem remained unsold but the entire inventory sold to Ceram had been sold to third parties.

(iv) Included in Ashanti's trade receivables is an amount due from its customer Kumasi of $128.85m. This relates to a sale which took place on 1 May 20X4, payable in three annual instalments of $50m commencing 30 April 20X5 discounted at a market rate of interest adjusted to reflect the risks of Kumasi of 8%. Based on previous sales where consideration has been received in annual instalments, the directors of Kumasi estimate a lifetime expected credit loss in relation to this receivable of $75.288m. The probability of default over next twelve months is estimated at 25%. For trade receivables containing a significant financing component, Ashanti chooses to follow the three stage approach for impairments (rather than always measuring the loss allowance at an amount equal to lifetime credit losses). The $128.85m was recorded in receivables and revenue, but no other accounting entries have been made.

(v) Ashanti sold $5 million of goods to a customer who recently made an announcement that it is restructuring its debts with its suppliers including Ashanti. It is probable that Ashanti will not recover the amounts outstanding. The goods were sold after the announcement was made although the order was placed prior to the announcement. Ashanti wishes to make an additional allowance of $8 million against the total receivable balance at the year end, of which $5 million relates to this sale.

(vi) Ashanti owned a piece of property, plant and equipment (PPE) which cost $12 million and was purchased on 1 May 20X3. It is being depreciated over ten years on the straight-line basis with zero residual value. On 30 April 20X4, it was revalued to $13 million and on 30 April 20X5, the PPE was revalued to $8 million. The whole of the revaluation loss had been posted to other comprehensive income and depreciation has been charged for the year. It is Ashanti's company policy to make all necessary transfers for excess depreciation following revaluation.

(vii) The salaried employees of Ashanti are entitled to 25 days paid leave each year. The entitlement accrues evenly over the year and unused leave may be carried forward for one year. The holiday year is the same as the financial year. At 30 April 20X5, Ashanti has 900 salaried employees and the average unused holiday entitlement is three days per employee. 5% of employees leave without taking their entitlement and there is no cash payment when an employee leaves in respect of holiday entitlement. There are 255 working days in the year and the total annual salary cost is $19 million. No adjustment has been made in the financial statements for the above and there was no opening accrual required for holiday entitlement.

(viii) As permitted by IFRS 9 *Financial instruments* all group companies have made an irrevocable election to recognise changes in the fair value of investments in equity instruments (excluding shares group entities) in in other comprehensive income (items that will not be reclassified to profit or loss).

(ix) Ignore any taxation effects of the above adjustments and the disclosure requirements of IFRS 5 *Non-current assets held for sale and discontinued operations.*

Required

(a) Prepare a consolidated statement of profit or loss and other comprehensive income for the year ended 30 April 20X5 for the Ashanti Group. **(35 marks)**

(b) Explain the factors which provide encouragement to companies to disclose social and environmental information in their financial statements, briefly discussing whether the content of such disclosure should be at the company's discretion. **(8 marks)**

(c) Discuss the nature of and incentives for 'management of earnings' and whether such a process can be deemed to be ethically acceptable. **(7 marks)**

(Total = 50 marks)

49 Preparation question: Foreign operation

BPP Note. In this question the proformas are given to you to help you get used to setting out your answer. You may wish to transfer them to a separate sheet, or alternatively use a separate sheet for your workings only.

Standard Co acquired 80% of Odense SA for $520,000 on 1 January 20X4 when the retained reserves of Odense were 2,100,000 Danish Krone.

An impairment test conducted at the year end revealed impairment losses of 168,000 Danish Krone relating to Odense's recognised goodwill. No impairment losses had previously been recognised.

The translation differences in the consolidated financial statements at 31 December 20X5 relating to the translation of the financial statements of Odense (excluding goodwill) were $27,000. Retained reserves of Odense in Odense's separate financial statements in the post-acquisition period to 31 December 20X5 as translated amounted to $138,000. The dividends charged to retained earnings in 20X6 were paid on 31 December 20X6.

It is the group's policy to value the non-controlling interest at acquisition at its proportionate share of the fair value of the subsidiary's net assets.

Exchange rates were as follows:

	Kr to $1
1 January 20X4	9.4
31 December 20X5	8.8
31 December 20X6	8.1
Average 20X6	8.4

Required

Prepare the consolidated statement of financial position, statement of profit or loss and other comprehensive income and statement of changes in equity extract for retained earnings of the Standard Group for the year ended 31 December 20X6.

Set out your answer below, using a separate sheet for workings.

STATEMENTS OF FINANCIAL POSITION AT 31 DECEMBER 20X6

	Standard	*Odense*	*Rate*	*Odense*	*Consol*
	$'000	Kr'000		$'000	$'000
Property, plant and equipment	1,285	4,400	8.1	543	
Investment in Odense	520	–		–	
Goodwill	–	–		–	
	1,805	4,400		543	
Current assets	410	2,000	8.1	247	
	2,215	6,400		790	
Share capital	500	1,000	9.4	106	
Retained reserves	1,115				
Pre-acquisition		2,100	9.4	224	
Post-acquisition			Bal	324	
	–	–			
	1,615	5,300		654	
Non-controlling interest					
Loans	200	300	8.1	37	
Current liabilities	400	800	8.1	99	
	600	1,100		136	
	2,215	6,400		790	

STATEMENT OF PROFIT OR LOSS AND OTHER COMPREHENSIVE INCOME FOR YEAR ENDED 31 DECEMBER 20X6

	Standard	*Odense*	*Rate*	*Odense*	*Consol*
	$'000	Kr'000		$'000	$'000
Revenue	1,125	5,200	8.4	619	
Cost of sales	(410)	(2,300)	8.4	(274)	
Gross profit	715	2,900		345	
Other expenses	(180)	(910)	8.4	(108)	
Impairment loss	–	–		–	
Dividend from Odense	40				
Profit before tax	575	1,990		237	
Income tax expense	(180)	(640)	8.4	(76)	
Profit for the year	395	1,350		161	
Other comprehensive income for the year:					
Items that may be reclassified to profit or loss					
Exchange differences on translation of foreign operation	–	–			
Total comprehensive income for the year	395	1,350			
Profit attributable to:					
Owners of the parent					
Non-controlling interest					
Total comprehensive income attributable to:					
Owners of the parent					
Non-controlling interest					

STATEMENTS OF CHANGES IN EQUITY FOR THE YEAR (EXTRACT FOR RETAINED RESERVES)

	Standard	*Odense*
	$'000	Kr'000
Balance at 1 January 20X6	915	3,355
Dividends paid	(195)	(405)
Total comprehensive income for the year	395	1,350
Balance at 31 December 20X6	1,115	4,300

CONSOLIDATED STATEMENT OF CHANGES IN EQUITY
FOR YEAR ENDED 31 DECEMBER 20X6 (EXTRACTS)

	Retained Earnings
	$'000
Balance at 1 January 20X6	1,065
Dividends paid	
Total comprehensive income for the year	
Balance at 31 December 20X6	

50 Aspire

49 mins

6/14

Aspire, a public limited company, operates many of its activities overseas. The directors have asked for advice on the correct accounting treatment of several aspects of Aspire's overseas operations. Aspire's functional currency is the dollar.

(a) Aspire has created a new subsidiary, which is incorporated in the same country as Aspire. The subsidiary has issued 2 million dinars of equity capital to Aspire, which paid for these shares in dinars. The subsidiary has also raised 100,000 dinars of equity capital from external sources and has deposited the whole of the capital with a bank in an overseas country whose currency is the dinar. The capital is to be invested in dinar denominated bonds. The subsidiary has a small number of staff and its operating expenses, which are low, are incurred in dollars. The profits are under the control of Aspire. Any income from the investment is either passed on to Aspire in the form of a dividend or reinvested under instruction from Aspire. The subsidiary does not make any decisions as to where to place the investments.

Aspire would like advice on how to determine the functional currency of the subsidiary. **(7 marks)**

(b) Aspire has a foreign branch which has the same functional currency as Aspire. The branch's taxable profits are determined in dinars. On 1 May 20X3, the branch acquired a property for 6 million dinars. The property had an expected useful life of 12 years with a zero residual value. The asset is written off for tax purposes over eight years. The tax rate in Aspire's jurisdiction is 30% and in the branch's jurisdiction is 20%. The foreign branch uses the cost model for valuing its property and measures the tax base at the exchange rate at the reporting date.

Aspire would like an explanation (including a calculation) as to why a deferred tax charge relating to the asset arises in the group financial statements for the year ended 30 April 20X4 and the impact on the financial statements if the tax base had been translated at the historical rate. **(6 marks)**

(c) On 1 May 20X3, Aspire purchased 70% of a multi-national group whose functional currency was the dinar. The purchase consideration was $200 million. At acquisition, the net assets at cost were 1,000 million dinars. The fair values of the net assets were 1,100 million dinars and the fair value of the non-controlling interest was 250 million dinars. Aspire uses the full goodwill method.

Aspire wishes to know how to deal with goodwill arising on the above acquisition in the group financial statements for the year ended 30 April 20X4. **(5 marks)**

(d) Aspire took out a foreign currency loan of 5 million dinars at a fixed interest rate of 8% on 1 May 20X3. The interest is paid at the end of each year. The loan will be repaid after two years on 30 April 20X5. The interest rate is the current market rate for similar two-year fixed interest loans.

Aspire requires advice on how to account for the loan and interest in the financial statements for the year ended 30 April 20X4. **(5 marks)**

Aspire has a financial statement year end of 30 April 20X4 and the average currency exchange rate for the year is not materially different from the actual rate.

Exchange rates	$1 = dinars
1 May 20X3	5
30 April 20X4	6
Average exchange rate for year ended 30 April 20X4	5.6

Required

Advise the directors of Aspire on their various requests above, showing suitable calculations where necessary.

Note. The mark allocation is shown against each of the four issues above.

Professional marks will be awarded in this question for clarity and quality of presentation **(2 marks)**

(Total = 25 marks)

51 Case study question: Bubble

98 mins

Sep/Dec 15

The following draft financial statements relate to Bubble, a public limited company and two other companies in which it owns investments.

DRAFT STATEMENTS OF FINANCIAL POSITION AS AT 31 OCTOBER 20X5

	Bubble $m	*Salt* $m	*Tyslar* Dinars m
Assets			
Non-current assets:			
Property, plant and equipment	280	105	390
Investment in Salt	110	–	–
Investment in Tyslar	46	–	–
Financial assets	12	9	98
	448	114	488
Current assets			
Inventories	20	12	16
Trade and other receivables	30	25	36
Cash and cash equivalents	14	11	90
	64	48	142
Total assets	512	162	630
Equity			
Equity shares	80	50	210
Retained earnings	230	74	292
Other components of equity	40	12	-
Total equity	350	136	502
Non-current liabilities	95	7	110
Current liabilities	67	19	18
	162	26	128
Total equity and liabilities	512	162	630

The following information is relevant to the preparation of the group statement of financial position.

(a) Bubble acquired 80% of the equity shares of Salt on 1 November 20X3 when Salt's retained earnings were $56m and other components of equity were $8m. The fair value of the net assets of Salt was $120m at the date of acquisition. This does not include a contingent liability which was disclosed in Salt's financial statements as a possible obligation of $5m. The fair value of the obligation was assessed as $1m at the date of acquisition and remained unsettled as at 31 October 20X5. $5m is still disclosed as a possible obligation with no change in its fair value. Any remaining difference in the fair value of the net assets at acquisition relates to non-depreciable land. The fair value of the non-controlling interest at acquisition was estimated as $25m. Bubble always adopts the full goodwill method under IFRS 3 *Business combinations.*

(b) Bubble also owns 60% of the equity shares of Tyslar, a company located overseas which uses the dinar as its functional currency. The shares in Tyslar were acquired on 1 November 20X4 at a cost of 368 million dinars. At the date of acquisition, retained earnings were 258 million dinars and Tyslar had no other components of equity. No fair value adjustments were deemed necessary in relation to the acquisition of Tyslar. The fair value of the non-controlling interest was estimated as 220 million dinars at acquisition.

An impairment review of goodwill was undertaken as at 31 October 20X5. No impairment was necessary in relation to Salt, but the goodwill of Tyslar is to be impaired by 20%. Neither Bubble, Salt nor Tyslar has issued any equity shares since acquisition.

(c) On 1 February 20X5, Bubble gave an interest-free loan to Tyslar for $10m. Tyslar recorded this correctly in its financial statements using the spot rate of exchange. Tyslar repaid $5m on 1 July 20X5 when the spot exchange rate was $1 to 10 dinars. Tyslar therefore reduced its non-current liabilities by 50 million dinars. No further entries were made in Tyslar's financial statements. The remaining balances remain within the financial assets of Bubble and the non-current liabilities of Tyslar.

(d) Bubble wished to expand its overseas operations and on 1 May 20X5 acquired an overseas property with a fair value of 58·5 million dinars. In exchange for the building, Bubble paid the supplier with land which Bubble had held but had yet to determine its use. The carrying amount of the land was $5m but it had an open market value of $7m. Bubble was unsure as to how to deal with this transaction and so has transferred $5m from investment properties to property, plant and equipment. The transaction has commercial substance.

In addition, Bubble spent $0·5m to help relocate staff to the new property and added this amount to the cost of the asset. Bubble has made no other entries in its financial statements in relation to the property. Bubble has a policy of depreciating properties over 35 years and follows the revaluation model under IAS 16 Property, Plant & Equipment. Due to a surge in the market, it is estimated that the fair value of the property is 75 million dinars as at 31 October 20X5.

(e) Bubble operates a defined benefit scheme for its employees but has yet to record anything for the current year except to expense the cash contributions which were $6m. The opening position was a net liability of $15m which is included in the non-current liabilities of Bubble in its draft financial statements. Current service costs for the year were $5m and interest rates on good quality corporate bonds fell from 8% at the start of the year to 6% by 31 October 20X5. In addition, a payment of $3m was made out of the cash of the pension scheme in relation to employees who left the scheme. The reduction in the pension scheme liability as a result of the curtailment was $4m. The actuary has assessed that the scheme is in deficit by $17m as at 31 October 20X5.

(f) The following exchange rates are relevant to the preparation of the group financial statements:

	Dinars to $
1 November 20X4	8
1 February 20X5	9
1 May 20X5	9
31 October 20X5	9.5
Average for year to 31 October 20X5	8.5

Required

(a) Prepare a consolidated statement of financial position of the Bubble Group at 31 October 20X5 in accordance with International Financial Reporting Standards. **(35 marks)**

(b) The directors of Bubble are not fully aware of the requirements of IAS 21 *The Effects of changes in foreign exchange rates* in relation to exchange rate differences. They would like advice on how exchange differences should be recorded on both monetary and non-monetary assets in the financial statements and how these differ from the requirements for the translation of an overseas entity. The directors also wish advice on what would happen to the exchange differences if Bubble were to sell all of its equity shares in Tyslar, and any practical issues which would arise on monitoring exchange differences if the remaining balance on the loan from Bubble to Tyslar was not intended to be repaid.

Required

Provide a brief memo for the directors of Bubble which identifies the correct accounting treatment for the various issues raised. **(9 marks)**

(c) The directors of Bubble are thinking of acquiring further overseas investments in the near future but the entity currently lacks sufficient cash to exploit such opportunities. They would prefer to raise finance from an equity issue as Bubble already has significant loans within non-current liabilities and they do not wish to increase Bubble's gearing any further. They are therefore keen to maximise the balance on the group retained earnings in order to attract the maximum level of investment possible. One proposal is that they may sell 5% of the equity interest in Tyslar during 20X6. This will improve the cash position but will enable Bubble to maintain control over Tyslar. In addition, the directors believe that the shares can be sold profitably to boost the retained earnings of Bubble and of the group. The directors intend to transfer the relevant proportion of the exchange differences on translation of the subsidiary to group retained earnings, knowing that this is contrary to accounting standards.

Required

Discuss why the proposed treatment of the exchange differences by the directors is not in compliance with International Financial Reporting Standards, explaining any ethical issues which may arise. **(6 marks)**

(Total = 50 marks)

52 Preparation question: Consolidated statement of cash flows

BPP Note. In this question, proformas are given to you to help you get used to setting out your answer. You may wish to transfer them to a separate sheet, or alternatively to use a separate sheet for your workings.

On 1 September 20X5 Swing Co acquired 70% of Slide Co for $5,000,000 comprising $1,000,000 cash and 1,500,000 $1 shares.

The statement of financial position of Slide Co at acquisition was as follows:

	$'000
Property, plant and equipment	2,700
Inventories	1,600
Trade receivables	600
Cash	400
Trade payables	(300)
Income tax payable	(200)
	4,800

The consolidated statement of financial position of Swing Co as at 31 December 20X5 was as follows:

	20X5	*20X4*
Non-current assets	$'000	$'000
Property, plant and equipment	35,500	25,000
Goodwill	1,400	–
	36,900	25,000
Current assets		
Inventories	16,000	10,000
Trade receivables	9,800	7,500
Cash	2,400	1,500
	28,200	19,000
	65,100	44,000
Equity attributable to owners of the parent		
Share capital	12,300	10,000
Share premium	5,800	2,000
Revaluation surplus	350	–
Retained earnings	32,100	21,900
	50,550	33,900
Non-controlling interest	1,750	–
	52,300	33,900
Current liabilities		
Trade payables	7,600	6,100
Income tax payable	5,200	4,000
	12,800	10,100
	65,100	44,000

The consolidated statement of profit or loss and other comprehensive income of Swing Co for the year ended 31 December 20X5 was as follows:

	20X5
	$'000
Profit before tax	16,500
Income tax expense	(5,200)
Profit for the year	11,300
Other comprehensive income (not reclassified to P/L)	
Revaluation surplus	500
Total comprehensive income for the year	11,800
Profit attributable to:	
Owners of the parent	11,100
Non-controlling interest	200
	11,300
Total comprehensive income for the year attributable to	
Owners of the parent	11,450
Non-controlling interest 200 + (500 × 30%)	350
	11,800

Notes:

1 Depreciation charged for the year was $5,800,000. The group made no disposals of property, plant and equipment.

2 Dividends paid by Swing Co amounted to $900,000.

It is the group's policy to value the non-controlling interest at its proportionate share of the fair value of the subsidiary's identifiable net assets.

Required

Prepare the consolidated statement of cash flows of Swing Co for the year ended 31 December 20X5. No notes are required.

CONSOLIDATED STATEMENT OF CASH FLOWS PROFORMA
STATEMENT OF CASH FLOWS FOR THE YEAR ENDED 31 DECEMBER 20X5

	$'000	$'000
Cash flows from operating activities		
Profit before tax		
Adjustments for:		
Depreciation		
Impairment losses		
Increase in trade receivables (W4)		
Increase in inventories (W4)		
Increase in trade payables (W4)		
Cash generated from operations		
Income taxes paid (W3)		
Net cash from operating activities		
Cash flows from investing activities		
Acquisition of subsidiary, net of cash acquired (W2)		
Purchase of property, plant & equipment (W1)		
Net cash used in investing activities		

	$'000	$'000
Cash flows from financing activities		
Proceeds from issue of share capital		
Dividends paid		
Dividends paid to non-controlling interest (W2)	———	
Net cash used in financing activities		———
Net decrease in cash and cash equivalents		
Cash and cash equivalents at the beginning of the period		
Cash and cash equivalents at the end of the period		

Workings

1 *Assets*

	Property, plant and equipment $'000	*Goodwill* $'000
b/d		–
OCI (revaluation)		
Depreciation/ Impairment		**(X)** β
Acquisition of sub/assoc		(W5)
Cash paid/(rec'd) β	**X**	–
c/d		

2 *Equity*

	Share capital $'000	*Share premium* $'000	*Retained earnings* $'000	*Non-controlling interest* $'000
b/d				–
P/L				
Acquisition of subsidiary				(W5)
Cash (paid)/rec'd β	**X**	**X**	**(X)***	**X**
c/d				

*Dividend paid is given in question but working shown for clarity.

3 *Liabilities*

	Tax payable $'000
b/d	
P/L	
Acquisition of subsidiary	
Cash (paid)/rec'd	**(X) β**
c/d	

4 *Working capital changes*

	Inventories $'000	*Receivables* $'000	*Payables* $'000
Balance b/d			
Acquisition of subsidiary			
Increase/(decrease) (balancing figure)	**X**	**X**	**X**
Balance c/d			

5 *Purchase of subsidiary*

	$'000
Cash received on acquisition of subsidiary	
Less cash consideration	
Cash outflow	**(X)**

Note. Only the **cash** consideration is included in the figure reported in the statement of cash flows. The **shares** issued as part of the consideration are reflected in the share capital working (W2) above.

Goodwill on acquisition (to show no impairment):

	$'000
Consideration	
Non-controlling interest	
Net assets acquired	
Goodwill	

53 Case study question: Weston

98 mins

Mar/Jun 16

The following information relates to the financial statements of the Weston Group.

WESTON GROUP
STATEMENT OF FINANCIAL POSITION AS AT 31 JANUARY

	20X6 $m	*20X5* $m
Assets		
Non-current assets		
Property, plant and equipment	352	386
Goodwill	4	19
Other intangible assets	37	27
Investment in associate	102	-
	495	432
Current assets		
Inventories	108	165
Trade and other receivables	106	104
Financial assets at amortised cost	19	-
Cash and cash equivalents	20	43
	253	312
	748	744
Equity and Liabilities		
Share capital	100	100
Retained earnings	377	270
Other components of equity	24	21
	501	391
Non-controlling interest	64	85
Total equity	565	476
Non-current liabilities		
Long-term borrowings	26	48
Retirement benefit liability	60	72
Net deferred tax liability	14	15
Total non-current liabilities	100	135
Current liabilities		
Trade and other payables	36	41
Current tax payable	47	92
Total current liabilities	83	133
Total liabilities	183	268
Total equity and liabilities	748	744

WESTON GROUP
STATEMENT OF PROFIT OR LOSS AND OTHER COMPREHENSIVE INCOME
FOR THE YEAR ENDED 31 JANUARY 20X6

	$m
Continuing operations	
Revenue	1,102
Cost of sales	(818)
Gross profit	284
Other income	14
Distribution costs	(45)
Administrative expenses	(63)
Finance costs	(23)
Share of profit of associate	16
Profit before tax	183
Income tax expense	(40)
Profit for the year from continuing operations	143
Discontinued operations	
Loss for the year from discontinued operations (Note (i))	(25)
Profit for the year	118
Other comprehensive income after tax (items that will not be reclassified to profit or loss)	
Remeasurement gains on defined benefit plan	3
Other comprehensive income for the year, net of tax	3
Total comprehensive income for the year	121
Profit/loss attributable to	
Owners of the parent	107
Non-controlling interest	11
	118
Total comprehensive income attributable to	
Owners of the parent	110
Non-controlling interest	11
	121

The following information relates to the financial statements of Weston.

(i) On 31 July 20X5, Weston disposed of their entire 80% equity holding in Northern for cash. The shares had been acquired on 31 July 20X1 for a consideration of $132m when the fair value of the net assets was $124m. This included a fair value uplift of $16m in relation to plant with a remaining useful life of eight years. Deferred tax at 25% on the fair value adjustment was also correctly provided for in the group accounts and is included within the fair value of net assets. The fair value of the non-controlling interest at acquisition was $28m. Goodwill, calculated under the full fair value method, was tested annually for impairment. At 31 January 20X5, goodwill relating to Northern had been impaired by 75%. A goodwill impairment charge has been included within administration expenses for the current year but does not relate to Northern.

The carrying values in the individual accounts of Northern at disposal are listed below. The fair value adjustment and subsequent deferred tax were not incorporated into the individual accounts of Northern.

	Carrying values $m
Property, plant and equipment	80
Inventory	38
Trade receivables	23
Trade and other payables	(10)
Deferred tax liability	(6)
Bank overdraft	(2)

(ii) The loss for the period from discontinued operations in the consolidated statement of profit or loss and other comprehensive income relates to Northern and can be analysed as follows.

	$m
Profit before tax	6
Income tax expense	(2)
Loss on disposal	(29)
	(25)

(iii) Weston purchased a 40% interest in an associate for cash on 1 February 20X5. The associate paid a dividend of $10m in the year ended 31 January 20X6.

(iv) The retirement benefit liability relates to Weston as other companies in the group operate defined contribution schemes. The latest actuarial valuation is as follows.

	$m
Net obligation at 1 February 20X5	72
Service cost component	11
Contributions to scheme	(19)
Remeasurements - actuarial gains	(4)
Net obligation at 31 January 20X6	60

The benefits paid in the period by the trustees of the scheme were $7m. Weston operates in a country which only allows tax relief when contributions are paid into the scheme. The tax base was therefore zero at 31 January 20X5 and 31 January 20X6. The tax rate paid by Weston is 25%. The defined benefit expense is included within administrative expenses.

(v) On 1 February 20X5, Weston commenced development expenditure on product Q. Product Q is expected to be launched during 20X7. $7m amortisation on other intangible assets is included within cost of sales.

(vi) There were no disposals of property, plant and equipment during the year except on the sale of Northern. Depreciation for the year was $20m and is included within the cost of sales.

(vii) The financial asset at amortised cost is a $20m two-year loan which Weston gave to an unconnected company on 1 February 20X5. Twelve month expected credit losses were estimated at $1m and have been charged to administrative expenses. The coupon and effective rate of interest were both 8%. Interest was received on 31 January 20X6 and recorded correctly in the consolidated financial statements despite a significant deterioration in economic conditions within the industry of the unconnected company. As a result, the investment is to be downgraded with an expected 40% chance of default on the remaining cash flows. No entry has yet been made to downgrade the investment in the consolidated financial statements.

(viii) Included within the trade and other payables at 31 January 20X5 was contingent consideration of $10m. A discount rate of 10% was used to measure the fair value of this obligation. This arose on the acquisition of Eastern, a subsidiary acquired several years ago. The consideration to be paid was contingent on the profits of Eastern. Eastern did not perform as well as expected during the year and Weston paid $7m in full and final settlement of the obligation on 31 January 20X6.

(ix) Weston did not pay a dividend to its shareholders during the year ended 31 January 20X6.

(a) *Required*

Prepare a group statement of cash flows for the Weston Group for the year ended 31 January 20X6 in accordance with the requirements of IAS 7 *Statements of cash flows.*

Note: Ignore deferred taxation other than where it is mentioned in the question. **(35 marks)**

(b) The directors of Weston have been reviewing the International Integrated Reporting Council's Framework for Integrated Reporting. The directors believe that International Financial Reporting Standards are already extensive and provide stakeholders with a comprehensive understanding of an entity's financial position and performance for the year. In particular, statements of cash flow enable stakeholders to assess the liquidity, solvency and financial adaptability of a business. They are concerned that any additional disclosures could be excessive and obscure the most useful information within a set of financial statements. They are therefore unsure as to the rationale for the implementation of a separate, or combined, integrated report.

Required

Discuss the extent to which statements of cash flow provide stakeholders with useful information about an entity and whether this information would be improved by the entity introducing an Integrated Report. **(8 marks)**

(c) Shortly before 31 January 20X6, Weston gave a $5m, zero interest, short-term loan to its subsidiary, Eastern. Eastern repaid the loan in full during February 20X6. Since the loan was repaid within Weston's usual credit terms of 30 days, it was classified as a trading item as at 31 January 20X6. Consequently Weston included the balance within trade and other receivables and Eastern included it within trade and other payables at the year end. Eastern has several bank loans with substantial debt covenants linked to both interest cover and its gearing ratio. The bank loans would have become immediately repayable should Eastern breach any of the terms of the covenants. Before receiving the loan, Eastern had a bank overdraft balance of $4·5m.

Required

Discuss the impact which the $5m loan would have on the debt covenants of Eastern and whether there are any ethical implications arising from the situation. You do not need to adjust your answer to part (a) in relation to this issue. **(7 marks)**

(Total = 50 marks)

54 Case study question: Angel — 98 mins

12/13

The following draft group financial statements relate to Angel, a public limited company:

ANGEL GROUP: STATEMENT OF FINANCIAL POSITION AS AT 30 NOVEMBER 20X3

	30 Nov 20X3	*30 Nov 20X2*
	$m	$m
Assets		
Non-current assets		
Property, plant and equipment	475	465
Goodwill	105	120
Other intangible assets	150	240
Investment in associate	80	–
Financial assets	215	180
	1,025	1,005
Current assets		
Inventories	155	190
Trade receivables	125	180
Cash and cash equivalents	465	355
	745	725
Total assets	1,770	1,730
Equity and liabilities		
Equity attributable to owners of the parent: to last million		
Share capital	850	625
Retained earnings	456	359
Other components of equity	29	20
	1,335	1,004
Non-controlling interest	90	65
Total equity	1,425	1,069

	30 Nov 20X3	30 Nov 20X2
	$m	$m
Non-current liabilities		
Long-term borrowings	26	57
Deferred tax	35	31
Retirement benefit liability	80	74
Total non-current liabilities	141	162
Current liabilities:		
Trade payables	155	361
Current tax payable	49	138
Total current liabilities	204	499
Total liabilities	345	661
Total equity and liabilities	1,770	1,730

ANGEL GROUP: STATEMENT OF PROFIT OR LOSS AND OTHER COMPREHENSIVE INCOME FOR THE YEAR ENDED 30 NOVEMBER 20X3

	$m
Revenue	1,238
Cost of sales	(986)
Gross profit	252
Other income	30
Administrative expenses	(45)
Other expenses	(50)
Operating profit	187
Finance costs	(11)
Share of profit of equity accounted investees (net of tax)	12
Profit before tax	188
Income tax expense	(46)
Profit for the year	142
Profit/loss attributable to	
Owners of the parent	111
Non-controlling interest	31
	142
Other comprehensive income for the year: items that will not be reclassified to profit or loss	
Financial assets	4
Revaluation of property, plant and equipment	8
Actuarial losses on defined benefit plan	(4)
Tax related to items not reclassified	(3)*
Other comprehensive income (net of tax) for the year	5
Total comprehensive income for the year	147
Total comprehensive income attributable to	
Owners of the parent	116
Non-controlling interest	31
	147

Note. Of the $3m tax, $1m relates to the financial assets.

ANGEL GROUP: STATEMENT OF CHANGES IN EQUITY FOR THE YEAR ENDED 30 NOVEMBER 20X3

	Share capital $m	*Retained earnings* $m	*Other components of equity: financial assets reserve* $m	*Other components of equity: revaluation reserve* $m	*Total* $m	*Non-controlling interest* $m	*Total equity* $m
Balance at 1 December 20X2	625	359	15	5	1,004	65	1,069
Share capital issued	225				225		225
Dividends for year		(10)			(10)	(6)	(16)
Total comprehensive income for the year		107	3	6	116	31	147
Balance at 30 November 20X3	850	456	18	11	1,335	90	1,425

The following information relates to the financial statements of the Angel Group.

(i) Angel decided to renovate a building which had a zero book value at 1 December 20X2. As a result, $3 million was spent during the year on its renovation. On 30 November 20X3, Angel received a cash grant of $2 million from the government to cover some of the refurbishment cost and the creation of new jobs which had resulted from the use of the building. The grant related equally to both job creation and renovation. The only elements recorded in the financial statements were a charge to revenue for the refurbishment of the building and the receipt of the cash grant, which has been credited to additions of property, plant and equipment (PPE). The building was revalued at 30 November 20X3 at $7 million.

Angel treats grant income on capital-based projects as deferred income.

(ii) On 1 December 20X2, Angel acquired all of the share capital of Sweety for $30 million. The book values and fair values of the identifiable assets and liabilities of Sweety at the date of acquisition are set out below, together with their tax base. Goodwill arising on acquisition is not deductible for tax purposes. There were no other acquisitions in the period. The tax rate is 30%. The fair values in the table below have been reflected in the year-end balances of the Angel Group.

	Carrying values $m	*Tax base* $m	*Fair values excluding deferred taxation* $m
Property, plant and equipment	12.0	10	14
Inventory	5.0	4	6
Trade receivables	3.0	3	3
Cash and cash equivalents	2.0	2	2
Total assets	22.0	19	25
Trade payables	(4.0)	(4)	(4)
Retirement benefit obligations	(1.0)		(1)
Deferred tax liability	(0.6)		
Net assets at acquisition	16.4	15	20

(iii) The retirement benefit is classified as a long-term borrowing in the statement of financial position and comprises the following.

	$m
Net obligation at 1 December 20X2	74
Net interest cost	3
Current service cost	8
Contributions to plan	(9)
Remeasurements – actuarial losses	4
Net obligation 30 November 20X3	80

The benefits paid in the period by the trustees of the plan were $6 million. Angel had included the obligation assumed on the purchase of Sweety in current service cost above, although the charge to administrative expenses was correct in the statement of profit and loss and other comprehensive income. There were no tax implications regarding the retirement benefit obligation. The defined benefit cost is included in administrative expenses.

(iv) The property, plant and equipment (PPE) comprises the following.

	$m
Carrying value at 1 December 20X2	465
Additions at cost including assets acquired on the purchase of subsidiary	80
Gains on property revaluation	8
Disposals	(49)
Depreciation	(29)
Carrying value at 30 November 20X3	475

Angel has constructed a machine which is a qualifying asset under IAS 23 *Borrowing costs* and has paid construction costs of $4 million. This amount has been charged to other expenses. Angel Group paid $11 million in interest in the year, which includes $1 million of interest which Angel wishes to capitalise under IAS 23. There was no deferred tax implication regarding this transaction.

The disposal proceeds were $63 million. The gain on disposal is included in administrative expenses.

(v) Angel purchased a 30% interest in an associate for cash on 1 December 20X2. The net assets of the associate at the date of acquisition were $280 million. The associate made a profit after tax of $40 million and paid a dividend of $10 million out of these profits in the year ended 30 November 20X3.

(vi) An impairment test carried out at 30 November 20X3 showed that goodwill and other intangible assets were impaired. The impairment of goodwill relates to 100% owned subsidiaries.

(vii) The following schedule relates to the financial assets owned by Angel.

	$m
Balance at 1 December 20X2	180
Less sales of financial assets at carrying value	(26)
Add purchases of financial assets	57
Add gain on revaluation of financial assets (investments in equity instruments)	4
Balance at 30 November 20X3	215

The sale proceeds of the financial assets were $40 million. Profit on the sale of the financial assets is included in 'other income' in the financial statements.

The financial assets included a mixture of financial assets measured at fair value through profit or loss and investments in equity instruments for which an irrevocable election had been made to hold them at fair value through other comprehensive income. All the financial assets at fair value through profit or loss were sold, with no revaluation gain arising in the year of sale before the date of sale.

(viii) The finance costs were all paid in cash in the period.

Required

(a) Prepare a consolidated statement of cash flows using the indirect method for the Angel Group plc for the year ended 30 November 20X3 in accordance with the requirements of IAS 7 *Statement of cash flows*.

Note. The notes to the statement of cash flows are not required. **(35 marks)**

(b) The directors of Angel are confused over several issues relating to IAS 7 *Statement of cash flows*. They wish to know the principles utilised by the International Accounting Standards Board in determining how cash flows are classified, including how entities determine the nature of the cash flows being analysed.

They have entered into the following transactions after the year end and wish to know how to deal with them in a cash flow statement, as they are unsure of the meaning of the definition of cash and cash equivalents.

Angel had decided after the year end to deposit the funds with the bank in two term deposit accounts as follows.

(i) $3 million into a 12-month term account, earning 3.5% interest. The cash can be withdrawn by giving 14 days' notice but Angel will incur a penalty, being the loss of all interest earned.

(ii) $7 million into a 12-month term account earning 3% interest. The cash can be withdrawn by giving 21 days' notice. Interest will be paid for the period of the deposit but if money is withdrawn, the interest will be at the rate of 2%, which is equivalent to the bank's stated rate for short-term deposits.

Angel is confident that it will not need to withdraw the cash from the higher-rate deposit within the term, but wants to keep easy access to the remaining $7 million to cover any working capital shortfalls which might arise.

Required

Discuss the principles behind the classifications in the statements of cash flows whilst advising Angel on how to treat the two transactions above. **(9 marks)**

(c) All accounting professionals are responsible for acting in the public interest, and for promoting professional ethics. The directors of Angel feel that when managing the affairs of a company the profit motive could conflict with the public interest and accounting ethics. In their view, the profit motive is more important than ethical behaviour and codes of ethics are irrelevant and unimportant.

Required

Discuss the above views of the directors regarding the fact that codes of ethics are irrelevant and unimportant. **(6 marks)**

(Total = 50 marks)

55 Case study question: Jocatt **98 mins**

12/10

The following draft group financial statements relate to Jocatt, a public limited company.

JOCATT GROUP
STATEMENT OF FINANCIAL POSITION AS AT 30 NOVEMBER

	20X2	*20X1*
	$m	$m
Assets		
Non-current assets		
Property, plant and equipment	327	254
Investment property	8	6
Goodwill	48	68
Intangible assets	85	72
Investment in associate	54	–
Investments in equity instruments	94	90
	616	490

	20X2	20X1
	$m	$m
Current assets		
Inventories	105	128
Trade receivables	62	113
Cash and cash equivalents	232	143
	399	384
	1,015	874
Equity and Liabilities		
Equity attributable to the owners of the parent:		
Share capital	290	275
Retained earnings	351	324
Other components of equity	15	20
	656	619
Non-controlling interest	55	36
Total equity	711	655
Non-current liabilities		
Long-term borrowings	67	71
Deferred tax	35	41
Long-term provisions: pension liability	25	22
Total non-current liabilities	127	134
Current liabilities		
Trade payables	144	55
Current tax payable	33	30
Total current liabilities	177	85
Total liabilities	304	219
Total equity and liabilities	1,015	874

JOCATT GROUP
STATEMENT OF PROFIT OR LOSS AND OTHER COMPREHENSIVE INCOME
FOR THE YEAR ENDED 30 NOVEMBER 20X2

	$m
Revenue	432.0
Cost of sales	(317.0)
Gross profit	115.0
Other income	25.0
Distribution costs	(55.5)
Administrative expenses	(36.0)
Finance costs paid	(6.0)
Gains on property	10.5
Share of profit of associate	6.0
Profit before tax	59.0
Income tax expense	(11.0)
Profit for the year	48.0

	$m
Other comprehensive income after tax (items that will not be reclassified to profit or loss)	
Gain on investments in equity instruments (IEI)	2.0
Losses on property revaluation	(7.0)
Remeasurement losses on defined benefit plan	(6.0)
Other comprehensive income for the year, net of tax	(11.0)
Total comprehensive income for the year	37.0
Profit attributable to	
Owners of the parent	38.0
Non-controlling interest	10.0
	48.0
Total comprehensive income attributable to	
Owners of the parent	27.0
Non-controlling interest	10.0
	37.0

JOCATT GROUP
STATEMENT OF CHANGES IN EQUITY FOR THE YEAR ENDED 30 NOVEMBER 20X2

	Share capital	*Retained earnings*	*Investments in equity instruments*	*Revaluation surplus (PPE)*	*Total*	*Non-controlling interest*	*Total equity*
	$m	$m	$m	$m	$m	$m	$m
Balance at 1 December 20X1	275	324	4	16	619	36	655
Share capital issued	15				15		15
Dividends		(5)			(5)	(13)	(18)
Rights issue						2	2
Acquisitions						20	20
Total comprehensive income for the year		32	2	(7)	27	10	37
Balance at 30 November 20X2	290	351	6	9	656	55	711

The following information relates to the financial statements of Jocatt.

(i) On 1 December 20X0, Jocatt acquired 8% of the ordinary shares of Tigret. Jocatt had treated this as an investment in equity instruments in the financial statements to 30 November 20X1 with changes in fair value taken to profit or loss for the year. There were no changes in fair value in the year to 30 November 20X1. On 1 January 20X2, Jocatt acquired a further 52% of the ordinary shares of Tigret and gained control of the company. The consideration for the acquisitions was as follows.

	Holding	*Consideration*
		$m
1 December 20X0	8%	4
1 January 20X2	52%	30
	60%	34

At 1 January 20X2, the fair value of the 8% holding in Tigret held by Jocatt at the time of the business combination was $5 million and the fair value of the non-controlling interest in Tigret was $20 million. The purchase consideration at 1 January 20X2 comprised cash of $15 million and shares of $15 million.

The fair value of the identifiable net assets of Tigret, excluding deferred tax assets and liabilities, at the date of acquisition comprised the following.

	$m
Property, plant and equipment	15
Intangible assets	18
Trade receivables	5
Cash	7

The tax base of the identifiable net assets of Tigret was $40 million at 1 January 20X2. The tax rate of Tigret is 30%.

(ii) On 30 November 20X2,Tigret made a rights issue on a 1 for 4 basis. The issue was fully subscribed and raised $5 million in cash.

(iii) Jocatt purchased a research project from a third party including certain patents on 1 December 20X1 for $8 million and recognised it as an intangible asset. During the year, Jocatt incurred further costs, which included $2 million on completing the research phase, $4 million in developing the product for sale and $1 million for the initial marketing costs. There were no other additions to intangible assets in the period other than those on the acquisition of Tigret.

(iv) Jocatt operates a defined benefit scheme. The current service costs for the year ended 30 November 20X2 are $10 million. Jocatt enhanced the benefits on 1 December 20X1. The total cost of the enhancement is $2 million. The net interest on net plan assets was $8 million for the year and Jocatt recognises remeasurement gains and losses in accordance with IAS 19 as revised in 2011.

(v) Jocatt owns an investment property. During the year, part of the heating system of the property, which had a carrying value of $0.5 million, was replaced by a new system, which cost $1 million. Jocatt uses the fair value model for measuring investment property.

(vi) Jocatt had exchanged surplus land with a carrying value of $10 million for cash of $15 million and plant valued at $4 million. The transaction has commercial substance. Depreciation for the period for property, plant and equipment was $27 million.

(vii) Goodwill relating to all subsidiaries had been impairment tested in the year to 30 November 20X2 and any impairment accounted for. The goodwill impairment related to those subsidiaries which were 100% owned.

(viii) Deferred tax of $1 million arose in the year on the gains on investments in equity instruments in the year where the irrevocable election was made to take changes in fair value through other comprehensive income

(ix) The associate did not pay any dividends in the year.

Required

(a) Prepare a consolidated statement of cash flows for the Jocatt Group using the indirect method under IAS 7 *Statements of cash flows.*

Note: Ignore deferred taxation other than where it is mentioned in the question. **(35 marks)**

(b) Jocatt operates in the energy industry and undertakes complex natural gas trading arrangements, which involve exchanges in resources with other companies in the industry. Jocatt is entering into a long-term contract for the supply of gas and is raising a loan on the strength of this contract. The proceeds of the loan are to be received over the year to 30 November 20X3 and are to be repaid over four years to 30 November 20X7. Jocatt wishes to report the proceeds as operating cash flow because it is related to a long-term purchase contract. The directors of Jocatt receive extra income if the operating cash flow exceeds a predetermined target for the year and feel that the indirect method is more useful and informative to users of financial statements than the direct method.

(i) Comment on the directors' view that the indirect method of preparing statements of cash flow is more useful and informative to users than the direct method. **(8 marks)**

(ii) Discuss the reasons why the directors may wish to report the loan proceeds as an operating cash flow rather than a financing cash flow and whether there are any ethical implications of adopting this treatment. **(7 marks)**

(Total = 50 marks)

56 Glowball

49 mins

ACR, Pilot paper

The directors of Glowball, a public limited company, had discussed the study by the Institute of Environmental Management which indicated that over 35% of the world's largest 250 corporations are voluntarily releasing green reports to the public to promote corporate environmental performance and to attract customers and investors. They have heard that their main competitors are applying the 'Global Reporting Initiative' (GRI) in an effort to develop a worldwide format for corporate environmental reporting. However, the directors are unsure as to what this initiative actually means. Additionally they require advice as to the nature of any legislation or standards relating to environmental reporting, as they are worried that any environmental report produced by the company may not be of sufficient quality and may detract and not enhance their image if the report does not comply with recognised standards. Glowball has a reputation for ensuring the preservation of the environment in its business activities.

Further the directors have collected information in respect of a series of events which they consider to be important and worthy of note in the environmental report but are not sure as to how they would be incorporated in the environmental report or whether they should be included in the financial statements.

The events are as follows.

(a) Glowball is a company that pipes gas from offshore gas installations to major consumers. The company purchased its main competitor during the year and found that there were environmental liabilities arising out of the restoration of many miles of farmland that had been affected by the laying of a pipeline. There was no legal obligation to carry out the work but the company felt that there would be a cost of around $150 million if the farmland was to be restored.

(b) Most of the offshore gas installations are governed by operating licenses which specify limits to the substances which can be discharged to the air and water. These limits vary according to local legislation and tests are carried out by the regulatory authorities. During the year the company was prosecuted for infringements of an environmental law in the USA when toxic gas escaped into the atmosphere. In 20X2 the company was prosecuted five times and in 20X1 eleven times for infringement of the law. The final amount of the fine/costs to be imposed by the courts has not been determined but is expected to be around $5 million. The escape occurred over the seas and it was considered that there was little threat to human life.

(c) The company produced statistics that measure their improvement in the handling of emissions of gases which may have an impact on the environment. The statistics deal with:

  (i) Measurement of the release of gases with the potential to form acid rain. The emissions have been reduced by 84% over five years due to the closure of old plants.

  (ii) Measurement of emissions of substances potentially hazardous to human health. The emissions are down by 51% on 20W8 levels.

  (iii) Measurement of emissions to water that removes dissolved oxygen and substances that may have an adverse effect on aquatic life. Accurate measurement of these emissions is not possible but the company is planning to spend $70 million on research in this area.

(d) The company tries to reduce the environmental impacts associated with the siting and construction of its gas installations. This is done in the way that minimises the impact on wild life and human beings. Additionally when the installations are at the end of their life, they are dismantled and are not sunk into the sea. The current provision for the decommissioning of these installations is $215 million and there are still decommissioning costs of $407 million to be provided as the company's policy is to build up the required provision over the life of the installation.

Required

Prepare a report suitable for presentation to the directors of Glowball in which you discuss the following elements:

(a) Current reporting requirements and guidelines relating to environmental reporting. **(10 marks)**

(b) The nature of any disclosure which would be required in an environmental report and/or the financial statements for the events (a)–(d) above. **(15 marks)**

(The mark allocation includes four marks for the style and layout of the report.) **(Total = 25 marks)**

57 Preparation question: Current issues

BPP Note. Current developments are mainly covered within individual topics, for example all the questions on leasing test the recent standard IFRS 16, those on revenue recognition test IFRS 15 and the question on the *Conceptual Framework* tests the recent exposure draft.

(a) In January 2016, the IASB published IFRS 16 *Leases.*

(i) Briefly list the key changes.

(ii) Briefly suggest the main likely effects of the new standard.

(b) On-Ice Co, a retailer of frozen food, leases freezers from Icicle Co for ten years at $30,000 per year. This payment includes servicing costs.

On-Ice could lease the same make and model of freezers from Icicle for $27,000 per year without the servicing, and get the servicing done by another company for $5,000 per year.

Required

How should On-Ice account for the payments to Icicle?

(c) Discuss the significance of debt/equity distinction.

(d) Explain the types of and significance of additional performance measures, and suggest potential problems with such measures.

(e) Explain what is meant by the IASB 'Disclosure Initiative'. Briefly summarise its proposals relating to materiality.

58 Fair values and IFRS 13 — 49 mins

Financial statements have seen an increasing move towards the use of fair values in accounting. Advocates of 'fair value accounting' believe that fair value is the most relevant measure for financial reporting whilst others believe that historical cost provides a more useful measure. Issues have been raised over the reliability and measurement of fair values, and over the nature of the current level of disclosure in financial statements in this area.

In 2011 the IASB published IFRS 13 *Fair value measurement,* which sets out to sets out to define fair value, set out in a single IFRS a framework for measuring fair value and require disclosure about fair value measurements.

Required

(a) Discuss the view that fair value is a more relevant measure to use in corporate reporting than historical cost. **(12 marks)**

(b) Discuss the main changes introduced by IFRS 13 *Fair value measurement.* **(9 marks)**

(c) Fairview holds shares in Greenfield, which it treats as an equity instrument (a financial asset). Sale of this financial asset is restricted by contract to qualifying investors.
How would the fair value of this instrument be measured? **(4 marks)**

(Total = 25 marks)

59 Mehran

49 mins

Mar/Jun 16

The directors of Mehran, a public limited company, have seen many different ways of dealing with the measurement and disclosure of the fair value of assets, liabilities and equity instruments. They feel that this reduces comparability among different entities' financial statements. They would like advice on several transactions where they currently use fair value measurement as they have heard that the introduction of IFRS 13 *Fair value measurement,* while not interfering with the scope of fair value measurement, will reduce the extent of any diversity and inconsistency.

(a) Mehran, a public limited company, has just acquired a company, which comprises a farming and mining business. Mehran wishes advice on how to fair value some of the assets acquired.

One such asset is a piece of land, which is currently used for farming. The fair value of the land if used for farming is $5m. If the land is used for farming purposes, a tax credit currently arises annually, which is based upon the lower of 15% of the fair market value of land or $500,000 at the current tax rate. The current tax rate in the jurisdiction is 20%.

Mehran has determined that market participants would consider that the land could have an alternative use for residential purposes. The fair value of the land for residential purposes before associated costs is thought to be $7.4m. In order to transform the land from farming to residential use, there would be legal costs of $200,000, a viability analysis cost of $300,000 and costs of demolition of the farm buildings of $100,000. Additionally, permission for residential use has not been formally given by the legal authority and because of this, market participants have indicated that the fair value of the land, after the above costs, would be discounted by 20% because of the risk of not obtaining planning permission.

In addition, Mehran has acquired the brand name associated with the produce from the farm. Mehran has decided to discontinue the brand on the assumption that it will gain increased revenues from its own brands. Mehran has determined that if it ceases to use the brand, then the indirect benefits will be $20m. If it continues to use the brand, then the direct benefit will be $17m. **(6 marks)**

(b) Mehran wishes to fair value the inventory of the entity acquired. There are three different markets for the produce, which are mainly vegetables. The first is the local domestic market where Mehran can sell direct to retailers of the produce. The second domestic market is one where Mehran sells directly to manufacturers of canned vegetables. There are no restrictions on the sale of produce in either of the domestic markets other than the demand of the retailers and manufacturers. The final market is the export market but the government limits the amount of produce which can be exported. Mehran needs a licence from the government to export its produce. Farmers tend to sell all of the produce that they can in the export market and, when they do not have any further authorisation to export, they sell the remaining produce in the two domestic markets.

It is difficult to obtain information on the volume of trade in the domestic market where the produce is sold locally direct to retailers but Mehran feels that the market is at least as large as the domestic market – direct to manufacturers. The volumes of sales quoted below have been taken from trade journals.

	Domestic market – direct to retailers	*Domestic market – direct to manufacturers*	*Export market*
Volume – annual	Unknown	20,000 tonnes	10,000 tonnes
Volume – sales per month	10 tonnes	4 tonnes	60 tonnes
Price per tonne	$1,000	$800	$1,200
Transport costs per tonne	$50	$70	$100
Selling agents' fees per tonne	-	$4	$6

(10 marks)

(c) Mehran owns a non-controlling equity interest in Erham, a private company, and wishes to fair value it as at its financial year end of 31 March 20X6. Mehran acquired the ordinary share interest in Erham on 1 April 20X4. During the current financial year, Erham has issued further equity capital through the issue of preferred shares to a venture capital fund.

As a result of the preferred share issue, the venture capital fund now holds a controlling interest in Erham. The terms of the preferred shares, including the voting rights, are similar to those of the ordinary shares, except that the preferred shares have a cumulative fixed dividend entitlement for a period of four years and the preferred shares rank ahead of the ordinary shares upon the liquidation of Erham. The transaction price for the preferred shares was $15 per share.

Mehran wishes to know the factors which should be taken into account in measuring the fair value of their holding in the ordinary shares of Erham at 31 March 20X6 using a market-based approach. **(7 marks)**

Required

Discuss the way in which Mehran should fair value the above assets with reference to the principles of IFRS 13 *Fair value measurement*.

Note. The mark allocation is shown against each of the three issues above.

Professional marks will be awarded in this question for clarity and quality of presentation **(2 marks)**

(25 marks)

60 Pod

49 mins

Mar/Jun 16

The introduction of a new accounting standard can have significant impact on an entity by changing the way in which financial statements show particular transactions or events. In many ways, the impact of a new accounting standard requires the same detailed considerations as is required when an entity first moves from local Generally Accepted Accounting Practice to International Financial Reporting Standards (IFRS).

A new or significantly changed accounting standard often provides the key focus for examination of the financial statements of listed companies by national enforcers who issue common enforcement priorities. These priorities are often highlighted because of significant changes to accounting practices as a result of new or changed standards or because of the challenges faced by entities as a result of the current economic environment. Recent priorities have included recognition and measurement of deferred tax assets and impairment of financial and non-financial assets.

Required

(a) (i) Discuss the key practical considerations, and financial statement implications which an entity should consider when implementing a move to a new IFRS. **(7 marks)**

(ii) Discuss briefly the reasons why regulators might focus on the impairment of non-financial assets and deferred tax assets in a period of slow economic growth, setting out the key areas which entities should focus on when accounting for these elements. **(8 marks)**

(b) Pod is a listed company specialising in the distribution and sale of photographic products and services. Pod's statement of financial position included an intangible asset which was a portfolio of customers acquired from a similar business which had gone into liquidation. Pod changed its assessment of the useful life of this intangible asset from 'finite' to 'indefinite'. Pod felt that it could not predict the length of life of the intangible asset, stating that it was impossible to foresee the length of life of this intangible due to a number of factors such as technological evolution, and changing consumer behaviour.

Pod has a significant network of retail branches. In its financial statements, Pod changed the determination of a cash generating unit (CGU) for impairment testing purposes at the level of each major product line, rather than at each individual branch. The determination of CGUs was based on the fact that each of its individual branches did not operate on a standalone basis as some income, such as volume rebates, and costs were dependent on the nature of the product line rather than on individual branches. Pod considered that cash inflows and outflows for individual branches did not provide an accurate assessment of the actual cash generated by those branches. Pod, however, has daily sales information and monthly statements of profit or loss produced for each individual branch and this information is used to make decisions about continuing to operate individual branches

Required

Discuss whether the changes to accounting practice suggested by Pod are acceptable under International Financial Reporting Standards. **(8 marks)**

Professional marks will be awarded in the question for clarity and quality of presentation. **(2 marks)**

(Total = 25 marks)

61 Gasnature **49 mins**

Sep/Dec 15

(a) Gasnature is a publicly traded entity involved in the production and trading of natural gas and oil. Gasnature jointly owns an underground storage facility with another entity, Gogas. Both parties extract gas from offshore gas fields, which they own and operate independently from each other. Gasnature owns 55% of the underground facility and Gogas owns 45%. They have agreed to share services and costs accordingly, with decisions regarding the storage facility requiring unanimous agreement of the parties. The underground facility is pressurised so that the gas is pushed out when extracted. When the gas pressure is reduced to a certain level, the remaining gas is irrecoverable and remains in the underground storage facility until it is decommissioned. Local legislation requires the decommissioning of the storage facility at the end of its useful life. Gasnature wishes to know how to treat the agreement with Gogas including any obligation or possible obligation arising on the underground storage facility and the accounting for the irrecoverable gas. **(9 marks)**

(b) Gasnature has entered into a ten-year contract with Agas for the purchase of natural gas. Gasnature has made an advance payment to Agas for an amount equal to the total quantity of gas contracted for 10 years which has been calculated using the forecasted price of gas. The advance carries interest of 6% per annum, which is settled by way of the supply of extra gas. Fixed quantities of gas have to be supplied each month and there is a price adjustment mechanism in the contract whereby the difference between the forecasted price of gas and the prevailing market price is settled in cash monthly. If Agas does not deliver gas as agreed, Gasnature has the right to claim compensation at the current market price of gas. Gasnature wishes to know whether the contract with Agas should be accounted for under IFRS 9 *Financial instruments.* **(6 marks)**

(c) Additionally, Gasnature is finalising its financial statements for the year ended 31 August 20X5 and has the following issues.

(i) Gasnature purchased a major refinery on 1 January 20X5 and the directors estimate that a major overhaul is required every two years. The costs of the overhaul are approximately $5m which comprises $3m for parts and equipment and $2m for labour. The directors proposed to accrue the cost of the overhaul over the two years of operations up to that date and create a provision for the expenditure. **(4 marks)**

(ii) From October 20X4, Gasnature had undertaken exploratory drilling to find gas and up to 31 August 20X5 costs of $5m had been incurred. At 31 August 20X5, the results to date indicated that it was probable that there were sufficient economic benefits to carry on drilling and there were no indicators of impairment. During September 20X5, additional drilling costs of $2m were incurred and there was significant evidence that no commercial deposits existed and the drilling was abandoned. **(4 marks)**

Required

Discuss, with reference to International Financial Reporting Standards, how Gasnature should account for the above agreement and contract, and the issues raised by the directors

Note. The mark allocation is shown against each of the items above.

Professional marks will be awarded in this question for clarity and quality of presentation. **(2 marks)**

(Total = 25 marks)

62 Lockfine

49 mins

6/11

Lockfine, a public limited company, operates in the fishing industry and has recently made the transition to International Financial Reporting Standards (IFRS). Lockfine's reporting date is 30 April 20X9.

(a) In the IFRS opening statement of financial position at 1 May 20X7, Lockfine elected to measure its fishing fleet at fair value and use that fair value as deemed cost in accordance with IFRS 1 *First time adoption of international financial reporting standards.* The fair value was an estimate based on valuations provided by two independent selling agents, both of whom provided a range of values within which the valuation might be considered acceptable. Lockfine calculated fair value at the average of the highest amounts in the two ranges provided. One of the agents' valuations was not supported by any description of the method adopted or the assumptions underlying the calculation. Valuations were principally based on discussions with various potential buyers. Lockfine wished to know the principles behind the use of deemed cost and whether agents' estimates were a reliable form of evidence on which to base the fair value calculation of tangible assets to be then adopted as deemed cost. **(6 marks)**

(b) Lockfine was unsure as to whether it could elect to apply IFRS 3 *Business Combinations* retrospectively to past business combinations on a selective basis, because there was no purchase price allocation available for certain business combinations in its opening IFRS statement of financial position.

As a result of a major business combination, fishing rights of that combination were included as part of goodwill. The rights could not be recognised as a separately identifiable intangible asset at acquisition under the local GAAP because a reliable value was unobtainable for the rights. The fishing rights operated for a specified period of time.

On transition from local GAAP to IFRS, the fishing rights were included in goodwill and not separately identified because they did not meet the qualifying criteria set out in IFRS 1, even though it was known that the fishing rights had a finite life and would be fully impaired or amortised over the period specified by the rights. Lockfine wished to amortise the fishing rights over their useful life and calculate any impairment of goodwill as two separate calculations. **(6 marks)**

(c) Lockfine has internally developed intangible assets comprising the capitalised expenses of the acquisition and production of electronic map data which indicates the main fishing grounds in the world. The intangible assets generate revenue for the company in their use by the fishing fleet and are a material asset in the statement of financial position. Lockfine had constructed a database of the electronic maps. The costs incurred in bringing the information about a certain region of the world to a higher standard of performance are capitalised. The costs related to maintaining the information about a certain region at that same standard of performance are expensed. Lockfine's accounting policy states that intangible assets are valued at historical cost. The company considers the database to have an indefinite useful life which is reconsidered annually when it is tested for impairment. The reasons supporting the assessment of an indefinite useful life were not disclosed in the financial statements and neither did the company disclose how it satisfied the criteria for recognising an intangible asset arising from development. **(6 marks)**

(d) The Lockfine board has agreed two restructuring projects during the year to 30 April 20X9:

Plan A involves selling 50% of its off-shore fleet in one year's time. Additionally, the plan is to make 40% of its seamen redundant. Lockfine will carry out further analysis before deciding which of its fleets and related employees will be affected. In previous announcements to the public, Lockfine has suggested that it may restructure the off-shore fleet in the future.

Plan B involves the reorganisation of the headquarters in 18 months time, and includes the redundancy of 20% of the headquarters' workforce. The company has made announcements before the year end but there was a three month consultation period which ended just after the year end, whereby Lockfine was negotiating with employee representatives. Thus individual employees had not been notified by the year end.

Lockfine proposes recognising a provision in respect of Plan A but not Plan B. **(5 marks)**

Professional marks will be awarded in this question for clarity and quality of discussion. **(2 marks)**

Required

Discuss the principles and practices to be used by Lockfine in accounting for the above valuation and recognition issues.

(Total = 25 marks)

63 Seltec **49 mins**

Seltec, a public limited company, processes and sells edible oils and uses several financial instruments to spread the risk of fluctuation in the price of the edible oils. The entity operates in an environment where the transactions are normally denominated in dollars. The functional currency of Seltec is the dollar.

(a) The entity uses forward and futures contracts to protect it against fluctuation in the price of edible oils. Where forwards are used the company often takes delivery of the edible oil and sells it shortly afterwards. The contracts are constructed with future delivery in mind but the contracts also allow net settlement in cash as an alternative. The net settlement is based on the change in the price of the oil since the start of the contract. Seltec uses the proceeds of a net settlement to purchase a different type of oil or purchase from a different supplier. Where futures are used these sometimes relate to edible oils of a different type and market than those of Seltec's own inventory of edible oil. The company intends to apply hedge accounting to these contracts in order to protect itself from earnings volatility. Seltec has also entered into a long-term arrangement to buy oil from a foreign entity whose currency is the dinar. The commitment stipulates that the fixed purchase price will be denominated in pounds sterling.

Seltec is unsure as to the nature of derivatives and hedge accounting techniques and has asked your advice on how the above financial instruments should be dealt with in the financial statements. **(14 marks)**

(b) Seltec has decided to enter the retail market and has recently purchased two well-known brand names in the edible oil industry. One of the brand names has been in existence for many years and has a good reputation for quality. The other brand name is named after a famous film star who has been actively promoting the edible oil as being a healthier option than other brands of oil. This type of oil has only been on the market for a short time. Seltec is finding it difficult to estimate the useful life of the brands and therefore intends to treat the brands as having indefinite lives.

In order to sell the oil, Seltec has purchased two limited liability companies from a company that owns several retail outlets. Each entity owns retail outlets in several shopping complexes. The only assets of each entity are the retail outlets. There is no operational activity and at present the entities have no employees.

Seltec is unclear as to how the purchase of the brands and the entities should be accounted for. **(9 marks)**

Required

Discuss the accounting principles involved in accounting for the above transactions and how the above transactions should be treated in the financial statements of Seltec.

Professional marks will be awarded in this question for clarity and quality of discussion. **(2 marks)**

The mark allocation is shown against each of the two parts above.

(Total = 25 marks)

64 Kayte **49 mins**

12/14

(a) Kayte operates in the shipping industry and owns vessels for transportation. In June 20X4, Kayte acquired Ceemone whose assets were entirely investments in small companies. The small companies each owned and operated one or two shipping vessels. There were no employees in Ceemone or the small companies. At the acquisition date, there were only limited activities related to managing the small companies as most activities were outsourced. All the personnel in Ceemone were employed by a separate management company. The companies owning the vessels had an agreement with the management company concerning assistance with chartering, purchase and sale of vessels and any technical management. The management company used a shipbroker to assist with some of these tasks.

Kayte accounted for the investment in Ceemone as an asset acquisition. The consideration paid and related transaction costs were recognised as the acquisition price of the vessels. Kayte argued that the vessels were only passive investments and that Ceemone did not own a business consisting of processes, since all activities regarding commercial and technical management were outsourced to the management company. As a result, the acquisition was accounted for as if the vessels were acquired on a stand-alone basis.

Additionally, Kayte had borrowed heavily to purchase some vessels and was struggling to meet its debt obligations. Kayte had sold some of these vessels but in some cases, the bank did not wish Kayte to sell the vessel. In these cases, the vessel was transferred to a new entity, in which the bank retained a variable interest based upon the level of the indebtedness. Kayte's directors felt that the entity was a subsidiary of the bank and are uncertain as to whether they have complied with the requirements of IFRS 3 *Business combinations* and IFRS 10 *Consolidated financial statements* as regards the above transactions.

(12 marks)

(b) Kayte's vessels constitute a material part of its total assets. The economic life of the vessels is estimated to be 30 years, but the useful life of some of the vessels is only 10 years because Kayte's policy is to sell these vessels when they are 10 years old. Kayte estimated the residual value of these vessels at sale to be half of acquisition cost and this value was assumed to be constant during their useful life. Kayte argued that the estimates of residual value used were conservative in view of an immature market with a high degree of uncertainty and presented documentation which indicated some vessels were being sold for a price considerably above carrying value. Broker valuations of the residual value were considerably higher than those used by Kayte. Kayte argued against broker valuations on the grounds that it would result in greater volatility in reporting.

Kayte keeps some of the vessels for the whole 30 years and these vessels are required to undergo an engine overhaul in dry dock every 10 years to restore their service potential, hence the reason why some of the vessels are sold. The residual value of the vessels kept for 30 years is based upon the steel value of the vessel at the end of its economic life. At the time of purchase, the service potential which will be required to be restored by the engine overhaul is measured based on the cost as if it had been performed at the time of the purchase of the vessel. In the current period, one of the vessels had to have its engine totally replaced after only eight years. Normally, engines last for the 30-year economic life if overhauled every 10 years. Additionally, one type of vessel was having its funnels replaced after 15 years but the funnels had not been depreciated separately. **(11 marks)**

Required

Discuss the accounting treatment of the above transactions in the financial statements of Kayte.

Note. The mark allocation is shown against each of the elements above.

Professional marks will be awarded in this question for clarity and quality of presentation. **(2 marks)**

(Total = 25 marks)

65 Ethan — 49 mins

6/12

Ethan, a public limited company, develops, operates and sells investment properties.

(a) Ethan focuses mainly on acquiring properties where it foresees growth potential, through rental income as well as value appreciation. The acquisition of an investment property is usually realised through the acquisition of the entity, which holds the property.

In Ethan's consolidated financial statements, investment properties acquired through business combinations are recognised at fair value, using a discounted cash flow model as approximation to fair value. There is currently an active market for this type of property. The difference between the fair value of the investment property as determined under the accounting policy, and the value of the investment property for tax purposes results in a deferred tax liability.

Goodwill arising on business combinations is determined using the measurement principles for the investment properties as outlined above. Goodwill is only considered impaired if and when the deferred tax liability is reduced below the amount at which it was first recognised. This reduction can be caused both by a reduction in the value of the real estate or a change in local tax regulations. As long as the deferred tax liability is equal to, or larger than, the prior year, no impairment is charged to goodwill. Ethan explained its accounting treatment by confirming that almost all of its goodwill is due to the deferred tax liability and that it is normal in the industry to account for goodwill in this way.

Since 20X0, Ethan has incurred substantial annual losses except for the year ended 31 May 20X3, when it made a small profit before tax. In year ended 31 May 20X3, most of the profit consisted of income recognised on revaluation of investment properties. Ethan had announced early in its financial year ended 31 May 20X4 that it anticipated substantial growth and profit. Later in the year, however, Ethan announced that the expected profit would not be achieved and that, instead, a substantial loss would be incurred. Ethan had a history of reporting considerable negative variances from its budgeted results. Ethan's recognised deferred tax assets have been increasing year-on-year despite the deferred tax liabilities recognised on business combinations. Ethan's deferred tax assets consist primarily of unused tax losses that can be carried forward which are unlikely to be offset against anticipated future taxable profits. **(11 marks)**

(b) Ethan wishes to apply the fair value option rules of IFRS 9 *Financial instruments* to debt issued to finance its investment properties. Ethan's argument for applying the fair value option is based upon the fact that the recognition of gains and losses on its investment properties and the related debt would otherwise be inconsistent. Ethan argued that there is a specific financial correlation between the factors, such as interest rates, that form the basis for determining the fair value of both Ethan's investment properties and the related debt. **(7 marks)**

(c) Ethan has an operating subsidiary, which has in issue A and B shares, both of which have voting rights. Ethan holds 70% of the A and B shares and the remainder are held by shareholders external to the group. The subsidiary is obliged to pay an annual dividend of 5% on the B shares. The dividend payment is cumulative even if the subsidiary does not have sufficient legally distributable profit at the time the payment is due.

In Ethan's consolidated statement of financial position, the B shares of the subsidiary were accounted for in the same way as equity instruments would be, with the B shares owned by external parties reported as a non-controlling interest. **(5 marks)**

Required

Discuss how the above transactions and events should be recorded in the consolidated financial statements of Ethan.

Note. The mark allocation is shown against each of the three transactions above.

Professional marks will be awarded for the quality of the discussion. **(2 marks)**

(Total = 25 marks)

66 Preparation question: Reconstruction scheme

Contemplation is a company that carries on business as film processors. For the past few years it has been making losses owing to the low price competition.

The company's statement of financial position as at 30 June 20X2 was as follows.

	$'000
Non-current assets	3,600
Current assets	4,775
	8,375
Equity	
Ordinary shares of $1 each fully paid	10,000
Retained earnings	(9,425)
	575
Non-current liabilities	
8% cumulative preference shares ((2,500,000 shares of $1 each)	3,300
11% Loan notes redeemable 20X9	3,500
Current liabilities	1,000
	8,375

The company has changed its marketing strategy and is now aiming at the specialist portrait print market. It is expected that the company will earn annual profits after tax of $1,500,000 for the next five years; the figure is before an interest charge. Income tax is assumed to be at a rate of 35%.

The directors are proposing to reconstruct the company and have produced the following proposal for discussion.

(a) To cancel the existing ordinary shares.

(b) The 11% loan notes are to be retired and the loan note holders issued in exchange with:

(i) $3,000,000 14% redeemable loan notes 20Y5; and
(ii) 2,000,000 ordinary shares of 25c each, fully paid up.

(c) The carrying value of the preference share capital above includes four years of dividends arrears. Assume that the IAS 32 definition of a liability is met. The preference shareholders are to be issued with 2,000,000 ordinary shares of 25c each fully paid up in exchange for the cancellation of these dividends arrears.

(d) The existing ordinary shareholders will be issued with 3,500,000 ordinary shares of 25c each, fully paid up.

In the event of a liquidation, it is estimated that the net realisable value of the assets would be $3,100,000 for the non-current assets and $3,500,000 for the net current assets.

Required

(a) Prepare a statement of financial position as at 1 July 20X2 after the reconstruction has been effected.

(b) Prepare computations to show the effect of the proposed reconstruction scheme on each of the loan note holders, preference shareholders and ordinary shareholders.

(c) Write a brief report to advise a shareholder who owns 10% of the issued ordinary share capital on whether to agree to the reconstruction as proposed. The shareholder has informed you that he feels the proposals are unfair.

(d) In your capacity as adviser to the shareholder, write a brief report to the directors suggesting any amendments you consider advisable.

Guidance notes

1 Layout a proforma statement of financial position for part (a) and fill in numbers as you work them out. Clearly label and cross reference workings.

2 The acceptability of any scheme to the major parties involved will be the main issue in such reconstructions. You must weigh up how much each group has to lose or gain and then reach a compromise.

67 Plans **29 mins**

X, a public limited company, owns 100% of companies Y and Z which are both public limited companies. The X group operates in the telecommunications industry and the directors are considering two different plans to restructure the group. The directors feel that the current group structure is not serving the best interests of the shareholders and wish to explore possible alternative group structures.

The statements of financial position of X and its subsidiaries Y and Z at 31 May 20X7 are as follows:

	X	*Y*	*Z*
	$m	$m	$m
Property, plant and equipment	600	200	45
Cost of investment in Y	60		
Cost of investment in Z	70		
Net current assets	160	100	20
	890	300	65
Share capital – ordinary shares of $1	120	60	40
Retained earnings	770	240	25
	890	300	65

X acquired the investment in Z on 1 June 20X1 when the company's retained earnings balance was $20 million. The fair value of the net assets of Z on 1 June 20X1 was $60 million. Company Y was incorporated by X and has always been a 100% owned subsidiary. The fair value of the net assets of Y at 31 May 20X7 is $310 million and of Z is $80 million. The fair values of the net current assets of both Y and Z are approximately the same as their book values.

The directors are unsure as to the impact or implications that the following plans are likely to have on the individual accounts of the companies and the group accounts.

Local companies legislation requires that the amount at which share capital is recorded is dictated by the nominal value of the shares issued and if the value of the consideration received exceeds that amount, the excess is recorded in the share premium account. Shares cannot be issued at a discount. In the case of a share for share exchange, the value of the consideration can be deemed to be the book value of the investment exchanged.

The two different plans to restructure the group are as follows:

Plan 1

Y is to purchase the whole of X's investment in Z. The purchase consideration would be 50 million $1 ordinary shares of Y.

Plan 2

The same scenario as Plan 1, but the purchase consideration would be a cash amount of $75 million.

Required

Discuss the key considerations and the accounting implications of the above plans for the X group. Your answer should show the potential impact on the individual accounts of X, Y and Z and the group accounts after each plan has been implemented. **(15 marks)**

68 Decany **49 mins**

12/11

Decany owns 100% of the ordinary share capital of Ceed and Rant. All three entities are public limited companies. The group operates in the shipbuilding industry, which is currently a depressed market. Rant has made losses for the last three years and its liquidity is poor. The view of the directors is that Rant needs some cash investment. The directors have decided to put forward a restructuring plan as at 30 November 20X1. Under this plan:

(a) Ceed is to purchase the whole of Decany's investment in Rant. The purchase consideration is to be $98 million payable in cash to Decany and this amount will then be loaned on a long-term unsecured basis to Rant.

(b) Ceed will purchase land with a carrying amount of $10 million from Rant for a total purchase consideration of $15 million. The land has a mortgage outstanding on it of $4 million. The total purchase consideration of $15 million comprises both five million $1 nominal value non-voting shares issued by Ceed to Rant and the $4 million mortgage liability which Ceed will assume.

(c) A dividend of $25 million will be paid from Ceed to Decany to reduce the accumulated reserves of Ceed.

The statements of financial position of Decany and its subsidiaries at 30 November 20X1 are summarised below.

	Decany	*Ceed*	*Rant*
	$m	$m	$m
Non-current assets			
Property, plant and equipment at cost/valuation	600	170	45
Cost of investment in Ceed	130		
Cost of investment in Rant	95		
Current assets	155	130	20
	980	300	65

	Decany $m	Ceed $m	Rant $m
Equity and reserves			
Share capital	140	70	35
Retained earnings	750	220	5
	890	290	40
Non-current liabilities			
Long-term loan	5		12
Current liabilities			
Trade payables	85	10	13
	980	300	65

As a result of the restructuring, several of Ceed's employees will be made redundant. According to the detailed plan, the costs of redundancy will be spread over two years with $4 million being payable in one year's time and $6 million in two years' time. The market yield of high quality corporate bonds is 3%. The directors feel that the overall restructure will cost $2 million.

Required

(a) (i) Prepare the individual entity statements of financial position after the proposed restructuring plan. **(13 marks)**

(ii) Set out the requirements of IAS 27 (Revised) *Separate financial statements* as regards the reorganisation and payment of dividends between group companies, discussing any implications for the restructuring plan. **(5 marks)**

(b) Discuss the key implications of the proposed plans for the restructuring of the group. **(5 marks)**

Professional marks will be awarded in Part (b) for clarity and expression of your discussion. **(2 marks)**

(Total = 25 marks)

69 Lucky Dairy — 49 mins

ACR, 6/02, amended

The Lucky Dairy, a public limited company, produces milk for supply to various customers. It is responsible for producing twenty five per cent of the country's milk consumption. The company owns 150 farms and has a stock of 70,000 cows and 35,000 heifers which are being raised to produce milk in the future. The farms produce 2.5 million kilograms of milk per annum and normally hold an inventory of 50,000 kilograms of milk (Extracts from the draft accounts to 31 May 20X2).

The herds comprise at 31 May 20X2:

70,000 – 3 year old cows (all purchased on or before 1 June 20X1)
25,000 – heifers (average age 1½ years old – purchased 1 December 20X1)
10,000 – heifers (average age 2 years – purchased 1 June 20X1)

There were no animals born or sold in the year. The per unit values less estimated point of sale costs were as follows.

	$
2 year old animal at 1 June 20X1	50
1 year old animal at 1 June 20X1 and 1 December 20X1	40
3 year old animal at 31 May 20X2	60
1½ year old animal at 31 May 20X2	46
2 year old animal at 31 May 20X2	55
1 year old animal at 31 May 20X2	42

The company has had a difficult year in financial and operating terms. The cows had contracted a disease at the beginning of the financial year which had been passed on in the food chain to a small number of consumers. The publicity surrounding this event had caused a drop in the consumption of milk and as a result the dairy was holding 500,000 kilograms of milk in storage.

The government had stated, on 1 April 20X2, that it was prepared to compensate farmers for the drop in the price and consumption of milk. An official government letter was received on 6 June 20X2, stating that $1.5 million will be paid to Lucky on 1 August 20X2. Additionally on 1 May 20X2, Lucky had received a letter from its lawyer saying that legal proceedings had been started against the company by the persons affected by the disease. The company's lawyers have advised them that they feel that it is probable that they will be found liable and that the costs involved may reach $2 million. The lawyers, however, feel that the company may receive additional compensation from a government fund if certain quality control procedures had been carried out by the company. However, the lawyers will only state that the compensation payment is 'possible'.

The company's activities are controlled in three geographical locations, Dale, Shire and Ham. The only region affected by the disease was Dale and the government has decided that it is to restrict the milk production of that region significantly. Lucky estimates that the discounted future cash income from the present herds of cattle in the region amounts to $1.2 million, taking into account the government restriction order. Lucky was not sure that the fair value of the cows in the region could be measured reliably at the date of purchase because of the problems with the diseased cattle. The cows in this region amounted to 20,000 in number and the heifers 10,000 in number. All of the animals were purchased on 1 June 20X1. Lucky has had an offer of $1 million for all of the animals in the Dale region (net of point of sale costs) and $2 million for the sale of the farms in the region. However, there was a minority of directors who opposed the planned sale and it was decided to defer the public announcement of sale pending the outcome of the possible receipt of the government compensation. The board had decided that the potential sale plan was highly confidential but a national newspaper had published an article saying that the sale may occur and that there would be many people who would lose their employment. The board approved the planned sale of Dale farms on 31 May 20X2.

The directors of Lucky have approached your firm for professional advice on the above matters.

Required

Advise the directors on how the biological assets and produce of Lucky should be accounted for under IAS 41 *Agriculture* and discuss the implications for the published financial statements of the above events.

(Candidates should produce a table which shows the changes in value of the cattle stock for the year to 31 May 20X2 due to price change and physical change excluding the Dale region, and the value of the herd of the Dale region as at 31 May 20X2. Ignore the effects of taxation. Heifers are young female cows.)

(25 marks)

70 Yanong **49 mins**

6/15

The directors of Yanong, a public limited company, have seen many different ways of dealing with the measurement and disclosure of the fair value of assets, liabilities and equity instruments. They feel that this reduces comparability among different entities' financial statements. They would like advice on several transactions where they currently use fair value measurement as they have heard that the introduction of IFRS 13 *Fair value measurement,* while not interfering with the scope of fair value measurement, will reduce the extent of any diversity and inconsistency.

(a) Yanong owns several farms and also owns a division which sells agricultural vehicles. It is considering selling this agricultural retail division and wishes to measure the fair value of the inventory of vehicles for the purpose of the sale. Three markets currently exist for the vehicles. Yanong has transacted regularly in all three markets. At 30 April 20X5, Yanong wishes to find the fair value of 150 new vehicles, which are identical. The current volume and prices in the three markets are as follows:

Market	*Sales price – per vehicle ($)*	*Historical volume – vehicles sold by Yanong*	*Total volume of vehicles sold in market*	*Transaction costs – per vehicle ($)*	*Transport costs to the market – per vehicle*
Europe	40,000	6,000	150,000	500	400
Asia	38,000	2,500	750,000	400	700
Africa	34,000	1,500	100,000	300	600

Yanong wishes to value the vehicles at $39,100 per vehicle as these are the highest net proceeds per vehicle, and Europe is the largest market for Yanong's product. Yanong would like advice as to whether this valuation would be acceptable under IFRS 13 *Fair value measurement* **(6 marks)**

(b) The company uses quarterly reporting for its farms as they grow short-lived crops such as maize. Yanong planted the maize fields during the quarter to 31 October 20X4 at an operating cost of $10 million. The fields originally cost $20 million. There is no active market for partly grown fields of maize and therefore Yanong proposes to use a discounted cash flow method to value the maize fields. As at 31 October 20X4, the following were the cash flow projections relating to the maize fields:

	3 months to 31 January 20X5	*3 months to 30 April 20X5*	*Total*
	$m	$m	$m
Cash inflows		80	80
Cash outflows	(8)	(19)	(27)
Notional rental charge for land usage	(1)	(1)	(2)
Net cash flows	(9)	60	51

In the three months to 31 January 20X5, the actual operating costs amounted to $8 million and at that date Yanong revised its future projections for the cash inflows to $76 million for the three months to April 20X5. At the point of harvest at 31 March 20X5, the maize was worth $82 million and it was sold for $84 million (net of costs to sell) on 15 April 20X5. In the measurement of fair value of the maize, Yanong includes a notional cash flow expense for the 'rent' of the land where it is self-owned.

The directors of Yanong wish to know how they should have accounted for the above biological asset at 31 October 20X4, 31 January 20X5, 31 March 20X5 and when the produce was sold. Assume a discount rate of 2% per quarter as follows:

	Factor
Period 1	0.980
Period 2	0.961

(6 marks)

(c) On 1 May 20X2, Yanong granted 500 share appreciation rights (SARs) to its 300 managers. All of the rights vested on 30 April 20X4 but they can be exercised from 1 May 20X4 up to 30 April 20X6. At the grant date, the value of each SAR was $10 and it was estimated that 5% of the managers would leave during the vesting period. The fair value of the SARs is as follows:

	Fair value of SAR
30 April 20X3	$9
30 April 20X4	$11
30 April 20X5	$12

All of the managers who were expected to leave employment did leave the company as expected before 30 April 20X4. On 30 April 20X5, 60 managers exercised their options when the intrinsic value of the right was $10·50 and were paid in cash.

Yanong is confused as to whether to account for the SARs under IFRS 2 *Share-based payment* or IFRS 13 *Fair value measurement,* and would like advice as to how the SARs should have been accounted for from the grant date to 30 April 20X5. **(6 marks)**

(d) Yanong uses the revaluation model for its non-current assets. Yanong has several plots of farmland which are unproductive. The company feels that the land would have more value if it were used for residential purposes. There are several potential purchasers for the land but planning permission has not yet been granted for use of the land for residential purposes. However, preliminary enquiries with the regulatory authorities seem to indicate that planning permission may be granted. Additionally, the government has recently indicated that more agricultural land should be used for residential purposes.

Yanong has also been approached to sell the land for commercial development at a higher price than that for residential purposes.

Yanong would like advice on how to measure the fair value of the land in its financial statements. **(5 marks)**

Required

Advise Yanong on how the above transactions should be dealt with in its financial statements with reference to relevant International Financial Reporting Standards.

Note. The mark allocation is shown against each of the four issues above.

Professional marks will be awarded in this question for clarity and quality of presentation **(2 marks)**

Note. Ignore any deferred tax implications of the transactions above.

(25 marks)

71 IFRSs and SMEs 49 mins

ACR, 6/06, amended

International Financial Reporting Standards (IFRSs) are primarily designed for use by publicly listed companies and in many countries the majority of companies using IFRSs are listed companies. In other countries IFRSs are used as national Generally Accepted Accounting Practices (GAAP) for all companies including unlisted entities. It has been argued that the same IFRSs should be used by all entities or alternatively a different body of standards should apply to small and medium entities (SMEs) and recently the IASB published an IFRS for SMEs.

Required

(a) Discuss whether it was necessary to develop a set of IFRSs specifically for SMEs. **(7 marks)**

(b) Discuss the nature of the following issues in developing IFRSs for SMEs.

   (i) The purpose of the standards and the type of entity to which they should apply. **(7 marks)**
   (ii) How existing standards could be modified to meet the needs of SMEs. **(6 marks)**
   (iii) How items not dealt with by an IFRS for SMEs should be treated. **(5 marks)**

(Total = 25 marks)

72 Whitebirk 43 mins

12/10, amended

(a) The main argument for separate SME accounting standards is the undue cost burden of reporting, which is proportionately heavier for smaller firms.

   Required

   Discuss the main differences and modifications to IFRS which the IASB made to reduce the burden of reporting for SME's, giving specific examples where possible and include in your discussion how the Board has dealt with the problem of defining an SME. **(9 marks)**

   Professional marks will be awarded in part (a) for clarity and quality of discussion. **(2 marks)**

(b) Whitebirk has met the definition of a SME in its jurisdiction and wishes to comply with the *IFRS for Small and Medium-sized Entities*. The entity wishes to seek advice on how it will deal with the following accounting issues in its financial statements for the year ended 30 November 20X2. The entity already prepares its financial statements under full IFRS.

   (i) Whitebirk purchased 90% of Close, a SME, on 1 December 20X1. The purchase consideration was $5.7 million and the value of Close's identifiable assets was $6 million. The value of the non-controlling interest at 1 December 20X1 was measured at $0.7 million. Whitebirk has used the full goodwill method to account for business combinations and the life of goodwill cannot be estimated with any accuracy. Whitebirk wishes to know how to account for goodwill under the *IFRS for SMEs*.

   (ii) Whitebirk has incurred $1 million of research expenditure to develop a new product in the year to 30 November 20X2. Additionally, it incurred $500,000 of development expenditure to bring another product to a stage where it is ready to be marketed and sold.

(iii) Whitebirk purchased some properties for $1.7m on 1 December 20X1 and designated them as investment properties under the cost model. No depreciation was charged as a real estate agent valued the properties at $1.9m at the year end.

(iv) Whitebirk has an intangible asset valued at $1m on 1 December 20X1. The asset has an indefinite useful life, and in previous years had been reviewed for impairment. As at 30 November 20X2, there are no indications that the asset is impaired.

Required

Discuss how the above transactions should be dealt with in the financial statements of Whitebirk, with reference to the *IFRS for Small and Medium-sized Entities.* **(11 marks)**

(Total = 22 marks)

Answers

1 Conceptual framework

Text reference. Conceptual framework is covered in Chapter 1 of your Study Text.

Top tips. Although this question is rather general, it is a good idea to mention the IASB documents, covered in your BPP Study Text. This question and answer has been amended since it was set.

Easy marks. Part (a) is fairly open ended. This does not mean you can waffle, but it does give scope for different approaches and credit will be given for valid points well expressed.

Examiner's comment. The ACCA examination/examining team was disappointed that more candidates did not answer this question better. The IASB and FASB, and the ASB see the current conceptual framework project as being a key current development, and there has been a significant amount of coverage in the accountancy press. Students must read the accountancy press in order to gain an insight into current issues. The answers to Part (a) were often quite narrow with little discussion of the practical use of a conceptual framework. Good answers considered the reasons for differences in accounting.

Marking scheme

		Marks
(a)	Subjective	14
(b)	Up to 3 marks per key issue	5
	(i) Derecognition	
	(ii) Prudence	
(c)	1 mark per valid point	4
	Appropriateness and quality of discussion	2
	Maximum	25

(a) **The need for a conceptual framework**

The financial reporting process is concerned with providing information that is useful in the business and economic decision-making process. Therefore a conceptual framework will form the theoretical basis for determining which events should be accounted for, how they should be measured and how they should be communicated to the user.

Although it is theoretical in nature, a conceptual framework for financial reporting has highly practical final aims.

The **danger of not having a conceptual framework** is demonstrated in the way some countries' standards have developed over recent years; standards tend to be produced in a **haphazard and fire-fighting approach**. Where an agreed framework exists, the standard-setting body act as an architect or designer, rather than a fire-fighter, building accounting rules on the foundation of sound, agreed basic principles.

The lack of a conceptual framework also means that fundamental principles are tackled more than once in different standards, thereby producing contradictions and inconsistencies in basic concepts, such as those of prudence and matching. This leads to ambiguity and it affects the true and fair concept of financial reporting.

Another problem with the lack of a full conceptual framework has become apparent in the USA. The large number of highly detailed standards produced by the Financial Accounting Standards Board (FASB) has created a financial reporting environment governed by specific rules rather than general principles. FASB has 'concept statements' but a full conceptual framework would be better.

A conceptual framework can also bolster standard setters against political pressure from various 'lobby groups' and interested parties. Such pressure would only prevail if it was acceptable under the conceptual framework.

Can it resolve practical accounting issues?

A framework cannot provide all the answers for standard setters. It can provide **basic principles** which can be used when deciding between alternatives, and can narrow the range of alternatives that can be considered. In the UK, the *Statement of Principles* has provided **definitions that have formed the basis of definitions in accounting standards,** as has the IASB's conceptual framework in areas such as financial instruments and provisions. A framework can also provide guidance in the absence of an accounting standard. For example, there is no IFRS dealing specifically with off balance sheet finance, so the IASB *Conceptual Framework* must form the basis for decisions.

However, a conceptual framework is **unlikely**, on past form, to **provide all** the **answers to practical accounting problems**. There are a number of reasons for this:

(i) Financial statements are intended for a variety of users, and it is not certain that a single conceptual framework can be devised which will suit all users.

(ii) Given the diversity of user requirements, there may be a need for a variety of accounting standards, each produced for a different purpose (and with different concepts as a basis).

(iii) It is not clear that a conceptual framework makes the task of preparing and then implementing standards any easier than without a framework.

The IASB's *Conceptual Framework for Financial Reporting* was criticised by the UK Accounting Standards Board at least partly on grounds of practical utility – it is thought to be **too theoretical,** and also for focusing on **some users (decision makers) at the expense of others (shareholders).** Perhaps it is not possible to satisfy all users.

(b) **ED *Conceptual Framework for Financial Reporting***

(i) **Derecognition of assets and liabilities**

Guidance on derecognition is new to this proposed version of the *Conceptual Framework.* The **guidance is driven by the requirement of faithful representation.** A faithful representation must be provided of:

(1) The **assets and liabilities retained after a transaction** or other event that led to derecognition, and

(2) The **change in the entity's assets and liabilities as a result of that transaction** or other event.

Decisions about derecognition are generally straightforward. However, in some cases the two aims described above conflict with each other, making the decisions more difficult. The discussion in the Exposure Draft focuses on these cases.

(ii) **Prudence**

Chapter 2 *The Qualitative Characteristics of Useful Financial Information* was finalised in the 2010 version of the *Conceptual Framework,* and so there are generally only limited changes from that version. However, one change that could be regarded as important is the introduction of an **explicit reference to the idea of prudence.** Prudence is described as the **exercise of caution when making judgements under conditions of uncertainty.** It is explicitly stated that prudence is important in achieving **neutrality,** and therefore in achieving **faithful representation.** Prudence had been removed from the *Conceptual Framework* in 2010 on the grounds that it conflicted with neutrality, carrying a bias in favour of caution.

The IASB has further clarified that prudence works both ways: assets and liabilities should be neither overstated nor understated.

(c) **Possible criticisms of the proposals**

Possible criticisms include the following, tentatively raised by the Accounting Council of the Financial Reporting Council at a meeting in 2015.

(i) **Prudence**. The ED does not reflect the notion of 'asymmetric prudence'—the recognition of losses and liabilities at a lower level of likelihood (and hence often earlier) than gains and assets. This notion is mentioned in the Basis for Conclusions, but ought to be part of the Conceptual Framework itself.

(ii) **Neutrality.** Prudence is a way of achieving 'neutrality', defined as 'without bias'. However, the FRC believe that 'unbiased' would be a clearer word.

(iii) **Reliability.** The description of faithful representation given in the Exposure Draft does not include the idea, which was in the discussion of reliability in a previous version of the Conceptual Framework, that the information 'can be depended upon by users'. The idea of reliability needs to be reinstated.

(iv) **Statement of profit or loss.** Terms such as 'profit', 'return' and 'performance' need to be defined, and the significance of recycling adjustments needs to be explained.

(v) **Elements**. The Exposure Draft does not propose to define elements for the statement of cash flows.

2 Lizzer

Text reference. Disclosure and usefulness of reports are covered in Chapter 10of the Study Text. Disclosures relating to financial instruments are covered in Chapter 7.

Top tips. Part (a) asks for a discussion about the optimal level of disclosure, and barriers to reducing disclosure. Arguments both for and against extensive disclosure could be made, as well as the case that too much disclosure means that the user cannot see the wood for the trees. Part (b) asks for application of specific disclosures, namely those in IFRS 7 relating to financial instruments.

You would be advised to do a quick answer plan before you start, otherwise there is a danger of rambling.

Easy marks. There are no obvious easy marks as such. However, Part (a) is rather open ended, so the trick is to keep on writing and backing up your arguments.

Examiner's comments. In answering Part (a) of this question, candidates were able to draw upon their own experiences and examples. However, this was not always forthcoming and thus it demonstrated the lack of wider reading by candidates. Having stated this fact the question was quite well answered. Part b required candidates to apply their knowledge of this area in determining whether disclosure should be made in two instances where the directors' view was that no further information regarding the two instances should be disclosed in the financial statements because it would be 'excessive'. The instances concerned IFRS 7*Financial instruments: disclosures.* This is not a frequently examined part of the syllabus but candidates did not require a detailed knowledge of the IFRS to be able to answer the question. Marks could be gained for a logical discussion of the scenario involved. This question was well answered in the main.

Marking scheme

			Marks
(a)	Subjective: disclosure		9
	barriers		6
(b)	Subjective		8
	Professional marks		2
		Available	25

(a) (i) **Optimal level of disclosure**

Users of financial statements need **as much relevant information as possible** in order to make or retain wise investments and to avoid less prudent uses of capital. Companies also benefit from providing this information as it means that they do not take on debt that they cannot afford. There are, then, obvious advantages to increased disclosure.

(1) **Lenders** need to know if a company has **liquidity problems**. Disclosure of reasons for a large bank overdraft, or changes in gearing, may help allay any concerns, or alternatively may help the lender avoid a bad decision.

(2) Users need to know the full extent of **any risk** they are taking on in investing in – or indeed trading with – a company. Risk is not automatically a bad thing, if potential returns are good, and information on both profitability and gearing can help the decision-making process along. A venture capitalist may be more willing to take on risk than a high street bank, but both will need full disclosure of relevant information. A better understanding of risk may lower the cost of capital.

(3) **Investors** and potential investors will need to know which companies are the most **profitable**, and whether those profits are sustainable. Their job is to maximise returns. It is not in the long-term interests of either companies or potential investors to withhold information.

(4) **Other stakeholders,** such as employees, customers, suppliers and environmentalists need to be informed of issues that concern them.

However, the key word here is **relevant. Too much disclosure can obscure**, rather than inform, as the key points are buried under excessive detail and less important points. Information overload may even mean that users stop reading altogether. Clear presentation helps – a summary of key points with cross references to more detailed analysis can save the user from the need to read through information that is not relevant to his or her needs.

Preparers of annual reports **do not, however, have full discretion** over how the reports are presented, because they are subject to the following **constraints**.

(1) Legal requirements, such as the Companies Acts in the UK
(2) International Financial Reporting Standards and local financial reporting standards
(3) Corporate governance codes
(4) Listing requirements, both local and overseas for companies with an overseas listing
(5) *Management Commentary,* although this has more flexibility than the others

These requirements have been **developed for different purposes,** which may add to the disclosure burden because entities must make **separate sets of disclosures on the same topic**. For example, an international bank in the UK may have to disclose credit risk under IFRS 7 *Financial instruments: disclosures,* the Companies Acts, the Disclosure and Transparency Rules, the SEC rules and Industry Guide 3, and the Basel Accords.

While the IASB has **reduced the level of disclosures for small and medium-sized enterprises** with the *IFRS for SMEs,* in general the **tendency** has been for **annual reports to expand**, and this is set to continue as stakeholders become increasingly demanding.

(ii) **Barriers to reducing disclosure**

Companies are sometimes reluctant to reduce the level of disclosure. These barriers are behavioural and include the following.

(1) **The perception that disclosing everything will satisfy all interested parties.** Many of the disclosures will not be applicable to the needs of any one user.

(2) **The threat of criticism or litigation.** Preparers of financial statements err on the side of caution rather than risk falling foul of the law by omitting a required disclosure. Removing disclosures is seen as creating a risk of adverse comment and regulatory challenge.

(3) **Cut and paste mentality.** If items were disclosed in last year's annual report and the issue is still on-going, there is a tendency to copy the disclosures into this year's report. It is thought that, if such disclosures are removed, stakeholders may wonder whether the financial statements still give a true and fair view. Disclosure is therefore the safest option and the default position.

(4) **Standard disclosures should be easy to find.** It has been suggested that the 'clutter' problem could be alleviated by segregating standing data in a separate section of the annual report (an appendix) or putting it on the company's website. A valid objection to this approach, however, is that even though explanatory information does not change much from year to year, its inclusion remains necessary to an understanding of aspects of the report. Users will benefit from being able to find all this information in one place in the hard copy, rather than having to go to a website to gain a full understanding of a particular point. An appendix may not be the best place for the standing information, as the reader has to hunt in the small print in order to understand a point.

(5) **Not all users have access to the internet.** Relegating points of detail or standing information to the company's website would disadvantage such users.

(6) **Segregation of information may appear arbitrary.** Preparers (and users) may disagree as to what is important enough to be included in the main body of an annual report and what may be published in an appendix or on the website.

(7) **Checklist approach.** While materiality should determine what is disclosed, because what is material is what may influence the user, the assessment of what is material can be a matter of judgement. The purpose of checklists is to include all possible disclosures that could be material. Users may not be know which of the checklist disclosures is actually material in the context of their specific needs.

(b) (i) **Disclosure of debt risk**

It is not for Lizzer alone to determine who are the primary users of financial statements and what disclosures are necessary. The entity **needs to consider the requirements of IFRS 7** *Financial instruments: disclosures,* and apply them more broadly, to include debt-holders as well as just shareholders. More generally, IAS 1 *Presentation of financial statements* states that the objective of financial statements is to provide information about an entity's financial performance, financial position and cash flows that is useful to a wide range of users in making economic decisions. These users are defined by the *Conceptual Framework* as 'existing and potential investors, lenders and **other creditors**' which would **include debt-holders**.

The objective of IFRS 7 is to require entities to provide disclosures in their financial statements that enable users to evaluate:

(1) The significance of financial instruments for the entity's financial position and performance

(2) The nature and extent of risks arising from financial instruments to which the entity is exposed during the period and at the reporting date, and how the entity manages those risks

The disclosures required by IFRS 7 **show the extent to which an entity is exposed to different types of risk,** relating to both recognised and unrecognised financial instruments**. Credit risk** is one such risk, defined by the standard as:

'The risk that one party to a financial instrument will cause a financial loss for the other party by failing to discharge an obligation.'

Clearly disclosures about credit risk are important to debt-holders, Such disclosures are **qualitative** (exposure to risk and objectives, policies and processes for managing risk) and **quantitative**, based on the information provided internally to management personnel, enhanced if this is insufficient.

More important, in this context is **market risk**. The debtholders are exposed to the risk of the underlying investments whose value could go up or down depending on market value. Market risk is defined as:

'The risk that the fair value or future cash flows of a financial instrument will fluctuate because of changes in market prices. Market risk comprises three types of risk: currency risk, interest rate risk and other price risk.'

Disclosures required in connection with market risk are:

(1) **Sensitivity analysis**, showing the effects on profit or loss of changes in each market risk

(2) If the sensitivity analysis reflects interdependencies between risk variables, such as interest rates and exchange rates the method, **assumptions and limitations** must be disclosed

(ii) **Potential breach of loan covenants**

The applicable standards here are IFRS 7 Financial instruments: disclosures, and IAS 10 Events after the reporting period.

According to IFRS 7, Lizzer **should have included additional information** about the loan covenants **sufficient to enable the users of its financial statements to evaluate the nature and extent of risks arising from financial instruments** to which the entity is exposed at the end of the reporting period. Such disclosure is particularly important in Lizzer's case because there was considerable risk at the year end (31 January 20X3) that the loan covenants would be breached in the near future, as indicated by the directors' and auditors' doubts about the company continuing as a going concern. Information should have been given about the **conditions attached to the loans and how close the entity was at the year-end to breaching** the covenants.

IFRS 7 requires disclosure of additional information about the covenants relating to each loan or group of loans, including headroom (the difference between the amount of the loan facility and the amount required).

The **actual breach of the loan covenants** at 31 March 20X3 was a **material event after the reporting period** as defined in IAS 10. The breach, after the date of the financial statements but before those statements were authorised, represents a **non-adjusting event**, which should have given rise to further disclosures in accordance with IAS 10.

Although the breach is a non-adjusting event, there appears to be some **inconsistency** between the information in the directors' and auditors' reports (which express going-concern doubts) and the information in the financial statements, which are prepared on a going-concern basis. **If any of the figures** in the statement of financial position are **affected,** these will **need to be adjusted.**

3 Tang

Text reference. IFRS 15 *Revenue from contracts with customers* is covered in Chapter 1 of your Study Text.

Top tips. This is a typical current issues question with discussion followed by application to a scenario with some numbers. It is on the very topical issue of revenue recognition. Part (b)(ii) is somewhat challenging, given that this was the first time IFRS 15 has been tested. However this was only 6 of the 25 marks, so do not let this put you off in what is otherwise a very fair question. Read the question carefully in Part (a)(i) – it asks for criteria for a contract, so do not launch straight into the other criteria, but leave that till Part (a)(ii).

Easy marks. Part (a)(ii) is a 'gift', if you have learnt the revenue recognition steps, which you should have!

Examiner's comment. Part (a) required a reasonable knowledge of IFRS 15 but many candidates could only recite the 5 steps to revenue recognition without being able to elaborate on them. It is important that students read Student Accountant as articles on such topics as IFRS 15 appear regularly. Part(b) required the application of part (a) in terms of determining the impact of a significant financing component on a contract and also contract modifications. Candidates did not answer this part of the question very well. It is difficult when new standards are issued but there is a wealth of information available to tutors and students on such topics as IFRS 15, so it is important that candidates read widely on such a topic.

Marking scheme

		Marks
(a)	(i) 1 mark per point up to maximum	5
	(ii) 1 mark per point	8
(b)	(i) 1 mark per point up to maximum	4
	(ii) 1 mark per point up to maximum	6
Professional marks		2
		25

(a) (i) **Criteria for a contract under IFRS 15**

The definition of what constitutes a contract for the purpose of applying the standard is critical. The definition of contract is based on the definition of a contract in the USA and is similar to that in IAS 32 *Financial instruments: presentation.* A contract exists when an agreement between two or more parties creates enforceable rights and obligations between those parties. The agreement does not need to be in writing to be a contract but the decision as to whether a contractual right or obligation is enforceable is considered within the context of the relevant legal framework of a jurisdiction. Thus, whether a contract is enforceable will vary across jurisdictions. The performance obligation could include promises which result in a valid expectation that the entity will transfer goods or services to the customer even though those promises are not legally enforceable.

The first criteria set out in IFRS 15 is that the parties should have approved the contract and are committed to perform their respective obligations. It would be questionable whether that contract is enforceable if this were not the case. In the case of oral or implied contracts, this may be difficult but all relevant facts and circumstances should be considered in assessing the parties' commitment. The parties need not always be committed to fulfilling all of the obligations under a contract. IFRS 15 gives the example where a customer is required to purchase a minimum quantity of goods but past experience shows that the customer does not always do this and the other party does not enforce their contract rights. However, there needs to be evidence that the parties are substantially committed to the contract.

It is essential that each party's rights and the payment terms can be identified regarding the goods or services to be transferred. This latter requirement is the key to determining the transaction price.

The contract must have commercial substance before revenue can be recognised, as without this requirement, entities might artificially inflate their revenue and it would be questionable whether the transaction has economic consequences. Further, it should be probable that the entity will collect the consideration due under the contract. An assessment of a customer's credit risk is an important element in deciding whether a contract has validity but customer credit risk does not affect the measurement or presentation of revenue. The consideration may be different to the contract price because of discounts and bonus offerings. The entity should assess the ability of the customer to pay and the customer's intention to pay the consideration. If a contract with a customer does not meet these criteria, the entity can continually re-assess the contract to determine whether it subsequently meets the criteria.

Two or more contracts which are entered into around the same time with the same customer may be combined and accounted for as a single contract, if they meet the specified criteria. The standard provides detailed requirements for contract modifications. A modification may be accounted for as a separate contract or a modification of the original contract, depending upon the circumstances of the case.

(ii) **Four remaining IFRS 15 steps**

Step one in the five-step model requires the identification of the contract with the customer. After a contract has been determined to fall under IFRS 15, the following steps are required before revenue can be recognised.

Step two requires the identification of the separate performance obligations in the contract. This is often referred to as 'unbundling', and is done at the beginning of a contract. The key factor in identifying a separate performance obligation is the distinctiveness of the good or service, or a bundle of goods or services. A good or service is distinct if the customer can benefit from the good or service on its own or together with other readily available resources and is separately identifiable from other elements of the contract. IFRS 15 requires a series of distinct goods or services which are substantially the same with the same pattern of transfer, to be regarded as a single performance obligation. A good or service, which has been delivered, may not be distinct if it cannot be used without another good or service which has not yet been delivered. Similarly, goods or services which are not distinct should be combined with other goods or services until the entity identifies a bundle of goods or services which is distinct. IFRS 15 provides indicators rather than criteria to determine when a good or service is distinct within the context of the contract. This allows management to apply judgement to determine the separate performance obligations which best reflect the economic substance of a transaction.

Step three requires the entity to determine the transaction price, which is the amount of consideration which an entity expects to be entitled to in exchange for the promised goods or services. This amount excludes amounts collected on behalf of a third party, for example, government taxes. An entity must determine the amount of consideration to which it expects to be entitled in order to recognise revenue.

The transaction price might include variable or contingent consideration. Variable consideration should be estimated as either the expected value or the most likely amount. Management should use the approach which it expects will best predict the amount of consideration and should be applied consistently throughout the contract. An entity can only include variable consideration in the transaction price to the extent that it is highly probable that a subsequent change in the estimated variable consideration will not result in a significant revenue reversal. If it is not appropriate to include all of the variable consideration in the transaction price, the entity should assess whether it should include part of the variable consideration. However, this latter amount still has to pass the 'revenue reversal' test.

Additionally, an entity should estimate the transaction price taking into account non-cash consideration, consideration payable to the customer and the time value of money if a significant financing component is present. The latter is not required if the time period between the transfer of goods or services and payment is less than one year. If an entity anticipates that it may ultimately accept an amount lower than that initially promised in the contract due to, for example, past experience of discounts given, then revenue would be estimated at the lower amount with the collectability of that lower amount being assessed. Subsequently, if revenue already recognised is not collectable, impairment losses should be taken to profit or loss.

Step four requires the allocation of the transaction price to the separate performance obligations. The allocation is based on the relative standalone selling prices of the goods or services promised and is made at inception of the contract. It is not adjusted to reflect subsequent changes in the standalone selling prices of those goods or services. The best evidence of standalone selling price is the observable price of a good or service when the entity sells that good or service separately. If that is not available, an estimate is made by using an approach which maximises the use of observable inputs. For example, expected cost plus an appropriate margin or the assessment of market prices for similar goods or services adjusted for entity-specific costs and margins or in limited circumstances a residual approach. When a contract contains more than one distinct performance obligation, an entity allocates the transaction price to each distinct performance obligation on the basis of the standalone selling price.

Where the transaction price includes a variable amount and discounts, consideration needs to be given as to whether these amounts relate to all or only some of the performance obligations in the contract. Discounts and variable consideration will typically be allocated proportionately to all of the performance obligations in the contract. However, if certain conditions are met, they can be allocated to one or more separate performance obligations.

Step five requires revenue to be recognised as each performance obligation is satisfied. An entity satisfies a performance obligation by transferring control of a promised good or service to the customer, which could occur over time or at a point in time. The definition of control includes the ability to prevent others from directing the use of and obtaining the benefits from the asset. A performance obligation is satisfied at a point in time unless it meets one of three criteria set out in IFRS 15. Revenue is recognised in line with the pattern of transfer.

If an entity does not satisfy its performance obligation over time, it satisfies it at a point in time and revenue will be recognised when control is passed at that point in time. Factors which may indicate the passing of control include the present right to payment for the asset or the customer has legal title to the asset or the entity has transferred physical possession of the asset.

(b) (i) **Existing printing machine**

The contract contains a significant financing component because of the length of time between when the customer pays for the asset and when Tang transfers the asset to the customer, as well as the prevailing interest rates in the market. A contract with a customer which has a significant financing component should be separated into a revenue component (for the notional cash sales price) and a loan component. Consequently, the accounting for a sale arising from a contract which has a significant financing component should be comparable to the accounting for a loan with the same features. An entity should use the discount rate which would be reflected in a separate financing transaction between the entity and its customer at contract inception. The interest rate implicit in the transaction may be different from the rate to be used to discount the cash flows, which should be the entity's incremental borrowing rate. IFRS 15 would therefore dictate that the rate which should be used in adjusting the promised consideration is 5%, which is the entity's incremental borrowing rate, and not 11·8%.

Tang would account for the significant financing component as follows:

Recognise a contract liability for the $240,000 payment received on 1 December 20X4 at the contract inception:

DEBIT Cash $240,000
CREDIT Contract liability $240,000

During the two years from contract inception (1 December 20X4) until the transfer of the printing machine, Tang adjusts the amount of consideration and accretes the contract liability by recognising interest on $240,000 at 5% for two years.

Year to 30 November 20X5

DEBIT Interest expense $12,000
CREDIT Contract liability $12,000

Contract liability would stand at $252,000 at 30 November 20X5.

Year to 30 November 20X6

DEBIT Interest expense $12,600
CREDIT Contract liability $12,600

Recognition of contract revenue on transfer of printing machine at 30 November 20X6 of $264,600 by debiting contract liability and crediting revenue with this amount.

(ii) **Constructed printing machine**

Tang accounts for the promised bundle of goods and services as a single performance obligation satisfied over time in accordance with IFRS 15. At the inception of the contract, Tang expects the following:

Transaction price $1,500,000

Expected costs $800,000

Expected profit (46·7%) $700,000

At contract inception, Tang excludes the $100,000 bonus from the transaction price because it cannot conclude that it is highly probable that a significant reversal in the amount of cumulative revenue recognised will not occur. Completion of the printing machine is highly susceptible to factors outside the entity's influence. By the end of the first year, the entity has satisfied 65% of its performance obligation on the basis of costs incurred to date. Costs incurred to date are therefore $520,000 and Tang reassesses the variable consideration and concludes that the amount is still constrained. Therefore at 30 November 20X5, the following would be recognised:

Revenue $975,000

Costs $520,000

Gross profit $455,000

However, on 4 December 20X5, the contract is modified. As a result, the fixed consideration and expected costs increase by $110,000 and $60,000, respectively. The total potential consideration after the modification is $1,710,000 which is $1,610,000 fixed consideration + $100,000 completion bonus. In addition, the allowable time for achieving the bonus is extended by six months with the result that Tang concludes that it is highly probable that including the bonus in the transaction price will not result in a significant reversal in the amount of cumulative revenue recognised in accordance with IFRS 15. Therefore the bonus of $100,000 can be included in the transaction price. Tang also concludes that the contract remains a single performance obligation. Thus, Tang accounts for the contract modification as if it were part of the original contract. Therefore, Tang updates its estimates of costs and revenue as follows:

Tang has satisfied 60·5% of its performance obligation ($520,000 actual costs incurred compared to $860,000 total expected costs). The entity recognises additional revenue of $59,550 [(60·5% of $1,710,000) – $975,000 revenue recognised to date] at the date of the modification as a cumulative catch-up adjustment. As the contract amendment took place after the year end, the additional revenue would not be treated as an adjusting event

4 Venue

Text reference. Revenue recognition is covered in Chapter 1 of your Study Text.

Top tips. This is a topical issue and the subject of a new standard, IFRS 15, which is covered in your Study Text. You should not just give the details of the new approach, but explain why it was needed. Our answer is longer than you would be expected to write in the examination. The ACCA examination/examining team has indicated that there will be a computational element in his current issues question. As here, it is not too complex. This question has been largely re-written to take account of the requirements of IFRS 15.

Easy marks. Credit will be given for valid arguments in Part (a), which has a generous mark allocation.

Examiner's comment. Part (a) of this question was well answered and discussions were good. However some candidates wrote general comments about recognition criteria for revenue and again these answers did not relate to the requirements of the question and were not in sufficient detail to justify full marks and the length and depth of the answers were often too short given the mark allocation for this question. Part (b) of the original question was well answered.

Marking scheme

		Marks
(a)	Main weaknesses of IAS 18 and IAS 11 – up to	8
	IFRS 15 improvements – up to	11
	Professional marks	2
(b)	Control not obtained by customer	3
	Option lapses	1
		25

(a) (i) **Main weaknesses of previous standards on revenue recognition**

The previous revenue recognition standards, IAS 18 *Revenue* and IAS 11 *Construction contracts*, were criticised because an entity applying the standards might recognise amounts in the financial statements that do not faithfully represent the nature of the transactions.

IAS 18 *Revenue* was criticised for being **vague** and this led to inconsistency in how it was applied by different entities. IAS 11 *Construction contracts* was also criticised, and there was sometimes uncertainty about which standard to apply. It was further argued that those standards were inconsistent with principles used in other accounting standards

Specifically, the weaknesses of the old standards were as follows.

(1) **Timing of revenue recognition.**

Many companies were uncertain about when they should recognise revenue because there is a lack of clear and comprehensive guidance in IAS 18 and IAS 11. This was particularly the case for goods and services because goods are sold at a point in time whereas services may be provided over time. This meant that the revenue recognised did not represent fairly the pattern of transfer to the customer of the goods and services.

(2) **Conflict with the IASB *Conceptual Framework***

Under the *Conceptual Framework*, income is recognised when an increase in future economic benefits related to an increase in an asset or a decrease of a liability has arisen that can be measured reliably. This means, in effect, that recognition of income occurs simultaneously with the recognition of increases in assets or decreases in liabilities (for example, the net increase in assets arising on a sale of goods or services or the decrease in liabilities arising from the waiver of a debt payable). It was not clear how this applied in the case of construction contracts.

(3) **Distinguishing between goods and services**

IAS 18 and IAS 11 did not clearly distinguish between goods and services, so some companies were not entirely sure whether to account for some transactions under IAS 18 or IAS 11. The standards are very different as regards the timing of recognition

(4) **Variable consideration**

Some contracts will have variable terms for the consideration paid to company by its customer. However, IAS 18 and IAS 11 did not include comprehensive guidance for measuring how much revenue should be recognised in such cases.

(5) **Multi-element arrangements**

Some transactions, often called multi-element arrangements, involve the delivery of more than one good or service. **The previous standards did not give sufficient guidance on dealing with such transactions.** IAS 18 stated that in certain circumstances the revenue recognition criteria must be applied to the separately identifiable components of a transaction. However, it did not explain the circumstances when a transaction could be broken down into separate components or the basis for identifying those components.

Under the standard proposed in the Exposure Draft *Revenue from contracts with customers*, distinct performance obligations would be accounted for separately. Goods or services are distinct if they are sold separately by the company, or if it provides benefits to the company's customer.

(6) **Disclosures**

Disclosures in current standards on revenue recognition were seen as inadequate when compared to disclosures in other standards.

(ii) **Improvements brought about by IFRS 15**

IFRS 15 was the result of a joint IASB and FASB project on revenue recognition. It seeks to strike a balance between the IASB rules in IAS 18, which were felt to be too general, leading to a lot of diversity in practice, and the FASB regulations, which were too numerous.

The core principle of IFRS 15 is that an entity should **recognise revenue to depict the transfer of promised goods or services to customers in an amount that reflects the consideration to which the entity expects to be entitled in exchange for those goods or services.**

To apply this core principle, IFRS 15 requires the following five step process:

(1) **Identify the contract with a customer.** A contract can be written, oral or implied by customary business practices.

(2) **Identify the separate performance obligations in the contract.** If a promised good or service is not distinct, it can be combined with others.

(3) **Determine the transaction price.** This is the amount to which the entity expects to be **'entitled'**. For variable consideration, the probability – weighted expected amount is used. The effect of any credit losses shown as a separate line item (just below revenue).

(4) **Allocate the transaction price to the separate performance obligations in the contract.** For multiple deliverables, the transaction price is allocated to each separate performance obligation in proportion to the **stand-alone selling price** at contract inception of each performance obligation.

(5) **Recognise revenue when (or as) the entity satisfies a performance obligation,** that is when the entity **transfers** a promised good or service to a customer. The good or service is only considered as transferred when the customer obtains **control** of it.

Addressing each of the criticisms in turn:

(1) **Timing of revenue recognition.**

IFRS 15 is clear about when revenue should be recognised. Revenue from a contract may be recognised in accordance with IFRS 15 *Revenue from contracts with customers* when all of the following criteria are met.

- The **parties** to the contract have **approved the contract.**
- **Each party's rights** in relation to the goods or services to be transferred **can be identified.**
- The **payment terms and conditions** for the goods or services to be transferred **can be identified.**
- The contract has **commercial substance.**
- The **collection of an amount of consideration** to which the entity is entitled to in exchange for the goods or services is **probable.**

(2) **Conflict with the IASB *Conceptual Framework***

IFRS 15 adopts an **asset/liability-driven approach**, consistent with the *Conceptual Framework*. Further, in the definition of ordinary activities. Reference is made to the description of revenue in the IASB's *Conceptual Framework.*

(3) **Distinguishing between goods and services**

Step 2 of the five-stage process above addresses this criticism by requiring the entity to **identify the separate performance obligations in the contract.** The key point is distinct goods or services. A contract includes promises to provide goods or services to a customer. Those promises are called performance obligations. A company would account for a performance obligation separately only if the promised good or service is distinct. A good or service is distinct if it is sold separately or if it could be sold separately because it has a distinct function and a distinct profit margin.

(4) **Variable consideration**

This criticism is addressed by Step 3 above, which requires the entity to **determine the transaction price**. The transaction price is the amount of consideration a company expects to be entitled to from the customer in exchange for transferring goods or services. The transaction price would reflect the company's probability-weighted estimate of **variable consideration** (including reasonable estimates of contingent amounts) in addition to the effects of the customer's credit risk and the time value of money (if material). Examples of where a variable consideration can arise include: discounts, rebates, refunds, price concessions, credits and penalties.

(5) **Multi-element arrangements**

Under IFRS 15, **distinct performance obligations must be accounted for separately**. Goods or services are distinct if they are sold separately by the company, or if it provides benefits to the company's customer.

(6) **Disclosures**

The disclosures in IFRS 15 are clear and comprehensive. Entities must disclose sufficient information to enable users of financial statements to understand the **nature, amount, timing and uncertainty of revenue and cash flows arising from contract with customers.**

(b) **Plant**

Reven does not obtain control of the plant, because the repurchase option means that it is limited in its ability to use and obtain benefit from the plant.

As **control has not been transferred**, Venue must account for the transaction as a **financing arrangement**, because the exercise price is above the original selling price. Venue must continue to recognise the plant and recognise the cash received as a financial liability. The difference of $50,000 is recognised as interest expense.

If, on 31 July 20X7, the **option lapses** unexercised, Reven will then obtain control of the plant. In this case, **Venue must will derecognise the plant and recognise revenue of $550,000** (the $500,000 already received plus the $50,000 charged to interest).

5 Preparation question: Sundry standards

(a) **Curtailment**

Statement of financial position extract	
	$'000
Non-current liabilities (4,115 – 4,540)	425
Statement of comprehensive income extract	$'000
Charged to profit or loss	
Current service cost	275
Net interest on net defined benefit liability (344 – 288)	56
Curtailment cost	58
	389
Other comprehensive income	
Actuarial gain on obligation	107
Return on plan assets (excluding amounts in net interest)	7
Reconciliation of pension plan movement	$'000
Plan deficit at 1 Feb 20X7 (3,600 – 4,300)	(700)
Company contributions	550
Profit or loss total	(389)
Other comprehensive income total (107 + 7)	114
Plan deficit at 31 Jan 20X8 (4,115 – 4,540)	(425)

	$'000
Changes in the present value of the defined benefit obligation	
Defined benefit obligation at 1 Feb 20X7	4,300
Interest cost @ 8%	344
Pensions paid	(330)
Curtailment	58
Current service cost	275
Remeasurement gain through OCI (bal. Fig.)	(107)
Defined benefit obligation at 31 Jan 20X8	4,540
Changes in the fair value of plan assets	
Fair value of plan assets at 1 Feb 20X7	3,600
Contributions	550
Pensions paid	(330)
Interest on plan assets 8% × 3,600	288
Remeasurement gain through OCI (295 – 288)	7
Fair value of plan assets at 31 Jan 20X8 (bal. fig.)	4,115

(b) **Settlement**

(i) *Calculation of net defined benefit liability*

Changes in the present value of the defined benefit obligation

	Obligation
	$'000
20X8 b/f	40,000
Interest at 8%	3,200
Current service cost	2,500
Past service cost	2,000
Benefits paid	(1,974)
	45,726
Remeasurement losses through OCI	274
20X8 c/f	46,000
	$'000
20X9 b/f	46,000
Interest at 9%	4,140
Current service cost	2,860
Settlement	(11,400)
Benefits paid	(2,200)
	39,400
Remeasurement losses	1,400
20X9 c/f	40,800

Changes in the fair value of plan assets

	Assets
	$'000
20X8 b/f	40,000
Interest at 8%	3,200
Benefits paid	(1,974)
Contributions paid in	2,000
	43,226
Remeasurement losses	(226)

20X8 c/f	43,000
20X9 b/f	43,000
Interest at 9%	3,870
Settlement	(10,800)
Benefits paid	(2,200)
Contributions paid in	2,200
	36,070
Remeasurement losses	(390)
20X9 c/f	35,680

- During 20X8, there is an improvement in the future benefits available under the plan and as a result there is a past service cost of $1million, being the increase in the present value of the obligation as a result of the change.
- During 20X9, Sion sells part of its operations and transfers the relevant part of the pension plan to the purchaser. This is a settlement. The overall gain on settlement is calculated as:

	$'000
Present value of obligation settled	11,400
Fair value of plan assets transferred on settlement	(10,800)
Cash transferred on settlement	(400)
Gain	200

(ii) *Financial statements extracts*

STATEMENT OF FINANCIAL POSITION

	20X8	*20X9*
	$'000	$'000
Net defined benefit liability:(46,000 – 43,000)/(40,800 – 35,680)	3,000	5,120

STATEMENT OF PROFIT OR LOSS AND OTHER COMPREHENSIVE INCOME

	20X8	*20X9*
	$'000	$'000
Profit or loss		
Current service cost	2,500	2,860
Past service cost	2,000	–
Gain on settlement	–	(200)
Net interest: (3,200 – 3,200)/(4,140 – 3,870)	–	270
Other comprehensive income		
Remeasurement loss on defined pension plan: (274 + 226)/(1,400 +390)	500	1,790

(c) **Classification of financial assets**

Bed's investment is a financial asset. According to IFRS 9 *Financial instruments*, financial assets are classified as measured at either amortised cost or fair value depending on:

(i) The entity's business model for managing the financial assets and
(ii) The contractual cash flow characteristics of the financial assets.

In particular, a financial asset is measured at amortised cost where:

(i) The asset is held within a business model where the objective is to hold assets in order to collect contractual cash flows

(ii) The contractual terms of the financial asset give rise on specified dates to cash flows that are solely payments of principal and interest on the principal outstanding.

For this purpose, interest is consideration for the time value of money and for the credit risk associated with the principal amount.

Embedded derivatives

Derivatives embedded within a host which is a financial asset within the scope of IFRS 9 are not separated out for accounting purposes; instead the entire hybrid contract is accounted for as one and classified as measured at amortised cost or fair value through profit or loss in accordance with the guidelines above.

Deposit with Em Bank

The deposit is considered a financial asset classified as held at amortised cost.

The additional 3% interest is an example of an embedded derivative. However, as the host contract is a financial asset, the derivative is not separated out for the purposes of accounting and the entire hybrid contract is accounted for together.

6 Key

Text reference. Impairment is covered in Chapter 3 of the BPP Study Text.

Top tips. A full question on impairment is unusual, although the topic itself comes up regularly. There are a lot of marks for discussion in Part (a), including 2 professional marks, so don't rush this bit. Part (b) says 'discuss with suitable computations', so do not make the mistake of expecting the calculations to speak for themselves. P2 is a preparation for the accountant's role as advisor – and explanations will be just as important in this role as computations.

Easy marks. These are available for bookwork in Part (a), and for the calculation of value in use in Part (b).

Examiner's comments. The ACCA examination/examining team was pleased with candidates' answers to the first part of the question, which asked them to discuss the main considerations which an entity should take into account when impairment testing non-current assets in a climate where there were credit limitations. However, many made the mistake of simply setting out the rules of impairment testing without relating it to the economic climate set out in the question. The second part of the question required candidates to set out how to account for any potential impairment in given circumstances. This was quite well answered. Some candidates had difficulties in discounting future cash flows and the treatment of the impairment loss and revaluation gain. Many did not discuss the key issues in sufficient depth, or simply calculated the accounting adjustments without sufficient discussion of the issues.

Marking scheme

		Marks
(a)	Impairment processes	4
	General considerations	4
	Professional marks	2
(b)	Non-current asset at cost	6
	Non-current asset at valuation	6
	Non-current asset held for sale	3
		25

(a) The basic principle of IAS 36 *Impairment of assets* is that an asset should be carried at no more than its recoverable amount, that is the amount to be recovered through use or sale of the asset. If an **asset's value** is **higher than its recoverable amount**, an **impairment loss** has occurred. The impairment loss should be **written off** against profit or loss for the year.

Entities must determine, **at each reporting date**, whether there are any indications that impairment has occurred. Indicators of impairment may be internal or external. Where it is not possible to measure impairment for individual assets, the loss should be measured for a **cash generating unit. Internal factors** may apply in any economic climate, and include such matters as physical damage, adverse changes to the methods of use of the asset, management restructuring and over-estimation of cash flows. In an adverse economic climate, additional, **external indicators** of impairment are more likely to be evident. Such factors include:

(i) A **significant decrease** in the **market** value of an asset in excess of **normal passage of time**
(ii) Significant **adverse changes** in the **markets** or **business** in which the asset is used
(iii) Adverse changes to the **technological, economic or legal environment** of the business
(iv) Increase in **market interest rates** likely to affect **the discount rate** used in calculating value in use
(v) Where **interest rates increase**, adversely affecting **recoverable amounts**
(vi) The **carrying amount** of an entity's assets exceeding its **market capitalisation**

The **recoverable amount** is **defined** as the **higher** of:

(i) The **asset's fair value less costs of disposal**. This is the price that would be received to sell the asset in an orderly transaction between market participants at the measurement date under current market conditions, net of costs of disposal.

(ii) The asset's **value in use**. This is the present value of estimated future cash flows (inflows minus outflows) generated by the asset, including its estimated net disposal value (if any) at the end of its useful life. A number of factors must be reflected in the calculation of value in use (variations, estimates of cash flows, uncertainty), but the most important is the **time value of money** as value in use is based on **present value calculations**.

Impairment testing is difficult whether the recoverable amount is based on fair value less costs of disposal, because of the uncertainties surrounding **assumptions** that must be made. IAS 36 requires that these **are 'reasonable and supportable'**. Cash flow projections up to five years should be based on the most recent budgets and financial forecasts, but in a recession, these **should not be overly optimistic**. Longer term cash flow projections should be based on a steady or declining growth rate. Discount rates should reflect the specific risks of the asset or cash generating unit.

In an adverse economic climate, the entity will need to **consider the market** in which it operates in making its assumptions about recoverable amounts, because the market affects recoverable amounts. If **comparable industries** are taking impairment losses, then the entity will need to **explain the absence of such impairment charges**. Industry analysts will expect this. The market also needs to be informed about how the entity is reflecting the economic downturn in its impairment calculations, and what market information is being used in the impairment testing.

Clearly, testing for impairment will be a **time-consuming activity**. Cash flow assumptions may need to be reassessed, and **discount rates** must be scrutinised to see if they are **still valid** in a time of rising risk premiums and poor liquidity. Detailed calculations must be made and revised as necessary. Estimates and calculations may also need to be **revised** in the light of **information** becoming available only **after the end of the reporting period**. Last but not least, **extensive disclosures** will be required of discount rates, long-term growth rate assumptions and the reasons behind such assumptions.

(b) **Impairment loss for year ended 31 May 20X4**

IAS 36 states that if an **asset's value** is **higher than** its **recoverable amount**, an **impairment loss** has occurred. The impairment loss should be written off to profit or loss for the year.

The carrying value of the non-current assets of Key at 31 May 20X4 is cost less depreciation:

$3m – ($3m ÷ 5) = $2.4m.

This needs to be compared to value in use at 31 May 20X4, which, using a discount rate of 5%, is calculated as:

Year ended	*31 May 20X5*	*31 May 20X6*	*31 May 20X7*	*31 May 20X8*	*Total*
Cash flows	280	450	500	550	
Discount factors	0.9524	0.9070	0.8638	0.8227	
Discounted cash flows ($'000)	267	408	432	452	1,559

The value in use of $1,559,000 is below the carrying value, so the carrying value must be written down, giving rise to an **impairment loss**:

$2,400,000 – $1,559,000 = $841,000

Value in use at 30 November 20X4

The directors wish to reverse the impairment loss calculated as at 31 May 20X4, on the grounds that, using the same cash flows, the value in use of the non-current assets is now above the carrying value. However, while IAS 36 requires an assessment at each reporting date of whether an impairment loss has decreased, this does not apply to the unwinding of the discount (or goodwill). Since the **same cash flows** have been used, the increase in value in use is **due to the unwinding of the discount, and so cannot be reversed**.

Government reimbursement

The treatment of compensation received in the form of reimbursements is governed by IAS 37 *Provisions, contingent liabilities and contingent assets.* Reimbursements from governmental indemnities are recorded in profit or loss for the year **when the compensation becomes receivable,** and the receipt is **treated as a separate economic event** from the item it was intended to compensate for. In this particular case, receipt is by no means certain, since the government has merely indicated that it may compensate.

Thus **no credit can be taken** for compensation of 20% of the impairment loss.

Revalued asset

When an **impairment loss occurs** for a **revalued asset**, the **impairment loss** should be first be charged to other comprehensive income (that is, treated as a **revaluation decrease**). Any **excess** is then charged to **profit or loss**.

The revaluation gain and impairment loss will be accounted for as follows:

	Revalued carrying value
	$m
1 December 20X1	10.0
Depreciation (10 × 2/10)	(2.0)
Revaluation (bal. fig.)	0.8
1 December 20X3	8.8
Depreciation (1 year) (8.8 × 1/8)	(1.1)
Impairment loss (bal. fig.)	(2.2)
Recoverable amount at 30 November 20X4	5.5

The impairment loss of $2.2m is charged to **other comprehensive income** until the revaluation surplus has been eliminated, and the rest is charged to profit or loss. Therefore the impairment **loss charged to other comprehensive income** will be **$0.8m.** The **remainder**, $2.2m – $0.8m = $1.4m will be **charged to profit or loss**.

It is possible that the company would transfer an amount from revaluation surplus to retained earnings to cover the excess depreciation of $0.1m. If so, the impairment loss charged to OCI would be $(0.8 – 0.1m) = $0.7m.

Property to be sold

The fact that management plans to sell the property because it is being under-utilised may be an **indicator** of **impairment**. Such assets (or cash generating units) must be tested for impairment when the decision to sell is made.

IFRS 5 *Non-current assets held for sale and discontinued operations* may apply in such cases, but the decision to sell the asset is generally made well before the IFRS 5 criteria are met. IFRS requires an asset or disposal group to be classified as held for sale where it is **available for immediate sale** in its **present condition** subject only to **terms that are usual** and customary and the sale is **highly probable**. For a sale to be highly probable:

- Management must be **committed** to the sale.
- An **active programme to locate a buyer** must have been initiated.
- The **market price** must be **reasonable** in relation to the asset's current fair value.
- The sale must be **expected to be completed within one year** from the date of classification.

An asset (or disposal group) that is held for sale should be measured at the **lower of** its **carrying amount** and **fair value less costs to sell**. Immediately before classification of the asset as held for sale, the entity must update any impairment test carried out. **Once** the asset has been **classified as held for sale**, any **impairment loss** will be based on the **difference between the adjusted carrying amounts and the fair value less cost to sell.** The impairment loss (if any) will be **recognised in profit or loss**.

A **subsequent increase** in fair value less costs of disposal may be **recognised** in profit or loss **only to the extent of any impairment previously recognised**.

In the case of the property held by Key, it is likely that **IFRS 5 would not apply** because **not all the criteria for a highly probable sale** have been met. Management is committed to the sale, and there is an active programme to locate a buyer. However, **Key has not reduced the price of the asset, which is in excess of its market value** – one of the IFRS 5 criteria is that the market price must be reasonable in relation to the asset's current fair value. In addition, the asset has remained unsold for a year, so it **cannot be assumed that the sale will be completed within one year** of classification.

The property does not meet the IFRS 5 criteria, so it **cannot be classified as held for sale**. However, an **impairment** has taken place and, in the circumstances, the **recoverable amount** would be **fair value less costs to sell**.

7 Emcee

Text reference. Intangible assets and borrowing costs are covered in Chapter 3 of the BPP Study Text. IFRS 13 is also covered in Chapter 3, and in more detail in Chapter 7. IFRS 5 is covered in Chapter 15 and IAS 24 in Chapter 11.

Top tips. This is a specialised industry question set in a sports organisation. The issues covered are borrowing costs (Part (a)), intangible assets, non-current assets held for sale and impairment of assets (Part (b)) and fair value measurement and related party transactions (Part (c).

Easy marks. No parts of this question are particularly easy - the main way to get the marks is to break down the scenario into its constituent parts and make sure you deal with each relevant standard.

Examiner's comment. The recommended approach is to discuss the principles and then apply them to the scenario. The mark allocation can vary between principles and application, although as a general rule the marks are split equally between the two elements of the answer.

Marking scheme

		Marks
(a)	1 mark per point up to maximum	6
(b)	1 mark per point up to maximum	10
(c)	1 mark per point up to maximum	7
Professional marks		2
Maximum		25

(a) **Borrowing costs**

The cost of an item of property, plant and equipment may include borrowing costs incurred for the purpose of acquiring or constructing it. IAS 23 *Borrowing costs* requires such borrowing costs to be capitalised if the asset takes a substantial period of time to be prepared for its intended use or sale. The definition of borrowing costs includes interest expense calculated by the effective interest method, finance charges on leases and exchange differences arising from foreign currency borrowings relating to interest costs. Borrowing costs should be capitalised during construction and include the costs of funds borrowed for the purpose of financing the construction of the asset, and general borrowings which would have been avoided if the expenditure on the asset had occurred. The general borrowing costs are determined by applying a capitalisation rate to the expenditure on that asset. The capitalisation rate will be the weighted average of the borrowing costs applicable to the general pool.

The weighted-average carrying amount of the stadium during the period is:

$(20 + 70 + 120 + 170)m/4, that is $95m,

The capitalisation rate of the borrowings of Emcee during the period of construction is 9% per annum, therefore the total amount of borrowing costs to be capitalised is the weighted-average carrying amount of the stadium multiplied by the capitalisation rate.

That is ($95m × 9% × 4/12) $2.85m.

(b) **Players' registrations**

IAS 38 *Intangible assets* states that an entity should recognise an intangible asset where it is probable that future economic benefits will flow to the entity and the cost of the asset can be measured reliably. Therefore, the costs associated with the acquisition of players' registrations should be capitalised at the fair value of the consideration payable. Costs would include transfer fees, league levy fees, agents' fees incurred by the club and other directly attributable costs. Costs also include the fair value of any contingent consideration, which is primarily payable to the player's former club with associated league levy fees, once payment becomes probable. Subsequent reassessments of the amount of contingent consideration payable would be also included in the cost of the player's registration. The estimate of the fair value of the contingent consideration payable requires management to assess the likelihood of specific performance conditions being met, which would trigger the payment of the contingent consideration. This assessment would be carried out on an individual player basis. The additional amount of contingent consideration potentially payable, in excess of the amounts included in the cost of players' registrations, would be disclosed. Costs would be fully amortised over the period covered by the player's contract.

Where a playing contract is extended, any costs associated with securing the extension are added to the unamortised balance at the date of the extension and the revised book value is amortised over the remaining revised contract life. Player registrations would be classified as assets held for sale under IFRS 5 *Non-current assets held for sale and discontinued operations* when their carrying value is expected to be recovered principally through a sale transaction and a sale is considered to be highly probable. Additionally, the registrations should be actively marketed by Emcee, which it appears that they are. It would appear that in these circumstances that management is committed to a plan to sell the registration, that the asset is available for immediate sale, that an active programme to locate a buyer is initiated by circulating clubs. In order to fulfil the last criteria of IFRS 5, it may be prudent to only class these registrations as available for sale where unconditional offers have been received prior to a period end. IFRS 5 requires that it is unlikely that the plan to sell the registrations will be significantly changed or withdrawn.

However, because of the subjectivity involved, in the case of player registrations these assets would be stated at the lower of the carrying amount and fair value less costs to sell, as the carrying amount will already be stated in accordance with IFRSs.

Gains and losses on disposal of players' registrations would be determined by comparing the fair value of the consideration receivable, net of any transaction costs, with the carrying amount and would be recognised in profit or loss within profit on disposal of players' registrations. Where a part of the consideration receivable is contingent on specified performance conditions, this amount is recognised in profit or loss when the conditions are met.

IAS 36 *Impairment of assets* states that entities should annually test their assets for impairment. An asset is impaired if its carrying amount exceeds its recoverable amount which is the higher of the asset's fair value less costs of disposal and its value in use. It is difficult to determine the value in use of an individual player in isolation as that player (unless via a sale or insurance recovery) cannot generate cash flows on his own. Whilst any individual player cannot really be separated from the single cash generating unit (CGU), being the basketball or football team, there may be certain circumstances where a player is taken out of the CGU, when it becomes clear that they will not play for the club again, for example, a player sustaining a career threatening injury or being permanently removed from the playing squad for another reason. If such circumstances arise, the carrying value of the player should be assessed against the best estimate of the player's fair value less any costs to sell and an impairment charge made in profit or loss, which reflects any loss arising. The playing registrations disposed of, subsequent to the year end, for $25m, with an associated net book value of $7m, would be disclosed as events after the reporting date.

(c) **Valuation of stadiums**

IFRS 13 *Fair value measurement* would value the stadiums at the price which would be received to sell the asset in an orderly transaction between market participants at the measurement date. The price would be the one which maximises the value of the asset or the group of assets using the principal of the highest and best use. The price would essentially use Level 2 inputs which are inputs other than quoted market prices included within Level 1 which are observable for the asset or liability, either directly or indirectly. Property naming rights present complications when valuing property. The status of the property dictates its suitability for inviting sponsorship attached to its name. It has nothing to do with the property itself but this can be worth a significant amount. Therefore Emcee could include the property naming rights in the valuation of the stadiums and write it off over three years.

IAS 24 *Related party disclosures* sets out the criteria for two entities to be treated as related parties. Such criteria include being members of the same group or where a person or a close member of that person's family is related to a reporting entity if that person has control or joint control over the reporting entity. IAS 24 deems that parties are not related simply because they have a director or key manager in common. In this case, there are two directors in common and it appears as though the entities are not related. However, the Regulator will need to establish whether the sponsorship deal is a related party transaction (RPT) for the purpose of the financial control provisions. There would need to be demonstrated that the airline may be expected to influence, or be influenced by, the club or a related party of the club. If the deal is deemed to be an RPT, the Regulator will consider whether the sponsorship is at fair value. If the Regulator considers the deal not to be at a fair value, Emcee may be fined and therefore the entity will have to make a provision or disclose a contingent liability for any potential fine under IAS 37 *Provisions, contingent liabilities and contingent assets.*

8 Scramble

Text reference. Intangible assets and impairment are covered in Chapter 3. IFRS 9 is covered in Chapter 7.

Top tips. Parts (a) and (b) were on impairment testing. You may have found Part (b), requiring determination of the discount rate to be used, rather difficult, and you may have needed to draw on your financial management studies. Part (c) was on intangible assets (agents' fees on transfer of players to the club and extension of players' contracts) and an IFRS 9 financial asset (rights to ticket sales of another football club).

Easy marks. There are no obviously easy marks in this question.

Examiner's comment. In Part (a) many candidates automatically assumed that the accounting treatments were incorrect but in this case the entity was correctly expensing maintenance costs, as these did not enhance the asset over and above original benefits. Similarly, the decision to keep intangibles at historical cost is a matter of choice and therefore the accounting policy outlined in the question was acceptable. In Part (b), candidates realised that the discount rate was not in accordance with IAS 36, but did not explain why. In Part (c) definition of an intangible asset was well expressed by students and candidates realised in most cases that the players' registration rights met the definition of intangible assets. However very few candidates stated that the agents' fees represented professional fees incurred in bringing the asset into use and therefore could be included in intangibles.

Marking scheme

	Marks
Intangible assets – subjective assessment	7
Cash generating units – subjective assessment	7
Intangible assets – subjective assessment	9
Professional	2
	25

(a) **Internally developed intangibles**

IAS 38 *Intangible assets* **allows internally developed intangibles such to be capitalised** provided certain criteria (technological feasibility, probable future benefits, intent and ability to use or sell the software, resources to complete the software, and ability to measure cost) are met. It is assumed, in the absence of information to the contrary, that they have; accordingly Scramble's treatment is correct in this respect.

Scramble is also correct in expensing the maintenance costs. These should not be capitalised as they do not enhance the value of the asset over and above the original benefits.

As regards subsequent measurement, IAS 38 requires that **an entity must choose either the cost model or the revaluation** model for each class of intangible asset. Scramble has chosen cost, and this is acceptable as an accounting policy.

Intangible assets **may have a finite or an indefinite useful life**. IAS 38 states that an entity may treat an intangible asset as having an indefinite useful life, when, having regard to all relevant factors there is no foreseeable limit to the period over which the asset is expected to generate net cash inflows for the entity.

'Indefinite' is not the same as 'infinite'. Computer software is mentioned in IAS 38 as an intangible that is prone to technological obsolescence and whose life may therefore be short. Its **useful life should be reviewed each reporting period** to determine whether events and circumstances continue to support an indefinite useful life assessment for that asset. If they do not, the change in the useful life assessment from indefinite to finite should be accounted for as a change in an accounting estimate.

The asset should also be **assessed for impairment in accordance with IAS 36** *Impairment of assets.* Specifically, the entity must test the intangible asset for impairment annually, and whenever there is an indication that the asset may be impaired. The asset is tested by **comparing its recoverable amount with its carrying amount**.

The **cash flows** used by Scramble to determine value in use for the purposes of impairment testing **do not comply with IAS 36**. Scramble does not analyse or investigate the differences between expected and actual cash flows, but this is an important way of testing the reasonableness of assumptions about expected cash flows, and IAS 36 requires such **assumptions to be reasonable and supported by evidence**.

Scramble is also **incorrect** to include in its estimate of future cash flows those **expected to be incurred in improving the games and the expected increase in revenue** resulting from that expense. IAS 36 requires cash flow projections to relate to the asset in its current condition. Nor should cash flow estimates include tax payments or receipts as here.

(b) **Discount rate for impairment**

While the cash flows used in testing for impairment are specific to the entity, the **discount rate is supposed to appropriately reflect the current market assessment of the time value of money and the risks specific to the asset or cash generating unit.** When a specific rate for an asset or cash generating unit is not directly available from the market, which is usually the case, the discount rate to be used is a surrogate. An estimate should be made of a **pre-tax rate that reflects the current market assessment of the time value of money and the risks specific to the asset** that have **not been adjusted** for in the estimate of future cash flows. According to IAS 36, this rate is the return that the investors would require if they chose an investment that would generate cash flows of amounts, timing and risk profile equivalent to those that the entity expects to derive from the assets.

Rates that should be considered are the entity's weighted average cost of capital, the entity's incremental borrowing rate or other market rates. The objective must be to obtain a rate which is sensible and justifiable. Scramble should not use the risk free rate adjusted by the company specific average credit spread of outstanding debt raised two years ago. Instead the credit spread input applied **should reflect the current market assessment of the credit spread at the time of impairment testing**, even though Scramble does not intend raising any more finance.

Disclosures

With regard to the impairment loss recognised in respect of each cash generating unit, IAS 36 would disclosure of:

- The amount of the loss
- The events and circumstances that led to the loss
- A description of the impairment loss by class of asset

It is **no defence** to maintain that this information was **common knowledge in the market**. The disclosures are still needed. It should be noted that IAS 1 requires disclosure of material items, so this information needs to be disclosed if the loses are **material,** with materiality determined using a suitable measure such as percentage of profit before tax.

(c) **Recognition of intangible assets**

Registration rights and agents' fees

The relevant standard here is IAS 38 *Intangible assets.* An **intangible asset may be recognised** if it gives control (the power to benefit from the asset), if it meets the identifiability criteria in IAS 38, if it is probable that future economic benefits attributable to the asset will flow to the entity and if its fair value can be measured reliably. For an intangible asset to be identifiable the asset must be separable or it must arise from contractual or other legal rights. It appears that these **criteria have been met**:

(i) The registration rights are contractual.

(ii) Scramble has control, because it may transfer or extend the rights.

(iii) Economic benefits will flow to Scramble in the form of income it can earn when fans come to see the player play.

IAS 38 specifies the items that make up the **cost** of separately acquired assets:

(i) Its purchase price, including import duties and non-refundable purchase taxes, after deducting trade discounts and rebates, and

(ii) Any directly attributable cost of preparing the asset for its intended use.

IAS 38 specifically mentions, as an example of directly attributable costs, 'professional fees arising directly from bringing the asset to its working condition'. In this business**, the players' registration rights meet the definition of intangible assets**. In addition, **Scramble is incorrect** in believing that the **agents' fees** paid on extension of players' contracts do not meet the criteria to be recognised as intangible assets. The fees are incurred to service the player registration rights, and **should therefore be treated as intangible assets**.

Rights to revenue from ticket sales

Whether Rashing can show these rights as intangible assets depends on whether the IAS 38 criteria have been met. Since Rashing has no discretion over the pricing of the tickets and cannot sell them, it cannot be said to control the asset. Accordingly, the rights **cannot be treated as an intangible asset**.

The entity is only entitled to cash generated from ticket sales, so the issue is one of a **contractual right to receive cash**. The applicable standard is therefore not IAS 38 but IFRS 9 *Financial instruments,* under which the rights to ticket revenue represent a **financial asset**.

IFRS 9 has two classifications for financial assets: amortised cost and fair value. Financial assets are classified as being at **amortised cost** if **both** of the following apply.

(i) The asset is held within a business model whose objective is to hold the assets to collect the contractual cash flows.

(ii) The contractual terms of the financial asset give rise, on specified dates, to cash flows that are solely payments of principal and interest on the principal outstanding.

All other financial assets are measured at fair value.

Rashing's receipts are regular cash flows, but they are based on ticket revenues, which are determined by match attendance. Therefore they are not solely payments of principal and interest, and **do not meet the criteria for classification at amortised cost**. Consequently, the financial asset should be classified as being **at fair value** under IFRS 9.

9 Estoil

Text reference. Impairment is covered in Chapter 3 of your Study Text.

Top tips. As Question 4 on the paper, this was different from the usual current issues question in the topic it tested (IAS 36), although not in structure, being a discussion followed by application to a scenario. While IAS 36 is brought forward knowledge from F7, the depth of discussion required is greater, and the scenario requires more thought. Part (a) required a discussion of factors to take account of in conducting an impairment test , followed by an application to a scenario in Part (b). The discussion required drew on your financial management knowledge (eg WACC).

Easy marks. There are no obvious easy marks in this question.

Examiner's comment. Candidates scored well on Part (a) of the question. Marks were gained for discussion of each of the issues based on one mark per point, which meant that candidates could score 10 marks by discussing only 2 points per issue. Part (b) dealt with issues have been identified by the IASB as being extremely judgemental and the cause of subjectivity in financial statements. The question was quite well answered by candidates.

Marking scheme

		Marks
(a)	Subjective – 1 mark per point	13
(b)	Subjective	10
Professional marks		2
		25

(a) Entities must determine, **at each reporting date**, whether there are any indications that impairment has occurred. Indicators of impairment may be internal or external. The following factors need to be considered when conducting an impairment test under IAS 36 *Impairment of assets.*

(i) **Changes in circumstances in the reporting period**

Circumstances may change due to internal factors, for example matters as physical damage, adverse changes to the methods of use of the asset, management restructuring and over-estimation of cash flows, and external factors, such as **adverse changes** in the **markets** or **business** in which the asset is used, or adverse changes to the **technological, economic or legal environment** of the business.

If such indicators come to light between the date of the impairment test and the end of the next reporting period, **more than one impairment test may be required** in the accounting period. In addition, tests for impairment of goodwill and some other intangible assets may be performed at any time during the accounting period, provided it is performed at the same time each year. Not all goodwill is tested at the year end – some entities test it at an interim period. Should impairment indicators arise after the annual impairment test has been performed, it may be necessary to test goodwill for impairment at the year end and at a subsequent interim reporting date as well.

A possible indicator of impairment is volatility in financial statements; for example sharp changes in commodity prices may cause the assets of mining and energy companies to be impaired. In such cases, the assets affected should be tested in the interim period.

(ii) **Market capitalisation**

A strong indicator of impairment is when the **carrying amount** of an entity's assets exceeds the entity's **market capitalisation,** suggesting that the entity is overvalued. However, there **may not be a direct correlation** between the market capitalisation and the impairment loss arising from a lower return generated on the entity's assets –the market may have taken other factors into account. The discrepancy does, however, **highlight the need for the entity to examine its cash-generating units, and possibly to test goodwill for impairment.** The reason for the shortfall must be examined and

understood, even though IAS 36 does not require a formal reconciliation between an entity's market capitalisation, its fair value less costs to sell and its value in use.

(iii) **Allocating goodwill to cash-generating units**

Goodwill arising on an acquisition is required to be allocated to each of the acquirer's cash-generating units (CGUs), or to a group of CGUs, that are expected to benefit from the synergies of the combination. **If CGUs are subsequently revised or operations disposed of, IAS 36 requires goodwill to be reallocated, based on relative values, to the units affected.**

The difficulty with this is that IAS 36 **does not give guidance as to what is meant by relative value.** While **fair value less costs to sell** (FVLCS) could be used, this is not mandated by the standard. However, the entity may still need to carry out a valuation process on the part retained. **Value in use**(VIU) is a possibility, but the measure needs to be one that can be applied equally to both the part retained and the part disposed of. VIU has the obvious problem that it will be much the same as FVLCS for the operations disposed of, but there could be significant differences between VIU and FVLCS for the part retained. Alternatively, there could be reasonable ways of estimating relative value by using an **appropriate industry or business surrogate**, for example revenue, profits, industry KPIs.

(iv) **Valuation issues**

The basic principle of IAS 36 *Impairment of assets* is that an asset should be carried at no more than its recoverable amount, that is the amount to be recovered through use or sale of the asset. If an **asset's value** is **higher than its recoverable amount**, an **impairment loss** has occurred. The impairment loss should be **written off** against profit or loss for the year.

The **recoverable amount** is **defined** as the **higher** of the **asset's fair value less costs of disposal** and the asset's **value in use**. Measuring both of these requires the use of **estimates and assumptions,** some of which **may be problematic**.

(1) **Fair value less costs of disposal** is defined as the price that would be received to sell the asset in an orderly transaction between market participants at the measurement date under current market conditions, net of costs of disposal. IAS 36 gives a 'hierarchy of evidence' for this, with 'price in a binding sale agreement' at the top, only likely to be available if the asset is held for sale, and allowing, in the absence of any active market, estimates based on **a discounted cash flow (DCF) model, which may not be reliable.**

(2) Determining the types of **future cash flows which should be included in the measurement of VIU can also be difficult**. Under IAS 36 an asset or CGU must be tested in its current status, not the status that management wishes it was in or hopes to get it into in the near future. Therefore, the standard requires VIU to be measured at the net present value of the future cash flows the entity expects to derive from the asset or CGU in its current condition over its remaining useful life. This means that it is not appropriate to take account of management plans for enhancing the performance of the asset or CGU, even though these may bring about an increase in value.

(3) While the cash flows used in testing for impairment are specific to the entity, the **discount rate is supposed to appropriately reflect the current market assessment of the time value of money and the risks specific to the asset or cash generating unit.** When a specific rate for an asset or cash generating unit is not directly available from the market, which is usually the case, the discount rate to be used is a surrogate. An estimate should be made of a **pre-tax rate that reflects the current market assessment of the time value of money and the risks specific to the asset** that have **not been adjusted** for in the estimate of future cash flows. According to IAS 36, this rate is the return that the investors would require if they chose an investment that would generate cash flows of amounts, timing and risk profile equivalent to those that the entity expects to derive from the assets.

Rates that should be considered are the entity's weighted average cost of capital (WACC), the entity's incremental borrowing rate or other market rates. The objective must be to obtain a rate which is sensible and justifiable.

(4) The test is further complicated by the **impact of taxation.** IAS 36 requires that VIU be measured using pre-tax cash flows and a pre-tax discount rate, but WACC is a post-tax rate, as are most observable equity rates used by valuers.

(5) There is a need for **consistency in determining the recoverable amount and carrying amount which are being compared.** For example, in the case of pensions, there can be significant differences between the measurement basis of the pension asset or (more likely) liability and the cash flows that relate to pensions.

(6) IAS 36 requires that **corporate assets** must be allocated to a cash-generating unit on a 'reasonable and consistent basis, but does not expand on this.

(v) **Disclosures**

With regard to the impairment loss recognised in respect of each cash generating unit, IAS 36 would disclosure of:

(1) The amount of the loss
(2) The events and circumstances that led to the loss
(3) A description of the impairment loss by class of asset

It is **no defence** to maintain that this information was **common knowledge in the market**. The disclosures are still needed.

(b) (i) **Discount rate**

Estoil has **not complied with IAS 36** *Impairment of assets* in its use of one discount rate for all cash-generating units (CGUs) regardless of the currency of the country in which the cash flows are generated. IAS 36 requires that **future cash flows must be estimated in the currency in which they will be generate**d and then discounted using a discount rate appropriate for that currency. The present value thus calculated must be **translated using the spot exchange rate at the date of the value in use calculation.**

The currency in which the estimated cash flows are denominated has an impact on many of the inputs to the weighted average cost of capital (WACC) calculation, including the risk-free interest rate. **Estoil was incorrect in using the ten-year government bond rate for its own jurisdiction** as the risk-free rate because government bond rates differ between countries due to different expectations about future inflation, and so there may be a discrepancy between the expected inflation reflected in the estimated cash flows and the risk-free rate.

IAS 36 requires that the **discount rate should appropriately reflect the current market assessment of the time value of money and the risks specific to the asset or cash generating unit.** Applying one discount rate for all the CGUs does not achieve this. The WACC of the CGU or of the company of which the CGU is currently part should generally be used to determine the discount rate. The company's WACC may only be used for all CGUS if the risks associated with the individual CGUs do not materially diverge from the remainder of the group, and this is **not evident** in the case of Estoil.

(ii) **Cash flow forecasts**

IAS 36 requires that any cash flow projections are based upon **reasonable and supportable assumptions** over a maximum period of five years unless it can be proven that longer estimates are reliable. The assumptions should **represent management's best estimate of the range of economic conditions expected to obtain over the remaining useful life of the asset.** Management must also assess the reasonableness of the assumptions by examining the reasons for any differences between past forecasted cash flows and actual cash flows. **The assumptions that form the basis for current cash flow projections must be consistent with past actual outcomes.**

Fariole has **failed to comply** with the requirements of IAS 36 in the preparation of its cash flow forecasts. Although the realised cash flow **forecasts for 20X4 were negative** and well below projected cash flows, **the directors significantly increased budgeted cash flows for 20X5**. This increase was **not justified,** and casts doubts on Fariole's ability to budget realistically.

IAS 36 requires estimates of future cash flows to include:

(1) Projections of cash inflows from the continuing use of the asset

(2) Projections of cash outflows which are necessarily incurred to generate the cash inflows from continuing use of the asset

(3) Net cash flows to be received (or paid) for the disposal of the asset at the end of its useful life.

Forecast cash outflows must include those relating to the day-to-day servicing of the asset. This will **include future cash outflows needed to maintain the level of economic benefits expected to be generated by the asset in its current condition.** Fariole has not taken into account expected changes in working capital and capital expenditure, but it is very likely that investments in working capital and capital expenditure would be necessary to maintain the assets of the CGUs in their current condition.

In conclusion, the **cash flow forecasts used by Fariole are not in accordance with IAS 36.**

10 Preparation question: Defined benefit plan

Statement of profit or loss and other comprehensive income notes

Defined benefit expense recognised in profit or loss

	$m
Current service cost	11
Past service cost	10
Net interest on the net defined benefit asset (10% × (110 + 10)) – (10% × 150)	(3)
	18

Other comprehensive income (items that will not be reclassified to profit or loss)
Remeasurement of defined benefit plans

	$m
Actuarial gain on defined benefit obligation	17
Return on plan assets (excluding amounts in net interest)	(22)
	(5)

Statement of financial position notes

Net defined benefit asset recognised in the statement of financial position

	31 December 20X1	*31 December 20X0*
	$m	$m
Present value of pension obligation	116	110
Fair value of plan assets	(140)	(150)
Net asset	(24)	(40)

Changes in the present value of the defined benefit obligation

	$m
Opening defined benefit obligation	110
Interest on obligation (10% × (110 + 10))	12
Current service cost	11
Past service cost	10
Benefits paid	(10)
Gain on remeasurement through OCI (balancing figure)	(17)
Closing defined benefit obligation	116

Changes in the fair value of plan assets

	$m
Opening fair value of plan assets	150
Interest on plan assets (10% × 150)	15
Contributions	7
Benefits paid	(10)
Loss on remeasurement through OCI (balancing figure)	(22)
Closing fair value of plan assets	140

11 Macaljoy

Text reference. Pensions are covered in Chapter 4; provisions in Chapter 5.

Top tips. Part (a)(i) is very straightforward, but make sure you relate your answer to the pension schemes of Macaljoy. Similarly in Part (b)(i), you need to write specifically about warranty provisions, as well as more generally about provisions. Note that IAS 19 was revised in 2011. Actuarial gains and losses must now be recognised immediately in other comprehensive income (not reclassified to profit or loss).

Easy marks. Two marks are available for presentation and communication, and would be silly marks to lose. Plus there are marks for straightforward bookwork that you can get even if you don't get all the calculations right.

Examiner's comments. The question was quite well answered and candidates often produced good quality answers. The ACCA examination/examining team was surprised to see that several candidates confused defined benefit and defined contribution schemes. Also at this level, it is important that candidates have an in depth knowledge of the differences between the two schemes rather than just a general view of the differences. Professional marks were awarded for the structure of the report and consideration of certain factors, that is:

(a) The intended purpose of the document
(b) Its intended users and their needs
(c) The appropriate type of document
(d) Logical and appropriate structure/format
(e) Nature of background information and technical language
(f) Detail required
(g) Clear, concise and precise presentation

Marking scheme

				Marks
(a)	Pensions	(i)	Explanation	7
		(ii)	Calculation	7
(b)	Provisions	(i)	Explanation	6
		(ii)	Calculation	3
Structure of report				2
Maximum				25

To: The Directors
Macaljoy

Date: 1 November 20X7

Subject: **Pension plans and warranty claims**

The purpose of this report is to explain the difference between defined benefit and defined contribution pension plans, and to show the accounting treatment of Macaljoy's pension schemes. It also discusses the principles of accounting for warranty claims and shows the accounting treatment of Macaljoy's warranty claims.

(a) (i) **Defined contribution plans and defined benefit plans**

With **defined contribution** plans, the employer (and possibly, as here, current employees too) pay regular contributions into the plan of a given or 'defined' amount each year. The contributions are invested, and the size of the post-employment benefits paid to former employees depends on how well or how badly the plan's investments perform. If the investments perform well, the plan will be able to afford higher benefits than if the investments performed less well.

The B scheme is a defined contribution plan. The employer's liability is limited to the contributions paid.

With **defined benefit** plans, the size of the post-employment benefits is determined in advance, ie the benefits are 'defined'. The employer (and possibly, as here, current employees too) pay contributions into the plan, and the contributions are invested. The size of the contributions is set at an amount that is expected to earn enough investment returns to meet the obligation to pay the post-employment benefits. If, however, it becomes apparent that the assets in the fund are insufficient, the employer will be required to make additional contributions into the plan to make up the expected shortfall. On the other hand, if the fund's assets appear to be larger than they need to be, and in excess of what is required to pay the post-employment benefits, the employer may be allowed to take a 'contribution holiday' (ie stop paying in contributions for a while).

The **main difference** between the two types of plans lies in **who bears the risk**: if the employer bears the risk, even in a small way by guaranteeing or specifying the return, the plan is a defined benefit plan. A defined contribution scheme must give a benefit formula based solely on the amount of the contributions.

A defined benefit scheme may be created even if there is no legal obligation, if an employer has a practice of guaranteeing the benefits payable.

The A scheme is a defined benefit scheme. Macaljoy, the employer, guarantees a pension based on the service lives of the employees in the scheme. The company's liability is not limited to the amount of the contributions. This means that the employer bears the investment risk: if the return on the investment is not sufficient to meet the liabilities, the company will need to make good the difference.

(ii) **Accounting treatment: B scheme**

No assets or liabilities will be recognised for this defined contribution scheme. The **contributions** paid by the company of $10m will be **charged to profit or loss**. The contributions paid by the employees will be part of the wages and salaries cost.

Accounting treatment: A scheme

The accounting treatment is as follows:

Statement of profit or loss and other comprehensive income notes

Expense recognised in profit or loss for the year ended 31 October 20X7

	$m
Current service cost	20.0
Net interest on the net defined benefit liability (10 – 9.5)	0.5
Net expense	20.5

Other comprehensive income: remeasurement of defined benefit plans (for the year ended 31 October 20X7)

	$m
Actuarial loss on defined benefit obligation	(29.0)
Return on plan assets (excluding amounts in net interest)	27.5
Net actuarial loss	(1.5)

STATEMENT OF FINANCIAL POSITION NOTES

Amounts recognised in statement of financial position

	31 October 20X7	*1 November 20X6*
	$m	$m
Present value of defined benefit obligation	240	200
Fair value of plan assets	(225)	(190)
Net liability	15	10

Change in the present value of the defined benefit obligation

	$m
Present value of obligation at 1 November 20X6	200
Interest on obligation: 5% × 200	10
Current service cost	20
Benefits paid	(19)
Loss on remeasurement through OCI (balancing figure)	29
Present value of obligation at 31 October 20X7	240

Change in the fair value of plan assets

	$m
Fair value of plan assets at 1 November 20X6	190.0
Interest on plan assets: 5% × 190	9.5
Contributions	17.0
Benefits paid	(19.0)
Gain on remeasurement through OCI (balancing figure)	27.5
Fair value of plan assets at 31 October 20X7	225.0

(b) **Warranty provisions**

(i) **Principles**

Under IAS 37 *Provisions, contingent liabilities and contingent assets,* provisions must be recognised in the following circumstances.

(1) There is a **legal** or **constructive obligation** to transfer benefits as a result of past events.
(2) It is probably that **an outflow of economic resources** will be required to **settle** the **obligation**.
(3) A **reasonable estimate** of the amount required to settle the obligation can be made.

If the company can **avoid expenditure by its future action, no provision** should be recognised. A legal or constructive obligation is one created by an **obligating event**. Constructive obligations arise when an entity is committed to certain expenditures because of a pattern of behaviour which the public would expect to continue.

IAS 37 states that the amount recognised should be the **best estimate of the expenditure required to settle the obligation at the end of the reporting period**. The estimate should **take the various possible outcomes into account** and should be the **amount that an entity would rationally pay** to settle the obligation at the reporting date or to transfer it to a third party. In the case of warranties, the provision will be made at a probability weighted expected value, taking into account the risks and uncertainties surrounding the underlying events.

The amount of the provision should be **discounted to present value** if the time value of money is material using a **risk adjusted rate**. If some or all of the expenditure is expected to be **reimbursed** by a third party, the reimbursement should be **recognised as a separate asset,** but only if it is virtually certain that the reimbursement will be received.

(ii) **Accounting treatment**

In Macaljoy's case, the past event giving rise to the obligation is the sale of the product with a warranty. A provision for the warranty will be made as follows:

	$
Re year 1 warranty	280,000
Re year 2 warranty	350,000
	630,000

If material, the provisions may be discounted:

	$
Re year 1 warranty	269,000
Re year 2 warranty	323,000
	592,000

Calculations are shown below.

Macaljoy may be able to **recognise the asset and income from the insurance claim,** but only if the insurance company has validated the claim and **receipt is virtually certain**. In general contingent assets are not recognised, but disclosed if an inflow of economic benefits is probable.

Calculations

Year 1: warranty

	Expected value $'000	*Discounted expected value (4%)* $'000
80% × Nil	0	
15% × 7,000 × $100	105	
5% × 7,000 × $500	175	
	280	$280,000/1.04 = $269,000*

Year 2: extended warranty

	Expected value $'000	*Discounted expected value (4%)* $'000
70% × Nil	0	
20% × 5,000 × $100	100	
10% × 5,000 × $500	250	
	350	$350,000/(1.04)^2 = $323,000*

***Note.** These figures are rounded

12 Ryder

Text reference. IAS 10 is in Chapter 5, IAS 36 in Chapter 3 and IFRS 5 in Chapter 15.

Top tips. This is a mixed standard question, of the kind that the ACCA examination/examining team generally likes.

Easy marks. Parts (a) and (b) are fairly straightforward. You should be familiar with IAS 10 and 36, even if you missed the IFRS 5 aspect.

Examiner's comment. This question was generally well answered. The question was quite discriminating as there was in most cases a correct answer rather than an issue to discuss. Surprisingly many candidates did not know how to deal with contingent consideration on the purchase of subsidiary. Candidates dealt well with the property intended for sale but many candidates did not realise that cash settled share based payments (share appreciation rights) are remeasured to fair value at each reporting date. There was some confusion in candidate's answers over what constitutes 'grant date' and 'vesting date' and the importance for the share based payment transactions. The question was quite discriminating as there was in most cases a correct answer rather than an issue to discuss. Surprisingly many candidates did not know how to deal with a proposed dividend or how to deal with contingent consideration on the purchase of subsidiary. Candidates dealt well with the property intended for sale but many candidates did not realise that cash settled share based payments (share appreciation rights) are remeasured to fair value at each reporting date. There was some confusion in candidate's answers over what constitutes 'grant date' and 'vesting date' and the importance for the share based payment transactions.

(a) **Disposal of subsidiary**

The issue here is the value of the subsidiary at 31 October 20X5. The directors have stated that there has been no significant event since the year end which could have resulted in a reduction in its value. This, taken together with the loss on disposal, indicates that the subsidiary had **suffered an impairment at 31 October 20X5**. IAS 10 requires the sale to be treated as an **adjusting event** after the reporting period as it provides **evidence of a condition that existed at the end of the reporting period**.

The assets of Krup should be **written down to their recoverable amount**. In this case this is the eventual sale proceeds. Therefore the value of the net assets and purchased goodwill of Krup should be **reduced by $11 million** (the loss on disposal of $9 million plus the loss of $2 million that occurred between 1 November 2005 and the date of sale). IAS 36 *Impairment of assets* states that an impairment loss should be allocated to goodwill first and therefore the **purchased goodwill of $12 million is reduced to $1 million**. The impairment loss of $11 million is **recognised in profit or loss**.

Because there was no intention to sell the subsidiary at 31 October 20X5, **IFRS 5 *Non current assets held for sale and discontinued operations* does not apply**. The disposal is **disclosed** in the notes to the financial statements in accordance with IAS 10.

(b) **Issue of shares at fair value**

IFRS 3 *Business combinations* (revised 2008) recognises that, by entering into an acquisition, the acquirer becomes obliged to make additional payments. The revised IFRS 3 **requires recognition of contingent consideration, measured at fair value, at the acquisition date**.

The treatment of **post-acquisition changes** in the fair value of the contingent consideration **depends on the circumstances**.

(i) If the change is due to **additional information** that affects the position at the acquisition date, **goodwill should be re-measured, as a retrospective adjustment**. The additional information must come to light **within the measurement period,** a maximum of one year after acquisition.

(ii) If the change is **due to events which took place after the acquisition date,** for example meeting earnings target, an **equity instrument is not re-measured**. Other instruments are re-measured, with changes to total comprehensive income.

Ryder has **correctly included** an estimate of the amount of consideration in the cost of the acquisition on 21 January 20X4. This would have been based on the fair value of the ordinary shares at that date of $10 per share, giving a total of 300,000 × $10 = $3,000,000:

DEBIT Investment	$3,000,000	
CREDIT Equity		$3,000,000

As the consideration is in the form of shares, and the change is due to an event which took place after the acquisition date (the rise in share price), **the consideration is not remeasured.**

The value of the contingent shares should be included in a **separate category of equity** in the statement of financial position at 31 October 20X5. They should be transferred to share capital and share premium after the actual issue of the shares on 12 November 20X5.

IAS 10 requires **disclosure of all material share transactions** or potential share transactions entered into after the reporting period end, excluding the bonus issue. Therefore **details of the issue of the contingent shares should be disclosed** in the notes to the financial statements.

(c) **Property**

The property appears to have been **incorrectly classified** as 'held for sale'. Although the company had always intended to sell the property, IFRS 5 states that in order to qualify as 'held for sale' an asset must be **available for immediate sale in its present condition**. Because **repairs were needed** before the property could be sold and these were **not completed until after the reporting period end**, this was clearly **not the case at 31 October 20X5**.

In addition, even if the property had been correctly classified, it has been **valued incorrectly**. IFRS 5 requires assets held for sale to be valued at **the lower of their carrying amount or fair value less costs to sell**. The property **should have been valued at its carrying amount of $20 million**, not at the eventual sale proceeds of $27 million.

The property **must be included within property, plant and equipment** and must be **depreciated**. Therefore its **carrying amount at 31 October 20X5 is $19 million** ($20 million less depreciation of $1 million). The **gain of $7 million** that the company has previously recognised **should be reversed**.

Although the property cannot be classified as 'held for sale' in the financial statements for the year ended 31 October 2005, it **will qualify for the classification after the end of the reporting period**. Therefore details of the sale should be **disclosed** in the notes to the financial statements.

(d) **Share appreciation rights**

The granting of share appreciation rights is a **cash settled share based payment transaction** as defined by IFRS 2 *Share based payment.* IFRS 2 requires these to be **measured at the fair value of the liability** to pay cash. The liability should be **re-measured at each reporting date and at the date of settlement**. Any **changes in fair value** should be **recognised in profit or loss** for the period.

However, the company has **not remeasured the liability since 31 October 20X4**. Because IFRS 2 requires the expense and the related liability to be recognised over the two-year vesting period, the rights should be measured as follows:

	$m
At 31 October 20X4: ($6 × 10 million × ½)	30
At 31 October 20X5 ($8 × 10 million)	80
At 1 December 20X5 (settlement date) ($9 × 10 million)	90

Therefore at 31 October 20X5 the liability **should be re-measured to $80 million** and an **expense of $50 million** should be recognised in profit or loss for the year.

The additional expense of $10 million resulting from the remeasurement at the settlement date is not included in the financial statements for the year ended 31 October 20X5, but is recognised the following year.

13 Royan

Text reference. Provisions and contingent liabilities are covered in Chapter 5 of your Study Text.

Top tips. This question has been amended as the project it tested has been put on hold since the question was set..

Easy marks. As the ACCA examination/examining team pointed out, 'there were several marks for simply spelling out current guidance, which is rote learning. Secondly; there are basic reasons why the IASB would wish to replace any standard. For example consistency with US standards, fitness for purpose, inappropriateness in the current business climate. Thus, candidates could have answered this part of the question with basic general knowledge of the standard setting process.'

Examiner's comment. There were a number of easy marks (see above). However, the question was not well answered. It is very important to read the scenario carefully as there are clues in the question which are there to help the candidate.

Marking scheme

	Marks
Existing guidance and critique	10
IAS 37 treatment	3
Communication skills	2
	15

(a) **Guidance in IAS 37**

Under IAS 37 *Provisions, contingent liabilities and contingent assets,* provisions must be recognised in the following circumstances.

(i) There is a **legal** or **constructive obligation** to transfer benefits as a result of past events.

(ii) It is **probable** that **an outflow of economic resources** will be required to **settle** the **obligation**.

(iii) The obligation can be **measured reliably**.

IAS 37 considers an outflow to be probable if the event is **more likely than not** to occur.

If the company can **avoid expenditure by its future action, no provision** should be recognised. A legal or constructive obligation is one created by an **obligating event**. Constructive obligations arise when an entity is committed to certain expenditures because of a pattern of behaviour which the public would expect to continue.

IAS 37 states that the amount recognised should be the **best estimate of the expenditure required to settle the obligation at the end of the reporting period**. The estimate should **take the various possible outcomes into account** and should be the **amount that an entity would rationally pay** to settle the obligation at the reporting date or to transfer it to a third party. Where there is **s large population of items,** for example in the case of warranties, the provision will be made at **a probability weighted expected value,** taking into account the risks and uncertainties surrounding the underlying events. Where there is a **single obligation, the individual most likely outcome** may be the best estimate of the liability.

The amount of the provision should be **discounted to present value** if the time value of money is material using a **risk adjusted rate**. If some or all of the expenditure is expected to be **reimbursed** by a third party, the reimbursement should be **recognised as a separate asset,** but only if it is virtually certain that the reimbursement will be received.

Why replace IAS 37?

IAS 37 has provided useful guidance over the years that it has been in force, and is generally consistent with the *Conceptual Framework*. However, for the following reasons, it has been considered necessary to replace it.

(i) IAS 37 requires recognition of a liability only if it is **probable,** that is more than 50% likely, that the obligation will result in an outflow of resources from the entity. This is **inconsistent with other standards,** for example IFRS 3 *Business combinations* and IFRS 9 *Financial instruments* which do not apply the probability criterion to liabilities. In addition, probability is not part of the *Conceptual Framework* definition of a liability.

(ii) There is **inconsistency with US GAAP** as regards how they treat the **cost of restructuring** a business. US GAAP requires entities to recognise a liability for individual costs of restructuring only when the entity has incurred that particular cost, while IAS 37 requires recognition of the total costs of restructuring when the entity announces or starts to implement a restructuring plan.

(ii) The **measurement rules** in IAS 37 are **vague and unclear**. In particular, 'best estimate' could mean a number of things: the mot likely outcome the most likely outcome, the weighted average of all possible outcomes or even the minimum/maximum amount in a range of possible outcomes. IAS 37 does not clarify which costs need to be included in the measurement of a liability, and in practice different entities include different costs. It is also unclear if 'settle' means 'cancel', 'transfer' or 'fulfil' the obligation.

(b) **Treatment under IAS 37**

The IAS 37 criteria for recognising a **provision** have been met as there is a present obligation to dismantle the oil platform, of which the present value has been measured at **$105m**. Because Royan cannot operate the oil without incurring an obligation to pay dismantling costs at the end of ten years, the expenditure also enables it to acquire **economic benefits** (income from the oil extracted). Therefore, Royan should **recognise an asset of $105m** (added to the 'oil platform' in property, plant and equipment) and this should be **depreciated** over the life of the oil platform, which is ten years. In addition, there will be an adjustment charged in profit or loss each year to the present value of the obligation for the **unwinding of the discount.**

14 Electron

Text reference. Environmental provisions are covered in Chapter 5; share schemes in Chapter 9.

Top tips. This is a multi-standard question on environmental provisions, leases, proposed dividend and a share option scheme. The question on the power station is similar to one you will have already met in this kit, and you have come across longer, more complicated questions on share-based payment, a favourite topic with this examiner.

Easy marks. The proposed dividend is straightforward, as is the explanation (if not the calculations) for the provision. The treatment of share options provides 4 easy marks for nothing much in the way of complications.

Marking scheme

	Marks
Oil contracts	4
Power station	7
Operating leases	5
Proposed dividend	3
Share options	4
Effective communication	2
Available/Maximum	25

REPORT

To: The Directors, Electron

Date: July 20X6

From: Accountant

Accounting treatment of transactions

Oil trading contracts

The first point to note is that the contracts always result in the delivery of the commodity. They are therefore correctly treated as normal sale and purchase contracts, **not financial instruments**.

The adoption of a policy of **deferring recognising revenue and costs is appropriate** in general terms because of the duration of the contracts. Over the life of the contracts, costs and revenues are equally matched. However, there is a mismatch between costs and revenues in the early stages of the contracts.

In the first year of the contract, 50% of revenues are recognised immediately. However, costs, in the form of amortisation, are recognised evenly over the duration of the contract. This means that **in the first year, a higher proportion of the revenue is matched against a smaller proportion of the costs**. It could also be argued that revenue is inflated in the first year.

IFRS 15 *Revenue from contracts with customers* should be applied. IFRS 15 has a **five-step process for** recognising revenue, of which Step 5 states: 'Recognise revenue when (or as) a performance obligation is satisfied.' Step 5 would treat this as a **performance obligation satisfied over time** because the oil is delivered over a contract period and therefore control is transferred over time. Revenue should therefore be recognised evenly over the duration of the contract.

Power station

IAS 37 *Provisions, contingent liabilities and contingent assets* states that a provision should be recognised if:

- There is a present obligation as a result of a past transaction or event and
- It is probable that an outflow of resources embodying economic benefits will be required to settle the obligation
- A reliable estimate can be made of the amount of the obligation

In this case, the obligating event is the **installation of the power station**. The **operating licence** has created a **legal obligation** to incur the cost of removal, the expenditure is **probable,** and a **reasonable estimate** of the amount can be made.

Because Electron cannot operate its power station without incurring an obligation to pay for removal, **the expenditure also enables it to acquire economic benefits** (income from the energy generated). Therefore Electron correctly **recognises an asset** as well as a provision, and **depreciates this asset over its useful life of 20 years.**

Electron should recognise a provision for the cost of removing the power station, but should not include the cost of rectifying the damage caused by the generation of electricity until the power is generated. In this case the cost of rectifying the damage would be 5% of the total discounted provision.

The accounting treatment is as follows:

STATEMENT OF FINANCIAL POSITION AT 30 JUNE 20X6 (EXTRACTS)

	$m
Property, plant and equipment	
Power station	100.0
Decommissioning costs (W)	13.6
	113.6
Depreciation (113.6 ÷ 20)	(5.7)
	107.9
Provisions	
Provision for decommissioning at 1 July 20X5	13.6
Plus unwinding of discount (13.6 × 5%)	0.7
	14.3
Provision for damage (0.7(W)÷20)	0.1
	14.4

STATEMENT OF PROFIT OR LOSS AND OTHER COMPREHENSVIE INCOME
FOR THE YEAR ENDED 30 JUNE 20X6 (EXTRACTS)

	$m
Depreciation	5.7
Provision for damage	0.1
Unwinding of discount (finance cost)	0.7

Working

	$m
Provision for removal costs at 1 July 20X5 (95% × (15 ÷ 1.05))	13.6
Provision for damage caused by extraction at 30 June 20X6 (5% (15 ÷ 1.05))	0.7

Operating lease

One issue here is the **substance** of the lease agreement. In the case of lessors (but not lessees), IFRS 16 *Leases* classifies leases as either finance leases or operating leases. A finance lease **transfers substantially all the risks and rewards of ownership to the lessee**, while an operating lease does not. The company **retains legal ownership of the equipment** and also **retains the benefits of ownership** (the equipment remains available for use in its operating activities). In addition, the **present value of the lease payments is only 57.1% of the fair value of the leased assets** ($40 million ÷ $70 million). For a lease to be a finance lease, the present value of the lease payments should be **substantially all** the fair value of the leased assets. Therefore the lease **appears to be correctly classified as an operating lease**.

A further issue is the **treatment of the fee received**. The company has recognised the whole of the net present value of the future income from the lease in profit or loss for the year to 30 June 20X6, despite the fact that only a deposit of $10 million has been received. In addition, the date of inception of the lease is 30 June 20X6, so **the term of the lease does not actually fall within the current period.** IFRS 16 para. 81 states that **income from operating leases should be recognised on a straight line basis over the lease term** unless another basis is more appropriate. IFRS 15 *Revenue from contracts with customers* applies here. It does not allow revenue to be recognised **before an entity has performed under the contract** and therefore **no revenue should be recognised** in relation to the operating leases for the current period.

Proposed dividend

The dividend was **proposed after the end of the reporting period** and therefore IAS 10 *Events after the reporting period* applies. This **prohibits the recognition of proposed dividends** unless these are declared before the end of the reporting period. The directors **did not have an obligation** to pay the dividend **at 31 October 20X5** and therefore there **cannot be a liability**. The directors seem to be arguing that their past record creates a constructive obligation as defined by IAS 37 *Provisions, contingent liabilities and contingent assets.* A constructive obligation may exist as a result of the proposal of the dividend, but this had **not arisen at the end of the reporting period**.

Although the proposed dividend is not recognised it was **approved before the financial statements were authorised for issue** and should be **disclosed** in the notes to the financial statements.

Share options

The share options granted on 1 July 20X5 are **equity-settled transactions**, and are governed by IFRS 2 *Share based payment.* The aim of this standard is to recognise the cost of share based payment to employees over the period in which the services are rendered. The options are generally **charged to profit or loss** on the basis of their **fair value at the grant date**. If the equity instruments are traded on an active market, market prices must be used. Otherwise an option pricing model would be used.

The conditions attached to the shares state that the share options will vest in three years' time provided that the employees remain in employment with the company. Often there are other conditions such as growth in share price, but here **employment is the only condition**.

The **treatment** is as follows:

- Determine the fair value of the options at grant date.
- Charge this fair value to profit or loss equally over the three year vesting period, making adjustments at each accounting date to reflect the best estimate of the number of options that will eventually vest. This will depend on the estimated percentage of employees leaving during the vesting period.

For the year ended 30 June 20X6, the charge to profit or loss is $3m × 94% × 1/3 = $940,000. Shareholders' equity will be increased by an amount equal to this profit or loss charge.

15 Panel

Text reference. Tax is covered in Chapter 6 of the text.

Top tips. This is a single topic question, which is a departure from the ACCA examination/examining team's usual mixed standard question. The IFRS 1 aspects are likely to become less frequent over time.

Easy marks. Part (b) (iii) and (iv) are easier than (i) and (ii), though they carry the same number of marks.

Examiner's comment. Part (a) was quite well answered albeit often in a very general way. Part (b) was answered far better than when this area was tested in June 2005. The other three areas were a leasing transaction, an inter company sale and an impairment of property plant and equipment. These elements of the question were quite well answered although the discussion of the topic areas was generally quite poor whilst the computations were quite good. Deferred tax is a key area and must be understood.

(a) (i) **The impact of changes in accounting standards**

IAS 12 *Income taxes* is based on the idea that all **changes in assets and liabilities** have unavoidable **tax consequences**. Where the recognition criteria in IFRS are different from those in tax law, the **carrying amount of an asset or liability in the financial statements is different from the amount at which it is stated for tax purposes (its 'tax base')**. These differences are known as **'temporary differences'**. The practical effect of these differences is that a transaction or event occurs in a different accounting period from its tax consequences. For example, income from interest receivable is recognised in the financial statements in one accounting period but it is only taxable when it is actually received in the following accounting period.

IAS 12 requires a company to make **full provision** for the tax effects of temporary differences. Where a change in an accounting standard results in a change to the carrying value of an asset or liability in the financial statements, the **amount of the temporary difference** between the carrying value and the tax base **also changes**. Therefore the amount of the deferred tax liability is affected.

(ii) **Calculation of deferred tax on first time adoption of IFRS**

IFRS 1 *First time adoption of International Financial Reporting Standards* requires a company to **prepare an opening IFRS statement of financial position** and to **apply IAS 12 to temporary differences** between the carrying amounts of assets and liabilities and their tax bases at that date. Panel prepares its opening IFRS statement of financial position sheet **at 1 November 20X3**. The carrying values of its assets and liabilities are **measured in accordance with IFRS 1** and **other applicable IFRSs** in force at 31 October 20X5. The deferred tax provision is based on **tax rates that have been enacted or substantially enacted by the end of the reporting period**. Any **adjustments** to the deferred tax liability under previous GAAP are **recognised directly in equity (retained earnings)**.

(b) (i) **Share options**

Under IFRS 2 *Share based payment* the company **recognises an expense** for the employee services received in return for the share options granted over the vesting period. The related tax deduction **does not arise until the share options are exercised**. Therefore a **deferred tax asset arises**, based on the difference between the intrinsic value of the options and their carrying amount (normally zero).

At 31 October 20X4 the tax benefit is as follows:

	$m
Carrying amount of share based payment	–
Less: tax base of share based payment (16 ÷ 2)	(8)
Temporary difference	(8)

The **deferred tax asset is $2.4 million** (30% × 8). This is recognised at 31 October 20X4 provided that taxable profit is available against which it can be utilised. Because the tax effect of the remuneration expense is greater than the tax benefit, the tax benefit is **recognised in profit or loss**. (The tax effect of the remuneration expense is 30% × $40 million ÷ 2 = $6 million.)

At 31 October 20X5 there is **no longer a deferred tax asset** because the options have been exercised. The **tax benefit receivable is $13.8 million** (30% × $46 million). Therefore the deferred tax asset of $2.4 million is no longer required.

(ii) **Leased plant**

Under IFRS 16 *Leases*, a **right-of-use asset is recognised,** and a **lease liability.** The lease liability is measured at the **present value of the lease payments** discounted using, if available, the interest rate implicit in the least . The right-of-use asset is measured at the amount of the initial measurement of the lease liability, plus certain other direct costs not incurred in this case, such as legal fees. Subsequent to initial measurement, the right-of-use asset is measured using the IAS 16 cost model unless it applies the IAS 16 revaluation model or the IAS 40 fair value model. In this case the cost model is applied, and the right-of-use asset is depreciated on a straight line basis over the five years.

The obligation to pay lease rentals is **recognised as a liability**. Each instalment payable is treated partly as interest and partly as repayment of the liability. The **carrying amount** of the plant for accounting purposes is the **net present value of the lease payments less depreciation**.

A **temporary difference** effectively arises between the value of the plant for accounting purposes and the equivalent of the outstanding obligations, as the annual rental payments quality for the relief. The tax base of the asset is the amount deductable for tax in future, which is zero. The tax base of the liability is the carrying amount less any future tax deductible amounts, which will give a **tax base of zero**.

Therefore at 31 October 20X5 a **net temporary difference** will be as follows:

	$m	$m
Carrying value in financial statements:		
Asset:		
Net present value of future lease payments at inception of lease	12	
Less depreciation (12 ÷ 5)	(2.4)	
		9.60
Less lease liability		
Liability at inception of lease	12.00	
Interest (8% × 12)	0.96	
Lease rental	(3.00)	
		(9.96)
		0.36
Less tax base		(0.00)
Temporary difference		0.36

A **deferred tax asset of $108,000** (30% × 360,000) arises.

(iii) **Intra-group sale**

Pins has **made a profit of $2 million** on its sale to Panel. Tax is **payable on the profits of individual companies**. Pins is liable for tax on this profit in the current year and will have provided for the related tax in its individual financial statements. However, **from the viewpoint of the group** the profit **will not be realised until the following year**, when the goods are sold to a third party and must be **eliminated** from the consolidated financial statements. Because the group **pays tax before the profit is realised** there is a **temporary difference of $2 million** and a **deferred tax asset of $600,000** (30% × $2 million).

(iv) **Impairment loss**

The impairment loss in the financial statements of Nails **reduces the carrying value** of property, plant and equipment, but is **not allowable for tax**. Therefore the **tax base** of the property, plant and equipment **is different from its carrying value** and there is a **temporary difference**.

Under IAS 36 *Impairment of assets* the impairment loss is allocated first to goodwill and then to other assets:

	Goodwill	Property, plant and equipment	Total
	$m	$m	$m
Carrying value at 31 October 20X5	1	6.0	7.0
Impairment loss	(1)	(0.8)	(1.8)
	–	5.2	5.2

IAS 12 states that **no deferred tax should be recognised on goodwill** and therefore **only the impairment loss relating to the property, plant and equipment affects the deferred tax position.**

The effect of the impairment loss is as follows:

	Before impairment	*After impairment*	*Difference*
	$m	$m	$m
Carrying value	6	5.2	
Tax base	(4)	(4.0)	
Temporary difference	2	1.2	0.8
Tax liability (30%)	0.6	0.36	0.24

Therefore the impairment loss reduces deferred the tax liability by $240,000.

16 Kesare

Text reference. Covered in Chapter 6 of the text.

Top tips. To state the obvious, this is a question best avoided unless you like deferred tax. However, if you do, or if you dislike other topics more, the question may be broken down into components where you can get a foothold. Layout is important to avoid getting muddled.

Easy marks. For those not fond of high speed number-crunching, there are some fairly easy marks in Part (a) available for a general discussion about concepts and the framework. In addition there are some easy marks for adjustments to the financial statements, most of which do not relate to the deferred tax aspects. In generally, however, this is not a question that lends itself to easy marks.

Marking scheme

			Marks
(a)	Quality of discussion		2
	Conceptual Framework		1
	Temporary difference		2
	Liability		1
	Weakness		1
			7
(b)	Adjustments:	Investment in equity instruments	2
		Convertible bond	2
		Defined benefit plan	2
		Property, plant and equipment	1
	Deferred tax:	Goodwill	1
		Other intangibles	1
		Financial assets	1
		Trade receivables	1
		Other receivables	1
		Long-term borrowings	1
		Employee benefits	1
		Trade payables	1
	Calculation		3

	Marks
	18
Available	25
Professional communication	2

(a) IAS 12 *Income taxes* is based on the idea that **all changes in assets and liabilities** have **unavoidable tax consequences**. Where the recognition criteria in IFRS are different from those in tax law, **the carrying amount of an asset or liability in the financial statements is different from its tax base** (the amount at which it is stated for tax purposes). These differences are known as **temporary differences**. The practical effect of these differences is that a transaction or event occurs in a different accounting period from its tax consequences. For example, depreciation is recognised in the financial statements in different accounting periods from capital allowances.

IAS 12 requires a company to make **full provision** for the tax effects of temporary differences. Both **deferred tax assets**, and **deferred tax liabilities** can arise in this way.

It may be argued that deferred tax assets and liabilities **do not meet the definition of assets and liabilities** in the IASB *Conceptual Framework for Financial Reporting.* Under the *Conceptual Framework* an asset is the right to receive economic benefits as a result of past events, and a liability is an obligation to transfer economic benefits, again as a result of past events.

Under IAS 12, the tax effect of transactions are recognised in the same period as the transactions themselves, but in practice, tax is paid in accordance with tax legislation when it becomes a legal liability. There is a **conceptual weakness** or inconsistency, in that only one liability, that is tax, is being provided for, and not other costs, such as overhead costs.

(b)

	$'000	*Adjustments to financial statements* $'000	*Adjusted financial statements* $'000	*Tax base* $'000	*Temporary difference* $'000
Property, plant and equipment	10,000		10,000	2,400	7,600
Goodwill	6,000		6,000	6,000	
Other intangible assets	5,000		5,000	0	5,000
Financial assets (cost)	9,000	1,500	10,500	9,000	1,500
Total non-current assets	30,000		31,500		
Trade receivables	7,000		7,000	7,500	(500)
Other receivables	4,600		4,600	5,000	(400)
Cash and cash-equivalents	6,700		6,700	6,700	–
Total current assets	18,300		18,300		
Total assets	48,300		49,800		
Share capital	(9,000)		(9,000)		
Other reserves	(4,500)	(1,500)	(6,400)		
		(400)			
Retained earnings	(9,130)	520	(8,610)		
Total equity	(22,630)		(24,010)		
Long term borrowings	(10,000)	400	(9,600)	(10,000)	400
Deferred tax liability	(3,600)		(3,600)	(3,600)	–
Employee benefits	(4,000)	(520)	(4,520)	(5,000)	480
Current tax liability	(3,070)		(3,070)	(3,070)	–
Trade and other payables	(5,000)		(5,000)	(4,000)	(1,000)
Total liabilities	(25,670)		(25,790)		13,080
Total equity and liabilities	48,300		49,800		

Deferred tax liability		$'000	$'000
Liability b/fwd (per draft SOFP)			3,600
Charge: OCI ($1,500 × 30%			
(note (i))		450	
P/L (bal. fig)		(126)	
			324
Deferred tax liability c/fwd	14,980 × 30%	4,494	
Deferred tax asset – c/fwd	1,900 × 30%	(570)	
Net deferred tax liability	13,080 × 30%		3,924

Notes on adjustments

(i) The investments in equity instruments are shown at cost. However, per IFRS 9, they should instead be valued at fair value, with the increase ($10,500 – $9,000 = $1,500) going to other comprehensive income (items that will not be reclassified to profit or loss) as per the irrevocable election.

(ii) IAS 32 states that convertible bonds must be split into debt and equity components. This involves reducing debt and increasing equity by $400.

(iii) The defined benefit plan needs to be adjusted to reflect the change. The liability must be increased by $520,000. The same amount is charged to retained earnings.

(iv) The development costs have already been allowed for tax, so the tax base is nil. No deferred tax is recognised on goodwill.

(v) The accrual for compensation is to be allowed when paid, ie in a later period. The tax base relating to trade and other payables should be reduced by $1m.

17 Chemclean

Text reference. IAS 38 is covered in Chapter 3 of your Study Text, IAS 1 in Chapter 10 and IFRS 3 and 10 in Chapter 12. IAS 12 is covered in Chapter 6.

Top tips. Part (a) deals with standards that should be familiar to you, but the issues require in-depth consideration. In particular, you need to consider how IAS 38 and IFRS 3 interact. This is not the first time the issue of what constitutes a business has been examined. Similarly, inventories and cost of sales in Part (b) may seem like basic knowledge, which is of course assumed, but you are having to consider it in the context of potential manipulation of the financial statements and the very topical issue of presentation. Finally deferred tax (Part (c)) requires you to question an accounting treatment, which could be aiming at presenting the results in an unrealistically favourable light.

Easy marks. There are marks for knowing the basics of the standards tested, but those marks will not get you a pass on this question.

Examiner's comment. In Part (a), candidates often discussed the recognition requirements for intangible assets, although some answers focused too long on issues relating to self-created intangible assets (not relevant in this case). Better answers focused on the implications of acquiring know-how, outlining the fact that the probability recognition criterion is always considered to be satisfied for intangible assets that are acquired separately or in a business combination. Very few candidates identified an acquisition of a shell company without employees (and hence without processes required to make it a 'business') as an asset acquisition as opposed to a business combination. In part (b), many candidates suggested inventory be valued at lower of cost or net realisable value, and incorrectly rejected the carrying value being at fair value after an acquisition (despite sometimes outlining IFRS 3 issues). Many answers were limited to a rejection of the treatment in the question without explaining why. Very few candidates discussed the issue with respect to IAS 1 *Presentation of financial statements,* which does not permit 'extraordinary items'. Part (c) was well answered, with most candidates providing good explanations of why the deferred tax asset should be derecognised.

Marking scheme

		Marks
(a)	1 mark per point up to maximum	8
(b)	1 mark per point up to maximum	6
(c)	1 mark per point up to maximum	9
Professional marks		2
		25

(a) **Intangible asset**

IAS 38 *Intangible assets* requires an entity to recognise an intangible asset, whether purchased or self-created (at cost) if, and only if:

(i) It is probable that the future economic benefits which are attributable to the asset will flow to the entity; and

(ii) The cost of the asset can be measured reliably.

This requirement applies whether an intangible asset is acquired externally or generated internally. IAS 38 includes additional recognition criteria for internally generated intangible assets.

The probability of future economic benefits must be based on reasonable and supportable assumptions about conditions which will exist over the life of the asset. The probability recognition criterion is always considered to be satisfied for intangible assets that are acquired separately or in a business combination. If an intangible item does not meet both the definition of and the criteria for recognition as an intangible asset, IAS 38 requires the expenditure on this item to be recognised as an expense when it is incurred. Research constitutes original and planned investigations undertaken with the prospect of gaining new scientific or technical knowledge and understanding. No intangible assets arising from research should be recognised. Expenditure on research should be recognised as an expense when it is incurred.

In this case, Chemclean should recognise an intangible asset for the use of Jomaster's technology. The right should be measured at its cost of $4m. The intangible asset should be amortised from the date it is available for use. The technology is available for use when the manufacturing of the compound begins. The amortisation should be presented as cost of sales in the statement of profit or loss if expenses are presented by function or as amortisation if expenses are presented by nature, as it is an expense directly related to the production of the compound. At the end of each reporting period, Chemclean is required to assess whether there is any indication that the asset may be impaired, that is its carrying amount may be higher than its recoverable amount.

The price an entity pays to acquire an intangible asset reflects expectations about the probability that the expected future economic benefits from the asset will flow to the entity. The effect of probability is therefore reflected in the cost of the asset.

Due to the nature of intangible assets, subsequent expenditure will only rarely meet the criteria for being recognised in the carrying amount of an asset. Thus Chemclean continues to expense its own internal development expenditure until the criteria for capitalisation are met and economic benefits are expected to flow to the entity from the capitalised asset. When the drug is sold, the royalty payments are presented in profit or loss.

IFRS 10 *Consolidated financial statements* defines control of an investee in terms of the following: 'An investor controls an investee when the investor is exposed, or has rights, to variable returns from its involvement with the investee and has the ability to affect those returns through its power over the investee'. Therefore it appears that Chemclean will control Conew.

IFRS 3 *Business combinations* defines a 'business' as 'an integrated set of activities and assets that is capable of being conducted and managed for the purpose of providing a return in the form of dividends, lower costs or other economic benefits directly to investors or other owners, members or participants'. A business consists of inputs and processes applied to those inputs which have the ability to create outputs.

Although businesses usually have outputs, outputs are not required for an integrated set to qualify as a business. Processes are defined in IFRS 3 as any system, standard, protocol, convention or rule that creates or has the ability to create output. Any transaction in which an entity obtains control of one or more businesses qualifies as a business combination and is subject to the measurement and recognition requirements of IFRS 3. Processes are included in the acquired group when intellectual property (IP) is accompanied by other resources such as assets or employees or other elements such as protocols and plans which will further help develop the IP to the next phase. The formation of a legal entity, which is involved in the transaction, is an irrelevance and the legal form of the transaction does not determine the accounting treatment. Here, the acquisition of an interest in Conew is an asset acquisition and should be accounted for under IAS 38 because Conew does not meet the definition of a business.

(b) **Presentation issues**

IAS 1 *Presentation of financial statements* provides little specific guidance on the presentation of line items in financial statements, such as the level of detail or number of line items that should be presented in the financial statements. Furthermore, IAS 1's objective is to set out 'the overall requirements for the presentation of financial statements, guidelines for their structure and minimum requirements for their content'. In doing so, IAS 1 sets out minimum levels of required items in the financial statements by requiring certain items to be presented on the face of, or in the notes to, the financial statements and in other required disclosures. The current requirements in IFRS do not provide a definition of 'gross profit' or 'operating results' or many other common subtotals. The absence of specific requirements arises from the fact that the guidance in IAS 1 relies on management's judgement about which additional line items, headings and subtotals:

(i) Are relevant to an understanding of the entity's financial position/financial performance; and

(ii) Should be presented in a manner which provides relevant, reliable, comparable and understandable information.

IAS 1 allows entities to include additional line items, amend descriptions and the ordering of items in order to explain the elements of financial performance due to various activities, which may differ in frequency and predictability.

In the case of Chemclean, the cost of the inventories sold should be presented as cost of goods sold and not split in the manner set out by Chemclean. IFRS 3 *Business combinations* requires an acquirer to measure the identifiable assets acquired in a business combination at their fair values at the date of acquisition. Therefore, the carrying amount of the inventories originating from the acquisition of the subsidiary is their acquisition-date fair value.

IAS 2 *Inventories* requires the carrying amount of inventories sold to be recognised as an expense in the period in which the related revenue is recognised. Cost of sales are costs previously included in the measurement of inventory which has now been sold plus unallocated production overheads and abnormal amounts of production costs of inventories. Consequently, the entire carrying amount of inventory, including the effects of the fair value step-up, should be presented as cost of sales. Transactions like business combinations may have a significant impact on profit or loss and these transactions are not necessarily frequent or regular. However, the practice of presenting non-recurring items may be interpreted as a way to present

'Extraordinary items' in the financial statements despite the fact that 'extraordinary items' are not allowed under IAS 1. It can also be argued that additional lines and subtotals, as permitted by IAS 1, may add complexity to the analysis of the financial statements, which may become difficult to understand if entities use sub-totals and additional headings to isolate the effects of non-recurring transactions from classes of expense or income.

(c) **Deferred tax**

(i) Chemclean should not have fully recognised the deferred tax asset arising from the carry forward of unused tax losses. It is recognisable only to the extent of its taxable temporary differences. IAS 12 *Income taxes* states that a deferred tax asset shall be recognised for the carry-forward of unused tax losses to the extent that it is probable that future taxable profit will be available against which unused tax losses can be utilised. IAS 12 explains that the existence of unused tax losses is strong evidence that future taxable profit may not be available. Therefore, when an entity has a history of recent losses, the entity recognises a deferred tax asset arising from unused tax losses only to the extent that the entity has sufficient taxable temporary differences or when there is convincing other evidence that sufficient taxable profit will be available against which the unused tax losses can be utilised by the entity.

Chemclean recognised losses during the previous five years. In order to use the deferred tax asset of $16m, Chemclean would have to recognise a profit of $53.3m at the existing tax rate of 30%. In comparison, the entity recognised an average loss of $19m per year during the five previous years. There should be convincing evidence showing that there would be taxable profits available in the future in order to recognise a deferred tax asset. A comparison of the budgeted results to its actual results for the previous two years indicated material differences relating to impairment losses. In the interim financial statements for the first half of the financial year to 30 June 20X4, Chemclean recognised impairment losses equal to budgeted impairment losses for the whole year. The unused tax losses appear to result from identifiable causes, which are likely to recur. IAS 12 states that in assessing the probability that taxable profit will be available against which the unused tax losses or unused tax credits can be utilised, a consideration is whether the unused tax losses result from identifiable causes which are unlikely to recur.

Chemclean's budgets and assumptions are not convincing other evidence because the entity does not appear to have been capable of making accurate forecasts in the past and there were material differences between the amounts budgeted and realised for the previous two years. Chemclean had presented future budgets primarily based on general assumptions about the development of key products and economic improvement indicators, rather than what was expected to influence the future income and therefore enable the use of the deferred tax asset. Finally, in its financial statements, Chemclean disclosed a material uncertainty about its ability to continue as a going concern. This would be a key factor when considering the recognition of a deferred tax asset.

Therefore no deferred tax asset or liability should be recognised. The liability of $3m relating to temporary differences can be offset against $3m of unused tax losses. No further tax losses should be recognised.

(ii) The IASB issued an amendment to IAS 12 in January 2016, clarifying that unrealised losses on debt instruments measured at fair value and measured at cost for tax purposes give rise to a deductible temporary difference regardless of whether the debt instrument's holder expects to recover the carrying amount of the debt instrument by sale or by use. The amendment also addresses the issue of what constitutes future taxable profits.

18 Preparation question: Financial instruments

(a) STATEMENT OF PROFIT OR LOSS AND OTHER COMPREHENSIVE INCOME

	$
Finance income	
(441,014 × (W1) 8%)	35,281
STATEMENT OF FINANCIAL POSITION	
Non-current assets	
Financial asset (441,014 + 35,281)	476,295

Working: Effective interest rate

$$\frac{600,000}{441,014} = 1.3605 \therefore \text{ from tables interest rate is 8\%}$$

(b) **Compound instrument**

Presentation

	$
Non-current liabilities	
Financial liability component of convertible bond (Working)	1,797,467
Equity	
Equity component of convertible bond (2,000,000 – (Working) 1,797,467)	202,533

Working

	$
Fair value of equivalent non-convertible debt	
Present value of principal payable at end of 3 years $(4{,}000 \times \$500 = \$2m \times \frac{1}{(1.09)^3})$	1,544,367
Present value of interest annuity payable annually in arrears for 3 years [(5% × $2m) × 2.531]	253,100
	1,797,467

19 Coatmin

Text reference. Related parties are covered in Chapter 11 of your Study Text and financial instruments are covered in Chapter 7.

Top tips. Part (c) has been amended to reflect the July 2014 version of IFRS 9. Part (a) tested an exemption from IAS 24 (for government-related activities), rather than the more mainstream aspect, but as the ACCA examination/examining team stated, you would have been given credit for discussion of the relevant principles. Part (b) also tested an exemption from the mainstream – financial guarantee contracts, which are not required to be classified as subsequently measured at amortised cost. Pay attention to 'clues' in the question – the fact that the guarantee is being measured at FVTPL suggests that it is a financial instrument rather than a provision. Part (d) on credit risk is topical, but candidates may have struggled with the interest rate swap in part (c) of the original question, now amended for IFRS 9.

Easy marks. There are marks for textbook explanations on hedging in Part (c), but in general this is a tricky question.

Examiner's comment. In Part (a), ccandidates who did not know the specific answer to this part of the question were given credit for discussion of the related principles and many candidates were scoring 4 out of 5 marks for this part of the question. Part (b) was not well answered by candidates but a client would expect a qualified member of a profession to understand the difference between a provision and a financial guarantee. It appeared from the answers that this distinction was not understood by many candidates even though the question did say that the guarantee was being measured at fair value through profit or loss, which would tend to indicate that the guarantee was a financial instrument. Part (c) should have been textbook knowledge, but candidates still struggled. Part (d) was quite well answered with candidates gaining marks for a discussion of the principles involved and for the accounting for the increase in the value of the liability.

Marking scheme

		Marks
(a)	IAS 24	5
(b)	IFRS 9 explanation	3
	Guarantee calculations	4
(c)	Hedging discussion	4
	Effectiveness discussion	3
(d)	Credit risk entries	4
Professional marks		2
		25

(a) **Related parties**

The applicable standard relating to the activities is IAS 24 *Related party disclosures.* The standard requires disclosure of transactions with related parties. The definition of related parties is very detailed and includes parents, subsidiaries, and key management personnel of the entity or of a parent of the entity. Post-employment benefit plans are also included.

Where related party transactions have taken place, management must disclose the following:

(i) The name of its **parent** and, if different, the **ultimate controlling party** irrespective of whether there have been any transactions.

(ii) Total **key management personnel compensation** (broken down by category)

(iii) **If the entity has had related party transactions**:

(1) nature of the related party **relationship**

(2) information about the **transactions and outstanding balances, including commitments and bad and doubtful debts** necessary for users to understand the potential effect of the relationship on the financial statements.

No disclosure is required of intragroup related party transactions in the consolidated financial statements (since they are eliminated).Items of a **similar** nature may be disclosed **in aggregate** except where separate disclosure is necessary for understanding purposes.

A **government-related entity** is an entity over which a government has control, joint control or significant influence. In the wake of the financial crisis, more financial institutions were caught by the rules, because the financial support provided by governments of many countries to banks and other financial institutions resulted in control or significant influence. In principle, a government-controlled bank such as Coatmin could be required to disclosed details of its transactions, deposits and commitments with the central bank and with other government-controlled banks.

However, an **exemption** is available from full disclosure of transactions, outstanding balances and commitments with the government or with other entities related to the same government.

If the exemption is applied, IAS 24 requires disclosure of:

(a) The **name of the government** and **nature of the relationship**, and

(b) The nature and amount of each **individually significant transaction** (plus a qualitative or quantitative indication of the extent of other transactions which are collectively, but not individually, significant).

These disclosures provide more meaningful information about the nature of the entity's relationship and transactions with government than do the usual IAS 24 disclosures.

(b) **Financial guarantee contract**

IFRS 9 *Financial instruments* (revised 2014) requires entities to classify all financial liabilities as subsequently measured at amortised cost using the effective interest method, with the following exceptions.

(i) Financial liabilities **at fair value through profit or loss**. Such liabilities, including derivatives that are liabilities, must be subsequently measured at fair value.

(ii) Financial liabilities that arise **when a transfer of a financial asset does not qualify for derecognition** or when the continuing involvement approach applies

(iii) **Financial guarantee contracts.** After initial recognition, an issuer of such a contract must subsequently measure it at the higher of:

(1) The amount of the loss allowance determined in accordance with the IFRS 9 rules on expected credit losses, and

(2) The amount initially recognised less, when appropriate, the cumulative amount of income recognised in accordance with the principles of IFRS 15 *Revenue from contracts with customers.*

If an entity chooses to measure a financial guarantee contract (or loan commitment) **at fair value through profit or loss,** as here, **all fair value movements go through profit or loss** with no transfer to other comprehensive income. Changes in the credit risk of liabilities relating to financial guarantee contracts are not required to be presented in other comprehensive income under IFRS 9 (revised July 2014).

Assuming that discounting is not material, the accounting entries will be as follows.

At 1 December 20X2

DEBIT	Profit or loss	$1.2m	
CREDIT	Financial liabilities		$1.2m

To record the loss incurred in giving the guarantee

At 30 November 20X3

DEBIT	Financial liabilities	$0.4m	
CREDIT	Profit or loss		$0.4m

To amortise the initial fair value over the life of the guarantee.

This reflects the reduction in exposure arising from the fact that the subsidiary has made the first repayment.

At 30 November 20X4

DEBIT	Profit or loss ($40m – ($1.2m – $0.4m))	$39.2m	
CREDIT	Financial liabilities		$39.2m

To provide for the calling of the guarantee

DEBIT	Financial liabilities ($40m – $0.4m)	$39.6m	
CREDIT	Profit or loss		$39.6m

To record movement from expected credit loss allowance to measurement at amortised initial value

The above change was made in the light of the subsidiary's receipt of the donation enabling it to make the second repayment, which means a change in probability that the guarantee will be called. This is an event after the reporting period which provides further evidence of conditions existing at the end of the reporting period, and so is an adjusting event.

(c) **Hedging**

IFRS 9 *Financial instruments* (revised 2014) allows hedge accounting but only if **all** of the following **conditions** are met.

(i) The hedging relationship consists **only of eligible hedging instruments and eligible hedged items**.

(ii) There must be **formal documentation** (including identification of the hedged item, the hedging instrument, the nature of the risk that is to be hedged and how the entity will assess the hedging instrument's effectiveness in offsetting the exposure to changes in the hedged item's fair value or cash flows attributable to the hedged risk).

(iii) The hedging relationship meets all of the IFRS 9 hedge effectiveness criteria.

IFRS 9 defines **hedge effectiveness** as the degree to which changes in the fair value or cash flows of the hedged item attributable to a hedged risk are offset by changes in the fair value or cash flows of the hedging instrument. The directors of Coatmin have asked whether hedge effectiveness can be calculated. It is possible that they have in mind the somewhat arbitrary 80%-125% 'bright line' test of IAS 39, the forerunner of IFRS 9. IFRS 9 replaces this with an **objective-based assessment** for hedge effectiveness, under which the following criteria must be met.

(i) There is an **economic relationship** between the hedged item and the hedging instrument, ie the hedging instrument and the hedged item have values that generally move in the opposite direction because of the same risk, which is the hedged risk;

(ii) The **effect of credit risk does not dominate the value** changes that result from that economic relationship, ie the gain or loss from credit risk does not frustrate the effect of changes in the underlyings on the value of the hedging instrument or the hedged item, even if those changes were significant; and

(iii) The **hedge ratio of the hedging relationship** (quantity of hedging instrument vs quantity of hedged item) is the same as that resulting from the quantity of the hedged item that the entity **actually hedges** and the quantity of the hedging instrument that the entity **actually uses** to hedge that quantity of hedged item.

While the above criteria will certainly involve calculations, the assessment is more sophisticated and arguably more realistic.

(d) **Liability**

IFRS 9 *Financial instruments* (revised 2014) requires that financial liabilities which are **designated as measured at fair value through profit or loss are treated differently**. In this case the gain or loss in a period must be classified into:

- Gain or loss **resulting from credit risk**, and
- **Other** gain or loss.

This provision of IFRS 9 was in response to an anomaly regarding changes in the credit risk of a financial liability.

Changes in a financial liability's credit risk affect the fair value of that financial liability. This means that when an entity's creditworthiness deteriorates, the fair value of its issued debt will decrease (and *vice versa*). IFRS 9 requires the gain or loss as a result of credit risk to be recognised in other comprehensive income, unless it creates or enlarges an **accounting mismatch**, in which case it is recognised in profit or loss. The other gain or loss (not the result of credit risk) is recognised in profit or loss.

On derecognition any gains or losses recognised in other comprehensive income are **not** transferred to **profit or loss**, although the cumulative gain or loss may be transferred within equity.

This is a decrease in the fair value of the liability, which is a fair value gain in the books of Coatmin. Coatmin should split the fair value decrease as follows:

STATEMENT OF PROFIT OR LOSS AND OTHER COMPREHENSIVE INCOME (EXTRACT)
FOR THE YEAR ENDED 30 NOVEMBER 20X4

Profit or loss for the year	
Liabilities at fair value	$'000
Fair value gain not attributable to change in credit risk	45
Profit (loss) for the year	45
Other comprehensive income (not reclassified to profit or loss)	
Fair value gain on financial liability attributable to change in credit risk	5
Total comprehensive income	50

20 Avco

Text reference. The distinction between debt and equity is covered in Chapter 7 of your Study Text.

Top tips. While this question, on the distinction between debt and equity, was quite narrow in focus, the topic has featured in an article by the examining team. The issue has been flagged by the examining team as topical. The distinction between debt and equity is fundamental to any set of financial statements, and it is essential that you can explain it with reference to such matters as debt being determined where redemption is at the option of the instrument holder, where there is a limited life to the instrument and dividends being non-discretionary. Part (b) required you to apply the principles in Part (a) to two scenarios, discussing whether the instruments were debt or equity. It was not possible, therefore, to do Part (b) if you could not do Part (a), because you need to understand the principles in order to apply them. Unless you were sure of your ground, you would have been advised to tackle another optional question, in which the parts were more standalone.

Easy marks. It is difficult to find much in the way of easy marks in this challenging question. However, if you had practised the December 2013 question Bental, you might have found that Part (a) dealt with some of the same arguments, and this might have made the question easier.

Examiner's comment. The key message from the ACCA examination/examining team is that the final decision as to whether the instrument was debt or equity was not as important as the ability to discuss the scenario. Obviously the answer should be correct but if candidates can discuss the relevant issues then they will score a good proportion of the marks.

Marking scheme

			Marks
(a)	(i)	1 mark per point up to maximum	9
	(ii)	Effects	5
(b)		1 mark per point up to maximum	9
Professional marks			2
			25

(a) (i) **Classification differences between debt and equity**

It is not always easy to **distinguish between debt and equity in an entity's** statement of financial position, partly because many financial instruments have elements of both.

IAS 32 *Financial instruments: presentation* brings clarity and consistency to this matter, so that the **classification is based on principles** rather than driven by perceptions of users.

IAS 32 defines an **equity instrument** as: 'any contract that evidences a residual interest in the assets of an entity after deducting all of its liabilities'. It must first be **established that an instrument is not a financial liability,** before it can be classified as equity.

A key feature of the **IAS 32 definition of a financial liability** is that it **is a contractual obligation to deliver cash or another financial asset to another entity**. The contractual obligation may arise from a requirement to make payments of principal, interest or dividends. The contractual obligation may be explicit, but it may be implied indirectly in the terms of the contract. An example of a debt instrument is a bond which requires the issuer to make interest payments and redeem the bond for cash.

A financial instrument is an **equity instrument** only if there is no obligation to deliver cash or other financial assets to another entity and if the instrument will or may be settled in the issuer's own equity instruments. An example of an equity instrument is **ordinary shares, on which dividends are payable at the discretion of the issuer.** A less obvious example is preference shares required to be converted into a fixed number of ordinary shares on a fixed date or on the occurrence of an event which is certain to occur.

An instrument may be classified as an equity instrument if it contains a **contingent settlement provision** requiring settlement in cash or a variable number of the entity's own shares **only on the occurrence of an event which is very unlikely to occur** – such a provision is **not considered to be genuine.** If the **contingent payment condition** is **beyond the control of** both the entity and the holder of the instrument, then the instrument is classified as a **financial liability**.

A **contract resulting in the receipt or delivery of an entity's own shares is not automatically an equity instrument.** The classification depends on the so-called **'fixed test'** in IAS 32. A contract which will be settled by the entity receiving or delivering a **fixed number of its own equity instruments in exchange for a fixed amount of cash is an equity instrument**. The reasoning behind this is that by fixing upfront the number of shares to be received or delivered on settlement of the instrument in concern, the holder is exposed to the upside and downside risk of movements in the entity's share price.

In contrast, if the **amount of cash or own equity shares to be delivered or received is variable**, then the contract is a **financial liability or asset.** The reasoning behind this is that using a variable number of own equity instruments to settle a contract can be similar to using own shares as 'currency' to settle what in substance is a financial liability. Such a contract does not evidence a residual interest in the entity's net assets. Equity classification is therefore inappropriate.

IAS 32 gives two **examples** of contracts where the number of own equity instruments to be received or delivered varies so that their fair value equals the amount of the contractual right or obligation.

(1) A contract to deliver a variable number of own equity instruments equal in value to a fixed monetary amount on the settlement date is classified as a financial liability.

(2) A contract to deliver as many of the entity's own equity instruments as are equal in value to the value of 100 ounces of a commodity results in liability classification of the instrument.

There are **other factors** which might result in an instrument being **classified as debt.**

(1) Dividends are non-discretionary.

(2) Redemption is at the option of the instrument holder.

(3) The instrument has a limited life.

(4) Redemption is triggered by a future uncertain event which is beyond the control of both the issuer and the holder of the instrument.

Other factors which might result in an instrument being **classified as equity** include the following.

(1) Dividends are discretionary.
(2) The shares are non-redeemable.
(3) There is no liquidation date.

(ii) **Significance of debt/equity classification for the financial statements**

The distinction between debt and equity is very important, since the classification of a financial instrument as either debt or equity **can have a significant impact on the entity's reported earnings and gearing ratio**, which in turn can affect debt covenants. Companies may wish to classify a financial instrument as **equity,** in order to give a **favourable impression of gearing,** but this may in turn have a **negative effect** on the perceptions of existing shareholders if it is seen **as diluting existing equity interests.**

The distinction is also relevant in the context of a **business combination** where an entity **issues financial instruments as part consideration, or to raise funds to settle a business combination in cash.** Management is often called upon to **evaluate different financing options**, and in order to do so must **understand the classification rules and their potential effects**. For example, **classification as a liability** generally means that **payments are treated as interest** and charged to profit or loss, and this may, in turn, **affect the entity's ability to pay dividends** on equity shares.

(b) (i) **Cavor**

B shares

The classification of Cavor's B shares will be made by applying **the principles-based definitions of equity and liability in IAS 32**, and considering the **substance,** rather than the legal form of the instrument. 'Substance' here relates only to consideration of the contractual terms of the instrument. Factors outside the contractual terms are not relevant to the classification. The following factors demonstrate that Cavor's B shares are **equity instruments.**

(1) **Dividends are discretionary** in that they need only be paid if paid on the A shares, on which there is no obligation to pay dividends. Dividends on the B shares will be paid at the same rate as on the A shares, which will be variable.

(2) Cavor has **no obligation to redeem** the B shares.

Share options

The 'fixed test' must be applied. If the amount of cash or own equity shares to be delivered is variable, then the contract is a debt instrument. Here, however, the contract is to be settled by Cavor issuing a fixed number of its own equity instruments for a fixed amount of cash. Accordingly there is **no variability, and the share options are classified as an equity instrument.**

(ii) **Lidan**

A financial liability under IAS 32 is **a contractual obligation to deliver cash or another financial asset to another entity**. The contractual obligation may arise from a requirement to make payments of principal, interest or dividends. The contractual obligation may be explicit, but it may be implied indirectly in the terms of the contract.

In the case of Lidan, the **contractual obligation is not explicit**. At first glance it looks as if Lidan has a choice as to how much it pays to redeem the B shares. However, the conditions of the financial instrument are such that the value of the **settlement in own shares is considerably greater than the cash settlement obligation.** The effect of this is that **Lidan is implicitly obliged to redeem the B shares at for a cash amount of $1 per share**. The own-share settlement alternative is uneconomic in comparison to the cash settlement alternative, and cannot therefore serve as a means of avoiding classification as a liability.

IAS 32 states further that where a derivative contract has settlement options, **all of the settlement alternatives must result in it being classified as an equity instrument**, otherwise it is a financial asset or liability.

In conclusion, **Lidan's B shares must be classified as a liability**.

21 Complexity

Text reference. Financial instruments are covered in Chapter 7 of the BPP Study Text.

Top tips. A regular topic – financial instruments – is examined in a current issues context. Recently the ACCA examination/examining team has started to insert a calculation element into his current issues question. On past form, the calculations have not been difficult, but have served to illustrate the impact of a change or proposed change. The 2008 Discussion Paper is not specifically examinable, and some of its arguments have been addressed by IFRS 9. However, IFRS 9 has complexities of its own, and many of the problems have not yet been solved.

Easy marks. The calculation is a good source of easy marks as it is straightforward. And there are marks for bookwork – listing the problems of complexity and advantages of fair value.

Examiner's comments. This question was quite well answered. In part (a) candidates were asked to discuss the measurement issues relating to financial instruments and how these issues would be alleviated if fair value were used for all financial instruments. However, many candidates simply quoted the measurement rules relating to financial instruments without setting out how these rules created confusion and complexity for users. Some simply set out the advantages and disadvantages of fair value accounting rather than discussing how the use of fair value might result in less complexity in financial statements. The calculations in part (b)of the question were quite well done although very few candidates saw that the although redemption amounts were the same, the carrying amounts were quite different.

Marking scheme

			Marks
(a)	(i)	1 mark per point up to maximum	9
	(ii)	1 mark per point up to maximum	9
	Professional marks		2
(b)	Identical payment		2
	Carrying amount		1
	Fair value		2
			25

(a) (i) Many users and preparers of accounts have found financial instruments to be **complex**. There are a number of reasons for this complexity and resulting confusion, many of which were covered in a Discussion Paper, *Reducing Complexity in Reporting Financial Instruments*, issued by the IASB as long ago as 2008.

The main reason for complexity in accounting for financial instruments is the **many different ways in which they can be measured**. The measurement method depends on:

(1) The **applicable financial reporting standard.** A variety of IFRS and IAS apply to the measurement of financial instruments. For example, financial assets may be measured using consolidation for subsidiaries (IFRS 10), the equity method for associates and joint ventures (IAS 28 and IFRS 11) or IFRS 9 for most other financial assets.

(2) The **categorisation of the financial instrument**. IAS 39 *Financial instruments: recognition and measurement* had four categories: fair value through profit or loss, available for sale financial assets, loans and receivables and held to maturity.

While IFRS 9 simplifies these categories so that financial assets are classified as measured at **either amortised cost or fair value,** the final (July 2014) introduced another category of **fair value through other comprehensive income,** in addition to fair value through profit or loss. A financial asset may only be classified as measured at amortised cost if the object of the business model in which it is held is to collect contracted cash flows and its contractual terms give rise on specified dates to cash flows that are solely payments of principal and interest.

(3) Whether **hedge accounting** has been applied. Hedge accounting is **complex**, for example when cash flow hedge accounting is used, gains and losses may be split between profit or loss for the year and other comprehensive income (items that may subsequently be reclassified to profit or loss). In addition, there may be mismatches when hedge accounting applies reflecting the underlying mismatches under the non-hedging rules.

Some measurement methods use an estimate of **current value, and others use historical cost.** Some include impairment losses, others do not.

The different measurement methods for financial instruments creates a number of **problems for preparers and users** of accounts:

(1) The treatment of a particular instrument **may not be the best**, but may be determined by other factors.

(2) Gains or losses resulting from different measurement methods may be combined in the same line item in the statement of profit or loss and other comprehensive income. **Comparability** is therefore compromised.

(3) Comparability is also affected when it is **not clear** what measurement method has been used.

(4) It is **difficult to apply the criteria** for deciding which instrument is to be measured in which way. As new types of instruments are created, the criteria may be applied in ways that are not consistent.

(ii) There is pressure to reduce complexity in accounting for financial instruments. One idea, put forward in the 2008 Discussion Paper, is that **fair value is the only measure that is appropriate for all types of financial instruments**, and that a full fair value model would be much simpler to apply than the current mixed model. A single measurement method would, it is argued:

(1) Significantly **reduce complexity in classification**. There would be no need to classify financial instruments into the four categories of fair value through profit or loss, available for sale financial assets, loans and receivables and held to maturity. This simplification has already been partially achieved by IFRS 9.

(2) **Reduce complexity in accounting**. There would be no need to account for transfers between the above categories, or to report how impairment losses have been quantified.

(3) **Eliminated measurement mismatches** between financial instruments and reduce the need for fair value hedge accounting.

(4) Eliminate the need to identify and separate **embedded derivatives**.

(5) **Better reflect the cash flows** that would be paid if liabilities were transferred at the re-measurement date.

(6) Make reported information **easier to understand**.

(7) **Improve the comparability** of reported information between entities and between periods.

However, while fair value has some obvious advantages, it has problems too. **Uncertainty** may be an issue for the following reasons

(1) Markets are not all liquid and transparent.

(2) Many assets and liabilities do not have an active market, and methods for estimating their value are more subjective.

(3) Management must exercise judgement in the valuation process, and may not be entirely objective in doing so.

(4) Because fair value, in the absence of an active market, represents an estimate, additional disclosures are needed to explain and justify the estimates. These disclosures may themselves be subjective.

(5) Independent verification of fair value estimates is difficult for all the above reasons.

(b) Different valuation methods bring comparability problems, as indicated in Part (a), and this can be seen with the examples in this part of the question.

Amortised cost

Using amortised cost, both the initial loan and the new loan result in **single payments that are almost identical** on 30 November 20X9:

Initial loan: \$47m × 1.05 for 5 years = \$59.98m

New loan: \$45m × 1.074 for 4 years = \$59.89m

However, the **carrying amounts at 30 November 20X5 will be different:**

Initial loan: \$47m + (\$47m × 5%) = \$49.35m

New loan: \$45m

Fair value

If the two loans were carried at fair value, both **the initial loan and the new loan would have the same value,** and be carried at \$45m. There would be a net profit of \$2m, made up of the interest expense of \$47m × 5% = \$2.35m and the unrealised gain of \$49.35m – \$45m = \$4.35m.

Arguably, since the obligation on 30 November 20X9 will be the same for both loans, fair value is a more appropriate measure than amortised cost.

22 Preparation question: Leases

(a) Interest rate implicit in the lease

PV = annuity × cumulative discount factor

250,000 = 78,864 × CDF

$\therefore$ CDF $= \dfrac{250{,}000}{78{,}864}$

= 3.170

$\therefore$ Interest rate is 10%

(b) At the inception of the lease, Sugar Co recognises a right-of-use asset and a lease liability. The right-of-use asset is measured at the amount of the lease liability, which is the present value of the lease payments discounted at the rate of interest implicit in the lease, here $250,000. At 31 December, the right-of-use asset is measured at cost less accumulated depreciation: $250,000 – $(250,000/4) = $187,500. The lease liability is measured by increasing the carrying amount to reflect interest on the lease liability and reducing the carrying amount to reflect the lease payments made.

STATEMENT OF FINANCIAL POSITION (EXTRACT)

Property, plant and equipment

Carrying amount of right-of-use asset is $187,500.

Non-current liabilities

	$
Lease liabilities (W)	136,886

Current liabilities

	$
Lease liabilities (W) (196,136 – 136,886)	59,250

STATEMENT OF PROFIT OR LOSS AND OTHER COMPREHENSIVE INCOME (PROFIT OR LOSS SECTION)

Depreciation on right-of-use asset	62,500
Finance charges	25,000

Working

		$
Year ended 31 December 20X1:		
1.1.20X1	Liability b/d	250,000
1.1.20X1 – 31.12.20X1	Interest at 10%	25,000
31.12.20X1	Instalment in arrears	(78,864)
31.12.20X1	Liability c/d	196,136
Year ended 31 December 20X2:		
1.1.20X2 – 31.12.20X2	Interest at 10%	19,614
31.12.20X2	Instalment in arrears	(78,864)
31.12.20X2	Liability c/d	136,886

23 Havanna

Text reference. Revenue recognition (the new IFRS 15) is covered in Chapter 1 of your Study Text, IFRS 5 in Chapter 15 and sale and leaseback in Chapter 8.

Top tips. Revenue recognition (Part (a)) is a popular topic with this examiner, partly because the rules have recently changed, and partly because it is an area in which preparers of accounts may wish to bend the existing rules to present the results in a favourable light. You need to explain why their proposed treatment is unacceptable, not just state that it is. IFRS 5 (Part (b)) requires clear, logical thinking: there are two potential impairments, the first in calculating the adjusted carrying value of the disposal group at the time of classification as held for sale, and then again on comparison of this adjusted carrying value with fair value less costs to sell. You are not given any figures for the provisions incorrectly charged to continued operations, but be aware that the adjusted carrying value and fair value less costs to sell would need to be further adjusted once these were treated correctly. In Part (c), you should be aware that sale and leaseback is now covered by IFRS 16, a new standard.

Easy marks. There are marks for textbook definitions in Part (a), and Part (c) gives pointers by using the different sales prices to help structure your answer.

Examiner's comment. The level of knowledge needed to answer Part (a) of this question was quite basic but candidates had to apply that knowledge to gain the marks and again this was where any problem arose. However, this part of the question was answered quite well. The main problem with answers to Part (b) was that candidates found reasons as to why the disposal group was incorrectly classified as such, when there was no evidence in the question of this fact. The main problem was the measurement of the disposal group but many candidates failed to recognise this fact. The main problem in Part (c) (sale and leaseback) was that some candidates simply showed the accounting entries without discussing the implications. However, candidates scored well on this part of the question.

Marking scheme

	Marks
(a) Revenue recognition up to	6
(b) IFRS 5 explanation	9
(c) Leases	8
Professional marks	2
	25

(a) **Contracts with sports organisations**

The applicable standard relating to the contracts is IFRS 15 *Revenue from contracts with customers.* This standard has a **five-step process for** recognising revenue.

(i) Identify the contract with the customer.
(ii) Identify the separate performance obligations.
(iii) Determine the transaction price.
(iv) Allocate the transaction price to the performance obligations.
(v) Recognise revenue when (or as)a performance obligation is satisfied.

It is assumed that (i) and (iii) are satisfied – the contracts are binding, and there is no indication in the question that the transaction price is undetermined. Step (ii) **'identify the separate performance obligations'** needs to be considered. Despite Havanna's claims, the performance obligation under IFRS 15 is **the provision of services.**)). Revenue should be recognised as the services are provided (step (v). Step (v) would treat this as a **performance obligation satisfied over time** because the customer simultaneously receives and consumes the benefits as the performance takes place.

A performance obligation satisfied over time meets the criteria in Step (v) above and, if it entered into more than one accounting period, as here for some of the contracts, would previously have been described as a long-term contract.

In this type of contract an entity has an enforceable right to payment for performance completed to date. The standard describes this as an amount that approximates the selling price of the goods or services transferred to date (for example recovery of the costs incurred by the entity in satisfying the performance plus a reasonable profit margin).

Methods of measuring the amount of performance completed to date encompass **output methods** and **input methods**.

(i) **Output methods** recognise revenue on the basis of the value to the **customer** of the goods or services transferred. They include surveys of performance completed, appraisal of units produced or delivered etc.

(ii) **Input methods** recognise revenue on the basis of the **entity's** inputs, such as labour hours, resources consumed, costs incurred. If using a cost-based method, the costs incurred must contribute to the entity's progress in satisfying the performance obligation.

Havanna argues that the **'limited obligations'** under the contracts (coaching and access to its membership database) **do not constitute rendering of services**, and that it is therefore acceptable to recognise the contract revenue in full. However, this treatment contravenes IFRS 15

In the case of these contracts, the services are performed by an indeterminate number of acts over a specified period of time. Under IFRS 15, the best measure of progress towards complete satisfaction of the performance obligation over time is a **time-based measure** and Havanna should recognise revenue on a **straight-line basis over the specified period.**

There is **no justification for Havanna's treatment**, that is recognising the contract income in full when the contract is signed. The 'limited obligations' argument is not supported by IFRS 15. Accordingly, Havanna **must apportion the income arising from the contracts over the period of the contracts**, as required by the standard.

(b) **Sale of division**

Impairment loss

The division to be sold meets the criteria in IFRS 5 *Non-current assets held for sale and discontinued operations* to be classified as held for sale, and has been classified as a **disposal group** under IFRS 5.

A disposal group that is held for sale should be measured at the **lower of** its **carrying amount** and **fair value less costs to sell**. Immediately before classification of a disposal group as held for sale, the entity must recognise impairment in accordance with applicable IFRS. Any impairment loss is generally recognised in profit or loss, but if the asset has been measured at a revalued amount under IAS 16 *Property, plant and equipment* or IAS 38 *Intangible assets,* the impairment will be treated as a revaluation decrease. **Once** the disposal group has been **classified as held for sale**, any **impairment loss** will be based on the **difference between the adjusted carrying amounts and the fair value less cost to sell**. The impairment loss (if any) will be **recognised in profit or loss**. For assets carried at fair value prior to initial classification, the requirement to deduct costs to sell from fair value will result in an immediate charge to profit or loss.

Havanna has calculated the impairment as $30m, being the difference between the carrying amount at initial classification and the value of the assets measured in accordance with IFRS.

Step 1 Calculate carrying value under applicable IFRS: $90m – $30m = $60m

Step 2 Classified as held for sale. Compare the adjusted carrying amount under applicable IFRS ($60m) with fair value less costs to sell ($40m). Measure at the lower of carrying value and fair value less costs to sell, here $40m.

Step 3 Determine whether any additional impairment loss is needed to write the division down to fair value less costs to sell. It is clear that an additional impairment loss is needed of $60m – $40m = $20m

Therefore **an additional impairment loss of $20m should be recognised.**

Other costs

Certain other costs relating to the division being sold are currently shown as provisions relating to continuing operations. This treatment is not correct:

(i) The trade receivable from Cuba Sports should have **been tested for impairment immediately before classification** of the division as held for sale. An **impairment loss** for the amount of the trade receivable should have been **recognised** and would have **reduced the carrying amount of the division on the initial classification as held for sale**. In addition, the division has guaranteed the sale proceeds to Havanna's Head Office, so as the amount owing has not been collected a **refund** would be needed, and the **sales price of the division** (and hence the fair value less costs to sell) would need to be **adjusted** to reflect the amount of the potential refund.

(ii) The discounting expense for the sales price of the disposal group reflects the fact that payment is deferred until 30 November 20X5. This **discount** should not have been recognised in continuing operations, but **should have been taken into account in calculating the fair value less costs to sell** of the disposal group.

(iii) The provision for **transaction costs** should not have been recognised in continuing operations. The costs (legal advice and lawyers' fees) should be considered as **part of 'costs to sell'** when calculating fair value less costs to sell.

All three items affect fair value less costs to sell, and item (i), the trade receivable, also affects the carrying value of the division on classification as held for sale.

(c) **Sale and leaseback**

(i) IFRS 16 *Leases* requires an initial assessment to be made regarding whether or not the transfer constitutes a sale. This is done by determining when the performance obligation is satisfied in accordance with IFRS 15 *Revenue from contracts with customers* (IFRS 16: para.98). In this case, we are told in the question that the IFRS 15 criteria have been met. IFRS 16 therefore requires that, at the start of the lease, Havanna should measure the right-of-use asset arising from the leaseback of the building at the proportion of the previous carrying amount of the building that relates to the right-of-use retained. This is calculated as carrying amount × discounted lease payments/fair value. The discounted lease payments were given in the question as $3.85m.

For Havanna, the right of use asset is therefore: $4.2m × $3.85m/$5m = $3,234,000.

Havanna only recognises the amount of gain that relates to the rights transferred. The gain on sale of the building is $800,000 ($5,000,000 – $4,200,000), of which:

$(800,000 × 3,850/5,000,000) = $616,000 relates to the rights retained.

The balance, $(800,000 – 616,000) = $184,000, relates to the rights transferred to the buyer.

At the commencement date the lessee accounts for the transaction as follows:

	Debit	*Credit*
	$	$
Cash	5,000,000	
Right-of-use asset	3,234,000	
Building		4,200,000
Financial liability		3,850,000
Gain on rights transferred		184,000
	8,234,000	8,234,000

The right-of-use asset will be depreciated over ten years, the gain will be recognised in profit or loss and the financial liability will be increased each year by the interest charge and reduced by the lease payments.

(ii) (1) **Sales price $6 million**

Here the **sales price would be above fair value**. IFRS 16 states that the excess over fair value should be accounted for as additional finance provided by the lessor, so the $1 million ($6m – $5m) above the fair value would be treated as an **additional liability, not as a gain on the sale.**

(2) **Sales price $4 million**

Here the **sales price is below fair value**. IFRS 16 requires that 'below market terms' should be accounted for a s a **prepayment of lease payments.** In other words, the shortfall in consideration received from the lessor is treated as a lease payment by the lessee.

24 William

Text reference. Sale and leaseback is covered in Chapter 8 of your BPP Study Text. Employee benefits are in Chapter 4. Share-based payment is covered in Chapter 9 and contingent liabilities in Chapter 5 and Chapter 12 (in the context of business combinations).

Top tips. Part (a), on sale and leaseback, is more straightforward than some of the past exam questions on this subject. Part (b) is on a defined benefit pension plan, a regular occurrence. Part (c) deals with a a cash-settled share-based payment, a popular topic with this examiner. Part (d) tested a contingent liability: candidates needed to know that the treatment is different in the individual financial statements of the acquiree and in the consolidated financial statements, where the liability is recognised whether or not it is probable that an outflow of economic benefits will take place.

Easy marks. The structure of the question, which is broken down into manageable chunks, should make it easy to pick up the first few marks on each topic.

Examiner's comment. In Part (a), candidates generally dealt correctly with the treatment of the lease. Answers to Part (c) were often confused. Part (d) was well answered on the whole, but some candidates were confused over the treatment of the two situations and stated that the treatment was the same in both scenarios.

Marking scheme

		Marks
(a)	Leaseback principle	2
	Accounting	3
	Presentation	2
(b)	Provision for relocation costs	3
	Curtailment (past service cost) of defined benefit pension plan	4
(c)	Cash-settled share-based payments	2
	Calculation	3
(d)	Contingent liability – discussion	4
Communication skills		2
		25

(a) **Sale and leaseback**

The **form** of this transaction is a **sale and leaseback.** IFRS 16 requires an initial assessment to be made regarding whether or not the transfer constitutes a sale. This is done by determining when the performance obligation is satisfied in accordance with IFRS 15 *Revenue from contracts with customers* (IFRS 16: para.98). In this case, we are told in the question that the IFRS 15 criteria have been met. IFRS 16 therefore requires that, at the start of the lease, William should measure the right-of-use asset arising from the leaseback of the building at the proportion of the previous carrying amount of the building that relates to the right-of-use retained. This is calculated as carrying amount × discounted lease payments/fair value. The discounted lease payments were given in the question as $5m, which is the lease liability.

For William, the right of use asset is therefore: $3.6m × $5m/$6m = $3m.

William only recognises the amount of gain that relates to the rights transferred. The gain on sale of the building is $2,400,000 ($6,000,000 – $3,600,000), of which:

$(2,400,000 × 5,000,000/6,000,000) = $2,000,000 relates to the rights retained.

The balance, $(2,400,000 – 2,000,000) = $400,000, relates to the rights transferred to the buyer.

At 1 June 20X2, the William should account for the transaction as follows:

	Debit	*Credit*
	$	$
Cash	6,000,000	
Right-of-use asset	3,000,000	
Building		3,600,000
Financial liability		5,000,000
Gain on rights transferred		400,000
	9,000,000	9,000,000

The right-of-use asset will be depreciated over 20 years, which is the shorter of the lease term and the remaining useful life, $3m ÷ 20 years = $0.15m:

DEBIT	Depreciation expense	$0.15m	
CREDIT	Accumulated depreciation		$0.15m

The financial liability will be increased each year by the interest charge and reduced by the lease payments.

The finance cost on the lease liability is charged at the implicit rate of 7% to profit or loss for the year ended 31 May 20X3. The amount is calculated as follows:

Lease liability	
	$m
1 June 20X2 b/f	5.000
Finance cost: 5m × 7%	0.350
Instalment	(0.441)
31 May 20X3 c/f	4.909
Finance cost: 4.909m × 7%	0.344
Instalment	(0.441)
31 May 20X4 c/f	4.812

The lease liability at 31 May 20X3 is split between current and non-current:

	$m
Non-current liability (owed at 31 May 20X4)	4.812
Current liability (bal. fig.) = instalment (0.441) less finance cost (0.344)	0.097
Total liability at 31 May 20X3	4.909

(b) **Relocation costs and reduction to net pension liability**

A **provision for restructuring** should be recognised in respect of the relocation of the provision during the year ended 31 May 20X3 in accordance with IAS 37 *Provisions, contingent liabilities and contingent assets.* This is because William's board of directors authorised a **detailed formal plan** for the relocation shortly before the year end (13 May 20X3) and William has **raised a valid expectation in affected employees** that it will carry out the restructuring by informing them of the main features of the plan. As the relocation is due to take within two months of the year end (July 20X3), the time value of money is likely to be immaterial. Therefore no discounting is required and a provision should be recognised at the estimated relocation costs of $50 million.

The reduction in the net pension liability as a result of the employees being made redundant and no longer accruing pension benefits is a **curtailment** under IAS 19 *Employee benefits (revised 2011)*. IAS 19 defines a curtailment as occurring when an entity significantly reduces the number of employees covered by a plan. It is **treated as a type of past service costs**. The past service cost may be negative (as is the case here) when the benefits are withdrawn so that the present value of the defined benefit obligation decreases. IAS 19 requires the past service cost to be **recognised in profit or loss** at the earlier of:

- When the plan curtailment occurs, and
- When the entity recognises the related restructuring costs.

Here the restructuring costs (and corresponding provision) are recognised in the year ended 31 May 20X3 and the plan curtailment will not take place until after the year end in July 20X3 when the employees are made redundant. Therefore the reduction in the net pension liability and corresponding income in profit or loss should be recognised at the earlier of these two dates, ie when the restructuring costs are recognised in the year ended 31 May 20X3.

Both the relocation costs and income from the reduction in the net pension liability are likely to require **separate disclosure** in the statement of profit or loss and other comprehensive income or in the notes to the accounts per IAS 1 *Presentation of financial statements* due to their materiality.

(c) **Share-based payment**

Share appreciation rights are **cash-settled share-based-payments**. IFRS 2 *Share-based payment* requires that the entity should measure the goods or services acquired and the liability incurred at the **fair value of the liability**. The fair value of the liability should be **measured at each reporting date** until the liability is settled and at the date of settlement. Any **changes** in fair value are recognised in profit or loss for the period.

	$
1 June 20X2 liability b/f: (20 – 3 (managers)) × 500 SARS × $14 (fair value) × 2/2 (vested)	119,000
Cash paid on exercise: 7 managers × 500 SARS × $21 (intrinsic value)	(73,500)
Expense (balancing figure)	74,500
31 May 20X3 liability c/f: (20 – 3 – 7 (managers)) × 500 SARS × $24 (fair value)	120,000

The expense for the year is accounted for as follows:

DEBIT Expense	(P/L)	$74,500	
CREDIT	Cash		$73,500
CREDIT	Liability		$1,000

(d) **Contingent liability**

The legal claim against Chrissy will be treated differently in Chrissy's individual financial statements as compared with the consolidated accounts of the William group.

Chrissy's individual financial statements

The legal claim against Chrissy **does not meet the definition of a provision** under IAS 37 *Provisions, contingent liabilities and contingent assets*. One of IAS 37's requirements for a provision is that an outflow of resources embodying economic benefits should be probable, and William believes that it is more likely than not that such an **outflow will not occur**.

However, the possible payment does fall within the IAS 37 definition of a **contingent liability,** which is:

- A possible obligation depending on whether some uncertain future event occurs, or
- A present obligation but payment is not probable or the amount cannot be measured reliably.

Therefore as **a contingent liability** the details of the claim and the $4 million estimated fair value of the contingent liability would be **disclosed** in the notes to the financial statements.

Consolidated financial statements

Under IFRS 3 *Business combinations*, an acquirer must allocate the cost of a business combination by recognising the acquiree's identifiable assets, liabilities and contingent liabilities that satisfy the recognition criteria at their **fair values** at the date of the acquisition. Contingent liabilities where there is only a possible obligation which, under IAS 37, depend on the occurrence or non-occurrence of some uncertain future event are not recognised under IFRS 3. However, the **IAS 37 probability criterion does not apply under IFRS 3**: a contingent liability is recognised **whether or not it is probable that an outflow** of economic benefits will take place, where there is a present obligation and its fair value can be measured reliably.

Consequently, William should **recognise the contingent liability as part of the business combination at its fair value** of $4 million. This will reduce net assets at acquisition, and therefore increase goodwill.

25 Leigh

Text reference. See Chapters 9 and 12 of the text.

Top tips. This was a difficult question, as all three parts included peripheral areas of the syllabus. This question dealt with several share-based payment transactions. However, not all such transactions were dealt with by a single accounting standard. Part (a) dealt with the cost of a business combination and the issue of shares as purchase consideration. It also dealt with shares given to employees as remuneration. The events are dealt with under the separate accounting standards IFRS 2 and IFRS 3. Part (b) dealt with the purchase of property, plant and equipment, and the grant of rights to a director when there is a choice of settlement. This part of the question was quite technically demanding. Part (c) dealt with the issue of shares to acquire an associate and the subsequent accounting for the associate.

Easy marks. It is difficult to identify easy marks for this question. Unless share-based payment is your 'pet topic', it would have been best avoided in an exam.

Examiner's comment. The question was poorly answered. Parts (a) and (c) were very straightforward but candidates did not seem to recognise the issues or accounting standards which should be used. The question required an application of some basic knowledge but candidates failed to do this. Part (b) required some detailed knowledge of IFRS 2 and again candidates did not have such knowledge. It appears that unless the ACCA examination/examining team details the accounting standard to be used in answering the question, candidates have difficulty in applying knowledge to scenarios.

Marking scheme

			Marks
(a)	Hash		7
	Employees		3
(b)	Property, plant and equipment		5
	Director		4
(c)	Handy		6
		Available/Maximum	25

(a) **Shares issued to the directors**

The three million $1 shares issued to the directors **on 1 June 20X6** as part of the **purchase consideration** for Hash are accounted for under **IFRS 3** *Business combinations* rather than under IFRS 2 *Share-based payment.* This is because they are not remuneration or compensation, but simply part of the purchase price of the company. The cost of the business combination will be the total of the fair values of the consideration given by Leigh plus any attributable costs. The total fair value here is $6m, of which $3m is share capital and $3m is share premium.

The **contingent consideration** – 5,000 shares per director to be received on 31 May 20X7 if the directors are still employed by Leigh – may, however, be seen as compensation and thus fall to be treated under IFRS 2. The fact that the additional payment of shares is **linked to continuing employment** suggests that it is a compensation arrangement, and therefore **IFRS 2 will apply**.

Under IFRS 2, the fair value used is that at the **grant date,** rather than when the shares vest. The market value of each share at that date is $2. (Three million shares are valued at $6m.) So the total value of the compensation is 5 × 5,000 × $2 = **$50,000**.

The $50,000 is charged to profit or loss with a corresponding increase in equity.

Shares issued to employees

These shares are remuneration and are **accounted for under IFRS 2**.

The fair value used is that at the **date of issue,** as the grant date and issue date are the same, **that is $3 per share**. Because the shares are given as a bonus they vest immediately and are presumed to be consideration for past services.

The total of $3m would be changed to profit or loss and included in equity.

(b) **Purchase of property, plant and equipment**

Under IFRS 2, the purchase of property, plant and equipment would be treated as a share-based payment in which the counterparty has a **choice of settlement**, in shares or in cash. Such transactions are **treated as cash-settled** to the extent that the entity has incurred a **liability**. It is treated as the issue of a compound financial instrument, with a debt and an equity element.

Similar to IAS 32 *Financial instruments: presentation,* IFRS 2 requires the **determination of the liability element and the equity element**. The fair value of the equity element is the fair value of the goods or services (in this case the property) less the fair value of the debt element of the instrument. The fair value of the property is $4m (per question). The share price of $3.50 is the expected share price in three months' time (assuming cash settlement). The fair value of the liability component at 31 May 20X7 is its present value: 1.3 × $3 = $3.9.

The journal entries are:

DEBIT	Property, plant and equipment	$4m	
CREDIT	Liability		$3.9m
CREDIT	Equity		$0.1m

In three months' time, the debt component is remeasured to its fair value. Assuming the estimate of the future share price was correct at $3.50, the liability at that date will be 1.3 million × $3.5 = $4.55. An adjustment must be made as follows:

DEBIT	Expense (4.55 – 3.9)	$0.65m	
CREDIT	Liability		$0.65m

Choice of share or cash settlement

The share-based payment to the new director, which offers a choice of cash or share settlement, is also treated as the issue of a compound instrument. In this case, the **fair value of the services is determined by the fair value of the equity instruments given**. The fair value of the equity alternative is $2.50 × 50,000 = $125,000. The cash alternative is valued at 40,000 × $3 = $120,000. The **difference** between these two values – $5,000 – is deemed to be the **fair value of the equity component**. At the settlement date, the liability element would be measured at fair value and the method of settlement chosen by the director would determine the final accounting treatment.

At 31 May 20X7, the accounting entries would be:

DEBIT	Profit or loss – directors' remuneration	$125,000	
CREDIT	Liability		$120,000
CREDIT	Equity		$5,000

In effect, the director surrenders the right to $120,000 cash in order to obtain equity worth $125,000.

(c) **Investment in Hardy**

The investment in Hardy should be treated as an **associate under** IAS 28 *Investments in associates and joint ventures.* Between 20% and 50% of the share capital has been acquired, and significant influence may be exercised through the right to appoint directors. Associates are accounted for as cost plus post acquisition change in net assets, **generally cost plus share of post-acquisition retained earnings**. The cost is the fair value of the shares in Leigh exchanged for the shares of Handy. However, negative goodwill arises because the fair value of the net assets of Hardy exceeds this. The negative goodwill must be added back to determine the cost to be used for the carrying value, and, following a reassessment, credited to profit or loss. (Dr Cost 0.2, Cr P/L 0.2)

	$m
Cost: 1m × $2.50	2.5
Add back negative goodwill: (2.5 + (9 × 70% 'NCI') – 9)	0.2
	2.7
Post acquisition profits: (5 – 4) × 30%	0.3
Carrying value at 31 May 20X7	3.0

Note. The 0.2 is not part of post acquisition retained earnings. It is adjustment to the original cost to remove the negative goodwill.

Because negative goodwill has arisen, the investment must be **impairment tested**. A comparison must be made with the estimated recoverable amount of Hardy's net assets. The investment must not be carried above the recoverable amount:

Recoverable amount at 31 May 20X7: $11m × 30% = $3.3m

The recoverable amount is above the carrying value, so the investment at 31 May 20X7 will be shown at $3m.

26 Zack

Text reference. IAS 8 *Accounting policies, changes in accounting estimates and errors* is covered in Chapter 10 of your study text. IAS 23 *Borrowing costs* is covered in Chapter 3.

Top tips. As Question 4 on the paper, this was different from the usual current issues question in the topic it tested (IAS 8), although not in structure, being a discussion followed by application to a scenario. While IAS 8 is brought forward knowledge from F7, the depth of discussion required is greater, and the scenario requires more thought.

Easy marks. There are marks available for textbook knowledge of IAS 8 and IAS 23, which you should have from your earlier studies, and also the fact that there is much subjectivity in the marking scheme means a variety of valid arguments may be acceptable. Note the word 'valid', however: you **must** apply the knowledge to the scenario and you will get no credit for 'waffle'.

Examiner's comment. The question asked for discussion and examples and the marking scheme reflected these requirements. The weighting of the marks was heavily towards the discursive aspect of the question and many candidates failed to gain these marks, particularly as regards the examples as very few practical examples were given. This question demonstrates the difference in knowledge and application between paper F7 and P2.The preamble to the question also gave candidates guidance as to how to answer the question by saying 'Entities also often consider the acceptability of the use of hindsight in their reporting' but often this guidance was ignored. Part (b) was well answered. However, it was interesting that in Part (a) there were very few examples given of prior period errors etc even though there were examples given in Part (b) which could have been used in the correct context in Part (a).

Marking scheme

		Marks
(a)	Subjective	15
(b)	Subjective	8
Professional marks		2
		25

(a) (i) **Judgement and materiality in selecting accounting policies**

The selection of accounting policies in the preparation of financial statements is important in providing consistency, comparability and clarity to users of those statements. In general entities do not have a great deal of discretion, but must follow the accounting policies required by IFRS that are relevant to the particular circumstances of the entity. In certain circumstances, however, IFRS offers a choice or does not give guidance. In these situations, management should select appropriate accounting policies.

Judgement

Management is required to exercise judgement in developing and applying an accounting policy that results in information that is relevant and reliable. If there is **no IFRS** standard or interpretation that is specifically applicable, management should consider the applicability of the requirements in IFRS on **similar and related issues**, and then the definitions, recognition criteria and measurement concepts for assets, liabilities, income and expenses in the **Conceptual Framework**. Management may also consider the most recent pronouncements of **other standard-setting bodies** that use a similar conceptual framework to develop accounting standards, other accounting literature and accepted industry practices, to the extent that these do not conflict with IFRS.

Unless a standard permits or requires otherwise, accounting policies should be applied **consistently** to similar transactions and events. For example, it is permissible to carry some items of property, plant and equipment at fair value and some at historical cost, but items within any one class of property, plant and equipment must be treated in the same way.

Management's judgement will be constrained as regards its selection of accounting policies (or changes in accounting policies or estimates) by the need to **follow the requirements of IAS 8** *Accounting policies, changes in accounting estimates and errors.*

Materiality

IAS 8 states that omissions or misstatements of items 'are material if they could, by their size or nature, individually or collectively, influence the economic decisions of users taken on the basis of the financial statements'.

In general, IFRS **only apply to material items,** and an accounting policy need not be applied if its effect would be immaterial. Similarly, a **change** in accounting policy or estimate **would only be necessary if the item was material.** Specifically in the context of IAS 8 and errors, materiality 'depends on the size and nature of the omission or misstatement judged in the surrounding circumstances. The size or nature of the item, or a combination of both, could be the determining factor'.

In addition, IAS 8 notes that it is **inappropriate to make, or leave uncorrected, immaterial departures** from IFRSs to **achieve a particular presentation**, so the principle of materiality cannot be abused to present the results in an artificially favourable light.

(ii) **Change in accounting policy**

IAS 8 allows a change in accounting policy **only where required by a standard** or if it results in financial statements providing reliable and **more relevant information** about the effects of transactions, other events or conditions on the entity's financial position, financial performance, or cash flows. Changes in accounting policy **should be very rare,** because IFRS specifies the accounting policies for most of the transactions an entity will make. Changes in accounting **estimates**, on the other hand, will be **more frequent**. A change in accounting estimate is 'an adjustment of the carrying amount of an asset or liability, or related expense, resulting from reassessing the expected future benefits and obligations associated with that asset or liability'. Such changes may be needed to estimate the figures correctly in order to comply with an accounting policy.

IAS 8 notes that changes in accounting policies **do not include applying an accounting policy to a kind of transaction or event that did not occur previously or were immaterial**. Such a policy would be applied **prospectively,** that is prior period figures would not be adjusted. For example, if an entity begins to let out its head office to residents to earn rental income, this change of use of the building would mean that it should be accounted for as an investment property under IAS 40. However, this is not a change of accounting policy, rather it is the application of a standard to an asset to which it did not apply previously, and so there would be no retrospective application.

If a change in accounting policy is required by a new IFRS or interpretation, the change is accounted for as required by that new pronouncement if the new pronouncement includes specific transition provisions. Not all new standards and interpretations include transition provisions, and if none are included then the change in accounting policy is applied retrospectively.

Retrospective application means that an entity **adjusts the opening balance of each component of equity that is affected for the earliest prior period presented in the financial statements**. It also adjusts the other comparative amounts, that is, amounts in the statement of profit or loss and other comprehensive income, and the statements of financial position, cash flows and changes in equity and related notes. The **comparative amounts** disclosed for each prior period presented **as if the new policy had always applied**. This rule applies except where it is impracticable to determine either the period-specific effects of the change or the cumulative effects of the change.

It is sometimes **difficult to compare** the current period with prior periods because there is **insufficient data** relating to the prior period. Perhaps it was not foreseen that such data would be needed. Even if the data is available, restatement of prior information often requires **complex and detailed estimates** to be made, although this does not mean that reliable adjustments cannot be made.

The further in the past the prior period adjustment relates to, the harder it is for estimates to reflect the circumstances existing at the time. Judgement may be clouded by hindsight, that is influenced by knowledge of events which have occurred since the prior period. **IAS 8 does not permit the use of hindsight** in estimations of amounts to be recognised, measured or disclosed in a prior period, or in making assumptions about management intentions at that time.

If it is impracticable to determine the cumulative effect, at the beginning of the current period, of applying a new accounting policy to all prior periods, an entity must adjust the comparative information to apply the new accounting policy prospectively from the **earliest date practicable**. This may in practice be the current period.

(iii) **IAS 8 and earnings management**

IAS 8 requires the correction of prior period errors to be carried out retrospectively by restating the comparative amounts for the prior period(s) presented in which the error occurred, or if the error occurred before the earliest prior period presented, restating the opening balances of assets, liabilities and equity for the earliest prior period presented. The effect is to restate the comparatives **as if the error had never occurred**. The impact of any prior period errors will not be included in the current period's profit or loss, but will be shown – or perhaps hidden – in retained earnings.

It could be argued that this gives managers an **incentive to use prior period corrections under IAS 8** as a form of **earnings management,** because it allows them to **manipulate current earnings**.

Expenses could be miscalculated and the correction treated as a prior period error in the following year, with an **adjustment through retained earnings rather than profit or loss**. Earnings per share could be miscalculated, or liabilities reported as non-current rather than current. IAS 8 allows such misstatements to be **corrected the following year without any long-term negative effects in the statement of financial position**.

While IAS 8 does not permit **hindsight,** in practice this may be **difficult to prove**, and inappropriate hindsight may be used to relegate bad news to prior periods once the bad news has passed. **Errors are not given the prominence** which users of financial statements might need in order to assess management's competence and integrity, as well as how good the results are. Use of reserves instead of profit or loss has long been seen as undesirable this very reason.

(b) (i) **Borrowing costs**

IAS 23 *Borrowing costs* requires that borrowing costs directly attributable to the acquisition, construction or production of a 'qualifying asset' (one that necessarily takes a substantial period of time to get ready for its intended use or sale) are included in the cost of the asset. Other borrowing costs are recognised as an expense.

IAS 23 would therefore require capitalisation of the borrowing costs of $3m incurred while the shopping centre is under construction. In the case of the borrowing costs of $2m incurred on the 20X2 asset, it has been found that there would be a material misstatement of the asset balance if borrowing costs were not capitalised, so IAS 23 requires capitalisation of those borrowing costs.

The accounting treatment previously used by Zack was incorrect because it did not comply with IAS 23. Consequently, the change to the new, correct policy is **the correction of an error rather than a change of accounting policy** as regards the 20X2 asset**.** This is a prior period error, which **must be corrected retrospectively**. This involves restating the financial statements for the year ended 30 November 20X2, when the contract was completed, and **restating the opening balances** for 20X3 so that the financial statements are presented as if the error had never occurred. In 20X3, the $3m of borrowing costs should be capitalised in accordance with IAS 23; this is compliance with IFRS rather than a change of accounting policy. It can be assumed that there will be no depreciation, as the asset is under construction.

The **effects of the restatement** for the year ended 30 November 20X2 are:

(1) The carrying amount of property, plant and equipment is **restated upwards** by $2m, less depreciation for the year.

(2) There is a corresponding **increase in profit or loss** for the year of the same amount.

(3) **Disclosures** are required relating to the prior period error:

- The nature of the prior period error
- For each prior period presented, to the extent practicable, the amount of the correction, for each financial statement line item affected, and for basic and diluted earnings per share
- The amount of the correction at the beginning of the earliest prior period presented
- If retrospective restatement is impracticable, an explanation and description of how the error has been corrected.

(ii) **Change in depreciation method**

Changing from straight line depreciation to reducing balance is a **change in accounting estimate, not a change in accounting policy**. A change in accounting estimate is 'an adjustment of the carrying amount of an asset or liability, or related expense, resulting from reassessing the expected future benefits and obligations associated with that asset or liability.'

Changes in accounting estimates are **not applied retrospectively** and accordingly, financial information presented for prior periods is not restated. Instead, the effect of a change in an accounting estimate is recognised **prospectively** (that is, from the date of change) by including it in profit or loss in the period of change, if the change affects only that period, or in the period of change and future periods, where the change also affects future periods.

Where the effect on future periods is not disclosed because it is not practicable, that fact should be disclosed.

The revision to the depreciation figures calculated by management are not correct, because they include an adjustment of **$5m for the year to 30 November 20X2**, that is a **retrospective adjustment.** The carrying amount as at 1 December 20X2 will be depreciated based on **prospective** reducing balance application.

(iii) **Accruals error**

This systems error would be treated as a **prior period error** in accordance with IAS 8. Zack must correct this by **restating the prior period information** for the year ended 30 November 20X2:

(1) Increase profit or loss for 20X2 by $2m.
(2) Adjust trade payables for 20X2 by $2m, to eliminate the overstatement.
(3) Restate the movement in reserves note.

This is the correction of an error, not an accounting estimate.

27 Minco

Text reference. Revenue recognition is covered in Chapter 1 of your Study Text. Intangible assets, property, plant and equipment, and impairment are covered in Chapter 3. IFRS 5 is covered in Chapter 15 and IAS 34 is covered in Chapter 10.

Top tips. This was a specialised industry question, set in the property industry. As the ACCA examination/examining team has stated, no specialist knowledge of the industry was required. The question covered a number of standards and issues (revenue, interim reporting, asset held for sale, provisions, intangibles and the treatment of an annual retainer). Both the question and the answer to Part (a) have been amended to reflect the different emphasis of the new IFRS 15 from its predecessor, IAS 18. Part (d) has also been amended.

Easy marks. Although IFRS 15 is new, there are some easy marks to be had in Part (a) for showing knowledge of the criteria for identifying the contract with a customer.

Examiner's comment. Most candidates had knowledge of revenue recognition and many applied their knowledge satisfactorily. However in Part (b), many candidates struggled to recognise the issues where a tennis player receives a signing bonus of $20,000, earns an annual amount of $50,000 and receives a bonus of 20% of the prize money won at a tournament. Many candidates did not recognise the intangible asset or the financial liability. Additionally, there was little discussion of the principles behind the accounting application. Part (c) required knowledge of two standards, IAS 16 and IAS 37.The scenarios that appear in this exam will often require multiple IFRSs to be applied to them. Often candidates chose to discuss the leasing standard. Part (d) also required the application of several standards: IAS 34, IFRS 5, IAS 16 and IAS 38. It was quite well done in terms of the calculations but was quite weak on the discursive element.

Marking scheme

		Marks
(a)	1 mark per point up to maximum	7
(b)	1 mark per point up to maximum	5
(c)	1 mark per point up to maximum	5
(d)	1 mark per point up to maximum	6
Professional marks		2
Maximum		25

(a) **Contract for sale of the building**

Revenue from a contract may be recognised in accordance with IFRS 15 *Revenue from contracts with customers* when all of the following criteria (Paragraph 9) are met.

(i) The **parties** to the contract have **approved the contract**.

(ii) **Each party's rights** in relation to the goods or services to be transferred **can be identified**.

(iii) The **payment terms and conditions** for the goods or services to be transferred **can be identified**.

(iv) The contract has **commercial substance**.

(v) The **collection of an amount of consideration** to which the entity is entitled to in exchange for the goods or services is **probable**.

Criteria (i) to (iv) have been met, but **criterion (v),** relating to Holistic Healthco's ability and intention to pay, is **in doubt.** The following factors need to be taken into consideration.

(i) Holistic Healthco's liability under the loan is limited because the **loan is non-recourse**. If the customer defaults Minco is not entitled to full compensation for the amount owed, but only has the right to repossess the building.

(ii) Holistic Healthco intends to repay the loan (which has a significant balance outstanding) primarily from income derived from its fitness and leisure centre. This is a **business facing significant risks** because of high competition in the industry and because of the customer's limited experience.

(iii) Holistic Healthco has **no other income or assets** that could be used to repay the loan.

It is therefore **not probable that Minco will collect the consideration** to which it is entitled in exchange for the transfer of the building and so the IFRS 15 (Paragraph 9) criteria have not been met. Minco must then consider whether either of the criteria in IFRS 15 Paragraph 15 have been met, that is:

(a) Has Minco has received **substantially all** of the consideration?
(b) Has Minco **terminated the contract?**

The answer to both of these is **no,** therefore, in accordance with Paragraph 16 of the standard, **Minco must account for the non-refundable $150,000 payment as a deposit liability.** Minco must continue to account for the initial deposit, as well as any future payments of principal and interest, as a deposit liability, until such time that the company concludes that the criteria in Paragraph 9 are met, specifically that it will recover the consideration owing, or until it has received substantially all of it, or terminated the contract. Minco must **continue to assess the situation** to see if these changes have occurred.

(b) **Promotional expenditure**

There are three types of payment involved in the arrangement with the tennis player. The question states that the payments are not interrelated, so the interactions between them do not need to be examined and the expense recognition pattern may be different for each.

Signing bonus

The contract is for advertising and promotional expenditure to improve Minco's brand image. IAS 38 *Intangible assets* requires **that these costs must be expensed when the services are received**. The signing bonus is paid in advance of the services being received, those services being wearing Minco's logo, taking part in a specified number of tournaments and attending photo/film sessions for advertising. The signing bonus of $20,000 is paid to the player at the start of the contract, but relates to the full three-year contract term. It must therefore be treated as a **prepayment at the start of the contract and expensed on a straight-line basis** over the three-year contract period.

If the **contract is terminated** before the end of the three-year period, Minco should **expense immediately any amount not recovered** from the player.

It has been assumed in specifying the above treatment that separate services cannot be identified. However, **if the terms of the contract allow separate services to be identified and measured reliably**, then Minco should **recognise the expense once the separate service is rendered.**

Annual retainer

Minco has also contracted to pay the player an annual retainer of $50,000 provided she has competed in all the specified tournaments for that year. IFRS 9 *Financial instruments* requires this arrangement to be treated as a **financial liability** because Minco has a **contractual obligation to deliver cash** to the player. The financial liability is recognised at the **present value of the expected cash flows.**

Minco incurs this obligation on the date **when the player has competed in all the specified tournaments** and it is at this point that the **liability should be recognised.**

Performance bonus

Minco must also pay a performance bonus to the player whenever she wins a tournament. These payments are **related to specific events,** and therefore they are treated as **executory contracts.** (An executory contract is a contract in which something remains to be done by one or both parties.) They are **accrued and expensed when the player has won** a tournament.

(c) **Head office**

Additional floor

IAS 16 *Property, plant and equipment* is the relevant standard here. The standard requires that Minco should capitalise the costs of the extra floor, which is an improvement to the building, and amortise these costs over the six-year lease period.

IAS 16 states that the initial cost of an asset **should include** the initial estimate of the **costs of dismantling and removing the item and restoring the site** where the entity has an obligation to do so. This is the case here: Minco has an obligation to remove the floor at the end of the lease because of the clause in the lease requiring the building's condition to be identical at the end of the lease to its condition at the beginning of the lease. A **present obligation exists**, as defined by IAS 37 *Provisions, contingent liabilities and contingent assets* and therefore the entity should also **recognise a provision** for that amount. The provision should be **discounted to its present value** and the unwinding of the discount recognised in profit or loss.

This arrangement is, in substance, a decommissioning liability. The **asset** recognised for the cost of removal should be **amortised over the six-year period of the lease**. Minco may recover the cost from the benefits generated by the new floor over the remainder of the lease.

General disrepair of the building

A **present obligation** arises for the repair costs under IAS 37 *Provisions, contingent liabilities and contingent assets* because the lease agreement states that the landlord can re-charge these costs to Minco. The **obligating event is the wear and t**ear to the building, which arises gradually over the period of the lease and which will result in an outflow of economic benefits. The **estimated costs should be spread over the six-year lease** period. A **reliable estimate** of the yearly obligation can be made, although this may not necessarily be one sixth per year, for example if exceptional wear and tear arises in any given year.

Roof repair

The lease states clearly that the landlord can re-charge any costs of repairing the roof immediately. Accordingly, **an obligation exists** and a **provision needs to be made for the whole of the roof repair work** on the date on which the requirement was identified.

(d) **Property**

IAS 34 requirement

In accordance with IAS 34 *Interim financial reporting,* an entity must apply the same accounting policies in its interim financial statements as in its annual financial statements. Measurements should be made on a 'year to date' basis. Minco's interim financial statements are for the six months to 30 November 20X3.

Minco must apply the provisions of IFRS 5 *Non-current assets held for sale and discontinued operations* to the valuation of the property.

Application of IFRS 5

In accordance with IFRS 5, an asset held for sale should be measured at the **lower of** its **carrying amount** and **fair value less costs to sell**. Immediately before classification of the asset as held for sale, the entity must recognise impairment in accordance with applicable IFRS. Any impairment loss is generally recognised in profit or loss, but if the asset has been measured at a revalued amount under IAS 16 *Property, plant and equipment* or IAS 38 *Intangible assets,* the impairment will be treated as a revaluation decrease. **Once** the asset has been **classified as held for sale**, any **impairment loss** will be based on the **difference between the adjusted carrying amounts and the fair value less cost to sell**. The impairment loss (if any) will be **recognised in profit or loss**.

A **subsequent increase** in fair value less costs to sell may be **recognised** in profit or loss **only to the extent of any impairment previously recognised**. To summarise:

Step 1 Calculate carrying value under applicable IFRS, here IAS 16:

Depreciation for the four months to 1 October 20X3, the date of classification as held for sale is calculated on the carrying amount net of the impairment loss incurred on 31 May 20X3, over the remaining useful life of eight years, ($1m is two years' depreciation out of 5m/0.5 – ten years):

(5m – 1m – 0.35m) ÷ 8 × 4/12 = $152,083

So the carrying value at 1 October 20X3 is 5m – 1m – 0.35m – 0.15m = $3.5m

Step 2 Classified as held for sale. Compare the carrying amount ($3.5m) with fair value less costs to sell ($3.4m). Measure at the lower of carrying value and fair value less costs to sell, here $3.4m, giving an initial write-down of $100,000.

Step 3 Determine fair value less costs to sell at the date of the interim financial statements, 1 December 20X3, here given as $3.52m and compare with carrying value of $3.4m. This gives a gain of $120,000.

The impairment previously recognised is: $350,000 + $100,000 = $450,000. The gain of $120,000 is less than this, and may therefore be credited to profit or loss, and the property is carried at $3.52m.

Step 4 On 31 May 20X4, fair value less costs to sell is $3.95m. The change in fair value less cost to sell is recognised but the gain recognised cannot exceed any impairment losses to date. Impairment losses to date are $350,000 + $100,000 – $120,000 = $330,000, and this is less than the change in fair value less costs to sell of $430,000. This restricted gain of $330,000 is recognised, and the property is carried at $3.85m.

Step 5 On 5 June 20X4, the property is sold for $4m, at which point a gain of $150,000 is recognised. If material, this sale would be a non-adjusting event under IAS 10 *Events after the reporting period.*

28 Alexandra

Text reference. IAS 1 and IAS 8 are covered in Chapter 10 of your Study Text. IFRS 15 is covered in Chapter 1. Related parties are covered in Chapter 11. Pension plans are covered in Chapter 4.

Top tips. Part (a) was on reclassification of long-term debt as current. Part (b) had a correction of an error (IAS 8) arising from an incorrect application of IFRS 15 *Revenue from contracts with customers.* Thus you have the interaction of two standards, so don't just concentrate on one. Part (c) was on related party disclosures for key management personnel, which needed to be broken down by category, and part (d) required candidates to explain why a pension plan needed to be accounted for as a defined benefit plan. As this is a multi-topic standard question, you can always have a respectable go at the parts where your knowledge is strongest. As the ACCA examination/examining team often says, all information in the question is included for a purpose, so there are plenty of pointers in Part (d).

Easy marks. Part (c) has some easy marks for reproducing definitions from IAS 24. Unusually, the employee benefits question (Part (d)) could be a source of easy marks, as it contains a number of hints, and gives you an opportunity to reproduce knowledge about the differences between the two types of plan without any complicated calculations.

Examiner's comment. In Part (a), only a few candidates mentioned that according to IAS 1 *Presentation of financial statements*, a liability should be classified as current if it is due to be settled within 12 months after the date of the statement of financial position. In Part (b), most candidates had a good understanding of the nature of the revenue standard (IAS 1, now IFRS 15), but few treated the change in accounting treatment as a correction of an error in accordance with IAS 8 *Accounting policies, changes in accounting estimates and errors.* The previous policy applied was not in accordance with the applicable standard. Most scored well on Part (c), realising that that the exclusion of the remuneration of the non-executive directors from key management personnel disclosures did not comply with the requirements of IAS 24 *Related party disclosures.* Part (d) was well answered, with most candidates coming to the right conclusion.

Marking scheme

		Marks
(a)	1 mark per question up to maximum	6
(b)	1 mark per question up to maximum	5
(c)	1 mark per question up to maximum	5
(d)	1 mark per question up to maximum	7
Professional marks		2
Maximum		25

(a) **Default on loan**

Under IAS 1 *Presentation of financial statements,* a **long-term financial liability** due to be **settled within twelve months** of the year end date should be classified as a **current liability**. Furthermore, a **long-term financial liability** that is payable on **demand** because the entity **breached** a **condition** of its loan agreement should be classified as **current** at the year end even if the **lender** has agreed **after the year end**, and **before** the financial statements are **authorised for issue**, **not** to **demand payment** as a consequence of the breach.

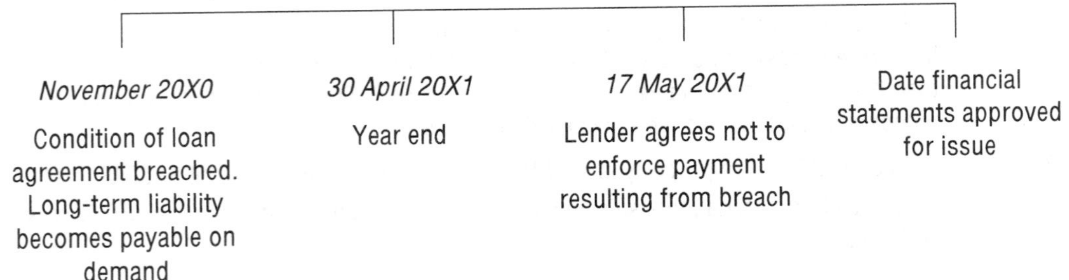

However, if the **lender** has **agreed** by the **year end** to provide a **period of grace** ending **at least twelve months after the year end** within which the entity can rectify the breach and during that time the lender cannot demand immediate repayment, the liability is classified as **non-current**.

In the case of Alexandra, the waiver was given before the year end, but only for the loan to be repaid a month after the year end, then a further waiver was agreed, but again only for a few weeks. It would **not therefore be appropriate for Alexandra to classify the bond as long-term debt** in the statement of financial position as at 30 April 20X1.

The fact that Alexandra has defaulted and sought two loan waivers may cast doubt on its ability to continue as a going concern, especially as the loan waivers may not be renewed. If there is uncertainty regarding Alexandra's going concern status, IAS 1 requires Alexandra to disclose these uncertainties. If Alexandra ceases to be a going concern, then the financial statements would need to be prepared on a break-up basis.

(b) **Maintenance contracts**

There are two aspects to consider:

(i) What is the correct way to recognise the revenue from the maintenance contracts?
(ii) What adjustments does Alexandra need to make, having changed its method of recognition?

Correct IFRS 15 treatment

IFRS 15 *Revenue from contracts with customers* has a five-stage process for recognising revenue. Step (ii) **'identify the separate performance obligations'** would classify the performance obligations in the maintenance contracts as the provision of services. Step (v)of the IFRS 15 process requires the entity to would treat this as a **performance obligation satisfied over time** because the customer simultaneously receives and consumes the benefits as the performance takes place.

Revenue should be recognised as the services are provided (step (v).

Under IFRS 15, the best measure of progress towards complete satisfaction of the performance obligation over time is a **time-based measure** and Alexander should recognise revenue on a **straight-line basis over the specified period.**

Accordingly, **the new treatment**, and the one used to date by Xavier Co, is the **correct** accounting treatment under IFRS 15, and the **previous treatment,** of recognising the revenue on invoicing at the beginning of the contract, was **incorrect**.

Adjustments under IAS 8

The accounting treatment previously used by Alexandra was incorrect because it did not comply with IFRS 15 *Revenue from contracts with customers*.. Consequently, the change to the new, correct policy is **the correction of an error rather than a change of accounting policy**.

IAS 8 *Accounting policies, changes in accounting estimates and errors* states that changes in accounting estimates result from changes in circumstances, new information or more experience, which is not the case here. This is a prior period error, which **must be corrected retrospectively**. This involves **restating the opening balances** for that period so that the financial statements are presented as if the error had never occurred.

In the opening balance of retained earnings, the maintenance contract income that was recognised in full in the year ended 30 April 20X0 must be split between the revenue due for that year (on an IFRS 15 basis as described above) and that which should be deferred to subsequence periods. There will be less revenue recognised in the prior year, resulting in a **net debit to opening retained earnings**.

In the year ended 30 April 20X1, the correct accounting policy has been applied. Since the maintenance contracts typically run for two years, it is likely that most of the **income deferred from the prior year relating to this period will also be recognised** in the current period. The effect of this for the year ended 30 April 20X1 is that the reduction in profits of $6m will be mitigated by the recognition of income deferred from last year.

(c) **Directors' remuneration**

The disclosures that Alexandra has provided are insufficient to comply with IAS 24 *Related party disclosures* on two counts:

(i) No breakdown of directors' remuneration
(ii) Exclusion of remuneration of non-executive directors

Breakdown of directors' remuneration

IAS 24 *Related party disclosures* requires that entities should **disclose** key management personnel compensation **not only in total** but also **for each of the** following **categories:**

- Short-term employee benefits
- Post-employment benefits
- Other long-term benefits
- Termination benefits
- Share-based payment

The remuneration for the directors of Alexandra fits into the categories of 'short-term benefits' (ie salary and bonus) and 'share-based payment' (ie share options), and should be disclosed accordingly. Only totals for each category need to be disclosed, not the earnings of individual board members, so no cultural protocol will be breached by these disclosures. However, Alexandra is a public limited company, and so local legislation and corporate governance rules may require more detailed disclosure.

Non-executive directors

By excluding the non-executive directors from the remuneration disclosures, **Alexander is in breach of IAS 24**.

IAS 24 defines **key management personnel** as those persons having authority and responsibility for planning, directing and controlling the activities of the entity, directly or indirectly, including any director (**whether executive or otherwise**) of that entity.

Thus, the remuneration of the non-executive directors, who are key management personnel, should have been disclosed along with that of the executive directors.

(d) **Pension plan**

Alexander wishes to account for its pension plan as a defined contribution scheme, probably because the accounting is more straightforward and the risk not reflected in the figures in the financial statements. These figures were material in the case of Alexandra. However, although the entity's plan has some features in common with a defined contribution plan, it needs to be considered whether this is really the case.

With **defined contribution** plans, the employer (and possibly, as here, current employees too) pay regular contributions into the plan of a given or 'defined' amount each year. The contributions are invested, and the size of the post-employment benefits paid to former employees depends on how well or how badly the plan's investments perform. If the investments perform well, the plan will be able to afford higher benefits than if the investments performed less well.

With **defined benefit** plans, the size of the post-employment benefits is determined in advance, ie the benefits are 'defined'. The employer (and possibly, as here, current employees too) pay contributions into the plan, and the contributions are invested. The size of the contributions is set at an amount that is expected to earn enough investment returns to meet the obligation to pay the post-employment benefits. If, however, it becomes apparent that the assets in the fund are insufficient, the employer will be required to make additional contributions into the plan to make up the expected shortfall. On the other hand, if the fund's assets appear to be larger than they need to be, and in excess of what is required to pay the post-employment benefits, the employer may be allowed to take a 'contribution holiday' (ie stop paying in contributions for a while).

The **main difference** between the two types of plans lies in **who bears the risk**: if the employer bears the risk, even in a small way by guaranteeing or specifying the return, the plan is a defined benefit plan. A defined contribution scheme must give a benefit formula based solely on the amount of the contributions.

Alexandra's is, in reality, a defined benefit plan. Alexandra, the employer, guarantees a pension based on the average pay of the employees in the scheme. The entity's liability is not limited to the amount of the contributions to the plan, but is supplemented by an insurance premium which the insurance company can increase if required in order to fulfil the plan obligations. The trust fund which the insurance company is building up, is in turn dependent on the yield on investments. If the insurer has insufficient funds to pay the guaranteed pension, Alexandra has to make good the deficit. Indirectly, through insurance premiums, the employer bears the investment risk. The employee's contribution, on the other hand is fixed.

A further indication that Alexander bears the risk is the provision that if an employee leaves Alexandra and transfers the pension to another fund, Alexandra is liable for, or is refunded the difference between the benefits the employee is entitled to and the insurance premiums paid. Alexandra thus **has a legal or constructive obligation** to make good the shortfall if the insurance company does not pay all future employee benefits relating to employee service in the current and prior periods.

In conclusion, even though the insurance company limits some of the risk, Alexandra, rather than its employees, bears the risk, so this is a **defined benefit plan**.

29 Klancet

Text reference. Specialised industries are covered in general terms in Chapter 20 of your Study Text. Segment reporting is covered in Chapter 10. Intangible assets are covered in Chapter 3.

Top tips. In Part (a), on segment reporting, the key was to argue that the second laboratory met the definition of an operating segment, while the first one did not. Part (b) covered two patents, one to be sold in return for shares of the acquirer and the other acquired through the issue of the entity's own shares. Part (c) covered the development of two drugs by an external provider, one where regulatory approval had been refused in the past and the other which was a variation of an existing drug, the key issue being whether these could be capitalised as development expenditure, which was the case for the latter, but not the former.

Easy marks. These are available for discussing the principles of IFRS 8 in Part (a) and for knowing the quantitative thresholds.

Examiner's comments. In Part (a), candidates often discussed the principles of IFRS 8 very well and many felt correctly that the second laboratory should be reported as a separate segment. However few students realised that the first laboratory was in fact simply supporting the business of the entity and was not actually a separate segment. In Part (b), few students discussed IFRS 9 in this context or IFRS 2.This part of the question was not well answered by candidates. Part (c) of the question was quite well answered as regards the principles but the application particularly in the case of the first contract was not well discussed. In this case, the payments were to a third party who was carrying out the development of the drug and should have been expensed.

Marking scheme

		Marks
(a)	1 mark per point up to maximum	8
(b)	1 mark per point up to maximum	7
(c)	1 mark per point up to maximum	8
Professional marks		2
		25

(a) **Segment reporting**

IFRS 8 *Operating segments* states that an operating segment is a component of an entity which engages in business activities from which it may earn revenues and incur costs. In addition, discrete financial information should be available for the segment and these results should be regularly reviewed by the entity's chief operating decision maker (CODM) when making decisions about resource allocation to the segment and assessing its performance. However, if a function is an integral part of the business, it may be disclosed as a segment even though it may not earn revenue.

Other factors should be taken into account when identifying the operating segments. These include the nature of the business activities of each component, the existence of managers responsible for them, and information presented to the board of directors.

IFRS 8 also has certain quantitative measures to identify a segment, although an entity can report segment information for smaller operating segments if there is a belief that the information is useful.

According to IFRS 8, an operating segment is one which meets any of the following quantitative thresholds:

(i) Its reported revenue, including both sales to external customers and intersegment sales or transfers, is 10% or more of the combined revenue, internal and external, of all operating segments.

(ii) The absolute amount of its reported profit or loss is 10% or more of the greater, in absolute amount, of (1) the combined reported profit of all operating segments which did not report a loss and (2) the combined reported loss of all operating segments which reported a loss.

(iii) Its assets are 10% or more of the combined assets of all operating segments.

As regards the two research and development laboratories, qualitative and quantitative factors should be considered in determining the operating segments. The qualitative factors will include whether the resultant operating segments are consistent with the principles of IFRS 8, whether the operating segments represent the level at which the CODM is assessing performance and allocating resources and whether the identified operating segments enable users of its financial statements to evaluate its activities and financial performance, and the business environment it operates in.

As a result of the application of the above criteria, the first laboratory will not be reported as a separate operating segment. The divisions have heads directly accountable to, and maintaining regular contact with, the CODM to discuss all aspects of their division's performance. The divisions seem to be consistent with the core principle of IFRS 8 and should be reported as separate segments. The laboratory does not have a separate segment manager and the existence of a segment manager is normally an important factor in determining operating segments. Instead, the laboratory is responsible to the divisions themselves, which would seem to indicate that it is simply supporting the existing divisions and not a separate segment. Additionally, there does not seem to be any discrete performance information for the segment, which is reviewed by the CODM.

The second laboratory should be reported as a separate segment. It meets the quantitative threshold for percentage of total revenues and it meets other criteria for an operating segment. It engages in activities which earn revenues and incurs costs, its operating results are reviewed by the CODM and discrete information is available for the laboratory's activities. Finally, it has a separate segment manager.

(b) **Patents**

All equity investments in the scope of IFRS 9 *Financial instruments* are to be measured at fair value in the statement of financial position, with value changes recognised in profit or loss, except for those equity investments for which the entity has elected to report value changes in 'other comprehensive income'. If an equity investment is not held for trading, an entity can make an irrevocable election at initial recognition to measure it at fair value through other comprehensive income with only dividend income recognised in profit or loss. Despite the fair value requirement for all equity investments, IFRS 9 contains guidance on when cost may be the best estimate of fair value and also when it might not be representative of fair value. IFRS 13 *Fair value measurement* defines fair value in this case which would be the price which would be received to sell an asset or paid to transfer a liability in an orderly transaction between market participants at the measurement date. Klancet would use level 1 inputs in this case, which are quoted prices in active markets.

Klancet's management should initially recognise the shares received at their fair value and should also derecognise the patent which is transferred to Jancy. Any gain or loss should also be recognised. The fair value of the shares received represents the amount of the consideration received according to IFRS 15 *Revenue from contracts with customers*. Revenue from royalties will be recognised on an accrual basis in accordance with the substance of the relevant agreement (IFRS 15)). As such, Klancet should not yet recognise any asset relating to the future royalty stream from the potential sales of the drug, because this stream of royalties is contingent upon the successful development of the drug.

With regards to the purchase of the patent, this is an equity settled, share-based payment transaction. The rules from IFRS 2 *Share-based payment* should be used. The entity should measure the goods purchased at the fair value of the goods received, unless that fair value cannot be estimated reliably. If Klancet cannot estimate reliably the fair value of the goods received, it should measure the value by reference to the fair value of the equity instruments granted. Klancet should recognise the patent at its fair value. The best indicator of fair value is the publicly traded price of the shares on the acquisition date.

(c) **Development of drugs**

IAS 38 *Intangible assets* requires an entity to recognise an intangible asset, whether purchased or self-created (at cost) if, and only if, it is probable that the future economic benefits which are attributable to the asset will flow to the entity and the cost of the asset can be measured reliably. This requirement applies whether an intangible asset is acquired externally or generated internally. IAS 38 includes additional recognition criteria for internally generated intangible assets. Development costs are capitalised only after technical and commercial feasibility of the asset for sale or use have been established. This means that the entity must intend and be able to complete the intangible asset and either use it or sell it and be able to demonstrate how the asset will generate future economic benefits.

If an entity cannot distinguish the research phase of an internal project to create an intangible asset from the development phase, the entity treats the expenditure for that project as if it were incurred in the research phase only. The price which an entity pays to acquire an intangible asset reflects its expectations about the probability that the expected future economic benefits in the asset will flow to the entity. The effect of probability is reflected in the cost of the asset and the probability recognition criterion above is always considered to be satisfied for separately acquired intangible assets. The cost of a separately acquired intangible asset can usually be measured reliably. This is particularly so when the purchase consideration is in the form of cash or other monetary assets. The cost of a separately acquired intangible asset comprises its purchase price and any directly attributable cost of preparing the asset for its intended use.

In the case of the first project, Klancet owns the potential new drug, and Retto is carrying out the development of the drug on its behalf. The risks and rewards of ownership remain with Klancet. By paying the initial fee and the subsequent payment to Retto, Klancet does not acquire a separate intangible asset, which could be capitalised. The payments represent research and development by a third party, which need to be expensed over the development period provided that the recognition criteria for internally generated intangible assets are not met. Development costs are capitalised only after technical and commercial feasibility of the asset for sale or use have been established. This means that the entity must intend and be able to complete the intangible asset and either use it or sell it and be able to demonstrate how the asset will generate future economic benefits. At present, this criterion does not appear to have been met as regulatory authority for the use of the drug has not been given and, in fact, approval has been refused in the past.

In the case of the second project, the drug has already been discovered and therefore the costs are for the development and manufacture of the drug and its slight modification. There is no indication that the agreed prices for the various elements are not at fair value. In particular, the terms for product supply at cost plus profit are consistent with Klancet's other supply arrangements. Therefore, Klancet should capitalise the upfront purchase of the drug and subsequent payments as incurred, and consider impairment at each financial reporting date. Regulatory approval has already been attained for the existing drug and therefore there is no reason to expect that this will not be given for the new drug. Amortisation should begin once regulatory approval has been obtained. Costs for the products have to be accounted for as inventory using IAS 2 *Inventories* and then expensed as costs of goods sold as incurred.

30 Cloud

Text reference. Integrated reporting is covered in Chapter 18 of the Study Text. Other aspects of performance reporting are covered in Chapter 10. Hedging is covered in Chapter 7 and transfers from revaluation are covered in Chapter 3.

Top tips. This question covered two topics: the issue of recognition of income and expenses in profit or loss vs other comprehensive income, reclassification between the two and integrated reporting. The ACCA examination/examining team's answer on P/L versus OCI has been amended slightly to reflect the publication of the recent Exposure Draft on the *Conceptual Framework*. Both topics were covered in recent *Student Accountant* articles by the examining team.

Easy marks. The Integrated Reporting question is straightforward textbook knowledge.

Examiner's comments. In Part (a), the arguments for and against reclassification adjustments were quite well answered by candidates as was the current presentation requirements of IAS 1.However the IIRC's *Framework*, which is a recent addition to the syllabus, was often confused with the IASB's *Conceptual Framework*, with the result that some candidates scored poorly on this part of the question. Part(b) required the application of part (a in terms of determining which elements of a profit or loss should be reported in OCI and which elements in profit or loss. The first part of this question dealt with a cash flow hedge and the treatment of gains and losses .The second part of the question dealt with the revaluation of property, plant and equipment and was very well answered by most candidates. The cash flow hedge was not as well answered.

Marking scheme

		Marks
(a)	(i) 1 mark per point up to maximum	4
	(ii) 1 mark per point up to maximum	5
	(iii) 1 mark per point up to maximum	8
(b)	1 mark per point up to maximum	6
	Professional marks	2
	Available	25

(a) (i) **Current presentation requirements**

IAS 1 *Presentation of financial statements* defines profit or loss as 'the total of income less expenses, excluding the components of other comprehensive income' and other comprehensive income as comprising 'items of income and expense (including reclassification adjustments) that are not recognised in profit or loss as required or permitted by other IFRSs'. IFRS currently requires the statement of profit or loss and other comprehensive income to be presented as either one statement, being a combined statement of profit or loss and other comprehensive income or two statements, being the statement of profit or loss and the statement of comprehensive income. An entity has to show separately in OCI, those items which would be reclassified (recycled) to profit or loss and those items which would never be reclassified (recycled) to profit or loss. The related tax effects have to be allocated to these sections.

IAS 1 states that profit or loss includes all items of income or expense (including reclassification adjustments) except those items of income or expense which are recognised in OCI as required or permitted by IFRS. IAS 1 further states that the other comprehensive income section is required to present line items which are classified by their nature, and grouped between those items which will or will not be reclassified to profit or loss in subsequent periods.

(ii) **Reclassification adjustments**

Reclassification adjustments are amounts recycled to profit or loss in the current period which were recognised in OCI in the current or previous periods. An example of items recognised in OCI which may be reclassified to profit or loss are foreign currency gains on the disposal of a foreign operation and realised gains or losses on cash flow hedges. Those items which may not be reclassified are changes in a revaluation surplus under IAS 16 *Property, plant and equipment*, and actuarial gains and losses on a defined benefit plan under IAS 19 *Employee benefits*. However, there is a general lack of agreement about which items should be presented in profit or loss and in OCI. The interaction between profit or loss and OCI is unclear, especially the notion of reclassification and when or which OCI items should be reclassified. A common misunderstanding is that the distinction is based upon realised versus unrealised gains.

There are several arguments for and against reclassification. If reclassification ceased, then there would be no need to define profit or loss, or any other total or subtotal in profit or loss, and any presentation decisions can be left to specific IFRSs. It is argued that reclassification protects the integrity of profit or loss and provides users with relevant information about a transaction which occurred in the period. Additionally, it can improve comparability where IFRS permits similar items to be recognised in either profit or loss or OCI.

Those against reclassification argue that the recycled amounts add to the complexity of financial reporting, may lead to earnings management and the reclassification adjustments may not meet the definitions of income or expense in the period as the change in the asset or liability may have occurred in a previous period.

The lack of a consistent basis for determining how items should be presented has led to an inconsistent use of OCI in IFRS. Opinions vary but there is a feeling that OCI has become a home for anything controversial because of a lack of clear definition of what should be included in the statement. Many users are thought to ignore OCI, as the changes reported are not caused by the operating flows used for predictive purposes.

A Discussion Paper on the *Conceptual Framework* sought to clarify what distinguishes recognised items of income and expense which are presented in profit or loss from items of income and expense presented in OCI. It further attempted to clarify why items presented in OCI in one period should be reclassified into profit or loss in the same period or a later period. It suggested that the *Conceptual Framework* should require a profit or loss total or subtotal which also results, or could result, in some items of income or expense being recycled and should limit the use of OCI to items of income or expense resulting from changes in current measures of assets and liabilities (remeasurements). However, not all such remeasurements would be eligible for recognition in OCI.

This approach was carried forward into the 2015 Exposure Draft *Conceptual Framework for Financial Reporting*.

The Discussion Paper proposed a **narrow and broad approach** to what should be included in other comprehensive income, but the IASB has not yet decided which approach it will use.

(1) **Narrow approach.** Other comprehensive income would **include bridging items and mismatched remeasurements.**

Bridging items are items of income or expense which represent the difference between measurement used in determining profit or loss and remeasurement used in the statement of financial position. An example would be investments in equity instruments with changes in fair value recorded in other comprehensive income. Such items would have to be **recycled as a consequence of the measurement basis presented in profit or loss.**

Mismatched remeasurements represent the effects of part of a linked set of assets, liabilities or past or planned transactions. It represents their effect so incompletely that, in the opinion of the IASB, the item provides little relevant information about the return that the entity has made on its economic resources in the period. An example would be a cash flow hedge, where fair value gains and losses are accumulated in other comprehensive income until the hedged transaction affects profit or loss. These amounts should **be recycled when the item can be presented with the matched item.**

(2) **Broad approach.** In addition to the narrow approach, this would also include transitory remeasurements. **Transitory remeasurements** are remeasurements of long-term assets and liabilities that are likely to reverse or significantly change over time. These items would be shown in OCI - for example, the remeasurement of a net defined pension benefit liability or asset. The IASB would **decide in each IFRS whether a transitory remeasurement should be subsequently recycled.**

The ED on the *Conceptual Framework* does not provide any guidance as to which of the above approaches it recommends.

(iii) **Integrated Reporting**

The International Integrated Reporting Council (IIRC) has released a framework for integrated reporting. The *Framework* establishes principles and concepts which govern the overall content of an integrated report. An integrated report sets out how the organisation's strategy, governance, performance and prospects can lead to the creation of value. The IIRC has set out a principles-based framework rather than specifying a detailed disclosure and measurement standard. This enables each company to set out its own report rather than adopting a checklist approach. The integrated report aims to provide an insight into the company's resources and relationships, which are known as the capitals and how the company interacts with the external environment and the capitals to create value. These capitals can be financial, manufactured, intellectual, human, social and relationship, and natural capital but companies need not adopt these classifications. Integrated reporting is built around the following key components:

(1) Organisational overview and the external environment under which it operates

(2) Governance structure and how this supports its ability to create value

(3) Business model

(4) Risks and opportunities and how they are dealing with them and how they affect the company's ability to create value

(5) Strategy and resource allocation

(6) Performance and achievement of strategic objectives for the period and outcomes

(7) Outlook and challenges facing the company and their implications

(8) The basis of presentation needs to be determined including what matters are to be included in the integrated report and how the elements are quantified or evaluated.

The *Framework* does not require discrete sections to be compiled in the report but there should be a high level review to ensure that all relevant aspects are included. An integrated report should provide insight into the nature and quality of the organisation's relationships with its key stakeholders, including how and to what extent the organisation understands, takes into account and responds to their needs and interests. Further, the report should be consistent over time to enable comparison with other entities.

The IIRC considered the nature of value and value creation. These terms can include the total of all the capitals, the benefit captured by the company, the market value or cash flows of the organisation and the successful achievement of the company's objectives. However, the conclusion reached was that the *Framework* should not define value from any one particular perspective because value depends upon the individual company's own perspective. It can be shown through movement of capital and can be defined as value created for the company or for others. An integrated report should not attempt to quantify value, as assessments of value are left to those using the report.

The report does not contain a statement from those 'charged with governance' acknowledging their responsibility for the integrated report. This may undermine the reliability and credibility of the integrated report. There has been discussion about whether the *Framework* constitutes suitable criteria for report preparation and for assurance. There is a degree of uncertainty as to measurement standards to be used for the information reported and how a preparer can ascertain the completeness of the report. The IIRC has stated that the prescription of specific measurement methods is beyond the scope of a principles-based framework. The *Framework* contains information on the principles-based approach and indicates that there is a need to include quantitative indicators whenever practicable and possible. Additionally, consistency of measurement methods across different reports is of paramount importance. There is outline guidance on the selection of suitable quantitative indicators.

There are additional concerns over the ability to assess future disclosures, and there may be a need for confidence intervals to be disclosed. The preparation of an integrated report requires judgement but there is a requirement for the report to describe its basis of preparation and presentation, including the significant frameworks and methods used to quantify or evaluate material matters. Also included is the disclosure of a summary of how the company determined the materiality limits and a description of the reporting boundaries.

A company should consider how to describe the disclosures without causing a significant loss of competitive advantage. The entity will consider what advantage a competitor could actually gain from information in the integrated report, and will balance this against the need for disclosure.

(b) At 30 April 20X5, Cloud should write down the steel, in accordance with IAS 2 *Inventories*, to its net realisable value of $6 million, therefore reducing profit by $2 million. Cloud should reclassify an equivalent amount of $2 million from equity to profit or loss. Thus there is no net impact on profit or loss from the write down of inventory. The gain remaining in equity of $1 million will affect profit or loss when the steel is sold. Therefore on 3 June 20X5, the gain on the sale of $0·2 million with be recognised in profit or loss, and the remaining gain of $1 million will be transferred to profit or loss from equity.

As regards the property, plant and equipment, at 30 April 20X4, there is a revaluation gain of $4 million being the difference between the carrying amount of $8 million ($10 million – $2 million) and the revalued amount of $12 million. This revaluation gain is recognised in other comprehensive income.

At 30 April 20X5 the asset's value has fallen to $4 million and the carrying amount of the asset is $9 million ($12 million – $3 million). The entity will have transferred $1 million from revaluation surplus to retained earnings, being the difference between historical cost depreciation of $2 million and depreciation on the revalued amount of $3 million. The revaluation loss of $5 million will be charged first against the revaluation surplus remaining in equity of ($4 million – $1 million), ie $3 million and the balance of $2 million will be charged against profit or loss.

IAS 1 requires an entity to present a separate statement of changes in equity showing amongst other items, total comprehensive income for the period, reconciliations between the carrying amounts at the beginning and the end of the period for each component of equity, and an analysis of other comprehensive income.

31 Calcula

Text reference

The concept of integrated reporting is covered in Chapter 18 of your BPP Study Text.

Top tips

Part (a): A good technique to answering part (a) was to consider the key differences between integrated reporting and traditional approaches to reporting performance. Remember the aim of integrated reporting is to show users how the company has created value using the resources at its disposal. By contrast traditional methods of reporting performance are focused on financial metrics such as profitability. Part (b): The second requirement builds upon part (a). Part (a) requires you to illustrate that you understand the theory of integrated reporting in general. There were easy marks going for this part of the question provided you had read Chapter 5 of your BPP Study Text which explores the role of integrated reporting. Part (b) required the application of these points to the scenario, with particular emphasis on how integrated reporting could help Calcula improve its strategic performance.

To score well on this requirement it is critical that your answer is related to Calcula. The scenario is provided to give you the opportunity to show two things. Firstly, that you understand the theory – ie what integrated reporting is – and secondly, for you to show that can apply your knowledge. A good approach to dealing with such questions is to set the scene by identifying what has gone wrong in the scenario. In this case stakeholders (shareholders and employees) are confused as to the strategic direction that Calcula is trying to pursue.

Next, use your knowledge to explain how integrated reporting can help Calcula to communicate its strategy. Integrated reporting places a strong emphasis on relaying what the company stands for through setting out its objectives and strategy to realise these. The introduction of integrated reporting would therefore provide the company with a great opportunity to convey Asha Alexander's new mission.

Easy marks: Three marks were available for incorporating a discussion of the finance director's views. Failure to comment on a particular matter when a question directs you – in this case, making reference to the finance director's statement – loses you easy marks.

Part (c): Was a fairly straightforward requirement. Provided you were able to generate a range of practical implications you should have picked up the 5 easy marks on offer.

Marking scheme

	Marks
Part a:	
Integrated reporting:	
Up to 2 marks for a discussion of how integrated reporting allows for a wider performance appraisal	2
Up to 3 marks for a discussion of value creation	3
Up to 2 marks for a discussion on how short term decisions have long term Implications	2
Up to 2 marks for a discussion of monetary values and the use of KPIs in integrated reporting	2
1 mark for a discussion of materiality	1
	10

Part b:	
1 mark for explaining the current stakeholder confusion at Calcula	1
Up to 3 marks for a discussing how integrated reporting may help communicate Strategy	3
Up to 3 marks for a discussion on how integrated reporting may improve Calcula's Performance	3
Up to 3 marks for a discussion of the finance director's comments	3
	10
Part c:	
1 mark per implication raised related to Calcula	5
	25

(a) **Integrated reporting**

Wider performance appraisal

Integrated reporting is concerned with conveying a wider message on an entity's performance. It is not solely centred on profit and the company's financial position but aims to focus on how the organisations activities interact to create value over the short, medium and long term. It is thought that by producing a holistic view of organisational performance that this will lead to improved management decision making as business decisions are not taken in isolation.

Value creation

In the context of integrated reporting an organisation's resources are referred to as 'capitals'. The International Integrated Reporting Council have identified six capitals which can be used to assess value creation. Increases or decreases in these capitals indicate the level of value created or lost over a period. Capitals cover various types of resources found in a standard organisation. These may include financial capitals, such as the entity's financial reserves, through to its intellectual capital which is concerned with intellectual property and staff knowledge.

Performance evaluation of the six capitals is central to integrated reporting. Throughout time these capitals continually interact with one another, an increase in one may lead to a decrease in another. A decision to purchase a new IT system would improve an entity's 'manufactured' capital while decreasing its financial capital. By contrast the decision to purchase a patent for a new production technology would increase intellectual capital and may also boost financial capital if it reduces costs and increases output. It is important to note that due to the voluntary nature of integrated reporting, organisations are free to report only on those 'capitals' felt to be most relevant.

Short term v long term

In many ways, integrated reporting forces management to balance its short term objectives against its longer term plans. Business decisions which are solely dedicated to the pursuit of increasing profit (financial capital) at the expense of building good relations with key stakeholders such as customers (social capital) are likely to hinder value creation in the longer term.

Performance measures

Integrated reporting is not aimed at attaching a monetary value to every aspect of the organisation's operations. It is fundamentally concerned with evaluating value creation, and uses qualitative and quantitative performance measures to help stakeholders assess how well an organisation is creating value.

The use of KPIs to convey performance is an effective way of reporting. For example, when providing detail on customer satisfaction, this can be communicated as the number of customers retained compared to the previous year. Best practice in integrated reporting requires organisations to report on both positive and negative movements in 'capital'. This ensures the entity's performance is fully communicated and not just those favourable movements. Stakeholders are likely to be as interested (if not more so) in understanding what an organisation has not done well as opposed to only considering the entity's achievements. Integrated reporting ensures that a balanced view of performance is presented.

Materiality

When preparing an integrated report, management should disclose matters which are likely to impact on an organisation's ability to create value. Internal weaknesses and external threats regarded as being materially important are evaluated and quantified. This provides users with an indication of how management intend to combat such instances should they materialise.

(b) **Integrated reporting at Calcula**

Confusion

As a result of the recent management changes at Calcula, the company has struggled to communicate its 'strategic direction' to key stakeholders. The company's annual accounts have made it hard for shareholders to understand Calcula's strategy which in turn has led to confusion. Uncertainty among shareholders and employees is likely to increase the risk of investors selling their shares and talented IT developers seeking employment with competitors.

Communicating strategy

The introduction of integrated reporting may help Calcula to overcome these issues as it places a strong focus on the organisation's future orientation. An integrated report should detail the company's mission and values, the nature of its operations, along with features on how it differentiates itself from its competitors.

Including Calcula's new mission to become the market leader in the specialist accountancy software industry would instantly convey what the organisation stands for.

In line with best practice in integrated reporting, Calcula could supplement its mission with how the board intend to achieve this strategy. Such detail could focus on resource allocations over the short to medium term. For example, plans to improve the company's human capital through hiring innovative software developers working at competing firms would help to support the company's long term mission. To assist users in appraising the company's performance, Calcula should provide details on how it will measure value creation in each 'capital'. 'Human capital' could be measured by the net movement in new joiners to the organisation compared to the previous year.

A key feature of integrated reporting focuses on the need for organisations to use non-financial customer-oriented performance measures (KPI's) to help communicate the entity's strategy. The most successful companies in Calcula's industry are committed to enhancing their offering to customers through producing innovative products. Calcula could report through the use of KPI's how it is delivering on this objective, measures could be set which for example measure the number of new software programs developed in the last two years or report on the number of customer complaints concerning newly released software programs over the period.

Improving long term performance

The introduction of integrated reporting may also help Calcula to enhance its performance. Historically, the company has not given consideration to how decisions in one area have impacted on other areas. This is clearly indicated by former CEO's cost cutting programme which served to reduce the staff training budget. Although, this move may have enhanced the company's short term profitability, boosting financial capital, it has damaged long term value creation.

The nature of the software industry requires successful organisations to invest in staff training to ensure that the products they develop remain innovative in order to attract customers. The decision to reduce the training budget will most likely impact on future profitability if Calcula is unable to produce software customers' demand.

Finance director's comments

As illustrated in the scenario, the finance director's comments indicate a very narrow understanding of how the company's activities and 'capitals' interact with each other in delivering value. To dismiss developments in integrated reporting as simply being a 'fad', suggest that the finance director is unaware of the commitment of ACCA in promoting its introduction. The ACCA's support for integrated reporting may lead to backing from other global accountancy bodies thereby reducing the scope for it be regarded as a passing 'fad'.

However, some critics refute this and argue that the voluntary nature of integrated reporting increases the likelihood that companies will choose not to pursue its adoption. Such individuals highlight that until companies are legally required to comply with integrated reporting guidelines, many will simply regard it as an unnecessary effort and cost.

The finance director's assertion regarding shareholders is likely to some degree to be correct. Investors looking for short term results from an investment might assess Calcula's performance based on improvements in profitability. However, many shareholders will also be interested in how the board propose to create value in the future. Ultimately, Calcula's aim to appease both groups is its focus on maximising shareholder value, the achievement of which requires the successful implementation of both short and long term strategies.

Furthermore, unlike traditional annual accounts, integrated reports highlight the importance of considering a wider range of users. Key stakeholder groups such as Calcula's customers and suppliers are likely to be interested in assessing how the company has met or not met their needs beyond the 'bottom line'. Integrated reporting encourages companies to report performance measures which are closely aligned to the concepts of sustainability and corporate social responsibility. This is implied by the different capitals used: consideration of social relationships and natural capitals do not focus on financial performance but instead are concerned, for example, with the impact an organisation's activities have on the natural environment.

Ultimately as integrated reporting provides senior management with a greater quantity of organisational performance data this should help in identifying previously unrecognised areas which are in need of improvement.

Clearly, a major downside to generating extensive additional data concerns determining which areas to report on. This is made especially difficult as there is no recognised criteria for determining the level of importance of each 'capital'. As we shall explore in part (c), the finance director's remark regarding the increase in the Calcula's workload to comply with integrated reporting practices may have some merit.

It is debatable as to whether the production of an integrated report necessarily leads to an improvement in organisational performance or whether it simply leads to an improvement in the reporting of performance. However, focusing management's attention on the non-financial aspects of Calcula's performance as well as its purely financial performance, could be expected to lead to performance improvements in those areas. For example, if innovation is highlighted as a key factor in sustaining Calcula's long term value, a focus on innovation could help to encourage innovation within the company.

(c) **Implications of implementing integrated reporting**

IT and IS costs

The introduction of integrated reporting at Calcula will most likely require significant upgrades to be made to the company's IT and information system infrastructure. Such developments will be needed to assist Calcula in capturing both financial and non-financial KPI data. Due to the broad range of business activities reported on using integrated reporting (customer, finance and human resources) the associated costs in improving the infrastructure to deliver relevant data about each area is likely to be significant. It may, however, be the case that Calcula's existing information systems are already capable of producing the required non-financial performance data needed in which case it is likely that the focus here will be on investigating which data sets should be included in the integrated report.

Time implications

The process of gathering and collating the data to include in an integrated report is likely to require a significant amount of staff time. This may serve to decrease staff morale especially if staff are expected to undertake this work in addition to completing existing duties. In some cases this may require Calcula to pay employees overtime to ensure all required information is published in the report on time.

Staff costs

To avoid overburdening existing staff the board may decide to appoint additional staff to undertake the work of analysing data for inclusion in the integrated report. This will invariably lead to an increase in staff costs.

Consultancy costs

As this will be Calcula's first integrated report the board may seek external guidance from an organisation which provides specialist consultancy on reporting. Any advice is likely to focus on the contents of the report. The consultant's fees are likely to be significant and will increase the associated implementation costs of introducing integrated reporting.

Disclosure

A potential downside of adopting integrated reporting centres on Calcula potentially volunteering more information about its operations than was actually needed. In the event that Calcula fully disclosed the company's planned strategies it is likely that this could be used by competitors. Such a move is likely to undermine any future moves to out-manoeuvre other industry players. In the event that Calcula have hired an external consultant to support the introduction of integrated reporting it is likely that the advice given by the consultant will stress the need to avoid disclosure of commercially sensitive information.

32 Egin Group

Text reference. Related parties are covered in Chapter 11 of the text.

Top tips. This question dealt with the importance of the disclosure of related party transactions and the criteria determining a related party. Additionally, it required candidates to identify related parties, and to account for goodwill and a loan made to one of the related parties which was a foreign subsidiary. Don't forget, from your group accounting knowledge, that goodwill relating to the foreign subsidiary is treated as a foreign currency asset and translated at the closing rate of exchange.

Easy marks. Part (a) should earn you five very easy marks, as it is basic knowledge. Part (b) is application, but very straightforward. This leaves only nine marks for the more difficult aspects.

Examiner's comment. The importance of related parties and their criteria was quite well answered, although candidates often quoted specific examples rather than the criteria for establishing related parties. The identification of related party relationships was well answered, but the accounting for the goodwill of the foreign subsidiary (and the loan made to it) were poorly answered.

Marking scheme

				Marks
(a)	(i)	Reasons and explanation		5
	(ii)	Egin		5
		Spade		3
		Atomic		3
(b)	Goodwill			5
	Loan			5
			Available	26
			Maximum	25

(a) (i) **Why it is important to disclose related party transactions**

The directors of Egin are correct to say that related party transactions are a normal feature of business. However, where entities are members of the same group, for example parent and subsidiary, the **financial performance and position of both entities can be affected**. An obvious instance of this is where one group company sells goods to another at artificially low prices. Even where there are no actual transactions between group companies, **a parent normally influences the way in which a subsidiary operates**. For example, a parent may instruct a subsidiary not to trade with particular customers or suppliers or not to undertake particular activities. In the absence of other information, users of the financial statements **assume that a company pursues its interests independently** and undertakes transactions on an **arm's length basis** on terms that could have been obtained in a transaction with a third party. Knowledge of related party relationships and transactions affects the way in which users assess a company's operations and the risks and opportunities that it faces. Therefore **details of an entity's controlling party and transactions with related parties should be disclosed**. Even if the company's transactions and operations have not been affected by a related party relationship, **disclosure puts users on notice that they may be affected in future**.

Under IAS 24 *Related party disclosures* a related party is a person or entity that is related to the entity that is preparing its financial statements (the 'reporting entity').

Persons

IAS 24 states that a person or a close member of that person's family is related to a reporting entity if that person:

(1) Has **control** or **joint control** over the reporting entity;

(2) Has **significant influence** over the reporting entity; or

(3) Is a member of the **key management personnel** of the reporting entity or of a parent of the reporting entity.

Entities

An entity is related to a reporting entity if any of the following conditions applies:

(1) The entity and the reporting entity are **members of the same group** (which means that each parent, subsidiary and fellow subsidiary is related to the others).

(2) One entity is an **associate* or joint venture*** of the other entity (or an associate or joint venture of a member of a group of which the other entity is a member).

(3) Both entities are **joint ventures* of the same third party**.

(4) One entity is a **joint venture* of a third entity** and the other entity is an **associate of the third entity**.

(5) The entity is a **post-employment benefit plan** for the benefit of employees of either the reporting entity or an entity related to the reporting entity.

(6) The entity is **controlled** or **jointly controlled** by a person identified in the definition above.

(7) A person identified above as having control or joint control over the reporting entity has **significant influence** over the entity or is a member of the **key management personnel** of the entity (or of a parent of the entity).

*Including subsidiaries of the associate or joint venture.

(ii) **Nature of related party relationships**

Within the Egin Group

Briars and Doye are related parties of Egin because they are **members of the same group** (both subsidiaries of Egin). For the same reason, as fellow subsidiaries, **Briars and Doye** are also **related parties of each other**. **Eye is also a related party of Egin** because it is an **associate of Egin.** (Egin has **significant influence** over Eye.)

Briars and Doye may be related parties of Eye. There is only one director in common and IAS 24 states that entities are not necessarily related simply because they have a director (or other member of key management personnel) in common, or because a member of key management personnel of one entity has significant influence over the other entity. However**, Eye is an associate of Egin**, and therefore **a member of the group** that Briars and Doye are members of (see (2) under 'Entities' above).

Although Tang was sold several months before the year end it was a **related party of Egin, Briars and Doye until then**. Therefore the related party relationship between Tang and the Egin group **should be disclosed** even though there were no transactions between them during the period.

Blue is a related party of Briars as a **director of Briars controls it.** Because the director is not on the management board of Egin it is **not clear whether Blue is also a related party of Egin group**. This would depend on whether the director is considered key management personnel at a group level. The director's services as a consultant to the group may mean that a related party relationship exists. The issue would depend on whether this role meant that this person was directing or controlling a major part of the group's activities and resources.

Between Spade and the Egin Group

Spade is a related party of Doye because it exertss **significant influence** over Doye. This means that the **sale** of plant and equipment **to Spade must be disclosed**. **Egin is not necessarily a related party of Spade** simply because both have an investment in Doye. A related party relationship will only exist if one party **exercises influence** over another **in practice**.

The directors have proposed that disclosures should state that prices charged to related parties are set on an **arm's length basis**. Because the transaction took place **between related parties** by definition it **cannot have taken place on an arm's length basis** and this description would be **misleading**. Doye sold plant and equipment to Spade at **normal selling prices** and this is the information that should be disclosed, provided the terms can be substantiated.

Between Atomic and the Egin Group

Atomic is a related party of Egin because it can exercise **significant influence** over it. Atomic's significant influence over Egin gives it **significant influence over Briars and Doye** as they are controlled by Egin. **Eye is not a related party of Atomic** as atomic has no ability to exercise control or significant influence over Eye

(b) **Goodwill arising on the acquisition of Briars**

IAS 21 *The effect of changes in foreign exchange rates* states that goodwill arising on the acquisition of a foreign subsidiary should be expressed in the functional currency of the foreign operation and **retranslated at the closing rate at each year-end**. Goodwill is calculated and translated as follows:

	Euros m	Rate	$m
Consideration transferred	50		25.0
Non-controlling interests (45 × 20%)	9	2	4.5
Less fair value of identifiable net assets at acquisition	(45)		(22.5)
Goodwill at acquisition	14		7.0
Impairment	(3)	2.5	(1.2)
Exchange loss (balancing figure)			(1.4)
At 31 May 20X6	11	2.5	4.4

Goodwill is measured at **$4.4 million** in the statement of financial position. An impairment loss of **$1.2 million** is **recognised in profit or loss** and an **exchange loss of $1.4 million** is **recognised in other comprehensive income (items that may subsequently be reclassified to profit or loss,** and taken to the translation reserve in equity.

Loan to Briars

The loan is a **financial liability measured at amortised cost**. The loan is measured at **fair value** on initial recognition. Fair value **the price that would be received to sell an asset or paid to transfer a liability in an orderly transaction between market participants at the measurement date**. This would normally be the actual transaction price. However, Egin and Briars are **related parties** and the transaction **has not taken place on normal commercial terms**.

IFRS 9 states that it is necessary to **establish what the transaction price would have been** in an orderly transaction between market participants at the measurement date. The amount that will eventually be repaid to Egin is $10 million and the normal commercial rate of interest is 6%. Therefore the fair value of the loan is its **discounted present value**, which is **retranslated at the closing rate** at each year-end.

Therefore the loan is measured at the following amounts in the statement of financial position:

	$'000	Rate	Euros 000
At 1/6/20X5 ($10 \times \frac{1}{1.06^2}$)	8,900	2	17,800
Interest (unwinding of discount) (8,900 × 6%)	534	2.3	1,228
Exchange loss			4,557
At 31/5/20X6 ($10 \times \frac{1}{1.06}$)	9,434	2.5	23,585

The **unwinding of the discount** is recognised as a **finance cost** in profit or loss for the year and the **exchange loss** is also **recognised in profit or loss.**

Note. It would also be possible to calculate the finance cost for the year ended 31 May 20X6 at the closing rate. This would increase the exchange loss and the total expense recognised in profit and loss would be the same.

33 Preparation question: Control

(a) IFRS 10 states that an investor **controls** an investee if and only if it has all of the following.

Power over the investee

(1) Exposure, or rights, to **variable returns** from its involvement with the investee, and
(2) The **ability to use its power** over the investee to affect the amount of the investor's returns.

Power is defined as **existing rights that give the current ability to direct the relevant activities of the investee**. There is no requirement for that power to have been exercised.

Relevant activities may include:

- Selling and purchasing goods or services
- Managing financial assets
- Selecting, acquiring and disposing of assets
- Researching and developing new products and processes
- Determining a funding structure or obtaining funding.

In some cases assessing power is straightforward, for example, where power is obtained directly and solely from having the majority of voting rights or potential voting rights, and as a result the ability to direct relevant activities.

(b)

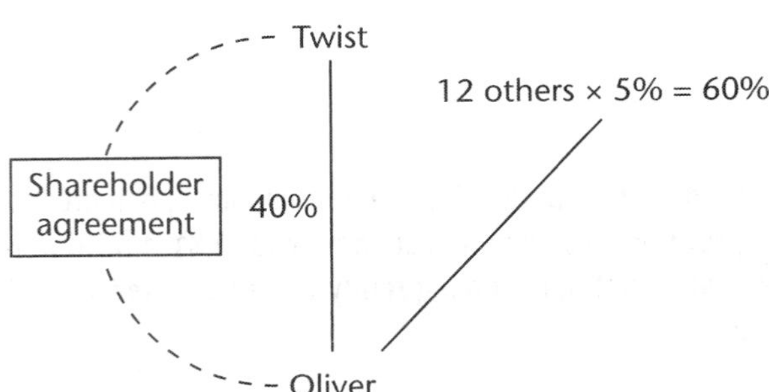

The absolute size of Twist's holding and the relative size of the other shareholdings alone are not conclusive in determining whether the investor has rights sufficient to give it power. However, the fact that Twist has **a contractual right to appoint, remove and set the remuneration of management** is sufficient to conclude that it **has power over Oliver**. The fact that Twist has not exercised this right is not a determining factor when assessing whether Twist has power. In conclusion, Twist does control Oliver, and should consolidate it.

(c)

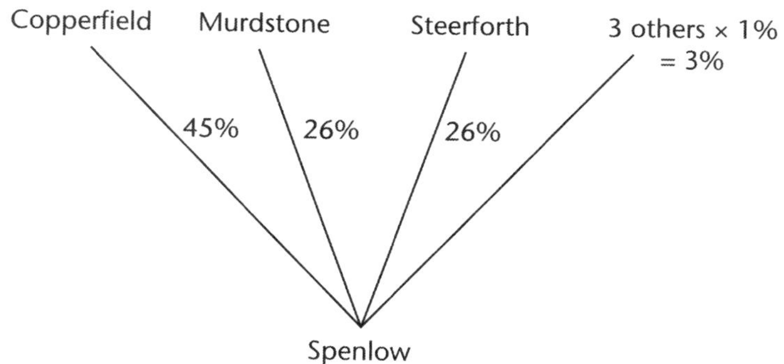

In this case, the size of Copperfield's voting interest and its size relative to the other shareholdings are sufficient to conclude that Copperfield **does not have power**. Only two other investors, Murdstone and Steerforth, would need to co-operate to be able to prevent Copperfield from directing the relevant activities of Spenlow.

(d)

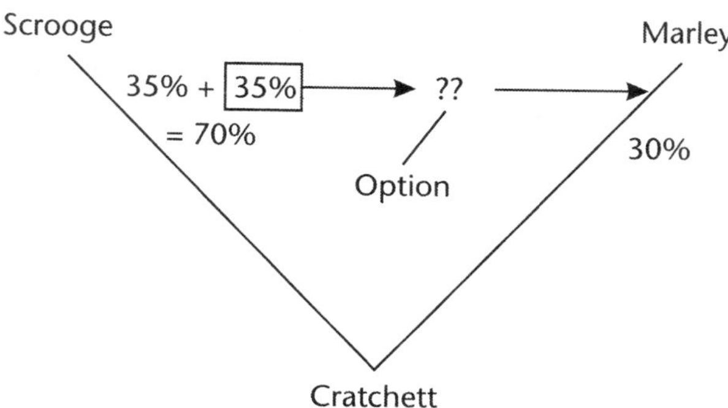

Scrooge holds a majority of the current voting rights of Cratchett, so is likely to meet the power criterion because it appears to have the current ability to direct the relevant activities. Although Marley has currently exercisable options to purchase additional voting rights (that, if exercised, would give it a majority of the voting rights in Cratchett), the terms and conditions associated with those options are such that the options are not considered substantive.

Thus voting rights, even combined with potential voting rights, may not be the deciding factor. Scrooge should consolidate Cratchett.

34 Marrgrett

Text reference. These topics are covered in Chapter 12 of the BPP Study Text, apart from disposals, which is covered in Chapter 14.

Top tips. This question required a discussion of the impact of the revisions to IFRS 3 *Business combinations* on various aspects of group accounting. These topics are covered in the BPP Study Text, but unless you were very familiar with the changes from old to new, you would not have been advised to attempt this question. That said, it was not technically demanding. Note that since this question was set there have been further revisions to group accounting, covered where relevant elsewhere in this kit.

Easy marks. There are no marks that are easier to gain than others – either you know the subject or you don't!

Examiner's comment. Answers were generally quite good but the main issue was that candidates found it difficult to assimilate relevant information.. Particular issues included failing to recognise that the existing 30% interest in the associate should be fair valued when control of the subsidiary is gained, also dealing with the payments to the subsidiary's directors created a problem and a minority of candidates stated that the full goodwill method was mandatory.

Marking scheme

		Marks
Consideration		6
IFRS 3 and consideration		5
Consideration		2
Intangible assets		2
NCI		5
Finalisation and reorganisation provision		2
IFRS 10		3
Professional marks		2
	Available	25

Revision of IFRS 3 Business combinations

IFRS 3 views **the group as an economic entity.** This means that it treats all providers of equity – including non-controlling interests – as shareholders in the group, even if they are not shareholders of the parent.

All business combinations are accounted for as **acquisitions**. The revisions to IFRS 3 affect both the consideration, and the business acquired. Specifically, **all consideration is now measured at fair value,** and there are implications for the valuation of the non-controlling interest.

Marrgrett is proposing to purchase additional shares in its associate, Josey. An increase from 30% to 70% will **give control,** as the holding passes the all-important 50% threshold. The changes to IFRS 3 have far-reaching implications for various aspects of the acquisition, which is what the standard calls a 'business combination achieved in stages'.

Equity interest already held

Consideration includes cash, assets, contingent consideration, equity instruments, options and warrants. It also includes the **fair value of any equity interest already held**, which marks a departure from the previous version of IFRS 3. This means that **the 30% holding must be re-measured to fair value** at the date of the acquisition of the further 40% holding. The revalued 30% stake, together with the consideration transferred in the form of cash and shares, is compared to the fair value of Josey's net assets at the date control was obtained, in order to arrive at a figure for goodwill.

Any **gain or loss** on the revaluation of the associate is taken to **profit or loss for the year**.

Transaction costs

The original IFRS 3 required fees (legal, accounting, valuation etc) paid in relation to a business acquisition to be included in the cost of the acquisition, which meant that they were measured as part of goodwill.

Under the revised IFRS 3 **costs relating to the acquisition must be recognised as an expense** at the time of the acquisition. They are not regarded as an asset. (Costs of issuing debt or equity are to be accounted for under the rules of IFRS 9.)

Share options

As an incentive to the shareholders and employees of Josey to remain in the business, Marrgrett has offered share options in Josey. These are conditional on them remaining in employment for two years after the acquisition, that is they are contingent on future events. The question arises of whether they are **contingent consideration**, for which the treatment is specified in the revised IFRS 3, **or as compensation** for services after the acquisition, for which the treatment is given in IFRS 2 Share-based payment.

The conditions attached to the share options are employment based, rather than contingent on, say, the performance of the company. Accordingly the options must be treated as **compensation and valued under the rules of IFRS 2. The charge will be to post-acquisition earnings**, since the options are given in exchange for services after the acquisition.

Contingent consideration

The additional shares being offered to Josey's shareholders to the value of $50,000 are contingent on the achievement of a certain level of profitability. These are contingent consideration, defined in IFRS 3 as:

> Usually, an obligation of the acquirer to transfer additional assets or equity interests to the former owners of an acquiree as part of the exchange for control of the acquiree if specified future events occur or conditions are met.

The original IFRS 3 required contingent consideration to be accounted for **only if it was probable that it would become payable** and could be measured reliably. Subsequent changes in the amount of the contingent consideration were accounted for as adjustments to the cost of the business combination, and therefore generally as changes to goodwill.

However, the revised IFRS 3 recognises that, by entering into an acquisition, the acquirer becomes obliged to make additional payments. Not recognising that obligation means that the consideration recognised at the acquisition date is not fairly stated. Accordingly, the revised IFRS 3 **requires recognition of contingent consideration, measured at fair value, at the acquisition date**.

The shares worth up to $50,000 meet the IAS 32 *Financial instruments: presentation* definition of a financial liability. This contingent consideration will be **measured at fair value,** and any **changes** to the fair value on subsequent re-measurement will be taken to **profit or loss for the year**.

Intangible assets

Josey's intangible assets, which include trade names, internet domain names and non-competition agreements, will be **recognised on acquisition** by Marrgrett of a controlling stake. IFRS 3 revised gives more detailed guidance on intangible assets than did the previous version; as a result, more intangibles may be recognised than was formerly the case. The more intangibles are recognised, the lower the figure for goodwill, which is consideration transferred less fair value of assets acquired and liabilities assumed.

Non-controlling interest

As indicated above, the revised IFRS views the group as an economic entity and so non-controlling shareholders are also shareholders in the group. This means that goodwill attributable to the non-controlling interest needs to be recognised.

The non-controlling interest now forms part of the calculation of goodwill. The question now arises as to how it should be valued.

The 'economic entity' principle suggests that the non-controlling interest should be valued at fair value. In fact, IFRS 3 gives a **choice**:

> For each business combination, the acquirer shall measure any non-controlling interest in the acquiree **either at fair value or at the non-controlling interest's proportionate share of the acquiree's identifiable net assets**. *(IFRS 3)*

IFRS 3 revised suggests that the closest approximation to fair value will be the market price of the shares held by the non-controlling shareholders just before the acquisition by the parent.

Non-controlling interest at fair value will be different from non-controlling interest at proportionate share of the acquiree's net assets. The difference is goodwill attributable to non-controlling interest, which may be, but often is not, proportionate to goodwill attributable to the parent.

Effect of type of consideration

The nature of the consideration transferred – cash, shares, contingent, and so on – **does not affect the goodwill**. However, the structure of the payments may affect post-acquisition profits. For example if part of the consideration is contingent (as here), changes to the fair value will be reflected in profit or loss for the year in future years.

Partial disposal

Under the revised IFRS 3, the treatment of a partial disposal depends on whether or not control is retained. Generally, control is lost when the holding is decreased to less than 50%.

On disposal of a controlling interest, any retained interest (an associate or trade investment) is measured at fair value on the date that control is lost. This fair value is used in the calculation of the gain or loss on disposal, and also becomes the carrying amount for subsequent accounting for the retained interest.

If the **50%** boundary is **not crossed**, as when the interest in a subsidiary is reduced, the event is treated as a **transaction between owners.**

Whenever the 50% boundary is crossed, the existing interest is revalued, and a gain or loss is reported in profit or loss for the year. If the 50% boundary is not crossed, no gain or loss is reported; instead there is an **adjustment to the parent's equity**.

Margrett intends to **retain control of the first subsidiary**, so in this case there will be no gain or loss, but an adjustment to the Margrett's equity to reflect the increase in non-controlling interest. In the case of the **second subsidiary,** however, **control is lost**. A **gain will be recognised on the portion sold, and also on the portion retained,** being the difference between the fair value and the book value of the interest retained.

Re-organisation provision

IFRS 10 *Consolidated financial statements* explains that a plan to restructure a subsidiary following an acquisition is not a present obligation of the acquiree at the acquisition date, unless it meets the criteria in IAS 37 *Provisions, contingent liabilities and contingent assets.* This is very unlikely to be the case at the acquisition date. Therefore, Margrett **should not recognise a liability** for the re-organisation of the group at the date of the acquisition.

This **prevents creative accounting**. An acquirer cannot set up a provision for restructuring or future losses of a subsidiary and then release this to profit or loss in subsequent periods in order to reduce losses or smooth profits.

35 Preparation question: Associate

J GROUP CONSOLIDATED STATEMENT OF FINANCIAL POSITION AS AT 31 DECEMBER 20X5

	$'000
Assets	
Non-current assets	
Freehold property (1,950 + 1,250 + 370 (W7))	3,570
Plant and equipment (795 + 375)	1,170
Investment in associate (W3)	480
	5,220
Current assets	
Inventories (575 + 300 – 20 (W6))	855
Trade receivables (330 + 290))	620
Cash at bank and in hand (50 + 120)	170
	1,645
	6,865
	$'000
Equity and liabilities	
Equity attributable to owners of the parent	
Issued share capital	2,000
Retained earnings	1,785
	3,785
Non-controlling interests (W5)	890
Total equity	4,675
Non-current liabilities	
12% debentures (500 + 100)	600
Current liabilities	
Bank overdraft	560
Trade payables (680 + 350)	1,030
	1,590
Total liabilities	2,190
	6,865

Workings

1 *Group structure*

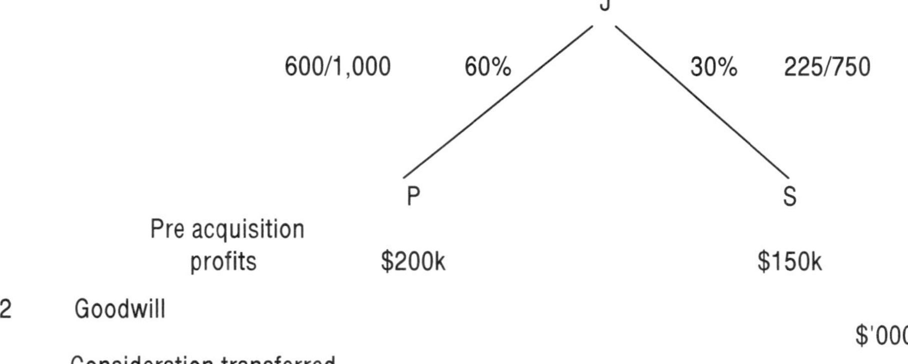

2 Goodwill

	$'000	$'000
Consideration transferred		1,000
NCI (at 'full' FV: 400 × $1.65)		660
Net assets acquired:		
Share capital	1,000	
Retained earnings at acquisition	200	
Fair value adjustment (W7)	400	
		(1,600)
		60
Impairments to date		(60)
Year-end value		–

3 *Investment in associate*

	$'000
Cost of associate	500.0
Share of post acquisition retained reserves (W4)	72.0
Less impairment of investment in associate	(92.0)
	480.0

4 *Retained earnings*

	J Co $'000	*P Co* $'000	*S Co* $'000
Retained earnings per question	1,460	885	390
Unrealised profit (W6)		(20)	
Fair value adjustment movement (W6)		(30)	
Retained earnings at acquisition		(200)	(150)
		635	240
P Co: share of post acquisition retained earnings 60% × 635	381		
S Co: share of post acquisition retained earnings 30% × 240	72		
Goodwill impairments to date			
P Co: 60 (W2) × 60%	(36)		
S Co	(92)		
	1,785		

5 *Non-controlling interests*

	$'000
NCI at acquisition (W2)	660
NCI share of post acq'n ret'd earnings ((W4) 635 × 40%)	254
NCI share of impairment losses ((W2) 60 × 40%)	(24)
	890

6 *Unrealised profit on inventories*

P Co ——→ J Co $100k × 25/125 = $20,000

7 Fair value adjustment table

	At acquisition	*Movement*	*At reporting date*	
	$'000	$'000	$'000	
Land	200		200	
Buildings	200	(30)	170	(200 × 34/40)
	400	(30)	370	

36 Preparation question: 'D'-shaped group

(a) BAUBLE GROUP
CONSOLIDATED STATEMENT OF FINANCIAL POSITION AS AT 31 DECEMBER 20X9

	$'000
Non-current assets	
Property, plant and equipment (720 + 60 + 70)	850
Goodwill (W2)	111
	961
Current assets (175 + 95 + 90)	360
	1,321
Equity attributable to owners of the parent	
Share capital – $1 ordinary shares	400
Retained earnings (W3)	600
	1,000
Non-controlling interest (W4)	91
	1,091
Current liabilities (120 + 65 + 45)	230
	1,321

Workings

1 *Group Structure*

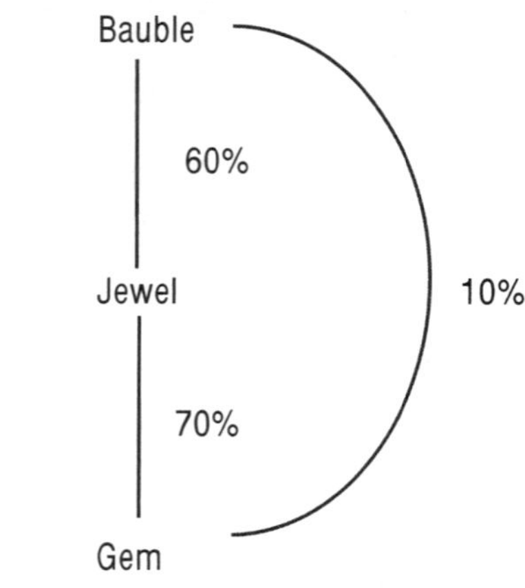

Bauble interest in Gem		
	– Direct	10%
	– Indirect (60% × 70%)	42%
		52%
Non-controlling interest in Gem		48%

2 *Goodwill*

		Jewel		*Gem*	
		$'000	$'000	$'000	$'000
Consideration transferred: Bauble			142		43.0
Consideration transferred: Jewel				(100 × 60%)	60.0
NCI	(145 × 40%)		58	(90 × 48%)	43.2
Net assets at acq'n as represented by:					
Share capital		100		50	
Ret'd earnings		45		40	
			(145)		(90.0)
Goodwill			55		56.2

Total goodwill = $111,200

3 *Consolidated retained earnings*

	B	*J*	*G*
	$'000	$'000	$'000
Per Q	560	90	65
Less: pre-acquisition ret'd earnings		(45)	(40)
		45	25
J – share of post acquisition ret'd earnings (45 × 60%)	27		
G – share of post acquisition ret'd earnings (25 × 52%)	13		
	600		

4 *Non-controlling interests*

	Jewel	*Gem*
	$'000	$'000
NCI at acquisition (W2)	58	43.2
NCI share of post acquisition retained earnings:		
Jewel ((W3) 45 × 40%)	18	
Gem ((W3) 25 × 48%)		12
NCI in investment in Gem (100 × 40%)	(40)	
	36	55.2
	91.2	

(b) **Goodwill**

		Jewel		*Gem*	
		$'000	$'000	$'000	$'000
Consideration transferred: Bauble			142		43.0
Consideration transferred: Jewel				(100 × 60%)	60.0
NCI	(160 × 40%)		64	(90 × 48%)	43.2
Net assets at acq'n as represented by:					
Share capital		100		50	
Ret'd earnings		60		40	
			(160)		(90)
Goodwill			46		56.2
			102.2		

37 Preparation question: Sub-subsidiary

Text reference. Complex groups are covered in Chapter 13.

Top tips. This question is quite straightforward as long as you remember how to calculate the NCI of a sub-subsidiary. Points to watch in this question are the treatment of intragroup transactions and the calculation of non-controlling interest.

Easy marks. With complex groups, remember to sort out the group structure first. There are enough straightforward marks available here if you remember your basic rules for consolidations. The consolidation is quite straightforward as long as you remember how to calculate the NCI of a sub-subsidiary.

(a) EXOTIC GROUP
CONSOLIDATED STATEMENT OF PROFIT OR LOSS AND OTHER COMPREHENSIVE INCOME
FOR THE YEAR ENDED 31 DECEMBER 20X9

	$'000
Revenue: 45,600 + 24,700 + 22,800 – (W6) 740	92,360
Cost of sales: 18,050 + 5,463 + 5,320 – (W6) 740+ (W6) 15 + (W6) 15(W6)	(28,123)
Gross profit	64,237
Distribution costs (3,325 + 2,137 + 1,900)	(7,362)
Administrative expenses (3,475 + 950 + 1,900)	(6,325)
Finance costs	(325)
Profit before tax	50,225
Income tax expense (8,300 + 5,390 + 4,241)	(17,931)
Profit for the year	32,294
Other comprehensive income for the year (items that will not be reclassified to P/L)	
Revaluation of property (200 + 100)	300
Total comprehensive income	32,594
Profit attributable to:	
Owners of the parent	28,581
Non-controlling interest (W4)	3,713
	32,294
Total comprehensive income attributable to:	
Owners of the parent	28,871
Non-controlling interest (W4)	3,723
	32,594

(b) EXOTIC GROUP
CONSOLIDATED STATEMENT OF FINANCIAL POSITION AS AT 31 DECEMBER 20X9

	$'000
Non-current assets	
Property, plant and equipment: 35,483 + 24,273 + 13,063 + (W7) 575	73,394
Goodwill (W2)	3,520
	76,914
Current assets :1,568 + 9,025 + 8,883 – (W6) 15 – (W6) 15	19,446
	96,360
Equity attributable to owners of the parent	
Share capital	8,000
Retained earnings (W3)	56,642
	64,642
Non-controlling interest (W4)	8,584
	73,226
Current liabilities (13,063 + 10,023 + 48)	23,134
	96,360

Workings

1 *Group structure*

Exotic
| 90%
Melon
| 80%
Kiwi

Effective interest (90% × 80%)	72%
∴ Non-controlling interest	28%
	100%

2 *Goodwill*

	Melon	*Kiwi*	
	$000	$000	$000
Consideration transferred	6,650	3,800 × 90%	3,420
Non-controlling interests (at 'full' fair value)	500		900
FV of identifiable net assets at acq'n:			
Per qu/ 2,000 (SC) + 950 (RE)	(5,000)		(2,950)
	2,150		1,370
		3,520	

3 *Retained earnings*

	Exotic	*Melon*	*Kiwi*
	$'000	$'000	$'000
Retained earnings per question	22,638	24,075	19,898
Less: PUP (W6)		(15)	(15)
Pre-acquisition retained earnings		(1,425)	(950)
		22,635	18,933
Share of Melon (22,635 × 90%)	20,372		
Share of Kiwi (18,933 × (W1) 72%)	13,632		
	56,642		

4 *Non-controlling interest (SOCI)*

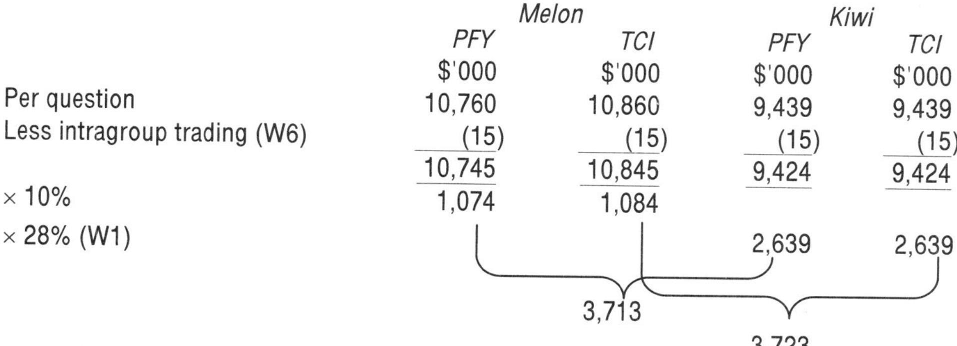

	Melon *PFY*	*Melon* *TCI*	*Kiwi* *PFY*	*Kiwi* *TCI*
	$'000	$'000	$'000	$'000
Per question	10,760	10,860	9,439	9,439
Less intragroup trading (W6)	(15)	(15)	(15)	(15)
	10,745	10,845	9,424	9,424
× 10%	1,074	1,084		
× 28% (W1)			2,639	2,639
	3,713		3,723	

5 *Non-controlling interests (statement of financial position)*

	Melon	*Kiwi*
	$000	$000
NCI at acquisition (W2)	500	900
NCI share of post acquisition retained earnings:		
Melon ((W3) 22,635 × 10%)	2,263.5	
Kiwi ((W3) 18,933 × (W1) 28%)		5,301.2
NCI in investment in Kiwi (3,800 × 10%)	(380)	
	2,383.5	6,201.2
	8,584.7	

6 *Intragroup trading*

(i) Cancel intragroup sale/purchase:

DEBIT group revenue (260 + 480)	$740,000	
CREDIT group cost of sales		$740,000

(ii) Unrealised profit

	$'000
Melon (60 × 25/100)	15
Kiwi (75 × 25/125)	15

Adjust in books of seller:

DEBIT Cost of sales/retained earnings

CREDIT Group Inventories

7 *Fair value adjustment*

Melon:	*At acqn 1Jan 20X5*	*Movement*	*At year end 31Dec 20X9*
	$'000	$'000	$'000
Land: 5,000.000 – (3,000,000 + 1,425,000)	575	–	575

8 *Revenue **

	$'000
Exotic	45,600
Melon	24,700
Kiwi	22,800
Less intragroup sales (W6)	(740)
	92,360

9 *Cost of sales **

	$'000
Exotic	18,050
Melon	5,463
Kiwi	5,320
Add PUP (W6): Melon	15
Kiwi	15
	28,123

* **Note**. Workings 8 and 9 are included for completeness. You should do the workings on the face of the SPLOCI.

38 Glove

Text reference. Complex groups are covered in Chapter 13.

Top tips. This question required the preparation of a consolidated statement of financial position of a group which contained a sub-subsidiary. In addition, candidates had to account for brand names, a retirement benefit plan, a convertible bond, and an exchange of plant. The question was a little easier than in previous exams, and you should not have been alarmed at getting both pensions and financial instruments, since only the straightforward aspects were being tested.

Easy marks. There are marks for standard consolidation calculations (goodwill, NCI, retained earnings) which should be familiar to you from your earlier studies, and for setting out the proforma, even if you didn't have time to do the fiddly adjustments. The convertible bond – don't be scared because it is a financial instrument! – is something you have covered at an earlier level.

Examiner's comment. The accounting for the sub-subsidiary was reasonably well answered but candidates found the application of the corridor approach a major problem. The convertible bond element was relatively straight-forward and would have sat quite well in a lower level paper. However, candidates found this element quite difficult.

The parameters of the syllabus in the area of financial instruments have been well documented, but candidates do not seem to be able to grasp the fundamentals of the subject. The treatment of the trade name was again not well answered with the principles of recognition seldom set out correctly. Overall, the consolidation element was quite well answered but the additional technical elements were poorly treated by candidates in their answers.

Marking scheme

		Marks
Equity		7
Reserves		6
Non-current liabilities		3
Defined benefit plan		4
Convertible bond		4
Plant		2
Trade name		3
	Available	29
	Maximum	25

GLOVE GROUP

CONSOLIDATED STATEMENT OF FINANCIAL POSITION AS AT 31 MAY 20X7

	$m
Non-current assets	
Property, plant and equipment	
260 + 20 + 26 + 6 (W6) + 5(W6) + 3 (W9)	320.0
Goodwill (W2)	10.1
Other intangibles: trade name (W6)	4.0
Investments in equity instruments	10.0
	344.1
Current assets: 65 + 29 + 20	114.0
Total assets	458.1
Equity and liabilities	
Equity attributable to owners of parent	
Ordinary shares	150.0
Other reserves (W4)	30.7
Retained earnings (W3)	150.9
Equity component of convertible debt (W8)	1.6
	333.2
Non-controlling interests (W5)	28.9
	362.1
Non-current liabilities (W10)	
45 + 2 + 3 + 0.1 (W7) – 30 + 28.9 (W8)	49.0
Current liabilities: 35 + 7 + 5	47.0
	96.0
Total equity and liabilities	458.1

Workings

1 *Group structure*

Glove			
1 June 20X5 — 80%		Retained earnings	$10m
		Other reserves	$4m
Body			
1 June 20X5 — 70%		Retained earnings	$6m
		Other reserves	$8m
Fit			

	%
Effective interest: 80% × 70%	56
∴ Non-controlling interest	44
	100

2 *Goodwill*

	Glove in Body		*Body in Fit*	
	$m	$m	$m	$m
Consideration transferred		60	(30 × 80%)	24.00
Non-controlling interests	(65 × 20%)	13	(39 × 44%)	17.16
Fair value of net assets at acq'n:				
Per question	60		39	
Trade name (W6)	5		–	
		(65)		(39.00)
		8		2.16
		10.16		

3 *Retained earnings*

	Glove	*Body*	*Fit*
	$m	$m	$m
Per question	135.00	25	10
Fair value movement (W6)	–	(1)	–
Convertible bonds (W8) (2.3 – 1.8)	(0.50)		
Assets exchange:			
Adjustment to plant (W9)	3.00		
Less pre-acquisition		(10)	(6)
		14	4
Share of Body			
80% × 14	11.20		
Share of Fit			
56% × 4	2.24		
	150.94		

4 *Other reserves*

	Glove	*Body*	*Fit*
	$m	$m	$m
Per question	30.0	5	8
Pension scheme (W7)	(0.1)		
Less pre-acquisition		(4)	(8)
		1	–
Share of body			
80% × 1	0.8		
Share of Fit			
56% × 0	0.0		
	30.7		

5 *Non-controlling interests*

	Body	Fit
	$m	$m
NCI at acquisition (W2)	13	17.16
NCI share of post acquisition retained earnings:		
Body ((W3) 14 × 20%)	2.8	
Fit ((W3) 4 × 44%)		1.76
NCI share of post acquisition other reserves:		
Body ((W4) 1 × 20%)	0.2	
Fit ((W4) 0 × 44%)		0
NCI in investment in Fit (30 × 20%)	(6)	
	10	18.92
	28.92	

6 *Fair value adjustments*

	At acquisition	Movement (2 years)	At reporting date (31 May 20X7)
	$m	$m	$m
Body			
Land: 60 – (40 + 10 + 4)	6	–	6
Brand name (note)	5	(1)	4
	11	(1)	10
Fit			
Land: 39 – (20 + 8 + 6)	5	–	5

Note. The trade name is an internally generated intangible asset. While these are not normally recognised under IAS 38 *Intangible assets*, IFRS 3 *Business combinations* allows recognition if the fair value can be measured reliably. Thus this Glove should recognise an intangible asset on acquisition (at 1 June 20X5). This will reduce the value of goodwill.

The trade name is amortised over ten years, of which two have elapsed: $5m × 2/10 = $1m.

So the value is $(5 – 1)m = $4m in the consolidated statement of financial position.

7 *Defined benefit pension scheme*

The amount to be recognised is as follows

	$m
Loss on remeasurement through OCI on defined benefit obligation	(1.0)
Gain on remeasurement through OCI on plan assets	0.9
	(0.1)

Accounting entries:

DEBIT	Other comprehensive income	$0.1m	
CREDIT	Net defined benefit liability		$0.1m

8 *Convertible bond*

Under IAS 32, the bond must be split into a liability and an equity component:

	$m	$m
Proceeds: 30,000 × $1,000		30
Present value of principal in three years' time		
$\$30m \times \frac{1}{1.08^3}$	23.815	
Present value of interest annuity		
$30m × 6% = $1,800,000		
$\times \frac{1}{1.08}$	1.667	
$\times \frac{1}{(1.08)^2}$	1.543	
$\times \frac{1}{(1.08)^3}$	1.429	
Liability component		(28.454)
∴ Equity component		1.546

Rounded to $1.6m

Balance of liability at 31 May 20X7

	$'000
Balance b/d at 1 June 20X6	28,454
Effective interest at 8%	2,276
Coupon interest paid at 6%	(1,800)
Balance c/d at 31 May 20X7	28,930

9 *Exchange of assets*

The cost of the plant should be measured at the fair value of the asset given up, rather than the carrying value. An adjustment must be made to the value of the plant, and to retained earnings.

	$
Fair value of land	7
Carrying value of land	(4)
∴ Adjustment required	3

DEBIT	Plant	$3m	
CREDIT	Retained earnings		$3m

10 *Non-current liabilities*

Note. This working is for additional information. To save time, you should do yours on the face of the consolidated position statement

	$m	$m
Non-current liabilities per question:		
Glove	45	
Body	2	
Fit	3	
		50.0
Unrecognised actuarial losses (W7)		0.1
Proceeds of convertible bond		(30.0)
Value of liability component		28.9
		49.0

39 Case study question: Jarvis

Text reference. Complex groups are covered in Chapter 14, pensions in Chapter 4, deferred tax in Chapter 6, financial instruments in Chapter 7 and environmental issues in Chapter 18.

Top tips. Part (a) is a consolidated statement of profit or loss and other comprehensive income for a complex group with the sub-subsidiary being acquired part way through the year. This part includes a number of adjustments including intra-group trading and unrealised profit, the sale of a financial asset, pension costs, a revaluation of a foreign currency asset, a hedge and deferred tax. A methodical step by step approach is key here. Note that question 1 often includes adjustments on pensions and financial instruments as in this case.

Part (b) requires a discussion of corporate responsibility and in particular social and environmental reporting. Part (c) requires consideration of the ethical factors involved in companies disclosing large amounts of narrative information in these areas but not viewing corporate responsibility as part of corporate strategy. Both of these topics have been identified as being likely to appear on a recurring basis in question 1 so make sure you are comfortable with answering discussion type questions.

Easy marks. There are some standard consolidation workings in Part (a), and you could slot in the caption for, say, 'gain on property revaluation' even if you get the calculation wrong. Leave enough time for Parts (b) and (c) – the ACCA examination/examining team has commented in the past that candidates often do not. Part (b) is straightforward knowledge and Part (c) allows scope for interpretation – it is more important that you show awareness of the issues than come up with a 'correct' answer.

Marking scheme

			Marks
(a)	Revenue and COS adjustment – intragroup sale	1	
	Unrealised profit	1	
	Deferred tax on unrealised profit (1 calc, 1 sign)	2	
	COS – pension adjustment	2	
	Elimination of dividend	1	
	Impairment loss (including 2 for goodwill and 2 for net assets of Whitehill)	7	
	Investment in equity instrument (and current tax adjustment)	3	
	Finance income (hedge)	1	
	Finance costs – pension adjustment	1	
	Non-controlling interests – PFY	2½	
	Non-controlling interests – TCI	2½	
	Gain on property revaluation (including 1 for deferred tax)	4	
	Actuarial losses on defined benefit pension plan	2	
	Cash flow hedge – effective portion to OCI	2	
	Basic consolidation (J + W + 9/12 C)	3	
			35
(b)	Explain corporate responsibility	2	
	Public interest	2	
	Shareholder value	2	
	Government/regulation	1	
	Lack of requirements	1	
	Quality of discussion	2	
			10

			Marks
(c)	Not part of strategy	2	
	Public relations	2	
	Possibly misleading	1	
			5
			50

(a) JARVIS GROUP
CONSOLIDATED STATEMENT OF PROFIT OR LOSS AND OTHER COMPREHENSIVE INCOME
FOR THE YEAR ENDED 31 DECEMBER 20X8

	$m
Revenue (4,500 + 2,800 + (1,800 × 9/12) – (W3) 400)	8,250
Cost of sales (3,200 + 2,000 + (1,200 × 9/12) – (W3) 400 + (W3) 20 – (W4) 11 + (W7) 40)	(5,749)
Gross profit	2,501
Other income (80 + 20 – (W5) 48 + (W9) 20)	72
Distribution costs (220 + 140 + (80 × 9/12))	(420)
Administrative expenses (180 + 110 + (60 × 9/12))	(335)
Finance income (W11)	2
Finance costs (40 + 20 + (12 × 9/12) + (W4) 8)	(77)
Profit before tax	1,743
Income tax expense (280 + 160 + (120 × 9/12) – (W3) 6 – (W9) 3)	(521)
Profit for the year	1,222
Other comprehensive income (items that will not be reclassified to profit or loss):	
Gains on property revaluation, net of tax (140 + 90 + (80 × 9/12) + (W10) 7 – (W10) 2)	295
Loss on remeasurement of defined benefit pension plan obligation ((W4) 9 – 6)	(3)
	292
Items that may subsequently be reclassified to profit or loss:	
Cash flow hedge (W11)	10
Other comprehensive income for the year:	302
Total comprehensive income for the year	1,524
Profit attributable to:	
Owners of the parent (1,222 – 202)	1,020
Non-controlling interests (W2)	202
	1,222
Total comprehensive income attributable to:	
Owners of the parent (1,524 – 251)	1,273
Non-controlling interests (W2)	251
	1,524

Workings

1 *Group structure*

Jarvis

1.1.20X7 ↓ 80%

Whitehill

1.4.20X8 ↓ 60%

Crow

Effective interest in Crow (80% × 60%)	48%
∴ Non-controlling interests	52%
	100%

Timeline

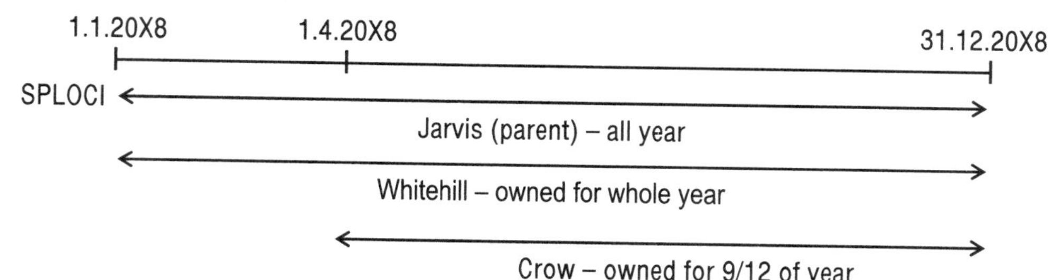

2 *Non-controlling interests*

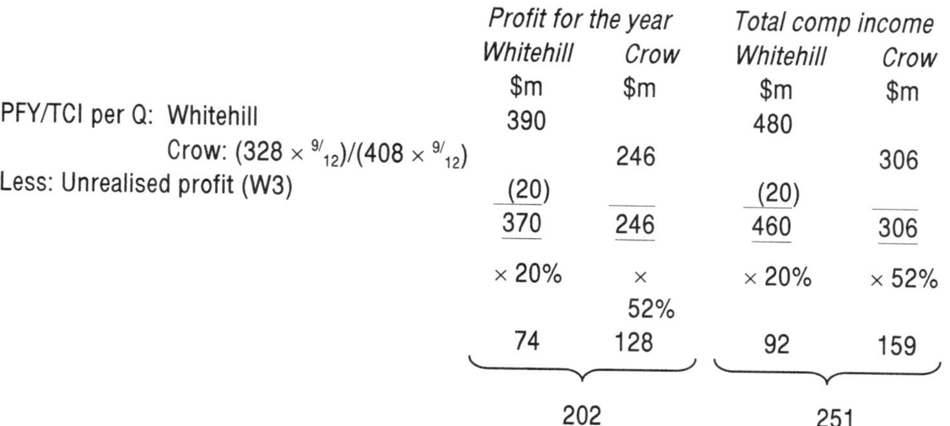

	Profit for the year		*Total comp income*	
	Whitehill	*Crow*	*Whitehill*	*Crow*
	$m	$m	$m	$m
PFY/TCI per Q: Whitehill	390		480	
Crow: $(328 \times {}^{9}/_{12})/(408 \times {}^{9}/_{12})$		246		306
Less: Unrealised profit (W3)	(20)		(20)	
	370	246	460	306
	× 20%	× 52%	× 20%	× 52%
	74	128	92	159
	202		251	

3 *Intragroup trading*

Cancel intragroup sale/purchase:

DEBIT	Revenue	$400m	
CREDIT	Cost of sales		$400m

Unrealised profit on intragroup sale:

Unrealised profit = $100m × 20%
= $20m

In Whitehill's (seller's) books:

DEBIT	Cost of sales	$20m	
CREDIT	Inventories		$20m

This is profit made by Whitehill therefore will be used to adjust for the non-controlling interests.

Deferred tax effect of unrealised profit:

Deductible temporary difference = $20m × 30%
= $6m

This is a deferred tax asset and therefore is a credit to the *group* income tax expense, as a consolidation adjustment:

DEBIT	Deferred tax asset	$6m	
CREDIT	Income tax expense (P/L)		$6m

The deferred tax does not affect the non-controlling interests, despite relating to a profit made by the subsidiary. This is because under IAS 12 *Income Taxes*, the deferred tax is deemed to be an issue related to the receiving company calculated at the receiving company's tax rate (as the receiving company will get a tax deduction at that rate when the temporary difference reverses). In this case, the receiving company is the parent and so the deferred tax does not affect the subsidiary or the non-controlling interests calculation.

4 *Defined benefit pension cost*

IAS 19 (Revised) *Employee Benefits* requires gains and losses on remeasurement of the asset or obligation to be recognised in other comprehensive income for the year. Therefore, the charge to cost of sales should simply be the current service cost of $12m. The net interest cost of $8m can also be reported in cost of sales or as a finance cost, but the company should be consistent with its past policy of recognising the net interest cost as a finance cost. This means that cost of sales requires a reduction of $11m ($23m – $12m).

Gains and losses on remeasurement of the asset or liability are reported in other comprehensive income for the year.

5 *Intragroup dividend*

Jarvis has a figure for other income of $80m. This includes its share of the dividend from Whitehill $48m ($60m × 80%) which must be removed on consolidation.

6 *Goodwill – Whitehill*

	$m
Consideration transferred	1,400
Non-controlling interests (1,500 × 20%)	300
Less: Net fair value of identifiable assets and liabilities at acq'n	(1,500)
	200

7 *Impairment loss*

	Whitehill
	$m
Notional goodwill ((W6) 200 × 100%/80%)	250
Carrying amount of net assets (W8)	2,300
	2,550
Recoverable amount	2,500
Impairment loss	50
Group share (Cost of sales) (50 × 80%)	40

8 *Carrying amount of net assets of Whitehill*

	$m
Fair value of net assets at 1 January 20X7	1,500
Total comprehensive income for year to 31 December 20X7	380
Total comprehensive income for year to 31 December 20X8	480
Dividend paid during 20X8	(60)
	2,300

Tutorial notes

No adjustment is made to the net assets for the unrealised profit (W3). This is because recoverable amount for the group financial statements would be based on the individual financial statements of Whitehill (ie 100% of cash flows for value in use or 100% of current fair value for the fair value less costs of disposal figure). So as the recoverable amount does not include a provision for unrealised profit (which is a consolidation adjustment), net assets do not need to be adjusted either when doing the group impairment test. An alternative would be to adjust both, although this would generate the same answer.

However, an adjustment would need to be made for any fair value adjustments at date of the impairment test. This is because fair value adjustments are taken into account in the goodwill calculation (reducing it) and therefore also need to be taken in account for the net assets (increasing them).

9 *Profit on sale of investment in equity instrument*

	$m
Proceeds	70
Carrying value at 31 December 20X7	(50)
	20

This figure (gross of tax) will be included in other income.

The current tax charge per question relating to the sale of the investment is on selling price less cost, and therefore includes not only the tax on the $20m gain on the sale, but also the tax on the previous revaluation gain of $10m. The tax on the $10m gain before 31 December 20X7 was previously recognised in profit or loss as deferred tax and is included in the deferred tax liability brought forward.

The following correcting entry is therefore required to eliminate the deferred tax liability b/d:

		$m	$m
DEBIT	Deferred tax liability (10 × 30%)	3	
CREDIT	Income tax expense (deferred tax) (P/L)		3

10 *Revaluation of land and buildings*

	Buildings	*Land*	*Total*	*Rate*	*Total*
	Corona m	Corona m	Corona m		$m
1 January 20X7	1,100	400	1,500	20	75
Depreciation 20X7 & 20X8 ((1,100 – 100)/50 × 2)	(40)	—	(40)	20	(2)
	1,060	400	1,460	20	73
Revaluation (balancing figure) (to OCI)	220	80	300		7
Revalued amount at 31 December 20X8	1,280	480	1,760	22	80

The land and buildings are a non-monetary asset held directly by Jarvis. They are recorded in Jarvis' books as the exchange rate at the date of purchase and depreciation is based on this value until they are revalued.

Deferred tax on the revaluation gain:

		$m	$m
DEBIT	Deferred tax (OCI) (7 × 30%)	2.1	
CREDIT	Deferred tax liability		2.1

11 *Hedge*

This is a cash flow hedge as the intention of the company is to have security over its cash outflows to purchase fuel.

At the year end the derivative must be valued at its fair value. The effective portion of the hedge (matching the expected increase in cash outflow to purchase the fuel) is recognised in other comprehensive income and the remainder in profit or loss:

		$m	$m
DEBIT	Derivative asset	12	
CREDIT	Other comprehensive income		10
CREDIT	Profit or loss ('finance income')		2

(b) Increasingly businesses are expected to be socially responsible as well as profitable. As investors become more aware of social and environmental issues affecting the globe, then social responsibility factors will increasingly be seen as affecting shareholder value. Strategic decisions by businesses, especially global businesses, nearly always have wider social consequences. In fact it could be argued that a company produces two outputs, the goods or services that it provides and the social consequences of its activities. These latter aspects are what is meant by corporate responsibility and two of the main areas are social reporting and environmental reporting.

Corporate responsibility also encompasses disclosure of areas that can be monitored: such as the level of the entity's carbon emissions or carbon 'footprint' as it is now often called, the level of community support, and the use of sustainable inputs, such as buying paper from suppliers that plant new trees.

There are many factors which should encourage companies to disclose information on their levels of corporate responsibility in terms of social and environmental reporting in their financial statements.

Probably the most important factor however is public interest, which is increasing rapidly. It is now widely recognised that although financial statements are primarily produced for investors there are also many other stakeholders in a company, including employees, customers, suppliers and the general public. All of these stakeholders are potentially interested in the way in which the company's business affects the community and the environment. Increasingly the end user customer is concerned about how the product is made and concerned about the use of cheap foreign labour. Equally the customer will be concerned about packaging and waste and the effects of this on the environment. If a company has a good reputation for care of its employees and care for the environment this will be an important marketing tool.

Companies now appreciate that their attitude to corporate responsibility also can have a direct effect on shareholder value. Their social and environmental policies are an important part of their overall performance and responsible practices in these areas and the provision of information in the annual report on these areas will have a positive effect on shareholder value if the company is perceived to be a good investment.

A further factor is the increasing influence of governments and professional bodies in their encouragement of disclosure and sustainable practices. In some countries there are awards for environmental and social reporting and the disclosures provided in the financial statements. In the UK the Prince of Wales set up the *Accounting for Sustainability* project which is designed to develop systems that will help both public and private sector organisations account more accurately for the wider social and environmental costs of their activities.

There are also a variety of published guidelines and codes of practice designed to encourage the practices of social and environmental reporting, such as the *Global Reporting Initiative.*

However what is missing is any substantial amount of legislation or accounting requirements in this area. The disclosure that is taking place is largely driven by the factors considered above, but the level and type of disclosure is then at the discretion of the company.

(c) The problem that has been noted with companies' disclosures regarding corporate responsibility is that although there is now widespread narrative disclosure in the annual report this tends not to be backed up with quantitative disclosures in the form of key performance indicators.

One of the reasons for this is that few companies identify aspects of corporate responsibility as strategic priorities. The ethical problem here is that the narrative reports are of extensive amounts of information that are not necessarily being actively managed within the business, giving perhaps a false impression of the extent of corporate responsibility at board level. The reporting itself has no clear links to the business performance and strategy and is therefore not necessarily a clear reflection of the company's thinking on these areas.

If social and environmental issues do not genuinely affect strategic and operational decisions such as the types of products developed, supply chain issues, brand positioning and corporate culture then it could be argued that these corporate responsibility disclosures are little more than a public relations exercise which could at worst mislead stakeholders in the company.

40 Preparation question: Part disposal

(a) ANGEL GROUP

CONSOLIDATED STATEMENT OF FINANCIAL POSITION AS AT 31 DECEMBER 20X8

	$'000
Non-current assets	
Property, plant and equipment	200.00
Investment in Shane (W3)	133.15
	333.15
Current assets (890 + 120 (cash on sale))	1,010.00
	1,343.15
Equity attributable to owners of the parent	
Share capital	500.00
Retained reserves (W4)	533.15
	1,033.15
Current liabilities	310.00
	1,343.15

ANGEL GROUP

CONSOLIDATED STATEMENT OF PROFIT OR LOSS AND OTHER COMPREHENSIVE INCOME FOR THE YEAR ENDED 31 DECEMBER 20X8

	$'000
Profit before interest and tax [100 + (20 × 6/12)]	110.00
Profit on disposal of shares in subsidiary (W6)	80.30
Share of profit of associate (12 × 35% × 6/12)	2.10
Profit before tax	192.40
Income tax expense [40 + (8 × 6/12)]	(44.00)
Profit for the year	148.40
Other comprehensive income (not reclassified to P/L) net of tax [10 + (6 × 6/12)]	13.00
Share of other comprehensive income of associate (6 × 35% × 6/12)	1.05
Other comprehensive income for the year	14.05
Total comprehensive income for the year	162.45
Profit attributable to:	
Owners of the parent	146.60
Non-controlling interests (12 × 6/12 × 30%)	1.80
	148.40
Total comprehensive income attributable to:	
Owners of the parents	159.75
Non controlling interests (18 × 6/12 × 30%)	2.70
	162.45

ANGEL GROUP

CONSOLIDATED RECONCILIATION OF MOVEMENT IN RETAINED RESERVES

	$'000
Balance at 31 December 20X7 (W5)	373.40
Total comprehensive income for the year	159.75
Balance at 31 December 20X8 (W4)	533.15

Workings

1 *Timeline*

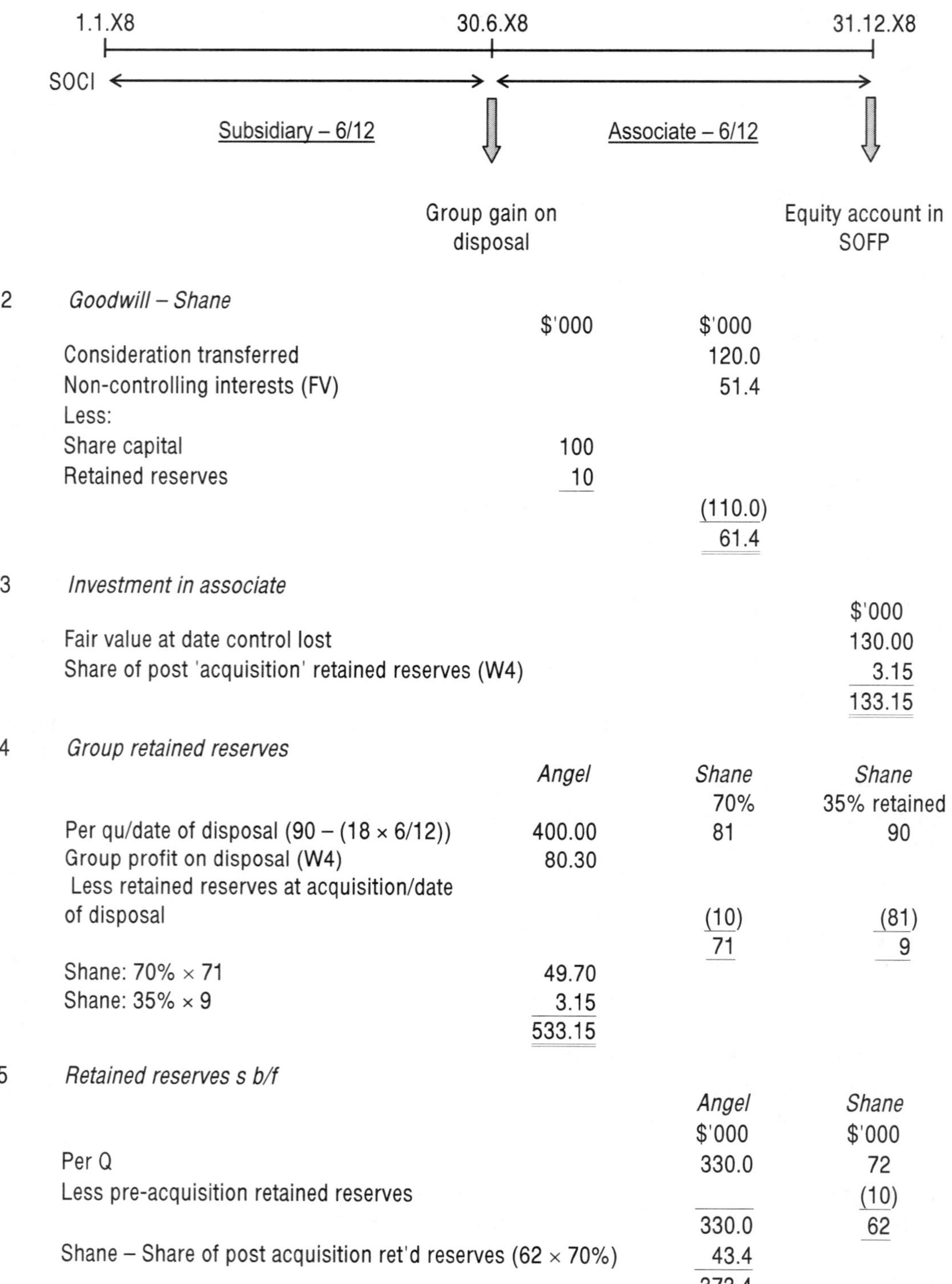

2 *Goodwill – Shane*

	$'000	$'000
Consideration transferred		120.0
Non-controlling interests (FV)		51.4
Less:		
Share capital	100	
Retained reserves	10	
		(110.0)
		61.4

3 *Investment in associate*

	$'000
Fair value at date control lost	130.00
Share of post 'acquisition' retained reserves (W4)	3.15
	133.15

4 *Group retained reserves*

	Angel	*Shane* 70%	*Shane* 35% retained
Per qu/date of disposal (90 – (18 × 6/12))	400.00	81	90
Group profit on disposal (W4)	80.30		
Less retained reserves at acquisition/date of disposal		(10)	(81)
		71	9
Shane: 70% × 71	49.70		
Shane: 35% × 9	3.15		
	533.15		

5 *Retained reserves s b/f*

	Angel $'000	*Shane* $'000
Per Q	330.0	72
Less pre-acquisition retained reserves		(10)
	330.0	62
Shane – Share of post acquisition ret'd reserves (62 × 70%)	43.4	
	373.4	

6 *Group profit on disposal of Shane*

	$'000	$'000
Fair value of consideration received		120.0
Fair value of 35% investment retained		130.0
Less share of carrying value when control lost		
Net assets 190 – (18 × 6/12)	181.0	
Goodwill (W2)	61.4	
Less non-controlling interests (W7)	(72.7)	
		(169.7)
		80.3

7 *Non-controlling interests at date of disposal*

	$'000	$'000
Non-controlling interest at acquisition (FV)		51.4
NCI share of post-acqn retained earnings (30% × 71(W4))		21.3
		72.7

(b) **Angel disposes of 10% of its holding**

If Angel disposes of 10% of its holding in Shane, Shane goes from being a 70% subsidiary to a 60% subsidiary. In other words **control is retained**. No accounting boundary has been crossed, and the event is treated as a transaction between owners.

The accounting treatment is as follows:

Statement of profit or loss and other comprehensive income

(i) The subsidiary is **consolidated in full** for the whole period.

(ii) The **non-controlling interest in the statement of profit or loss and other comprehensive income** will be based on percentage before and after disposal, ie time apportion.

(iii) There is **no profit or loss on disposal**.

Statement of financial position

(i) The **change (increase) in non-controlling interests** is shown as an **adjustment to the parent's equity**.

(ii) **Goodwill** on acquisition **is unchanged** in the consolidated statement of financial position.

In the case of Angel and Shane you would time apportion the non-controlling interest in the statement of profit or loss and other comprehensive income, giving 30% for the first half the year and 40% for the second half. You would also calculate the adjustment to the parent's equity as follows:

	$'000
Fair value of consideration received	X
Increase in NCI in net assets and goodwill at disposal	(X)
Adjustment to parent's equity	X

41 Preparation question: Purchase of further interest

(a) **RBE already controls DCA** with its 70% investment, so **DCA is already a subsidiary** and would be fully consolidated. In substance, this is **not an acquisition**. Instead, it is treated in the group accounts as a **transaction between the group shareholders** ie the parent has purchased a 20% shareholding from NCI. No goodwill is calculated on the additional investment.

The value of the NCI needs to be worked out at the date of the additional investment (1 October 20X2), and the **proportion purchased by the parent needs to be removed from NCI**. The difference between the consideration transferred and the amount of the reduction in the NCI is included as an **adjustment to parent equity**.

(b) RBE GROUP CONSOLIDATED STATEMENT OF CHANGES IN EQUITY
FOR THE YEAR ENDED 31 DECEMBER 20X2

	Equity attributable to owners of the parent $'000	*Non-controlling interest* $'000	*Total* $'000
Balance at 1 January 20X2	3,350	650	4,000
Total comprehensive income for the year (W2)	1,350	150	1,500
Share issue (2m × $1.30)	2,600	–	2,600
Dividends paid (100 × 30%)	(200)	(30)	(230)
Adjustment to equity (on additional purchase of 20% of DCA's shares) (W3 and 4)	(37)	(503)	(540)
Balance at 31 December 20X2	7,063	267	7,330

Workings

1 *Group structure*

RBE

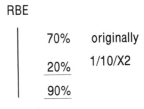

70%	originally
20%	1/10/X2
90%	

DCA

2 *Total comprehensive income*

NCI share:

	$'000
To 1 October 20X2 (30% × 600 × 9/12)	135
To 31 December 20X2 (10% × 600 × 9/12)	15
NCI share of TCI	150

Parent share:

	$'000
Parent share of TCI of DCA (600 – 150)	450
TCI of RBE	900
NCI share of TCI	1,350

3 *Decrease in NCI*

	$'000
NCI b/f 1 January 20X2	650
Share of TCI to 1 October 20X2 (W2)	135
Less share of dividend paid (April 20X2) (30% × 100)	(30)
NCI at 1 October 20X2	755
Decrease in NCI on transfer of shares to parent (755 × 20/30)	503

4 *Adjustment to equity*

	$'000
Consideration transferred	(540)
Decrease in NCI on acquisition (W3)	503
Adjustment to parent's equity	(37)

In RBE's individual statement of financial position, the purchase of the 20% in DCA would have been recorded as follows:

	$'000	$'000
DEBIT Investment	540	
CREDIT Cash		540

Then in the group accounts, the adjustment to equity would be recorded as follows:

	$'000	$'000
DEBIT (reduce) NCI	503	
DEBIT (reduce) Parent's retained earnings	37	
CREDIT(cancel) Investment *		540

42 Case study question: Marchant

Text references. Disposals are covered in Chapter 14 of your Study Text. Pensions are covered in Chapter 5 and share-based payment in Chapter 8. Fair value is covered in Chapters 7 and 12. Ethical issues are covered in Chapter 2.

Top tips. Question 1 part (a) was a consolidated statement of profit or loss and other comprehensive income, with two disposals, one where control was lost and one where control was retained. It is important that you know the difference in the treatment, so be sure to revise this if you had difficulty. Adjustments were required for intragroup sale of inventory (with a 'twist' in that the sale was at fair value so the unrealised loss was genuine), a pension plan, PPE, share-based payment and classification of a hedging loss.

You needed to know, at least in general terms, how to answer Part (a)(ii) in order to treat the gain on the sale of Nathan correctly in Part (a)(i).

Part 1(b) required a discussion of the extent to which fair values are used in IFRS and the impact of this on the usefulness of financial statements. Part (c), as usual, contained an ethical issue – as in a number of past questions, the issue concerned the tension between judgement and conflict of interest, in the (topical) context of recognising a lease in the statement of financial position classification. It is important to tailor your answer to the requirements in discussion parts of questions – ACCA examination/examining team has criticised candidates in the past for failure to *apply* their knowledge.

Easy marks. Once you have established the group structure, there are some very easy marks to be had for multiplying numbers given in the question by $^{6}/_{12}$. Part (b) allows for flexibility in the arguments made, and IFRS 13 *Fair value measurement,* is also topical, so you should have covered it in detail.

Examiner's comment. Once again, the ACCA examination/examining team stressed that candidates should show their workings: 'markers will look to see if there are recognisable figures in such a working but it is important to describe the calculation so that the marker can establish the principle'. Marks are given for correct principles with inaccurate calculations.

Candidates did not deal particularly well with the impairment of goodwill as they did not understand that any subsequent increase in the recoverable amount is likely to be internally generated goodwill rather than a reversal of purchased goodwill impairment. IAS 38 *Intangible assets* prohibits the recognition of internally generated goodwill, thus any reversal of impairment is not recognised. Candidates dealt successfully with the revaluation of non-current assets, the share option scheme and the wrong classification of a cash flow hedge.

In Part (a)(ii) of the question candidates were asked to explain, with suitable calculations, how the sale of the 8% interest in a subsidiary should be dealt with in the group statement of financial position at 30 April 2014. Marks were allocated for the explanation and the calculation. Thus if a candidate simply showed the calculation, marks were lost. Candidates generally answered this part of the question quite well.

Part (b) required candidates to answer across a range of standards and not just focus on IFRS 13. This part of the question was not well answered. In Part (c), candidates had to make reference to more than simply the rules as they had to comment on the fact that subjectivity and professional judgement were involved. The rest of the marks were allocated for the ethical discussion, which many candidates were quite poor at, choosing to spend a significant amount of time discussing the rules about leasing rather than using professional and ethical insight.

Marking scheme

		Marks
(a)	Impairment adjustment	4
	Nathan	6
	Option	6
	Inventory	1
	Share options	4
	PPE	3
	Employee benefits	4
	NCI	2
	Sale of equity interest in Nathan	5
		35
(b)	1 mark per valid point, maximum	9
(c)	1 mark per valid point, maximum	6
		50

(a)(i) MARCHANT GROUP

STATEMENT OF PROFIT OR LOSS AND OTHER COMPREHENSIVE INCOME
FOR THE YEAR ENDED 30 APRIL 20X4

	$m
Revenue: 400 + 115 + (70 × $^6/_{12}$) – 12 (W4)	538.00
Cost of sales: 312 + 65 + (36 × $^6/_{12}$) – 12 (W4)	(383.00)
Gross profit	155.00
Other income: 21 + 7 + (2 × $^6/_{12}$) – 5 (W3) + 22(W9) – 5.33 (W10)	40.67
Administrative expenses: 15 + 9 + (12 × $^6/_{12}$)	(30.00)
Other expenses: 35 + 19 + (8 × $^6/_{12}$) + 7.5 (W5) + 2.36 (W6) + 2.13 (W7)	(69.99)
Finance costs: 5 + 6 + (4 × $^6/_{12}$) – 3 (W8)	(10.00)
Finance income: 6 + 5 + (8 × $^6/_{12}$)	15.00
Share of profit of associate: 15 × $^6/_{12}$ × 20%	1.50
Profit before tax	102.18
Income tax expense: 19 + 9 + (5 × $^6/_{12}$)	(30.50)
Profit for the year	71.68
Other comprehensive income (items that will not be reclassified to profit or loss)	
Gain on property revaluation: 10 – 2.2 (W7)	7.80
Loss on investments in equity instruments: 5 (W10)	(5.00)
Remeasurement of defined benefit plan (W5)	(2.00)
	0.80
Other comprehensive income (items that may subsequently be reclassified to profit or loss)	
Cash flow hedge (W8)	(3.00)
Other comprehensive income for the year	(2.20)
Total comprehensive income for the year	69.48
Profit attributable to:	
Owners of the parent (bal. fig.)	59.88
Non-controlling interests (W2)	11.80
	71.68
Total comprehensive income attributable to:	
Owners of the parent	58.88
Non-controlling interests (W2)	10.60
	69.48

Workings

1 *Group structure*

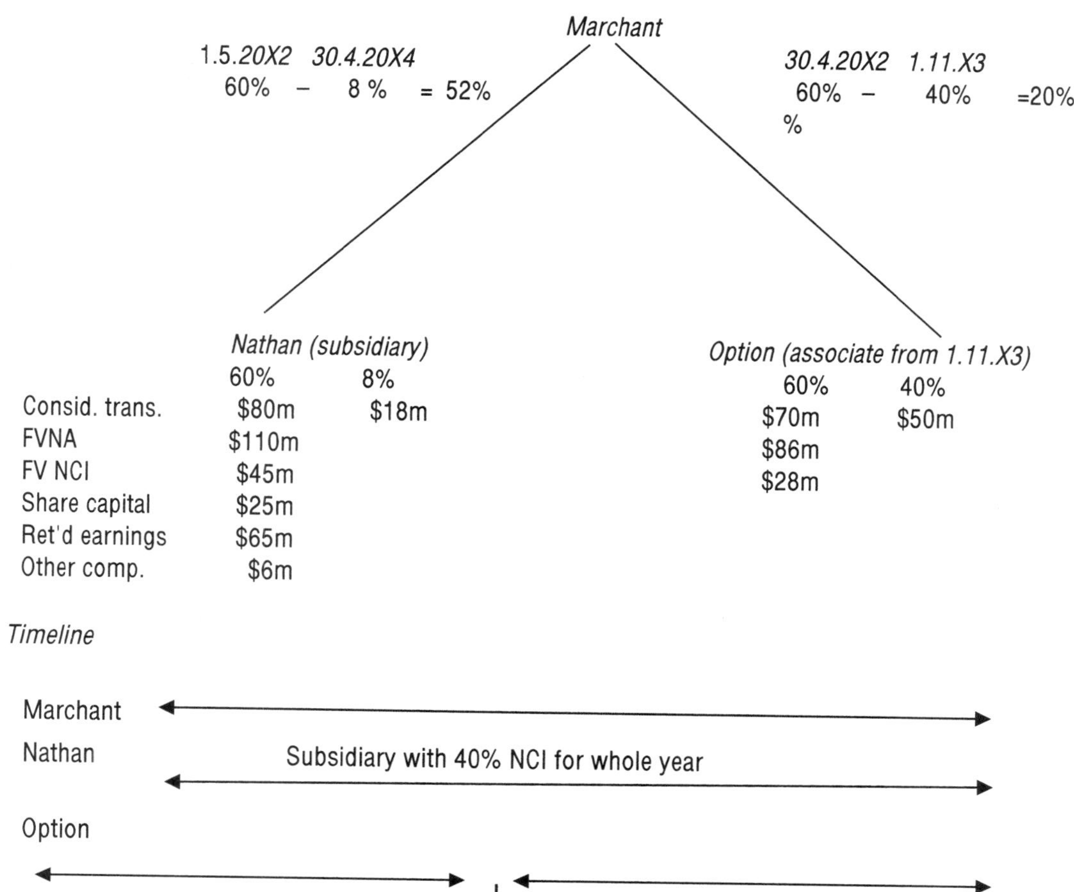

Timeline

Marchant ←——————————————→

Nathan — Subsidiary with 40% NCI for whole year ←——————————————→

Option

←——————→ Subsidiary with 40% NCI × 6/12 | ←——————→ 20% associate × 6/12

1.5.20X3 — *1.11.20X3* Sold 40% — *30.4.20X4*

2 *Non-controlling interests*

	Nathan		*Option*	
	Profit for year	*TCI*	*Profit for year*	*TCI*
	$m	$m	$m	$m
Per question	19.0	19.0		
15 × 6/12			7.5	
15 × 6/12				7.5
Reclassification of cash flow hedge (W8)	3.0	-	-	-
	22.0	19.0	7.5	7.5
NCI share	× 40%	× 40%	× 40%	× 40%
	8.8	7.6	3.0	3.0

Profit for year: 8.8 + 3.0 = $11.8

TCI: 7.6 + 3.0 = $10.6

3 *Goodwill*

	Nathan	*Option*
	$m	$m
Consideration transferred	80.0	70.0
Fair value of non-controlling interest	45.0	28.0
Fair value of net assets	(110.0)	(86.0)
	15.0	12.0
Impairment loss to 30.4.20X5: 44 × 5%	(3.0)	–
	12.0	12.0

Note. The impairment of the goodwill in Nathan had been reversed and the goodwill increased to $2m more than its original value, giving an increase of $(3m + 2m) = $5m. However, after the goodwill has been impaired, any subsequent increase is likely to be internally generated goodwill rather than a genuine reversal of goodwill impairment. The $3m uplift and $2m increase cannot be recognised and must be eliminated, so $5m is charged to profit or loss.

4 *Intragroup trading*

(i) Cancel intra group sales/purchases:

DEBIT	Revenue ($10m + $5m)	$12m	
CREDIT	Cost of sales (purchases)		$12m

(ii) Unrealised profit:

The unrealised loss on the sale of the inventory is not cancelled. The sale is at fair value, which indicates that the inventory was impaired. The loss on the sale is therefore genuine, and must remain realised. However, the revenue and cost of sales will be eliminated.

5 *Pension plan*

	$m
Net obligation b/d 1 May 20X3: 50 – 48	2.0
Past service costs	3.0
Net interest on net defined benefit obligation: (50 – 48 + 3*) × 10%	0.5
Current service cost	4.0
Remeasurement loss (balancing figure)	2.0
Net obligation c/d 30 April 20X4	11.5

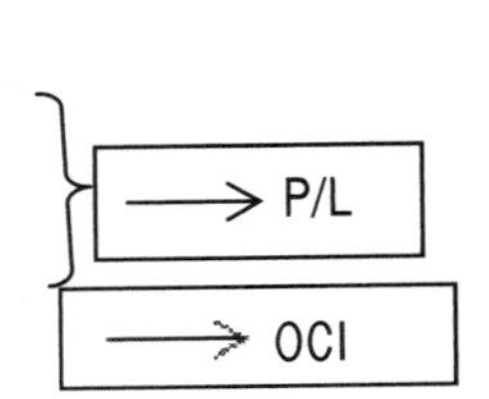

*Note that the interest includes interest on past service costs.

6 *Property, plant and equipment*

	$m	
At 1 May 20X2	12.00	
Depreciation: 12/10 years	(1.20)	
31 October 20X4 cash received (20 × 5%) ⟶ OCI	2.20	→ OCI
At 30 April 20X3	13.00	
		already accounted fo
Depreciation 20X3 to 20X4: 13/(10 – 1) years	(1.44)	
Revaluation loss	(4.56)	
	7.00	

DEBIT	Other comprehensive income	$2.20m	
DEBIT	Profit or loss	$2.36m	
CREDIT	Property, plant and equipment		$4.56m

7 *Share options*

	$m
30 April 20X3 Equity b/d: 8,000 × 4 × $100 × ⅓	1.07
Profit or loss (balancing figure)	2.13
30 April 20X4 Equity c/d: 8,000 × 6 × $100 × ⅔	3.20

8 *Cash flow hedge*

As the hedge is effective, the loss is taken to other comprehensive income:

DEBIT	Other comprehensive income	$3m	
CREDIT	Finance costs (profit or loss)		$3m

9 *Group profit on disposal of Option (control lost)*

	$m	$m
Fair value of consideration received		50
Fair value of 20% investment retained		40
Less share of consolidated carrying value when control lost		
Net assets	90	
Goodwill (W3)	12	
Less non-controlling interests	(34)	
		(68)
		22

10 *Investment in Nathan*

A fair value gain has been recorded on the investment in Nathan of $95m – $90m = $5m. This gain must be eliminated on consolidation because the calculation of goodwill is based on the fair value of the consideration at the date of acquisition, not at the date of the current financial statements. The double entry for the reversal is:

DEBIT	Other comprehensive income	$5m	
CREDIT	Investment in Nathan.		$5m

Reversal of fair value gain recognised in parent's separate financial statements

The sale of the 8% equity in Nathan does not result in loss of control, and is shown as a movement in equity in the consolidated financial statements, with no profit or loss arising. Accordingly, the gain on the sale recognised in the parent's separate financial statements must be reversed:

		$m	$m
DEBIT	Other income (18 – (95 × 8%/60%))	5.33	
DEBIT	Investment in Nathan (95 × 8%/60%)	12.67	
CREDIT	Other components of equity		18

Reversal of gain on sale recognised in parent's separate financial statements

(ii) **Sale of 8% interest in Nathan**

When Marchant disposed of 8% of its holding in Nathan, Nathan went from being a 60% subsidiary to a 52% subsidiary. In other words **control is retained**. No accounting boundary has been crossed, and the event is treated as a transaction between owners.

The accounting treatment is as follows:

Statement of profit or loss and other comprehensive income

(1) The subsidiary is **consolidated in full** for the whole period.

(2) The **non-controlling interest in the statement of profit or loss and other comprehensive income** is based on percentage before and after disposal, ie time apportion. In this case, the sale took place on the last day of the year, so there is a 40% non-controlling interest for the whole year.

(3) There is **no profit or loss on disposal**.

Statement of financial position

(1) The change (increase) in non-controlling interests is shown as an adjustment to the parent's equity.

(2) Goodwill on acquisition is unchanged in the consolidated statement of financial position.

The adjustment to the parent's equity is as follows:

Non-controlling interest at year end:

	$m
Non-controlling interest at acquisition	45.0
NCI share of post-acquisition reserves: 40% × $(120– (25 + 65 + 6))	9.6
Impairment	(1.2)
	53.4

Increase in NCI: $53.4m × 8%/40% = $10.68m

	$m
Fair value of consideration received	18.00
Increase in NCI in net assets and goodwill at disposal	(10.68)
Adjustment to parent's equity	7.32

(b) **Fair value in financial statements**

It is not entirely accurate to say that IFRS implement a fair value model. While IFRS use fair value (and present value) more than other accounting frameworks, and more than they, and the old IAS did in the past, it is **not a complete fair value system.** IFRS are based on the **business model of the entity** and on the probability of realising the asset- and liability-related cash flows through operations or transfers. In fact the IASB favours a mixed measurement system, with some items being measured at fair value and others at historical cost. Historical cost has a number of **advantages** over fair values, mainly as regards reliability.

(i) It is **easy to understand**.
(ii) It is grounded in **real transaction amounts**, and is therefore **objective** and objectively verifiable.
(iii) There is **less scope for manipulation**.

Before the publication of IFRS 13 *Fair value measurement* in 2011, there were a number of definitions of fair value, and there was considerable inconsistency. IFRS 13 was developed to solve some of these problems. 13 defines fair value as **'the price that would be received to sell an asset or paid to transfer a liability in an orderly transaction between market participants at the measurement date.'** The price which would be received to sell the asset or paid to transfer (not settle) the liability is described as **the 'exit price'.**

IFRS 13 has brought consistency to the definition and application of fair value, and this consistency is applied across other IFRS, which are generally required to measure fair value 'in accordance with IFRS 13'. This **does not mean, however, that IFRS requires all assets and liabilities to be measured at fair value**. On the contrary, many entities measure most items at depreciated historical cost, a notable exception being in the case of business combinations, where assets and liabilities are recorded at fair value at the acquisition date. In other cases, the use of fair value is restricted. For example:

(i) IAS 16 *Property, plant and equipment* **allows revaluation** through other comprehensive income, provided it is **carried out regularly**.

(ii) While IAS 40 *Investment properties* allows the **option** of measuring investment properties **at fair value** with corresponding changes in profit or loss, and this arguably reflects the business model of some property companies, **many companies still use historical cost.**

(iii) IAS 38 *Intangible assets* **permits the measurement of intangible assets at fair value** with corresponding changes in equity, but **only** if the assets can be measured reliably through the existence of an **active market** for them.

IFRS 9 *Financial Instruments*, issued in final form in July 2014, makes **more extensive use of fair value.** The standard requires that on initial recognition, financial assets are classified as measured at either:

(i) Amortised cost, or
(ii) Fair value through other comprehensive income, or
(ii) Fair value through profit or loss

A financial asset is classified as measured at amortised cost where:

(i) The objective of the business model within which the asset is held is to hold assets in order to collect contractual cash flows and

(ii) The contractual terms of the financial asset give rise on specified dates to cash flows that are solely payments of principal and interest on the principal outstanding.

An application of these rules means that **equity investments may not be classified as measured at amortised cost** and must be measured at fair value. This is because contractual cash flows on specified dates are not a characteristic of equity instruments. By default, gains and losses on equity investments within the scope of IFRS 9 are recognised in profit or loss for the year. However, if the equity investment is not held for trading **an irrevocable election can be made at initial recognition to measure it at fair value through other comprehensive income** with only dividend income recognised in profit or loss. The amounts recognised in OCI are not re-classified to profit or loss on disposal of the investment although they may be reclassified in equity.

A **debt instrument** may be classified as measured at either amortised cost or fair value **depending on whether it meets the criteria above**. Even where the criteria are met at initial recognition, a debt instrument may be classified as measured at fair value through profit or loss if doing so eliminates or significantly reduces a measurement or recognition inconsistency (sometimes referred to as an 'accounting mismatch') that would otherwise arise from measuring assets or liabilities or recognising the gains and losses on them on different bases. An example of this may be where an entity holds a fixed rate loan receivable that it hedges with an interest rate swap that swaps the fixed rates for floating rates. Measuring the loan asset at amortised cost would create a measurement mismatch, as the interest rate swap would be held at FVTPL. In this case, the loan receivable could be designated at FVTPL under the fair value option to reduce the accounting mismatch that arises from measuring the loan at amortised cost. In practice only banks make a limited use of such transactions.

A financial asset **must** be classified and measured **at fair value through other comprehensive income** (unless the asset is designated at fair value through profit or loss under the fair value option) if it meets both the following criteria:

(i) The financial asset is held within a business model whose objective is achieved by both collecting contractual cash flows and selling financial assets.

(ii) The contractual terms of the financial asset give rise on specified dates to cash flows that are solely payments of principal and interest on the principal amount outstanding.

This business model is **new to the July 2014 version of IFRS 9.**

All derivatives are measured at **fair value**. Most **derivatives**, for example swaps, options and futures contracts, do not have a cost when signed and their historical cost is not relevant. **Embedded derivatives** must be classified in their entirety as either amortised cost or fair value, depending on whether they meet the definition of a financial asset within the scope of the standard. Other embedded derivatives must be separated from their host contracts and each part considered separately.

While IFRS makes some use of fair values in the measurement of assets and liabilities, **financial statements prepared under IFRS are not,** as is sometimes believed, **intended to reflect the aggregate value of an entity.** On the contrary, the *Conceptual Framework for Financial Reporting* specifically states that general purpose financial reports are not designed to show the value of a reporting entity. Such an attempt would be incomplete, **since IFRS disallows the recognition of internally generated intangibles**. Rather, the objective identified by the IASB is to provide financial information about a reporting entity which is useful to existing and potential investors, lenders and other creditors in making decisions about providing resources to the entity.

It is only when an entity is **acquired by another entity and consolidated** in group accounts that an entity's **net assets are reported at market value.**

(c) **Treatment of lease**

IFRS 16 requires recognition of nearly all leases of over twelve months in the statement of financial position. (There is an exception for low value leases, but as this is the company's main premises, that does not apply.) The arrangement meets the IFRS 16 criteria for a lease in that there is an identifiable asset and the contract conveys the right to control the use of that asset for a period of time in exchange for consideration.

The difference of opinion has arisen between the financial controller and the managing director, and is best resolved by the **financial controller seeking expert, independent advice.**

The treatment chosen should be that which presents fairly the substance of the transaction, taking into account all the facts of the case and the advice taken. While under IFRS 16's predecessor, IAS 17, there was some subjectivity, that subjectivity has been removed by IFRS 16. There is now no choice, and in any case a choice of accounting treatment **should be driven by technical and professional standards, not by the desire to present a favourable picture for a particular purpose**. Thus, if the arrangement meets the IFRS 16 criteria for a lease, the lease should not be kept out of the statement of financial position in order to understate the liabilities of the entity for the purpose of raising a loan. If the managing director is **trying to compel the financial controller to change what would be the appropriate treatment because of business pressures**, then this presents the financial controller with an ethical dilemma. The pressure will be greater because the financial controller is new.

The **ACCA Code of Ethics** (or professional accountants' code of ethics) will be an essential point of reference in this situation, since it sets out boundaries outside which accountants should not stray. If the managing director refuses to allow the financial controller to apply the IFRS 16 treatment, then the financial controller **should disclose this to the appropriate internal governance authority**, and thus feel confident that his/her actions were ethical.

43 Ejoy

Text reference. Changes in group structure are covered in Chapter 14.

Top tips. This question required the production of a consolidated statement of profit or loss and other comprehensive income of a group. Candidates were expected to calculate and impairment test the investment in a subsidiary, to account for a joint venture, to deal with impairment and hedging of financial assets, and account for a discontinued operation.

Easy marks. Do not spend too long on the discontinued operation. You would not be penalised too heavily if you got this wrong and there are easy marks to be gained for adding across and other basic consolidation aspects.

Examiner's comment. Overall the question was quite well answered, with the majority of candidates achieving a pass mark. However, candidates answered the financial instruments part of the question quite poorly. The main problem seemed to be the application of knowledge; candidates could recite the principles of accounting for financial instruments but could not deal with the practical application thereof. The calculation of the goodwill was done well. However, the impairment testing of the investment in the subsidiary was poorly answered. Candidates need to understand this procedure as it will be a regular feature of future papers.

Marking scheme

		Marks
Goodwill		7
Joint venture		2
Financial assets		7
Statement of profit or loss and other comprehensive income		8
Tbay		4
Non-controlling interest		2
	Maximum	30

EJOY: CONSOLIDATED STATEMENT OF PROFIT OR LOSS AND OTHER COMPREHENSIVE INCOME FOR THE YEAR ENDED 31 MAY 20X6

	$m
Continuing operations	
Revenue (2,500 + 1,500)	4,000
Cost of sales (1,800 + 1,200 + 34 (W8))	(3,034)
Gross profit	966
Other income (70 + 10 – 3 (W11)	77
Distribution costs (130 + 120)	(250)
Administrative expenses (100 + 90)	(190)
Finance income (W6)	9
Finance costs (W7)	(137)
Profit before tax	475
Income tax expense (200 + 26)	(226)
Profit for period from continuing operations	249
Discontinued operations	
Profit for the year from discontinued operations ((30 × 6/12) – 2 (W8))	13
Profit for the year	262
Other comprehensive income for the year (not reclassified to P/L):	
Gain on property revaluation net of tax: 80 + 10 + (8 × 6/12)	94
Total comprehensive income for the year	356
Profit attributable to:	
Owners of the parent	257
Non-controlling interest (W2)	5
	262
Total comprehensive income for the year attributable to:	
Owners of the parent (bal. fig.)	348
Non-controlling interest (W2)	8
	356

Workings

1 *Group structure*

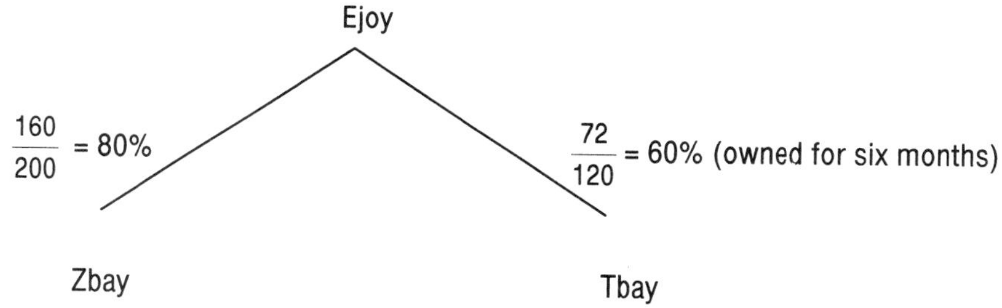

Tbay is a discontinued operation (IFRS 5).

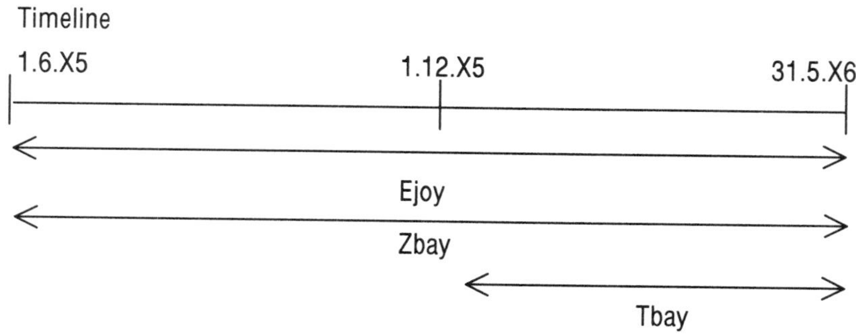

2 *Non-controlling interest*

	Profit for the year		Total comp income	
	Zbay	*Tbay*	*Zbay*	*Tbay*
	$m	$m	$m	$m
PFY/TCI per question	34.0		44	
(30 × 6/12)/(38 × 6/12)		15		19
Interest income on loan asset held by Zbay (W4)	4.5		4.5	
Interest on loss allowance during the year (Loan held by Zbay) (W4)	(0.1)		(0.1)	
Less impairment loss (loan asset) (W4)	(45.5)		(45.5)	
	(7.1)	15	2.9	19
	× 20%	×40%	× 20%	× 40%
	(1.4)	6	0.6	7.6
	4.6		8.2	

3 *Goodwill*

		Zbay		*Tbay*
		$m		$m
Consideration transferred		520		192
Non-controlling interests	(600 × 20%)	120	(310 × 40%)	124
Fair value of net assets at acquisition		(600)		(310)
		40		6

4 *Loan held by Zbay*

On 31 May 20X5, Zbay will have recognised, in accordance with IFRS 9, an allowance equivalent to twelve months' expected credit losses. This is the lifetime expected credit losses multiplied by the probability of default in the next twelve months: 10% × $25m = $2.5m. This is the brought down loss allowance at 1 June 20X5.

Interest of 4% will be recognised on this allowance of $2.5m during the year ended 31 May 20X6, which is the unwinding of the discount. This interest will be recognised in profit or loss for the year, and will increase the loss allowance by the same amount:

DEBIT Profit or loss (4% × $2.5m)	$0.1m	
CREDIT Loss allowance		$0.1m

The loss allowance at 31 May 20X6 is therefore $2.6m.

Interest income must also be recognised in profit or loss for the year ended 31 May 20X6 on the gross carrying amount of $100m: 4.5% × $100m = $4.5m.

By 31 May 20X6 there is objective evidence of impairment. Stage 3 of the IFRS 9 has been reached, and lifetime expected credit losses, now revised to $48.1m, must be recognised in full. This means that the loss allowance, including interest, of $2.6m must be increased to $48.1m, and the difference charged to profit or loss for the year ended 31 May 20X6:

DEBIT Profit or loss ($48.1m – $2.6m)	$45.5m	
CREDIT Loss allowance		$45.5m

5 *Hedged bond (Ejoy)*

	$m
1.6.X5	50.0
Interest income (5% × 50)	2.5
Interest received	(2.5)
Fair value loss (balancing figure)	(1.7)
Fair value at 31.5.X6 (per question)	48.3

Because the interest rate swap is 100% effective as a fair value hedge, it exactly offsets the loss in value of $1.7 million on the bond. The bond is classified at fair value through profit or loss. Both the gain on the swap and the loss on the bond are recognised in profit or loss as income and expense. The net effect on profit or loss is nil.

6 *Finance income*

	$m
Interest income on loan asset held by Zbay (W4)	4.5
Interest receivable on bond held by Ejoy (W5)	2.5
Interest received on interest rate swap held by Ejoy	0.5
Fair value gain on interest rate swap	1.7
	9.2

7 *Finance costs*

	$m
Per draft statements of profit or loss and other comprehensive income (50 + 40)	90.0
Interest on loss allowance during the year (Loan held by Zbay) (W4)	0.1
Increase in loss allowance (Loan held by Zbay) (W4)	45.5
Fair value loss on hedged bond (W5)	1.7
	137.3

8 *Impairment losses*

	Zbay $m	*Tbay* $m
Notional goodwill (40 × 100%/80%) (6 × 100%/60%) (W3)	50.0	10.0
Carrying amount of net assets (W9)/(W10)	622.9	329.0
	672.9	339.0
Recoverable amount	(630.0)	
Fair value less costs of disposal (344 – (5 × 100%/60%))		(335.7)
Impairment loss: gross	42.9	3.3
Impairment loss recognised: all allocated to goodwill (80% × 42.9)/(60% × 3.3)	34.3	2.0

9 *Carrying amount of net assets at 31 May 20X6 (Zbay)*

	$m
Fair value of identifiable assets and liabilities acquired (1 June 20X4)	600.0
TCI for year to 31 May 20X5	20.0
TCI for year to 31 May 20X6 per draft statement of profit or loss and other comprehensive income	44.0
Interest income on loan asset held by Zbay (W4)	4.5
Interest on loss allowance during the year (Loan held by Zbay) (W4)	(0.1)
Less impairment loss (loan asset) (W4)	(45.5)
	622.9

10 *Carrying amount of net assets (Tbay)*

	$m
Carrying value of investment in Tbay at 31 May 20X6:	
Fair value of net assets at acquisition (1 December 20X5)	310
Post acquisition TCI(38 × 6/12)	19
	329

11 *Joint venture*

	$m	$m
Elimination of Ejoy's share of gain on disposal (50% × 6)		3
DEBIT Other income	3	
CREDIT Investment in joint venture		3

44 Case study question: Traveler

Text reference. Business combinations achieved in stages are covered in Chapter 14. Employee benefits are covered in Chapter 4. Segment reporting is covered in Chapter 10. Ethical issues are covered in Chapter 2.

Top tips. This question has been amended to reflect the revision to IAS 19 in 2011. This is still one of the trickier adjustments in Part (a), together with the impairment of the loan. You should have recognised straightaway that one of the acquisitions is of a further controlling interest (going from 60% to 80%) so there will be an adjustment to parent's equity and no need to revalue the existing interest.

Easy marks. There are some standard consolidation workings here, and you could slot in the caption for, say, adjustment to parent's equity even if you get the calculation wrong. Leave enough time for Parts (b) and (c) – the ACCA examination/examining team has commented in the past that candidates often do not. Part (b) is straightforward knowledge and Part (c) allows a variety of valid points to be made .

Examiner's comment. In general, candidates demonstrated a good knowledge of the consolidation process together with calculation skills for the accounting adjustments needed to the parent's financial statements. Some candidates struggled with the impairment testing of the partial goodwill, forgetting to gross up for the non-controlling interest. Other common weaknesses in Part (a) of answers included ignoring the change in ownership interest, calculating impairment by simply comparing goodwill to recoverable amount without considering the net assets or fair value adjustment, not calculating a movement in equity for the non controlling interest change and including OCI changes in retained earnings rather than other components of equity. In addition, some candidates spent too long on Part (a) at the expense of readily available marks in Parts (b) and (c). Parts 1(b) and 1(c) can mean the difference between pass and fail.

Marking scheme

		Marks
(a)		
	Property, plant and equipment	4
	Goodwill	7
	Financial assets	4
	Defined benefit asset	4
	Current assets/total non-current liabilities	1
	Share capital	1
	Retained earnings	7
	Other components of equity	3
	Non-controlling interest	3
	Current liabilities	1
		35
(b)		
	Subjective assessment	8
	Up to 2 marks per element	
(c)		
	Subjective assessment	7
		50

(a) TRAVELER GROUP
CONSOLIDATED STATEMENT OF FINANCIAL POSITION
AS AT 30 NOVEMBER 20X1

	$m
Non-current assets	
Property, plant and equipment: 439 + 810 + 620 + 10(W6) + 22(W6) – 56(W7) – 2.7(W9)	1,842.3
Goodwill (W2)	69.2
Financial assets: 108 + 10 + 20 – 7.9(W8)	130.1
Net defined benefit asset (W10): 72 – 25 – 55 + 45 – 19	18.0
	2,059.6
Current assets: 995 + 781 + 350	2,126.0
Total assets	4,185.6
Equity and liabilities	
Equity attributable to owners of the parent	
Share capital	1,120.0
Retained earnings (W3)	973.4
Other components of equity (W4)	66.7
	2,160.1
Non-controlling interests (W5)	343.5
	2,503.6
Non-current liabilities: 455 + 323 + 73	851.0
Current liabilities: 274 + 199 + 313 + 45 (W10)	831.0
Total equity and liabilities	4,185.6

Workings

1 *Group structure*

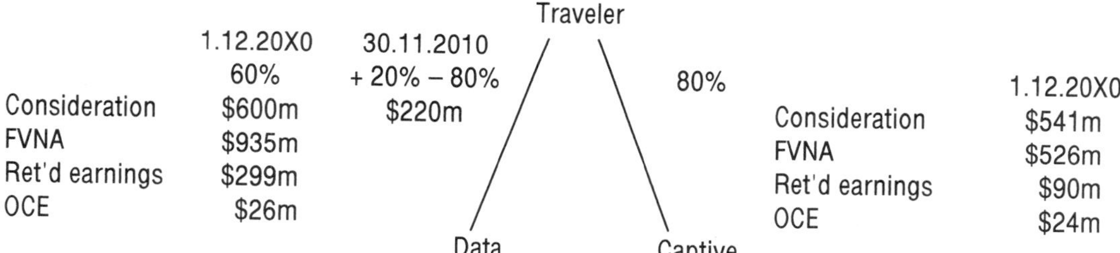

2 *Goodwill*

	Full method Data $m	*Partial method Captive* $m
Consideration transferred – for 60%	600	
Consideration transferred – for 80%		541.0
Non-controlling interests		
Fair value per qu	395	
526 × 20%		105.2
FV of identifiable net assets at acq'n:	(935)	526.0)
	60	120.2
Impairment losses (W12)	(50)	(61.0)
	10	59.2
	69.2	

3 *Retained earnings*

	Traveler	*Data*	*Captive*
	$m	$m	$m
Per question	1,066.0	442	169
Consideration (W7)	(56.0)		
Loss allowance on loan (W8)	(7.9)		
Depreciation of factory (W9)	(2.7)		
Defined benefit pension charge (W10)	(55.0)		
Pre-acquisition (W1)		(299)	(90)
		143	79
Group share			
Data: 143 × 60%	85.8		
Captive: 79 × 80%	63.2		
Impairment losses(W12) (50 × 80%) +61	(101.0)		
	992.4		

4 *Other components of equity*

	Traveler	*Data*	*Captive*
	$m	$m	$m
Per question	60.0	37	45
Loss on remeasurement of defined benefit plan (W10)	(25.0)		
Impairment of pension plan (W10)	(19.0)		
Pre-acquisition (W1)		(26)	(24)
		11	21
Group share post acqn:			
Data: 11 × 60 %	6.6		
Captive : 21 × 80%	16.8		
Adjustment to parent's equity (W11)	8.3		
	47.7		

5 *Non-controlling interests*

	Data	*Captive*
	$m	$m
At acquisition (FV/W2)	395.0	105.2
Post acquisition share of retained earnings		
Data: 143 (W3) × 40%	57.2	
Captive: 79 (W3) × 20%		15.8
Post acquisition share of other components of equity		
Data: 11 (W4) × 40%	4.4	
Captive: 21 (W4) × 20%		4.2
	456.6	125.2
Acquisition of additional 20% of Data (W11)	(228.3)	–
	228.3	125.2
Impairment losses: 50(W12) × 20%	(10.0)	–
	218.3	125.2
	343.5	

6 *Fair value adjustments*

Data:

	At acqn 1.10.20X0	*Movement*	*At year end 30.11.20X1*
	$m	$m	$m
Land: 935 – (600 + 299 + 26)	10	–	10
Captive:			
Land: 526– (390 + 90+ 24)	22	–	22

7 *Consideration transferred: Captive*

This has been incorrectly treated as:

DEBIT	Cost of investment in Captive	$541m	
CREDIT	Profit or loss		$64m
CREDIT	Cash		$477m

The land transferred as part of the consideration needs to be removed from non-current assets, the $64m sales proceeds removed from profit or loss and a gain on disposal calculated. The gain is $64m sale consideration, less carrying value of $56m = $8m. The correct entries should have been:

DEBIT	Cost of investment in Captive	$541m	
CREDIT	Profit or loss (gain on disposal		$8m
CREDIT	Land		$56m
CREDIT	Cash		$477m

To correct, the entries are:

DEBIT	Profit or loss	$56m	
CREDIT	Land		$56m

8 *Loan*

The loan is a financial asset held at amortised cost under IFRS 9 *Financial instruments.* Traveler wishes to value the loan at fair value. However, IFRS 9 states that the classification of an instrument is determined on initial recognition and that reclassifications, which are not expected to occur frequently, are permitted only if the entity's business model changes.

Financial assets are subsequently measured at amortised cost if **both** of the following apply.

(i) The asset is held within a business model whose objective is to hold the assets to collect the contractual cash flows.

(ii) The contractual terms of the financial asset give rise, on specified dates, to cash flows that are solely payments of principal and interest on the principal outstanding.

All other financial assets are measured at fair value.

Traveler's objective for holding the debt instrument has not changed, and so it cannot measure it at fair value but must continue to measure it at amortised cost.

The loan is in Stage 2, so lifetime expected credit losses must be recognised and the increase charged to profit or loss.

DEBIT	Loss allowance (and Traveler's retained earnings (W3)) 9.9 – 2	$7.9m	
CREDIT	Financial assets		$7.9m

9 *Depreciation of factory*

Traveler wishes to account for the factory as a single asset. However, the roof and the building must be treated separately for the purposes of depreciation. The roof will be depreciated over five years and the remainder of the factory will be depreciated over 25 years taking into account the residual value of $2m:

	Building	*Roof*	*Total*
	$m	$m	$m
Cost	45.0	5	50.0
Depreciation:			
(45 – 2) ÷ 25years/ 5 ÷ 5years	(1.7)	(1)	(2.7)
	43.3	4	47.3

DEBIT	Profit or loss (and Traveler's retained earnings (W3))	$2.7m	
CREDIT	Property, plant and equipment		$2.7m

10 *Defined benefit pension plan*

According to IAS 19 *Employee benefits* (revised 2011), losses on remeasurement of the net defined benefit asset (previously called actuarial losses) must be recognised immediately in other comprehensive income. There will also be a ceiling placed on the amount to be recognised as an asset, which is the present value of available future refunds and reductions in future contributions of $18m. The adjustments are as follows:

	$m		$m
Net defined benefit asset b/d	72 Dr		
Charges to profit or loss	(55) Cr	→	Dr Profit or loss (and retained earnings)
Loss on remeasurement of defined benefit asset	(25) Cr	→	Dr Other comprehensive income(and other components of equity)
Contributions	45 Dr	→	Cr Current liabilities
	37 Dr		
Impairment loss (β)	(19) Cr	→	Dr Other comprehensive income
Asset ceiling (see above)	18 Dr		

11 *Adjustment to parent's equity on acquisition of additional 20% of Data*

This is an increase in the controlling interest and therefore a reduction in the non-controlling interest, of 20%/40%:

DEBIT	Non-controlling interest (W5) $456.6m × 20%/40%	$228.3m	
CREDIT	Investment		$220m
CREDIT	Parents equity (other components of equity (W4))		$8.3m

12 *Impairment of goodwill*

	Data	*Captive*
	$m	$m
Net assets at year end per question	1,079	604.0
Fair value adjustments (W6)	10	22.0
	1,089	626.0
Goodwill (W2) Data 60, Captive 120.2 × 100%/80% (see note(i))	60	150.3
	1,149	776.3
Recoverable amount per question	(1,099)	(700.0)
Impairment loss gross	50	76.3
Impairment loss recognised (see note (ii)): 100%/80%	50	61.0

Notes

(i) Because the non-controlling interest in Data is at fair value, goodwill arises on this non-controlling interest, which bears its share of any impairment using the proportions in which profits and losses are shared at the year end when the impairment review arose, that is 20%. The gross impairment of $50m is taken to the goodwill working and the 20% ($10m) to the NCI working (W5). In the case of Captive, where the partial goodwill method is used, only 80% of the impairment is taken to the goodwill working.

(ii) Because the non-controlling interest in Data is at fair value, the goodwill is already grossed up, but Captive uses the partial goodwill method, so the goodwill needs to be grossed up for an unrecognised NCI of 20%.

(b) **Allocation of common costs under IFRS 8 *Operating segments***

If segment reporting is to fulfil a useful function, costs need to be appropriately assigned to segments. Centrally incurred expenses and central assets can be significant, and the basis chosen by an entity to allocate such costs **can therefore have a significant impact** on the financial statements. In the case of Traveler, head office management expenses, pension expenses, the cost of managing properties and interest and related interest bearing assets could be material amounts, whose misallocation could mislead users.

IFRS 8 *Operating segments* **does not prescribe a basis** on which to allocate common costs, but it does require that that basis should be **reasonable**. For example, it would not be reasonable to allocate the head office management expenses to the most profitable business segment to disguise a potential loss elsewhere. Nor would it be reasonable to allocate the pension expense to a segment with no pensionable employees.

A reasonable basis on which to allocate common costs for Traveler might be as follows:

(i) **Head office management costs.** These could be allocated on the basis of turnover or net assets. Any allocation might be criticised as arbitrary – it is not necessarily the case that a segment with a higher turnover requires more administration from head office – but this is a fairer basis than most.

(ii) **Pension expense.** A reasonable allocation might be on the basis of number of employees or salary expense of each segment.

(iii) **Costs of managing properties.** These could be allocated on the basis of the value of the properties used by each business segment, or the type and age of the properties (older properties requiring more attention than newer ones).

(iv) **Interest and interest-bearing assets.** These need not be allocated to the same segment – the interest receivable could be allocated to the profit or loss of one segment and the related interest bearing asset to the assets and liabilities of another.

The **amounts reported under IFRS 8 may differ from those reported in the consolidated financial statements** because IFRS 8 requires the information to be presented on the same basis as it is reported internally, even if the accounting policies are not the same as those of the consolidated financial statements. For example, segment information may be reported on a cash basis rather than an accruals basis. Such differences might include allocation of centrally incurred costs that are necessary for an understanding of the reported segment information.

IFRS 8 requires **reconciliations** between the segments' reported amounts and those in the consolidated financial statements. Entities must provide an explanation of such differences, and of the basis of accounting for transactions between reportable segments.

(c) **Ethical issues and conflict of interest**

Increasingly businesses are expected to be **socially responsible as well as profitable**. Strategic decisions by businesses, particularly global businesses nearly always have wider social consequences. It could be argued, as Henry Mintzburg does, that a company produces two outputs: goods and services, and the social consequences of its activities, such as pollution.

The requirement to be a **good corporate citizen goes beyond the normal duty of ethical behaviour** in the preparation of financial statements. To act ethically, the directors must put the interests of the company and its shareholders first, for example they must not mislead users of financial statements and must exercise competence in their preparation. Corporate citizenship, on the other hand, is concerned with a company's **accountability to a wide range of stakeholders**, not just shareholders. There may well be a **conflict of interest between corporate social responsibility and maximising shareholder wealth**; for example it may be cheaper to outsource abroad, but doing so may have an adverse effect on the local economy.

In the context of **disclosure**, a company might prefer not to give information – for example segment information – away, as it could be useful to competitors and have a negative impact on profit and bonuses.

However, the two goals **need not conflict**. It is possible that being a good corporate citizen can **improve business performance. Customers may buy from a company that they perceive as environmentally friendly,** or which avoids animal testing, and **employees may remain loyal** to such a company, and both these factors are likely to increase shareholder wealth in the long term. If a company engages constructively with the country or community in which it is based, it may be seen by shareholders and potential shareholders as being a **good long- term investment** rather than in it for short-term profits. As regards disclosure, a company that makes **detailed disclosures,** particularly when these go beyond what is required by legislation or accounting standards, will be seen as **responsible and a good potential investment**.

45 Case study question: Joey

Text reference. Business combinations achieved in stages are covered in Chapter 14 of the text. IFRS 5 is covered in Chapter 15. Share-based payment is covered in Chapter 9. Ethics is covered in Chapter 2.

Top tips. Business combinations achieved in stages appear regularly on this paper. It is important to get the group structure right – here you have an associate becoming a subsidiary. The other subsidiary is very straightforward, the only unusual aspect being that it is a gain on a bargain purchase. The main complication is the joint operation becoming a joint venture. There are five marks for this, and you will get at least two of these for identifying the change from joint operation to joint venture – there are clear pointers in the question – and briefly stating the accounting treatment. Add some correct numbers and you're nearly there – so do not spend too long on this at the expense of easier marks.

Don't skimp on Parts (b) and (c) – there are 15 marks, and the ACCA examination/examining team recently commented that candidates' performance on these parts of Question 1 often indicate whether they will pass the paper!

Easy marks. These are available for setting out the proforma and workings, and also for valid points made Part (c) on ethical matters. Do not spend too much time on the fiddly joint venture working at the expense of these much easier marks.

Examiner's comment. Candidates dealt with the group structure quite well and the calculations of goodwill /'negative goodwill 'arising on acquisition were generally accurate. Candidates invariably calculate retained earnings and non-controlling interest inaccurately but the marking guide gives credit for candidates own figures as long as the principle is correct. For example, marks are allocated for calculating NCI as long as candidates are using the correct share of the subsidiaries' post acquisition earnings. Candidates struggled with the joint arrangement, but they should realise that there are marks available for the correct identification of the issue even if their accounting treatment is not totally accurate. In the written parts, candidates **must** apply the principles to the scenario.

Marking scheme

		Marks
(a)	Property, plant and equipment	5
	Goodwill	6
	Assets held for sale	5
	Current assets/total non-current liabilities	1
	Retained earnings	6
	Other components of equity	3
	Non-controlling interest	3
	Current liabilities	1
	Joint venture	5
		35
(b)	Subjective assessment of discussion – up to 2 marks per element	8
(c)	Subjective assessment – 1 mark per point	7
	Available	50

(a) JOEY GROUP

CONSOLIDATED STATEMENT OF FINANCIAL POSITION AS AT 30 NOVEMBER 20X4

	$m
Assets	
Non-current assets	
Property, plant and equipment: 3,295 + 2,000 + 1,200 – 38 (W2) + 266 (W7) – 14 (W2)	6,709.00
Goodwill (W2)	89.00
Intangible asset: franchise right (W7)	15.00
Joint venture (W9)	0.75
	6,813.75
Current assets: 985 + 861 + 150 + 15.3 (W8)	2,011.30
Total assets	8,825.05
Equity and liabilities	
Equity attributable to owners of the parent	
Share capital	850.00
Retained earnings (W3)	3,450.25
Other components of equity (W5)	258.50
	4,558.75
Non-controlling interests (W6)	908.10
	5,466.85
Non-current liabilities: 1,895 + 675 + 200	2,770.00
Current liabilities: 320 + 106 + 160 + 0.7 (W9) + 1.5 (W9)	588.20
Total equity and liabilities	8,825.05

Workings

1 *Group structure*

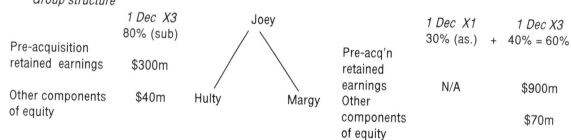

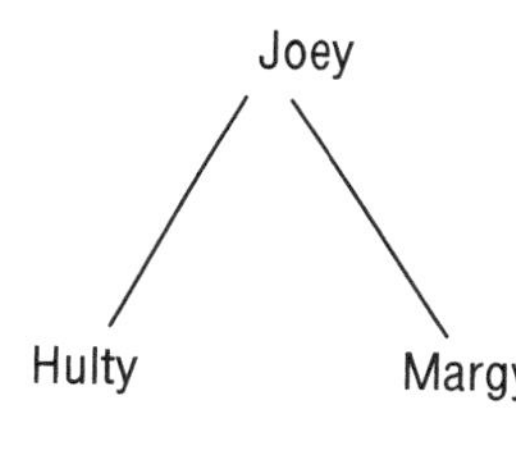

	1 Dec X3 80% (sub)			*1 Dec X1* 30% (as.)	+	*1 Dec X3* 40% = 60%
Pre-acquisition retained earnings	$300m		Pre-acq'n retained earnings	N/A		$900m
Other components of equity	$40m		Other components of equity			$70m

2 *Goodwill*

		Hulty		*Margy*
	$m	$m	$m	$m
Consideration transferred		700		975
Non-controlling interest (at fair value)		250		620
Fair value of previously held equity interest				705
Less fair value of net assets at acquisition				
Share capital	600		1,020	
Retained earnings	300		900	
Other components of equity	40		70	
Fair value adjustments:				
Land (W7)	-		266	
Contingent liability (note 3)	-		(6)	
Franchise right (W7)	20		–	
		(960)		(2,250)
Gain on bargain purchase (note (i))		(10)*		50
Add decrease in FV of buildings (note (ii))				40
Measurement period adjustment – contingent liability: $6m – $5m (note (iii))				(1)
Goodwill				89

Notes

(i) This is a gain on a bargain purchase and should be recorded in profit or loss for the year attributable to the parent (W3).

(ii) The carrying amount of property, plant and equipment as of 30 November 20X4 is decreased by \$40m less excess depreciation charged of \$2m, ie \$38m. This will increase the carrying amount of goodwill by \$40m and depreciation expense for 20X4 is decreased by \$2m. The decrease in depreciation is split between the retained earnings of the parent (\$1·4m) and NCI (\$0·6m).

(iii) In accordance with IFRS 3 *Business combinations,* contingent liabilities subsequent to the date of acquisition must be measured at the higher of the amount that would be recognised under IAS 37 *Provisions, contingent liabilities and contingent assets* and the amount initially recognised, less any cumulative amortisation. These requirements apply only for the period in which the item is considered to be a contingent liability. In this case the contingent liability has subsequently met the requirements to be classified as a provision and will be measured in accordance with IAS 37, rather than IFRS 3.

3 *Retained earnings*

	Joey	*Hulty*	*Margy*
	\$m	\$m	\$m
Per question	3,340.00	350	980
Fair value movement: depn. reduction (W7)			2
amortisation (W7)		(5)	
Liability adjustment			5
Gain on bargain purchase (W2)	10.00		
Profit on derecognition of associate (W4)	5.00		
Asset held for sale: 0.2 – 0.1 – 0.3 (W8)	(0.20)		
Joint operation (W9)	(0.70)		
Joint venture: 0.75 – 1.5 (W9)	(0.75)		
Pre-acquisition		(300)	(900)
		45	87
Group share			
Hulty: 80% × 45	36.00		
Margyy: 70% × 87	60.90		
	3,450.25		

4 *Profit on derecognition of 30% associate*

	\$m
Fair value at date control obtained (per question	705
Carrying amount of associate: 600 cost + 90 (post-acqn. RE) + 10 (post acqn OCE)	(700)
	5

5 *Other components of equity*

	Joey	*Hulty*	*Margy*
	\$m	\$m	\$m
Per question	250.0	40	80
Asset held for sale	1.5		
Pre-acquisition		(40)	(70)
:		0	10
Group share post acqn			
Hulty: 80% × 0	0.0		
Margyy: 70% × 10	7.0		
	258.5		

6 *Non-controlling interests*

	Hulty	Margy
	$m	$m
At date of control (FV)	250	620.0
Post-acquisition share of retained earnings		
Hulty: 45 (W3) × 20%	9	
Margy: 87 (W3) × 30%		26.1
Post-acquisition share of other components of equity		
Hulty: 0(W5) × 20%	0	
Margy: 10(W5) × 30%		3.0
	259	649.1
	908.1	

7 *Fair value adjustments*

Hulty:

	At acqn 1 Dec 20X3 $m	Movement (over 4 years) $m	At year end 30 Nov 20X4 $m
Franchise: 960 – (600 + 300 + 40)	20	(5)	15

Margy:

	At acqn 1 Dec 20X3	Movement (reduced depn.)	At year end 30 Nov 20X4
Land: 2,250 – (1,020 + 900 + 70) + 6*	266	-	266
Property, plant & equipment	(40)	2	(38)
	Goodwill (FV of NA)	Retained earnings	PPE in year end

*Contingent liability

8 *Asset held for sale*

At 31 March 20X4, the criteria in IFRS 5 *Non-current assets held for sale and discontinued operations* have been met, and the property may be classified as held for sale. In accordance with IFRS 5, an asset held for sale should be measured at the **lower of** its **carrying amount** and **fair value less costs to sell**. Immediately before classification of the asset as held for sale, the entity must recognise impairment in accordance with applicable IFRS. Any impairment loss is generally recognised in profit or loss. The steps are as follows.

Step 1 Calculate carrying value under applicable IFRS, here IAS 16 *Property, plant and equipment*.

At 31 March 20X4, the date of classification as held for sale, depreciation to date is calculated as $300,000 × 4/12 = $100,000. The carrying value of the property is therefore $13.9m. The journal entries are:

DEBIT	Profit or loss (W3)	$0.1m	
CREDIT	PPE		$0.1m

The difference between the carrying value and the fair value at 31 March 20X4 is material, so the property is revalued to its fair value of $15.4m

DEBIT	PPE $(15.4 – 13.9)m	$1.5m	
CREDIT	Other comprehensive income (W5)		$1.5m

Step 2 Consider whether the property is impaired by comparing its carrying amount, the fair value of $15.4m, with its recoverable amount. The recoverable amount is the higher of value in use (given as $15.8m) and fair value less costs to sell ($15.4m – $3m = $15.1m.) The property is not impaired because the recoverable amount (value in use) is higher than the carrying amount (fair value). No impairment loss is recognised.

Step 3 Classify as held for sale. Compare the carrying amount ($15.4m) with fair value less costs to sell ($15.1m). Measure at the lower of carrying value and fair value less costs to sell, here $15.1m, giving an initial write-down of $300,000.

DEBIT	Profit or loss (W3)	$0.3m	
CREDIT	PPE		$0.3m

Step 4 On 30 November 20X4, the property is sold for $15.6m, which, after deducting costs to sell of $0.3m gives a profit or $0.2m.

DEBIT	Receivables	$15.3m	
CREDIT	PPE		$15.1m
CREDIT	Profit or loss (W3)		$0.2m

9 *Joint operation and joint venture*

The arrangement with Content Publishing qualifies as a joint arrangement under IFRS 11 *Joint arrangements,* because key strategic and marketing decisions are taken jointly. For the period to 31 May 20X4, the arrangement is not structured through a separate vehicle, and so must be classified under IFRS 11 as a joint operation.

The treatment of the joint operation is set out in IFRS 11. Joey must recognise on a line-by-line basis its assets, liabilities, revenues and expenses plus its share of the joint assets, liabilities, revenue and expenses. The figures are calculated as follows:

Profit or loss of joint operation for the six months ending 31 May 20X4:

	$m
Revenue: 5 × 6/12	2.50
Cost of sales: 2 × 6/12	(1.00)
Gross profit	1.50

Joey's share is therefore:

	$m
Revenue: 90% × $2.5m	2.25
Cost of sales: printing, binding, platform maintenance, all Joey	(1.00)
Gross profit	1.25
Profit royalty to CP: 30% × $1.5m	(0.45)
Net profit	0.80

Joey must adjust the profit for the period to 31 May 20X4 by the amounts owing to CP as follows:

DEBIT	Profit or loss (0.45 + (2.5 × 10%)	$0.7m	
CREDIT	Accounts payable (CP)		$0.7m

From 1 June 20X4 the arrangement qualifies as a joint venture under IFRS 11, since Joey has a share of the net assets rather than rights to the individual assets and liabilities. The profit of the new entity must be removed as follows:

DEBIT	Profit or loss	$1.5m	
CREDIT	CR JCP – profit for the period (current liabilities)		$1.5m

Joey's share of JCP's profit must be equity accounted as follows:

DEBIT	Investment in joint venture ((\$5m – \$2m) × 6/12 × 50%)	$0.75m	
CREDIT	Profit or loss		$0.75m

(b) **Share-based payment**

This arrangement will be governed by IFRS 2 *Share-based payment,* which includes within its scope **transfers of equity instruments of an entity's parent in return for goods or services.** Clear guidance is given in the standard as to **when to treat group share-based payment transactions as equity settled and when to treat them as cash settled.**

To determine the accounting treatment, the group entity receiving the goods and services must **consider its own rights and obligations as well as the awards granted.** The amount recognised by the group entity receiving the goods and services will not necessarily be consistent with the amount recognised in the consolidated financial statements.

Group share-based payment transactions **must be treated as equity** settled if either of the following apply:

(i) The entity **grants rights to its own equity instruments**.
(ii) The entity has **no obligation to settle the** share-based payment transactions.

Treatment in consolidated financial statements

Because the group receives all of the services in consideration for the group's equity instruments, the transaction is treated as **equity settled**. The fair value of the share-based payment at the grant date is **charged to profit or loss over the vesting period with a corresponding credit to equity.**

Treatment in subsidiaries' financial statements

The subsidiaries do not have an obligation to settle the awards, so the grant is treated as an **equity settled** transaction. The fair value of the share-based payment at the grant date is **charged to profit or loss over the vesting period with a corresponding credit to equity.** The parent, Joey, is compensating the employees of the subsidiaries, Margy and Hulty, with no expense to the subsidiaries, and therefore the **credit in equity is treated as a capital contribution**. Because the shares vest immediately, the expense recognised in Margy and Hulty's statement of profit or loss will be the full cost of the fair value at grant date.

Treatment in parent's separate financial statements

There are no employees providing services to the parent, Joey, and therefore there is **no share-based payment charge**. Joey should recognised an increase in its investment in the subsidiaries and a credit to equity.

Potential IAS 24 disclosures

Joey should consider whether any of the employees are **key management personnel**. If so, the disclosure requirements of IAS 24 *Related party disclosures* should be applied.

(c) **Ethical issue and potential conflict of interest**

Ethical standards are important to accountants **because ethics have practical application in the accountant's professional life.**

Company directors are understandably **motivated by profit** – it is what the company's shareholders expect – and there may appear to be a conflict of interest between profit and ethics, including social ethics. Excessive focus on profit has led in some cases to **aggressive earnings management**, whereby directors use creative accounting techniques to present the results in a favourable light, or to **questionable business practices**, such as outsourcing to countries with poor health and safety records, or which use child labour.

Ethical codes cannot provide ready-made solutions to all potential conflicts, but it **can provide a set of principles on which to base judgements**. A vague wish to 'do the right thing' will be of little use when faced with a decision to report a colleague or member of the client's staff who is acting unethically. The study of ethics can direct the accountant's thinking and reasoning and help him or her make the right decision, even if it does not make that decision any easier. An example of ethical guidance serving this purpose is the ACCA's *Code of Ethics and Conduct,* which requires its members to adhere to a set of fundamental principles in the course of their professional duty, such as confidentiality, objectivity, professional behaviour, integrity, professional competence and due care.

In this particular case there is a **twofold conflict of interest:**

(i) The chief accountant is under pressure to provide the bank with a projected cash flow statement that will meet the bank's criteria when in fact the projections do not meet the criteria. The chief accountant's financial commitments mean that that he cannot afford to lose his job. **His ethical and professional standards are at odds with the pressures of his personal circumstances.**

(ii) The **directors have a duty to the company's shareholders and employees, and a duty to present fairly any information the bank may rely on**. Joey's need for a significant injection of capital, arising from the directors' wish to modernise plant and equipment is at odds with this. In fact it could be argued that there is a **conflict between the short-term interests of the company** (the need to modernise) **and its long-term interests** (the detriment to the company's reputation if its directors do not act ethically).

The **chief accountant is faced with an immediate ethical dilemma** and must apply his moral and ethical judgement. As a professional, he has a responsibility to present the truth fairly, and not to indulge in 'creative accounting' in response to pressure. **He should therefore put the interests of the company and professional ethics first,** and insist that the report to the bank is an honest reflection of the current financial position.

46 Case study question: Kutchen

Text reference. Business combinations achieved in stages and disposals are covered in Chapter 14. Employee benefits are covered in Chapter 4 and deferred tax in Chapter 6. Fair values are covered in Chapters 7 and 12. Financial instruments are covered in Chapter 7. Ethical issues are covered in Chapter 2.

Top tips. Part (a) required the preparation of a consolidated statement of financial position with one subsidiary acquired at the beginning of the year, one part way through the year and a third subsidiary disposed of on the last day of the year. As usual, a number of adjustments were required. In questions like this with a number of changes in group structure, it is important to think carefully about the group structure before launching into the question. Part (b) covered a practical scenario of whether some contingent payments should be accounted for as debt or equity. This is a recurring theme on Paper 2. Part (c), on 'rules-based' versus 'principles-based' accounting standards, was sufficiently open ended to earn marks, provided the case is argued clearly. Waffle will earn no marks.

Easy marks. In Part (a), there are plenty of marks for standard consolidation workings, so it is important not to be put off by the 'twists', such as the calculation of NCI using the PE ratio: if it isn't clear, just put in a figure and get on with the rest of the question.

Examiner's comments. In Part (a), Candidates seemed to be able to calculate NCI using market prices but struggled with the calculation involving the PE ratio. The understanding of the PE ratio is fundamental to corporate reporting. In addition to the purchase and disposal of subsidiaries, the holding company also decided to restructure one of its business segments which affected the employees' pension benefits in two locations. Candidates were expected to show the impact on profit or loss of the restructuring. This part of the question was quite well done, as was the calculation of the impairment loss and the deferred tax asset, which arose because of the impairment. It is imperative that candidates not only understand group accounting techniques but also complete the workings for goodwill, retained earnings, other comprehensive income (OCI) and NCI. Many candidates struggled with the difference between debt and equity in Part (b). In Part (c), Candidates were given due credit for relevant opinion on the subject matter of the question.

Marking scheme

		Marks
(a)		
	Property, plant and equipment	4
	Goodwill	7
	Non-current liabilities	2
	Finance lease (lessor)	3
	Deferred tax	2
	Current assets	1
	Pensions	3
	Retained earnings	6
	Other components of equity	2
	Non-controlling interest	3
	Current liabilities	2
		35
(b)		
	1 mark per point up to maximum	8
(c)		
	Philosophy	3
	Ethical considerations	4
		50

(a) KUTCHEN GROUP
CONSOLIDATED STATEMENT OF FINANCIAL POSITION
AS AT 31 MARCH 20X5

	$m
Non-current assets	
Property, plant and equipment: 216 + 41 + 38 + 14 (W6) + 13 (W6) – 3 (W8) – 5 (W12)	314.00
Goodwill (W2)	26.06
Finance lease receivable: 50 + 14 + 8 – 0.2 (W11)	71.80
	411.86
Current assets: 44 + 25 + 64	133.00
Total assets	544.86
Equity and liabilities	
Equity attributable to owners of the parent	
Share capital: 43 + 20 (W7)	63.00
Retained earnings (W3)	50.05
Other components of equity (W4)	25.40
	138.45
Non-controlling interests (W5)	33.06
	171.51
Non-current liabilities: 67 + 12 + 28 – 2 (W10) – 2.4 (W10) – 1.25 (W12)	101.35
Current liabilities: 199 + 26 + 37 + 4 (W10) + 6 (W10)	272.00
Total equity and liabilities	544.86

Workings

1 *Group structure*

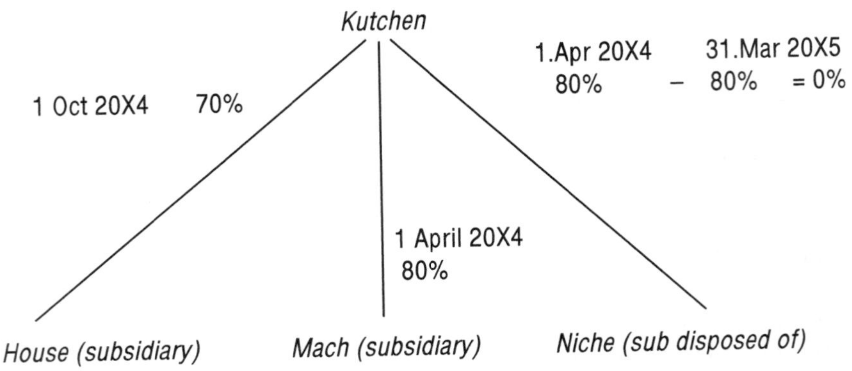

	Kutchen		
	1 Oct 20X4 70%	1 April 20X4 80%	1.Apr 20X4 80% – 31.Mar 20X5 80% = 0%
	House (subsidiary)	*Mach (subsidiary)*	*Niche (sub disposed of)*
Consid. trans.			
Shares	20m × $2		
Contingent	5m × $2 × 20%		
Cash		$52m	$40m
Land		$5m	
FVNA	$48m	$55m	$44m

2 *Goodwill*

	House $m	*Match* $m	*Niche* $m
Consideration transferred (W7)/ (52 + 5 (W8))/Per qu	42.00	57.00	40.0
Non-controlling interests (at FV) (13m × 30% × $4.20)/(W8)	16.38	13.68	
Non-controlling interests: 44 × 20%			8.8
Less fair value of net assets acquired	(48.00)	(55.00)	(44.0)
	10.38	15.68	4.8
Impairment losses	(-)	(-)	(2.0)
	10.38	15.68	2.8
	26.06		
Derecognised on disposal (W9)			(2.8)
			–

3 *Retained earnings*

	Kutchen $m	*House* $m	*Mach* $m
Per question	41.00	24	15
Gain on transfer of land (W8)	2.00		
Transfer of post acq'n. profit of Niche (W9)	10.00		
Pension gain (W10)	2.00		
Pension loss (W10)	(1.60)		
Restructuring provision (W10)	(6.00)		
Lease adjustment (W11)	(0.20)		
Impairment of building (W12)	(5.00)		
Deferred tax (W12)	1.25		
Pre-acquisition (W1)		(18)	(12)
		6	3
Group share			
House: 6 × 70%	4.20		
Mach: 3 × 80%	2.40		
	50.05		

4 *Other components of equity*

	Kutchen $m	House $m	Mach $m
Per question	12.0	5	4
Purchase of House			
Share premium	20.0		
Contingent consideration	2.0		
Transfer of post acq'n. profit of Niche (W9)	(10.0)		
Pre-acquisition (W1)		(3)	(4)
		2	0
Group share post acqn:			
House: 2 × 70 %	1.4		
Mach : 0 × 80%	0.0		
	25.4		

5 *Non-controlling interests*

	House $m	Mach $m
At acquisition (/W2)	16.38	13.68
Post acquisition share of retained earnings		
House: 6(W3) × 30%	1.80	
Mach: 3 (W3) × 20%		0.60
Post acquisition share of other components of equity		
House: 2 (W4) × 30%	0.60	
Mach: 0 (W4) × 20%		0.00
	18.78	14.28
	33.06	

6 *Fair value adjustments*

House:

	At acqn 1.10.20X4 $m	Movement $m	At year end 31.3.20X5 $m
Land: 48 – (13 + 18 + 3)	14	–	14

Mach:

	At acqn 1.4.20X4	Movement	At year end 31.3.20X5
Land: 55 – (26 + 12+ 4)	13	–	13

7 *Cost of investment in House*

The journal entries for the consideration transferred are:

DEBIT	Cost of investment in House	$42m		
CREDIT	Share capital of Kutchen (20m × $1)		$20m	
CREDIT	Share premium of Kutchen (20m × ($2 – $1))		$20m	
CREDIT	Share premium of Kutchen (5m × 20% × $2)			$2m

8 Cost of investment in Mach

The journal entry for the cash paid for the shares (already recorded) is:

DEBIT	Cost of investment in Mach	$52m	
CREDIT	Cash		$52m

The land transferred as part of the purchase consideration should be valued at its acquisition fair value of $5m. The increase of $2m over the carrying amount should be credited to profit or loss (retained earnings):

DEBIT	Cost of investment in Mach	\$5m	
CREDIT	Land of Kutchen		\$3m
CREDIT	Profit or loss (retained earnings)		\$2m

Net profit of Mach for the year to 31 March 20X4 is \$3.6 million. The P/E ratio (adjusted) is 19. Therefore the fair value of Mach is 19 × \$3.6 million, ie \$68.4 million. The NCI has a 20% holding; therefore the fair value of the NCI is \$13.68 million.

9 *Sale of Niche*

	\$m	\$m
Consideration received		50.0
Fair value of remaining interest		0.0
Less carrying amount at date of disposal		
Net assets	60.0	
Goodwill (W2)	2.8	
Less NCI: 60 × 20%	(12)	
		(50.8)
Loss on disposal		(0.8)
Post acq'n profit (was held at cost): (60 – 44) × 80%		12.8
Impairment loss		(2.0)
		10.0

The gain on the sale in Kutchen's individual company financial statements was recorded in other components of equity. This should be corrected as follows in the consolidated financial statements.

DEBIT	Other components of equity	\$10m	
CREDIT	Retained earnings		\$10m

10 *Restructuring and defined benefit pension plan*

Location 1:

After restructuring, the present value of the pension liability in location 1 is reduced to \$8 million. Thus there will be a negative past service cost in this location of \$(10 – 8) million, ie \$2 million. The adjustments are as follows:

DEBIT	Defined benefit pension plan obligation	\$2m	
CREDIT	Profit or loss and retained earnings		\$2m

Location 2:

There is a settlement and a curtailment as all liability will be extinguished by the payment of \$4 million. Therefore there is a loss of \$(2·4 – 4) million, ie \$1·6 million. The adjustments are as follows:

DEBIT	Defined benefit pension plan obligation	\$2.4m	
DEBIT	Profit or loss and retained earnings (balance)	\$1.6m	
CREDIT	Current liabilities		\$4m

And, since the company has started to implement the plan:

DEBIT	Profit or loss and retained earnings	\$6m	
CREDIT	Provision		\$6m

11 *Lessor finance lease*

This should be corrected as follows:

Kutchen's entries were:

DEBIT	Cost of sales	\$40m	
CREDIT	Property, plant and equipment		\$40m

DEBIT	Lease receivable	$50m	
CREDIT	Revenue		$50m

Kutchen's entries should have been:

DEBIT	Cost of sales	$40m	
CREDIT	Property, plant and equipment		$40m
DEBIT	Lease receivable (47 + 2.8)	$49.8m	
CREDIT	Revenue		$49.8m

To correct:

DEBIT	Revenue	$0.2m	
CREDIT	Lease receivable		$0.2m

12 *Impairment of building and deferred tax*

	$m
Cost at 1 January 20X4: 25 million dinars/2	12.5
Depreciation to 31 March 20X5	(0.5)
	12.0
∴ Impairment loss	(5.0)
Recoverable amount	7.0

DEBIT	Profit or loss (retained earnings)	$5m	
CREDIT	Property, plant and equipment		$5m

Deferred tax:

The tax base and carrying amount of the non-current assets are the same before the impairment charge. After the impairment charge, there will be a difference of $5 million. This will create a deferred tax asset of $5 million × 25%, ie $1·25 million. As Kutchen expects to make profits for the foreseeable future, this can be recognised in the financial statements.

Accounting carrying amount	*Less*	*Tax base*	=	*Temporary difference*	*× 25%*	=	*Deferred tax (asset)*
$m		$m		$m			$m
7		12		(5)	× 25%		(1.25)

DEBIT	Deferred tax asset	$1.25m	
CREDIT	Deferred tax (P/L)		$1.25m

(b) **Contingent payment**

The *Conceptual Framework* defines a liability as a present obligation, arising from past events and there is an expected outflow of economic benefits. IAS 32 *Financial instruments: presentation* establishes principles for presenting financial instruments as liabilities or equity. IAS 32 does not classify a financial instrument as equity or financial liability on the basis of its legal form but the substance of the transaction. The key feature of a financial liability is that the issuer is obliged to deliver either cash or another financial asset to the holder. An obligation may arise from a requirement to repay principal or interest or dividends. In contrast, equity has a residual interest in the entity's assets after deducting all of its liabilities. An equity instrument includes no obligation to deliver cash or another financial asset to another entity. A contract which will be settled by the entity receiving or delivering a fixed number of its own equity instruments in exchange for a fixed amount of cash or another financial asset is an equity instrument. However, if there is any variability in the amount of cash or own equity instruments which will be delivered or received, then such a contract is a financial asset or liability as applicable.

The contingent payments should not be treated as contingent liabilities but they should be recognised as financial liabilities and measured at fair value at initial recognition. IAS 37 *Provisions, contingent liabilities and contingent assets*, excludes from its scope contracts which are executory in nature, and therefore prevents the recognition of a liability. Additionally, there is no onerous contract in this scenario.

Contingent consideration for a business must be recognised at the time of acquisition, in accordance with IFRS 3 *Business combinations*. However, IFRS do not contain any guidance when accounting for contingent consideration for the acquisition of a NCI in a subsidiary. The contract for contingent payments does meet the definition of a financial liability under IAS 32. Kutchen has an obligation to pay cash to the vendor of the NCI under the terms of a contract. It is not within Kutchen's control to be able to avoid that obligation. The amount of the contingent payments depends on the profitability of Mach, which itself depends on a number of factors which are uncontrollable. IAS 32 states that a contingent obligation to pay cash which is outside the control of both parties to a contract meets the definition of a financial liability which shall be initially measured at fair value. Since the contingent payments relate to the acquisition of the NCI, the offsetting entry would be recognised directly in equity.

(c) **Rules-based or principles-based?**

The IASB emphasises the fundamental importance of standards which focus on principles, drawn clearly from the IASB's *Conceptual Framework,* rather than on detailed rules. This approach requires both companies and their auditors to exercise professional judgement in the public interest, by requiring preparers to develop financial statements which provide a faithful representation of all transactions and requiring auditors to resist client pressures. The US financial reporting model is based largely on principles, but supplemented by extensive rules and regulations. Companies want detailed guidance because those details eliminate uncertainties about how transactions should be structured, and auditors want specificity because those specific requirements limit the number of difficult disputes with clients and may provide defence in litigation.

The IASB has indicated that a body of detailed guidance encourages a rulebook mentality and it often helps those who are intent on finding ways around standards. The detailed guidance may obscure, rather than highlight, the underlying principles, since the emphasis is often on compliance with the 'letter' of the rule rather than on the 'spirit' of the accounting standard.

Moving from a rules-based system of accounting standards to a principles-based system could create ethical challenges for accountants. More professional judgement would be needed, which could be perceived as creating potential ethical grey areas. However, whilst IFRS tend to use more of a principles-based approach, this, in turn, requires accountants to have a complete understanding of ACCA's ethical principles and possess an ability to apply those principles effectively using a personal decision-making process. Accountants are required to appreciate the critical role ethics serves in the accounting profession and work continually in improving their process for recognising and thinking through ethical issues. The ethical conduct of an accountant should not be influenced by the nature of the accounting principles and practices, which are being complied with.

Convergence of accounting principles is an important part of the IASB's work plan and road map for adoption of a single set of high quality globally accepted accounting standards. It follows therefore that there should be global convergence on the subject of an independent accountant's ethical responsibility for assuring that financial statements do in fact fairly present economic reality.

There is no doubt that where a rules-based system has been in operation, there is likely to be an expansion of ethical challenges for both accountants and auditors involved with the financial statements of public companies if a principles-based approach was adopted. For example, the litigious atmosphere which businesses face in the US could lead to poor application of IFRS because of pressures relating to potential litigation. However, it is up to the accounting profession to ensure that ethical practices ensure high quality financial statements. Initially, accountants may face ethical pressures from management to develop and follow a rationale for seeing the financial results of their organisation in absolutely the most favourable light, because of the apparent elimination of accounting rules. However, IFRS are a robust set of accounting standards and it is unrealistic to assume that these standards could not replace those based around rules.

47 Case study question: Robby

Text reference. Business combinations achieved in stages are covered in Chapter 14. Non-current assets are covered in Chapter 3. Joint operations are covered in Chapter 13 and financial instruments in Chapter 7.

Top tips. Part (a) required a consolidated statement of financial position with two subsidiaries, one of which was acquired in stages. Included in this part of the question was a joint operation, and there were adjustments for the revaluation of property, plant and equipment, impairment of receivables and sale and repurchase of land. The joint operation was fiddly and time-consuming, although not conceptually difficult as you are told what kind of joint arrangement it was. If you struggled with the details of the step acquisition of Zinc given in Note (b) of the question, look carefully at our goodwill calculation in (W3). The investment in Zinc was made up of the 55% investment at its cost and the 5% investment at its 31 May 20X2 fair value, with a gain on revaluation of the 5% taking place in the current year (to 31 May 20X3). Part (b)(i) was textbook knowledge of a topical issue. Note the ACCA examination/examining team's comment for Part (b)(ii) on the ethical implications of the sale of land just before the year end. This type of question is in line with the ACCA examination/examining team's pattern of applying ethical principles to transactions that might be designed to manipulate the financial statements. It is not enough just to discuss the accounting treatment without considering the ethical issues.

Easy marks. There are some standard consolidation workings here, and you could slot in the caption for, say, joint operation, even if you get the calculation wrong or do not have time to do it all. Leave enough time for Part (b) – the ACCA examination/examining team has commented in the past that candidates often do not.

Examiner's comment. In Part 1(a), candidates showed themselves to be very good at preparing group accounts using the full goodwill method, and coped well with the impairment of the PPE. However, they had problems determining the fair value of the consideration as some candidates did not take into account the increase in the fair value of the equity interest. They also struggled with the joint operation. In Part 1(b), candidates did not seem to know the de-recognition rules of IFRS 9 and often described the nature of a financial instrument, when a financial instrument should be recognised and the valuation methods utilised, which was correct but did not answer the question. Answers to Part 1(b)(ii) were good, although many candidates spent a disproportionate amount of time discussing the accounting treatment with little time spent on the ethical aspect of the transaction.

Marking scheme

		Marks
(a)		
	Property, plant and equipment	6
	Goodwill	6
	Non-controlling interest	4
	Financial assets	1
	Current assets	3
	Other components of equity	3
	Retained earnings	6
	Non-current liabilities	2
	Current liabilities	4
		35
(b)		
	(i) 1 mark per point up to max	9
	(ii) Manipulation	2
	Ethical discussion	4
		50

(a) ROBBY GROUP
CONSOLIDATED STATEMENT OF FINANCIAL POSITION AS AT 31 MAY 20X3

	$m
Assets	
Non-current assets	
Property, plant and equipment: 112 + 60 + 26 + 24 (W8) + 3.6 (W9) + 6.12 (W10) – 2.59 (W11) + 12 (W13)	241.13
Goodwill: 5 (W2) + 1 (W3)	6.00
Financial assets: 9 + 6 + 14	29.00
Jointly controlled operation: 6 – 6 (W10)	–
	276.13
Current assets: 5 + 7 + 12 + 8 (W10) + 4 (W12)	36.00
Total assets	312.13
Equity and liabilities	
Equity attributable to owners of the parent	
Ordinary shares	25.00
Other components of equity (W4)	2.00
Retained earnings (W5)	81.45
	108.45
Non-controlling interests (W6)	27.64
	136.09
Non-current liabilities: 53 + 20 + 21 + 0.84 (W10)	94.84
Current liabilities: 47 + 6 + 2 +6.6 (W10) + 3.6 (W12) + 16 (W13)	81.20
Total equity and liabilities	312.13

Workings

1 *Group structure*

		Robby			
	1 June X1 80% (sub)		*1 June X0* 5% (IEI)	+	*1 Dec X2* 55% = 60%
Pre-acquisition retained earnings	$16m		Pre-acquisition retained earnings	N/A	$15m
	Hail		Zinc		

2 *Goodwill (Hail)*

	$m
Consideration transferred	50*
Non-controlling interest (fair value per question)	15
FV of identifiable net assets at acq'n	(60)
	5

***Note.** Hail is valued at $55m as at 31 May 20X3, so there is a revaluation gain of $55m – $50m = $5m which needs to be reversed out in the calculation of consolidated other components of equity (W4).

3 *Goodwill (Zinc)*

	$m
Consideration transferred – for 55%	16
Non-controlling interest at fair value (per question)	9
Fair value of previously held interest (for 5% at 1 December 20X2)	5*
FV of identifiable net assets at acq'n: 26 + 3	(29)
	1

***Note.** There will be a revaluation gain on the previously held interest, calculated as follows:

	$m
Fair value of 5% at date control achieved (1 December 20X2)	5
Fair value of 5% per SOFP, ie at 31 May 20X2: $19m per Robby's SOFP, less $16m consideration for 55%	(3)
Revaluation gain (1 June 20X2 to 1 December 20X2)	2

This gain on revaluation of the previously held interest is taken to profit or loss for the year, and hence to retained earnings (W5).

4 *Other components of equity*

	$m
Robby (per question)	11.00
Dividend income from Hail transferred to retained earnings (W7)	(2.00)
Reserve transfer on property, plant and equipment (W11)	(0.11)
Impairment loss on property, plant and equipment (W11)	(1.89)
Revaluation gain on investment in Hail (W2)	(5.00)
Pre-acquisition (W1)	2.00

5 *Retained earnings*

	Robby	*Hail*	*Zinc*
	$m	$m	$m
Per question	70.00	27.0	19.0
Gain on revaluation of 5% investment in Zinc (W3)	2.00		
Dividend income from Hail (W7)	2.00		
Fair value depreciation (W9)	–		(0.4)
Profit from joint operation (W10)	0.68		
Reserve transfer on PPE (W11)	0.11		
Impairment loss on PPE (W11)	(0.70)		
Reverse loss on debt factoring (W12)	0.40		
Reverse gain on sale and repurchase (W13)	(4.00)		
Pre-acquisition (W1)		(16.0)	(15.0)
		11.0	3.6
Group share of post-acquisition profits of:			
Hail: 11 × 80%	8.80		
Zinc: 3.6 × 60%	2.16		
	81.45		

6 *Non-controlling interests*

	Hail	*Zinc*
	$m	$m
At acquisition (W2/W3)	15.0	9.00
Post acquisition share of retained earnings		
Hail: 11 (W5) × 20%	2.2	
Zinc: 3.6 (W5) × 40%		1.44
	17.2	10.44
	27.64	

7 *Dividend*

The $2m dividend income has been incorrectly recorded in other comprehensive income for the year, and therefore in other components of equity. It should have been recorded in profit or loss for the year, and therefore in retained earnings.

To correct, the entries are:

DEBIT Other components of equity	$2m	
CREDIT Retained earnings		$2m

8 *Fair value adjustment: Hail*

Hail:

	At acqn 1June 20X1	*Movement (2 years)*	*At year end 31 May 20X3*
	$m	$m	$m
Land: 60 – (20 + 16)	24	–	24
	Goodwill (FV of NA)	Retained earnings	PPE in year end

9 *Fair value adjustment: Zinc*

Hail:

	At acqn 1 Dec 20X2	*Movement (6 months)*	*At year end 31 May 20X3*
	$m	$m	$m
PPE: (26 + 3) – (10 + 15)	4	(0.4)	3.6
	Goodwill (FV of NA)	Retained earnings	PPE in year end

***Note.** The fair value movement is the additional depreciation caused by the fair valuing for consolidation purposes: $4m × 1/5 × 6/12 = $0.4m

10 *Joint operation (in Robby's books)*

The treatment of the joint operation is set out in IFRS 11 *Joint arrangements.* Robby must recognise on a line-by-line basis its assets, liabilities, revenues and expenses plus its share (40%) of the joint assets, liabilities, revenue and expenses. The figures are calculated as follows:

Statement of financial position

	$m
Property, plant and equipment:	
1 June 20X2 cost: gas station (15 × 40%)	6.00
dismantling provision (2 × 40%)	0.80
	6.80
Accumulated depreciation: 6.8/10	(0.68)
31 May 20X3 NBV	6.12
Trade receivables (from other joint operator): 20 (revenue) × 40%	8.00
Trade payables (to other joint operator): 16 + 0.5 (costs) × 40%	6.60
Dismantling provision:	
At 1 June 20X2	0.80
Finance cost (unwinding of discount): 0.8 × 5%	0.04
At 31 May 20X3	0.84

Profit or loss for the year

	$m
Revenue: 20 × 40%	8.00
Cost of sales: 16 × 40%	(6.40)
Operating costs: 0.5 × 40%	(0.20)
Depreciation	(0.68)
Finance cost (unwinding of discount)	(0.04)
Profit from joint operation (to retained earnings (W10)	0.68

Robby has accounted only for its share of the construction cost of $6m. The journals to correct this are therefore as follows:

		$m	$m
DEBIT	Property, plant and equipment	6.12	
DEBIT	Trade receivables	8.00	
CREDIT	Joint operation		6.00
CREDIT	Trade payables		6.60
CREDIT	Provision		0.84
CREDIT	Retained earnings (Robby)		0.68

11 *Property, plant and equipment*

		Carrying amount $m	*Revaluation surplus* $m
1 June 20X0	Cost	10.00	
	Acc. depreciation $\frac{2}{10} \times 10$	(1.00)	
		9.00	
	Revaluation gain(bal. fig)	2.00	2.00
31 May 20X2	Revalued PPE c/d	11.00	
	Depreciation for year $\frac{1}{18} \times 11$	(0.61)	
	Transfer to retained earnings: 0.61 – 0.50		(0.11)
31 May 20X3	Balance	10.39	1.89
	Impairment loss (bal. fig.)	(2.59)	
	Recoverable amount	7.80	

The impairment loss is charged to other comprehensive income and therefore to other components of equity to the extent of the revaluation surplus. The remainder is taken to profit or loss and therefore to retained earnings. Thus $1.89 is taken to other components of equity and $2.59 – $1.89 = $0.7 to retained earnings.

Journals in Robby's books

Reserve transfer:

DEBIT	Other components of equity	$0.11m	
CREDIT	Retained earnings		$0.11m

Impairment loss:

DEBIT	Other components of equity	$1.89m	
DEBIT	Retained earnings	$0.70	
CREDIT	Property, plant and equipment		$2.89m

12 *Debt factoring*

Robby should not have derecognised the receivables because the risks and rewards of ownership have not been transferred. The receivables must therefore be reinstated and the loss reversed:

DEBIT	Trade receivables	$4.0m	
CREDIT	Current liabilities		$3.6m
CREDIT	Retained earnings (to reverse loss)		$0.4m

13 *Sale and repurchase of land*

Robby should not have derecognised the land from the financial statements because the risks and rewards of ownership have not been transferred. The substance of the transaction is a loan of $16m, and the 5% 'premium' on repurchase is effectively an interest payment. This is an attempt to manipulate the financial statements in order to show a more favourable cash position. The sale must be reversed and the land reinstated at its carrying amount before the transaction. The repurchase, ie the repayment of the loan takes place one month after the year end, and so this is a current liability:

DEBIT	Property, plant and equipment	$12m	
DEBIT	Retained earnings (to reverse profit on disposal (16 – 12)	$4m	
CREDIT	Current liabilities		$16m

(b) (i) **Derecognition of a financial asset**

Derecognition is the removal of a previously recognised financial instrument from an entity's statement of financial position.

An entity should derecognise a **financial asset** when:

(1) The **contractual rights** to the cash flows from the financial asset **expire**, or

(2) The entity **transfers the financial asset or substantially all the risks and rewards of ownership** of the financial asset to another party.

IFRS 9 gives **examples of where an entity has transferred substantially all the risks and rewards of ownership**. These include:

(1) An unconditional sale of a financial asset

(2) A sale of a financial asset together with an option to repurchase the financial asset at its fair value at the time of repurchase.

The standard also **provides examples of situations where the risks and rewards of ownership have not been transferred**:

(1) A sale and repurchase transaction where the repurchase price is a fixed price or the sale price plus a lender's return

(2) A sale of a financial asset together with a total return swap that transfers the market risk exposure back to the entity

(3) A sale of short-term receivables in which the entity guarantees to compensate the transferee for credit losses that are likely to occur.

It is possible for only **part** of a financial asset or liability to be derecognised. This is allowed if the part comprises:

(1) Only specifically identified cash flows, or

(2) Only a fully proportionate (pro rata) share of the total cash flows

For example, if an entity holds a bond it has the right to two separate sets of cash inflows: those relating to the principal and those relating to the interest. It could sell the right to receive the interest to another party while retaining the right to receive the principal.

In the case of Robby, the substance of the transaction needs to be considered rather than its legal form. Robby has transferred the receivables to the factor in exchange for $3.6m cash, but it is liable for any shortfall between $3.6m and the amount collected. In principle, Robby is liable for the whole $3.6m, although it is unlikely that the default would be as much as this. **Robby therefore retains the credit risk.** In addition, Robby is entitled to receive the benefit (less interest) of repayments in excess of $3.6m once the $3.6m has been collected. Therefore for amounts in excess of $3.6m Robby also retains the late payment risk. **Substantially all the risks and rewards** of the financial asset **therefore remain with Robby**, and the receivables should **continue to be recognised.**

(ii) **Sale of land**

Ethical behaviour in the preparation of financial statements, and in other areas, is of **paramount importance**. This applies equally to preparers of accounts, to auditors and to accountants giving advice to directors. Financial statements may be manipulated for all kinds of reasons, for example to enhance a profit-linked bonus. In this case, the purpose of the sale and repurchase is **to present a misleadingly favourable picture of the cash position**, which **hides** the fact that the Robby Group **has severe liquidity problems**. The extent of the liquidity problems can be seen in the current ratio of $36m/$81.2m = 0.44:1, and the gearing ratio of 0.83, calculated as follows:

53 + 20 + 21 (non-current liabilities) + 3.6 (factored receivables) + 16 (land option)	=	113.60	= 0.83
Equity interest (including NCI)		136.09	

The effect of the sale just before the year end was to **eliminate the bank overdraft** and improve these ratios, although once the sale of land has been correctly accounted for as a loan, there is no improvement in gearing. The sale as originally accounted for might forestall proceedings by the bank, but as the substance of the transaction is a loan, it does not alter the true position and gives a **misleading impression** of it.

Company accountants act unethically if they use 'creative' accounting in accounts preparation to make the figures look better. To act ethically, the directors must put the interests of the company and its shareholders first, and must also have regard to other stakeholders such as potential investors or lenders. **If a treatment does not conform to acceptable accounting practice, it is not ethical.** Acceptable accounting practice includes conformity with the qualitative characteristics set out in the *Conceptual Framework* particularly fair presentation and verifiability. Conformity with the *Conceptual Framework* precludes **window-dressing transactions** such as this, and so the land needs to be reinstated in the accounts and a current liability set up for the repurchase.

48 Case study question: Ashanti

Text references. Complex groups are covered in Chapter 13 of your Study Text. Disposals are covered in Chapter 14. Financial instruments are covered in Chapter 7. Management of earnings is covered in Chapter 10 and also in Chapter 1 in the context of revenue recognition.

Top tips. This is an exceptionally demanding question, so don't worry too much if you didn't get it all. However, it is really important that you get the group structure. It is complicated. First you have a complex group. Then there are two disposals, one where control is lost (sub-subsidiary to sub-associate) and one where control is retained (70% to 60% subsidiary). In fact the adjustment on the disposal of the interest in Bochem does not belong in the statement of profit or loss and other comprehensive income, but we include it for completeness.

There are also a number of adjustments, some of which relate to financial instruments.

In Part (b), don't be tempted to waffle.

Easy marks. There are a surprising number of easy marks for such a complicated question. First there are the usual straightforward consolidation aspects – adding across, intragroup trading, setting up workings, revaluation of property. And part (c) is reasonably flexible, with credit available for sensible comments.

Examiner's comment. Candidates generally did well on this question. They showed a good understanding of the full goodwill method. Some made the mistake of showing a gain on disposal of the interest in Bochem in the statement of profit or loss and other comprehensive income, when it should be an adjustment to equity. The ACCA examination/examining team stressed the importance of showing workings in a clear, concise manner, so that marks can be allocated for principles and method, even if mistakes are made in the calculations.

Marking scheme

		Marks
(a)	Consolidated statement of profit or loss and other comprehensive income	5
	Bochem	8
	Ceram	6
	Inventory	2
	Bond	4
	PPE	3
	Impairment of customer	2
	Employee benefits	2
	NCI	3
		35

		Marks
(b)	1 mark per valid point, maximum	8
(c)	Description of management of earnings	4
	Moral/ethical considerations	3
		7
		50

(a) ASHANTI GROUP
STATEMENT OF PROFIT OR LOSS AND OTHER COMPREHENSIVE INCOME
FOR THE YEAR ENDED 30 APRIL 20X5

	$m
Revenue: 810 + 235 + (142 × $^6/_{12}$) – 15 (W4) – 5 (W6)	1,096.00
Cost of sales: 686 + 137 + (84 × $^6/_{12}$) – 15 (W4) + 1 (W4)	(851.00)
Gross profit	245.00
Other income: 31 + 17 + (12 × $^6/_{12}$) + 3.8 (W10)	57.80
Distribution costs: 30 + 21 + (26 × $^6/_{12}$)	(64.00)
Administrative expenses: 55 + 29 + (12 × $^6/_{12}$) + 2 (W3) + 1.6 (W7) + 0.21 (W8) + 2.2 (W9)	(96.01)
Finance income (W5)	10.31
Finance costs: 8 + 6 + (8 × $^6/_{12}$) + 20.328 (W5) + 8 (W6)	(46.33)
Share of profit of associate: 14 × $^6/_{12}$ × 30%	2.10
Profit before tax	108.87
Income tax expense: 21 + 23 + (10 × $^6/_{12}$)	(49.00)
Profit for the year	59.87
Other comprehensive income (items that will not be reclassified to profit or loss)	
Gain on investments in equity instruments: 20 + 9 + (6 × $^6/_{12}$)	32.00
Gain/loss on property revaluation: 12 + 6 + 1.6 (W7)	19.60
Actuarial loss on defined benefit plan: 14	(14.00)
Share of other comprehensive income of associate: 6 × $^6/_{12}$ × 30%	0.90
Other comprehensive income for the year net of tax	38.5
Total comprehensive income for the year	98.37
Profit attributable to:	
Owners of the parent (bal. fig.)	45.48
Non-controlling interests (W2)	14.39
	59.87
Total comprehensive income attributable to:	
Owners of the parent (bal. fig.)	77.89
Non-controlling interests (W2)	20.48
	98.37

Workings

1 *Group structure*

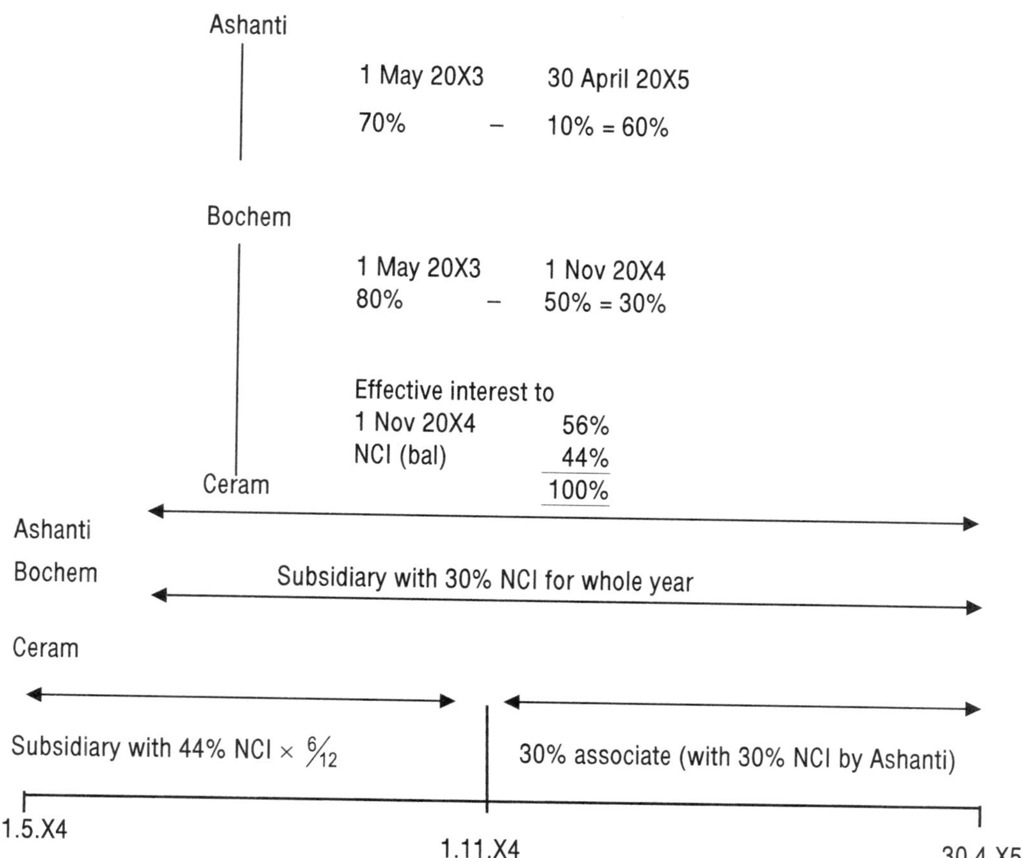

Ashanti

Bochem — Subsidiary with 30% NCI for whole year

Ceram

Subsidiary with 44% NCI × $\frac{6}{12}$ | 30% associate (with 30% NCI by Ashanti)

1.5.X4 — 1.11.X4 — 30.4.X5

2 *Non-controlling interests*

	Bochem		*Ceram*	
	Profit for year	*TCI*	*Profit for year*	*TCI*
	\$m	\$m	\$m	\$m
Per question	36.0	51.0		
14 × $\frac{6}{12}$			7.0	
20 × $\frac{6}{12}$				10
Depreciation of fair value adjustment (W3)	(2.0)	(2.0)		
Impairment of 'full' goodwill	(2.2)	(2.2)		
Profit on disposal of Ceram (W10)	3.8	3.8		
Share of profit of associate				
14 × $\frac{6}{12}$ × 30%	2.1			
Share of TCI of associate (6 × $\frac{6}{12}$ × 30%) + 2.1		3.0		

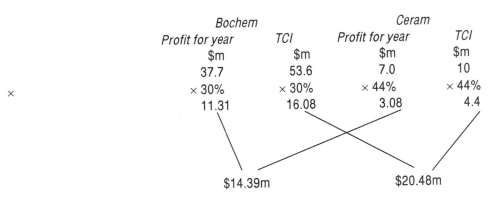

	Bochem Profit for year	TCI	Ceram Profit for year	TCI
	$m	$m	$m	$m
	37.7	53.6	7.0	10
×	× 30%	× 30%	× 44%	× 44%
	11.31	16.08	3.08	4.4

$14.39m (11.31 + 3.08) $20.48m (16.08 + 4.4)

Note. There is no profit on the part disposal of Bochem because control is not lost.

3 *Fair value adjustments*

Bochem	*At acquisition 1 May 20X3*	*Movement 20X4*	*Movement 20X5*	*At year end 30 April 20X5*
	$m	$m	$m	$m
Plant (160 – (55 + 85 + 10))	10	$^{10}/_{5}$ = (2)	(2)	6
		(4)		
Ceram 115 – 115	–	–		–

4 *Intragroup trading*

(i) Cancel intra group sales/purchases:

DEBIT	Revenue ($10m + $5m)	$15m	
CREDIT	Cost of sales (purchases)		$15m

(ii) Unrealised profit:

Note. The inventory sold to Ceram has been sold to third parties, so the unrealised profit arises only on the unsold inventory of Bochem.

DEBIT	Cost of sales (10 × ½ × 20%)	$1m	
CREDIT	Investment in associate (SOFP)		$1m

5 *Trade receivable*

Interest on the trade receivable is $128.85m × 8% = $10.308m.

A loss allowance for the trade receivable should be recognised at an amount equal to twelve months' expected credit losses. Although IFRS 9 offers an option for the loss allowance for trade receivables with a financing component to always be measured at the lifetime expected losses, Ashanti has chosen instead to follow the three stage approach of IFRS 9.

The twelve-month expected credit losses are calculated by multiplying the probability of default in the next twelve months by the lifetime expected credit losses that would result from the default. Here this amounts to $18.822million ($75.288m × 25%). Because this allowance is recognised at 1 May 20X4, the discount must be unwound by one year: $18.822m × 8% = $1.506m.

Overall adjustment:

DEBIT Finance costs (impairment of receivable) (18.822 + 1.506)	$20.328m	
CREDIT Loss allowance		$20.328m

6 *Allowance for receivables*

The revenue of $5m was correctly recorded as control of the goods was transferred to the customer so the performance obligation was satisfied (IFRS 15).

The full allowance for expected credit losses should therefore be recognised.

DEBIT	Finance costs (impairment of receivable)	$8m	
CREDIT	Allowance for doubtful debts		$8m

7 *Property, plant and equipment*

		SOFP $m	Revaluation surplus $m	
1 May 20X3	Cost	12.000		
	Depreciation 12/10	(1.200)		
	Revaluation (bal. fig)	2.200	2.2	To OCI (not re-classified on disposal)
30 April 20X4	Revalued PPE c/d	13.000		
	Depreciation for year 13/9	(1.444)		
	Transfer to retained earnings: 1.444 – 1.2		(0.244)	
			1.956	
	Revaluation loss (bal. fig.)	(3.556)	(1.956)	and 1.6 to P/L
30 April 20X5	Revalued PPE c/d	8.000	0.000	

Original entries:

DEBIT	Other comprehensive income	$3.56m	
CREDIT	Property, plant and equipment		$3.56m

Correct entries:

DEBIT	Other comprehensive income	$1.96m	
DEBIT	Profit or loss (bal. fig.)	$1.6m	
CREDIT	Property, plant and equipment		$3.56m

To correct:

DEBIT	Profit or loss	$1.6m	
CREDIT	Other comprehensive income		$1.6m

8 *Holiday pay accrual*

IAS 19 *Employee benefits* requires that an accrual be made for holiday entitlement carried forward to next year.

Number of days c/fwd: $900 \times 3 \times 95\% = 2,565$ days

Number of working days: $900 \times 255 = 229,500$

$$\text{Accrual} = \frac{2,565}{229,500} \times \$19\text{m} = \$0.21\text{m}$$

DEBIT	Administrative expenses	$0.21m	
CREDIT	Accruals		$0.21m

9 *Goodwill*

	Bochem $m	Ceram $m
Consideration transferred: per question/136 × 70%	150.0	95.2
Fair value of non-controlling interest	54.0	26.0
Fair value of net assets	(160.0)	(115.0)
	44.0	6.2
Impairment loss to 30.4. 20X4: 44 × 15%	(6.6)	(–)
	37.4	
Impairment loss to 30.4.20X5: 44 × 5%	(2.2)	
	35.2	6.2

10 *Profit on sale of Ceram*

	$m	$m
Fair value of consideration received		90.0
Fair value of equity interest retained		45.0
Consolidated value of Ceram at date of disposal		
Net assets	160.0	
Goodwill	6.2	
	166.2	
Less NCI per question	(35.0)	
		(131.2)
		3.8

11 *Sale of 10% of Bochem*

As control is not lost, there is **no effect on the consolidated statement of profit or loss and other comprehensive income**. The sale is, in effect, a **transfer between owners** (Ashanti and the non-controlling interest). It is accounted for as an equity transaction directly in equity, and only reflected in the statement of changes in equity.

DEBIT	Cash	$34m	
CREDIT	Non-controlling interest (251.2 * × 10%)		$25.12m
CREDIT	Adjustment to parent's equity (not OCI)		$8.88m

* Net assets of Bochem at date of sale:

	$m
Net assets at 30 April 20X5	210.0
FV adjustments (W3)	6.0
	216.0
Goodwill (W9)	35.2
	251.2

BPP note. Because there is no effect on the consolidated statement of profit or loss and other comprehensive income, it was not necessary to do this working in order to obtain full marks. Nevertheless, it is good practice, so we have included it for completeness.

(b) **Social and environmental information**

There are a number of factors which encourage companies to disclose social and environmental information in their financial statements.

Public interest in corporate social responsibility is steadily increasing. Although financial statements are primarily intended for investors and their advisers, there is growing recognition that companies actually have **a number of different stakeholders**. These include **customers, employees and the general public,** all of whom are **potentially interested** in the way in which a company's operations affect the natural environment and the wider community. These stakeholders can have a **considerable effect on a company's performance**. As a result many companies now deliberately attempt to build a **reputation for social and environmental responsibility**. Therefore the disclosure of environmental and social information is essential. There is also growing recognition that **corporate social responsibility is actually an important part of an entity's overall performance.** Responsible practice in areas such as reduction of damage to the environment and recruitment **increases shareholder value**. Companies that act responsibly and make social and environmental disclosures are **perceived as better investments** than those that do not.

Another factor is **growing interest by governments and professional bodies**. Although there are **no IFRSs** that specifically require environmental and social reporting, it may be required by **company legislation**. There are now a number of **awards for environmental and social reports** and high quality disclosure in financial statements. These provide further encouragement to disclose information.

At present companies are normally able to disclose **as much or as little information as they wish in whatever manner that they wish**. This causes a number of **problems**. Companies tend to disclose information **selectively** and it is difficult for users of the financial statements to **compare the performance of different companies**. However, there are **good arguments** for continuing to allow companies a certain amount of freedom to determine the information that they disclose. If detailed rules are imposed, **companies are likely to adopt a 'checklist' approach** and will **present information in a very general and standardised way**, so that it is of very little use to stakeholders.

(c) **Management of earnings**

'Earnings management' involves exercising judgement with regard to financial reporting and structuring transactions so as to give a **misleadingly optimistic picture** of a company's performance. This is done with the intention, whether consciously or not, of **influencing outcomes that depend on stakeholders' assessments**. For example, a bank, or a supplier or customer may decide to do business with a company on the basis of a favourable performance or position. A director may wish to delay a hit to profit or loss for the year in order to secure a bonus that depends on profit. Indeed earnings management, sometimes called 'creative accounting' may be described as manipulation of the financial reporting process for private gain.

A director may also wish to present the company favourably in order to maintain a **strong position within the market**. The motive is not directly private gain – he or she may be thinking of the company's stakeholders, such as employees, suppliers or customers – but in the long term earnings management is not a substitute for sound and profitable business, and cannot be sustained.

'Aggressive' earnings management is a form of fraud and differs from reporting error. Nevertheless, all forms of earnings management may be **ethically questionable**, even if not illegal.

A more positive way of looking at earnings management is to consider the **benefits of not manipulating earnings:**

(I) Stakeholders can rely on the data. Word gets around that the company 'tells it like it is' and does not try to bury bad news.

(ii) It encourages management to safeguard the assets and exercise prudence.

(iii) Management set an example to employees to work harder to make genuine profits, not arising from the manipulation of accruals.

(iv) Focus on cash flow rather than accounting profits keeps management anchored in reality.

Earnings management goes against **the principle of corporate social responsibility**. Companies have duty not to mislead stakeholders, whether their own shareholders, suppliers, employees or the government. Because the temptation to indulge in earnings management may be strong, particularly in times of financial crisis, it is important to have **ethical frameworks and guidelines** in place. The letter of the law may not be enough.

49 Preparation question: Foreign operation

CONSOLIDATED STATEMENT OF FINANCIAL POSITION

	Standard	*Odense*	*Rate*	*Odense*	*Consol*
	$'000	Kr'000		$'000	$'000
Property, plant and equipment	1,285	4,400	8.1	543	1,828
Inv in Odense	520	–		–	–
Goodwill (W2)	–	–		–	277
	1,805	4,400		543	2,105
Current assets	410	2,000	8.1	247	657
	2,215	6,400		790	2,762
Share capital	500	1,000	9.4	106	500
Retained earnings (W3)	1,115				1,395
Pre-acq'n		2,100	9.4	224	
Post acq'n	–	2,200	Bal fig	324	
	1,615	5,300		654	1,895
Non-controlling interest (W6)					131
					2,026
Loans	200	300	8.1	37	237
Current liabilities	400	800	8.1	99	499
	600	1,100		136	736
	2,215	6,400		790	2,762

CONSOLIDATED STATEMENT OF PROFIT OR LOSS AND OTHER COMPREHENSIVE INCOME

	Standard	*Odense*	*Rate*	*Odense*	*Consol*
	$'000	Kr'000		$'000	$'000
Revenue	1,125	5,200	8.4	619	1,744
Cost of sales	(410)	(2,300)	8.4	(274)	(684)
Gross profit	715	2,900		345	1,060
Other expenses	(180)	(910)	8.4	(108)	(288)
Impairment loss (W2)					(21)
Dividend from Odense	40				–
Profit before tax	575	1,990		237	751
Income tax expense	(180)	(640)	8.4	(76)	(256)
Profit for the year	395	1,350		161	495
OTHER COMPREHENSIVE INCOME					
Items that may subsequently be reclassified to profit or loss					
Exchange difference on translating foreign operations (W4)	–	–		–	72
TOTAL COMPREHENSIVE INCOME FOR THE YEAR	395	1,350		161	567
Profit attributable to:					
Owners of the parent					463
Non-controlling interest (161 × 20%)					32
					495
Total comprehensive income for the year attributable to:					
Owners of the parent					525
Non-controlling interest (161 + 48) × 20%					42
					567

CONSOLIDATED STATEMENT OF CHANGES IN EQUITY (EXTRACT)

	Retained earnings
	$'000
Balance at 20X5	1,065
Dividends paid	(195)
Total comprehensive income for the year (per SPLOCI)	525
Balance at 31/12/X6 (W3)/(W5)	1,395

Workings

1 *Group structure*

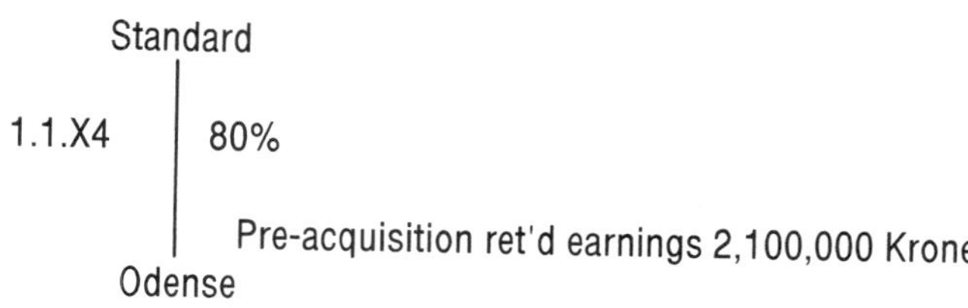

2 *Goodwill*

	Kr'000	Kr'000	Rate	$'000
Consideration transferred (520 × 9.4)		4,888		520
Non-controlling interests (3,100 × 20%)		620		66
Share capital	1,000		9.4	
Reserves	2,100			
		(3,100)		(330)
		2,408		256
Exchange differences 20X4-20X5		–	β	18
At 31.12.X5		2,408	8.8	274
Impairment losses 20X6		(168)	8.1	(21)
Exchange differences 20X6		–	β	24
At 31.12.X6		2,240	8.1	277

3 *Consolidated retained earnings carried forward*

	Standard
	$'000
Standard	1,115
Group share of post acquisition reserves at Odense (324 × 80%)	259
	1,374
Less goodwill impairment losses (W2)	(21)
Exchange on differences on goodwill (18 + 24)	42
	1,395

4 *Consolidated retained earnings b/f proof*

	$'000
Standard	915
Add post-acquisition retained earnings of Odense (4,355 @ 8.8 – 3,100 @ 9.4) × 80%	132
Less goodwill impairment losses (W2)	0
Exchange differences on goodwill (W2)	18
	1,065

5 *Exchange differences*

	$'000	$'000
On translation of net assets:		
Closing NA @ CR	654	
Opening NA @ OR (5,300 – 1,350 + 405 = 4,355 @ 8.8)	(495)	
Less retained profit as translated (161 (SOCI) – 405 @ 8.1)	(111)	
Exchange gain		48
On goodwill (W2)		24
		72

6 *Non-controlling interests (statement of financial position)*

	$'000
NCI at acquisition (W2)	66
NCI share of post acquisition reserves of Odense (324 × 20%)	65
	131

50 Aspire

Text reference. Foreign currency transactions are covered in Chapter 16 of your Study Text, and deferred tax is covered in Chapter 6.

Top tips. This question dealt with a number of foreign transactions (functional currency, goodwill, deferred tax and a loan), and contained a balanced mixture of discussion and computation. Unusually, this was not in the group accounts case study question, but as this topic is not covered at F7, it is to be expected that it will come up quite regularly in P2. Part (b), on deferred tax issues, was somewhat tricky. The treatment of goodwill (Part (c)) is fundamental to the understanding of accounting for an overseas subsidiary. Goodwill arising on acquisition of foreign operations and any fair value adjustments are both treated as the foreign operation's assets and liabilities. They are expressed in the foreign operation's functional currency and translated at the closing rate. Exchange differences arising on the retranslation of foreign entities' financial statements are recognised in other comprehensive income and accumulated as a separate component of equity.

Easy marks. There are some easy marks in Part (a) for a discussion of how to determine the functional currency – this issue has been examined in the past questions Ribby and Rose.

Examiner's comment. In Part (a), it was important for candidates to use the information in the question. The decision as to the functional currency was subjective and was based upon the candidate's interpretation of the information in the question. Candidates scored well on this part. Many found Part (b) difficult, ignoring the fact that a discussion was required and simply calculating the deferred taxation amount. In Part (c), candidates often calculated goodwill correctly but found the retranslation of goodwill quite difficult. Part (d) (loan and interest) were dealt with satisfactorily by most candidates.

Marking scheme

		Marks
(a)	1 mark per point up to maximum	7
(b)	1 mark per point up to maximum	6
(c)	1 mark per point up to maximum	5
(d)	1 mark per point up to maximum	5
Professional marks		2
Maximum		25

(a) **Factors to consider in determining functional currency of Aspire**

IAS 21 *The effects of changes in foreign exchange rates* defines functional currency as 'the currency of the primary economic environment in which the entity operates'. Each entity, whether an individual company, a parent of a group, or an operation within a group, should determine its functional currency and **measure its results and financial position in that currency**. If it is not obvious what the functional currency is, management will need to use its judgement in determining the currency which most faithfully represents the economic effects of the underlying transactions, events and conditions.

An entity should generally consider the following factors:

(i) What is the currency that mainly **influences sales prices** for goods and services (this will often be the currency in which sales prices for its goods and services are denominated and settled)?

(ii) What is the currency of the country whose **competitive forces and regulations** mainly determine the sales prices of its goods and services?

(iii) What is the currency that **mainly influences labour, material and other costs** of providing goods or services? (This will often be the currency in which such costs are denominated and settled.)

Other factors may also provide evidence of an entity's functional currency:

(i) It is the currency in which **funds from financing activities** are generated.
(ii) It is the currency in which **receipts from operating activities** are usually retained.

Aspire's subsidiary does not make investment decisions; these are under Aspire's control, and consideration of the currency which influences sales and costs is not relevant. Costs are incurred in dollars, but these are low and therefore not material in determining which is the subsidiary's functional currency. It is necessary, therefore to consider other factors in order to determine the functional currency of the subsidiary and whether its functional currency is the same as that of Aspire.

(i) The **autonomy** of a foreign operation from the reporting entity
(ii) The **level of transactions** between the reporting entity and the foreign operation
(iii) Whether the foreign operation **generates sufficient cash flows** to meet its cash needs
(iv) Whether **its cash flows directly affect those of the reporting entity**

The **subsidiary has issued 2 million dinars of equity to Aspire. Although this is in a different currency from that of Aspire, Aspire has controlled how the proceeds were to be invested** – in dinar-denominated bonds, suggesting that the **subsidiary is merely a vehicle for Aspire to invest in dinar-related investments.** Only 100,000 dinars of equity capital is from external sources, and this amount is insignificant compared to the equity issued to Aspire. The lack of autonomy of the subsidiary is confirmed by the fact that income from investments is either remitted to Aspire, or reinvested on instructions from Aspire, and by the fact that the subsidiary does not have any independent management or significant numbers of staff.

It appears that the subsidiary **is merely an extension of Aspire's activities rather than an autonomous entity.** Its purpose may have been to avoid reporting Aspire's exposure to the dinar/dollar exchange rate in profit or loss – it would be reported in other comprehensive income through the translation of the net investment in the subsidiary. These matters would lead to the conclusion that the **subsidiary's functional currency is the dollar.**

Operations are financed in dinars, and any income not remitted to Aspire is in dinars, and so the dinar represents the currency in which the subsidiary's economic activities are primarily carried out. However, in the absence of the benefit of presenting the dollar/dinar exchange rate fluctuations in other comprehensive income, Aspire could have invested the funds directly, and **so Aspire's functional currency should determine that of the subsidiary.**

(b) **Deferred tax charge**

Investments in foreign branches (or subsidiaries, associates or joint arrangements) are affected by **changes in foreign exchange rates**. In this case, the branch's taxable profits are determined in dinars, and changes in the dinar/dollar exchange rate may give rise to temporary differences. These differences can arise where the carrying amounts of the non-monetary assets are translated at historical rates and the tax base of those assets are translated at the closing rate. The **closing rate** may be used to translate the tax base because the resulting figure is an **accurate measure of the amount that will be deductible in future periods. The deferred tax is charged or credited to profit or loss.**

The deferred tax arising will be calculated **using the tax rate in the foreign branch's jurisdiction**, that is **20%.**

Property	*Dinars ('000)*	*Exchange rate*	*Dollars (($'000)*
Carrying amount:			
Cost	6,000	5	1,200
Depreciation for the year	(500)		(100)
Carrying amount	5,500		1,100
Tax base:			
Cost	6,000		
Tax depreciation	(750)		
Carrying amount	5,250	6	875
Temporary difference			225
Deferred tax at 20%			45

The **deferred tax charge in profit or loss will therefore increase by $45,000.**

If the tax base had been translated at the historical rate, the tax base would have been $(5.25m ÷ 5m) = $1.05m. This gives a temporary difference of $1.1m - $1.05m = $50,000, and therefore a deferred tax liability of $50,000 × 20% = $10,000. This is considerably lower than when the closing rate is used.

(c) **Goodwill on acquisition**

Goodwill on acquisition of a foreign subsidiary or group, and any fair value adjustments, are treated as **assets and liabilities of the foreign entity**. They are expressed in the foreign operation's functional currency and translated at the closing rate. This means that an exchange difference will arise between goodwill translated at the opening rate and at the closing rate. Even though the goodwill arose through a consideration paid in dollars, it is treated as a foreign currency asset, which means that it is translated into dinars at the rate ruling on the date of acquisition and then re-translated at the year-end rate.

Any **gain or loss** on translation is taken to **other comprehensive income**.

	Dinars (m)	*Rate*	$m
Consideration transferred			200
Non-controlling interests translated at 1 May 20X3	250	5	50
Less fair value of net assets at acq'n translated at 1 May 20X3	(1,100)	5	(220)
Goodwill			30
Exchange loss to other comprehensive income	-	ß	(5)
Goodwill as re-translated at 30 April 20X4: 30 × 5 ÷ 6	150	6	25

The exchange loss of $5m is recognised in other comprehensive income with the corresponding credit entries to a separate translation reserve (70%) and non-controlling interest (30%) in the statement of financial position:

DEBIT	Other comprehensive income	$5m	
CREDIT	Translation reserve (SOFP): $5m × 70%		$3.5m
CREDIT	Non-controlling interest (SOFP): $5m × 30%		$1.5m

(d) **Foreign currency loan**

On 1 May 20X3

On initial recognition (at 1 May 20X3), the loan is measured at the transaction price translated into the functional currency (the dollar), because the interest is at a market rate for a similar two-year loan. The loan is translated at the rate ruling on 1 May 20X3.

DEBIT	Cash 5m ÷ 5	$1m	
CREDIT	Financial liability (loan payable)		$1m

Being recognition of loan

As a monetary item, the loan balance at the year-end is translated at the spot rate at the year end.

Year ended 30 April 20X4

Because there are no transaction costs, the effective interest rate is 8%. Interest on the loan is translated at the average rate because this is an approximation for the actual rate

DEBIT	Profit or loss (interest expense): 5m × 8% ÷ 5.6	$71,429	
CREDIT	Financial liability (loan payable)		$71,429

Being recognition of interest payable for the year ended 30 April 20X4

On 30 April 20X4

The interest is paid and the following entry is made, using the rate on the date of payment of $1 = 6 dinars

DEBIT	Financial liability (loan payable)5m × 8% ÷ 6	$66,667	
CREDIT	Cash		$66,667

Being recognition of interest payable for the year ended 30 April 20X4

In addition, as a monetary item, the loan balance at the year-end is translated at the spot rate at the year end: 5m dinars ÷ 6 = $833,333. This gives rise to an exchange gain of £1,000,000 - $833,333 = $166,667. There is a further exchange gain on the interest paid of $71,429 - $66,667 = $4,762. This gives a total exchange gain of $4,762 + $166,667 = $171,429.

51 Case study question: Bubble

Text reference. Foreign currency transactions are covered in Chapter 16 of the text. Ethics is covered in Chapter 2, and pensions in Chapter 4.

Top tips. In Part (a), you were asked to prepare a consolidated statement of financial position for a simple group structure involving an overseas subsidiary and several adjustments for an intra-group loan, an exchange of assets and a pension plan. It is important to grab the easy marks for basic consolidation workings, and not get bogged down in the adjustments. Part of your workings will be the translation of Tyslar's, which is very straightforward. It is a good idea to provide a brief explanation of the adjustments, in case the figures are wrong.

In the ACCA examination/examining team's answer, which BPP has adapted for its own workings, the exchange differences on translation of the foreign subsidiary have been split out into a separate translation reserve, a requirement of IAS 21. However, credit would be given if you merged the differences into retained earnings, which the examining team have stated in the past is permitted in the context of the exam.

Part (b) consists mainly in describing the principles of IAS 21. Do not worry too much if you did not know the answer to the last part of the question, relating to the potential disposal of shares in Tyslar – you can score a pass on this part of the question without getting it all right. Note that Part (c) requires some basic knowledge of disposals where control is retained, ie that it is a transaction between shareholders, but it is basically an ethical question about manipulation, and there are standard arguments relating to this.

Easy marks. These are available for simply translating the statement of financial position at the correct rate, and setting out the proforma and the basic workings for group structure, non-controlling interest and retained earnings. If the asset exchange and the pensions adjustments worry you, ignore them and make a figure up – if you make a good attempt at the easy bits you will still pass comfortably.

Examiner's comment. The examiner emphasised the importance of clear workings and of referencing workings logically. This is because of the 'own figure rule', whereby mistakes are only penalised once. The translation and goodwill of the overseas subsidiary constituted an important part of the answer and carried a significant number of marks. Candidates generally performed quite well in dealing with the purchase of an overseas property and the defined benefit scheme. Candidates seemed to be able to show a statement reconciling the opening and closing liability for the defined benefit scheme but then found the detailed accounting problematical. Also, candidates often calculated the net interest cost on the defined benefit liability using the closing instead of opening rate of interest.

In Part (b), Many candidates did not read the question properly and did not discuss the treatment of monetary and non-monetary items but simply wrote about the translation of an overseas entity. Several candidates did not even attempt to answer the part of the question dealing with the sale of the equity holding even though this knowledge is fundamental to IAS 21. The main issue in answers to Part (c) was that candidates did not spend sufficient time discussing the ethical requirements of the question. Question 1c is an ethics based question and therefore candidates must spend time discussing the ethical problem in the question if they are to gain good marks.

Marking scheme

			Marks
(a)	Share capital		1
	Goodwill: Salt		1
	Intra-group loan		2
	Translation and exchange differences: Tyslar		6
	Pension		4
	Property, plant and equipment		3
	Inventories		1
	Intra-group Balances		2
	Other components of equity		3
	Retained earnings		6
	Non-controlling interest		3
	Non-current liabilities		2
	Current liabilities		1
			35
(b)	1 mark per sensible comment		9
(c)	1 mark per sensible comment		6
		Maximum	50

(a) BUBBLE GROUP

CONSOLIDATED STATEMENT OF FINANCIAL POSITION AS AT 31 OCTOBER 20X5

	$m
Non-current assets	
Goodwill: 16 (W3) + 10.1 (W4)	26.1
Property, plant and equipment: 280 + 105 + 41.1 (W2) + 6 (W8) + 1.5 (W10) – 0.1 + 1	434.5
Financial assets: 12 + 9 + 10.3 (W2) – 5 (W9)	26.3
	486.9
Current assets	
Inventories: 20 + 12 + 1.7 (W2)	33.7
Trade and other receivables: 30 + 25 + 3.8 (W2)	58.8
Cash and cash equivalents: 14 + 11 + 9.5 (W2)	34.5
	127.0
	613.9
Equity	
Equity shares	80.0
Retained earnings (W5)	239.8
Other components of equity (W7)	41.4
	361.2
Non-controlling interests (W6)	52.4
	413.6

	$m
Non-current liabilities	
95 + 7 + 12.4 (W2) – 5 (W9)) + 2 (W11)	111.4
Current liabilities	
67 + 19 + 1.9 (W2) + 1 (W8)	88.9
	613.9

Workings

1 *Group structure*

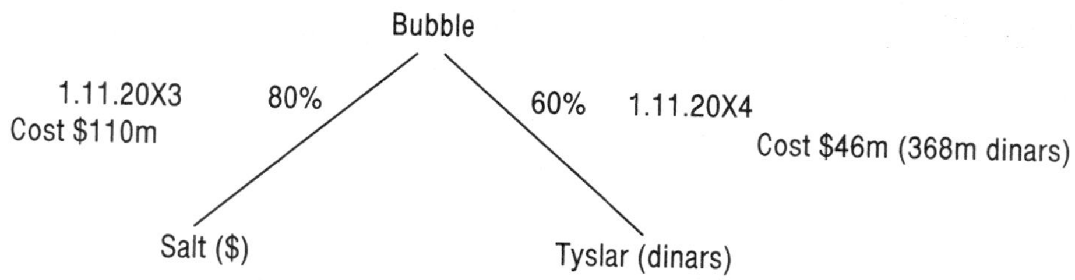

Salt ($)	Tyslar (dinars)
Retained earnings: $56m	Retained earnings: 258m dinars
Other components of equity: $8m	Other components of equity: n/a
Fair value NA: $120m	Fair value NA: n/a
Fair value NA: $120m	

2 *Translation of SOFP of Tyslar at 31 October 20X5*

	Dinars (m)	*Dinars (m) loan adj*	*Rate*	$m
Property, plant and equipment	390		9.5	41.1
Financial assets	98		9.5	10.3
Inventories	16		9.5	1.7
Trade and other receivables	36		9.5	3.8
Cash and cash equivalents	90		9.5	9.5
	630			66.4
Share capital	210		8	26.3
Retained earnings				
Pre-acqn	258		8	32.3
Post-acqn. (ß)				(6.5)
				25.8
Non-current liabilities 40 + 8 (W8)	110	7.5(W9)	9.5	12.4
Current liabilities	18		9.5	1.9
	630			66.4

3 *Goodwill: Salt*

	$m	$m
Consideration transferred (for 80%)		110
Non-controlling interests at fair value		25
Fair value of identifiable assets acquired and liabilities assumed		
Share capital	50	
Retained earnings	56	
Other components of equity	8	
Fair value adj.t re non-depreciable land (W8)	6	
Contingent liability at fair value (W8)	(1)	
		(119)
		16

4 *Goodwill: Tyslar*

	Dinars (m)	Rate	$m
Consideration transferred	368		46.0
Non-controlling interests	220		27.5
	588	8	
Less fair value of net assets at acq'n: 210m + 258m	(468)		(58.5)
At 1 November 20X4	120		15.0
Impairment loss	(24)	8.5	(2.8)
			12.2
Exchange loss	–		(2.1)
At 31 October 20X5	96	9.5	10.1

Since goodwill is under the fair value method, both the impairment and the exchange loss will be apportioned 60:40 between the shareholders of the parent and non-controlling interest respectively. Any goodwill arising on the acquisition of a foreign operation is treated as an asset of the foreign operation and retranslated at the closing rate.

In summary:

Goodwill for consolidated SFP will be ($16m (W1) + $10·1m) = $26·1m.

The impairment is $2·8m of which 60% ($1·7m) will be charged against group retained earnings and 40% ($1.1m) will be charged to the NCI.

5 *Retained earnings*

	Bubble	*Salt*	*Tyslar*
	$m	$m	$m
Per question/as translated (W2)	230.0	74.0	25.8
Adjustments			
Property, plant and equipment (W10)	1.5		
Depreciation of PPE (W10)	(0.1)		
Pension plan (W11)	0.8		
Impairment of goodwill of Tyslar (W4)	(1.7)		
Share of exchange loss on goodwill 2.1(W2) × 60%	(1.2)		
Pre-acquisition: per question		(56.0)	
as translated (W2)			(32.3)
		18	(6.5)
Group share: Salt: 18 × 80%	14.4		
Tyslar: ((6.5) × 60%	(3.9)		
	239.8		

6 *Other components of equity*

	Bubble	*Salt*
	$m	$m
Per question	40.0	12
Adjustments		
Revaluation gain (W10)	1.0	
Pension plan (W11)	(2.8)	
Pre-acquisition: per question		(8)
		4
Group share: Salt: 4 × 80%	3.2	
	41.4	

7 *Non-controlling interests*

	Salt	Tyslar
	$m	$m
NCI at acquisition	25.0	27.5
NCI share of post acquisition retained earnings:		
Salt ((W5) 18 × 20%)	3.6	
Tyslar ((W5) ((6.5 × 40%)		(2.6)
NCI share of post acquisition OCE:		
Salt ((W6) 4 × 20%)	0.8	-
Impairment of goodwill: 2.8(W4) × 40%		(1.1)
Exchange loss on goodwill: 2.1(W2) × 40%		(0.8)
	29.4	23.0
	52.4	

8 *Fair value adjustments*

Salt:

	Acquisition 1 November 20X3	Movement 2 years	Year end 31 October 20X5
	$m	$m	$m
Contingent liability	(1)	–	(1)
Land: 120 – (50 (SC) + 56 (RE) + 8 (OCE))	6	–	6
	5		5

9 *Intragroup loan*

The loan is a foreign currency monetary item in Tyslar's financial statements which means it needs to be retranslated at the closing rate of exchange. The exchange differences should have been recorded through Tyslar's profit or loss and will therefore affect retained earnings.

	$m	Exchange rate	Dinars m
1 February 2015	10	9 dinars:$1	90
Cash paid 1 July 2015	(5)	10 dinars:$1	(50)
			40
Exchange rate loss – balancing figure 31 October 2015			7.5
	5	9.5 dinars:$1	47.5

To correct, increase Tyslar's non-current liabilities by 7·5m dinars and reduce retained earnings by a corresponding amount. In addition, after retranslation, $5m will be cancelled from both financial assets and non-current liabilities as an intra-group adjustment.

DEBIT Profit or loss (retained earnings) and	7.5 dinars (to W2)	
CREDIT Non-current liabilities		7.5 dinars (to W2)

The intra-group loan will be eliminated from the consolidated SOFP.

DEBIT Non-current liabilities	$5m	
CREDIT Financial assets		$5m

10 *Exchange of assets*

The transaction has commercial substance and so the cost of the property acquired should be measured at the fair value of the asset given up. Therefore, the property should have been recorded at $7m rather than $5m. A profit on disposal should have arisen of $2m which will need to be credited to retained earnings. The $0·5m spent on staff relocation is not directly attributable to the property and so should have been expensed. Depreciation should be charged of $7m/35 × 6/12 = $100,000. This would leave a carrying amount before revaluation at 31 October 20X5 of $6·9m. The fair value at this date is 75m dinars/9·5 = $7·9m. A revaluation gain should be recorded in other components of equity of $1m.

To correct:

DEBIT	PPE (2 – 0.5)	$1.5m	
CREDIT	Profit or loss (ret'd earnings)		$1.5m

Being correction to cost of property (to FV of the asset given up)

DEBIT	Profit or loss (ret'd earnings)	$0.1m	
CREDIT	PPE (7/35 × 6/12)		$0.1m

Being depreciation of property

DEBIT	PPE	$1m	
CREDIT	Other components of equity		$1m

Being revaluation gain on property

11 *Pension plan*

	$
Opening liability	15.0
Net interest cost ($15m × 8%)	1.2
Current service cost	5.0
Gain on curtailment ($4m – $3m)	(1.0)
Cash contributions into the scheme	(6.0)
	14.2
Loss on remeasurement (β)	2.8
Closing liability	17.0

The cash contributions of $6m will need to be reversed from profit or loss and will reduce the net obligation on the pension scheme. The interest costs of $1·2m and the current service cost of $5m must be expensed and the gain on curtailment of the pension scheme credited to profit or loss (and so to retained earnings). The remeasurement loss of $2·8m should be deducted from other comprehensive income (and so to other components of equity). The net effect on the pension scheme is an increase in the liability of $2m to $17m.

To correct:

DEBIT	OCI (and OCE)	$2.8m	
CREDIT	P/L (ret'd earnings) : 1.2 + 5 – 6 – 1		$0.8m
CREDIT	Non-current liabilities		$2m

Being adjustments to record pension plan

12 *Translation reserve*

	$m
Translation of net assets (W2)	(9.5)
Translation of goodwill (W4)	(2.1)
	11.6

Group share: $11.6m × 60% = $7m

(b) **IAS 21 issues**

Monetary items are units of currency held and assets and liabilities to be received or paid in a fixed or determinable number of units of currency. This would include foreign bank accounts, receivables, payables and loans. Non-monetary items are other items which are in the statement of financial position. For example, non-current assets, inventories and investments.

Monetary items are retranslated using the closing exchange rate (the year-end rate). The exchange differences on retranslation of monetary assets must be recorded in profit or loss. IAS 21 *The effects of changes in foreign exchange rates*, is not specific under which heading the exchange gains and losses should be classified.

Non-monetary items which are measured in terms of historical cost in a foreign currency are translated using the exchange rate at the date of the transaction; and non-monetary items which are measured at fair value in a foreign currency are translated using the exchange rates at the date when the fair value was measured. Exchange differences on such items are recorded consistently with the recognition of the movement in fair values. For example, exchange differences on an investment property, a fair value through profit and loss financial asset, or arising on an impairment, will be recorded in profit or loss. Exchange differences on property, plant and equipment arising from a revaluation gain would be recorded in other comprehensive income.

When translating a foreign subsidiary, the exchange differences on all the net assets, including goodwill, are recorded within other comprehensive income. The proportion belonging to the shareholders of the parent will usually be held in a separate translation reserve. The proportion belonging to the non-controlling interest is not shown separately but subsumed within the non-controlling interest figure in the consolidated financial statements. If Bubble were to sell all of its equity shares in Tyslar, the cumulative exchange differences belonging to the equity holders of Bubble will be reclassified from equity to profit or loss. In addition, the cumulative exchange differences attributable to the non-controlling interest shall be derecognised but shall not be reclassified to profit or loss.

When a monetary item relating to a foreign operation is not intended to be settled, the item is treated as part of the entity's net investment in its subsidiary. There will be no difference in the accounting treatment in the individual accounts of Tyslar and hence exchange differences on the loan would remain in profit or loss. However, in the consolidated financial statements such differences should initially be recorded in other comprehensive income. These will be reclassified from equity to profit or loss on subsequent disposal of the subsidiary. This can cause practical issues in terms of monitoring all of the individual exchange differences to ensure that they are all correctly classified in the consolidated financial statements.

(c) **Compliance and ethical issues**

If Bubble were to sell the shares profitably a gain would arise in its individual financial statements which would boost retained earnings. However, if only 5% of the equity shares in Tyslar were sold, it would still hold 55% of the equity and presumably control would not be lost. The International Accounting Standards Board views this as an equity transaction (i.e. transactions with owners in their capacity as owners). This means that the relevant proportion of the exchange differences should be re- attributed to the non-controlling interest rather than to the retained earnings. The directors appear to be motivated by their desire to maximise the balance on the group retained earnings. It would appear that the directors' actions are unethical by overstating the group's interest in Tyslar at the expense of the non-controlling interest.

The purpose of financial statements is to present a fair representation of the company's position and if the financial statements are deliberately falsified, then this could be deemed unethical. Accountants have a social and ethical responsibility to issue financial statements which do not mislead the public. Any manipulation of the accounts will harm the credibility of the profession since the public assume that professional accountants will act in an ethical capacity. The directors should be reminded that professional ethics are an integral part of the profession and that they must adhere to ethical guidelines such as the ACCA's Code of Ethics and Conduct. Deliberate falsification of the financial statements would contravene the guiding principles of integrity, objectivity and professional behaviour. The directors' intended action appears to be in direct conflict with the code by deliberating overstating the parent company's ownership interest in the group in order to maximise potential investment in Bubble.

Stakeholders are becoming increasingly reactive to the ethical stance of an entity. Deliberate falsification would potentially harm the reputation of Bubble and could lead to severe, long-term disadvantages in the market place. The directors' intended action will therefore not be in the best interests of the stakeholders in the business. There can be no justification for the deliberate falsification of an entity's financial statements.

52 Preparation question: Consolidated statement of cash flows

STATEMENT OF CASH FLOWS FOR THE YEAR ENDED 31 DECEMBER 20X5

	$'000	$'000
Cash flows from operating activities		
Profit before tax	16,500	
Adjustments for:		
Depreciation	5,800	
Impairment losses (W1)	240	
	22,540	
Increase in trade receivables (W4)	(1,700)	
Increase in inventories (W4)	(4,400)	
Increase in trade payables (W4)	1,200	
Cash generated from operations	17,640	
Income taxes paid (W3)	(4,200)	
Net cash from operating activities		13,440
Cash flows from investing activities		
Acquisition of subsidiary net of cash acquired	(600)	
Purchase of property, plant and equipment (W1)	(13,100)	
Net cash used in investing activities		(13,700)
Cash flows from financing activities		
Proceeds from issue of share capital (W2)	2,100	
Dividends paid (W2)	(900)	
Dividends paid to non-controlling interest (W2)	(40)	
Net cash from financing activities		1,160
Net increase in cash and cash equivalents b/f		900
Net increase in cash and cash equivalents c/f		900
Cash and cash equivalents at the beginning of the period		1,500
Cash and cash equivalents at the end of the period		2,400

Workings

1 *Assets*

	Property, plant and equipment $'000	*Goodwill* $'000
b/d	25,000	–
OCI (revaluation)	500	
Depreciation/ Impairment	(5,800)	**(240)** β
Acquisition of sub/assoc	2,700	1,640 (W5)
Cash paid/(rec'd) β	**13,100**	–
c/d	35,500	1,400

2 *Equity*

	Share capital $'000	*Share premium* $'000	*Retained earnings* $'000	*Non-controlling interest* $'000
b/d	10,000	2,000	21,900	–
SPLOCI			11,100	350
Acquisition of subsidiary	1,500	2,500		1,440 (W5)
Cash (paid)/rec'd β	**800**	**1,300**	**(900)***	**(40)**
c/d	12,300	5,800	32,100	1,750

*Dividend paid is given in question but working shown for clarity.

3 *Liabilities*

	Tax payable
	$'000
b/d	4,000
P/L	5,200
Acquisition of subsidiary	200-
Cash (paid)/rec'd	**(4,200) β**
c/d	5,200

4 *Working capital changes*

	Inventories	*Receivables*	*Payables*
	$'000	$'000	$'000
Balance b/d	10,000	7,500	6,100
Acquisition of subsidiary	1,600	600	300
	11,600	8,100	6,400
Increase/(decrease) (balancing figure)	**4,400**	**1,700**	**1,200**
Balance c/d	16,000	9,800	7,600

5 *Purchase of subsidiary*

	$'000
Cash received on acquisition of subsidiary	400
Less cash consideration	(1,000)
Cash outflow	(600)

Note. Only the **cash** consideration is included in the figure reported in the statement of cash flows. The **shares** issued as part of the consideration are reflected in the share capital working (W2) above.

Goodwill on acquisition (before impairment):

	$'000
Consideration: 55 + 695 (W3) + 120 (W2) + 216	5,000
Non-controlling interest: 4,800 × 30%	1,440
Net assets acquired	(4,800)
Goodwill	1,640

53 Case study question: Weston

Text reference. Group statements of cash flow are covered in Chapter 17 of the text. Integrated reporting is covered in Chapter 18. Ethics is covered in Chapter 3.

Top tips. The preparation of a statement of cash flows is all about good technique. There are many straightforward, non-group aspects to this group statement of cash flows, so make sure you don't get bogged down in the detailed adjustments at the expense of these. Take care with the cash flow from investing activities. This will normally require complex workings. In particular, there will always be an acquisition or disposal of a subsidiary, as this is not tested at F7. The proceeds of disposal calculation is a little tricky, but the best way to approach it is to set out the working as for a profit/loss on disposal and find the proceeds as a balancing figure. We have set up workings for some cash payments and receipts even though the amounts are given to you in the question. It is good practice to set up standard workings in case there is something missing from the information in the question, or you have to calculate the figures from scratch.

Don't skimp on Parts (b) on the usefulness of statements of cash flows versus integrated reporting and (c) on ethics. There are marks for valid points.

Easy marks. The cash flow from financing section is a good source of easy marks, for example repayment of borrowings, cash arising on the issue of shares and dividends paid to the NCI.These are available for setting out the proforma and workings, and also for valid points made in Part (b) on the usefulness of the statement of cash flows and the integrated report is also a good source of marks.

Examiner's comment. The ACCA examining team stresses the importance of showing all workings. Even the simplest of calculations should be shown. For example sometimes, candidates can inaccurately sum two figures. If there were a correct working, then candidates would not be penalised for the summation error. While there are complex elements to all consolidates statement of cash flow questions, there are some basic marks too, and candidates nearly always get those. The 'movements in working capital' section of the statement is generally well answered by candidates but often problems arise with the signage of the movements with the result that positive movements are inaccurately shown as negative movements. Candidates receive no credit for inaccurate calculations in this regard even though the numbers used in the calculation may be correct. Generally, candidates find the investing activities section quite difficult. This is particularly so as regards the purchase of PPE. Regarding Part (b), Candidates need to come to the examination with an understanding of the limitations of corporate reporting as well as the nature of it. The various elements of corporate reporting are not distinct but are interrelated. Thus the information content of a statement of cash flows can be compared to the information content of an Integrated Report and candidates should be capable of giving a view on the two reports. In Part (c), some candidates focused on the reporting issues to the detriment of the ethical issues. Unless otherwise told you should assume that the marks are split equally.

Marking scheme

		Marks
(a)		
	Cash flows from operating activities	
	Profit/finance cost and associate's profit	3
	Pension scheme	2
	Depreciation and amortisation	2
	Impairment of financial asset	1
	Contingent consideration	1
	Goodwill and intangibles	2
	Working capital movements	4
	Finance cost paid	1
	Tax paid	3
	Cash flows from investing activities	
	Property, plant and equipment	2
	Intangibles	1
	Associate	2
	Disposal of Northern	5
	Amortised cost asset	1
	Contingent cash	1
	Cash flows from financing activities	
	Long-term borrowings	1
	Dividends paid to NCI	2
	Cash and cash equivalents	1
		35
(b)	1 mark per valid point, maximum	8
(c)	1 mark per valid point, maximum	7
		50

(a) WESTON GROUP

STATEMENT OF CASH FLOWS FOR THE YEAR ENDED 31 JANUARY 20X6

	$m	$m
Cash flow from operating activities		
Profit for the year: 183 + 6 – ((20 × 40%) – 1)	182.0	
Finance costs	23.0	
Finance income (W9)	(1.6)	
Share of profit of associate	(16.0)	
Service cost component of retirement benefit liability	11.0	
Cash paid to pension scheme	(19.0)	
Depreciation	20.0	
Impairment on amortised cost asset (W9) (1 + 7)	8.0	
Gain on contingent consideration (W10)	(4.0)	
Impairment of goodwill (W1)	6.0	
Amortisation of intangible assets (W1)	7.0	
	216.4	
Movements in working capital		
Increase in trade receivables(W4)	(25.0)	
Decrease in inventories (W4)	19.0	
Increase in trade payables(W4)	15.0	
Cash generated from operating activities	225.4	
Finance costs paid: 23 – (10 (W10) × 10%)	(22.0)	
Income taxes paid (W3)	(81.0)	
Net cash from operating activities		122.4
Cash flows from investing activities		
Purchase of property, plant and equipment (W1)	(74.0)	
Purchase of intangible assets	(17.0)	
Interest received	1.	
Dividends received from associate (W1)	4.0	
Purchase of associate (W1)	(90.0)	
Proceeds on disposal of Northern: 85.4 (W5) + 2	87.4	
Acquisition of amortised cost asset (per question)	(20.0)	
Settlement of contingent cash (W10)	(7.0)	
Net cash used in investing activities		(115.0)
Cash flows from financing activities		
Repayment of long-term borrowings (W3)	(22.0)	
Dividends paid to non-controlling shareholders (W2)	(8.4)	
Net cash generated by financing activities		(30.4)
Net increase in cash and cash equivalents		(23.0)
Cash and cash equivalents at beginning of year		43.0
Cash and cash equivalents at end of year		20.0

Workings

1 *Assets*

	PPE	*Goodwill*	*Intangible assets*	*Associate*	*Financial assets*
	$m	$m	$m	$m	$m
b/d	386	19	27	0	0
P/L				16	20 × 8% 1.6
OCI					
Dep'n/ Amort'n/Impairment (non-cash)	(20)	**(6)** β	(7)		(1) (7)
Acquisition/disposal of sub/assoc (W7)	(88)	(W5) (9)		**90β**	
Disposals/derecognition	0				
Cash rec'd (div. from assoc)				10 × 40%	
Cash paid/(rec'd)	**74** β	–	**17 β**	**(4)**	20 (1.6)
c/d	352	4	37	102	19 – 7 = 12

2 *Equity*

	Share capital	*Retained earnings*	*OCE*	*NCI*
	$m	$m	$m	$m
b/d	100	270	21	85.0
P/L		107	(4 – 1)	} 11.0
OCI			3	
Disposal of sub				(W6) (23.6)
Cash (paid)/rec'd	-	0	-	**(8.4)** β
c/d	100	377	24	64.0

3 *Liabilities*

	Long-term borrowings	*Retirement benefit*	*Tax payable*
	$m	$m	$m
b/d	48	72	(15 + 92) 107
P/L		11	(40 + 2) 42
OCI		(4)	(4 × 25%) 1
Disposal of subsidiary			(W7)(8)
Cash (paid)/rec'd	**(22)** β	(19)*	**(81)** β
c/d	26	80	61 (14 + 47)

** Cash flow given in question, but working shown for clarity*

4 *Working capital changes*

	Inventories	*Trade & other receivables*	*Trade & other payables*
	$m	$m	$m
b/d	165	104	41
Disposal of subsidiary	(38)	(23)	(10)
Contingent (W10)			+ 1 – 11
∴ **Increase/(decrease)**	**(19)** β	**25** β	**15** β
c/d	108	106	36

5 *Goodwill on acquisition of Northern*

	$m
Consideration transferred	132
Fair value of non-controlling interest	28
	160
Fair value of net assets at acqn.	(124)
Goodwill at acquisition	36
Impairment (75%)	(27)
Carrying value of goodwill at disposal	9

*Deferred tax:

6 *Loss on disposal of Northern*

	$'000	$'000
Fair value of consideration received β		85.4
Less share of carrying value when control lost		
Net assets (W7)	129.0	
Goodwill (W5)	9.0	
Less non-controlling interests (W8)	(23.6)	
		(114.4)
Loss on disposal per question		(29.0)

Note. The fair value of consideration received of $85.4m, calculated as a balancing figure, is adjusted on the face of the group statement of cash flows for the bank overdraft of $2m, which is added back to arrive at the proceeds on disposal.

7 *Net assets at date of disposal*

The fair value of the property, plant and equipment at disposal will be $80m as per the question plus $16m fair value uplift less 4/8 depreciation = $88m. A deferred tax liability on the fair value adjustment would arise of (25% x $16m) = $4m. This will be released in line with the extra depreciation, so the carrying value at disposal will be only $2m ($4m – ($4m x 4/8)). The carrying value of the entire deferred tax liability at disposal is therefore $8m ($6m per question + $2m).

	$'000
Property, plant and equipment (W1)	88
Inventory	38
Trade receivables	23
Trade and other payables	(10)
Deferred tax	(8)
Bank overdraft	(2)
	129

8 *Non-controlling interests at date of disposal*

	$'000
Non-controlling interest at acquisition (FV)	28.0
NCI share of post-acqn ret. Earnings: 20% × (129 – 124 (W5))	1.0
NCI share of goodwill impairment (20% × 27(W5))	(5.4)
	23.6

9 *Impairment of financial asset*

The financial asset has only one year to run at 31 January 20X6. The remaining cash flows to be received are therefore $21.6m (($20m + (8% × $20m)). Since there is a 40% chance of default, the expected cash flow at present value would be $12m (60% × $21.6m/1.08). A further impairment of $7m ($19m – $12m) is required against profits.

The expected credit loss could also be calculated as 40% of the present value of the expected cash flows less the $1m expected credit losses already charged to profit or loss: (40% × $21.6m/1·08) – $1m = $7m

Additionally, the overall impairment charged for the year of $8m, including the expected 12-month credit loss of $1m, should be added back to operating profits within the operating activities reconciliation.

(**Note.** The carrying value of the investment is $19m which is after $1m impairment for 12 months expected credit losses.)

Interest received (finance income) of $1.6m (8% × $20m) should be deducted from operating profits within the operating activities reconciliation and added to the cash from investing activities section.

10 *Contingent consideration and finance costs paid*

($10m x 10%) charged to finance cost. A gain on settlement therefore arises of $4m ($10m + $1m – $7m). The finance cost per P&L is $23m.

Cash paid is therefore $23m less $1m unwinding = $22m.

(b) **Statements of cash flows and the integrated report**

Statements of cash flows provide valuable information to stakeholders on the financial adaptability of an entity. Cash flows are objective and verifiable and so are more easily understood than profits. Profits can be manipulated through the use of judgement or choice of a particular accounting policy. Operating cash flows are therefore useful at highlighting the differences between cash and profits. The cash generated from operations is a useful indication of the quality of the profits generated by a business. Good quality profits will generate cash and increase the financial adaptability of an entity. Cash flow information will also have some predictive value. It may assist stakeholders in making judgements on the amount, timing and degree of certainty on future cash flows.

Cash flow information should be used in conjunction with the rest of the financial statements. The adjustment of non-cash flow items within operating activities may not be easily understood. The classification of cash flows can be manipulated between operating, investing and financing activities. It is important therefore not to examine the cash flow information in isolation. It is only through an analysis of the statement of financial position, statement of comprehensive income and notes, together with cash flow, that a more comprehensive picture of the entity's position and performance develops.

It is true that International Financial Reporting Standards are extensive and their required disclosures very comprehensive. This has led to criticism that the usefulness may be limited where the most relevant information is obscured by immaterial disclosures. An integrated reporting system would increase disclosure as well as imposing additional time and cost constraints on the reporting entity. However, integrated reporting will provide stakeholders with valuable information which would not be immediately accessible from an entity's financial statements.

Financial statements are based on historical information and may lack predictive value. They are essential in corporate reporting, particularly for compliance purposes but do not provide meaningful information regarding business value. The primary purpose of an integrated report is to explain to providers of capital how the organisation generates value over time. This is summarised through an examination of the key activities and outputs of the organisation whether they be financial, manufactured, intellectual, human, social or natural.

An integrated report seeks to examine the external environment which the entity operates within and to provide an insight into the entity's resources and relationships to generate value. It is principles based and should be driven by materiality, including how and to what extent the entity understands and responds to the needs of its stakeholders. This would include an analysis of how the entity has performed within its business environment, together with a description of prospects and challenges for the future. It is this strategic direction which is lacking from a traditional set of financial statements and will be invaluable to stakeholders to make a more informed assessment of the organisation and its prospects.

(c) **Impact of loan and ethical issues**

It is not unusual for members of a group to provide financial assistance in the form of loans or acting as a guarantor between one another. Provided that the loan was not issued to manipulate the financial statements and that there was full disclosure as a related party transaction, then no ethical issues may arise. However, this would appear to be unlikely in this scenario.

Since the loan is interest free, the loan will have no impact on the interest cover of Eastern. Neither profits nor finance expenses will be affected. The impact on the gearing ratio of Eastern is unclear and would depend on how debt was classified within the terms of the covenants. Should the overdraft be included within debt, the loan would substantially improve the gearing ratio through the elimination of the Eastern overdraft. Accountants have the responsibility to issue financial statements which do not mislead the stakeholders of the business. It would appear that the financial statements are being deliberately misrepresented, which would be deemed unethical. The cash received would improve the liquidity of Eastern and may enable them to avoid a breach on the debt covenants. Accountants should be guided by ACCA's Code of Ethics. Deliberate overstatement of the entity's liquidity would contravene the principles of integrity, objectivity and professional behaviour.

The timing and nature of the loan may provide further evidence that the rationale for the loan was to ensure no breach of the covenants took place. The loan is for an unusually short period given that it was repaid within 30 days. In addition, the timing is very suspicious given that it was issued just prior to the 31 January 20X6 year end. In any case, the classification of the loan within the trade and other receivables and trade and other payables balances would be misleading. The loan is not for trading purposes and a fairer representation would to be to include the loan within the current asset investments of Weston and as a short-term loan within the current liabilities of Eastern. This would ensure that the loan would be treated as debt within the gearing calculation of Eastern and would not be misleading for the bank when assessing whether a breach of the debt covenants had taken place.

54 Case study question: Angel

Text reference. Group statements of cash flow are covered in Chapter 17 of the text. Retirement benefits are covered in Chapter 4 and deferred tax in Chapter 6. Ethics is covered in Chapter 3.

Top tips. This question has been slightly amended from the original. There are many straightforward, non-group aspects to this group statement of cash flows, so make sure you don't get bogged down in the detailed adjustments at the expense of these. The adjustments to the net profit before tax include retirement benefit expense because only the contributions paid are included in the SOCF. We have set up workings for some cash payments and receipts even though the amounts are given to you in the question. It is good practice to set up standard workings in case there is something missing from the information in the question, or you have to calculate the figures from scratch.

Don't skimp on Part (b) – it has nine marks.

Easy marks. These are available for setting out the proforma and workings, and also for valid points made in Part (b) on cash flow and Part (c) on ethical matters. Do not spend too much time on the fiddly PPE working at the expense of these much easier marks.

Examiner's comment. The ACCA examination/examining team stresses the importance of showing all workings. For example, very few candidates correctly calculated the income taxes paid figure but there were several marks for this calculation, which were often awarded in the workings in the scripts. Several candidates did not adjust for the purchase of the subsidiary .This of course affects several items in the consolidated statement of cash flows. However the marking scheme treated the non-adjustment of the various balances as a single error. While there are complex elements to all consolidates statement of cash flow questions, there are some basic marks too, and candidates nearly always get those. Candidates found Part (b) of this question difficult to answer satisfactorily as many candidates simply outlined the headings in the statement rather than discussing the cause or reason for the classification. Part (c) required candidates to discuss a comment by the Directors of Angel that codes of ethics were irrelevant and unimportant. Worryingly, some candidates actually agreed with the directors' comment, stating that the profit motive was more important than ethical behaviour. This shows a lack of knowledge or a failure to apply the knowledge. This part of the question normally attracts high marks if candidates apply their knowledge and therefore it is a part of the paper, which should never be omitted.

Marking scheme

		Marks
(a)	Net profit before taxation	4
	Cash generated from operations	16
	Cash flow from investing activities	10
	Cash flow from financing activities	5
		35
(b)	Subjective assessment of discussion	9
(c)	Subjective assessment – 1 mark per point	6
	Available	50

(a) ANGEL GROUP
STATEMENT OF CASH FLOWS FOR THE YEAR ENDED 30 NOVEMBER 20X3

	$m	$m
Operating activities		
Profit before tax (W1)/Note 2	197.0	
Adjustments for		
Profit on sale of financial assets ($40m –$26m)	(14.0)	
Retirement benefit expense (W6)	10.0	
Depreciation	29.0	
Profit on sale of property plant and equipment: $63m – $49m	(14.0)	
Share of profit of associate (W1)	(12.0)	
Impairment of goodwill and intangible assets (W1): $26.5m + $90m	116.5	
Interest expense: $11m less $1m capitalised	10.0	
	322.5	
Decrease in trade receivables(W4)	58.0	
Decrease in inventories (W4)	41.0	
Decrease in trade payables(W4)	(210.0)	
Cash generated from operations	211.5	
Retirement benefit contributions*(W3)	(9.0)	
Interest paid: $11m less $1m capitalised	(10.0)	
Income taxes paid (W2)	(135.5)	
Net cash from operating activities c/f		57
Net cash from operating activities b/f		57
Investing activities		
Purchase of property, plant and equipment (W1)	(76)	
Proceeds from sale of property, plant and equipment	63	
Cash grant for property, plant and equipment (W2)	1	
Proceeds from sale of financial assets (per question)	40	
Acquisition of subsidiary, net of cash acquired: $30m – $2m	(28)	
Purchase of financial assets (per question/(W1))	(57)	
Acquisition of associate (W1)	(71)	
Dividend received from associate (W1)	3	
Net cash used in investing activities		(125)
Financing activities		
Proceeds from issue of share capital (W2)	225	
Repayment of long-term borrowings (W3)	(31)	
Dividends paid (W2)	(10)	
Dividends paid to non-controlling shareholders (W2)	(6)	
Net cash generated by financing activities		178
Net increase in cash and cash equivalents		110
Cash and cash equivalents at beginning of year		355
Cash and cash equivalents at end of year		465

Notes

1 *Building renovation*

The building renovation has been incorrectly accounted for, and this needs to be corrected in order to produce the workings for the statement of cash flows. The correcting entries are:

DEBIT	Property, plant and equipment	$3m	
CREDIT	Revenue		$3m

Being revaluation of building and correction of charge to revenue.

Angel treats grant income on capital-based projects as deferred income. However, the grant of $2m needs to be split equally between renovation (capital) and job creation (revenue). The correcting entries for this are:

DEBIT	Property, plant and equipment	$2m	
CREDIT	Retained earnings		$1m
CREDIT	Deferred income		$1m

2 *Adjustments to profit before tax*

Profit before tax needs to be adjusted to take account of the correcting entries for the building refurbishment and grant.

The construction costs for the machine have been incorrectly charged to other expenses, and the interest needs to be capitalised: Correcting entries are:

DEBIT	Property, plant and equipment	$4m	
CREDIT	Profit or loss		$4m

Being correction of construction costs charge

DEBIT	Property, plant and equipment	$1m	
CREDIT	Profit or loss		$1m

Being capitalisation of interest

Profit before tax

	$m
Per question	188
Correction of rebuilding costs	3
Share of cash grant	1
Correction of construction costs	4
Capitalisation of interest	1
	197

Workings

1 *Assets*

	PPE	*Goodwill*	*Intangible assets*	*Associate*	*Financial assets*
	$m	$m	$m	$m	$m
b/d	465	120.0	240	0	180
P/L				40 × 30% 12	4
OCI (8 – 3)	5				
Dep'n/Impairment/Amort'n (non-cash)	(29)	**(26.5)** β	**(90)** β		
Acquisition of sub/assoc	14	(W4) 11.5		**71** β	
Disposals/derecognition	(49)				(26)
Cash paid/(rec'd)	**76** β	0.0		40 × 30% (3)	57
c/d	482	105.0	150	80	215

2 *Equity*

	Share capital	*Retained earnings*	*NCI*
	$m	$m	$m
b/d	625	359	65
P/L		111	31
OCI		(4)	
Cash (paid)/rec'd	**225** *	(10) *	(6) *
c/d	850	456	90

* *cash flow given in question, but working shown for clarity*

3 *Liabilities*

	Long-term borrowings	*Tax payable*	*Retirement benefit*	*Deferred income*
	$m	$m	$m	$m
b/d	57	(31 + 138) 169.0	74	0
P/L		46.0	(W6) 10	
OCI		(2 + 1) 3.0	4	
Acquisition of subsidiary		(W5)1.5	1	
Cash (paid)/rec'd	**(31)** β	**(135.5)** β	(9)*	2 × 50% 1
c/d	26	84.0 (35 + 33)	80	1

* *cash flow given in question, but working shown for clarity*

4 *Working capital changes*

	Inventories	*Trade receivables*	*Trade payables*
	$m	$m	$m
b/d	190	180	361
Acquisition of subsidiary	6	3	4
∴ **Increase/(decrease)**	**(41)** β	**(58)** β	**(210)** β
c/d	155	125	155

5 *Goodwill on acquisition of Sweety*

	$m	$m
Consideration transferred		30.0
Fair value of net assets (net of deferred tax)	20.0	
	(1.5)	
Deferred tax*		(18.5)
		11.5

*Deferred tax:

	$m
Fair values of Sweety's identifiable net assets excluding deferred tax $15m + $15m	20
Tax base	(15)
Temporary difference arising on acquisition	5

Temporary difference arising on acquisition: $5m × 30% = $1.5m

6 *Retirement benefit*

The total net pension cost charged to profit or loss is:

	$m
Current service cost	8
Net interest cost	3
Less obligation assumed on the purchase of Sweety	(1)
	10

The remeasurement (actuarial) losses are charged to other comprehensive income. The amounts paid by the trustees are not included, because they are not paid by the company.

(b) **Classification of cash flows**

IAS 7 *Statement of cash flows* requires the classification of cash flows under three main headings: operating activities, investing activities and financing activities. The classification is, however, **not always straightforward**. Some cash flows which look similar may be **classified differently, depending on the nature of the business**. For example, an investment company might classify dividends received as a cash inflow from operating activities because investment is its operation, whereas a retail company would classify dividends received as an investing activity.

IAS 7 favours classification which **reflects the nature of an entity's activities** over classification in accordance with the underlying item in the statement of financial position.

To identify the nature of the cash inflow or outflow, the following questions should be considered:

(i) Why is the cash flow being paid or received?
(ii) Who receives or pays the cash flow?
(iii) What is the source of the cash flow?
(iv) Does the cash flow result from a transactions which determine a profit or a loss.

The statement of cash flows shows the **movement in cash and cash equivalents** between the start of the period and the end of the period. Cash is generally considered to be a straightforward item to determine; cash equivalents less so. IAS 7 defines them as 'short-term, highly liquid investments that are readily convertible to known amounts of cash and which are subject to an insignificant risk of changes in value'. The standard does not define 'short-term' but does state that 'an investment normally **qualifies as a cash equivalent only when it has a short maturity** of, say, three months or less from the date of acquisition'.

Three months would not generally be long enough for a significant change in value, and is also consistent with the **purpose of meeting short-term cash commitments**. In limited circumstances, a longer-term deposit with an early withdrawal penalty may be treated as a cash equivalent. The terms of the arrangement need to be considered in each case:

(i) The **$3m** on deposit for twelve months can be withdrawn early, but the penalty – loss of all interest earned – is so significant as to indicate that the cash is not intended to meet short term cash commitments. Therefore this investment would **not qualify as a cash equivalent.**

(ii) The $7m deposit also has a twelve-month maturity period, and can be withdrawn with 21 days' notice. There is a penalty for early withdrawal, but this is much less severe than the first deposit, being only a reduction in the rate of interest from 3% to 2%. This is normal for short-term deposits, as stated by the bank, indicating that the entity wishes to keep the funds available for short-term needs. Therefore this deposit **does meet the IAS 7 definition of cash equivalents**.

(c) **Professional ethics and conflict of interest**

Ethical codes are important to accountants **because ethics have practical application in the accountant's professional life**. The directors of Angel have been dismissive of the importance of ethics, but their arguments can be countered as follows.

Company directors are understandably **motivated by profit** – it is what the company's shareholders expect – and there may appear to be a conflict of interest between profit and ethics, including social ethics. Excessive focus on profit has led in some cases to **aggressive earnings management**, whereby directors use creative accounting techniques to present the results in a favourable light, or to **questionable business practices**, such as outsourcing to countries with poor health and safety records, or which use child labour.

Ethical codes cannot provide ready-made solutions to all potential conflicts, but it **can provide a set of principles on which to base judgements**. A vague wish to 'do the right thing' will be of little use when faced with a decision to report a colleague or member of the client's staff who is acting unethically. The study of ethics can direct the accountant's thinking and reasoning and help him or her make the right decision, even if it does not make that decision any easier. An example of ethical guidance serving this purpose is the ACCA's *Code of Ethics and Conduct,* which requires its members to adhere to a set of fundamental principles in the course of their professional duty, such as confidentiality, objectivity, professional behaviour, integrity, professional competence and due care.

The two goals – profit maximisation and ethical behaviour – **need not conflict**. It is possible that an ethical approach by companies can **improve business performance. Customers may buy from a company that they perceive as environmentally friendly,** or which avoids animal testing, and **employees may remain loyal** to such a company, and both these factors are likely to increase shareholder wealth in the long term. If a company engages constructively with the country or community in which it is based, it may be seen by shareholders and potential shareholders as being a **good long- term investment** rather than in it for short-term profits. As regards manipulation and creative accounting, in the long term, relationships with stakeholders are built on **trust and honesty,** eg, a company that provides transparent **disclosures,** particularly when these go beyond what is required by legislation or accounting standards, will be seen as **responsible and a good potential investment**.

55 Case study question: Jocatt

Text reference. Group statements of cash flow are covered in Chapter 17. Ethical issues are covered in Chapter 2.

Top tips. In tackling part (a), remember that time management is the key to cash flow questions. Set out your proforma and workings and do not spend too long on the fiddly bits. The question also required candidates to understand how a business combination achieved in stages would work under the revised IFRS 3 – you need to know that the fair value of the previously held interest in Tigret, and the fair value of the non-controlling interest in Tigret as a subsidiary, go in the goodwill calculation. Other complications include a retirement benefit scheme, a rights issue and goodwill impairment (because the goodwill is more fiddly, being a piecemeal acquisition). Make sure you allow adequate time for Part (b)(i) and (ii). The ACCA examination/examining team has recently stressed that students often don't – you can't hope to do well if you don't answer the whole question. There are 15 marks here for Part (b).

Easy marks. In Part (a) these are available for basic cash flow aspects – working capital calculations, non-controlling interest, tax and investment property additions. Follow our order for the workings – the easy ones come first. In Part (b), don't be tempted to write all you know about the direct method and how it works. The question is quite specific. Part (ii) follows on from Part (i), because one of the key problems with the indirect method is manipulation, and this has ethical implications.

Examiner's comment. Candidates generally performed well on this part of the question. The main areas where candidates found difficulties were: ensuring that the purchase of the subsidiary was dealt with in calculating cash flows across the range of assets and liabilities; the treatment of the past service costs relating to the defined benefit scheme; The calculation of the cash flow on taxation, although many candidates made a good attempt at this calculation

The first part of Part (b) on the indirect method of preparing cash flow statements was poorly answered. However, candidates performed well on the ethical aspects.

Marking scheme

		Marks
(a)		
	Net profit before tax	1
	Retirement benefit expense	2
	Depreciation on PPE	1
	Depreciation on investment property	1
	Amortisation of intangible assets	1
	Profit on exchange of land	1
	Loss on replacement of investment property	1
	Associate's profit	1
	Impairment of goodwill	4
	Gain on revaluation of investment in equity instruments (Tigret) prior to derecognition	1
	Finance costs	1
	Decrease in trade receivables	1
	Decrease in inventories	1
	Increase in trade payables	1
	Cash paid to retirement benefit scheme	1
	Finance costs paid	1
	Income taxes paid	2
	Purchase of associate	1
	Purchase of PPE	2
	Purchase of subsidiary	1
	Additions – investment property	1
	Proceeds from sale of land	1
	Intangible assets	1
	Purchase of investments in equity instruments	1
	Repayment of long-term borrowings	1
	Rights issue NCI	1
	Non-controlling interest dividend	1
	Dividends paid	1
	Net increase in cash and cash equivalents	1
		35
(b)		
	(i) Subjective	8
	(ii) Subjective	7
		50

(a) JOCATT GROUP

STATEMENT OF CASH FLOWS FOR YEAR ENDED 30 NOVEMBER 20X2

	$m	$m
Cash flows from operating activities		
Profit before taxation	59.0	
Adjustments for:		
Depreciation	27.0	
Amortisation (W1)	17.0	
Impairment of goodwill (W1)	31.5	
Profit on exchange of land*: 15 + 4 – 10	(9.0)	
Gain on investment property* (W1)	(1.5)	
Loss on replacement of investment property	0.5	
Gain on revaluation of investment in equity instruments (Tigret – fair value on derecognition less fair value at 1 December 20X1: 5 – 4)	(1.0)	
Retirement benefit expense (W7)	4.0	
Cash paid to defined benefit plan **(W3)**	(7.0)	
Share of profit of associate (per question)	(6.0)	
Interest expense (per question)	6.0	
	120.5	
Decrease in trade receivables (W4)	56.0	
Decrease in inventories (W4)	23.0	
Increase in trade payables (W4)	89.0	
Cash generated from operations	288.5	
Interest paid	(6.0)	
Income taxes paid (W3)	(16.5)	
Net cash from operating activities		266
Cash flows from investing activities		
Acquisition of subsidiary, net of cash acquired: 15 – 7	(8.0)	
Acquisition of associate (W1)	(48.0)	
Purchase of property, plant and equipment (W1)	(98.0)	
Purchase of investment property (per question)	(1.0)	
Purchase of intangible assets **(W6)**	(12.0)	
Purchase of investments in equity instruments (W1)	(5.0)	
Proceeds from sale of land	15.0	
Net cash used in investing activities		(157)
Cash flows used in financing activities		
Proceeds from issue of share capital (W2)	0.0	
Repayment of long-term borrowings (W3)	(4.0)	
Rights issue to non-controlling shareholders (from SOCIE)	2.0	
Dividends paid (from SOCIE or (W2))	(5.0)	
Dividends paid to non-controlling interest shareholders (from SOCIE or (W2))	(13.0)	
Net cash used in financing activities		(20)
Net increase in cash and cash equivalents		89
Cash and cash equivalents at the beginning of the year		143
Cash and cash equivalents at the end of the year		232

***Note.** The statement of profit or loss and other comprehensive income in the question shows 'gains on property' of $10.5m, which need to be added back to profit in arriving at cash generated from operations. This is made up of $1.5m gain on investment property (W2) and $9m gain on the exchange of surplus land for cash and plant (Note (vi) of the question. The double entry for the exchange is:

DEBIT	Cash	$15m	
DEBIT	Plant	$4m	
CREDIT	Land		$10m
CREDIT	Profit or loss		$9m

Separate from this, also shown in W2, is an impairment loss on the old heating system, for which the double entries are:

DEBIT	Profit or loss (old heating system)	$0.5m	
CREDIT	Investment property (old heating system)		$0.5m
DEBIT	Investment property (new heating system)	$1m	
CREDIT	Cash		$1m

Workings

1 *Assets*

	PPE	*Investment property*	*Goodwill*	*Intangible assets*	*Associate*	*Investments in equity instruments*
	$m	$m	$m	$m	$m	$m
b/d	254	6.0	68.0	72	0	90
P/L		**1.5 β**			6	1
OCI	(7)					3 *
Dep'n/ Amort'n/ Impairment	(27)		**(31.5) β**	**(17) β**		
Acquisition of sub/assoc	15		(W5) 11.5	18	48 β	
Non-cash additions	4					
Disposals/derecognition	(10)	(0.5)				(5)
Cash paid/(rec'd) β	**98**	1.0	0.0	(W6) 12	(0)	**5**
c/d	327	8.0	48.0	85	54	94

* Grossed up for related tax: $2m + $1m

2 *Equity*

	Share capital	*Retained earnings*	*NCI*
	$m	$m	$m
b/d	275	324	36
P/L		38	10
OCI		(6)	
Acquisition of subsidiary	15		20
Rights issue (5 × 40%)			2
Cash (paid)/rec'd β	**0**	**(5)** *	**(13)** *
c/d	290	351	55

* **Note.** Cash flow given in question, but working shown for clarity.

3 *Liabilities*

	Long-term borrowings	*Tax payable*	*Pension liability*
	$m	$m	$m
		(41 + 30)	
b/d	71	71.0	22
P/L		11.0	(W7) 4
OCI		1.0	6
Acquisition of subsidiary		(W5)1.5	
Cash (paid)/rec'd β	**(4)**	**(16.5)**	**(7)**
c/d	67	68.0	25
		(35 + 33)	

4 *Working capital changes*

	Inventories	*Trade receivables*	*Trade payables*
	$m	$m	$m
b/d	128	113	55
Acquisition of subsidiary		5	
∴ **Increase/(decrease)**	**(23)**	**(56)**	**89**
c/d	105	62	144

5 *Goodwill on acquisition of Tigret*

	$m	$m
Consideration transferred: $15m + $15m		30.0
Fair value of non-controlling interests		20.0
Fair value of previously held equity interest		5.0
		55.0
Identifiable net assets: 15 + 18 + 5 + 7	45.0	
Deferred tax: ($45m – $40m) × 30%	(1.5)	
		(43.5)
		11.5

6 *Intangible assets*

The research costs of $2m and the marketing costs of $1m are charged to profit or loss for the year.

The $8m cost of the patents and the $4m development costs = $12m are cash outflows to acquire intangible assets.

7 *Pension costs*

The total net pension cost charged to profit or loss is:

	$'m
Current service cost	10
Past service cost (recognised immediately)	2
Net interest income on plan assets	(8)
	4

(b) (i) **Use of the indirect method of preparing statements of cash flow**

The **direct method** of preparing cash flow statements discloses **major classes of gross cash receipts and gross cash payments**. It shows the items that affected cash flow and the size of those cash flows. Cash received from, and cash paid to, specific sources such as customers and suppliers are presented. This contrasts with the indirect method, where accrual-basis net income (loss) is converted to cash flow information by means of add-backs and deductions.

An important **advantage** of the direct method is that the users can see and understand the actual **cash flows,** and how they relate to items of income or expense. For example, payments of expenses are shown as cash disbursements and are deducted from cash receipts. In this way, the **user is able to recognise the cash receipts and payments** for the period.

From the point of view of the **user, the direct method is preferable**, because it discloses information, not available elsewhere in the financial statements, which could be of use in estimating future cash flow.

The **indirect method** involves **adjusting the net profit or loss** for the period for:

(1) Changes during the period in inventories, operating receivables and payables

(2) Non-cash items, eg depreciation, provisions, profits/losses on the sales of assets

(3) Other items, the cash flows from which should be classified under investing or financing activities

From the point of view of the **preparer of accounts, the indirect method is easier to use,** and **nearly all companies use it in practice**. The main argument companies have for using the indirect method is that the **direct method is too costly**. The **disadvantage** of the indirect method is that **users find it difficult to understand** and it is therefore more **open to manipulation**. This is particularly true with regard to classification of cash flows. Companies may wish to classify cash inflows as operating cash flows and cash outflows as non-operating cash flows.

The directors' proposal to report the loan proceeds as operating cash flow may be an example of such manipulation. For Jocatt, the indirect method would **not,** as is claimed, **be more useful and informative to users** than the direct method. IAS 7 allows both methods, however, so the indirect method would still be permissible.

(ii) **Reporting the loan proceeds as operating cash flow**

The directors of Jocatt have an **incentive to enhance operating cash flow**, because they receive extra income if operating cash flow exceeds a predetermined target. Accordingly, their proposal to classify the loan proceeds as operating cash flow should come under scrutiny.

Their proposal should first of all be considered in the light of their claim that the indirect method is more useful to users than the direct method. The opposite is the case, so while both methods are allowed, the directors' **motivation for wishing to use the method that is less clear to users** should be questioned.

The IAS 7 indirect method allows some leeway in classification of cash flows. For example, dividends paid by the entity can be shown as financing cash flows (showing the cost of obtaining financial resources) or operating cash flows (so that users can assess the entity's ability to pay dividends out of operating cash flows). However, the **purpose of such flexibility is to present the position as fairly as possible**. Classifying loan proceeds as operating cash flow does not do this.

Ethical behaviour in the preparation of financial statements, and in other areas, is of **paramount importance**. Directors act unethically if they use 'creative' accounting in accounts preparation to make the figures look better, in particular if their presentation is determined not by finding the best way to apply International Financial Reporting Standards, but, as here, by **self-interest**.

To act ethically, the directors must put the interests of the company and its shareholders first, and must also have regard to other stakeholders such as the loan provider. Accordingly, the **loan proceeds should be reported as cash inflows from financing activities,** not operating activities.

56 Glowball

Text reference. Covered in Chapter 18 of your text.

Top tips. This is a comprehensive question covering most aspects of environmental reporting that are likely to come up. Learn our answer and apply it to many questions on this topics.

Marking scheme

			Marks
(a)	Current reporting requirements		10
(b)	Restoration		5
	Infringement of law		4
	Emissions		4
	Decommissioning activities		4
	Report		4
		Available	31
		Maximum	25

REPORT

To: The Directors
Glowball

Date: 8 June 20X3

From: Ann Accountant

Environmental Reporting

Introduction

The purpose of this report is to provide information about current reporting requirements and guidelines on the subject of environmental reporting, and to give an indication of the required disclosure in relation to the specific events which you have brought to my attention. We hope that it will assist you in preparing your environmental report.

Current reporting requirements and guidelines

Most businesses have generally ignored environmental issues in the past. However, the use and **misuse** of **natural resources** all lead to environmental costs generated by businesses, both large and small.

There are very few rules, legal or otherwise, to ensure that companies disclose and report environmental matters. Any **disclosures tend to be voluntary**, unless environmental matters happen to fall under standard accounting principles. Environmental matters may be reported in the accounts of companies in the following areas.

IFRS and environmental reporting

There are **no required disclosures** under IFRS. However, if environmental matters fall within the scope of specific accounting principles they must be dealt with under the relevant standard. In particular:

- IAS 1 (revised) *Presentation of financial statements* requires disclosure of facts material to a proper understanding of financial statements.
- IAS 37 *Provisions, contingent liabilities and contingent assets* requires provisions for environmental damage to be recognised.

National and legal requirements

In the UK, the Companies Act 2006 requires disclosure of environmental matters in the Expanded Business Review, now incorporated into the Operating and Financial Review as best practice in Reporting Statement 1. Other countries require environmental reporting under national law.

Voluntary disclosure: sustainability

Most environmental disclosure is voluntary, although lists of companies in particular are under a great deal of pressure to make such disclosures. There have been a number of **initiatives** in the past (CERES, Friends of the Earth Charter) but the most important of these is the **Global Reporting Initiative (GRI)**.

The GRI is a long-term, multi-stakeholder international not-for-profit organisation, with many stakeholders. Its aim is to develop and disseminate globally applicable **Sustainability Reporting Guidelines** for voluntary use. These guidelines cover a number of areas (economic, environmental and social), and the latest guidelines (G4) were published in 2013.

The Guidelines set out the **framework of a sustainability report** and offer two options: the **Core option** and the **Comprehensive option**.

(a) The **Core option** contains the **essential elements** of a sustainability report. It provides the background against which an organisation communicates the impacts of its economic, environmental and social and governance performance and impacts.

(b) The **Comprehensive option** builds on the Core option by requiring **additional disclosures**

Organisations choosing the Core option have to disclose **at least one indicator** related to each 'identified material aspect', while organisations choosing the Comprehensive option have to disclose all indicators related to each 'identified material aspect'. For environmental reporting the indicators are: materials; energy; water; biodiversity; emissions; effluents and waste; products and services; compliance; transport; supplier environmental assessment; environmental grievance mechanisms.

Comments on 'environmental events'

(a) Of relevance to the farmland restoration is IAS 37 *Provisions, contingent liabilities and contingent assets.* Provisions for environmental liabilities should be recognised where there is a **legal or constructive obligation** to rectify environmental damage or perform restorative work. The mere existence of the restorative work does not give rise to an obligation and there is no legal obligation. However, it could be argued that there is a constructive obligation arising from the company's approach in previous years, which may have given rise to an **expectation** that the work would be carried out. If this is the case, a provision of $150m would be required in the financial statements. In addition, this provision and specific examples of restoration of land could be included in the environmental report.

(b) The treatment of the **fine** is straightforward: it is an obligation to transfer economic benefits. An estimate of the fine should be made and a **provision** set up in the financial statements for $5m. This should be mentioned in the environmental report. The report might also **put the fines in context** by stating how many tests have been carried out and how many times the company has passed the tests. The directors may feel that it would do the company's reputation no harm to point out the fact that the number of prosecutions has been falling from year to year.

(c) These statistics are good news and need to be covered in the environmental report. However, the emphasis should be on **accurate factual reporting** rather than boasting. It might be useful to provide target levels for comparison, or an industry average if available. The emissions statistics should be split into three categories:

- Acidity to air and water
- Hazardous substances
- Harmful emissions to water

As regards the aquatic emissions, the $70m planned expenditure on **research** should **be mentioned in the environmental report**. It shows a commitment to benefiting the environment. However, **IAS 37 would not permit a provision** to be made for this amount, since an obligation does not exist and the **expenditure is avoidable**. Nor does it qualify as development expenditure under IAS 38.

(d) The environmental report should mention the steps the company is taking to minimise the harmful impact on the environment in the way it sites and constructs its gas installations. The report should also explain the policy of dismantling the installations rather than sinking them at the end of their useful life.

Currently the company builds up a provision for decommissioning costs over the life of the installation. However, IAS 37 does not allow this. Instead, the **full amount must be provided** as soon as there is an

obligation arising as a result of **past events**, the **settlement** of which is **expected** to result in an **outflow of resources**. The obligation exists right at the beginning of the installation's life, and so the full $407m must be provided for. A corresponding asset is created.

57 Preparation question: Current issues

(a) (i) **Key changes in IFRS 16 *Leases***

(1) The most important change from its predecessor, IAS 17, is that nearly **all leases must be reported in the statement of financial position.** The distinction between finance and operating leases no longer applies for lessees, although it does for lessors.

(2) The are exceptions for leases of low value and leases of under twelve months.

(3) A lessee must measure the **lease liability** similarly to other financial liabilities and recognise **interest** on the liability.

(4) Lease assets (right-of-use assets) and liabilities are initially measured on a **present value** basis.

(5) Requirements for **lessors** are essentially **unchanged.**

(6) There are **extensive disclosure requirements** for both lessees and lessors.

(ii) **Key likely effects of IFRS 16**

(1) Companies will be required to report **larger amounts of assets and liabilities** in their statements of financial position. This will particularly affect companies that currently have much of their leasing commitments off balance sheet in the form of operating leases. An example of this is airlines, many of which do not show any asset or liability in respect of their aircraft. Under IFRS 16, an airline entering into a lease for an aircraft would show an asset for the 'right to use' the aircraft and an equal liability based on the current value of the lease payments it has promised to make.

(2) As a result of bringing lease liabilities onto the statement of financial position, **loan covenants may be breached** and need to be renegotiated.

(3) For companies that currently hold material operating leases, the **pattern of expenses will change**. Specifically, the **lease expense will be 'front-loaded'**. This is because IFRS 16 replaces the IAS 17 straight-line operating lease expense with a depreciation charge for leased assets, included within operating costs and an interest expense on lease liabilities included within financing costs. The total expense will generally be the same but there will be a **difference in expense profile** between IFRS 16 and IAS 17, with a consequent effect on EBITDA and operating profit.

(4) With regard to the statement of cash flows, IFRS 16 will generally change the **presentation of cash flows** in respect of leases previously accounted for as operating leases.

Operating cash outflows, which is where operating lease payments are reported under IAS 17, will **reduce**. However, there will be a corresponding **increase in financing cash outflows**. This is because repayments of the capital component of a lease liability are included within financing activities.

(b) IFRS 16 *Leases* requires entities to **account for the lease component of the contract separately from the non-lease component.** The entity must split the rental or lease payment and:

- Account for the lease component under IFRS 16, and
- Account for the service element separately, generally as an expense in profit or loss

The consideration in the contract is **allocated on the basis of the stand-alone prices** of the lease component(s) and the non-lease component(s).

On-Ice Co should allocate $25,313, ($30,000 × $27,000 ÷ $(27,000 + 5,000) to the lease element and account for that as a lease under IFRS 16.

On-Ice Co should allocate $4,687 ($30,000 × $5,000 ÷ $(27,000 + 5,000) to the servicing element and recognise it in profit or loss as an expense.

(c) **Significance of debt/equity distinction**

The distinction between debt and equity is very important, since the classification of a financial instrument as either debt or equity **can have a significant impact on the entity's reported earnings and gearing ratio**, which in turn can affect debt covenants. Companies may wish to classify a financial instrument as **equity,** in order to give a **favourable impression of gearing,** but this may in turn have a **negative effect** on the perceptions of existing shareholders if it is seen **as diluting existing equity interests.**

The distinction is also relevant in the context of a **business combination** where an entity **issues financial instruments as part consideration, or to raise funds to settle a business combination in cash.** Management is often called upon to **evaluate different financing options**, and in order to do so must **understand the classification rules and their potential effects**. For example, **classification as a liability** generally means that **payments are treated as interest** and charged to profit or loss, and this may, in turn, **affect the entity's ability to pay dividends** on equity shares.

Although the distinction was discussed at some length in a 2013 Discussion Paper on the *Conceptual Framework,* the topic was **not explored in the 2015 exposure draft.** Instead, it is **part of a separate project.**

(d) **Additional performance measures**

Additional performance measures (APMs) can take the form of additional key performance indicators or providing more information on the individual items within the financial statements. Users have driven the demand for APMs because financial statements, prepared in accordance with applicable financial reporting standards, have been restricted in the amount of information that can be provided.

Preparers of financial statements may wish to report **'sustainable' earnings**. This means, in effect, that certain items of income and expense are excluded because they are considered irrelevant as regards their impact on future years' performance. Examples of such items include fair value gains or losses on financial instruments.

Common APMs include the following:

(i) **Normalised profit.** This may be defined in various ways, but principally means profit per IFRS (or other applicable standards) excluding non-recurring items such as disposals of business, and other items such as amortisation of intangibles.

(ii) **EBIT.** This means earnings before interest and tax.

(iii) **EBITDA.** This stands for earnings before interest, tax, depreciation and amortisation.

(iv) **Net financial debt.** This is gross financial debt less cash and cash equivalents and other financial assets, and is a useful indicator of an entity's ability to meet its financial obligations.

In general, APMs are any measures of financial performance not specifically defined by the applicable financial reporting framework.

The **problematic nature** of some APMs may be seen in the case of EBITDA. This is a proxy for operating cash flows, although it is not the same. It takes operating profit and strips out depreciation, amortisation and (normally) any separately-disclosed items such as exceptional items.

EBITDA is not a cash flow ratio as such, but it is a widely used, and sometimes misused, approximation. Particular reservations include:

(i) EBITDA is not a cash flow measure and, while it excludes certain subjective accounting practices, it is still subject to accounting manipulation in a way that cash flows would not be. Examples would include revenue recognition practices and items that have some unusual aspects but are not disclosed separately and, therefore, not added back.

(ii) EBITDA is not a sustainable figure as there is no charge for capital replacement such as depreciation in traditional profit measures or CAPEX (capital expenditure) as in free cash flow.

More generally, APMs are sometimes used by issuers to present an **overly favourable picture** of an entity's financial performance by stripping out the negative aspects

(e) (i) The IASB's disclosure initiative is a broad-based undertaking exploring how disclosures in IFRS financial reporting can be improved. It is made up of a number of projects, the second of which was completed in January 2016.

The disclosure initiative was formally begun in 2012. Subsequently IASB undertook a constituent survey on disclosure and held a disclosure forum designed to bring together securities regulators, auditors, investors and preparers. This led to issued Feedback Statement Discussion Forum – Financial Reporting Disclosure in May 2013, which outlined the IASB's intention to consider a number of further initiatives, including short-term and research projects.

The disclosure initiative is intended to **complement the work being done on the *Conceptual Framework* project.**

(ii) In October 2015, a Draft Practice Statement was issued as part of the Disclosure Initiative. The Statement was developed in response to concerns with the level of uncertainty over the application of the concept of materiality, which can result in excessive disclosure of immaterial information while important information can be obscured or even missed out of the financial statements. It provides non-mandatory guidance to assist with the application of the concept of materiality to financial statements prepared in accordance with IFRS. The statement is divided into the following three key areas:

(1) Characteristics of materiality

(2) How to apply the concept of materiality when making decisions about presenting and disclosing information in the financial statements

(3) How to assess **whether omissions and misstatements of information are material** to the financial statements.

58 Fair values and IFRS 13

Text reference. Current issues are covered in Chapter 19. Fair value is covered where relevant in Chapters 3, 4, 12 and elsewhere briefly.

Top tips. IFRS 13 was issued a few years ago, but is still very topical.

Easy marks. Part (a) is fairly open ended, and credit will be given for valid points if you back up your arguments.

(a) **Fair value measurement or historical cost**

The debate between historical cost accounting and fair value measurement centres on **reliability versus relevance**. Very broadly speaking, fair values are perceived as relevant but not reliable. Historical cost accounting is perceived as reliable but not relevant.

Fair value can be said to be more relevant than historical cost because it is based on current market values rather than a value that is in some cases many years out of date. Fair values for an entity's assets, it is argued, will be give a closer approximation to the value of the entity as a whole, and are more useful to a decision maker or an investor.

If there is **more standardisation in fair valuing** – IFRS 13 *Fair value measurement* is a step towards this – then in the future, if not immediately, fair value measurement will have the advantage of being both relevant and reliable.

Historical cost accounting traditionally matches cost and revenue. The objective has been to match the cost of the asset with the revenue it earns over its useful life. It has a number of **disadvantages**.

(i) If the historical cost differs from its fair value on initial recognition, the **matching process in future periods becomes arbitrary**.

(ii) Non-current asset **values are unrealistic**, particularly those of property.

(iii) **Holding gains on inventory are included in profit.** During a period of high inflation the **monetary value of inventories held may increase significantly** while they are being processed. The conventions of historical cost accounting lead to the **realised part of this holding gain** (known as *inventory appreciation*) being **included** in **profit** for the year.

(iv) **Comparisons over time are unrealistic**, because they do not take account of inflation.

(v) **Costs incurred before an asset is recognised are not capitalised.** This is particularly true of development expenditure, and means that the historical cost does not represent the fair value of the consideration given to create the asset.

However, historical cost has a number of **advantages** over fair values, mainly as regards reliability.

(i) It is **easy to understand**.
(ii) It is grounded in **real transaction amounts**, and is therefore **objective** and objectively verifiable.
(iii) There is **less scope for manipulation**.

Until there is **more uniformity and objectivity in fair valuing**, it is likely that historical cost accounting will continue to be used.

(b) **IFRS 13 changes**

(i) **Definition.** With the publication of IFRS 13, IFRS and US GAAP now have the same definition of fair value and the measurement and disclosure requirements are now aligned. IFRS 13 defines fair value as **'the price that would be received to sell an asset or paid to transfer a liability in an orderly transaction between market participants at the measurement date.'**

The previous definition used in IFRS was 'the amount for which an asset could be exchanged, or a liability settled, between knowledgeable, willing parties in an arm's length transaction'.

The price which would be received to sell the asset or paid to transfer (not settle) the liability is described as the 'exit price' and this is the definition used in US GAAP. Although the concept of the 'arm's length transaction' has now gone, the market-based current exit price retains the notion of an exchange between unrelated, knowledgeable and willing parties.

(ii) **Measurement.** Fair value is a market-based measurement, not an entity-specific measurement. It focuses on assets and liabilities and on exit (selling) prices. It also takes into account market conditions at the measurement date. In other words, it looks at the amount for which the holder of an asset could sell it and the amount which the holder of a liability would have to pay to transfer it. It can also be used to value an entity's own equity instruments.

Because it is a market-based measurement, fair value is measured using the assumptions that market participants would use when pricing the asset, taking into account any relevant characteristics of the asset.

It is assumed that the transaction to sell the asset or transfer the liability takes place either:

(1) In the **principal market** for the asset or liability; or

(2) In the absence of a principal market, in the **most advantageous market** for the asset or liability. The principal market is the market which is the most liquid (has the greatest volume and level of activity) for that asset or liability. The most advantageous market is the market that maximises the amount that would be received to sell the asset or minimizes the amount that would be paid to transfer the liability (after taking into account transaction costs and transport costs). **In most cases the principal market and the most advantageous market will be the same.**

IFRS 13 acknowledges that when market activity declines an entity must use a valuation technique to measure fair value. In this case the emphasis must be on whether a transaction price is based on an orderly transaction, rather than a forced sale.

(iii) **Non-financial assets.** For non-financial assets the fair value measurement looks at the use to which the asset can be put. It takes into account the ability of a market participant to generate economic benefits by using the asset in its highest and best use.

(iv) **Valuation techniques.** IFRS 13 states that valuation techniques must be those which are appropriate and for which sufficient data are available. Entities should maximise the use of relevant **observable inputs** and minimise the use of **unobservable inputs**. The standard establishes a three-level hierarchy for the inputs that valuation techniques use to measure fair value:

Level 1 Quoted prices (unadjusted) in active markets for identical assets or liabilities that the reporting entity can access at the measurement date

Level 2 Inputs other than quoted prices included within Level 1 that are observable for the asset or liability, either directly or indirectly, eg quoted prices for similar assets in active markets or for identical or similar assets in non active markets or use of quoted interest rates for valuation purposes

Level 3 Unobservable inputs for the asset or liability, ie using the entity's own assumptions about market exit value

(v) **Disclosure.** For assets and liabilities that are measured at fair value on a recurring or non-recurring basis, an entity must disclose the valuation techniques and inputs used to develop those measurements. For recurring fair value measurements using significant **unobservable inputs** (Level 3), it must disclose the effect of the measurements on profit or loss or other comprehensive income for the period.

(c) **Investment in Greenfield**

The illustrative examples booklet accompanying IFRS 13 mentions the case of a financial asset for which sale is legally or contractually restricted for a specified period. The restriction is a characteristic of the instrument and, therefore, would be transferred to market participants. In this case the fair value of the instrument would be measured on the basis of the quoted price for an otherwise identical unrestricted equity instrument of the same issuer that trades in a public market, adjusted to reflect the effect of the restriction. The adjustment would reflect the amount market participants would demand because of the risk relating to the inability to access a public market for the instrument for the specified period. The adjustment will vary depending on:

(i) The nature and duration of the restriction

(ii) The extent to which buyers are limited by the restriction (eg there might be a large number of qualifying investors)

(iii) Qualitative and quantitative factors specific to both the instrument and the issuer

59 Mehran

Text reference. IFRS 13 is covered in Chapter 3 of the BPP Study Text and in more detail in Chapter 7. IFRS 9 is covered in Chapter 7.

Top tips. Most of this question is on IFRS 13 *Fair value measurement,* which has been examinable for several sittings. As well as the fair value hierarchy, it is important to be familiar the principles behind the standard, particularly the 'highest and best use' principle, and that of the 'principal and most advantageous market'.

Easy marks. Working out the most advantageous market is quite straightforward. The numbers are given to you for a reason! If you have practiced Q2(a) from June 2015, you would have been familiar with the requirements of IFRS 13: the relevance of the principal market and most advantageous market, and what costs are included within a fair value calculation.

Examiner's comment. Candidates often simply quote the valuation hierarchy without really understanding the nature of it. Candidates need to understand exactly what Level 1,2 and 3 inputs actually are. This question also required a valuation of unquoted investments essentially using the principles of IFRS 13.The prospect of answering such a question may seem quite daunting but if candidates use their general knowledge and experience in answering such a question is not quite so problematical. For example, if a fair valuation were to be placed upon a motor car, the market prices for a similar car would be used and adjusted if the mileage on the car was significantly different. The same principle applies to shares. That is, look at an equivalent transaction price for a similar share and use that as a starting point. A significant minority of candidates were distracted by the information on the preferred shares, and focused on the treatment of this, rather than the equity interest held by the entity.

Marking scheme

	Marks
(a) 1 mark per point up to maximum	6
(b) 1 mark per point up to maximum	10
(c) 1 mark per point up to maximum	7
Professional marks	2
Maximum	25

(a) **Land and brand name**

IFRS 13 *Fair value measurement* requires the fair value of a non-financial asset to be measured based on its highest and best use from a market participant's perspective. This requirement does not apply to financial instruments, liabilities or equity. The highest and best use takes into account the use of the asset which is physically possible, legally permissible and financially feasible. The highest and best use of a non-financial asset is determined by reference to its use and not its classification and is determined from the perspective of market participants. It does not matter whether the entity intends to use the asset differently. IFRS 13 allows management to presume that the current use of an asset is the highest and best use unless market or other factors suggest otherwise.

In this case, the agricultural land appears to have an alternative use as market participants have considered its alternative use for residential purposes. If the land zoned for agricultural use is currently used for farming, the fair value should reflect the cost structure to continue operating the land for farming, including any tax credits which could be realised by market participants. Thus the fair value of the land if used for farming would be $(5 + (20% of 0·5)) million, ie $5·1 million.

If used for residential purposes, the value should include all costs associated with changing the land to the market participant's intended use. In addition, demolition and other costs associated with preparing the land for a different use should be included in the valuation. These costs would include the uncertainty related to whether the approval needed for changing the usage would be obtained, because market participants would take that into account when pricing value of the land if it had a different use. Thus the fair value of the land if used for residential purposes would be $(7·4 – 0·2 – 0·3 – 0·1) million × 80%, ie $5·44m. Therefore the value of the land would be $5·44m on the highest and best use basis. In this situation, the presumption that the current use is the highest and best use of the land has been overridden by the market factors which indicate that residential development is the highest and best use. A use of an asset need not be legal at the measurement date, but it must not be legally prohibited in the jurisdiction.

In the absence of any evidence to the contrary, Mehran should value the brand on the basis of the highest and best use. The fair value is determined from the perspective of a market participant and is not influenced by the Mehran's decision to discontinue the brand. Therefore the fair value of the brand is $17m.

(b) **Fair value of inventory**

IFRS 13 sets out the concepts of principal market and most advantageous market. Transactions take place in either the principal market, which is the market with the greatest volume and level of activity for the inventory, or in the absence of a principal market, the most advantageous market. The most advantageous market is the market which maximises the amount which would be received to sell the inventory, after taking into account transaction costs and transportation costs. The price used to measure the inventory's fair value is not adjusted for transaction costs although it is adjusted for transport cost. The principal market is not necessarily the market with the greatest volume of activity for the particular reporting entity. The principle is based upon the importance of the market from the participant's perspective. However, the principal market is presumed to be the market in which the reporting entity transacts, unless there is evidence to the contrary. In evaluating the principal or most advantageous markets, IFRS 13 restricts the eligible markets to only those which can be accessed at the measurement date. If there is a principal market for the asset or liability, IFRS 13 states that fair value should be based on the price in that market, even if the price in a different market is higher. It is only in the absence of the principal market that the most advantageous market should be used. An entity does not have to undertake an exhaustive search of all possible markets in order to identify the principal or most advantageous market. It should take into account all information which is readily available.

There is a presumption in the standard that the market in which the entity normally transacts to sell the asset or transfer the liability is the principal or most advantageous market unless there is evidence to the contrary.

In this case, the greatest volume of transactions is conducted in the domestic market – direct to manufacturers. There is no problem with obtaining data from trade journals but the problem for Mehran is that there is no data to substantiate the volume of activity in the domestic market – direct to retailers even though Mehran feels that it is at least 20,000 tonnes per annum. The most advantageous market is the export market where after transport and transaction costs the price per tonne is $1,094.

	Domestic market – direct to retailers	*Domestic market – direct to manufacturers*	*Export market*
	$	$	$
Price per tonne	1,000	800	1,200
Transport costs per tonne	50	70	100
Selling agents' fees per tonne	-	4	6
Net price per tonne	950	726	1,094

It is difficult to determine a principal market because of the lack of information. It could be argued that the domestic market – direct to manufacturers has the highest volume for the produce, and is therefore the principal market by which Mehran should determine fair value of $730 ($800 – $70). However, because of the lack of information surrounding the domestic market – direct to retailers, the principal or most advantageous market will be presumed to be the market in which Mehran would normally enter into transactions which would be the export market. Therefore the fair value would be $1,100 ($1,200 – $100) per tonne.

(c) **Investment in Erham**

Measuring the fair value of individual unquoted equity instruments which constitute a non-controlling interest in a private company falls within the scope of IFRS 9 *Financial Instruments* in accordance with the principles set out in IFRS 13. There is a range of commonly used valuation techniques for measuring the fair value of unquoted equity instruments within the market and income approaches as well as the adjusted net asset method. IFRS 13 states that fair value is a market-based measurement, although it acknowledges that in some cases observable market transactions or other market information might not be available. IFRS 13 does not contain a hierarchy of valuation techniques nor does it prescribe the use of a specific valuation technique for meeting the objective of a fair value measurement. However, IFRS 13 acknowledges that, given specific circumstances, one valuation technique might be more appropriate than another. The market approach takes a transaction price paid for an identical or a similar instrument in an investee and adjusts the resultant valuation. The transaction price paid recently for an investment in an equity instrument in an investee which is similar, but not identical, to an investor's unquoted equity instrument in the same investee would be a reasonable starting point for estimating the fair value of the unquoted equity instrument.

Mehran would take the transaction price for the preferred shares and adjust it to reflect certain differences between the preferred shares and the ordinary shares. There would be an adjustment to reflect the priority of the preferred shares upon liquidation.

Mehran should acknowledge the benefit associated with control. This adjustment relates to the fact that Mehran's individual ordinary shares represent a non-controlling interest whereas the preferred shares issued reflect a controlling interest. There will be an adjustment for the lack of liquidity of the investment which reflects the lesser ability of the ordinary shareholder to initiate a sale of Erham relative to the preferred shareholder. Further, there will be an adjustment for the cumulative dividend entitlement of the preferred shares. This would be calculated as the present value of the expected future dividend receipts on the preferred shares, less the present value of any expected dividend receipts on the ordinary shares. The discount rate used should be consistent with the uncertainties associated with the relevant dividend streams.

Mehran should review the circumstances of the issue of the preferred shares to ensure that its price was a valid benchmark. Mehran must, however, use all information about the performance and operations of Erham which becomes reasonably available to it after the date of initial recognition of the ordinary shares up to the measurement date. Such information can have an effect on the fair value of the unquoted equity instrument at 31 March 20X6. In addition, Mehran should consider the existence of factors such as whether the environment in which Erham operates is dynamic, or whether there have been changes in market conditions between the issue of the preferred shares and the measurement date.

60 Pod

Text reference. Implementation of a new IFRS is covered in Chapter 19 of the Study Text. Intangible assets and impairment are covered in Chapter 3. Deferred tax is in Chapter 6.

Top tips. Part (a) (i) of this question required a discussion of the key practical considerations and financial statement implications when implementing a move to a new IFRS. There are a number of valid points that may be made, for example, the impact on performance-related pay, covenants, the need for communication with stakeholders and resourcing issues. Part (a)(ii) was more specific, and students should avoid the temptation to make general points about slow economic growth. The key point with regard to deferred tax assets is whether there will continue to be sufficient profits (otherwise you can't recognise them). An important point to mention with regard to impairment concerns the accuracy of cash flow projections. Part (b) of this question required a discussion of whether two proposed changes were acceptable. The first was a proposal to change the useful life of an intangible asset (a portfolio of customers acquired from a competitor) to 'indefinite', because of an inability to predict the asset's life. You need to consider the precise meaning of 'indefinite' – it means no foreseeable limit. The second proposal was to alter a cash-generating unit to the product line level rather than individual retail branch level. You needed a thorough knowledge of the criteria for a cash-generating unit and the ability to apply them to the scenario.

Easy marks. Part (a)(i) is fairly open ended when it comes to earing marks.

Examiner's comments. Both sections of Part (a) were well answered. The second section of Part (b) was well answered, but not the first. Although some candidates did argue that a customer's relationship will change over time, very few made reference to the need for maintenance costs in order for cash inflows to continue for an unlimited period of time, under IAS 38 *Intangible assets.*

Marking scheme

			Marks
(a)	(i)	1 mark per point up to maximum	7
	(ii)	1 mark per point up to maximum	8
(b)		1 mark per point up to maximum	8
		Professional marks	2
		Available	25

(a) (i) **Move to a new IFRS**

The entity itself should prepare an impact assessment and project plan relating to the introduction of the new IFRS. There may be significant changes to processes, systems and controls and management should communicate the impact to investors and other stakeholders. This would include plans for disclosing the effects of new accounting standards which are issued but not yet effective. The entity should chose a path to implementation and establish responsibilities and deadlines. This may help to determine the accountability of the implementation team and allow management to identify gaps in resources.

Further, IFRS-based financial statements are used in contracts or regulation. Banking agreements often specify maximum debt levels or financial ratios which refer to figures prepared in accordance with IFRS. New financial reporting requirements can affect those ratios, with potential breach of those contracts. Many jurisdictions have regulation which restricts the amount which can be paid out in dividends, by reference to accounting profit. Further, some governments use IFRS numbers for statistical and economic planning purposes and the data as evidence to place constraints on profitability in regulated industries.

It is important that the entity communicates the effects of a move to a new IFRS to the markets and analysts. On application of the new IFRS, investors will be provided with different information upon which to base their decisions. Investors' assessment of how management has discharged its stewardship responsibilities may be changed and this could affect the investors' investment decision. Further, new financial reporting requirements may disclose information which is of competitive advantage to third parties and this is a cost to the entity.

A change in an accounting standard could cause some entities to no longer invest in certain assets or it may change how they contract for some activities. For example, now that, under IFRS 16 *Leases*, most leases formerly accounted for as operating leases must be shown on the statement of financial position, this could have adverse economic impacts on certain sectors. Additionally, the new standard could affect the calculation of performance-related pay.

Where there is the introduction of a new accounting standard, the financial statements will need to reflect the new recognition, measurement and disclosure requirements which, in turn, will mean that entities will need to consider the requirements of IAS 8 *Accounting policies, changes in accounting estimates and errors*. IAS 8 contains a requirement that changes in accounting policies are fully applied retrospectively unless there are specific transitional provisions. Further, IAS 8 requires the disclosure of a number of matters as regards the new IFRS. Additionally, IAS 1 *Presentation of financial statements* requires a third statement of financial position to be presented if the entity retrospectively applies an accounting policy, restates items, or reclassifies items, and those adjustments had a material effect on the information in the statement of financial position at the beginning of the comparative period.

IAS 33 *Earnings per share* requires basic and diluted EPS to be adjusted for the impacts of adjustments resulting from changes in accounting policies accounted for retrospectively and IAS 8 requires the disclosure of the amount of any such adjustments. Taxation is often calculated on the profit measured for financial reporting purposes. For jurisdictions using IFRS as the basis for income tax, a change in a standard can change the tax base. The economic consequences of the link of accounting with tax liabilities can be significant.

(ii) **Impairment of non-financial and deferred tax asset**

A continuous period of slow economic growth could indicate to regulators that non-financial assets will continue to generate lower than expected cash flows, especially in those industries experiencing a downturn in fortunes. Particular attention should be paid to the valuation of goodwill and intangible assets with indefinite life spans. The entity should focus on certain specific areas including cash flow projections, disclosure of key assumptions and judgements, and appropriate disclosure of sensitivity analysis for material goodwill and intangible assets with indefinite useful lives.

In measuring value-in-use, cash flow projections should be based on reasonable and supportable assumptions which represent the best estimate of the range of future economic conditions. IAS 36 *Impairment of assets* points out that greater weight should be given to external evidence when determining the best estimate of cash flow projections. Each key assumption should be consistent with external sources of information, or there should be disclosure of how these assumptions differ from experience or external sources of information.

Such an economic climate could result in the recognition of tax losses or the existence of deductible temporary differences where perhaps impairments are not yet deductible for tax purposes. The recognition of deferred tax assets requires detailed consideration of the carry forward of unused tax losses, whether future taxable profits exist, and the need for disclosing judgements made in these circumstances.

IAS 12 *Income taxes* limits the recognition of a deferred tax asset to the extent that it is probable that future taxable profits will be available against which the deductible temporary difference can be utilised. IAS 12 states that the existence of unused tax losses is strong evidence that future taxable profit might not be available. Therefore, recent losses make the recognition of deferred tax assets conditional upon the existence of convincing other evidence. The probability that future taxable profit will be available to utilise the unused tax losses will need to be reviewed and if convincing evidence is available, there should be disclosure of the amount of a deferred tax asset and the nature of the evidence supporting its recognition. It is particularly relevant to disclose the period used for the assessment of the recovery of a deferred tax asset as well as the judgements made.

(b) **Indefinite useful life and cash-generating unit**

Under IAS 38 *Intangible assets,* an intangible asset has an indefinite useful life only if there is no 'foreseeable' limit to its useful life as in the case of a brand name. In the case of Pod, the customer relationship is with individuals and therefore there is by definition a time limit to that relationship. Difficulties in accurately determining an intangible asset's useful life do not provide a basis for regarding that useful life as indefinite. Where the cash flows are expected to continue for a finite period, the useful life of the asset is limited to that period, whereas if the cash flows are expected to continue indefinitely, the useful life is indefinite. The concept of indefinite not meaning infinite life refers to the fact that for intangible assets with an indefinite useful life, maintenance costs are necessary in order that cash inflows may continue for an unlimited period of time. For example, brand names do not have an infinite useful life if no investment is made in them. This argument does not apply to the circumstances of this case and therefore Pod is in contravention of IAS 38.

According to IAS 36 *Impairment of assets,* a CGU is defined as the smallest identifiable group of assets generating cash inflows which are largely independent of the cash inflows from other assets or groups of assets. In accordance with IAS 36, one factor to be considered is the monitoring of the entity's operations. Pod used the daily sales information and monthly statements of profit or loss of each individual branch to monitor its operations and to make decisions about continuing or disposing of its assets and operations. Each individual branch generates cash inflows which are largely independent of those generated by the other individual branches. Therefore, each branch should be identified as a separate CGU because Pod monitors and makes decisions about its assets and operations at the individual branch level.

61 Gasnature

Text reference. Specialised industries are covered in general terms in Chapter 20 of your Study Text. IFRS 11 is covered in Chapters 12 and 13. IAS 10 is covered in Chapter 5 and IFRS 9 in Chapter 7.

Top tips. In specialised industry questions, the standards examined will not necessarily be specialised, but the context may be unfamiliar, and it is important not to be thrown by this. Part (a) is a good example of applying mainstream syllabus topics (IAS 16) to an unusual situation ('irrecoverable gas'). Part (b) on 'own use' contracts has come up before, and the case could be argued either way. If the arguments seem complex, the good news is that there are only six marks for this part of the question, and you can make up the marks in Part (c), which is more mainstream.

Easy marks. Part (c) is relatively straightforward, and you should by now be familiar with the IFRS 11 criteria for distinguishing joint ventures from joint operations.

Examiner's comment. In Part (a), many candidates realised that there was a joint arrangement but could not distinguish between joint control and a joint venture, often using the terms interchangeably. Many candidates did not recognise the fact there would be a contingent liability to the other party to a joint arrangement arising on the decommissioning a site and also few were able to determine that the irrecoverable gas should be treated as PPE as it is a permanent asset until the site is decommissioned. Part (b), on IFRS 9, was not answered well, though it deals with some fundamental principles concerning whether a contract is a financial contract or an executory contract for the purchase of goods. Part (c) was quite well answered by candidates although there was some confusion over whether the overhaul component should be depreciated and over what time period.

Marking scheme

			Marks
(a)	1 mark per point up to maximum		9
(b)	1 mark per point up to maximum		6
(c)	(i)	1 mark per point up to maximum	4
	(ii)	1 mark per point up to maximum	4
Professional marks			2
			25

(a) **Joint arrangement**

The classification of a joint arrangement as a joint operation or a joint venture depends upon the rights and obligations of the parties to the arrangement (IFRS 11 *Joint arrangements*). A joint arrangement occurs where two or more parties have joint control. The contractually agreed sharing of control of an arrangement exists only when decisions about the relevant activities require the unanimous consent of the parties sharing control. The structure and form of the arrangement determines the nature of the relationship. However, regardless of the purpose, structure or form of the arrangement, the classification of joint arrangements depends upon the parties' rights and obligations arising from the arrangement. A joint arrangement which is not structured through a separate vehicle is a joint operation. In such cases, the contractual arrangement establishes the parties' rights and obligations. A joint operator accounts for the assets, liabilities, revenues and expenses relating to its involvement in a joint operation in accordance with the relevant IFRSs. The arrangement with Gogas is a joint operation as there is no separate vehicle involved and they have agreed to share services and costs with decisions regarding the platform requiring unanimous agreement of the parties. Gasnature should recognise its share of the asset as property, plant and equipment.

Under IAS 16 *Property, plant and equipment* (PPE), the cost of an item of property, plant and equipment includes the initial estimate of the costs of dismantling and removing the item and restoring the site on which it is located. IAS 37 *Provisions, contingent liabilities and contingent assets* contains requirements on how to measure decommissioning, restoration and similar liabilities. Where the effect of the time value of money is material, the amount of a provision should be the present value of the expenditures expected to be required to settle the obligation. Thus costs incurred by an entity in respect of obligations for dismantling, removing and restoring the site on which an item of property, plant and equipment is located are recognised and measured in accordance with IAS 16 and IAS 37. Thus Gasnature should recognise 55% of the cost of decommissioning the underground storage facility. However, because Gasnature is a joint operator, there is also a contingent liability for 45% of the decommissioning costs and there is a possible obligation for the remainder of the costs depending on whether some uncertain future event occurs, that is Gogas goes into liquidation and cannot fund the decommissioning costs. Therefore Gasnature, should also disclose a contingent liability relating to the Gogas's share of the obligation to the extent that it is contingently liable for Gogas's share.

IAS 16 states that property, plant and equipment are tangible items which:

(i) Are held for use in the production or supply of goods or services, for rental to others, or for administrative purposes, and

(ii) Are expected to be used during more than one period.

Thus Gasnature should classify and account for its share of the irrecoverable gas as PPE. The irrecoverable gas is necessary for the storage facility to perform its function as a gas storage facility. It is therefore part of the storage facility and should be capitalised as a component of the storage facility asset. The irrecoverable gas should be depreciated to its residual value over the life of the storage facility. However, if the gas is recoverable in full when the storage facility is decommissioned, then depreciation will be recorded against the irrecoverable gas component only if the estimated residual value of the gas decreases below cost during the life of the facility. When the storage facility is decommissioned and the cushion gas extracted and sold, the sale of the irrecoverable gas is accounted for as the disposal of an item of PPE in accordance with IAS 16 and the gain or loss recognised in profit or loss. The natural gas in excess of the irrecoverable gas which is injected into the facility should be treated as inventory in accordance with IAS 2 Inventories.

(b) **Contract with Agas**

IFRS 9 *Financial instruments* applies to those contracts to buy or sell a non-financial item which can be settled net in cash with the exception of contracts which are held for the purpose of the receipt or delivery of a non-financial item in accordance with the entity's expected purchase, sale or usage requirements (own use contract). In other words, it will result in physical delivery of the commodity. Contracts which are for an entity's 'own use' are exempt from the requirements of IFRS 9. Such a contract can be irrevocably designated as measured at fair value through profit or loss even if it was entered into for the above purpose. This designation is available only at inception of the contract and only if it eliminates or significantly reduces a recognition inconsistency (sometimes referred to as an 'accounting mismatch') which would otherwise arise from not recognising that contract because it is excluded from the scope of IFRS 9. There are various ways in which a contract to buy or sell a non-financial item can be settled net in cash or another financial instrument or by exchanging financial instruments. These include:

(i) When the terms of the contract permit either party to settle it net in cash

(ii) When the ability to settle net in cash is not explicit in the terms of the contract, but the entity has a practice of settling similar contracts net in cash

(iii) When, for similar contracts, the entity has a practice of taking delivery of the underlying and selling it within a short period after delivery, for the purpose of generating a profit

(iv) When the non-financial item which is the subject of the contract is readily convertible to cash.

A written option to buy or sell a non-financial item which can be settled net in cash is within the scope of IFRS 9. Such a contract cannot be entered into for the purpose of the receipt or delivery of the non-financial item in accordance with the entities expected purchase, sale or usage requirements. Contracts to buy or sell a non-financial item, such as a commodity, which can be settled net in cash or another financial instrument, or by exchanging financial instruments, are within the scope of IFRS 9. They are accounted for as derivatives. A level of judgement will be required in this area as net settlements caused by unique events beyond management's control may not necessarily prevent the entity from applying the 'own use' exemption to all similar contracts.

The contract entered into by Gasnature with Agas seems to be an own use contract which falls outside IFRS 9 and therefore would be treated as an executory contract. However, it could be argued that the contract is net settled because the penalty mechanism requires Agas to compensate Gasnature at the current prevailing market price. Further, if natural gas is readily convertible into cash in the location where the delivery takes place, the contract could be considered net settled. Additionally, if there is volume flexibility, then the contract could be regarded as a written option, which falls within the scope of IFRS 9.

However, the contract will probably still qualify as 'own use' as long as it has been entered into and continues to be held for the expected counterparties' sales/usage requirements. Additionally, the entity has not irrevocably designated the contract as measured at fair value through profit or loss, thus adding weight to the 'own use' designation.

(c) (i) It is not acceptable to accrue the costs of the overhaul. The entity does not have a constructive obligation to undertake the overhaul. Under IFRS, costs related to major inspection and overhaul are recognised as part of the carrying amount of property, plant and equipment if they meet the asset recognition criteria in IAS 16 *Property, plant and equipment*. The major overhaul component will then be depreciated on a straight-line basis over its useful life (i.e. over the period to the next overhaul) and any remaining carrying amount will be derecognised when the next overhaul is performed. Costs of the day-to-day servicing of the asset (i.e. routine maintenance) are expensed as incurred. Therefore the cost of the overhaul should have been identified as a separate component of the refinery at initial recognition and depreciated over a period of two years. This will result in the same amount of expense being recognised in profit or loss over the same period as the proposal to create a provision

(ii) Since there were no indicators of impairment at the period end, all costs incurred up to 31 August 20X5 amounting to $5m should remain capitalised by the entity in the financial statements for the year ended on that date. However, if material, disclosure should be provided in the financial statements of the additional activity during the subsequent period which determined the exploratory drilling was unsuccessful. This represents a non-adjusting event as defined by IAS 10 *Events after the reporting period* as an event which is indicative of a condition which arose after the end of the reporting period. The asset of $5m and additional drilling costs of $2m incurred subsequently would be expensed in the following year's financial statements.

62 Lockfine

Text reference. IFRS 1 and IFRS 13 are covered in Chapter 19 and 7 of your Study Text. IFRS 3 is covered in Chapter 12.

Top tips. This was a specialised industry question, set in the fishing industry. As the ACCA examination/examining team has stated, no specialist knowledge of the industry was required. The question was broken down into four almost equal parts. Parts (a) and (b) covered IFRS 1 *First-time adoption of International Financial Reporting Standards* in respect of fair value measurement and transition to IFRS 3 *Business combinations.* Part (c) was on intangible assets, and part (d) covered restructuring plans and provisions.

Easy marks. There are some relatively easy marks in Part (d) for listing out the IAS 37criteria for a constructive obligation to restructure.

Examiner's comment. In Part (a), the treatment of deemed cost was not well answered by candidates. Fair value becomes the 'deemed cost' going forward under the IFRS cost model. In Part (b) candidates recognised that if an entity during the transition process to IFRS, decides to retrospectively apply IFRS3 to a certain business combination then it must apply that decision consistently to all business combinations. However the key point often missed was that the decision to apply IFRS 3 cannot be made selectively. Part (c) was very well answered, with the main omission being the fact that under IAS 1 *Presentation of financial statements* an entity should disclose accounting policies relevant to an understanding of its financial statements. Part (d) was also answered well. Candidates were well versed in the principles behind how a constructive obligation to restructure arises under. IAS 37, *Provisions, contingent liabilities and contingent assets.*

Marking scheme

		Marks
(a)	1mark per question up to maximum	6
(b)	1mark per question up to maximum	6
(c)	1mark per question up to maximum	6
(d)	1mark per question up to maximum	5
Professional marks		2
Maximum		25

(a) **IFRS 1 and deemed cost**

IFRS 1 *First time adoption of International Financial Reporting Standards* states that an entity may elect to measure an item of property, plant and equipment at the **date of transition to IFRS** at fair value and **use that fair value as its deemed cost at that date**. Fair value is defined in IFRS 1 as amended by IFRS 13 *Fair value measurement* as:

'the price that would be received to sell an asset or paid to transfer a liability in an orderly transaction between market participants at the measurement date.'

An entity adopting IFRS for the first time may, under IFRS 1 as amended by IFRS 13, elect **to use a previous GAAP revaluation** of an item of property, plant and equipment at or before the date of transition to IFRS as deemed cost at the date of the revaluation under the following conditions.

(i) The revaluation was broadly comparable to fair value.

(ii) The revaluation was broadly comparable to cost or depreciated cost in accordance with IFRS, adjusted to reflect, for example, changes in a general or specific price index.

In addition, IFRS 1 does not give detailed rules about determining fair value, and first-time adopters who use fair value as deemed cost **must only provide limited disclosures**, not a full description of the methods and assumptions used.

In the case of Lockfine, the question to be decided is whether the selling agents' estimates can be used as the fair value to be used, in turn, as deemed cost under IFRS 1.

The selling agents' estimates provide only limited information about the valuation methods and assumptions, and it is doubtful that they can be relied upon for determining fair value in accordance with IAS 16 *Property, plant and equipment* and IFRS 13 *Fair value measurement.* Under IAS 16 measurement of fair value must be **reliable**. While it is correct to use independent valuers, IAS 16 requires that the reporting entity know the **assumptions** that have been made in assessing reliability. In addition, using the average of the highest amounts may not be prudent.

IFRS 1 allows more latitude than IAS 16. Lockfine is **not in breach of IFRS 1 which does not specify detailed rules for this particular case**, and allows fair value as determined on the basis of selling agents' estimates. This is a cost effective approach for entities that do not perform a full retrospective application of the requirements of IAS 16.

(b) **Fishing rights**

IFRS 1 requires that if an entity which is in the process of adopting IFRS decides to apply IFRS 3 retrospectively to a business combination, it **cannot do so selectively,** but must apply IFRS 3 **consistently to all business combinations** that occur between the date on which it decides to adopt.

IFRS 3 and the date of transition. An entity must have regard to **similar transactions in the period**. When allocating values to the assets and liabilities of the acquired company, the entity needs to have documentation to support its purchase price allocation. Without this, use of other methods of price allocation is not permitted unless the methods are strictly in accordance with IFRS.

Lockfine was **unable to recognise** the fishing rights of the business combination as separately identifiable because it **could not obtain a reliable value** for the rights, so it included the rights within goodwill.

IAS 38 has two criteria, both of which must be met for an entity to recognise an intangible asset, whether purchased or internally generated:

(i) It is probably that the future economic benefits attributable to the asset will flow to the entity.
(ii) The cost of the asset can be measured reliably.

The fishing rights **satisfy the first, but not the second of these criteria**. Accordingly the fishing rights were **correctly subsumed within goodwill**. As long as the goodwill presented under the first IFRS financial statements did not require a write down for impairment, it should be the net carrying amount at the date of transition.

Although the fishing rights have a finite life, **they will not be amortised over the period** specified by the rights, because they are included within goodwill. Instead, **the goodwill is reviewed annually for impairment** in accordance with IAS 36 *Impairment of assets.*

(c) **Electronic map data**

The standard that applies here is IAS 38 *Intangible assets.* Under IAS 38, an intangible asset is an asset with the following characteristics.

(i) It meets the standard's **identifiability criteria**. This means it must be separable or must arise from contractual or other legal rights

(ii) It is probable that **future economic benefits** attributable to the asset will flow to the entity. These could be in the form of increased revenues or cost savings.

(iii) The entity has **control**, that is the power to obtain benefits from the asset.

(iv) Its cost can be **measured reliably**.

It appears that the capitalised expenses of the acquisition and production of the electronic map data **meet these criteria**.

(i) The electronic maps are identifiable because they are capable of being separated from the entity as a whole and sold (or transferred or licensed), regardless of whether the entity intends to do this.

(ii) They are controlled by Lockfine.

(iii) It is probable that benefits attributable to the maps will flow to the entity because the electronic maps will generate revenue when used by the fishing fleet.

(iv) Their value can be measured reliably – Lockfine has a record of the costs.

The **electronic maps** will therefore be **recognised as an intangible asset at cost**. Generally they will subsequently be carried at cost less any amortisation and impairment losses.

Regarding the **database**, Lockfine believes that this has an indefinite useful life and, by implication, should not be amortised but should be tested annually for impairment. IAS 38 regards an intangible asset as having an indefinite useful life when, based on analysis of all the relevant factors, there is no foreseeable limit to the period over which the asset is expected to generate net cash inflows for the entity.

Indefinite does not mean the same as infinite and in the context of IAS 38 has specific implications. In particular, the indefinite useful life should not depend on future planned expenditure in excess of that required to maintain the asset. In this respect, **Lockfine complies with IAS 38**.

In addition, IAS 38 identifies certain factors that may affect the useful life, changing it in this instance from indefinite to finite. These include technological or commercial obsolescence and actions by competitors.

There is no specific requirement for an entity to disclose the IAS 38 criteria for recognition of an intangible asset arising from development, although it does require disclosure of assets which have an indefinite useful life (the carrying amount and reasons for assessing the useful life as indefinite). However, under IAS 1 *Presentation of financial statements,* entities **must disclose accounting policies that are relevant for an understanding of their financial statements**. The electronic maps and the data base constitute a material amount of total assets, so the accounting policies, including the IAS 38 criteria for development expenditure, need to be disclosed.

(d) **Restructuring plans**

IAS 37 criteria

IAS 37 *Provisions, contingent liabilities and contingent assets* **contains specific requirements** relating to **restructuring provisions**. The general recognition criteria apply and IAS 37 also states that **a provision should be recognised** if an entity has a **constructive obligation** to carry out a restructuring. A constructive obligation exists where **management has a detailed formal plan** for the restructuring, identifying **as a minimum:**

(i) The business or part of the business being restructured

(ii) The principal locations affected by the restructuring

(iii) The location, function and approximate number of employees who will be compensated for the termination of their employment

(iv) The date of implementation of the plan

(v) The expenditure that will be undertaken.

In addition, the plan must have raised a **valid expectation** in those affected that the entity will carry out the restructuring. To give rise to such an expectation and, therefore, a constructive obligation, the **implementation must be planned to take place as soon as possible**, and the timeframe must be such as to make changes to the plan unlikely.

Plan A

Lockfine proposes recognising a provision in respect of the plan to sell 50% of its off-shore fleet in a year's time and to make 40% of the seamen redundant. However, although the plan has been communicated to the public, the above criteria are not met. **The plan is insufficiently detailed**, and various aspects are not finalised. The figure of 40% is tentative as yet, the **fleets and employees affected have not been identified**, and a decision has not been made on whether the off-shore fleet will be restructured in the future. Some of these issues await further analysis.

The proposal does not, therefore, meet the IAS 37 criteria for a detailed formal plan and an announcement of the plan to those affected by it. Lockfine cannot be said to be committed to this restructuring and so **a provision should not be recognised**.

Plan B

Lockfine has not proposed recognising a provision for the plan to reorganise its headquarters and make 20% of the headquarters' workforce redundant. However, it is likely that this treatment is incorrect, because the plan appears to meet the IAS 37 criteria above:

(i) The locations and employees affected have been **identified**.

(ii) An **announcement** has been made and employee representatives notified – it is not necessary to notify individual employees as their representatives have been told.

(iii) The conclusion of the three month consultation period indicates that the above announcement is sufficiently detailed to give rise to a **valid expectation** that the restructuring will take place, particularly if the discussions have been about the terms of the redundancy.

It will be necessary to c**onsider the above negotiations** – provided these are about details such as the terms of redundancy rather than about changing the plan, then the IAS 37 criteria have been met. Accordingly, a provision needs to be recognised.

63 Seltec

Text references. Financial instruments are covered in Chapter 7, brands in Chapter 3, and business combinations in Chapters 12 to 17. This is a specialised industry question – other specialised industries are covered in Chapter 20 of your text.

Top tips. Note that IFRS 9 simplifies the treatment of embedded derivatives that are financial assets within the scope of the standard – these no longer need to be separated from their host contract. However, the more complex rules still apply to embedded derivatives that are not assets. In Part (b), you need to think carefully about what constitutes a business combination – substance is more important than form.

Easy marks. These are available for the definition of embedded derivatives and basic principles of intangible assets.

Examiner's comment. The ACCA examination/examining team was satisfied in the main with candidates' answers, but disappointed that few recognised the embedded derivative. Answers to the final part of the question, on business combinations, were disappointing, the main weakness being the application of the knowledge and the understanding of the nature of the purchase of the entities.

Marking scheme

	Marks
Hedge accounting	5
Futures	5
Embedded derivative	4
Brands	5
Business combinations	4
Professional marks	2
	25

(a) **Financial instruments**

Derivatives

IAS 32 *Financial instruments: presentation* and IFRS 9 *Financial instruments* define a **derivative** as a financial instrument or other contract that has all three of the following characteristics.

(i) Its value changes in response to the change in a specified interest rate, financial instrument price, commodity price, foreign exchange rate, index of prices or rates, credit rating or credit index, or other variable (sometimes called the 'underlying').

(ii) It requires no initial net investment or an initial net investment that is smaller than would be required for other types of contracts that would be expected to have a similar response to changes in market factors.

(iii) It is settled at a future date.

A contract is **not considered to be a derivative where its purpose is to take physical delivery** in the normal course of business, unless the entity has a practice of settling the contracts on a net basis.

In the case of Seltec, while the company often takes physical delivery of the edible oil, it does so only to sell shortly afterwards, and usually settles on a net basis. Thus the **contracts will be considered to be derivative** contracts rather than contracts for purchase of inventory. Derivatives are accounted for at fair value through profit or loss, unless hedge accounting applies.

Hedge accounting

The rules on hedge accounting are set out in IFRS 9 *Financial instruments* (revised 2014). Before a hedging relationship qualifies for hedge accounting, **all** of the following **conditions** must be met.

(i) The hedging relationship consists **only of eligible hedging instruments and eligible hedged items**.

(ii) There must be **formal documentation** (including identification of the hedged item, the hedging instrument, the nature of the risk that is to be hedged and how the entity will assess the hedging instrument's effectiveness in offsetting the exposure to changes in the hedged item's fair value or cash flows attributable to the hedged risk).

(iii) The hedging relationship meets all of the following hedge effectiveness criteria

(1) There is an **economic relationship** between the hedged item and the hedging instrument, ie the hedging instrument and the hedged item have values that generally move in the opposite direction because of the same risk, which is the hedged risk;

(2) The **effect of credit risk does not dominate the value** changes that result from that economic relationship, ie the gain or loss from credit risk does not frustrate the effect of changes in the underlyings on the value of the hedging instrument or the hedged item, even if those changes were significant; and

(3) The **hedge ratio of the hedging relationship** (quantity of hedging instrument vs quantity of hedged item) is the same as that resulting from the quantity of the hedged item that the entity **actually hedges** and the quantity of the hedging instrument that the entity **actually uses** to hedge that quantity of hedged item.

There are two kinds of hedging that Seltec may consider: fair value hedging and cash flow hedging.

A **fair value hedge** is a hedge of the exposure to changes in the fair value of a recognised asset or liability, or an identified portion of such an asset or liability, that is attributable to a particular risk and could affect profit or loss. The **gain or loss** resulting from **re-measuring** the hedging instrument at fair value is **recognised in profit or loss**. The gain or loss on the hedged item attributable to the **hedged risk** should **adjust the carrying amount** of the hedged item and be **recognised in profit or loss**.

A **cash flow hedge**: a hedge of the exposure to variability in cash flows that:

(i) Is attributable to a particular risk associated with a recognised asset or liability (such as all or some future interest payments on variable rate debt) or a highly probable forecast transaction (such as an anticipated purchase or sale), and that

(ii) Could affect profit or loss.

The portion of the gain or loss on the hedging instrument that is determined to be an **effective** hedge must be **recognised in other comprehensive income(items that may subsequently be reclassified to profit or loss)** and transferred to profit or loss when the hedged item is recognised in profit or loss. The **ineffective portion** of the gain or loss on the hedging instrument must be **recognised in profit or loss**.

The rules for cash flow hedges are particularly restrictive because it is difficult to isolate and measure the cash flows attributable to the specific risks for the non-financial items. Cash flow hedging results in higher volatility in earnings, so, provided the documentation and other requirements are met, **Seltec may prefer to use fair value hedging**. Seltec must take into account all changes in the price of edible oil of all types and geographical locations that it processes and sells and these must be compared with the changes in the value of the future. The hedge will be ineffective if the contracts have different prices. However, a hedge does not need to be fully effective, and hedge accounting may still be used provided the criteria above are met.

Embedded derivative

Certain contracts that are not themselves derivatives (and may not be financial instruments) include derivative contracts that are 'embedded' within them. These non-derivatives are called **host contracts** IFRS 9 defines an embedded derivative as a derivative instrument that is combined with a non-derivative host contract to form a single hybrid instrument. Some of the cash flows of the instrument vary in a way that is similar to a stand-alone derivative.

Ordinary derivatives must be accounted for at fair value in the statement of financial position with changes recognised through profit or loss.

IFRS 9 treatment

Where the host contract is a financial asset within the scope of the IFRS 9, the classification and **measurement rules of the standard are applied to the entire hybrid contract**. However, in this case the contract is a financial liability, not a financial asset within the scope of IFRS 9. Accordingly, the following rules apply:

The embedded derivative must be **separated from its host contract** and accounted for as a derivative, provided the following conditions are met.

(i) The economic characteristics and risks of the embedded derivative are not closely related to the economic characteristics and risks of the host contract.

(ii) A separate instrument with the same terms as the embedded derivative would meet the definition of a derivative.

(iii) The hybrid (combined) instrument is not measured at fair value with changes in fair value recognised in the profit or loss (a derivative embedded in a financial asset or financial liability need not be separated out if the entity holds the combined instrument at fair value through profit or loss).

If the embedded derivative is separated from its host contract, the **host contract is accounted for under the applicable IFRS**. A contract denominated in a foreign currency contains an embedded derivative unless:

(i) The foreign currency denominated in the contract is the currency of one of the parties to the contract.

(ii) The foreign currency is that commonly used in the market in which such transactions take place.

(iii) The foreign currency is that in which the related goods or services are denominated in routine commercial transactions.

In the case of Seltec, **none of the above three exceptions apply**. Seltec's trade in edible oil is generally in dollars, not pound sterling, the pound is not the functional currency of either party, and it is not the currency normally used in transactions in the business environment in which Seltec operates. Finally, the economic characteristics and risks of the embedded derivative are not closely related to the economic characteristics and risks of the host contract, since changes in the price of oil and currency fluctuations have different risks.

In conclusion, IFRS 9 would treat Seltec's contracts as containing an embedded derivative. The currency derivative must be accounted for at fair value through profit or loss.

(b) **Intangible assets**

An entity should **assess** the useful life of an intangible asset, which may be **finite or indefinite**. An intangible asset has an indefinite useful life when there is **no foreseeable limit** to the period over which the asset is expected to generate net cash inflows for the entity.

Seltec wishes to treat both brands as having indefinite useful lives. However, this may not be appropriate, and there are certain factors that need to be considered:

(i) Does the brand have long-term potential? The first brand has a proven track record, but the second, named after a famous film star, may last only as long as the film star's popularity, which will not be indefinite.

(ii) Is Seltec committed to supporting the brand? In the case of the first, it is, but the second is a relatively new product, and it is not clear that Seltec is in for the long haul.

If, as is likely, the **useful life of the second brand is considered to be finite**, its cost less residual should be amortised on a systematic basis over its useful life, using the straight-line method as an approximation if the pattern of benefits cannot be determined reliably.

The **first brand**, which is correctly said to have an **indefinite useful life**, should not be amortised. Its useful life should be reviewed at each reporting period to determine whether the assessment of the useful life as indefinite is still applicable. If not, the change, from indefinite to finite would be accounted for as a change in accounting estimate as per IAS 8. It should also be assessed for impairment in accordance with IAS 36, and otherwise accounted for like the second brand.

Purchase of entities

IFRS 3 *Business combinations* defines a business combination as 'a transaction or event in which an acquirer obtains control of one or more businesses. A business is defined as an integrated set of activities and assets that is capable of being conducted and managed for the purpose of providing a return directly to investors or other owners, members or participants'. Such a return may be in the form of cash, dividends or lower costs.

The two limited liability **companies do not meet the IFRS 3 definition of a business** because they are not self-sustaining and do not generate revenue independently of Seltec. The acquisition **should be treated as a purchase of property**.

64 Kayte

Text reference. Specialised industries are covered in general terms in Chapter 20 of your Study Text. IFRS 3 and IFRS 10 (control) are covered in Chapter 12. IAS 16 is covered in Chapter 3.

Top tips. Part (b) required candidates to consider the IFRS 3 definition of a business, which has not been tested before, although there were pointers in the scenario to suggest that the accounting treatment was incorrect, and that IFRS 3 principles of control, well within the mainstream, should have been applied. Part (b) was more demanding. While covering IAS 16, a standard that will be assumed knowledge for P2, the application was challenging, but fair.

Easy marks. The discussion of control should have presented few problems.

Examiner's comment. Generally candidates answered the question quite well. Componentisation regularly features in this examination as it is a major problem for entities worldwide. Marks were allocated on a basis of one mark per valid point which indicates that there is a minimum amount which candidates need to write in order to gain a pass mark in this question

Marking scheme

	Marks
(a) IFRS 3/IFRS 10 – 1 mark per point up to	12
(b) IAS 16 and application – 1 mark per point up to	11
Professional marks	2
	25

(a) **Acquisition of Ceemone**

Compliance with IFRS 3

Kayte has accounted for its investment in Ceemone as an asset acquisition, but this is **incorrect**. The investment **should have been accounted for as a business combination** in accordance with IFRS 3 *Business combinations.* This has the following implications.

(i) Transaction costs must be expensed.

(ii) The vessels must be recognised at fair value.

(iii) Any deferred tax must be recognised at nominal value.

(iv) Goodwill must be recognised, being the difference between the fair value of the consideration transferred and the fair value of the identifiable assets acquired and the liabilities assumed.

IFRS 3 gives a **definition of a business**, which needs to be applied in determining whether a transaction is a business combination:

> 'An integrated set of activities and assets that is capable of being conducted and managed for the purpose of providing a return in the form of dividends, lower costs or other economic benefits directly to investors or other owners, members or participants.'

A business generally has three elements.

(i) **Inputs**. An economic resource (e.g. non-current assets, intellectual property) that creates outputs when one or more processes are applied to it. In the case of Ceemone, the inputs would be shares in vessel-owning companies, charter arrangements, outsourcing arrangements with a management company and relationships with a shipping broker.

(ii) **Process**. A system, standard, protocol, convention or rule that when applied to an input or inputs, creates outputs (e.g. strategic management, operational processes, resource management). For

Ceemone, this would encompass financing the business, purchases and sales of the vessels and activities relating to chartering and operating the vessels.

(iii) **Outputs**. The result of inputs and processes applied to those inputs. The charter agreements would enable Ceemone to generate revenue and other economic benefits for Kayte. (IFRS 3 states that outputs are not required in order to qualify as a business.)

It is **not relevant that some activities were outsourced** to the management company. IFRS 3 states:

> 'Determining whether a particular set of assets and activities is a business should be based on whether the integrated set is capable of being conducted and managed as a business by a market participant. Thus, in evaluating whether a particular set is a business, it is not relevant whether a seller operated the set as a **business** or whether the acquirer intends to operate the set as a business.'

Ceemone could choose to conduct and manage the integrated set of assets and activities as a business. In summary, **the acquisition includes all the elements which constitute a business** in accordance with IFRS 3 and must be accounted for as a business combination.

IFRS 10 and control

The directors of Kayte believe that the entity to which the vessels have been transferred and in which the bank holds a variable interest is a **subsidiary of the bank**. In determining this, IFRS 10 *Consolidated financial statements* looks at the substance of the transaction rather than its legal form. The key point is whether an investor has **control** over an investee.

IFRS 10 *Consolidated financial statements* requires an acquirer to be identified in all business combinations, even where the business combination looks like a merger of equals. The acquirer is the combining entity which obtains **control** of the entity with which it is combined. It is not always easy to determine which party is the acquirer, and IFRS 10 gives guidance on the matter. The key point is **control,** rather than mere ownership, but this may not be easy to assess.

IFRS 10 states that an investor **controls** an investee if and only if it has all of the following.

(i) **Power** over the investee
(ii) Exposure, or rights, to **variable returns** from its involvement with the investee, and
(iii) The **ability to use its power** over the investee to affect the amount of the investor's returns.

Power is defined as **existing rights that give the current ability to direct the relevant activities of the investee**. There is no requirement for that power to have been exercised.

It is likely that the bank has power over the entity, and it may be exposed to variable returns from its involvement with the entity. The bank's interest depends on the entity's level of indebtedness, and so it can be said to have the ability to use its power to effect the amount of the investor's returns. The **bank may therefore be regarded as having a measure of control.** However, the extent of this control is not clear and will depend on the constitution of the entity.

(b) **Vessels**

Vessels sold at ten years old

Kayte's estimate of the residual life of these vessels is **based on acquisition cost.** This is **unacceptable** under IAS 16 *Property, plant and equipment.* IAS 16 defines residual value as:

> 'The estimated amount that an entity would currently obtain from disposal of the asset, after deducting the estimated costs of disposal, if the asset were already of the age and in the condition expected at the end of its useful life.'

IAS 16 requires that property, plant and equipment must be depreciated so that its depreciable amount is allocated on a systematic basis over its useful life. Depreciable amount is the cost of an asset less its residual value. IAS 16 stipulates that the **residual value must be reviewed at least each financial year-end** and, if expectations differ from previous estimates, any change is accounted for prospectively as a change in estimate under IAS 8 *Accounting policies, changes in accounting estimates and errors.*

Kayte's model implies that the residual value of the vessels remains constant through the vessels' useful life. However, the **residual value should be adjusted,** particularly as the date of sale approaches and the residual value approaches proceeds of disposal less costs of disposal at the end of the asset's useful life.

Following IAS 16, if the residual value is greater than an asset's carrying amount, the depreciation charge is zero until such time as the residual value subsequently decreases to an amount below the asset's carrying amount. The residual value should be the value at the reporting date as if the vessel were already of the age and condition expected at the end of its useful life. Depreciable amount is affected by an increase in the residual value of an asset because of past events, but not by expectation of changes in future events, other than the expected effects of wear and tear.

In this case it appears that the **useful life of the vessels (ten years) is shorter than the economic life (30 years)**. IAS 16 does not give guidance about the appropriate treatment in such cases. In the absence of such guidance, **broker valuations could be used**. The resulting volatility is not an argument against the use of such valuations.

Vessels kept for 30 years

Kayte **correctly uses a residual value for these vessels based upon the scrap value of steel.** The depreciable amount of the vessels is therefore the cost less the scrap value of steel, and the vessels should be depreciated over the 30-year period.

The **engine does not need to be treated as a separate component** of the asset, because as long as it is maintained every ten years, it will have the same 30-year life as the vessel. The **cost of major, planned maintenance is likely to increase over the life of the vessel** because of its age and the effects of inflation. This cost will need to be capitalised as incurred, and as a result the depreciation charge may be greater in the later years of the assets' useful life.

The **cost of the engine overhaul**, as major planned maintenance, needs to be **capitalised as a new asset**. It is then **depreciated over the ten years until the next overhaul**. Generally the depreciation of the original amount capitalised in respect of the vessel will be **calculated to have a net book value of nil when the overhaul is undertaken.**

Vessel with engine completely replaced after eight years

In the case of this vessel, work was required earlier than expected. The **overhaul costs and any remaining net book value** of the old engine should be **expensed immediately.**

Funnels

In determining which parts of the vessel, if any, to treat as separate components, the entity needs to consider all major maintenance events that are likely to occur. It may not always be possible to identify these until later, when it may transpire that **not all components were identified.** This is true of the funnels, which were not initially identified as separate components. They now need to be thus identified and it will be necessary to **determine what the net book value would have been had they been initially identified.** The initial cost of the funnels can be determined by reference to replacement cost, and the associated depreciation charge determined using the rate for the vessel (over thirty years). There will therefore be a significant net book value to be written off at the time the replacement funnels are capitalised.

65 Ethan

Text reference. Deferred tax is covered in Chapter 6 of your BPP Study Text. Investment property and impairment are covered in Chapter 3, and financial instruments and fair value are covered in Chapter 7.

Top tips. In Part (a), our answer focuses on IFRS 13, because by the time you take your exam, this IFRS will have been examinable for at least two years. Part (b) required application of the fair value option in IFRS 9 *Financial Instruments.* The option is used where such application would eliminate or significantly reduce a measurement or recognition inconsistency between the debt liabilities and the investment properties to which they were related in this question. In Part (c), candidates needed to recognise that, in classifying the B shares as equity rather than as a liability, the entity had not complied with IAS 32 *Financial instruments: presentation.* There were pointers to the shares being classified as a liability, in particular the fact that entity was obliged to pay an annual cumulative dividend on the B shares and did not have discretion over the distribution of such dividend.

Easy marks. There are no obviously easy marks in this question.

Examiner's comment. In Part (a), credit was given if candidates answered the part on fair value in terms of IAS 40 rather than the new IFRS 13. Answers to this question varied in standard, and candidates did not seem to be able to identify the key issues. The nature of the technical knowledge in this question was not high but the need to apply that knowledge was crucial to a good answer. Candidates had difficulty in understanding the nature of the option in Part (b), and yet it is used often in practice, which means it is an important element of the syllabus. In Part (c), few candidates realised that certain characteristics of the B shares indicated that they should be classified as a liability.

Marking scheme

	Marks
Impairment testing	5
Deferred taxation	6
Fair value option – IFRS 9	7
Financial liability	5
Communication skills	2
	25

(a) **Fair value**

The **fair value** of an asset is the price that would be received to sell an asset or paid to transfer a liability in an orderly transaction between market participants at the measurement date (IFRS 13 *Fair value measurement).* IFRS 13 states that valuation techniques must be those which are appropriate and for which sufficient data are available. Entities should maximise the use of relevant **observable inputs** and minimise the use of **unobservable inputs**. The standard establishes a three-level hierarchy for the inputs that valuation techniques use to measure fair value.

Level 1 Quoted prices (unadjusted) in active markets for identical assets or liabilities that the reporting entity can access at the measurement date

Level 2 Inputs other than quoted prices included within Level 1 that are observable for the asset or liability, either directly or indirectly, eg quoted prices for similar assets in active markets or for identical or similar assets in non-active markets or use of quoted interest rates for valuation purposes

Level 3 Unobservable inputs for the asset or liability, ie using the entity's own assumptions about market exit value

Although an active market exists for Ethan's investment properties, Ethan uses a discounted cash flow model to measure fair value. This is **not in accordance with IFRS 13**. As the fair value hierarchy suggests, IFRS 13 favours Level 1 inputs, that is market-based measures, over unobservable (Level 3) inputs such as discounted cash flows.

Goodwill and deferred tax

If the **fair value** of the investment properties **is not measured correctly** in accordance with IFRS 13, this means that the **deferred tax liability** on investment properties **may also be incorrect**. In addition, as goodwill is calculated as consideration transferred less fair value of net assets, **goodwill may be incorrect**. This is because deferred tax is calculated on the difference between the carrying amount of the asset and its tax base. So if the carrying amount is incorrect, the deferred tax will be incorrect. The goodwill calculation uses the fair value of **all** net assets, not just the investment properties and the related deferred tax liability, so it is **incorrect to use an increase in the deferred tax liability** as the **basis** for assessing whether goodwill is impaired.

The reasoning behind Ethan's approach is that as the deferred tax liability decreases, the fair value of net assets increases, thereby decreasing goodwill. However, this method of determining whether goodwill is impaired **does not accord with IAS 36** *Impairment of assets.* IAS 36 requires that goodwill should be **reviewed for impairment annually** for any indicators of impairment, which may be internal or external, and are not confined to changes in the deferred tax liability. Where it is not possible to measure impairment for individual assets, the loss should be measured for a **cash generating unit**.

The **recoverable amount** is **defined** as the **higher** of:

(i) The **asset's fair value less costs to sell**. This is the price that would be received to sell the asset in an orderly transaction between market participants at the measurement date under current market conditions, net of costs of disposal.

(ii) The asset's **value in use**. This is the present value of estimated future cash flows (inflows minus outflows) generated by the asset, including its estimated net disposal value (if any) at the end of its useful life.

If an **asset's carrying amount** is **higher than its recoverable amount**, an **impairment loss** has occurred. The impairment loss should be **written off against profit or loss** for the year, and the corresponding credit (write-off) applied first to goodwill, then to the investment properties, then to other assets pro-rata.

Deferred tax assets on losses

In theory, unused tax losses give rise to a deferred tax asset. However, IAS 12*Income taxes* states that **deferred tax assets should only be recognised to the extent that they are regarded as recoverable**. They should be regarded as recoverable to the extent that on the basis of all the evidence available it is **probable that there will be suitable taxable profits against which the losses can be recovered**. It is unlikely that future taxable profits of Ethan will be sufficient to realise all of the tax loss because of:

(i) The announcement that a substantial loss will be incurred this year instead of the expected profit
(ii) Considerable negative variances against budgets in the past

Consequently, **Ethan should not recognise the deferred tax asset**.

(b) **IFRS 9 fair value option**

Generally under IFRS 9 *Financial instruments*, the debt issued to finance its investment properties would be accounted for using **amortised cost,** while the properties themselves are at fair value. This is an **accounting mismatch,** that is a recognition or measurement inconsistency between the debt liability and the asset to which it relates. The asset and liability, and the gains and losses arising on them, would be measured on different bases.

The IFRS 9 **fair value option** allows an entity to **designate a liability at initial recognition as being at fair value through profit or loss** if using this option would **eliminate or significantly reduce** an accounting mismatch. Ethan has argued that the basis of measurement of the debt and the investment properties is **similar**, particularly as regards **interest rates**. This argument holds good in respect of the interest, and so the **fair value option would be allowed**.

However, IFRS 9 stipulates that if a liability is designated as being at fair value through profit or loss, **changes in the fair value that are due to changes in the liability's credit risk must be recognised directly in other comprehensive income** rather than profit or loss. Such **changes may not be re-classified** to profit or loss in subsequent years, although a **reserves transfer** is permitted from other components of equity to retained earnings. On the other hand, **if changes in the fair value attributable to the credit risk** of the liability **create or enlarge an accounting mismatch in profit or loss**, then all fair value movements are **recognised in profit or loss**.

(c) **B shares of subsidiary**

Ethan's accounting treatment of the B shares (as equity instruments) does not comply with IAS 32 *Financial instruments: presentation.* The IAS 32 definition of a financial liability includes any liability that is **a contractual obligation to deliver cash or another financial asset to another entity**. A financial instrument may only be classified as an equity instrument rather than a liability if the instrument does not include an obligation to deliver cash or other financial asset to another entity, or to exchange financial instruments with another entity under conditions that are potentially unfavourable.

In the **subsidiary's books,** the B shares would be treated as a **financial liability.** They contain an **obligation** to deliver cash in the form of a fixed dividend. The dividend is cumulative and must be paid whether or not the subsidiary has sufficient legally distributable profits when it is due, and so **the subsidiary cannot avoid this obligation**.

In the **consolidated financial statements,** the B shares would also be treated as a financial liability, **the intragroup element of this liability (70%) would cancel against the investment in B shares in the parent's (Ethan's) statement of financial position**. The shares **owned by external parties would not cancel;** they would remain **a financial liability**. It **is incorrect to treat them as non-controlling interest** because they are **not equity**.

66 Preparation question: Reconstruction scheme

Text reference. This topic is covered in Chapter 20 of the Study Text.

Top tips. In part (b), the changes to be considered are in the *market* value (or income stream) rather than the *nominal* value of each investor class. You only have sufficient information to look at future income (which will anyway have a considerable influence on market value) so you should look at that. It is also essential to recognise that the ordinary shareholders stand to lose control of the company under the current proposals.

(a) STATEMENT OF FINANCIAL POSITION OF CONTEMPLATION GROUP
AS AT 1 JULY 20X2 AFTER RECONSTRUCTION

	$'000
Non-current assets	3,600
Current assets	4,775
	8,375
Ordinary 25c shares (W3)	1,875
8% preference shares of $1 each, fully paid ($3.3m – $0.8m dividend in arrears)	2,500
Reserves (W1)	–
14% 20Y5 loan notes	3,000
Current liabilities	1,000
	8,375

Workings

1 *Reserves*

	$'000
Reserves at 30 June 20X2	(9,425)
Cancellation of previous ordinary shares	10,000
Net effect of issue of ordinary shares to preference shareholders in lieu of accrued arrears of dividend (W2)	300
Issue of new ordinary shares to holders of previous ordinary shares	(875)
	Nil

2 *Net effect of elimination of accrued preference dividend arrears*

	$'000
Cancellation of dividend arrears (8% × 4 × $2.5m)	800
Issue of new shares	500
Net effect: loss in nominal value of holding	300

3 *Ordinary shares*

	No	$'000
Issued to loan note holders	2,000,000	500
Issued to preference shareholders	2,000,000	500
Issued to existing ordinary shareholders	3,500,000	875
	7,500,000	1,875

Note. The purpose of the reconstruction is to eliminate the negative reserves and allow the company to start again. The table below shows the effect of each of the four adjustments ((a) to (d) in the question) in achieving this.

Ref	*Item*	*Debit* $'000	*Credit* $'000
(a)	Ordinary share capital cancelled	10,000	
(b)	11% loan notes retired	3,500	
	14% loan notes issued		3,000
	2,000,000 25c shares issued		500
(c)	Cancellation of dividend arrears (8% × 4 × $2.5m)	800	
	Issue of new shares		500
(d)	Issue of shares to existing shareholders 3.5m × 25c		875
	Elimination of negative reserves balance		9,425
		14,300	14,300

(b) (i) **Loan note holders**

	$'000
Cancellation of previous loan notes	3,500
Issue of new loan notes	3,000
Issue of new shares	500
Net effect on nominal value of holding	Nil

Loan note interest (before tax is paid by the recipient) would be $385,000 pa ($3.5m × 11%) if no reconstruction was effected and $420,000 ($3m × 14%) if the scheme is agreed. In addition, the loan note holders would be entitled to a share of earnings from their ordinary shares. (Maximum $273,867: see below.)

Loan note holders as fixed chargeholders would be repaid in full in the event of a liquidation and must therefore balance the risk of the company's failure in the future, when its assets may have declined in value, thus reducing their usefulness as security, against the forecast increase in return. They must also assess the effect of an extra few years' delay in redemption, which increases the risk. If loan note holders have confidence in the new strategy, then they are better off under the reconstruction.

(ii) **Preference shareholders**

	$'000
Cancellation of dividend arrears (8% × 4 × $2.5m)	800
Issue of new shares	500
Net effect: loss in nominal value of holding	300

No preference dividend could be paid if the reconstruction scheme does not go ahead as all profits for the foreseeable future would be applied in reducing retained losses. If the scheme is agreed, the annual dividend could be restored immediately and, as above, there would be an equity interest with a maximum dividend of $273,867 (see below).

Preference shareholders are assured of repayment of their capital at the moment but may not be in the future if losses are made again. If they are prepared to accept the risk that the new strategy may fail, then they are better off under the reconstruction.

(iii) **Existing ordinary shareholders**

	$'000
Cancellation of previous shares	(10,000)
Cancellation of previous negative reserves: 9,425 – 800*	8,625
Issue of new shares	875
Net effect: loss of nominal value of equity	(500)

Note. The $800,000 accrued arrears of preference dividends has been excluded from the figure for negative reserves because they are dealt with in (ii) above and do not affect the ordinary shareholders.

Ordinary shareholders will receive no dividend for many years if the scheme is not accepted. If it is accepted, then for the first few years, earnings will be as follows.

	$
Post-tax profits before interest	1,500,000
Loan note interest (less tax relief) 14% × 65% × $3m	273,000
	1,227,000
Preference dividend	200,000
Earnings	1,027,000

However, of this 1,000/(1,000 + 875) (part (a) (W3)) will be attributable to the new shares issued to loan note holders and preference shareholders (500/1,875 × $1,027,000 = $273,867 each). Therefore, the existing shareholders will receive a maximum dividend of 875/(1,875) × $1,027,000 = $479,267. It is, of course, exceedingly unlikely that the company will distribute its entire post-tax profit, and so the actual dividend would probably be lower.

(c) To: A Grieved
From: Financial Adviser
Date: 28 June 20X2
Subject: *Proposed scheme of reconstruction*

You have commented that you feel the proposed scheme is 'unfair': presumably you mean to the existing ordinary shareholders. This claim can be examined by looking at the outcome for you as an ordinary shareholder in each of the three options open to the directors:

(i) To liquidate the company;
(ii) To continue without reconstructing;
(iii) To adopt the proposed reconstruction.

(i) If the company is liquidated, the net assets would amount to the following.

	$'000
Realisation of assets (gross) ($3.1m + $3.5m)	6,600
Less loan notes	3,500
Less arrears of preference dividends	800
Net assets	2,300

This would be entirely absorbed by the claims of the preference shareholders ($2.5m). Thus there would be nothing left over for distribution to ordinary shareholders.

(ii) If no reconstruction takes place the profits after tax and interest will amount to approximately $1.25m ($1.5m profit before interest – [65% × 11% × $3.5m) interest) per annum. Thus it will be some seven years before the deficit on the profit and loss account is cleared and a further year to clear the arrears of preference dividends. Thus, the ordinary shareholders cannot expect a dividend for over eight years. The present value of such a dividend stream is minimal.

(iii) The net interest of the original ordinary shareholders in the reconstructed company is: 3,500,000 shares × 25c = $875,000.

There are no reserves.

In addition, the original shareholders can expect to receive dividends or a share in retained earnings from the time of the reconstruction.

So, while the original ordinary shareholders have given up more than the preference shareholders and the loan note holders (who have lost nothing) the reconstruction offers more than the possible alternative options.

Thus, from the point of view of income, the proposed scheme seems the best option under discussion.

However, you should also consider the fact that your control over the company has been seriously diluted. Over half the equity after the reconstruction ie 54% (4m shares/7.5m shares (W3) would be owned by the loan note holders and preference shareholders, who would also still own their loan notes and preference shares. The scheme could be amended so that control remains in the hands of the existing shareholders, who are, after all, not cushioned by holding loan notes or preference shares. If preference shareholders were given fewer ordinary shares, the scheme would be more equitable. The loan note holders would be unlikely to agree to any scaling down of their share allocation.

Nevertheless, with this proviso, it seems that the scheme is fair to ordinary shareholders who otherwise have no hope of dividends or repayment of capital in the event of a liquidation.

Please let me have your comments on the attached draft letter to the directors of Swanee as soon as possible. If they can be persuaded to agree to the suggested scaling down of new equity, then I would advise you to accede to the proposal.

(d) The Directors
Contemplation Limited
Anytown

28 June 20X2

Dear Sirs,

We are acting for A Grieved, the holder of 10% of the ordinary capital of Contemplation Limited, and refer to the proposals for reconstructing the company.

We consider that this proposal is unfairly advantageous to the existing shareholders. The loan note holders would increase their return from their investment from $385,000 pa (interest only) to $693,867 ($420,000 interest plus $273,867 share of the projected earnings).

The preference shareholders' return will also increase dramatically from a notional $200,000 pa (unlikely to be paid in the foreseeable future) to $473,867 pa ($200,000 preference dividend and $273,867 share of earnings).

This seems excessive in view of the reduced financial and business risk which would result from the reconstruction. We would suggest that an increase in return of 50% to $577,500 would adequately compensate the loan note holders for the additional risk of holding equity rather than loans. Consequently we would suggest that, in addition to the new 14% loan notes an issue of 1,150,193 shares would be more appropriate.

In view of the power of loan note holders, we accept that they may not accept a revision to the scheme that reduces the total nominal value of their investment in the company. The preference shareholders, however, are in a different category. There seems no justification for issuing to them such a high proportion of the new 25c shares. If they were to be given 730,282 shares (assuming the above scaling down was not accepted), their projected return would still increase by 50% and the existing ordinary shareholders would retain control of the company.

We look forward to your comments on the above suggestions.

Yours faithfully,

F Adviser & Co

67 Plans

Text reference. This topic is covered in Chapter 20 of the Study Text.

Top tip. The ACCA examination/examining team has mentioned internal reconstructions as an area he may test.

Key considerations and accounting impacts

There are a number of reasons why a group may re-organise, for example:

- Companies may be transferred to another business during a **divisionalisation process**
- To **create efficiencies** of group structure for **tax purposes**

The impact of each of the proposed structures is discussed below.

Plan 1: share for share exchange

If the purchase consideration is in the form of shares, then a share premium account will need to be set up in the books of Y. This share premium account must comprise the minimum premium value, which is the excess of the book value of the investment over the nominal value of the shares issued: $70m – $50m = $20m.

The impact on the individual company accounts and on the group accounts is as follows:

	Note	*X*	*Y*	*Z*	*Group*
		$m	$m	$m	$m
Property, plant and equipment		600	200	45	845
Goodwill					10
Cost of investment in Y	1	130			
Cost of investment in Z	2		70		
Net current assets		160	100	20	280
		890	370	65	1,135

	Note	*X*	*Y*	*Z*	*Group*
		$m	$m	$m	$m
Share capital	3	120	110	40	120
Share premium	4		20		
Retained earnings	5	770	240	25	1,015
		890	370	65	1,135

Notes

1 *Cost of investment in Y*

This is increased by the total value of the shares issued: $50m + $20m = $70m.

2 *Cost of investment in Z*

Transferred to Y. The book value of the investment is preserved.

3 *Share capital*

Y's share capital is increased by the nominal value of the shares issued, $50m.

4 *Share premium*

This is as discussed above.

5 *Retained earnings*

Goodwill arising on the purchase of Z is \$10m (\$70m – (\$40m + \$20m)). The group retained earnings are calculated as follows.

	X	Y	Z
	\$m	\$m	\$m
Per question	770	240	25
Retained earnings at acquisition		–	(20)
	770	240	5
Share of post-acquisition retained earnings of Y (240 × 100%)	240		
Share of post-acquisition retained earnings of Z (5 × 100%)	5		
	1,015		

Plan 2: cash purchase

The group accounts are not affected by the change as the reorganisation is internal. It has no impact on the group as a single entity.

If the purchase consideration is in the form of cash, a gain or loss on the sale of Z will arise in the books of X. This does not count as a distribution as the cash price of \$75m is not in excess of the fair value of the net assets of Z, \$80m. The effect on the accounts would be as follows:

	Note	X	Y	Z	Group
		\$m	\$m	\$m	\$m
Property, plant and equipment		600	200	45	845
Goodwill					10
Cost of investment in Y		60			
Cost of investment in Z	1		75		
Net current assets	2	235	25	20	280
		895	300	65	1,135
Share capital		120	60	40	120
Retained earnings	3	775	240	25	1,015
		895	300	65	1,135

Notes

1 *Cost of investment in Z*

This is the cash consideration of \$75m.

2 *Net current assets*

X's cash increases by \$75m and Y's cash decreases by \$75m.

3 *Retained earnings*

X's retained earnings have been increased by \$5m, being the profit on the sale of the investment in Z. This is eliminated on consolidation as it is an intragroup transaction. The consolidated retained earnings are calculated in exactly the same way as in the share for share exchange.

Summary and conclusion

There are advantages and disadvantages to each of the two plans. Before we could make a recommendation we would need more information about **why** the group wishes to restructure.

Neither plan changes the group financial statements. From an internal point of view it results in a closer relationship between Y and Z. This may be advantageous if Y and Z are close geographically or in terms of similarity of business activities. Alternatively, it might be advantageous for tax reasons.

68 Decany

Text reference. Group reorganisations are covered in Chapter 14. IAS 27 is covered in Chapter 12. IAS 37 is covered in Chapter 5.

Top tips. This question tested group reorganisations for the first time under the revised syllabus. In part (a)(i) you had to process the effects of the group reorganisation in the three affected companies of the group, which was straightforward. This part of the question did not require detailed knowledge of IFRS but the ability to apply accounting techniques. The preparation of the group financial statements was not required, and you should not have wasted time trying to do this. Part (a)(ii) required a specialist knowledge of IAS 27, now called *Separate financial statements.* Note that the ACCA examination/examining team has said this could come up again. Part (b) is a likely common add-on to this type of question.

Easy marks. Don't be put off by the fact that this is a re-construction scheme. There are some fairly straightforward accounts preparation aspects.

Examiner's comment. Candidates performed quite well on the numerical part of the question but often seemed to find it difficult to apply the requirements and often made basic mistakes due to not reading the question thoroughly. For example, the holding company sold an investment in a subsidiary to another subsidiary. Many candidates left the investment sold in the financial statements of the holding company. Part (a)(ii) was poorly answered. The distinction between pre- and post-acquisition profits is no longer required and the payment of such dividends requires the entity to consider whether there is an indicator of impairment. This is a point fundamental to the preparation of group accounting and will be examined again. Answers to Part (b) were disappointing because many candidates did not realise that the reconstruction only masked the problem facing the group. It did not solve or alter the business risk currently being faced by the group.

Marking scheme

			Marks
(a)	(i)	Decany	5
		Ceed	5
		Rant	3
			13
	(ii)	IAS 27	5
(b)	Discussion – subjective		5
	Professional marks		2
			25

(a) (i) **Individual entity statements of financial position after the restructuring plan**

	Note	Decany	Ceed	Rant
		$m	$m	$m
Non-current assets				
Property, plant and equipment at depreciated cost/valuation		600	170 + 15 = 185.0	45 – 10 = 35
Cost of investment in Ceed		130		11
Cost of investment in Rant	1		98.0	
Loan receivable	2	98		
Current assets	2	155 + 25 = 180	130 – 98 = 32.0	20 + 98 = 118
		1,008	315.0	164
Equity and reserves				
Share capital		140	70 + 5 = 75.0	35
Share premium	3		6.0	
Retained earnings	5	776	185.5	10
		916	266.5	45
Non-current liabilities				
Long-term loan	6	5	4.0	106
Provisions	7	2	9.5	
Current liabilities				
Dividend payable			25.0	
Trade payables		85	10.0	13
		1,008	315.0	164

Notes

1 *Sale of shares in Rant*

In Creed's books:

DEBIT	Investment in Rant	$98m	
CREDIT	Cash		$98

This is the cash consideration of $98m.

Decany has made a profit on the sale of rant of $98m – $95m = $3m, which is added to Decany's retained earnings. In Decany's books:

DEBIT	Cash	$98m	
CREDIT	Investment in Rant		$95m
CREDIT	Profit or loss (and retained earnings)		$3m

2 *Loan receivable*

Decany now has a loan receivable of $98m and Ceed's cash decreases by $98m. In Decany's books:

DEBIT	Loan receivable	$98m	
CREDIT	Cash (current assets)		$98m

In Rant's books:

DEBIT	Cash (current assets)	$98m	
CREDIT	Loan payable		$98m

3 *Sale of land by Rant to Creed/calculation of share premium*

The value of the shares issued to Decany is the land less the mortgage, ie $11m. The difference between this and the nominal value is the share premium.

In Ceed's books:

DEBIT	Land	$15m	
CREDIT	Mortgage liability (long-term loan)		$4m
CREDIT	Share capital		$6m
CREDIT	Share premium (balancing figure)		$5m

In Rant's books:

DEBIT	Investment in Ceed	$11m	
DEBIT	Mortgage liability (long-term loan)	$4m	
CREDIT	Land		$10m
CREDIT	Profit or loss (and retained earnings)		$5m

4 *Dividend payable by Ceed to Decany*

In Creed's books:

DEBIT	Retained earnings	$25m	
CREDIT	Dividend payable		$25m

In Creed's books:

DEBIT	Dividend receivable (current assets)	$25m	
CREDIT	Retained earnings		$25m

5 *Retained earnings*

	Decany	*Ceed*	*Rant*
	$m	$m	$m
Per question	750	220.0	5
Dividend from Ceed to Decany	25	(25.0)	–
Profit on sale of Rant	3	–	–
Profit on sale or land			5
Provision for restructuring (note 6)	(2)	(9.5)	–
	776	185.5	10

6 *Long-term loan (Rant)*

	$m
Per question	12
Loan payable (note 2)	98
Mortgage liability (note 3)	(4)
	106

7 *Redundancy costs and provision for restructuring*

The fact that there is a detailed plan for restructuring with employees identified for redundancy creates a constructive obligation under IAS 37 *Provisions, contingent liabilities and contingent assets*, and accordingly a provision should be made for redundancy costs and restructuring. Creed will incur the redundancy costs, which should be recognised in its financial statements at the present value of the future cash flows:

	$m
4m × 1/1.03	3.9
6m × $1/1.03^2$	5.6
	9.5

The provision of $9.5m will be shown in Creed's financial statements, and the overall restructuring provision of $2m in the financial statements of Decany.

(ii) **IAS 27 rules on reorganisation and payment of dividends between group companies**

IAS 27 *Separate financial statements* was revised in 2011 and effectively allows the **cost of an investment in a subsidiary to be based on the previous carrying amount of the subsidiary rather than on its fair value**. This is only allowed when a new parent (Ceed) is inserted above an existing parent of a group or entity (Rant), and where the following **criteria** are satisfied.

(1) The new parent (Ceed) obtains control of the original parent or entity (Rant) by issuing equity instruments in exchange for existing equity instruments of the original parent or entity.

(2) The assets and liabilities of the new group and the original group are the same immediately before and after the reorganisation.

(3) The owners of the original parent or entity (Decany) before the reorganisation have the same absolute and relative interests in the net assets of the original group and the new group immediately before and after the reorganisation.

The reorganisation of the Decany group appears to meet all the above criteria. (In respect of (3), Rant has not acquired a further interest in Ceed as a result of the transfer of land because the shares in Ceed issued to Rant are non-voting.)

A further amendment made in the revised IAS 27 was the removal of the 'cost method'. This required an entity to recognise distributions as income only if they came from post-acquisition retained earnings. Distributions received in excess of such retained earnings were regarded as a recovery of investment and were recognised as a reduction in the cost of the investment. Now, however, IAS 27 requires all dividends **in profit or loss in its separate financial statements when its right to receive the dividend is established**. The distinction between pre- and post-acquisition profits, which had been problematic, is no longer required.

If such dividends are paid, the entity is required to consider whether there is has been an **impairment**. Applying IAS 36 *Impairment of assets,* impairment is indicated in the following cases.

(1) The dividend exceeds the total comprehensive income of the subsidiary, jointly controlled entity or associate in the period the dividend is declared.

(2) The carrying amount of the investment in the separate financial statements exceeds the carrying amounts in the consolidated financial statements of the investee's net assets, including associated goodwill.

Neither of these apply in the case of Creed, and so there is no indication that Creed is impaired.

(b) **Impact of reconstruction plan**

The reconstruction plan has no impact on the group financial statements as all the intra-group transactions will be eliminated on consolidation. From an internal point of view it results in **a closer relationship between Creed and Rant**. This may be advantageous if Creed and Rant are close geographically or in terms of similarity of business activities. Alternatively, it might be advantageous for tax reasons.

Regarding the restructuring plan, IAS 37 *Provisions, contingent liabilities and contingent assets* **contains specific requirements** relating to **restructuring provisions**. The general recognition criteria apply and IAS 37 also states that **a provision should be recognised** if an entity has a **constructive obligation** to carry out a restructuring. A constructive obligation exists where **management has a detailed formal plan** for the restructuring, identifying **as a minimum:**

(i) The business or part of the business being restructured

(ii) The principal locations affected by the restructuring

(iii) The location, function and approximate number of employees who will be compensated for the termination of their employment

(iv) The date of implementation of the plan

(v) The expenditure that will be undertaken.

It appears that these criteria have been met. However, the amount of $2m in Decany's financial statements seems rather large, considering that the redundancy is provided separately in the accounts of Ceed, and the restructuring does not involve any relocation.

The plan shows the companies in a **more favourable light** in that Rant's **short-term cash flow problem is eliminated**. Rant now has cash available. However, it is showing a much increased long-term loan. In the financial statements of Rant, the investment in Ceed must be accounted as a financial asset under IFRS 9 *Financial instruments.*

It is possible that the purchase consideration for rant of $98m could be seen as **a transaction at an overvalue**. It creates a profit of $3m, which could be seen as artificial. The question also arises as to whether this $3m should be recognised, and of whether it should be viewed as a distribution. Should problems arise in connection with local legislation, a share exchange might be a less problematic plan than a cash purchase.

The question may also arise as to whether Ceed has effectively **made a distribution**. This could happen where the purchase consideration was well in excess of the fair value of Rant. An alternative to a cash purchase would be a share exchange. In this case, local legislation would need to be reviewed in order to determine the requirements for the setting up of any share premium account.

69 Lucky Dairy

Text reference. IAS 41 is covered in Chapter 20 of your Study Text. IAS 37 is covered in Chapter 5 and IFRS 5 in Chapter 15.

Top tips. In this question you were required to deal with a scenario that had as its main theme IAS 41 *Agriculture*. You should not, however, make the mistake of thinking that this question is just about IAS 41; it required a knowledge of several other standards including IAS 37 and IFRS 5.

Examiner's comment. Some candidates had not studied the area and guessed at the answer which generally led to poor marks. However, many candidates produced excellent answers although some seemed to think that the question was solely on IAS 41.

The dairy herd

The dairy herd is a **biological asset** as defined by IAS 41 *Agriculture*. IAS 41 states that a biological asset should be **measured at fair value less estimated point of sale costs** unless its fair value cannot be measured reliably. **Gains and losses** arising from a change in fair value should be **included in profit or loss** for the period.

In this case, fair value is based on market price and point of sale costs are the costs of transporting the cattle to the market. Cattle stock for the Ham and Shire regions is valued on this basis.

IAS 41 encourages companies to **analyse the change in fair value** between the movement due to **physical changes** and the movement due to **price changes** (see the table below). It also encourages companies to provide a quantified description of each group of biological assets. Therefore the value of the cows and the value of the heifers should be **disclosed separately** in the balance sheet.

Valuing the dairy herd for the Dale Region is less straightforward as its **fair value cannot be measured reliably at the date of purchase**. In this situation IAS 41 requires the herd to be valued at **cost less any impairment losses**. The standard also requires companies to provide an **explanation of why** fair value cannot be measured reliably and the **range of estimates** within which fair value is likely to fall.

Valuation of cattle stock, excluding Dale region

	Cows	*Heifers*	*Total*
	$'000	$'000	$'000
Fair value of herd at 1 June 20X1 (50,000 × 50)	2,500		2,500
Purchase 1 December 20X1 (25,000 × 40)		1,000	1,000
Increase in fair value less estimated point of sale costs due to price change:			
(50,000 × (55 – 50)/25,000 × (42 – 40))	250	50	300
Increase in fair value less estimated point of sale costs due to physical change:			
(50,000 × (60 – 55)/25,000 × (46 – 42))	250	100	350
Fair value less estimated point of sale costs at 31 May 20X2 (50,000 × 60/25,000 × 46)	3,000	1,150	4,150

Valuation of cattle stock in Dale Region

	$'000
Cost at 1 June 20X1	
Cows (20,000 × 50)	1,000
Heifers (10,000 × 40)	400
	1,400
Less impairment loss	(200)
	1,200

Note. The herd is impaired because its recoverable amount is $1.2 million. This is the higher of fair value less costs to sell of $1 million (the amount that the Lucky Dairy has been offered) and value in use of $1.2 million (discounted value of the milk to be produced).

	$'000
Estimated fair value at 31 May 20X2 (for disclosure only):	
Cows (20,000 × 60)	1,200
Heifers (10,000 × 55)	550
	1,750

Milk

The milk is **agricultural produce** as defined by IAS 41 and should normally be measured at **fair value less estimated point of sale costs at the time of milking**. In this case the company is holding ten times the amount of inventory that it would normally hold and it is probable that much of this milk is unfit for consumption. The company should estimate the amount of milk that will not be sold and **write down** the inventory accordingly. The write down should be disclosed separately in the income statement as required by IAS 1 *Presentation of financial statements.*

Government grant

Under IAS 41, the government grant should be recognised as income **when it becomes receivable**. As it was only on 6 June 20X2 that the company received official confirmation of the amount to be paid, the income **should not be recognised in the current year**. The amount may be sufficiently material to justify disclosure as a non-adjusting event after the balance sheet date.

Legal proceedings and additional compensation

The lawyers have indicated that the company will probably be found liable for passing on the disease to consumers. There is a **present obligation as the result of a past obligating event** and therefore a **provision for $2 million should be recognised**, as required by IAS 37 *Provisions, contingent liabilities and contingent assets.*

IAS 37 states that **reimbursement** should only be recognised when it is **virtually certain** to be received. It is **only possible** that the company will receive compensation for the legal costs and therefore this **cannot be recognised**. However, the compensation should be **disclosed** as a contingent asset in the financial statements.

Planned sale of Dale farms

The Board of Directors has **approved the planned closure**, but there has **not yet been a public announcement**. Despite the fact that a local newspaper has published an article on the possible sale, the company **has not created a valid expectation** that the sale will take place and in fact **it is not certain** that the sale will occur. Therefore, there is **no 'constructive obligation'** and under IAS 37 **no provision should be made** for redundancy or any other costs connected with the planned sale.

Under IFRS 5 *Non-current assets held for sale and discontinued operations* Dale must be treated as a **continuing operation** for the year ended 31 May 20X2 as the sale has not taken place. As management are **not yet fully committed** to the sale **neither the operation as a whole nor any of the separate assets of Dale can be classified as 'held for sale'.**

70 Yanong

Text reference. Agriculture is covered in Chapter 20 of your Study Text. Fair value measurement is covered in Chapter 7 and 12. Share-based payment is covered in Chapter 9.

Top tips. The determination of the fair value of the agricultural vehicles (Part (a)) was similar to the first time IFRS 13 was examined in December 2012, which is in this kit. The fair value measurement of the maize (Part (b) was challenging as it was the first time biological assets have been examined in this way. Balancing this, the cash-settled share-based payment (Part (c)) and valuation of a non-financial asset (the farmland, Part (d)) were more straightforward.

Easy marks. These could be gained by focusing on the parts of the question more familiar to the student, which is likely to be Parts (c) and (d), but all parts of the question must be attempted.

Examiner's comments. Answers to Part (a) were quite disappointing considering the fact that the market definitions are the cornerstone of IFRS 13. The principles involved in this part of the question were quite basic and fundamental to the standard. Part (b) of the question was not well answered. Valuation techniques are used extensively in corporate reporting and therefore candidates must become accustomed to using such techniques in answering questions. Part (c) of the question was well answered. It involved calculating and discussing the valuation of share appreciation rights (SARs) under IFRS 2 *Share-based Payment* and not IFRS 13. However part (d) of the question was surprisingly poorly answered. One of the fundamental principles of IFRS 13 is that of 'highest and best use' as long as the alternate uses are physically, legally and financially permissible. In this question, the non-current asset had more value if it were used for residential purposes rather than for farmland providing that planning permission was granted. A discussion of this principle and its application was required but was seldom forthcoming from candidates.

Marking scheme

		Marks
(a)	1 mark per point up to maximum	6
(b)	1 mark per point up to maximum	6
(c)	1 mark per point up to maximum	6
(d)	1 mark per point up to maximum	5
Professional marks		2
		25

(a) **Fair value of agricultural vehicles**

IFRS 13 says that fair value is an exit price in the principal market, which is the market with the highest volume and level of activity. It is not determined based on the volume or level of activity of the reporting entity's transactions in a particular market. Once the accessible markets are identified, market-based volume and activity determines the principal market. There is a presumption that the principal market is the one in which the entity would normally enter into a transaction to sell the asset or transfer the liability, unless there is evidence to the contrary. In practice, an entity would first consider the markets it can access. In the absence of a principal market, it is assumed that the transaction would occur in the most advantageous market. This is the market which would maximise the amount which would be received to sell an asset or minimise the amount which would be paid to transfer a liability, taking into consideration transport and transaction costs. In either case, the entity must have access to the market on the measurement date. Although an entity must be able to access the market at the measurement date, IFRS 13 does not require an entity to be able to sell the particular asset or transfer the particular liability on that date. If there is a principal market for the asset or liability, the fair value measurement represents the price in that market at the measurement date regardless of whether that price is directly observable or estimated using another valuation technique and even if the price in a different market is potentially more advantageous.

The principal (or most advantageous) market price for the same asset or liability might be different for different entities and therefore, the principal (or most advantageous) market is considered from the entity's perspective which may result in different prices for the same asset.

In Yanong's case, Asia would be the principal market as this is the market in which the majority of transactions for the vehicles occur. As such, the fair value of the 150 vehicles would be $5,595,000 ($38,000 – $700 = $37,300 x 150). Actual sales of the vehicles in either Europe or Africa would result in a gain or loss to Yanong when compared with the fair value, ie $37,300. The most advantageous market would be Europe where a net price of $39,100 (after all costs) would be gained by selling there and the number of vehicles sold in this market by Yanong is at its highest. Yanong would therefore utilise the fair value calculated by reference to the Asian market as this is the principal market.

The IASB decided to prioritise the price in the most liquid market (ie the principal market) as this market provides the most reliable price to determine fair value and also serves to increase consistency among reporting entities.

IFRS 13 makes it clear that the price used to measure fair value must not be adjusted for transaction costs, but should consider transportation costs. Yanong has currently deducted transaction costs in its valuation of the vehicles. Transaction costs are not deemed to be a characteristic of an asset or a liability but they are specific to a transaction and will differ depending on how an entity enters into a transaction. While not deducted from fair value, an entity considers transaction costs in the context of determining the most advantageous market because the entity is seeking to determine the market which would maximise the net amount which would be received for the asset.

(b) **Accounting treatment of maize**

Where reliable market-based prices or values are not available for a biological asset in its present location and condition, fair value should be measured using a valuation technique. Relevant observable inputs should be maximised whilst unobservable inputs should be minimised (IFRS 13 *Fair value measurement*). An appropriate valuation technique would be the present value of expected net cash flows from the asset, discounted at a current market-based rate. In the measurement of fair value of growing crops, a notional cash flow expense should be included for the 'rent' of the land where it is owned in order that the value is comparable to an entity which rents its land. The fair value of the biological asset is separate from the value of the land on which it grows.

	3 months to 31 January 20X5	*3 months to 30 April 20X5*	*Total*
$m	$m	$m	$m
Cash inflows		80	80
Cash outflows	(8)	(19)	(27)
Notional rental charge for land	(1)	(1)	(2)
Net cash flows	(9)	60	51
Discounted at 2%	(8·82)	57·67	48·85

Thus in the quarterly accounts at 31 October 20X4, the maize fields should be recognised at $68·85 million ($20 million land plus $48·85 million maize). A fair value gain of $48·85 million should be shown in profit or loss less the operating costs of $10 million.

At 31 January, Yanong has revised its projections for cash inflows to $76 million, which means that the net cash flows at that date were projected to be $(76 – 19 – 1) million, ie $56 million. Discounted at 2%, this amounts to $54·9 million. Thus a fair value gain of $(54·9 – 48·85) million, ie $6·05 million, should be shown in profit or loss together with the actual operating costs of $8 million.

At the point of harvest, on 31 March 20X5, the maize is valued at $82 million which means that a fair value gain of $(82 – 54·9) million, ie $27·1 million, is recognised in profit or loss and the maize is classified as inventory. The actual operating costs for the quarter would also be shown in profit or loss. When the maize is sold, a further profit of $(84 – 82) million, ie $2 million, is made on sale.

(c) **Share-based payment**

IFRS 13 applies when another IFRS requires or permits fair value measurements or disclosures about fair value measurements (and measurements, such as fair value less costs to sell, based on fair value or disclosures about those measurements). IFRS 13 specifically excludes transactions covered by certain other standards including share-based payment transactions within the scope of IFRS 2 *Share-based payment* and leasing transactions within the scope of IFRS 16 *Leases*.

Thus share-based payment transactions are scoped out of IFRS 13.

For cash settled share-based payment transactions, the fair value of the liability is measured in accordance with IFRS 2 initially, at each reporting date and at the date of settlement using an option pricing model. The measurement reflects all conditions and outcomes on a weighted average basis, unlike equity settled transactions. Any changes in fair value are recognised in profit or loss in the period. Therefore, the SARs would be accounted for as follows:

Year	*Expense*	*Liability*	*Calculation*	
	$	$		
30 April 20X3	641,250	641,250	$285 \times 500 \times \$9 \times \frac{1}{2}$	Time-apportioned over vesting period. Using the estimated (300 × 95%) 285 managers.
30 April 20X4	926,250	1,567,500	$285 \times 500 \times \$11$	Expense is difference between liabilities at 30 April 2014 and 30 April 2013
30 April 20X5	97,500	1,350,000	$225 \times 500 \times \$12$	Cash paid is 60 x 500 x $10.50, ie $315,000. The liability has reduced by $217,500 and therefore the expense is the difference of $97,500

The fair value of the liability would be $1,350,000 at 30 April 20X5 and the expense for the year would be $97,500.

Tutorial note.

SARs exercised:

30 April 20X5: 60 x $10·50 x 500 = $315,000

30 April 20X4: 60 x $11 x 500 = $330,000 Therefore a gain of $15,000 is made on these SARs.

Unexercised SARs:

30 April 20X5: 225 x $12 x 500 = $1,350,000

30 April 20X4: 225 x $11 x 500 = $1,237,500

Therefore a loss of $112,500 is made on the remaining unexercised SARs.

This results in an overall charge to profit or loss for the year ended 30 April 20X5 of $97,500.

(d) **Farmland**

A fair value measurement of a non-financial asset takes into account a market participant's ability to generate economic benefits by using the asset in its highest and best use or by selling it to another market participant who would use the asset in its highest and best use. The maximum value of a non-financial asset may arise from its use in combination with other assets or by itself. IFRS 13 requires the entity to consider uses which are physically possible, legally permissible and financially feasible. The use must not be legally prohibited. For example, if the land is protected in some way by law and a change of law is required, then it cannot be the highest and best use of the land. In this case, Yanong's land for residential development would only require approval from the regulatory authority and that approval seems to be possible, so this alternative use could be deemed to be legally permissible. Market participants would consider the probability, extent and timing of the approval which may be required in assessing whether a change in the legal use of the non-financial asset could be obtained.

Yanong would need to have sufficient evidence to support its assumption about the potential for an alternative use, particularly in light of IFRS 13's presumption that the highest and best use is an asset's current use. Yanong's belief that planning permission was possible is unlikely to be sufficient evidence that the change of use is legally permissible. However, the fact the government has indicated that more agricultural land should be released for residential purposes may provide additional evidence as to the likelihood that the land being measured should be based upon residential value. Yanong would need to prove that market participants would consider residential use of the land to be legally permissible. Provided there is sufficient evidence to support these assertions, alternative uses, for example, commercial development which would enable market participants to maximise value, should be considered, but a search for potential alternative uses need not be exhaustive. In addition, any costs to transform the land, for example, obtaining planning permission or converting the land to its alternative use, and profit expectations from a market participant's perspective should also be considered in the fair value measurement.

If there are multiple types of market participants who would use the asset differently, these alternative scenarios must be considered before concluding on the asset's highest and best use. It appears that Yanong is not certain about what constitutes the highest and best use and therefore IFRS 13's presumption that the highest and best use is an asset's current use appears to be valid at this stage.

71 IFRSs and SMEs

Text reference. SMEs are covered in Chapter 21 of your Study Text.

Top tips. This question required candidates to discuss the need to develop a set of IFRSs especially for small to medium-sized enterprises (SMEs). Do not be tempted to waffle or repeat yourself. Since this question was set, the IASB has published an IFRS for SMEs.

Easy marks. This is a knowledge-based question, so all marks are easy if you know it.

Examiner's comment. This question was generally well answered and the topic will feature in future exams.

Marking scheme

		Marks
(a)	Subjective	7
(b)	Purpose	3
	Definition of entity	4
	How to modify	6
	Items not dealt with	3
	Full IFRS	3
Available		26
Maximum		25

(a) Originally, International Accounting Standards (IASs) issued by the International Accounting Standards Committee (IASC) were **designed to be suitable for all types of entity**, including small and medium entities (SMEs) and entities in developing countries. Large listed entities based their financial statements on national GAAP which normally **automatically complied** with those IASs due to choices permitted in the past. In recent years, IASs and IFRSs have become **increasingly complex and prescriptive**. They are now designed **primarily** to meet the information needs of **institutional investors in large listed entities** and their advisers. In many countries, IFRSs are **used mainly by listed companies**.

There is a case for continued use of full IFRSs by SMEs. It can be argued that the **main objectives** of general purpose financial statements **are the same for all types of company**, of whatever size. Compliance with full IFRSs ensures that the financial statements of SMEs **present their financial performance fairly** and gives them greater **credibility**. It also ensures their **comparability** with those of other entities.

There were also many arguments for developing a separate set of standards for SMEs, and these have been taken into account (see below) Full IFRSs have become very **detailed and onerous** to follow. The **cost** of complying may **exceed the benefits** to the entity and the users of its financial statements. At present, an entity cannot describe their financial statements as IFRS financial statements unless they have complied with every single requirement.

SME financial statements are normally **used by a relatively small number of people**. Often, the **investors** are also **involved in day to day management**. The **main external users** of SME financial statements tend to be **lenders and the tax authorities**, rather than institutional investors and their advisers. These users have **different information needs** from those of investors. For these users, the accounting treatments and the detailed disclosures required may sometimes **obscure the picture** given by the financial statements. In some cases, **different, or more detailed information may be needed**. For example, related party transactions are often very significant in the context of SME activities and expanded disclosure may be appropriate.

The *IFRS for Small and Medium-Sized Entities* (IFRS for SMEs) was published in July 2009, and therefore falls to be examinable in 2010. It is only 230 pages, and has **simplifications** that reflect the needs of users of SMEs' financial statements and cost-benefit considerations. It is designed to facilitate financial reporting by small and medium-sized entities in a number of ways:

(i) It provides significantly **less guidance** than full IFRS.

(ii) Many of the **principles** for recognising and measuring assets, liabilities, income and expenses in full IFRSs are **simplified**.

(iii) Where full IFRSs allow accounting policy choices, the IFRS for SMEs **allows only the easier** option.

(iv) **Topics not relevant** to SMEs are **omitted**.

(v) Significantly **fewer disclosures** are required.

(vi) The standard has been written in **clear language** that can easily be translated.

(b) **Issues in developing IFRSs for SMEs**

(i) **The purpose of the standards and type of entity to which they should apply**

The main objective of accounting standards for SMEs is that they should provide the users of SME financial statements with **relevant, reliable and understandable information**. The standards should be **suitable for SMEs globally** and should **reduce the financial reporting burden** on SMEs. It is generally accepted that SME standards should be built on the **same conceptual framework** as full IFRSs.

It could also be argued that SME standards should **allow for easy transition** to full IFRS as some SMEs will become listed entities or need to change for other reasons. This would mean that SME standards **could not be separately developed from first principles** (as many would prefer) but instead would be a **modified version of full IFRS**. Some argue that ease of transition is not important as relatively few SMEs will need to change to IFRS in practice.

The **definition** of an SME could be based on **size** or on **public accountability** or on a combination of the two. There are several disadvantages of basing the definition on size limits alone. Size limits are **arbitrary** and **different limits are likely to be appropriate in different countries**. Most people believe that SMEs are **not simply smaller versions of listed entities**, but differ from them in more fundamental ways.

The most important way in which SMEs differ from other entities is that they are **not usually publicly accountable**. Using this as the basis of a definition raises other issues: which types of company are publicly accountable? Obviously the **definition would include** companies which have **issued shares** or other instruments **to the public**. It has been suggested that this category should also include companies **holding assets in a fiduciary capacity** (such as banks or providers of pensions), companies that provide **essential public services** (utility companies) and any entity with **economic significance in its country** (which in turn would have to be defined). This would mean that SME standards could potentially be used by a very large number of entities covering a very large range in terms of size.

There is a case for allowing **national standard setters** to **impose size limits** or otherwise **restrict** the types of entities that could use SME standards. There is also a case for allowing national standard setters to **define 'publicly accountable'** in a way that is appropriate for their particular jurisdiction.

The *IFRS for SMEs* published in July 2009 does not use size or quantitative thresholds, but qualification is determined by public accountability. It is up to legislative and regulatory authorities and standard-setters in individual jurisdictions to decide who may or must use the IFRS for SMEs.

(ii) **How existing standards could be modified to meet the needs of SMEs**

The starting point for modifying existing standards should be the most likely **users** of SME financial statements and their **information needs**. SME financial statements are mainly used by **lenders** and **potential lenders, the tax authorities** and **suppliers**. In addition, the **owners and management** (who are often the same people) may be dependent on the information in the financial statements. SME financial statements must **meet the needs** of their users, but the **costs** of providing the information **should not outweigh the benefits**.

There is considerable scope for **simplifying disclosure and presentation requirements**. Many of the existing requirements, for example those related to financial instruments, discontinued operations and earnings per share, are **not really relevant** to the users of SME financial statements. In any case, lenders and potential lenders are normally able to ask for additional information (including forecasts) if they need it.

The SME standards are a **simplified version of existing standards**, using only those principles that are likely to be relevant to SMEs. The IASB has proposed that the **recognition and measurement principles** in full IFRSs should **remain unchanged** unless there is a good argument for modifying them. Clearly the SME standards will have to be sufficiently rigorous to produce information that is relevant and reliable. However, many believe that there is a **case for simplifying** at least some of the more **complicated measurement requirements** and that it will be difficult to reduce the financial reporting burden placed on SMEs otherwise.

(iii) **How items not dealt with by SME standards should be treated**

Because SME standards **do not cover all possible transactions** and events, there will be occasions where an SME has to **account for an item that the standards do not deal with**. There are several alternatives.

(1) The entity is **required to apply the relevant full IFRS**, while still following SME standards otherwise.

(2) Management can **use its judgement** to develop an accounting policy based on the relevant full IFRS, or the *Framework*, or other IFRSs for SMEs and the other sources of potential guidance cited in IAS 8.

(3) The entity could continue to follow its **existing practice**.

In theory, the **first alternative is the most appropriate** as this is the most likely to result in relevant, reliable and comparable information. The argument against it is that SMEs may then effectively have to comply with **two sets of standards**.

Another issue is whether an SME should be able to **opt to comply** with a specific full IFRS or IFRSs while still following SME standards otherwise. There is an argument that SMEs should be able to, for example, make the additional disclosures required by a full IFRS if there is a good reason to do so. The argument against optional reversion to full IFRSs is that it would lead to **lack of comparability**. There would also need to be safeguards against entities attempting to 'pick and mix' accounting standards.

72 Whitebirk

Text reference. Small and medium-sized entities are covered in Chapter 21 of your Study Text.

Top tips. This is a topical issue and was the subject of a March 2010 *Student Accountant* article by the ACCA examination/examining team. Part (a) on the main differences between the *IFRS for SMEs* and full IFRS, was reasonably straightforward. Part (b) required you to apply the standard to specific areas: goodwill, research and development expenditure, investment property and impairment.

Easy marks. This was a rich source of easy marks for the well-prepared candidate. Make sure your arguments are well-structured in order to earn those two marks for clarity and quality of discussion.

Examiner's comment. Part (a) was very well answered. Answers to Part (b) were more variable. Some were unclear about how to account for the transactions and used full IFRS.

Marking scheme

			Marks
(a)		Subjective assessment including professional	11
(b)	(i)	Business combination	4
	(ii)	Research and development expenditure	3
	(iii)	Investment property	2
	(iv)	Intangible	2
			22

(a) **Modifications to reduce the burden of reporting for SMEs**

The *IFRS for SMEs* is only 230 pages, and has **simplifications** that reflect the needs of users of SMEs' financial statements and cost-benefit considerations. It is designed to facilitate financial reporting by small and medium-sized entities in a number of ways:

(i) It provides significantly **less guidance** than full IFRS. A great deal of the guidance in full IFRS would not be relevant to the needs of smaller entities.

(ii) Many of the **principles** for recognising and measuring assets, liabilities, income and expenses in full IFRSs are **simplified**. For example, goodwill and intangibles are always amortised over their estimated useful life (or ten years if it cannot be estimated). Research and development costs must be expensed. With defined benefit pension plans, all actuarial gains and losses are to be recognised immediately in other comprehensive income. All past service costs are to be recognised immediately in profit or loss. To measure the defined benefit obligation, the projected unit credit method must be used.

(iii) Where full IFRSs allow accounting policy choices, the *IFRS for SMEs* **allows only the easier option**. Examples of alternatives not allowed in the *IFRS for SMEs* include: revaluation model for intangible assets and property, plant and equipment, proportionate consolidation for investments in jointly-controlled entities and choice between cost and fair value models for investment property (measurement depends on the circumstances).

(iv) **Topics not relevant** to SMEs are **omitted**: earnings per share, interim financial reporting, segment reporting, insurance and assets held for sale.

(v) Significantly **fewer disclosures** are required.

(vi) The standard has been written in **clear language** that can easily be translated.

The above represents a considerable reduction in reporting requirements – perhaps as much as 90% – compared with listed entities. Entities will naturally wish to use the *IFRS for SMEs* if they can, but **its use is restricted**.

The restrictions are **not related to size**. There are several disadvantages of basing the definition on size limits alone. Size limits are **arbitrary** and **different limits are likely to be appropriate in different** countries. Most people believe that SMEs are **not simply smaller versions of listed entities**, but differ from them in more fundamental ways.

The most important way in which SMEs differ from other entities is that they are **not usually publicly accountable**. Accordingly, there are **no quantitative thresholds** for qualification as a SME; instead, the scope of the IFRS is determined by a **test of public accountability**. The IFRS is suitable for all entities except those whose securities are publicly traded and financial institutions such as banks and insurance companies.

Another way in which the use of the *IFRS for SMEs* is restricted is that **users cannot cherry pick** from this IFRS and full IFRS. If an entity adopts the *IFRS for SMEs,* it **must adopt it in its entirety**.

(b) (i) **Business combination**

IFRS 3 *Business combinations* allows an entity to adopt the full or partial goodwill method in its consolidated financial statements. The *IFRS for SMEs* **only allows the partial goodwill method**. This avoids the need for SMEs to determine the fair value of the non-controlling interests not purchased when undertaking a business combination.

In addition, IFRS 3 *Business combinations* requires goodwill to be tested annually for impairment. The *IFRS for SMEs* **requires goodwill to be amortised instead**. This is a much simpler approach and the *IFRS for SMEs* specifies that if an entity is unable to make a reliable estimate of the useful life, it is presumed to be ten years, simplifying things even further.

Goodwill on Whitebirk's acquisition of Close will be calculated as:

	$'000
Consideration transferred	5,700
Non-controlling interest: 10% × $6m	600
	6,300
Less fair value of identifiable net assets acquired	(6,000)
Goodwill	300

This goodwill of $0.3m will be amortised over ten years, that is $30,000 per annum.

(ii) **Research and development expenditure**

The *IFRS for SMEs* requires all internally generated research and development expenditure to be **expensed through profit or loss.** This is simpler than full IFRS – IAS 38 *Intangible Assets* requires internally generated assets to be capitalised if certain criteria (proving future economic benefits) are met, and it is often difficult to determine whether or not they have been met.

Whitebirk's total expenditure on research ($0.5m) and development ($1m) must be written off to profit or loss for the year, giving a charge of $1.5m.

(iii) **Investment property**

Investment properties must be held at fair value through profit or loss under the *IFRS for SMEs* where their fair value can be measured without undue cost or effort, which appears to be the case here, given that an estate agent valuation is available. Consequently a gain of $0.2m ($1.9m – $1.7m) will be reported in Whitebirk's profit or loss for the year.

(iv) **Intangible asset**

IAS 36 *Impairment of assets* requires annual impairment tests for indefinite life intangibles, intangibles not yet available for use and goodwill. This is a complex, time-consuming and expensive test.

The *IFRS for SMEs* only requires impairment tests where there are indicators of impairment. In the case of Whitebirk's intangible, there are no indicators of impairment, and so an impairment test is not required.

Mock exams

ACCA

Paper P2

Corporate Reporting (International)

Mock Examination 1

Time allowed: 3 hours 15 minutes

This question paper is divided into two sections:

Section A – this ONE question is compulsory and MUST be attempted

Section B – TWO questions ONLY to be attempted

Do NOT open this question paper until instructed by the supervisor.

Do NOT record any of your answers on the question paper.

This question paper must not be removed from the examination hall.

SECTION A – This ONE question is compulsory and MUST be attempted

Question 1

12/08

The following draft group financial statements relate to Warrburt, a public limited company:

WARRBURT GROUP: STATEMENT OF FINANCIAL POSITION AS AT 30 NOVEMBER 20X8

	30 Nov 20X8	*30 Nov 20X7*
	$m	$m
Assets		
Non-current assets		
Property, plant and equipment	350	360
Goodwill	80	100
Other intangible assets	228	240
Investment in associate	100	–
Investment in equity instruments	142	150
	900	850
Current assets		
Inventories	135	198
Trade receivables	92	163
Cash and cash equivalents	288	323
	515	684
Total assets	1,415	1,534
Equity and liabilities		
Equity attributable to owners of the parent: to last million		
Share capital	650	595
Retained earnings	367	454
Other components of equity	49	20
	1,066	1,069
Non-controlling interest	46	53
Total equity	1,112	1,122
Non-current liabilities		
Long-term borrowing	20	64
Deferred tax	28	26
Long-tem provisions	100	96
Total non-current liabilities	148	186
Current liabilities:		
Trade payables	115	180
Current tax payable	35	42
Short-term provisions	5	4
Total current liabilities	155	226
Total liabilities	303	412
Total equity and liabilities	1,415	1,534

WARRBURT GROUP: STATEMENT OF PROFIT OR LOSS AND OTHER COMPREHENSIVE INCOME FOR THE YEAR ENDED 30 NOVEMBER 20X8

	$m
Revenue	910
Cost of sales	(886)
Gross profit	24
Other income	7
Distribution costs	(40)
Administrative expenses	(35)
Finance costs	(9)
Share of profit of associate	6
Loss before tax	(47)
Income tax expense	(29)
Loss for the year from continuing operations	(76)
Loss for the year	(76)
Other comprehensive income for the year (after tax, not reclassified to P/L)	
Investment in equity instruments (IEI)	27
Gains on property revaluation	2
Actuarial losses on defined benefit plan	(4)
Other comprehensive income for the year (after tax)	25
Total comprehensive income for the year	(51)
Profit/loss attributable to:	
Owners of the parent	(74)
Non-controlling interest	(2)
	(76)
Total comprehensive income attributable to:	
Owners of the parent	(49)
Non-controlling interest	(2)
	(51)

WARRBURT GROUP: STATEMENT OF CHANGES IN EQUITY FOR THE YEAR ENDED 30 NOVEMBER 20X8

	Share capital	*Retained earnings*	*IEI*	*Revaluation surplus*	*Total*	*Non-controlling interest*	*Total equity*
	$m	$m	$m	$m	$m	$m	$m
Balance at 1 December 20X7	595	454	16	4	1,069	53	1,122
Share capital issued	55				55		55
Dividends		(9)			(9)	(5)	(14)
Total comprehensive income for the year		(78)	27	2	(49)	(2)	(51)
Balance at 30 November 20X8	650	367	43	6	1,066	46	1,112

NOTE TO STATEMENT OF CHANGES IN EQUITY:

	$m
Profit/loss attributable to owners of parent	(74)
Actuarial losses on defined benefit plan	(4)
Total comprehensive income for year – retained earnings	(78)

The following information relates to the financial statements of Warrburt.

(i) Warrburt holds investments in equity instruments (IEI) which are owned by the parent company. At 1 December 20X7, the total carrying amount of those investments was $150m. In respect of $112m of this $150m, Warrburt had made an irrevocable election under IFRS 9 for changes in fair value to go through other comprehensive income (items that will not be reclassified to profit or loss). The remaining $38m related to an investment in the shares of Alburt, in respect of which changes in fair value had been taken to profit or loss for the year. During the year, the investment in Alburt was sold for $45m, with the fair value gain shown in 'other income' in the financial statements. The following schedule summarises the changes:

	Alburt	*Other*	*Total*
	$m	$m	$m
Carrying value at 1 December 20X7	38	112	150
Add gain on derecognition/revaluation of IEI	7	30	37
Less sales of IEI at fair value	(45)	–	(45)
Carrying value at 30 November 20X8	–	142	142

Deferred tax of $3 million arising on the $30m revaluation gain above has been taken into account in 'other comprehensive income' for the year.

(ii) The retirement benefit liability is shown as a long-term provision in the statement of financial position and comprises the following:

	$m
Liability at 1 December 20X7	96
Expense for period	10
Contributions to scheme (paid)	(10)
Actuarial losses	4
Liability at 30 November 20X8	100

Warrburt recognises remeasurement gains and losses in other comprehensive income in the period in which they occur, in accordance with IAS 19 (revised 2011). The benefits paid in the period by the trustees of the scheme were $3 million. There is no tax impact with regards to the retirement benefit liability.

(iii) The property, plant and equipment (PPE) in the statement of financial position comprises the following:

	$m
Carrying value at 1 December 20X7	360
Additions at cost	78
Gains on property revaluation	4
Disposals	(56)
Depreciation	(36)
Carrying value at 30 November 20X8	350

Plant and machinery with a carrying value of $1 million had been destroyed by fire in the year. The asset was replaced by the insurance company with new plant and machinery which was valued at $3 million. The machines were acquired directly by the insurance company and no cash payment was made to Warrburt. The company included the net gain on this transaction in 'additions at cost' and as a deduction from administrative expenses.

The disposal proceeds were $63 million. The gain on disposal is included in administrative expenses. Deferred tax of $2 million has been deducted in arriving at the 'gains on property revaluation' figure in 'other comprehensive income (items that will not be reclassified to profit or loss)'.

The remaining additions of PPE comprised imported plant and equipment from an overseas supplier on 30 June 20X8. The cost of the PPE was 380 million dinars with 280 million dinars being paid on 31 October 20X8 and the balance to be paid on 31 December 20X8.
The rates of exchange were as follows:

	Dinars to $1
30 June 20X8	5
31 October 20X8	4.9
30 November 20X8	4.8

Exchange gains and losses are included in administrative expenses.

(iv) Warrburt purchased a 25% interest in an associate for cash on 1 December 20X7. The net assets of the associate at the date of acquisition were $300 million. The associate made a profit after tax of $24 million and paid a dividend of $8 million out of these profits in the year ended 30 November 20X8.

(v) An impairment test had been carried out at 30 November 20X8, on goodwill and other intangible assets. The result showed that goodwill was impaired by $20 million and other intangible assets by $12 million.

(vi) The short term provisions relate to finance costs which are payable within six months.

Warrburt's directors are concerned about the results for the year in the statement of profit or loss and other comprehensive income and the subsequent effect on the statement of cash flows. They have suggested that the proceeds of the sale of property, plant and equipment and the sale of investments in equity instruments should be included in 'cash generated from operations'. The directors are afraid of an adverse market reaction to their results and of the importance of meeting targets in order to ensure job security, and feel that the adjustments for the proceeds would enhance the 'cash health' of the business.

Required

(a) Prepare a group statement of cash flows for Warrburt for the year ended 30 November 20X8 in accordance with IAS 7 *Statement of cash flows*, using the indirect method. **(35 marks)**

(b) Discuss the key issues which the statement of cash flows highlights regarding the cash flow of the company. **(10 marks)**

(c) Discuss the ethical responsibility of the company accountant in ensuring that manipulation of the statement of cash flows, such as that suggested by the directors, does not occur. **(5 marks)**

(Total = 50 marks)

SECTION B – TWO questions ONLY to be attempted

Question 2

12/12

Coate, a public limited company, is a producer of ecologically friendly electrical power (green electricity).

(a) Coate's revenue comprises mainly the sale of electricity and green certificates. Coate obtains green certificates under a national government scheme. Green certificates represent the environmental value of green electricity. The national government requires suppliers who do not produce green electricity to purchase a certain number of green certificates. Suppliers who do not produce green electricity can buy green certificates either on the market on which they are traded or directly from a producer such as Coate. The national government wishes to give incentives to producers such as Coate by allowing them to gain extra income in this way.

Coate obtains the certificates from the national government on satisfactory completion of an audit by an independent organisation, which confirms the origin of production. Coate then receives a certain number of green certificates from the national government depending on the volume of green electricity generated. The green certificates are allocated to Coate on a quarterly basis by the national government and Coate can trade the green certificates.

Coate is uncertain as to the accounting treatment of the green certificates in its financial statements for the period ended 30 November 20X2 and how to treat the green certificates which were not sold at the end of the reporting period. **(7 marks)**

(b) During the year ended 30 November 20X2, Coate acquired an overseas subsidiary whose financial statements are prepared in a different currency to Coate. The amounts reported in the consolidated statement of cash flows included the effect of changes in foreign exchange rates arising on the retranslation of its overseas operations. Additionally, the group's consolidated statement of cash flows reported as a loss the effect of foreign exchange rate changes on cash and cash equivalents as Coate held some foreign currency of its own denominated in cash. **(5 marks)**

(c) Coate also sold 50% of a previously wholly owned subsidiary, Patten, to a third party, Manis. Manis is in the same industry as Coate. Coate has continued to account for the investment in Patten as a subsidiary in its consolidated financial statements. The main reason for this accounting treatment was the agreement that had been made with Manis, under which Coate would exercise general control over Patten's operating and financial policies. Coate has appointed three out of four directors to the board. The agreement also stated that certain decisions required consensus by the two shareholders.

Under the shareholder agreement, consensus is required with respect to:

(i) Significant changes in the company's activities

(ii) Plans or budgets that deviate from the business plan

(iii) Accounting policies; acquisition of assets above a certain value; employment or dismissal of senior employees; distribution of dividends or establishment of loan facilities

Coate feels that the consensus required above does not constitute a hindrance to the power to control Patten, as it is customary within the industry to require shareholder consensus for decisions of the types listed in the shareholders' agreement. **(6 marks)**

(d) In the notes to Coate's financial statements for the year ended 30 November 20X2, the tax expense included an amount in respect of 'Adjustments to current tax in respect of prior years' and this expense had been treated as a prior year adjustment. These items related to adjustments arising from tax audits by the authorities in relation to previous reporting periods.

The issues that resulted in the tax audit adjustment were not a breach of tax law but related predominantly to transfer pricing issues, for which there was a range of possible outcomes that were negotiated during 20X2 with the taxation authorities. Further at 30 November 20X1, Coate had accounted for all known issues arising from the audits to that date and the tax adjustment could not have been foreseen as at 30 November 20X1, as the audit authorities changed the scope of the audit. No penalties were expected to be applied by the taxation authorities. **(5 marks)**

Required

Discuss how the above events should be accounted for in the individual or, as appropriate, the consolidated financial statements of Coate.

Note. The mark allocation is shown against each of the four events above.

Professional marks will be awarded in Question 2 for the clarity and quality of the presentation and discussion.

(2 marks)

(Total = 25 marks)

Question 3

12/12, amended

Blackcutt is a local government organisation whose financial statements are prepared using International Financial Reporting Standards.

(a) Blackcutt wishes to create a credible investment property portfolio with a view to determining if any property may be considered surplus to the functional objectives and requirements of the local government organisation. The following portfolio of property is owned by Blackcutt.

Blackcutt owns several plots of land. Some of the land is owned by Blackcutt for capital appreciation and this may be sold at any time in the future. Other plots of land have no current purpose as Blackcutt has not determined whether it will use the land to provide services such as those provided by national parks or for short-term sale in the ordinary course of operations.

The local government organisation supplements its income by buying and selling property. The housing department regularly sells part of its housing inventory in the ordinary course of its operations as a result of changing demographics. Part of the inventory, which is not held for sale, is to provide housing to low-income employees at below market rental. The rent paid by employees covers the cost of maintenance of the property. **(7 marks)**

(b) Blackcutt has outsourced its waste collection to a private sector provider called Waste and Co and pays an annual amount to Waste and Co for its services. Waste and Co purchases the vehicles and uses them exclusively for Blackcutt's waste collection. The vehicles are painted with the Blackcutt local government organisation name and colours. Blackcutt can use the vehicles and the vehicles are used for waste collection for nearly all of the asset's life. If a vehicle breaks down or no longer functions, Waste and Co must provide replacement vehicles fitted with the same waste disposal containers and equipment and painted with the local government organisations name and colours. **(6 marks)**

(c) Blackcutt owns a warehouse. Chemco has leased the warehouse from Blackcutt and is using it as a storage facility for chemicals. The national government has announced its intention to enact environmental legislation requiring property owners to accept liability for environmental pollution. As a result, Blackcutt has introduced a hazardous chemical policy and has begun to apply the policy to its properties. Blackcutt has had a report that the chemicals have contaminated the land surrounding the warehouse. Blackcutt has no recourse against Chemco or its insurance company for the clean-up costs of the pollution. At 30 November 20X6, it is virtually certain that draft legislation requiring a clean up of land already contaminated will be enacted shortly after the year end. **(4 marks)**

(d) On 1 December 20X0, Blackcutt opened a school at a cost of $5 million. The estimated useful life of the school was 25 years. On 30 November 20X6, the school was closed because numbers using the school declined unexpectedly due to a population shift caused by the closure of a major employer in the area. The school is to be converted for use as a library, and there is no expectation that numbers using the school will increase in the future and thus the building will not be reopened for use as a school. The current replacement cost for a library of equivalent size to the school is $2.1 million. Because of the nature of the non-current asset, value-in-use and net selling price are unrealistic estimates of the value of the school. The change in use would have no effect on the estimated life of the building. **(6 marks)**

Required

Discuss how the above events should be accounted for in the financial statements of Blackcutt.

Note. The mark allocation is shown against each of the four events above.

Professional marks will be awarded in Question 3 for the clarity and quality of the presentation and discussion.

(2 marks)

(Total = 25 marks)

Question 4

12/12

The International Accounting Standards Board has recently completed a joint project with the Financial

Accounting Standards Board (FASB) on fair value measurement by issuing IFRS 13 *Fair value measurement.* IFRS 13 defines fair value, establishes a framework for measuring fair value and requires significant disclosures relating to fair value measurement.

The IASB wanted to enhance the guidance available for assessing fair value in order that users could better gauge the valuation techniques and inputs used to measure fair value. There are no new requirements as to when fair value accounting is required, but the IFRS gives guidance regarding fair value measurements in existing standards. Fair value measurements are categorised into a three-level hierarchy, based on the type of inputs to the valuation techniques used. However, the guidance in IFRS 13 does not apply to transactions dealt with by certain specific standards.

Required

(a) (i) Discuss the main principles of fair value measurement as set out in IFRS 13. **(7 marks)**

(ii) Describe the three-level hierarchy for fair value measurements used in IFRS 13. **(6 marks)**

(b) Jayach, a public limited company, is reviewing the fair valuation of certain assets and liabilities in light of the introduction of IFRS 13.

It carries an asset that is traded in different markets and is uncertain as to which valuation to use. The asset has to be valued at fair value under International Financial Reporting Standards. Jayach currently only buys and sells the asset in the Australasian market. The data relating to the asset are set out below.

Year to 30 November 20X2	*Asian market*	*European market*	*Australasian market*
Volume of market – units	4 million	2 million	1 million
Price	$19	$16	$22
Costs of entering the market	$2	$2	$3
Transaction costs	$1	$2	$2

Additionally, Jayach had acquired an entity on 30 November 20X2 and is required to fair value a decommissioning liability. The entity has to decommission a mine at the end of its useful life, which is in three years' time. Jayach has determined that it will use a valuation technique to measure the fair value of the liability. If Jayach were allowed to transfer the liability to another market participant, then the following data would be used.

Input	*Amount*
Labour and material cost	$2 million
Overhead	30% of labour and material cost
Third party mark-up – industry average	20%
Annual inflation rate	5%
Risk adjustment – uncertainty relating to cash flows	6%
Risk-free rate of government bonds	4%
Entity's non-performance risk	2%

Jayach needs advice on how to fair value the liability.

Required

Discuss, with relevant computations, how Jayach should fair value the above asset and liability under IFRS 13. **(10 marks)**

Professional marks will be awarded in question 4 for the clarity and quality of the presentation and discussion. **(2 marks)**

(Total = 25 marks)

Answers

DO NOT TURN THIS PAGE UNTIL YOU HAVE COMPLETED THE MOCK EXAM

A PLAN OF ATTACK

If this were the real Corporate Reporting exam and you had been told to turn over and begin, what would be going through your mind?

The answer may be 'I can't do this to save my life'! You've spent most of your study time on groups and current issues (because that's what your tutor/BPP Study Text told you to do), plus a selection of other topics, and you're really not sure that you know enough. The good news is that this may get you through. The first question, in Section A, is very likely to be on groups. In Section B you have to choose three out of four questions, and at least one of those is likely to be on current issues – a new IFRS, ED or discussion paper. So there's no need to panic. First spend **five minutes or so looking at the paper**, and develop a **plan of attack**.

Looking through the paper

The compulsory question in Section A is, as a case study on groups, in this case a group statement of cash flows. You also have a fairly easy bit on interpretation. In Section B you have three questions on a variety of topics:

- Question 2 is a scenario question covering IAS 20, IAS 7, IFRS 10 definition of control and adjustment for tax liability.
- Question 3 is a specialised industry question covering investment property, leasing, provisions and impairment.
- Question 4 is on the topical issue of fair value measurement under IFRS 13.

You only have to answer two out of these three questions. You don't have to pick your optional questions right now, but this brief overview should have convinced you that you have enough choice and variety to have a respectable go at Section B. So let's go back to the compulsory question in Section A.

Compulsory question

Question 1 requires you to **prepare a consolidated statement of cash flows**. Don't be put off by the foreign currency aspects – the translation process is actually quite mechanical. However, there are easy marks to be gained for basic consolidation techniques and basic cash flow techniques from F7. Part (b) is a good source of easy marks too.

Optional questions

Deciding between the optional questions is obviously a personal matter – it depends how you have spent your study time.

In our opinion, Questions 3 and 4 are more straightforward than Question 2. Question 4 allows plenty of scope for earning marks through textbook knowledge of principles, and question 3 has the advantage over Question 2 covering more mainstream topics. Question 2 has a rather obscure Part (b), although you could make up the marks elsewhere. The secret is to plan your answer; break it down into bite sized subsections, clearly labelled to help your marker to quickly conclude you understand the problem and have a logical answer.

Allocating your time

BPP's advice is always allocate your time **according to the marks for the question** in total and for the parts of the question. But **use common sense.** If you're doing Question 4 but have no idea about the numbers for fair value, jot down something (anything!) and spent more time on Part (a), where most of the easy marks are to be gained.

Forget about it!

And don't worry if you found the paper difficult. More than likely other candidates will too. The paper is marked fairly leniently and always has a good pass rate. If this were the real thing, you would need to **forget** the exam the minute you left the exam hall and **think about the next one**. Or, if it's the last one, **celebrate**!

Question 1

Text reference. Group statements of cash flow are covered in Chapter 17 of the text. Foreign currency transactions are covered in Chapter 16. Ethics is covered in Chapter 2.

Top tips. This question has been amended from the original. There are many straightforward, non-group aspects to this group statement of cash flows, so make sure you don't get bogged down in the detailed adjustments at the expense of these. The adjustments to the net loss before tax include some more unusual ones, such as the profit on the investment in equity instruments and the exchange loss. (Note that the realised loss of $1.1m would not normally be adjusted, but it is here, because it is not an operating item and so must be transferred to the 'purchase of property, plant and equipment' caption.) We have set up workings for impairment on goodwill and intangibles, even though the amounts are given to you in the question. It is good practice to set up standard workings in case there is something missing from the information in the question, or you have to calculate the figures from scratch.

Don't skimp on Part (b) – it has ten marks.

Easy marks. These are available for setting out the proforma and workings, and also for valid points made in Part (b) on interpretation and Part (c) on ethical matters. Do not spend too much time on the fiddly foreign exchange working at the expense of these much easier marks.

Examiner's comments. Candidates generally performed well on Part (a) of the question producing good answers, which were rewarded with good marks on this part. The main issues, which caused problems, were the new IAS 1 format of the financial statements, which many candidates were not familiar with and the treatment of the benefits paid by the trustees of the defined benefit scheme, which had no cash flow effect. The calculation of the exchange loss on the PPE was problematical for some candidates from the viewpoint of how to treat it in the statement of cash flows. Also the calculation of trade payables often failed to take into account the creditor for the purchase of plant. In Part (b), Many candidates did not use the information in the first part of the question in answering this part but gave general advantages and disadvantages of statements of cash flows. Part (c) question was quite well answered. However, candidates should develop a greater understanding of ethical principles rather than simply the ability to reiterate the ethical codes.

Marking scheme

			Marks
(a)	Net loss before tax		1
	Investment in equity instruments		4
	Retirement benefit		3
	Property, plant and equipment		6
	Insurance proceeds		2
	Associate		4
	Goodwill and intangibles		1
	Finance costs		2
	Taxation		4
	Working capital		4
	Proceeds of share issue		1
	Repayment of borrowings		1
	Dividends		1
	Non-controlling interest		1
			35
(b)	Operating cash flow and discussion		10
(c)	Discussion		5
		Available	50

(a) WARRBURT GROUP

STATEMENT OF CASH FLOWS FOR THE YEAR ENDED 30 NOVEMBER 20X8

	$m	$m
Operating activities		
Net loss before tax	(47)	
Adjustments for		
Gain on revaluation of investment in equity instruments		
(Alburt – fair value on disposal less fair value at 1 December 20X7(W1)	(7)	
Retirement benefit expense	10	
Depreciation	36	
Profit on sale of property plant and equipment: \$63m – \$56m	(7)	
Profit on insurance claim: \$3m – \$1m	(2)	
Foreign exchange loss (W6) \$1.1m + \$0.83m	2	
Share of profit of associate	(6)	
Impairment losses: \$20m + \$12m	32	
Interest expense	9	
	20	
Decrease in trade receivables (W4)	71	
Decrease in inventories (W4)	63	
Decrease in trade payables (W4)	(86)	
Cash generated from operations	68	
Retirement benefit contributions*	(10)	
Interest paid (W5)	(8)	
Income taxes paid (W3)	(39)	
Net cash from operating activities		11
Investing activities		
Purchase of property, plant and equipment: \$56m (W1) + \$1.1m (W6)	(57)	
Proceeds from sale of property, plant and equipment	63	
Proceeds from sale of investments in equity instruments	45	
Acquisition of associate (W1)	(96)	
Dividend received from associate: (W1)	2	
Net cash used in investing activities		(43)
Financing activities		
Proceeds from issue of share capital (W2)	55	
Repayment of long-term borrowings (W3)	(44)	
Dividends paid	(9)	
Dividends paid to non-controlling shareholders (W3)	(5)	
Net cash used in financing activities		(3)
Net decrease in cash and cash equivalents		(35)
Cash and cash equivalents at beginning of year		323
Cash and cash equivalents at end of year		288

***Note.** Only the contributions paid are reported in the cash flow, because this is the only movement of cash. The amounts paid by the trustees are not included, because they are not paid by the company.

Workings

1 *Assets*

	PPE	*Goodwill*	*Intangible assets*	*Associate*	*Investment in equity instruments*
	$m	$m	$m	$m	$m
b/d	360	100	240	0	150
P/L				6	
OCI (revaluation)	4				30**
Fair value gain on investment in Alburt					7
Dep'n/Impairment/	(36)	**(20)** β	**(12)** β		
Acquisition of associate				**96** β	
Asset destroyed	(1)				
Replacement from insurance company (at fair value)	3				
Disposals	(56)				
Non-cash additions (on credit)*	20				
				8 × 25%	
Cash paid/(rec'd)	**56**	0	0	(2)	**(45)**
c/d	350	80	228	100	142

Notes

* The additions are translated at the historic rate. Adjustment for exchange rate differences are dealt with in (W9).

	$m
Additions (cash) $\frac{280}{5}$ =	56
Additions (credit) $\frac{100}{5}$	20
Total (excluding destroyed assets replaced): 78 – (3 – 1)	76

** This is the gain on revaluation, which is shown in the statement of profit or loss and other comprehensive income net of deferred tax of $3m (W3), that is at $27m. The gross gain is therefore $30m and is the amount reflected in this working.

2 *Equity*

	Share capital	*Retained earnings*	*NCI*
	$m	$m	$m
b/d	595	454	53
P/L		(74)	(2)
OCI		(4)*	
Cash (paid)/rec'd	**55** β	(9) **	(5) **
c/d	650	367	46

*Actuarial loss

* *Cash flow given in question, but working shown for clarity

3 *Liabilities*

	Long-term borrowings	*Tax payable*	*Retirement benefit liability*
	$m	$m	$m
b/d	64	(26 + 42) 68	96
P/L		29	10
OCI		3 + 2 (W1)* 5	4
Cash (paid)/rec'd	**(44)** β	**(39)** β	**(10)****
c/d	20	63 (28+ 35)	100

* On revaluation gain on PPE + revaluation gain on investments in equity interests

** Only the contributions paid are reported in the cash flow, because this is the only movement of cash. The amounts paid by the trustees are not included, because they are not paid by the company.

4 *Working capital changes*

	Inventories	*Trade receivables*	*Trade payables*
	$m	$m	$m
b/d	198	163	180.00
Acquisition of subsidiary	–	–	–
Exchange loss (W6)			20.83
∴ Increase/(decrease)	**(63)** β	**(71)** β	**(85.83)** β
c/d	135	92	115

5 *Interest payable*

	$m
Balance b/fwd (short-term provisions)	4
Profit or loss for year	9
Cash paid (balancing figure)	**(8)**
Balance c/fwd (short-term provisions)	5

6 *Exchange loss*

At 30 June 20X8:

DEBIT	Property, plant and equipment (W1) $\frac{380}{5}$	$76m	
CREDIT	Payables $\frac{380}{5}$		$76m

To record purchase of property, plant and equipment

At 31 October 20X8;

DEBIT	Payables $\frac{280}{5}$	$56m	
DEBIT	Profit/loss (loss)	$1.1m	
CREDIT	Cash $\frac{280}{4.9}$		$57.1m

Being payment of 280 million dinars

At 30 November 20X8:

DEBIT	P/L (loss)	$0.83	
CREDIT	Payables $\left(\frac{100}{4.8}=20.83\right)-\left(\frac{100}{5}=20\right)$		$0.83m

Being loss on re-translation of payable at the year end.

Notes

1 The $20.83m was wrongly included in trade payables, so must be removed from the decrease in trade payables in the SOCF.

2 The unrealised loss on retranslation of the payable ($0.83m) must always be adjusted. The realised loss on the cash payment of $1.1 would not normally be adjusted, but it relates to a non-operating item, so is transferred to 'purchase of PPE'.

(b) **Key issues arising from the statement of cash flows**

The statement of financial position and the statement of profit or loss and other comprehensive income, and the ratios associated with these statements, can provide useful information to users, but it is the **statement of cash flows** which gives the **key insight** into a company's liquidity. Cash is the life-blood of business, and less able to be manipulated than profit. It is particularly important to look at where the cash has come from. If the cash is from trading activity, it is a healthy sign.

Although Warrburt has made a loss before tax of $23m, net cash from operating activities is a modest but healthy $11m. Before working capital changes, the cash generated is $20m. The question arises, however, as to **whether this cash generation can continue if profitability does not improve**.

Of some concern is the fact that **a large amount of cash has been generated by the sale of investments in equity instruments**. This source of cash generation is not sustainable in the long term.

Operating cash flow **does not compare favourably with liabilities** ($115m). In the long term, operating cash flow should finance the repayment of long-term debt, but in the case of Warrburt, working capital is being used to **for investing activities,** specifically the purchase of an associate and of property, plant and equipment. It remains to be seen whether these investments generate future profits that will sustain and increase the operating cash flow.

The company's **current ratio** (515/155 = 3.3) and **acid test ratio** (380/155 = 2.45) are **sound;** it appears that cash is tied up in long-term, rather than short-term investment. An encouraging sign, however, is that the cash used to repay long-term loans has been nearly replaced by cash raised from the issue of share capital. This means that **gearing will reduce**, which is particularly important in the light of possible problems sustaining profitability and cash flows from trading activities.

(c) **Ethical responsibility of accountant**

Directors may, particularly in times of falling profit and cash flow, wish to **present a company's results in a favourable light.** This may involve manipulation by creative accounting techniques such as window dressing, or, as is proposed here, an **inaccurate classification**.

If the proceeds of the sale of investments in equity instruments and property, plant and equipment are presented in the cash flow statement as part of 'cash generated from operations', the picture is **misleading**. Operating cash flow is crucial, in the long term, for the survival of the company, because it derives from trading activities, which is what the company is there to do. **Sales of assets generate short term cash flow,** and cannot be repeated year-on-year, unless there are to be no assets left to generate trading profits with.

As **a professional, the accountant has a duty,** not only to the company he works for, but to his professional body, stakeholders in the company, and to **the principles of independence and fair presentation of financial statements**. It is essential that the accountant **tries to persuade the directors not to proceed with the adjustments**, which he or she must know violates IAS 7, and may well go against the requirements of local legislation. If, despite his protests, the directors insist on the misleading presentation, then the accountant has a duty to **bring this to the attention of the auditors**.

Question 2

Text reference. Government grants are covered in Chapter 3, statements of cash flow in Chapter 17, IFRS 10 in Chapter 12, IAS 12 in Chapter 6 and IAS 8 in Chapter 10.

Top tips. Part (a), on the treatment of 'green certificates' effectively tested IAS 20 on government grants, a standard familiar from your F7 studies. It is important to explain **why** the certificates need to be accounted for as government grants. Part (b) was on exchange differences in statements of cash flows. This topic is usually tested as an adjustment in a statement of cash flows question. The key point is that the exchange differences are not cash flows but reconciling items. Part (c) tested the topical issue of control as per IFRS 10, with the slightly unusual scenario that the parent wished to continue to consolidate an investment that it did not control. (Usually such questions are based on a parent not wishing to consolidate an investment it does control.) Part (d) dealt with the issue of whether a correction to the tax provision in a previous year should be dealt with as a prior period adjustment. It shouldn't, as it is a change in accounting estimate.

Easy marks. In Part (c), IFRS 10 is topical and you will get marks for textbook knowledge of the definition of control. Part (d) draws on basic knowledge of the presentation of current tax.

Examiner's comment. In Part (a) of this question, candidates should not have simply discussed IAS 20 but widened the discussion to include the potential impact of other standards on the entity. The surprising thing about Part (b) of the question was the number of candidates who ignored the cash flow implications and simply discussed the accounting in the group statement of financial position. It is important for candidates to read the scenario the question. Marks will not be gained for irrelevant discussions. Part (c) involved the discussion yet again of more than a single IFRS. There are a number of IFRS which deal with group accounting and candidates should look at these standards in conjunction with each other. In this question control was determined by looking at IFRS 10 but additionally, if an entity is not a subsidiary then other standards should be consulted such as IFRS 11 for joint control implications and IAS 28 for equity accounting possibilities. A narrow answer dealing with IFRS 10 would have restricted the marks. This part of the question was quite well answered. Part (d) required candidates to look at adjustments to current tax in respect of prior years' and whether this expense should be been treated as a prior year adjustment. These items related to adjustments arising from tax audits by the authorities in relation to previous reporting periods. In this and the above part of the question the issues set out in the question were critical to a good answer.

Marking scheme

		Marks
(a)	1 mark per point up to maximum	7
(b)	1 mark per point up to maximum	5
(c)	1 mark per point up to maximum	6
(d)	1 mark per point up to maximum	5
Professional marks		2
		25

(a) **Green certificates**

The applicable standard relating to the green certificates is IAS 20 *Accounting for government grants and disclosure of government assistance.*

The principle behind the standard is that of accruals or matching: the **grant received must be matched with the related costs**.

Government grants are assistance by government in the form of transfers of resources to an entity in return for past or future compliance with certain conditions relating to the operating activities of the entity. A government grant is recognised only when there is reasonable assurance that the entity will comply with the conditions attaching to it and the grants will be received. In the case of the green certificates, the condition that must be complied with is the environmentally friendly production of electricity, as verified by the an independent audit.

There are two main types of grants:

(i) **Grants related to assets.** These are grants whose primary condition is that an entity qualifying for them should purchase, construct or otherwise acquire long-term assets. Subsidiary conditions may also be attached restricting the type or location of the assets or the periods during which they are to be acquired or held.

(ii) **Grants related to income.** These are government grants other than grants related to assets.

Since Coate can trade the green certificates, they are not long-term assets, and therefore fall into the category of **grants related to income**. They must be matched against the related costs of production of 'green electricity', as they are a form of government compensation for these costs.

There are two possible ways of presenting the grants (green certificates).

(i) As a credit in profit or loss, either separately or under a general heading such as 'other income', or
(ii) As a deduction from the related expense.

The **green certificates** are items held for sale in the ordinary course of business, and therefore should be recognised as **inventories** in accordance with IAS 2 *Inventories.* Green certificates that are unsold at the end of the reporting period are included in inventory and charged to production as **part of the cost of sales.**

A **deferred income approach** is used to match the grant to the related cost as follows.

To record the quarterly receipt of the grant

DEBIT	Certificate (SOFP)	$ Fair value of certificate at receipt	
CREDIT	Deferred income (SOFP)		$ Fair value of certificate at receipt

On the sale of a certificate: contribution to cost of production

When the certificate is sold its fair value may be recognised in profit or loss. It is treated as a deduction from cost of sales because it is a contribution to the cost of generating the 'green electricity'.

DEBIT	Deferred income (SOFP)	$ Fair value of certificate at receipt	
CREDIT	Cost of sales (SPLOCI)		$ Fair value of certificate at receipt

On the sale of a certificate: surplus/deficit

The certificate may be sold for more or less than its fair value at the time it was received from the government. This surplus/deficit is taken to/deducted from revenue in the SPLOCI.

DEBIT	Bank/receivable (SOFP)	$ Fair value of trade	
CREDIT	Certificate (SOFP)		$ Fair value of certificate at receipt
DEBIT/CREDIT	Revenue (SPLOCI)		$ Balance (deficit/surplus)

Following IAS 1 *Presentation of financial statements,* Coates is required to **disclose its accounting policy** in relation to government grants. IAS 20 specifically requires disclosure of **the nature and extent of the government assistance given and any conditions not yet fulfilled or related contingencies**. The disclosures of unfulfilled conditions are unlikely to be extensive because an audit must be completed to show that the conditions have been fulfilled.

(b) **Foreign exchange and cash flows**

According to IAS 7 *Statement of cash flows*, **unrealised foreign exchange gains and losses are not cash flows**. However, IAS 7 requires that the components making up the total opening and closing balances of cash and cash equivalents in the statement of cash flows should be disclosed in order to **reconcile cash and cash equivalents at the beginning and end of the period**.

Individual accounts (foreign cash balances)

Coates holds **foreign currency cash and cash equivalent** balances. As these are **monetary items**, IAS 21 *The effects of changes in foreign exchange rates* requires them to be **retranslated at the closing rate** at the reporting date. Exchange **gains and losses are recorded in profit or loss** in Coates's **individual** financial statements

In the **consolidated statement of cash flows**, if the **indirect method** is adopted, these exchange differences are **removed from profit before tax** as an adjustment within 'operating activities'. Instead they are shown at the foot of the consolidated statement of cash flows (as a separate heading from operating, investing and financing activities) as **part of the reconciliation** between opening and closing cash and cash equivalent balances.

Group accounts (overseas subsidiary)

IAS 21 requires the **assets and liabilities** (both monetary and non-monetary) of the overseas subsidiary to be **translated at the closing rate in the consolidated financial statements**. **Income and expenses** are translated at the rate ruling at the date of the transaction or the **average rate** as a close approximation. **Exchange differences** arising on retranslation of opening net assets and profit are recorded in **other comprehensive income** and then held as a separate component of equity. **On disposal** of the subsidiary, the gains or losses are **reclassified from other comprehensive income to profit or loss for the year**.

As the subsidiary was acquired during the current year, its cash and cash equivalents at the date of acquisition would have been recorded as a **cash flow within 'investing activities'**. As its year end cash and cash equivalents balance would have also been included in the closing cash and cash equivalents balance at the foot of the group statement of cash flows translated at the closing rate, the exchange difference arising from the **movement in exchange rates** between the acquisition date and the year-end will have to be shown **separately at the foot of the statement of cash flows** as part of the movement in cash and cash equivalents.

(c) **Treatment of former subsidiary**

Coate wishes to continue to consolidate its investment in Patten, of which it has sold 50% to Manis. The requirement (or in this case permission) to consolidate an investment is determined by **control**, not merely by ownership. In most cases, this will involve the parent company owning a majority of the ordinary shares in the subsidiary (to which normal voting rights are attached). There are circumstances, however, when the parent may own an equal share or only a minority of the voting power in the subsidiary, **but** the parent still has control. Coate is arguing that it still has control over Patten because of the agreement made with Manis that Coate would exercise general control over Patten's operating and financial policies. Whether this is the case will be determined in accordance with IRS 10 *Consolidated financial statements.*

IFRS 10 states that an investor **controls** an investee if and only if it has all of the following.

(i) **Power** over the investee
(ii) Exposure, or rights, to **variable returns** from its involvement with the investee, and
(iii) The **ability to use its power** over the investee to affect the amount of the investor's returns.

Power is defined as **existing rights that give the current ability to direct the relevant activities of the investee**. In some cases assessing power is straightforward, for example, where power is obtained directly and solely from having the majority of voting rights or potential voting rights, and as a result the ability to direct relevant activities. In other cases, assessment is more complex and more than one factor must be considered. Coate has only 50% of the voting rights of Patten, and so other factors come into play here.

IFRS 10 gives the following examples of **rights**, other than voting or potential voting rights, which individually, or alone, can give an investor power.

(i) Rights to appoint, reassign or remove key management personnel who can direct the relevant activities

(ii) Rights to appoint or remove another entity that directs the relevant activities

(iii) Rights to direct the investee to enter into, or veto changes to transactions for the benefit of the investor

(iv) Other rights, such as those specified in a management contract

Coates does not appear to have these rights over Patten. While the shareholder agreement gives Coates influence over Patten, the requirement for consensus with Manis relates to **decisions made in the ordinary course of business,** such as significant changes in the company's activities or budgets, appointment and dismissal of senior employees. Coates argues that it is customary within the industry to require shareholder consensus for such decisions, but the **extent of the restrictions precludes control by Coates**. Rather, the consensus requirements suggest **joint control,** and indicate that this is a joint arrangement, as per IFRS 11 *Joint arrangements.* IFRS 11 defines joint control as:

> The contractually agreed sharing of control of an arrangement, which exists only when decisions about the relevant activities require the unanimous consent of the parties sharing control

There are two types of joint arrangements: joint ventures and jointly controlled entities. Patten is a **separate vehicle**. As such, it could be either a joint operation or joint venture, so other facts must be considered.

There are no facts that suggest that Coates and Manis have rights to the assets of Patten in the consolidated financial statements nor an obligation for its liabilities. Therefore, as each party has an interest in the **net assets** of Patten, Patten should be treated as a **joint venture** (rather than a joint operation). Manis must be **de-consolidated from the Coates group,** and **equity accounted for** as a **joint venture** instead.

(d) **Tax adjustment**

According to IAS 12 *Income taxes* the tax expense in the statement of profit or loss and other comprehensive income includes the tax charge for the year, any under or overprovision of income tax from the previous year and any increase or decrease in the deferred tax provision:

	$
Current tax expense	X
Under/overprovisions relating to prior periods	X/(X)
Increases/decreases in the deferred tax balance	X/(X)
	X

While the correction of an over or under provision relates to a prior period, this is **not a prior period adjustment** as defined in IAS 8 *Accounting policies, changes in accounting estimates and errors* and as assumed by Coates. Rather, it is a **change in accounting estimate**.

Changes in accounting estimates result from new information or new developments and, accordingly, are **not corrections of errors**. A prior period error, which would require a prior period adjustment is **an omission or misstatement arising form failure to use reliable information** that was available or could have been obtained at the time of the authorisation of the financial statements. This is **not the case here**. Coates had accounted for all known issues at the previous year end (30 November 20X1), and could not have foreseen that the tax adjustment would be required. No penalties were applied by the taxation authorities, indicating that there were no fundamental errors in the information provided to them. Correction of an over- or under-provision for taxation is routine, since taxation liabilities are difficult to estimate.

The effect of a change in accounting estimate must be **applied by the company prospectively** by including it in profit or loss in the period of change, with separate disclosure of the adjustment in the financial statements.

Question 3

Text reference. Specialised industries are covered in general terms in Chapter 20 of your Study Text. Investment property and impairment are covered in Chapter 3, leases are covered in Chapter 8 and provisions in Chapter 5.

Top tips. This question has been amended following the introduction of IFRS 16 *Leases.* As usual, this specialised industry question does not require knowledge the sector concerned. However, the fact that this is a local government organisation partly affects the use to which the properties are put in Parts (a) and (d). Part (a) requires application rather than just knowledge, but the issues are uncontroversial. Part (b) requires knowledge and application of a new standard, IFRS 16 *Leases.* Now that the distinction between operating and finance leases has been abolished for lessees (though not for lessors), you can expect to see more questions on whether an arrangement is or contains a lease.

Easy marks. Part (a) on investment property should be familiar to you from your F7 studies, and Part (c) is a very straightforward test of IAS 37.

Examiner's comment. Part (a) dealt with investment property and property held as part of the organisation's housing inventory. Thus the key standards were IAS 40 and IAS 16.Candidates needed a basic understanding of the two standards and the ability to apply their knowledge. The question was quite well answered but again several candidates did not use the information in the question such as the fact that the rent paid only covered the cost of the maintenance of the property. The rental revenue was incidental to the purpose for which the property was held, thus the property was not treated as an investment property. In Part (b), the key skill required here was the application of knowledge. Very few candidates discussed who obtained the benefit from the asset. Generally, this part of the question was well answered. Part (c) dealt with a scenario that many accountants face in practice. Many candidates felt that there was an obligating event but because the legislation was not yet enacted, they felt that there should be disclosure of a contingent liability instead of correctly stating that a provision should be made. There were three elements to Part (d) of the question. Knowledge of the standard, application of the standard and completion of the calculations. Candidates performed quite well on the knowledge aspect of the question. When applying the knowledge, reference to the question is essential and this is where candidates have problems, as they are not used to using information in this way. The knowledge should be second nature, it should not require very much thought, as it is the application in a question such as this, which requires the thought time. Very few candidates calculated the impairment loss correctly but overall the question was quite well answered.

Marking scheme

	Marks
(a) 1 mark per point up to maximum	7
(b) 1 mark per point up to maximum	6
(c) 1 mark per point up to maximum	4
(d) 1 mark per point up to maximum	6
Professional marks	2
	25

(a) **Investment property**

IAS 40 *Investment property* applies to the accounting for property (land and/or buildings) **held to earn rentals or for capital appreciation or both**. Examples of investment property given in the standard include, but are not limited to:

(i) Land held for **long-term capital appreciation**

(ii) Land held for **undetermined future use**

Assets which IAS 40 states are not investment property, and which are therefore **not covered** by the standard include:

(i) Property held for use in the **production or supply of goods or services** or for administrative purposes

(ii) Property held for **sale in the ordinary course of business** or in the process of construction of development for such sale

Owner-occupied property, property being **constructed on behalf of third parties** and property leased to a third party **under a finance lease** are also specifically **excluded** by the IAS 40 definition. (Note that finance leases still exist for lessors, though not for lessees.)

If the entity provides **ancillary services** to the occupants of a property held by the entity, the appropriateness of classification as investment property is determined by the significance of the services provided. If those services are a relatively insignificant component of the arrangement as a whole (for instance, the building owner supplies security and maintenance services to the lessees), then the entity may treat the property as investment property. **Where the services provided are more significant** (such as in the case of an owner-managed hotel), the property should be classified as **owner-occupied**.

Applying IAS 40 to Blackcutt's properties, **the land owned for capital appreciation** and which may be sold any time in the future **will qualify as investment property**. Likewise, the **land whose use has not yet been determined** is also covered by the IAS 40 definition of investment property: as it has no current purpose it is deemed to be held for capital appreciation.

Investment property should be recognised as an asset where it is probable that the future economic benefits associated with the property will flow to the entity and the value can be measured reliably. IAS 40 permits an entity to choose between the cost model and the fair value model. Where the fair value model applies, the property is valued in accordance with IFRS 13 *Fair value measurement.* Gains or losses arising from changes in the fair value of investment property are recognised in profit or loss for the year.

The **houses routinely bought and sold** by Blackcutt in the ordinary course of its operations will **not qualify as investment property**, but will be treated under IAS 2 *Inventories.*

The **part of the housing inventory** not held for sale but **used to provide housing to low-income employees does not qualify as investment property** either. The properties are **not held for capital appreciation**, and because the rent is **below market rate** and only covers the maintenance costs, **they cannot be said to be held for rentals**. The **rental income is incidental** to the purposes for which the property is held, which is to provide housing services. As with the example of the owner-managed hotel above, the services are significant, and the property should be classified as **owner occupied**. Further indication that it is owner occupied is provided by the fact that it is rented out to **employees of the organisation**. It will be accounted for under IAS 16 *Property, plant and equipment.*

(b) **Lease**

The issue here is whether the arrangement with the private sector provider Waste and Co is, or contains, a lease, even if it does not take the legal form of a lease. The **substance of the arrangement should be considered** in connection with the IFRS 16 *Leases.* Key factors to consider are as follows.

(i) Is there an **identifiable asset?**

(ii) Does the customer have the right to **obtain substantially all the economic benefits** from use of the asset throughout the period of use?

(iii) Who has the **right to direct how and for what purpose the asset is used**?

(iv) Does the customer **have the right to operate the asset throughout the period of use** without the supplier having the right to change those operating instructions?

The answer in each case is yes.

(i) The vans are an identifiable asset. Although Waste and Co can substitute another vehicle if one of the existing vehicles needs repairing or no longer works, this substitution right is not substantive because of the significant costs involved in fitting out the vehicle for use by Blackcutt.

(ii) Blackcutt can use the vehicles and uses them exclusively for waste collection for nearly all their life. It therefore has a right to obtain substantially all the economic benefits from the use of the asset.

(iii) Blackcutt controls the vehicles, since it stipulates how they are painted, and ostensibly owns them because they must be painted with Blackcutt's name. It therefore has the right to direct how and for what purpose the asset is used.

(iv) As indicated in (ii) above, Blackcutt has the right to operate the asset throughout the period of use, although it has outsourced the driving to Waste and Co.

The arrangement is **a lease**. A **right-of-use asset** should be recorded, and a **lease liability** set up, equal to the present value of the lease payments . The **service element** relating to the waste collection must be considered as a **separate component** and charged to profit or loss.

(c) **Provision**

Under IAS 37 *Provisions, contingent liabilities and contingent assets,* provisions must be recognised in the following circumstances, and must not be recognised if they do not apply.

(i) There is a **legal** or **constructive obligation** to transfer benefits as a result of **past events**.
(ii) It is probably that **an outflow of economic resources** will be required to **settle** the **obligation**.
(iii) A **reliable estimate** of the amount required to settle the obligation can be made.

A legal or constructive obligation is one created by an **obligating event.** Here the obligating event is the **contamination of the land**, because of the virtual certainty of legislation requiring the clean-up. As Blackcutt has no recourse against Chemco or its insurance company this past event will certainly give rise to a **transfer of economic benefits from** Blackcutt.

Consequently, Blackcutt **must recognise a provision** for the best estimate of the clean-up costs. It should **not set up a corresponding receivable**, since no reimbursement may be obtained from Chemco or its insurance company.

(d) **Impairment of building**

The basic principle of IAS 36 *Impairment of assets* is that an asset should be carried at no more than its recoverable amount, that is the amount to be recovered through use or sale of the asset. If an **asset's value** is **higher than its recoverable amount**, an **impairment loss** has occurred. The impairment loss should be **written off** against profit or loss for the year.

Entities must determine, at each reporting date, whether there are any indications that impairment has occurred. In this case, **impairment is indicated** because the use to which the building is to be put has changed significantly (from a school to a library), a situation which will continue for the foreseeable future.

The **recoverable amount** is **defined** as the **higher** of the **asset's fair value less costs to sell** and the asset's **value in use.** However, these values are unavailable because of the specialised nature of the asset, and the only information available is depreciated replacement cost. Using a **depreciated replacement cost approach**, the impairment loss would be calculated as follows.

Asset	*Cost/replacement cost*	*Accumulated depreciation 6/25*	*Carrying amount/ replacement cost*
	$'000	$'000	$'000
School	5,000	(1,200)	3,800
Library	2,100	(504)	(1,596)
Impairment loss			2,204

Blackcutt should therefore recognise an **impairment loss of $2.204m** in profit or loss for the year.

Question 4

Text reference. Fair value measurement under IFRS 13 is covered in Chapter 7 of your Study Text with more detail on business combination aspects in Chapter 12. The IFRS 13 definition of fair value occurs throughout the text and is relevant to many topics.

Top tips. Fair value measurement is a topical issue and the subject of a recent standard. In recent sittings there has been a computational element in the current issues question. This time it is more detailed and technical than in previous settings. However, students would do well to apply common sense to the information in the scenario, even if not confident in their knowledge, bearing in mind the ACCA examination/examining team's comment to a previous paper: 'often the content of the scenario will help students answer the question as the scenario gives candidates direction in terms of their answers.'

Easy marks. Credit will be given for textbook knowledge in Part (a) of the principles of IFRS 13 *Fair value measurement* and its three-level hierarchy, which candidates should have found straightforward.

Examiner's comment. Surprisingly, this question was not as popular as was anticipated. The standard has been the subject of an article in student accountant, which is not always indicative of an exam question being set in the area. Candidates who answered the question did well. Several candidates did not read the question carefully enough and answered part (a)(ii) in part (a)(i). The marking guide allows some leeway in this regard. Part (b) required candidates to apply the principles set out in part (a) in two scenarios. The first was the fair valuation of an asset and the second was the fair valuation of a decommissioning liability. Both are common examples of fair valuation but candidates struggled to produce meaningful answers. It appears as though there was little understanding of the principles in the standard. For example, the nature of the principal and most advantageous markets for the asset was generally poorly applied. Similarly in the case of the decommissioning liability, the fair value of the liability assumes that it is transferred to a market participant at the measurement date. Often there will be no observable market in this case. These points were seldom raised.

Marking scheme

		Marks
(a)	(i) 1 mark per point up to maximum	7
	(ii) IFRS 13 hierarchy	6
(b)	1 mark per point up to maximum	6
	Calculations	4
Professional marks		2
		25

(a) (i) **IFRS 13 principles of fair value measurement**

IFRS 13 *Fair value measurement* defines fair value as **'the price that would be received to sell an asset or paid to transfer a liability in an orderly transaction between market participants at the measurement date.'**

The previous definition used in IFRS was 'the amount for which an asset could be exchanged, or a liability settled, between knowledgeable, willing parties in an arm's length transaction'.

The price which would be received to sell the asset or paid to transfer (not settle) the liability is described as the 'exit price', the definition also used in US GAAP. Although the concept of the 'arm's length transaction' has now gone, the market-based current exit price retains the notion of an exchange between unrelated, knowledgeable and willing parties.

Fair value is a **market-based measurement,** not an entity-specific measurement. It **focuses on assets and liabilities and on exit (selling) prices**. It also takes into account market conditions at the measurement date. In other words, it looks at the amount for which the holder of an asset could sell it and the amount which the holder of a liability would have to pay to transfer it. It can also be used to value an entity's own equity instruments.

Because it is a market-based measurement, fair value is measured using the assumptions that market participants would use when pricing the asset, taking into account any relevant characteristics of the asset.

It is assumed that the transaction to sell the asset or transfer the liability takes place either:

(1) In the **principal market** for the asset or liability; or

(2) In the absence of a principal market, in the **most advantageous market** for the asset or liability.

The **principal market** is the market which is the **most liquid** (has the greatest volume and level of activity for that asset or liability). In most cases the principal market and the most advantageous market will be the same.

Fair value is **not adjusted for transaction costs.** Under IFRS 13, these are **not a feature of the asset or liability,** but may be taken into account when **determining the most advantageous market.**

Fair value measurements are based on an asset or a liability's **unit of account**, which is specified not by IFRS 13, but by each IFRS where a fair value measurement is required. For most assets and liabilities, the unit of account is the individual asset or liability, but in some instances may be a group of assets or liabilities.

IFRS 13 acknowledges that when **market activity declines**, an entity must use a **valuation technique** to measure fair value. In this case the emphasis must be on whether a transaction price is based on an orderly transaction, rather than a forced sale.

The IFRS identifies **three valuation approaches**.

(1) **Market approach.** A valuation technique that uses prices and other relevant information generated by market transactions involving identical or comparable (ie similar) assets, liabilities or a group of assets and liabilities, such as a business.

(2) **Cost approach.** A valuation technique that reflects the amount that would be required currently to replace the service capacity of an asset (often referred to as current replacement cost).

(3) **Income approach.** Valuation techniques that convert future amounts (eg cash flows or income and expenses) to a single current (ie discounted) amount. The fair value measurement is determined on the basis of the value indicated by current market expectations about those future amounts.

For **non-financial assets** the fair value measurement looks at the use to which the asset can be put. It takes into account the ability of a market participant to generate economic benefits by using the asset in its **highest and best use**.

(ii) **IFRS 13 three-level hierarchy for fair value measurement**

IFRS 13 states that valuation techniques must be those which are appropriate and for which sufficient data are available. Entities should maximise the use of relevant **observable inputs** and minimise the use of **unobservable inputs**. The standard establishes a three-level hierarchy for the inputs that valuation techniques use to measure fair value:

Level 1 **Quoted prices** (unadjusted) in active markets for identical assets or liabilities that the reporting entity can access at the measurement date. If there is a quoted price in an active market, an entity uses that rice without adjustment to measure fair value. An example is prices on a stock exchange. Active markets are ones where transactions take place with sufficient frequency and volume for pricing information to be provided.

Level 2	**Inputs other than quoted prices** included within Level 1 that are observable for the asset or liability, either directly or indirectly, eg quoted prices for similar assets in active markets or for identical or similar assets in non-active markets or use of quoted interest rates for valuation purposes.
Level 3	**Unobservable inputs** for the asset or liability, ie using the entity's own assumptions about market exit value. For example, cash flow forecasts may be used to value an entity that is not listed.

Each fair value measurement is categorized based on the lowest level input that is significant to it.

Entities may use more than one valuation technique to measure fair value in a given situation. A **change of valuation technique** is **considered to be a change of accounting estimate** in accordance with IAS 8. However, the disclosures in IAS 8 for a change in accounting estimate are **not required** for revisions resulting from a change in valuation technique or its application.

(b) (i) **Fair value of asset**

Year to 30 November 20X2	*Asian market*	*European market*	*Australasian market*
Volume of market – units	4m	2m	1m
	$		$
Price	19	16	22
Costs of entering the market	(2)	(2)	n/a*
Potential fair value	17	14	22
Transaction costs	(1)	(2)	(2)
Net profit	16	12	20

***Notes**

(1) Because Jayach currently buys and sells the asset in the Australasian market, the **costs of entering that market** are not incurred and therefore **not relevant**.

(2) Fair value is **not adjusted for transaction costs.** Under IFRS 13, these are not a feature of the asset or liability, but may be taken into account when determining the most advantageous market.

(3) The **Asian market is the principal market** for the asset because it is the market with the greatest volume and level of activity for the asset. If information about the Asian market is available and Jayach can access the market, then Jayach should base its fair value on this market. Based on the Asian market, the **fair value of the asset would be $17**, measured as the price that would be received in that market ($19) less costs of entering the market ($2) and ignoring transaction costs.

(4) If **information** about the Asian market is **not available**, or if Jayach **cannot access the market**, Jayach must measure the fair value of the asset using the price in the **most advantageous market**. The most advantageous market is the market that maximises the amount that would be received to sell the asset, after taking into account both transaction costs and usually also costs of entry, that is the net amount that would be received in the respective markets. The most advantageous market here is therefore the **Australasian market**. As explained above, costs of entry are not relevant here, and so, based on this market, the **fair value would be $22**.

It is assumed that market participants are independent of each other and knowledgeable, and able and willing to enter into transactions.

(ii) **Fair value of decommissioning liability**

Because this is a business combination, Jayach must measure the liability at fair value in accordance with IFRS 13, rather than using the best estimate measurement required by IAS 37 *Provisions, contingent liabilities and contingent assets.* In most cases there will be no observable market to provide pricing information. If this is the case here, Jayach will use **the expected present value technique** to measure the fair value of the decommissioning liability. If Jayach were contractually committed to transfer its decommissioning liability to a market participant, it would conclude that a market participant would use the inputs as follows, arriving at a **fair value of $3,215,000**.

Input	*Amount*
	$'000
Labour and material cost	2,000
Overhead: 30% × 2,000	600
Third party mark-up – industry average: 2,600 × 20%	520
	3120
Inflation adjusted total (5% compounded over three years): 3,120 × 1.05^3	3,612
Risk adjustment – uncertainty relating to cash flows: 3,612 × 6%	217
	3,829
Discount at risk-free rate plus entity's non-performance risk (4% + 2% = 6%): 3,829 ÷ 1.06^3	3,215

ACCA
Paper P2
Corporate Reporting (International)

Mock Examination 2

Time allowed: 3 hours 15 minutes

This question paper is divided into two sections:

Section A – this ONE question is compulsory and MUST be attempted
Section B – TWO questions ONLY to be attempted

Do NOT open this question paper until instructed by the supervisor.

Do NOT record any of your answers on the question paper.

This question paper must not be removed from the examination hall.

SECTION A – This ONE question is compulsory and MUST be attempted

Question 1

6/09

Bravado, a public limited company, has acquired two subsidiaries and an associate. The draft statements of financial position are as follows at 31 May 20X9.

	Bravado	*Message*	*Mixted*
	$m	$m	$m
Assets			
Non-current assets			
Property, plant and equipment	265	230	161
Investments in subsidiaries:			
Message	300		
Mixted	133		
Investment in associate: Clarity	20		
Investment in equity instruments	51	6	5
	769	236	166
Current assets			
Inventories	135	55	73
Trade receivables	91	45	32
Cash and cash equivalents	102	100	8
	328	200	113
	1,097	436	279
Total assets			
Equity and liabilities			
Share capital	520	220	100
Retained earnings	240	150	80
Other components of equity	17	4	7
Total equity	777	374	187
Non-current liabilities:			
Long-term borrowings	120	15	5
Deferred tax	25	9	3
Total non-current liabilities	145	24	8
Current liabilities			
Trade and other payables	115	30	60
Current tax payable	60	8	24
Total current liabilities	175	38	84
Total liabilities	320	62	92
Total equity and liabilities	1,097	436	279

The following information is relevant to the preparation of the group financial statements.

(a) On 1 June 20X8, Bravado acquired 80% of the equity interests of Message, a private entity. The purchase consideration comprised cash of $300 million. The fair value of the identifiable net assets of Message was $400 million, including any related deferred tax liability arising on acquisition. The owners of Message had to dispose of the entity for tax purposes by a specified date, and therefore sold the entity to the first company to bid for it, which was Bravado. An independent valuer has stated that the fair value of the non-controlling interest in Message was $86 million on 1 June 20X8. Bravado does not wish to measure the non-controlling interest in subsidiaries on the basis of the proportionate interest in the identifiable net assets, but wishes to use the 'full goodwill' method. The retained earnings of Message were $136 million and other components of equity were $4 million at the date of acquisition. There had been no new issue of capital by Message since the date of acquisition and the excess of the fair value of the net assets is due to an increase in the value of non-depreciable land.

(b) On 1 June 20X7, Bravado acquired 6% of the ordinary shares of Mixted. Bravado had treated this as an as investment in equity instruments at fair value in the financial statements to 31 May 20X8, and had made an irrevocable election (see note (d)) to recognise changes in fair value in other comprehensive income. There were no changes in the fair value of Mixted in the year to 31 May 20X9. On 1 June 20X8, Bravado acquired a further 64% of the ordinary shares of Mixted and gained control of the company. The consideration for the acquisitions was as follows.

	Holding	*Consideration*
		$m
1 June 20X7	6%	10
1 June 20X8	64%	118
	70%	128

Under the purchase agreement of 1 June 20X8, Bravado is required to pay the former shareholders 30% of the profits of Mixted on 31 May 20Y0 for each of the financial years to 31 May 20X9 and 31 May 20Y0. The fair value of this arrangement was measured at $12 million at 1 June 20X8 and at 31 May 20X9 this value had not changed. This amount has not been included in the financial statements.

At 1 June 20X8, the fair value of the equity interest in Mixted held by Bravado before the business combination was $15 million, and the fair value of the non-controlling interest in Mixted was $53 million. The fair value of the identifiable net assets at 1 June 20X8 of Mixted was $170 million (excluding deferred tax assets and liabilities), and the retained earnings and other components of equity were $55 million and $7 million respectively. There had been no new issue of share capital by Mixted since the date of acquisition and the excess of the fair value of the net assets is due to an increase in the value of property, plant and equipment (PPE).

The fair value of the PPE was provisional pending receipt of the final valuations for these assets. These valuations were received on 1 December 20X8 and they resulted in a further increase of $6 million in the fair value of the net assets at the date of acquisition. This increase does not affect the fair value of the non-controlling interest. PPE is depreciated on the straight-line basis over seven years. The tax base of the identifiable net assets of Mixted was $166 million at 1 June 20X8. The tax rate of Mixted is 30%.

(c) Bravado acquired a 10% interest in Clarity, a public limited company, on 1 June 20X7 for $8 million. The investment was accounted for as an investment in equity instruments and at 31 May 20X8, its value was $9 million. On 1 June 20X8, Bravado acquired an additional 15% interest in Clarity for $11 million and achieved significant influence. Clarity made profits after dividends of $6 million and $10 million for the years to 31 May 20X8 and 31 May 20X9. An irrevocable election was made to take changes in fair value through other comprehensive income (items that will not be reclassified to profit or loss).

(d) Bravado has made an irrevocable election to hold its investments in Message, Mixted and Clarity at fair value with changes in fair value recognised in other comprehensive income. There were no changes in fair value during the year ended 31 May 20X9.

(e) On 1 June 20X7, Bravado purchased an equity instrument of 11 million dinars which was its fair value. On that date an election was made to hold it at fair value through other comprehensive income. The relevant exchange rates and fair values were as follows:

	$ to dinars	*Fair value of instrument – dinars*
1 June 20X7	4.5	11
31 May 20X8	5.1	10
31 May 20X9	4.8	7

Bravado has not recorded any change in the value of the instrument since 31 May 20X8. The reduction in fair value as at 31 May 20X9 is deemed to be as a result of impairment.

(f) Bravado manufactures equipment for the retail industry. The inventory is currently valued at cost. There is a market for the part completed product at each stage of production. The cost structure of the equipment is as follows.

	Cost per unit	Selling price per unit
	$	$
Production process: 1st stage	1,000	1,050
Conversion costs: 2nd stage	500	
Finished product	1,500	1,700

The selling costs are $10 per unit, and Bravado has 10,000 units at the first stage of production and 20,000 units of the finished product at 31 May 20X9. Shortly before the year end, a competitor released a new model onto the market which caused the equipment manufactured by Bravado to become less attractive to customers. The result was a reduction in the selling price to $1,450 of the finished product and $950 for 1st stage product.

(g) The directors have included a loan to a director of Bravado in cash and cash equivalents of $1 million. The loan has no specific repayment date on it but is repayable on demand. The directors feel that there is no problem with this accounting entry as there is a choice of accounting policy within International Financial Reporting Standards (IFRS) and that showing the loan as cash is their choice of accounting policy as there is no IFRS which says that this policy cannot be utilised.

(h) There is no impairment of goodwill arising on the acquisitions.

Required

(a) Prepare a consolidated statement of financial position as at 31 May 20X9 for the Bravado Group. **(35 marks)**

(b) Calculate and explain the impact on the calculation of goodwill if the non-controlling interest was calculated on a proportionate basis for Message and Mixted. **(9 marks)**

(c) Discuss the view of the directors that there is no problem with showing a loan to a director as cash and cash equivalents, taking into account their ethical and other responsibilities as directors of the company. **(6 marks)**

(Total = 50 marks)

SECTION B – TWO questions ONLY to be attempted

Question 2

6/13

(a) In its annual financial statements for the year ended 31 March 20X3, Verge, a public limited company, had identified the following operating segments.

(i) Segment 1 local train operations
(ii) Segment 2 inter-city train operations
(iii) Segment 3 railway constructions

The company disclosed two reportable segments. Segments 1 and 2 were aggregated into a single reportable operating segment. Operating segments 1 and 2 have been aggregated on the basis of their similar business characteristics, and the nature of their products and services. In the local train market, it is the local transport authority which awards the contract and pays Verge for its services. In the local train market, contracts are awarded following a competitive tender process, and the ticket prices paid by passengers are set by and paid to the transport authority. In the inter-city train market, ticket prices are set by Verge and the passengers pay Verge for the service provided. **(5 marks)**

(b) Verge entered into a contract with a government body on 1 April 20X1 to undertake maintenance services on a new railway line. The total revenue from the contract is $5 million over a three-year period. The contract states that $1 million will be paid at the commencement of the contract but although invoices will be subsequently sent at the end of each year, the government authority will only settle the subsequent amounts owing when the contract is completed. The invoices sent by Verge to date (including $1 million above) were as follows:

Year ended 31 March 20X2	$2.8 million
Year ended 31 March 20X3	$1.2 million

The balance will be invoiced on 31 March 20X4. Verge has only accounted for the initial payment in the financial statements to 31 March 20X2 as no subsequent amounts are to be paid until 31 March 20X4. The amounts of the invoices reflect the work undertaken in the period. Verge wishes to know how to account for the revenue on the contract in the financial statements to date.

Market interest rates are currently at 6%. **(6 marks)**

(c) In February 20X2, an inter-city train did what appeared to be superficial damage to a storage facility of a local company. The directors of the company expressed an intention to sue Verge but in the absence of legal proceedings, Verge had not recognised a provision in its financial statements to 31 March 20X2. In July 20X2, Verge received notification for damages of $1.2m, which was based upon the estimated cost to repair the building. The local company claimed the building was much more than a storage facility as it was a valuable piece of architecture which had been damaged to a greater extent than was originally thought. The head of legal services advised Verge that the company was clearly negligent but the view obtained from an expert was that the value of the building was $800,000. Verge had an insurance policy that would cover the first $200,000 of such claims. After the financial statements for the year ended 31 March 20X3 were authorised, the case came to court and the judge determined that the storage facility actually was a valuable piece of architecture. The court ruled that Verge was negligent and awarded $300,000 for the damage to the fabric of the facility. **(6 marks)**

(d) Verge was given a building by a private individual in February 20X2. The benefactor included a condition that it must be brought into use as a train museum in the interests of the local community or the asset (or a sum equivalent to the fair value of the asset) must be returned. The fair value of the asset was $1.5 million in February 20X2. Verge took possession of the building in May 20X2. However, it could not utilise the building in accordance with the condition until February 20X3 as the building needed some refurbishment and adaptation and in order to fulfil the condition. Verge spent $1 million on refurbishment and adaptation.

On 1 July 20X2, Verge obtained a cash grant of $250,000 from the government. Part of the grant related to the creation of 20 jobs at the train museum by providing a subsidy of $5,000 per job created. The remainder of the grant related to capital expenditure on the project. At 31 March 20X3, all of the new jobs had been created. **(6 marks)**

Required

Advise Verge on how the above accounting issues should be dealt with in its financial statements for the years ending 31 March 20X2 (where applicable) and 31 March 20X3.

Note. The mark allocation is shown against each of the four issues above.

Professional marks will be awarded in this question for clarity and quality of presentation. **(2 marks)**

(Total = 25 marks)

Question 3

6/13, amended

Janne is a real estate company, which specialises mainly in industrial property. Investment properties including those held for sale constitute more than 60% of its total assets. It also owns and operates a number of hotels.

(a) Janne measures its industrial investment property using the fair value method, which is measured using the 'new-build value less obsolescence'. Valuations are conducted by a member of the board of directors. In order to determine the obsolescence, the board member takes account of the age of the property and the nature of its use. According to the board, this method of calculation is complex but gives a very precise result, which is accepted by the industry. There are sales values for similar properties in similar locations available as well as market rent data per square metre for similar industrial buildings. **(6 marks)**

(b) Janne operates through several subsidiaries and reported a subsidiary as held for sale in its annual financial statements for both 20X2 and 20X3. On 1 January 20X2, the shareholders had, at a general meeting of the company, authorised management to sell all of its holding of shares in the subsidiary within the year. Janne had shown the subsidiary as an asset held for sale and presented it as a discontinued operation in the financial statements at 31 May 20X2. This accounting treatment had been continued in Janne's 20X3 financial statements.

Janne had made certain organisational changes during the year to 31 May 20X3, which resulted in additional activities being transferred to the subsidiary. Also during the year to 31 May 20X3, there had been draft agreements and some correspondence with investment bankers, which showed in principle only that the subsidiary was still for sale. **(6 marks)**

(c) (i) One of the hotels owned by Janne is a hotel complex which includes a theme park and a casino as well as a hotel. The theme park, casino, and hotel were sold in the year ended 31 May 20X3 to Conquest, a public limited company, for $200 million but the sale agreement stated that Janne would continue to operate and manage the three businesses for their remaining useful life of fifteen years. The residual interest in the business reverts back to Janne after the fifteen year period. Janne would receive 75% of the net profit of the businesses as operator fees and Conquest would receive the remaining 25%. Janne has guaranteed to Conquest that the net minimum profit paid to Conquest would not be less than $15 million. **(5 marks)**

(ii) Janne has recently started issuing vouchers to customers when they stay in its hotels. The vouchers entitle the customers to a $30 discount on a subsequent room booking within three months of their stay. Historical experience has shown that only one in five vouchers are redeemed by the customer. At the company's year end of 31 May 20X3, it is estimated that there are vouchers worth $20 million which are eligible for discount. The income from room sales for the year is $300 million and Janne is unsure how to report the income from room sales in the financial statements. **(6 marks)**

Required

Advise Janne on how the above accounting issues should be dealt with in its financial statements.

Note. The mark allocation is shown against each of the three issues above.

Professional marks will be awarded in this question for clarity and quality of presentation. **(2 marks)**

(Total = 25 marks)

Question 4

The transition to International Financial Reporting Standards (IFRSs) involves major change for companies as IFRSs introduce significant changes in accounting practices that were often not required by national generally accepted accounting practice. It is important that the interpretation and application of IFRSs is consistent from country to country. IFRSs are partly based on rules, and partly on principles and management's judgement. Judgement is more likely to be better used when it is based on experience of IFRSs within a sound financial reporting infrastructure. It is hoped that national differences in accounting will be eliminated and financial statements will be consistent and comparable worldwide.

Required

(a) Discuss how the changes in accounting practices on transition to IFRSs and choice in the application of individual IFRSs could lead to inconsistency between the financial statements of companies. **(17 marks)**

(b) Discuss how management's judgement and the financial reporting infrastructure of a country can have a significant impact on financial statements prepared under IFRS. **(6 marks)**

Appropriateness and quality of discussion. **(2 marks)**

(Total = 25 marks)

Answers

DO NOT TURN THIS PAGE UNTIL YOU HAVE COMPLETED THE MOCK EXAM

A PLAN OF ATTACK

Managing your nerves

As you turn the pages to start this exam a number of thoughts are likely to cross your mind. At best, examinations cause anxiety so it is important to stay focused on your task for the next three hours and fifteen minutes! Developing an awareness of what is going on emotionally within you may help you manage your nerves. Remember, you are unlikely to banish the flow of adrenaline, but the key is to harness it to help you work steadily and quickly through your answers.

Working through this mock exam will help you develop the exam stamina you will need to keep going for three hours.

Managing your time

Planning and time management are two of the key skills which complement the technical knowledge you need to succeed. To keep yourself on time, do not be afraid to jot down your target completion times for each question, perhaps next to the title of the question on the paper.

Focusing on scoring marks

When completing written answers, remember to communicate the critical points, which represent marks, and avoid padding and waffle. Sometimes it is possible to analyse a long sentence into more than one point. Always try to maximise the mark potential of what you write.

As you read through the questions, jot down on the question paper, any points you think you might forget. There is nothing more upsetting than coming out of an exam having forgotten to write a point you knew!

Also remember you can only score marks for what is on paper; you must write down enough to help the ACCA examination/examining team to give you marks!

Structure and signpost your answers

To help you answer the ACCA examination/examining team's requirements, highlight as you read through the paper the key words and phrases in the ACCA examination/examining team's requirements.

Also, where possible try to use headings and subheadings, to give a logical and easy-to-follow structure to your response. A well structured and signposted answer is more likely to convince the ACCA examination/examining team that you know your subject.

Your approach

This paper has two sections. The first section contains one question which is compulsory. The second has three questions and you must answer two of them.

You have a choice.

- Read through and answer the Section A question before moving on to Section B.
- Go through Section B and select the two questions you will attempt. Then go back and answer the question in Section A first.
- Select the two questions in Section B, answer them and then go back to Section A.

Time spent at the start of each question confirming the requirements and producing a plan for the answers is time well spent.

Question selection

When selecting the two questions from Section B make sure that you read through all of the requirements. It is painful to answer part (a) of a question and then realise that parts (b) and (c) are beyond you, by then it is too late to change your mind and do another question.

When reviewing the requirements look at how many marks have been allocated to each part. This will give you an idea of how detailed your answer must be.

Generally, you need to be aware of your strengths and weaknesses and select accordingly.

Doing the exam

Actually doing the exam is a personal experience. There is not a single *right way*. As long as you submit complete answers to question 1 and any two from questions 2 to 4 after the three hours are up, then your approach obviously works.

Looking through the paper

The compulsory case study question is, as will always be the case, on groups, in this case a business combination achieved in stages. You also have an associate, some foreign currency, debt factoring and ethical issues. In Section B you have three questions on a variety of topics:

- Question 2 (international and UK) is a four-part scenario involving a train operator, testing segment reporting, revenue recognition, provisions and property-related matters (IAS 16, IAS 20 and IAS 1).
- Question 3, the specialised industry question, is set in the property industry. It tested a discontinued operation, consideration of fair value of an investment property (IFRS 13) and revenue recognition.
- Question 4 is on the challenges of a move to IFRS.

You only have to answer three out of these four questions. You don't have to pick your optional questions right now, but this brief overview should have convinced you that you have enough choice and variety to have a respectable go at Section B. So let's go back to the compulsory question in Section A.

Compulsory question

Question 1 requires you to prepare a consolidated statement of financial position for a group in which there has been a business combination achieved in stages. Additional adjustments include debt factoring, a provision, capitalisation of leasehold expenses and a foreign currency contract. The key with this question, which you cannot avoid doing, is not to panic. There is a lot of number crunching, and you might not be able to complete the question. The thing to do is to set out your proformas and then patiently, but briskly, work through the workings, doing as much as you can. By using a strategy of picking the low hanging 'fruit' you could get 80% of the group aspects right which enables you to put 22 marks in the bank!

Optional questions

Deciding between the optional questions is obviously a personal matter – it depends how you have spent your study time.

Question 3 is rather more difficult than Question 2, in our opinion, because of the greater depth required for Part (c) on revenue recognition (nearly half the marks for the whole question).

One thing is clear – the optional questions all contain a discursive element and are all based around a scenario. The ACCA examination/examining team has said that the emphasis in this paper is on giving advice in a practical situation.

The secret is to plan your answer; break it down into bite sized subsections, clearly labelled to help your examiner to quickly conclude you understand the problem and have a logical answer.

Allocating your time

The golden rule is always allocate your time according to the marks for the question in total and for the parts of the question. But be sensible. If (for example) you have committed yourself to answering Question 5, but can think of nothing to say about fair value, you may be better off trying to pick up some extra marks on the questions you can do.

Afterwards

Don't be tempted to do a post mortem on the paper with your colleagues. It will only worry you and them and it's unlikely you'll be able to remember exactly what you wrote anyway. If you really can't resist going over the topics covered in the paper, allow yourself a maximum of half an hour's 'worry time', then put it out of your head! Relax as it's all out of your hands now!

Question 1

Text reference. Business combinations achieved in stages are covered in Chapter 14. Ethics are covered in Chapter 2.

Top tips. This question required the preparation of a consolidated statement of financial position where the non-controlling interest on acquisition was at fair value. This is often called the full goodwill method. There was also a calculation and explanation of the impact on the calculation of goodwill if the non-controlling interest was calculated on a proportionate basis and a discussion of the ethics of showing a loan to a director as cash and cash equivalents. The main body of the question required candidates to deal with the calculation of goodwill in a simple situation, the calculation of goodwill where there was a prior holding in the subsidiary, an investment in an associate, a foreign currency transaction, deferred tax and impairment of inventory. Don't be put off by the fact that the goodwill on Message is negative (gain on a bargain purchase). This is unusual, and can sometimes mean your calculation is wrong, but you don't lose many marks for arithmetical mistakes

Easy marks. Part (b) is very generously marked, since the calculation is similar to that in part (a) – you just need the NCI share of the subsidiary's net assets. If you're pushed for time you should ignore the foreign currency investment, as it's fiddly and only carries 3 marks.

Examiner's comment. In general the basic calculation of goodwill under the full goodwill method was well done by candidates. However, they dealt less well with the business combination achieved in stages, the contingent consideration and the deferred tax. Many candidates did not complete the retained earnings calculation and often there was doubt over where the gain on bargain purchase should be recorded. (Group retained profits) The calculation of the impairment of inventories was dealt with quite well by candidates, as was the increase in the value of PPE and land. Often the increase in the depreciation charge as a result of the revaluation of PPE was not calculated correctly, nor was the deferred taxation effect. Many candidates got muddled with Part (b) and omitted Part (c) altogether, but those who attempted Part (c) did well on it.

Marking scheme

			Marks
(a)	Message		5
	Mixted		6
	Clarity		4
	Investment in equity instrument		4
	Retained earnings		3
	Post acquisition reserves		2
	Other components of equity		2
	Current liabilities		1
	NCI		2
	Inventories		2
	PPE		2
	Deferred tax		1
	Trade receivables		1
			35
(b)	Message		3
	Mixted		3
	Explanation		3
			9
(c)	Subjective		6
		Available	50

(a) BRAVADO GROUP
CONSOLIDATED STATEMENT OF FINANCIAL POSITION AS AT 31 MAY 20X9

	$m
Non-current assets	
Property, plant and equipment: 265 + 230 + 161 + 40 (W7) + 12 (W7)	708.0
Goodwill (W2)	25.0
Investment in associate (W3)	22.5
Investment in equity instruments: 51 + 6 + 5 – 17.4 (W8)	44.6
	800.1
Current assets	
Inventories: 135 + 55 + 73 – 1.8 (W9)	261.2
Trade receivables: 91 + 45 + 32	168.0
Director's loan (W10)	1.0
Cash and cash equivalents: 102 + 100 + 8 – 1 (W10)	209.0
	639.2
	1,439.3
Equity attributable to owners of the parent	
Share capital	520.0
Retained earnings (W4)	282.3
Other components of equity (W5)	(0.4)
	801.9
Non-controlling interests (W6)	148.8
	950.7
Non-current liabilities	
Long-term borrowings: 120 + 15 + 5	140.0
Deferred tax: 25 + 9 + 3 + 2.6 (W7)	39.6
	179.6
Current liabilities	
Trade and other payables: 115 + 30 + 60 + 12 (W2)	217.0
Current tax payable: 60 + 8 + 24	92.0
	309.0
	1,439.3

Workings

1 *Group structure*

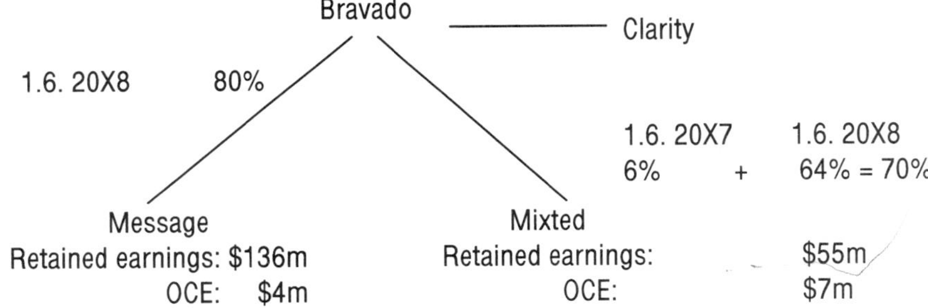

2 *Goodwill*

	Message		Mixted	
	$m	$m	$m	$m
Consideration transferred				
Cash		300		118
Contingent (at FV)		–		12
		300		130
Non-controlling interest (at fair value)		86		53
Fair value of previously held equity interest				15
Less fair value of net assets at acquisition				
Per question/170 + 6	400		176	
Deferred tax liability (W7)	–		(3)	
		(400)		(173)
(Gain on bargain purchase)/Goodwill		(14)*		25

***Note**. This is a gain on a bargain purchase and should be recorded in profit or loss for the year attributable to the parent (W4).

3 *Investment in associate*

	$m
Cost = fair value at date significant influence achieved: $9m + $11m	20.0
Share of post 'acquisition' retained earnings $10m* × 25%	2.5
	22.5

***Note.** The profit for the year to 31 May 20X9 is the relevant figure, as the investment only became an associate at the beginning of that year.

4 *Retained earnings*

	Bravado	Message	Mixted
	$m	$m	$m
Per question	240.0	150	80.0
Fair value movement (W7)			(1.6)
Loss on inventory (W10)	(1.8)		
Gain on bargain purchase (W2)	14.0		
Pre-acquisition		(136)	(55.0)
		14	23.4
Group share			
Message: 80% × 14	11.2		
Mixted: 70% × 23.4	16.4		
Clarity: 25% × 10*	2.5		
	282.3		

***Note.** The $10m profit for the year to 31 May 20X9 is the post-acquisition figure as Clarity became an associate on 1 June 20X8.

5 *Other components of equity*

	Bravado	Message	Mixted
	$m	$m	$m
Per question	17.0	4	7
Foreign IEI (W9)	(17.4)		
Pre-acquisition		(4)	(7)
Group share post acqn: Message	0.0	0	0
Mixted	0.0		
	(0.4)		

6 *Non-controlling interests*

	Message	Mixted
	$m	$m
At date of control (FV/W2)	86.0	53
Post acquisition share of reserves		
Message: 14 (W4) × 20%	2.8	
Mixted: 23.4 (W4) × 30%		7
	88.8	60
	148.8	

7 *Fair value adjustments*

Message:

	At acqn 1.6.X8	Movement	At year end 31.5 X9
	$m	$m	$m
Land: 400 – (220 + 136 + 4)	40	–	40

Mixted:

	At acqn 1.6.X8	Movement	At year end 31.5 X9
		$\left(\frac{1}{7}\right)$	
Property, plant & equipment: 170 + 6 – (100 + 55 + 7)	14	(2.0)	12.0
Deferred tax liability: (176 – 166) × 30%	(3)	0.4	(2.6)
	11	(1.6)	9.4

8 *Foreign currency investment in equity instrument*

	$m
Value on initial recognition: 11m dinars × 4.5 =	49.50
Value at 31 May 20X8: 10m dinars × 5.1 =	51.00
Gain	1.50

At 31 May 20X8, this gain would be recorded in other comprehensive income (not reclassified to profit or loss).

DEBIT	Investment in equity instrument	$1.5m	
CREDIT	Other components of equity (via OCI)		$1.5m

	$m
Value at 31 May 20X8	51.00
Value at 31 May 20X9: 7 × 4.8	(33.60)
Impairment	17.40

This is recorded as follows		$m	$m
DEBIT	Other components of equity (via OCI)	17.4	
CREDIT	Investment in equity instrument		17.4

9 *Inventories*

	$m	$m
Cost in financial statements		
1st stage (10,000 × 1,000)	10.0	
2nd stage (20,000 × 1,500)		30.0
Net realisable value		
1st stage (10,000 × (950 – 10))	(9.4)	
2nd stage (20,000 × (1,450 – 10))		(28.8)
	(0.6)	(1.2)
	(1.8)	

10 *Director's loan*

DEBIT	Loan receivable	$1m	
CREDIT	Cash		$1m

(b) **Goodwill if non-controlling interest is calculated on a proportionate basis**

	Message		*Mixted*	
	$m	$m	$m	$m
Consolidated transferred				
Cash		300		118.0
Contingent (at FV)		–		12.0
		300		130.0
Non-controlling interest (20% × 400)/(30% × 173)		80		51.9
Fair value of previously held equity interest				15.0
Less fair value of net assets at acquisition				
Per question	400		176	
Deferred tax liability (W7)	–		(3)	
		400		(173.0)
(Gain on bargain purchase)/goodwill		(20)		23.9

In the case of **Message**, if non-controlling interest is valued on a **proportionate basis**, the **gain on the bargain purchase is greater**. This is logical if the fair value of the non-controlling interest is seen as part of the cost of the acquisition, and the fair value of this NCI is greater than the NCI's proportionate share of the subsidiary's net assets.

In the case of **Mixted**, the **goodwill is less** because, as for Message, Bravado has 'paid' less. The non-controlling interest is, as for Message, seen as part of the cost of the acquisition.

(c) **Treatment of loan to director**

Although there is no specific prohibition against this treatment in IFRS, there is a requirement not to be misleading. The treatment is in **breach of the two fundamental qualitative characteristics** prescribed in the IASB's *Conceptual Framework for Financial Reporting,* namely:

(i) **Relevance.** The information should be disclosed separately as it is relevant to users.

(ii) **Faithful representation**: Information must be **complete, neutral** and **free from error.** Clearly this is not the case if a loan to a director is shown in cash.

The treatment is also in breach of the *Conceptual Framework's* key **enhancing qualitative characteristics:**

(i) **Understandability.** If the loan is shown in cash, it hides the true nature of the practices of the company, making the financial statements less understandable to users.

(ii) **Verifiability.** Verifiability helps assure users that information faithfully represents the economic phenomena it purports to represent. It means that different knowledgeable and independent observers could reach consensus that a particular depiction is a faithful representation. The treatment does not meet this benchmark as it reflects the subjective bias of the directors.

(iii) **Comparability.** For financial statements to be comparable year-on-year and with other companies, transactions must be correctly classified, which is not the case here. If the cash balance one year includes a loan to a director and the next year it does not, then you are not comparing like with like.

It could be argued that the loan should be treated as a financial asset under IFRS 9 *Financial instruments.* Further information would be needed, for example, is the $1 million the fair value? A case could even be made that, since the loan may never be repaid, it is in fact remuneration, and so should be treated as an expense. In addition, since the director is likely to fall into the category of key management personnel, related party disclosures under IAS 24 are likely to be necessary.

In some countries, loans to directors are **illegal**, with directors being personally liable. Even if this is not the case, there is a potential **conflict of interest** between that of the director and that of the company, which is why separate disclosure is required as a minimum. Directors are responsible for the financial statements required by statute, and thus it is their responsibility to put right any errors that mean that the financial statements do not comply with IFRS. There is generally a legal requirement to maintain proper accounting records, and recording a loan as cash conflicts with this requirement.

There is, in addition, an **ethical aspect**. In obscuring the nature of the transaction, it is possible that the directors are **motivated by personal interest**, and are thus failing in their duty to act honestly and ethically. If one transaction is misleading, it casts doubt on the credibility of the financial statements as a whole.

In conclusion, the treatment is problematic and **should be rectified**.

Question 2

Text reference. Segment reporting and IAS 1 are covered in Chapter 10 of the Study Text, and revenue recognition is covered in Chapter 1. Provisions and contingencies are covered in Chapter 5 and government grants in Chapter 3. This could also be viewed as a specialised industry question, as covered in Chapter 20 of the text.

Top tips. Part (a) requires you to apply the criteria in IFRS 8 to determine whether the company was correct in aggregating two reportable segments. There is plenty of information in the scenario to suggest otherwise. Part (b) needs some thought as possible confusion may arise about the $1m payment in advance, which is also included in an invoice. However, even if you missed this, you could still get good marks for seeing that the payments needed to be discounted in order that revenue should be recognised at fair value, and for seeing that the incorrect accounting treatment applied needed to be corrected retrospectively following IAS 8. You have met provisions (Part (c)) in your earlier studies, but at P2 questions go into more depth. The information you require is in the scenario, but you need to think about applying the standard. Part (d) asks you to consider the interaction of two property-related standards you have met before at F7, but again in a less straightforward context.

Easy marks. These are available for identifying which standards apply and outlining the principles applicable, and you will gain these marks whether or not you come to the correct conclusion about the accounting treatment. There are also some easy marks for definitions in Parts (a) and (c).

Examiner's comment. Part (a) dealt with IFRS 8 *Operating segments.* Candidates had to discuss how different segments should be treated in the financial statements. Candidates often set out the rules of aggregation of one or more operating segments into a single reportable segment. In Part (b), candidates had to discuss how the revenue was to be apportioned over the life of the contract. Candidates understood the requirements of IFRS 15 that the revenue should be measured at the fair value of the consideration received or receivable but few mentioned the requirement of the Framework regarding recognition .The calculation of the revenue's fair value was not well done by candidates nor was the unwinding of the discount. Several candidates did not realise that this was a prior period error. In Part (c), candidates understood the requirements of IAS 37 but did not always apply them correctly. This question required the use of judgment and opinion and therefore candidates who did not fully answer in accordance with the model answer could still score well. The majority of the marks were for the application of IAS 37 and not for the reproduction of the standard. Part (d) required knowledge of IAS 1, IAS 16 and IAS 20. IAS 16 states that the recognition criteria for PPE are based on the probability that future benefits will flow to the entity from the asset and that cost can be measured reliably. The above normally occurs when the risks and rewards of the asset have passed to the entity. Normally the risks and rewards are assumed to transfer when an unconditional and irrevocable contract is put in place. These facts were not known by several. The treatment of the government grant was well known by candidates. On the whole the question was well answered but candidates should always show the accounting entries where this is possible from the question and this was not always the case in this question.

Marking scheme

			Marks
(a)	Segment explanation up to		5
(b)	IFRS 15 explanation and calculation		6
(c)	IAS 37 explanation and calculation		6
(d)	IAS 1/16/20 explanation and calculation		6
	Professional marks		2
		Available	25

(a) **Operating segments**

IFRS 8 *Operating segments* requires operating segments as defined in the standard to be reported separately if they exceed at least one of certain qualitative thresholds. Two or more operating segments **below** the thresholds may be **aggregated** to produce a reportable segment if the segments have **similar economic characteristics,** and the segments are similar in a **majority** of the following aggregation criteria:

(i) The nature of the products and services
(ii) The nature of the production process
(iii) The type or class of customer for their products or services
(iv) The methods used to distribute their products or provide their services
(v) If applicable, the nature of the regulatory environment

Verge has aggregated segments 1 and 2, but this aggregation may not be permissible under IFRS 8. While the products and services are similar, the **customers for those products and services are different.** Therefore the fourth aggregation criteria has not been met.

In the local market, the decision to award the contract is in the hands of the local authority, which also sets prices and pays for the services. The **company is not exposed to passenger revenue risk**, since a contract is awarded by competitive tender. It could be argued that the local authority is the major customer in the local market.

By contrast, in the inter-city train market, the **customer ultimately determines whether a train route is economically viabl**e by choosing whether or not to buy tickets. Verge sets the ticket prices, but will be influenced by customer behaviour or feedback. The **company is exposed to passenger revenue risk**, as it sets prices which customers may or may not choose to pay.

It is possible that the fifth criteria, regulatory environment, is not met, since the local authority is imposing a different set of rules to that which applies in the inter-city market.

In conclusion, the two segments have different economic characteristics and so **should be reported as separate segments** rather than aggregated.

(b) **Maintenance contract**

The applicable standards here are IFRS 15 *Revenue from contracts with customers* and IAS 8 *Accounting policies, changes in accounting estimates and errors.*

Recognition of revenue from the maintenance contract

IFRS 15 *Revenue from contracts with customers* states that the entity must **determine the transaction price** (Step (iii) of the IFRS 15 five-step process for revenue recognition). The transaction price is the amount of consideration a company expects to be entitled to from the customer in exchange for transferring goods or services and must take account of the time value of money, if material.

Under IFRS 15, an entity must **adjust the promised amount of consideration for the effects of the time value of money if the timing of payments** agreed to by the parties to the contract (either explicitly or implicitly) **provides the customer or the entity with a significant benefit of financing** the transfer of goods or services to the customer. In those circumstances, the contract contains a **significant financing component**. A significant financing component may exist regardless of whether the promise of financing is explicitly stated in the contract or implied by the payment terms agreed to by the parties to the contract.

Where the inflow of cash or cash equivalents is **deferred,** the amount of the inflow must be **discounted** because the fair value is less than the nominal amount. In effect, this is partly a financing transaction, with Verge providing interest-free credit to the government body. The **market rate of interest**, here 6%, must be used to calculate the discounted amount, and the difference between this and the cash eventually received recognised as interest income.

IFRS 15 revenue recognition process (Step (v)) would treat this as a **performance obligation satisfied over time** because the customer simultaneously receives and consumes the benefits as the performance takes place. Verge must therefore **recognise revenue from the contract as the services are provided,** that is.

as work is performed throughout the contract's life, and not as the cash is received. The invoices sent by Verge reflect the work performed in each year, but the amounts must be **discounted in order to report the revenue at fair value**. The exception is the $1 million paid at the beginning of the contract. This is paid in advance and therefore not discounted, but it is invoiced and recognised in the year ended 31 March 20X2. The remainder of the amount invoiced in the year ended 31 March 20X2 ($2.8m – $1m = $1.8m) is discounted at 6% for two years.

In the year ended 31 March 20X3, the invoiced amount of $1.2m will be discounted at 6% for only one year. There will also be interest income of $96,000, which is the **unwinding of the discount** in 20X2.

Recognised in y/e 31 March 20X2

	$m
Initial payment (not discounted)	1.0
Remainder invoiced at 31 March 20X2: $1.8 \times \frac{1}{1.06^2}$	1.6
Revenue recognised	2.6

Recognised in y/e 31 March 20X3

Revenue: $\$1.2m \times \frac{1}{1.06} = \$1.13m$

Unwinding of the discount on revenue recognised in 20X2 $1.6m × 6% = $96,000

Correction of prior period error

The accounting treatment previously used by Verge was incorrect because it did not comply with IFRS 15 *Revenue from contracts with customers*. Consequently, the change to the new, correct policy is **the correction of an error rather than a change of accounting policy**.

Prior period errors, under IAS 8 *Accounting policies, changes in accounting estimates and errors*, result from failure to use or misuse of information that:

(i) Was available when financial information for the period(s) in question was available for issue; and

(ii) Could reasonably be expected to have been obtained and taken into account in the preparation and presentation of those financial statements.

IAS 8 includes the effects of mistakes in applying accounting policies, mathematical mistakes and oversights. Only including $1m of revenue in the financial statements for the year ended 31 March 20X2 is clearly a mistake on the part of Verge. As a prior period error, it **must be corrected retrospectively**. This involves **restating the comparative figures** in the financial statements for 20X3 (ie, the 20X2 figures) and **restating the opening balances** for 20X3 so that the financial statements are presented as if the error had never occurred.

(c) **Legal claim**

A **provision** is defined by IAS 37 *Provisions, contingent liabilities and contingent assets* as **a liability of uncertain timing or amount.** IAS 37 states that a provision should only be recognised if:

- There is a **present obligation** as the result of a **past event**
- An **outflow of resources embodying economic benefits is probable**, and
- A **reliable estimate** of the amount can be made

If these conditions apply, a provision must be recognised.

The past event that gives rise, under IAS 37, to a present obligation, is known as the **obligating event.** The obligation may be legal, or it may be constructive (as when past practice creates a valid expectation on the part of a third party). The entity must have **no realistic alternative but to settle** the obligation.

Year ended 31 March 20X2

In this case, the obligating event is the damage to the building, and it took place in the year ended 31 March 20X2. As at that date, no legal proceedings had been started, and the damage appeared to be superficial. While Verge should recognise an obligation to pay damages, at 31 March 20X2 **the amount of any provision would be immaterial**. It would a best estimate of the amount required to settle the obligation at that date, taking into account all relevant risks and uncertainties, and at the year end the amount does not look as if it will be substantial.

Year ended 31 March 20X3

IAS 37 requires that **provisions should be reviewed at the end of each accounting period for any material changes** to the best estimate previously made. The legal action will cause such a material change, and Verge will be required to reassess the estimate of likely damages. While the local company is claiming damages of $1.2m, Verge is not obliged to make a provision for this amount, but rather should **base its estimate on the legal advice** it has received and the opinion of the expert, both of which put the value of the building at $800,000. This amount should be provided for as follows.

DEBIT	Profit or loss for the year	$800,000	
CREDIT	Provision for damages		$800,000

Some or all of the expenditure needed to settle a provision may be expected to be recovered form a third party, in this case the insurance company. If so, the **reimbursement should be recognised only when it is virtually certain that reimbursement will be received if the entity settles the obligation**.

- The reimbursement should be treated as a **separate asset,** and the amount recognised should **not be greater than the provision itself**.
- The provision and the amount recognised for reimbursement **may be netted off in profit or loss** for the year.

There is no reason to believe that the insurance company will not settle the claim for the first $200,000 of damages, and so the company **should accrue for the reimbursement** as follows.

DEBIT	Receivables	$200,000	
CREDIT	Profit or loss for the year		$200,000

Verge lost the court case and is required to pay $300,000. This was after the financial statements were authorised, however, and so it is **not an adjusting event** per IAS 10 *Events after the reporting period.* Accordingly the amount of the provision as at 31 March 20X3 does not need to be adjusted.

(d) **Gift of building**

The applicable standards here are IAS 16 *Property, plant and equipment,* and IAS 20 *Accounting for government grants and disclosure of government assistance,* within the framework of IAS 1 *Presentation of financial statements.* IAS 1 requires that all items of income and expense recognised in a period should be included in profit or loss for the period unless a standard or interpretation requires or permits a different treatment.

IAS 16: recognition of building

IAS 16 states that the **cost** of an item of property, plant and equipment should be **recognised when two conditions** have been fulfilled:

- It is probable that future economic benefits associated with the item will flow to the entity.
- The cost of the item can be measured reliably.

These conditions are normally fulfilled when the risks and rewards have transferred to the entity, and they may be assumed to transfer **when the contract is unconditional and irrevocable**. As at 31 March 20X2, the condition of use has **not been complied** with and Verge has not taken possession of the building.

The building may, however, be recognised in the year ended 31 March 20X3, as the conditions of donation were met in February 20X3. The **fair value** of the building of $1.5m must be recognised as income in **profit or loss** for the year, as it was a gift. The **refurbishment and adaptation cost must also be included** as part of the cost of the asset in the statement of financial position, because, according to IAS 16, the cost includes **directly attributable costs of bringing the asset to the location and condition necessary** for it to be capable of operating in a manner intended by management. The transactions should be recorded as follows.

DEBIT	Property, plant and equipment	$2.5m	
CREDIT	Profit or loss for the year		$1.5m
CREDIT	Cash/payables		$1m

In addition, the building would be depreciated in accordance with the entity's accounting policy, which could (depending on the policy) involve time-apportioning over one or two months (February and March 20X3), depending on when in February the building came into use as a museum.

IAS 20: Government grant

The principle behind IAS 20 *Accounting for government grants and disclosure of government assistance* is that of accruals or matching: the **grant received must be matched with the related costs** on a systematic basis. Grants receivable as compensation for costs already incurred, or for immediate financial support with no future related costs, should be recognised as income in the period in which they are receivable.

Government grants are assistance by government in the form of transfers of resources to an entity in return for past or future compliance with certain conditions relating to the operating activities of the entity. There are two main types of grants:

(i) **Grants related to assets**: grants whose primary condition is that an entity qualifying for them should purchase, construct or otherwise acquire long-term assets.

(ii) **Grants related to income**: These are government grants other than grants related to assets.

It is not always easy to match costs and revenues, but in this case the terms of the grant are explicit about the expense to which the grant is meant to contribute. **Part of the grant** relates to the **creation of jobs** and this amount (20 × \$5,000 = \$100,000) should be **taken to income.**

The **rest of the grant** (\$250,000 – \$100,000 = \$150,000) should be recognised as **capital-based grant** (grant relating to assets). IAS 20 would **two possible approaches** for the capital-based portion of the grant.

(i) Match against the depreciation of the building using a deferred income approach.
(ii) Deduct from the carrying value of the building, resulting in a reduced depreciation charge.

The double entry would be:

DEBIT	Cash	\$250,000	
CREDIT	Profit or loss		\$100,000
CREDIT	Deferred income/PPE (depending on the accounting policy)		\$150,000

If a deferred income approach is adopted, the **deferred income would be released over the life of the building and matched against depreciation**. Depending on the policy, both may be time-apportioned because conditions were only met in February 20X3.

Question 3

Text reference. Investment property and fair value measurement are covered in Chapter 34, with more detail on fair values in Chapter 7. Discontinued operations are covered in Chapter 15. Revenue recognition is covered in Chapter 1. This is also a specialised industry question, as covered in Chapter 20 of the text.

Top tips. Although this question is set in a specialised industry, it draws on principles relating to fair values, discontinued operations and revenue recognition that are applicable in most industries. IFRS 13 (Part (a)) is a relatively recent standard, and you are asked to show how it applies in the context of investment property (IAS 40). The key message is that there is now guidance to replace what could be a subjective approach. IFRS 5 (Part (b)) has been tested in numerical questions, but here you are required to provide an analysis of whether the classification is correct, so do not waste time writing about the accounting treatment. As always, use the pointers in the scenario – they are there for a reason. Revenue recognition (Part (c))has been specifically flagged by this examiner as being important, and is the subject of a recent standard, IFRS 15.

Easy marks. Easy marks are few and far between, as you need to think in depth about applying the standards. However, although IFRS 13 *Fair value measurement* is a recent standard, Part (a) offers some scope for giving explanations and definitions straight from the standard, even if you come to a different conclusion.

Examiner's comment. Part (a) was well answered by most candidates as regards knowledge of IFRS 13 but again the application of IFRS 13 to the scenario was generally not well done. Part (b) was well answered by candidates. Part (c) was also answered well, with candidates applying their knowledge of the then current revenue recognition standard. Again it is important to note that only a portion of the marks is allocated to knowledge of the standard itself and the rest to application. It then becomes obvious why candidates do not score well as many simply set out the requirements of the IFRS without application to the scenario.

Marking scheme

			Marks
(a)	Investment properties explanation		6
(b)	IFRS 5 explanation		6
(c)	(i)	IFRS 15 explanation –1 mark per valid point up to	5
	(ii)	IFRS 15 explanation and calculations – 1 mark per valid point up to	6
Professional marks			2
		Available	25

(a) **Fair value**

IAS 40 *Investment property* allows two methods for valuing investment property: the fair value model and the cost model. If the fair value method is adopted, **then the investment property must be valued in accordance with IFRS 13** *Fair value measurement.* This is a recent standard, giving a common framework for guidance on measuring fair value. It defines fair value as: 'the price that would be received to sell an asset or paid to transfer a liability in an orderly transaction between market participants at the measurement date'.

Fair value is a market-based measurement rather than specific to the entity, so a company is not allowed to choose its own way of measuring fair value. IFRS 13 states that valuation techniques must be those which are appropriate and for which sufficient data are available. Entities should maximise the use of relevant **observable inputs** and minimise the use of **unobservable inputs**. The standard establishes a three-level hierarchy for the inputs that valuation techniques use to measure fair value.

Level 1 Quoted prices (unadjusted) in active markets for identical assets or liabilities that the reporting entity can access at the measurement date

Level 2 Inputs other than quoted prices included within Level 1 that are observable for the asset or liability, either directly or indirectly, eg quoted prices for similar assets in active markets or for identical or similar assets in non-active markets or use of quoted interest rates for valuation purposes

Level 3 Unobservable inputs for the asset or liability, ie using the entity's own assumptions about market exit value

Although the directors claim that 'new-build value less obsolescence' is accepted by the industry, it **may not be in accordance with IFRS 13**. As the fair value hierarchy suggests, IFRS 13 favours Level 1 inputs, that is market-based measures, over unobservable (Level 3) inputs. Due to the nature of investment property, which is often unique and not traded on a regular basis, fair value measurements are likely to be categorised as Level 2 or Level 3 valuations.

IFRS 13 mentions three valuation techniques: the market approach, the income approach and the cost approach. A market or income approach would usually be more appropriate for an investment property than a cost approach. The 'new-build value less obsolescence' (cost approach) does not take account of the Level 2 inputs such as sales value (market approach) and market rent (income approach). Nor does it take account of reliable estimates of future discounted cash flows, or values of similar properties.

In conclusion, **Janne must apply IFRS 13** to the valuation of its investment property, taking account of Level 2 inputs.

(b) **Disposal group held for sale**

IFRS 5 classifies a disposal group as held for sale where its carrying amount will be recovered principally through sale rather than use. The held for sale criteria in IFRS 5 *Non-current assets held for sale and discontinued operations* are very strict, and often decision to sell an asset or disposal group is made well before they are met.

IFRS requires an asset or disposal group to be classified as held for sale where it is **available for immediate sale** in its **present condition** subject only to **terms that are usual** and customary and the sale is **highly probable**.

The standard does not give guidance on **terms that are usual and customary** but the guidance notes give examples. Such terms may include, for example, a specified period of time for the seller to vacate a headquarters building that is to be sold, or it may include contracts or surveys. However, they would not include terms imposed by the seller that are not customary, for example, a seller could not continue to use its headquarters building until construction of a new headquarters building had taken place.

For a sale to be **highly probable:**

- Management must be **committed** to the sale.
- An **active programme to locate a buyer** must have been initiated.
- The asset must be **marketed at a price** that is **reasonable in relation to its own fair value**
- The sale must be **expected to be completed within one year** from the date of classification.
- It is **unlikely** that **significant changes** will be made to the plan **or the plan withdrawn**.

In **exceptional circumstances**, a disposal group may be classified as held for sale or **discontinued after a period of 12 months:**

(i) Circumstances arose during the initial twelve-month period that were previously considered unlikely, and the disposal group was not sold.

(ii) During the twelve-month period, the entity took steps to respond to the change in circumstances by actively marketing the disposal group at a price that is reasonable in the light of the change in circumstances, and the held-for-sale criteria are met.

The draft agreements and correspondence with bankers are **not specific enough** to prove that the subsidiary met the IFRS 5 criteria at the date it was classified. In addition, the **organisational changes** made by Janne in the year to 31 May 20X3 are a **good indication that the subsidiary was not available for sale in its present condition at the point of classification**. Additional activities have been transferred to the subsidiary, which is not an insignificant change.

Finally, the shareholders' authorisation was given for a year from 1 January 20X2. There is **no evidence that this authorisation was extended beyond 1 January 20X3**. The **subsidiary should therefore be treated as a continuing operation** in the financial statements for the year ended 31 May 20X2 and 31 May 20X3.

(c) (i) **Sale of hotel complex**

The issue here is one of **revenue recognition**, and the accounting treatment is governed by IFRS 15 *Revenue with contracts from customers.* Stage (v) of the standard's revenue recognition process requires that **revenue is recognised when (or as)a performance obligation is satisfied.** The entity satisfies a performance obligation by transferring **control** of a promised good or service to the customer. A performance obligation can be satisfied **at a point in time**, such as when goods are delivered to the customer, or **over time**. In the case of the hotel transfer, the issue is that of a performance obligation **satisfied at a point in time.** One of the IFRS 15 indicators of control is that significant risks and rewards of ownership have been transferred to the customer.

It can be argued in some cases where property is sold that the seller, by continuing to be involved, has **not satisfied the performance obligation by transferring control,** partly because the seller has not transferred the risks and rewards of ownership. In such cases, the **sale is not genuine**, but is often in substance a **financing arrangement**. IFRS 15 requires that the substance of a transaction is determined by looking at the transaction as a whole. If two or more transactions are linked, they should be treated as one transaction to better reflect the commercial substance.

Janne continues to operate and manage the hotel complex, receiving the bulk (75%) of the profits, and the residual interest reverts back to Janne; effectively, Janne **retains control** by retaining the risks and rewards of ownership. Conquest does not bear any risk: its minimum annual income is guaranteed at $15m. **The sale should not be recognised**. In substance it is a **financing transaction.** The **proceeds** should be treated as a **loan**, and the payment of **profits** as **interest**.

(ii) **Discount vouchers**

The treatment of the vouchers is governed by IFRS 15 *Revenue with contracts from customers.* The principles of the standard require that

(1) The voucher should be accounted for as a **separate component** of the sale.

(2) The promise to provide the discount is a **performance obligation.**

(3) The entity must estimate the **stand-alone selling price** of the discount voucher in accordance with paragraph B42 of IFRS 15. The That estimate must reflect the discount that the customer would obtain when exercising the option, adjusted for both of the following:

(1) Any discount that the customer could receive without exercising the option
(2) The likelihood that the option will be exercised.

The vouchers are issued as part of the sale of the room and redeemable against future bookings. The substance of the transaction is that **the customer is purchasing both a room and a voucher**.

Vouchers worth $20 million are eligible for discount as at 31 May 20X3. However, based on past experience, it is likely that only one in five vouchers will be redeemed, that is vouchers worth $4 million. Room sales are $300 million, **so effectively, the company has made sales worth $(300m + 4m) = $304 million in exchange for $300 million**. The **stand-alone price would give a total of $300m for the rooms and $4m for the vouchers.**

To **allocate the transaction price**, step (iv) of IFRS 15's five-step process for revenue recognition, the proceeds need to be split proportionally **pro-rata the stand-alone prices**, that is the discount of $4 million needs to be allocated between the room sales and the vouchers, as follows:

Room sales: $\frac{300}{304} \times \$300\text{m} = \$296.1\text{m}$

Vouchers (balance) = $3.9m

The $3.9 million attributable to the vouchers is only recognised when the performance obligations are fulfilled, that is when the vouchers are redeemed.

Question 4

Text reference. Current developments and international issues are covered in Chapter 19 of the Study Text.

Top tips. With this kind of question, it is advisable to do a quick answer plan to structure your answer, otherwise you run the risk of rambling. Part (a) deals with the transition to IFRS, whether this has brought greater consistency to financial statements. Part (b), on management judgement and the regulatory framework, is even more open-ended, so it is important not to waffle.

Easy marks. These are available for valid points backed up by arguments. The marking scheme below gives an outline of the kind of issues you might cover, but is not definitive.

Examiner's comment. The ACCA examination/examining team noted that surprisingly few chose this question, but that those who did answered it well. Answers to Part (a) were better than those for Part (b), which tended to dwell too much on the issue of fair values.

Marking scheme

			Marks
(a)	Changes from national GAAP		2
	Complexity		1
	Recognition, measurement, disclosure		2
	Alternative forms of presentation		1
	Inconsistent principles		2
	Alternative accounting treatments		3
	Little industry related guidance		1
	IFRS I		2
	Interpretation of IFRS		2
	Adoption date		1
			17
(b)	Management judgements		2
	Disclosure of sensitivity		1
	Regulatory infrastructure		2
	Training/markets		1
	Communication		2
			8
		Maximum	25

(a) **The challenge**

Implementation of International Financial Reporting Standards entails **a great deal of work** for many companies, particularly those in countries where local GAAP has not been so onerous. For example, many jurisdictions will not have had such detailed rules about recognition, measurement and presentation of financial instruments, and many will have had no rules at all about share-based payment.

A challenge for preparers of financial statements is also **a challenge for users**. When financial statements become far more complex under IFRS than they were under local GAAP, users may find them hard to understand, and consequently of little relevance.

Presentation

Many developed countries have legislation requiring set formats and layouts for financial statements. For example, in the UK there is the Companies Act 2006. IFRS demands that presentation is in accordance with IAS 1 *Presentation of financial statements,* but this standard allows alternative forms of presentation. In choosing between alternatives, **countries tend to adopt the format that is closest to local GAAP**, even if this is not necessarily the best format. For example, UK companies are likely to adopt the two-statement format for the statement of profit or loss and other comprehensive income, because this is closest to the old profit and loss account and statement of total recognised gains and losses.

Concepts and interpretation

Although later IAS and IFRS are based to an extent on the IASB *Conceptual Framework,* there is **no consistent set of principles** underlying them. The *Conceptual Framework* itself is being revised, and there is controversy over the direction the revision should take. Consequently, preparers of accounts are likely to think in terms of the conceptual frameworks – if any – that they have used in developing local GAAP, and these may be different from that of the IASB. German accounts, for example, have traditionally been aimed at the tax authorities.

Where IFRS themselves give clear guidance, this may not matter, but where there is uncertainty, preparers of accounts will fall back on their traditional conceptual thinking.

Choice of accounting treatment

Although many so-called 'allowed alternatives' have been eliminated from IFRS in recent years, choice of treatment remains. For example, IAS 16 *Property, plant and equipment* gives a choice of either the cost model or the revaluation model for a class of property, plant or equipment.

It could be argued that choice is a good thing, as companies should be able to select the treatment that most fairly reflects the underlying reality. However, in the context of change to IFRS, there is a danger that companies **will choose the alternative that closely matches the approach followed under local GAAP, or the one that is easier to implement**, regardless of whether this is the best choice.

Choice of recognition or measurement method

An example of **potential inconsistency** is IAS 21 *The effects of changes in foreign exchange rates.* The identification of the functional currency under this standard can be a subjective process, with arguments on either side. Revenue recognition is also an aspect of accounting that can cause considerable variation between companies and between countries, although less so than in the past following the 2014 introduction of the comprehensive standard IFRS 15 *Revenue from contracts with customers.*

Inconsistency of timing and exemptions taken

IFRSs have provision for early adoption, and this can affect comparability, although impact of a new standard must be disclosed under IAS 8 *Accounting policies, changes in accounting estimates and errors.* Further, IFRS 1 *First time adoption of International Financial Reporting Standards* permits a number of exemptions during the periods of transition to IFRS. This gives scope for manipulation, if **exemptions are 'cherry-picked'** to produce a favourable picture.

(b) **Impact of management judgement on IFRS financial statements**

The extent of the impact will vary, depending on how developed local GAAP was before the transition. However, in general it is likely that **management judgement will have a greater impact** on financial statements prepared under IFRS than under local GAAP. The main reasons for this are as follows.

(i) The **volume** of rules and number of areas addressed by IFRS is likely to be greater than that under local GAAP.

(ii) Many issues are perhaps **addressed for the first time**, for example share-based payment.

(iii) IFRSs are likely to be **more complex** than local standards.

(iv) IFRSs allow **choice** in many cases, which leads to subjectivity.

(v) Selection of **valuation method** requires judgement, and many IFRS leave the choice of method open. This affects areas such as pensions, impairment, intangible assets acquired in business combinations, onerous contracts and share-based payment.

Financial reporting infrastructure

As well as sound management judgement, implementation of IFRS requires a sound financial reporting infrastructure. Key aspects of this include the following.

(i) A **robust regulatory framework**. For IFRS to be successful, they must be rigorously enforced.

(ii) **Trained and qualified staff**. Many preparers of financial statements will have been trained in local GAAP and not be familiar with the principles underlying IFRS, let alone the detail. Some professional bodies provide conversion qualifications – for example, the ACCA's Diploma in International Financial Reporting – but the availability of such qualifications and courses may vary from country to country.

(iii) **Availability and transparency of market information**. This is particularly important in the determination of fair values, which are such a key component of many IFRSs.

(iv) **High standards of corporate governance and audit**. This is all the more important in the transition period, especially where there is resistance to change.

Overall, there are significant advantages to the widespread adoption of IFRS, but if the transition is to go well, there must be a realistic assessment of potential challenges.

ACCA

Paper P2

Corporate Reporting (International)

Mock Examination 3

September/December 2016

Time allowed: 3 hours 15 minutes

This question paper is divided into two sections:

Section A – this ONE question is compulsory and MUST be attempted
Section B – TWO questions ONLY to be attempted

Do NOT open this question paper until instructed by the supervisor.

Do NOT record any of your answers on the question paper.

This question paper must not be removed from the examination hall.

SECTION A – This ONE question is compulsory and MUST be attempted

Question 1

The following draft financial statements relate to Zippy, a public limited company. Zippy is a manufacturing company but also has a wide portfolio of investment properties. Zippy has investments in Ginny and Boo, both public limited companies.

DRAFT STATEMENTS OF PROFIT OR LOSS AND OTHER COMPREHENSIVE INCOME
FOR THE YEAR ENDED 30 JUNE 20X6

	Zippy	*Ginny*	*Boo*
	$m	$m	$m
Revenue	420	132	90
Cost of sales	(304)	(76)	(72)
Gross profit	116	56	18
Investment income	42	19	5
Administrative costs	(22)	(12)	(18)
Other expenses	(34)	(18)	(15)
Operating profit	102	45	(10)
Net finance costs	(2)	(6)	(9)
Profit before tax	100	39	(19)
Income tax expense	(30)	(7)	3
Profit for the year	70	32	(16)
Other comprehensive income			
Items that will not be reclassified to profit or loss:			
Gain on property revaluation	14	16	–
Total comprehensive income for year	84	48	(16)

The following information is relevant to the preparation of the group statement of profit or loss and other comprehensive income.

(i) On 1 July 20X4, Zippy acquired 60% of the equity interests of Ginny, a public limited company. The purchase consideration comprised cash of $90 million and the fair value of the identifiable net assets acquired was $114 million at that date. Zippy uses the 'full goodwill' method for all acquisitions and the fair value of the non-controlling interest (NCI) in Ginny was $50 million on 1 July 20X4. Goodwill had been reviewed annually for impairment and no impairment was deemed necessary.

(ii) Zippy disposed of a 20% equity interest in Ginny on 31 March 20X6 for a cash consideration of $44 million. The remaining 40% holding had a fair value of $62 million and Zippy exercised significant influence over Ginny following the disposal. Zippy accounts for investments in subsidiaries at cost and has included a gain in investment income of $14 million within its individual financial statements to reflect the disposal. The net assets of Ginny had a fair value of $118 million at 1 July 20X5 and this was reflected in the carrying amounts of the net assets. All gains and losses of Ginny have accrued evenly throughout the year. The disposal is not classified as a separate major line of business or geographical operation.

(iii) Zippy acquired 80% of the equity interests of Boo, a public limited company, on 30 June 20X4. The purchase consideration was cash of $60 million. The fair value of the NCI was calculated as $12 million at this date. Due to a tight reporting deadline, the fair value of the identifiable net assets at acquisition had not been finalised by the time the financial statements for the year ended 30 June 20X4 were published. Goodwill of $28 million was calculated using the carrying amount of the net assets of Boo. The fair value of the identifiable net assets of Boo was finalised on 31 December 20X4 as $54 million. The excess of the fair value of the identifiable net assets at acquisition is due to plant which had a remaining useful life of five years at the acquisition date.

Due to the losses of Boo, an impairment review was undertaken at 30 June 20X6. It was decided that goodwill had reduced in value by 10%. Goodwill impairments are charged to other expenses.

(iv) Zippy holds properties for investment purposes. At 1 July 20X5, Zippy held a 10-floor office block at a fair value of $90 million with a remaining useful life of 15 years. The first floor was occupied by Zippy's staff and the second floor was let to Boo free of charge. The other eight floors were all let to unconnected third parties at a normal commercial rent. It was estimated that the fair value of the office block was $96 million at 30 June 20X6. Zippy has a policy of restating all land and buildings to fair value at each reporting date. The only accounting entries for the year ended 30 June 20X6 in relation to this office block have been to correctly include the rental income in profit or loss. It can be assumed that each floor is of equal size and value. Depreciation is charged to administrative costs.

(v) On During April 20X6, an explosion at a different office block caused substantial damage and it was estimated that the fair value fell from $20 million at 30 June 20X5 to $14 million at 30 June 20X6. Zippy has estimated that costs of $3 million would be required to repair the block but is unsure whether to carry out the repairs or whether to sell the block for a reduced price. The property has been left in the financial statements at a value of $20 million. A provision of $3 million for the repair costs was charged to other expenses.

(vi) The following information relates to Zippy's defined benefit pension scheme:

	$m
Net plan assets at 30 June 20X5	14
Service cost for year ended 30 June 20X6	10
Contributions into the scheme	8
Discount rate at 1 July 20X5	10%
Discount rate at 1 30 June 20X6	12%
Re-measurement gains in year ended 30 June 20X6	4

No entries have been entered in the financial statements except that the contributions into the scheme have been correctly added to the pension scheme's assets.

(vii) On 1 January 20X6, Zippy entered into a contract to sell 10,000 units of a new product, the Whizoo, to a customer for $1,000 per unit. It was agreed that if the customer ordered an additional 5,000 units, a volume discounted price of $950 per unit would apply. 6,000 units were manufactured and delivered in the four months to 30 April 20X6.

Minor defects were discovered in the first 6,000 units due to an error in the manufacturing process and it was agreed that a credit note of $40 per unit would be issued as compensation. Zippy and the customer agreed to net this amount off against subsequent payments for future orders. A further 7,000 units had been manufactured and delivered by 30 June 20X6 without any defects. Zippy has included $6 million in revenue (6,000 x $1,000) for the first 6,000 units but has not recorded any additional revenue, as the directors are unsure of the correct accounting treatment.

Required

(a) Prepare the consolidated statement of comprehensive income for the Zippy Group for the year ended 30 June 20X6. **(35 marks)**

(b) Zippy The directors of Zippy have heard that under alternative accounting practices actuarial gains and losses (the remeasurement component) can be immediately recognised in profit or loss or deferred using an applicable systematic method. Additionally, they have heard that past service cost can be recognised initially in other comprehensive income and then recycled to profit or loss. The directors are unsure as to the differences between other comprehensive income and profit or loss and the rationale as to why some gains can be and others cannot be recycled.

Required

With reference to pension schemes, discuss the differences between other comprehensive income and profit or loss and the rationale as to why some gains and losses can be and others cannot be recycled to equity. Include in your answer a brief discussion of the benefits of immediate recognition of the remeasurement component under IAS 19 *Employee benefits*. **(8 marks)**

(c) On 1 July 20X6, there was an amendment to Zippy's defined benefit scheme whereby the promised pension entitlement was increased from 10% of final salary to 15%. A bonus is paid to the directors each year which is based upon the operating profit margin of Zippy. The directors of Zippy are unhappy that there is inconsistency on the presentation of gains and losses in relation to defined benefit schemes. Additionally, they believe that as the pension scheme is not an integral part of the operating activities of Zippy, it is misleading to include the gains and losses in profit or loss. They therefore propose to change their accounting policy so that all gains and losses on the pension scheme are recognised in other comprehensive income. They believe that this will make the financial statements more consistent, more understandable and can be justified on the grounds of fair presentation.

Required

Discuss the accounting and ethical implications arising from the proposed change of accounting policy on Zippy's defined benefit scheme. **(7 marks)**

(Total = 50 marks)

Section B – TWO questions ONLY to be attempted

Question 2

(a) Suntory, a private limited company, has two overseas subsidiaries, Maior and Minor. Suntory is based in a country which has a currency of the dollar. Maior is based in Japan where the currency is the yen. Minor is based in Portugal which has the currency of the euro. Suntory and Minor sell golf clothing and Maior sells golf equipment. Maior and Minor are financed by the provision of long-term loans at market interest rates in dollars from Suntory.

Suntory's sales are mainly in its own jurisdiction, and are priced and collected in dollars. The legal requirements and the business environment in Suntory's jurisdiction determines the pricing of Suntory's products. Goods and services are sourced locally and paid in dollars but occasionally the entity trades in small amounts in other currencies.

Maior conducts its business with significant autonomy from Suntory as it manufactures golf equipment which it sells mainly in Japan in yen. Local management determines prices based upon the local legal and business conditions. Most raw materials and labour are sourced from local suppliers with a small amount of specialised material sourced from China. Maior sells a small amount of golf clothing, which it purchases from Suntory and pays in dollars.

Minor imports golf clothing manufactured by Suntory and pays Suntory in dollars. All other operating expenses are paid in euros. Suntory gives Minor a discount on the normal selling price of its products. Minor sells its products mainly in Portugal in euros. The local legal and business conditions and the cost of the product from Suntory dictate the pricing of products but all prices have to be agreed by Suntory. At the month end, an intra-group dividend is paid in cash to Suntory in euros which amounts to the net profit made by Minor for the month.

The directors require advice on the determination of each of the functional currencies of Suntory, Maior and Minor.

(9 marks)

(b) On 1 December 20X2, Suntory acquired a trademark, Golfo, for a line of golf equipment for $3 million. Initially, Suntory expected to continue marketing and receiving cash flows from the golf product-line indefinitely. However, because of the difficulty in determining its useful life, Suntory decided to amortise the trademark over a 10-year life, using the straight-line method. In December 20X5, a competitor unexpectedly revealed a technological breakthrough which is expected to result in a product which, when launched, will significantly reduce the demand for the Golfo product-line. The demand for the Golfo product-line is expected to remain high until May 20X8, when the competitor is expected to launch its new product.

At 30 November 20X6, the end of the financial year, Suntory assessed the recoverable amount of the trademark at $500,000 and intends to continue manufacturing Golfo products until 31 May 20X8.

The directors of Suntory require advice as to how to deal with the trademark in the financial statements for the year ended 30 November 20X6. **(7 marks)**

(c) In At 30 November 20X6, three people own the shares of Suntory. The finance director owns 60%, and the operations director owns 30%. The third owner is a passive investor who does not help manage the entity. All ordinary shares carry equal voting rights. The wife of the finance director is the sales director of Suntory. Their son is currently undertaking an internship with Suntory and receives a salary of $30,000 per annum, which is normal compensation.

The finance director and sales director have set up an investment company, Baleel. They jointly own Baleel and their shares in Baleel will eventually be transferred to their son when he has finished the internship with Suntory.

In addition, on 1 June 20X6 Suntory obtained a bank loan of $500,000 at a fixed interest rate of 6% per annum. The loan is to be repaid on 30 November 20X7. Repayment of the principal and interest is secured by a guarantee registered in favour of the bank against the private home of the finance director.

The directors of Suntory require advice on the identification and disclosure of the company's related parties in preparing its separate financial statements for the year ending 30 November 20X6.margin. **(7 marks)**

Required

Discuss the advice which should be given to Suntory in each of the above cases with reference to relevant International Financial Reporting Standards.

Note. The mark allocation is shown against each of the three issues above.

Professional marks will be awarded in Question 2 for clarity and quality of the presentation. **(2 marks)**

(Total = 25 marks)

Question 3

(a) Evolve is a real estate company, which is listed on the stock exchange and has a year end of 31 August. On 21 August 20X6, Evolve undertook a scrip (bonus) issue where the shareholders of Evolve received certain rights. The shareholders are able to choose between:

(i) Receiving newly issued shares of Evolve, which could be traded on 30 September 20X6, or

(ii) Transferring their rights back to Evolve by 10 September 20X6 for a fixed cash price which would be paid on 20 September 20X6

In the financial statements at 31 August 20X6, Evolve believed that the criteria for the recognition of a financial liability as regards the second option were not met at 31 August 20X6 because it was impossible to reliably determine the full amount to be paid, until 10 September 20X6. Evolve felt that the transferring of the rights back to Evolve was a put option on its own equity, which would lead to recording changes in fair value in profit or loss in the next financial year. Evolve disclosed the transaction as a non-adjusting event after the reporting period.

(8 marks)

(b) At 31 August 20X6, Evolve controlled a wholly owned subsidiary, Resource, whose only assets were land and buildings, which were all measured in accordance with International Financial Reporting Standards. On 1 August 20X6, Evolve published a statement stating that a binding offer for the sale of Resource had been made and accepted and, at that date, the sale was expected to be completed by 31 August 20X6. The non-current assets of Resource were measured at the lower of their carrying amount or fair value less costs to sell at 31 August 20X6, based on the selling price in the binding offer. This measurement was in accordance with IFRS 5 *Non-current assets held for sale and discontinued operations*. However, Evolve did not classify the non-current assets of Resource as held for sale in the financial statements at 31 August 20X6 because there were uncertainties regarding the negotiations with the buyer and a risk that the agreement would not be finalised. There was no disclosure of these uncertainties and the original agreement was finalised on 20 September 20X6. **(9 marks)**

(c) Evolve operates in a jurisdiction with a specific tax regime for listed real estate companies. Upon adoption of this tax regime, the entity has to pay a single tax payment based on the unrealised gains of its investment properties. Evolve purchased Monk whose only asset was an investment property for $10 million. The purchase price of Monk was below the market value of the investment property, which was $14 million, and Evolve chose to account for the investment property under the cost model. However, Evolve considered that the transaction constituted a 'bargain purchase' under IFRS 3 *Business combinations*. As a result, Evolve accounted for the potential gain of $4 million in profit or loss and increased the 'cost' of the investment property to $14 million. At the same time, Evolve opted for the specific tax regime for the newly acquired investment property and agreed to pay the corresponding tax of $1 million. Evolve considered that the tax payment qualifies as an expenditure necessary to bring the property to the condition necessary for its operations, and therefore was directly attributable to the acquisition of the property. Hence, the tax payment was capitalised and the value of the investment property was stated at $15 million.

(6 marks)

Required

Advise Evolve on how the above transactions should be correctly dealt with in its financial statements with reference to relevant International Financial Reporting Standards.

Note. The mark allocation is shown against each of the three issues above.

Professional marks will be awarded in Question 3 for clarity and quality of presentation. **(2 marks)**

(Total = 25 marks)

Question 4

The International Accounting Standards Board (IASB) is undertaking a broad-based initiative to explore how disclosures in IFRS financial reporting can be improved. The Disclosure Initiative is made up of a number of implementation and research projects. The IASB has decided that the project should include a discussion on whether the definition of materiality should be changed and whether IAS 1 *Presentation of financial statements* should include additional guidance which clarifies the key characteristics of materiality. Materiality is a matter which has been debated extensively in the context of many forms of reporting, including the International Integrated Reporting Framework. There are difficulties in applying the concept of materiality in practice when preparing the financial statements and it is thought that these difficulties contribute to a disclosure problem, namely, that there is both too much irrelevant information in financial statements and not enough relevant information. Further, the IASB has published for public comment an Exposure Draft of proposed amendments to IAS 7 *Statement of cash flows*. The proposal responds to requests from investors for improved disclosures about an entity's financing activities and its cash and cash equivalents balances.

Required

(a) (i) Discuss the current definition of materiality and how the current application of the concept of materiality may be leading to a reduction in the clarity and understandability of financial statements. **(7 marks)**

(ii) Discuss how the concepts of materiality would be used in applying the International Integrated Reporting Framework. **(4 marks)**

(iii) Discuss the current issues with IAS 7 *Statement of cash flows* and briefly describe the proposed amendments to IAS 7 set out in the recent Exposure Draft. **(7 marks)**

Professional marks will be awarded in Part (a) for clarity and quality of presentation. **(2 marks)**

(b) Sanchera, a listed company, has prepared a statement of cash flows for the year ended 31 August 20X6. In financing activities, it has shown an increase in long-term borrowings to $140 million and an increase in the capital element of lease liabilities to $17 million. At 1 September 20X5, Sanchera had shown in its financial statements long-term borrowings of $50 million and the capital element of lease liabilities at $5 million. During the financial year, Sanchera has taken out a long-term loan with a financial institution of $55 million and had acquired Pecuna, a listed company, for $150 million on 1 July 20X6. Pecuna had a long-term loan of $35 million at acquisition. Further, Sanchera had taken out lease liabilities totalling $15 million and had paid $3 million off the capital element of the lease liabilities. Sanchera showed interest paid on lease liabilities of $5 million in operating activities. Finally, Sanchera had an overdraft with the bank of $2 million.

Required

Show the note to the statement of cash flows, which would be required under the Exposure Draft of proposed amendments to IAS 7, which sets out the components of financing activities. **(5 marks)**

(Total = 25 marks)

Answers

DO NOT TURN THIS PAGE UNTIL YOU HAVE COMPLETED THE MOCK EXAM

A PLAN OF ATTACK

Managing your nerves

As you turn the pages to start this exam a number of thoughts are likely to cross your mind. At best, examinations cause anxiety so it is important to stay focused on your task for the next three hours and fifteen minutes! Developing an awareness of what is going on emotionally within you may help you manage your nerves. Remember, you are unlikely to banish the flow of adrenaline, but the key is to harness it to help you work steadily and quickly through your answers.

Working through this mock exam will help you develop the exam stamina you will need to keep going for three hours and fifteen minutes.

Managing your time

Planning and time management are two of the key skills which complement the technical knowledge you need to succeed. To keep yourself on time, do not be afraid to jot down your target completion times for each question, perhaps next to the title of the question on the paper.

Focusing on scoring marks

When completing written answers, remember to communicate the critical points, which represent marks, and avoid padding and waffle. Sometimes it is possible to analyse a long sentence into more than one point. Always try to maximise the mark potential of what you write.

As you read through the questions, jot down on the question paper, any points you think you might forget. There is nothing more upsetting than coming out of an exam having forgotten to write a point you knew!

Also remember you can only score marks for what is on paper; you must write down enough to help the ACCA examination/examining team to give you marks!

Structure and signpost your answers

To help you answer the ACCA examination/examining team's requirements, highlight as you read through the paper the key words and phrases in the ACCA examination/examining team's requirements.

Also, where possible try to use headings and subheadings, to give a logical and easy-to-follow structure to your response. A well structured and signposted answer is more likely to convince the ACCA examination/examining team that you know your subject.

Your approach

This paper has two sections. The first section contains one long case study question which is compulsory. The second has three questions and you must answer two of them.

You have a choice.

- Read through and answer the Section A question before moving on to Section B.
- Go through Section B and select the two questions you will attempt. Then go back and answer the question in Section A first.
- Select the two questions in Section B, answer them and then go back to Section A.

Time spent at the start of each question confirming the requirements and producing a plan for the answers is time well spent.

Question selection

When selecting the two questions from Section B make sure that you read through all of the requirements. It is painful to answer part (a) of a question and then realise that parts (b) and (c) are beyond you, by then it is too late to change your mind and do another question.

When reviewing the requirements look at how many marks have been allocated to each part. This will give you an idea of how detailed your answer must be.

Generally, you need to be aware of your strengths and weaknesses and select accordingly.

Doing the exam

Actually doing the exam is a personal experience. There is not a single *right way*. As long as you submit complete answers to question 1 and any two from questions 2 to 4 after the three hours are up, then your approach obviously works.

Looking through the paper

The compulsory question is a case study. It involves the preparation of a statement of profit or loss and other comprehensive income with a disposal and various adjustments. There are also written questions on recognition in the statements of financial performance and ethics. In Section B you have three questions on a variety of topics:

- Question 2 is a scenario question covering foreign currency, intangibles and related parties.
- Question 3 is a specialised industry question set in the property industry, and covering purchase of own equity, asset held for sale and investment property.
- Question 4 was the usual current issues question, this time covering materiality and changes to the statement of cash flows.

You only have to answer two out of these three questions. You don't have to pick your optional questions right now, but this brief overview should have convinced you that you have enough choice and variety to have a respectable go at Section B. So let's go back to the compulsory question in Section A.

Compulsory question

Part (a) requires a consolidated statement of profit or loss and other comprehensive income with a disposal (subsidiary to associate) part-way through the year and adjustments for fair values, investment property, defined benefit pension plan and revenue recognition. There is plenty of opportunity to pass, even if you don't get all the complexities. The main thing is to get the group structure right. Just keep going, set out your workings clearly, and above all make sure you complete the question. Part (b) is a discussion question on recognition in profit or loss versus other comprehensive income. Part (c) is an ethical question on manipulation of financial statements. Make sure you write something even if you're unsure, as credit will be given for valid arguments.

Optional questions

Deciding between the optional questions is obviously a personal matter – it depends how you have spent your study time.

In our opinion, you should choose Question 2, which is a gift. Part (a) in particular is a straightforward application of the IAS 21 functional currency principles. Question 3 is much harder, testing obscure topics in a challenging way, and best avoided. That leaves Question 4. Part (b) is challenging, requiring detail of a Exposure Draft, but you are given the figures you need to produce a reconciliation, even if it is not quite right. In part (a) there is more scope to grab some easy marks as it is fairly subjective.

Use the information in the scenario

It is there for a purpose! Many students lose marks because they do not do this.

Allocating your time

The golden rule is always allocate your time according to the marks for the question in total and for the parts of the question. But be sensible. If, for example, you have committed yourself to answering Question 2, but are stuck on the impairment, you may be better off trying to pick up some extra marks on the questions you can do.

Afterwards

Don't be tempted to do a post mortem on the paper with your colleagues. It will only worry you and them and it's unlikely you'll be able to remember exactly what you wrote anyway. If you really can't resist going over the topics covered in the paper, allow yourself a maximum of half an hour's 'worry time', then put it out of your head! Relax as it's all out of your hands now!

Question 1

Text references. Disposals are covered in Chapter 14 of your Study Text. Pensions are covered in Chapter 4 and revenue in Chapter 1. Fair value is covered in Chapters 7 and 12. Ethical issues are covered in Chapter 2.

Top tips. Question 1 part (a) was a consolidated statement of profit or loss and other comprehensive income with a disposal part-way through the year in which control is lost but significant influence retained. It is important to get the group structure right. Adjustments were required for the disposal (including goodwill and loss on disposal calculations), fair values, investment property, defined benefit pension plan and revenue recognition. You also needed to 'work backwards' with regard to the goodwill on the other subsidiary to determine what the net assets acquired would have been, and then move on to calculate what it should have been.

Part 1(b) required a discussion of recognition in OCI versus profit or loss, specifically in the context of pension plans. It is very important that you relate your answer to pension plans, rather than producing a general discussion only, although some general points need to be made. Part (c), as usual, contained an ethical issue – as in a number of past questions, the issue concerned the potential manipulation of financial statements to achieve a result that would maximise a bonus. Again, the context was the pension plan. It is important to tailor your answer to the requirements in discussion parts of questions – ACCA examination/examining team has criticised candidates in the past for failure to *apply* their knowledge.

Easy marks. Once you have established the group structure, there are some very easy marks to be had for multiplying numbers given in the question by $^9/_{12}$. Part (b) allows for flexibility in the arguments made, and manipulation of financial statements (Part (c)) has been tested frequently, so you should have been able to make enough valid arguments to secure a pass.

Examiner's comment. This was not available at the time of writing.

Marking scheme

		Marks
(a)	Revenue	6
	Cost of sales	2
	Investment income	5
	Ginny disposal	6
	Ginny associate	2
	Boo and impairment	3
	Provision	2
	Pension	4
	Non-controlling interest	4
	Presentation of OCI into reclassified/not reclassified to profit or loss	1
		35
(b)	1 mark for each point to a maximum of	8
(c)	1 mark for each point to a maximum of	7
		50

(a) ZIPPY GROUP
STATEMENT OF PROFIT OR LOSS AND OTHER COMPREHENSIVE INCOME
FOR THE YEAR ENDED 30 JUNE 20X6

	$m
Revenue: 420 + (132 × $^9/_{12}$) + 90 + 6.8 (W9) – 0.2 (W9)	615.60
Cost of sales: 304 + (76 × $^9/_{12}$) + 72 + 2 (W4)	(435.00)
Gross profit	180.60
Investment income: 42 + (19 × $^9/_{12}$) + 5 – 14 (W3) + 4.8 (W6) – 6 (W7)	46.05
Administrative costs: 22 + (12 × $^9/_{12}$) + 18 + 10(W8) + 1.2 (W6)	(60.20)
Other expenses: 34 + (18 × $^9/_{12}$) + 15 + 1.8 (W4) – 3 (W7)	(61.30)
Operating profit	105.15
Net finance costs: 2 + (6 × $^9/_{12}$) + 9 + 1.4 (W8)	(16.90)
Group loss on disposal (W3)	(8.00)
Share of profit of associate: 32 × $^3/_{12}$ × 40%	3.20
Profit before tax	83.45
Income tax expense: 30 + (7 × $^9/_{12}$) – 3	(32.25)
Profit for the year	51.20
Other comprehensive income (items that will not be reclassified to profit or loss)	
Gain on property revaluation: 14 + (16 × $^9/_{12}$) + 2.4 (W6)	28.40
Remeasurement of defined benefit pension plan (W8)	4.00
Share of profit of other comprehensive income of associate: 16 × $^3/_{12}$ × 40%	1.60
Other comprehensive income for the year	34.00
Total comprehensive income for the year	85.20
Profit attributable to:	
Owners of the parent (bal. fig.)	45.60
Non-controlling interests (W2)	5.60
	51.20
Total comprehensive income attributable to:	
Owners of the parent	74.80
Non-controlling interests (W2)	10.40
	85.20

Workings

1 *Group structure*

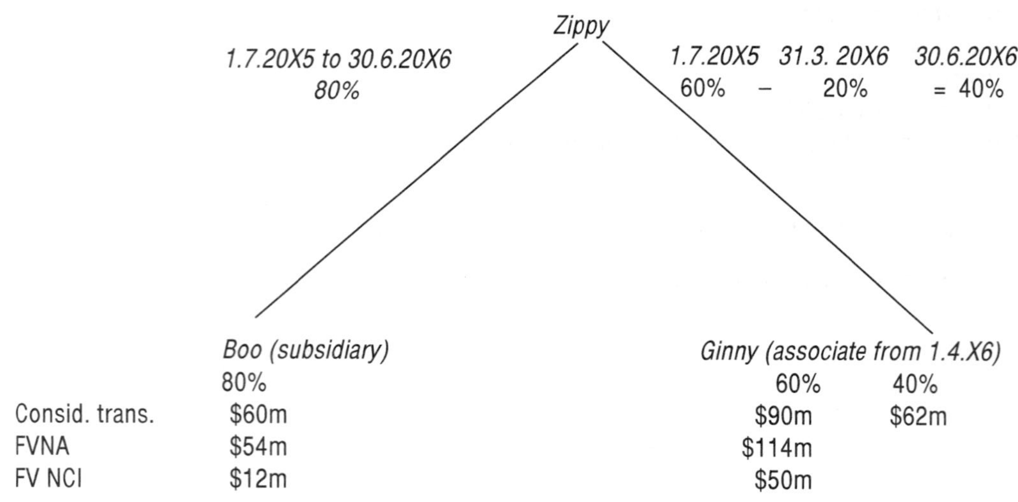

Timeline

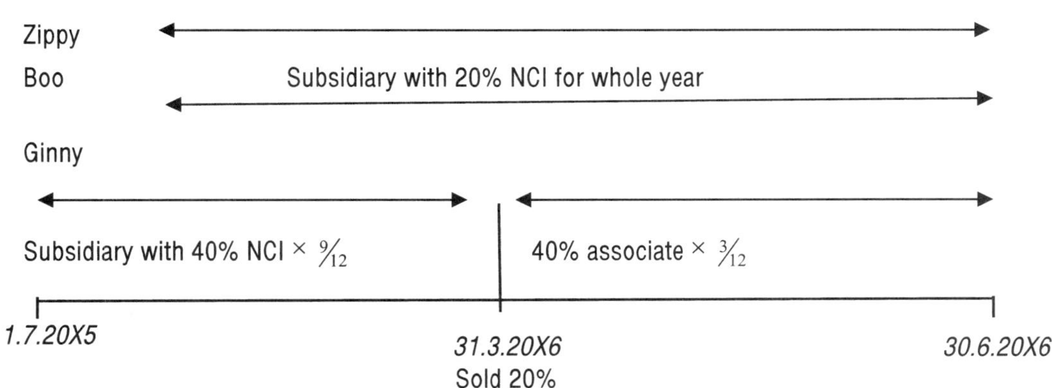

Gain/loss on disposal

2 *Non-controlling interests*

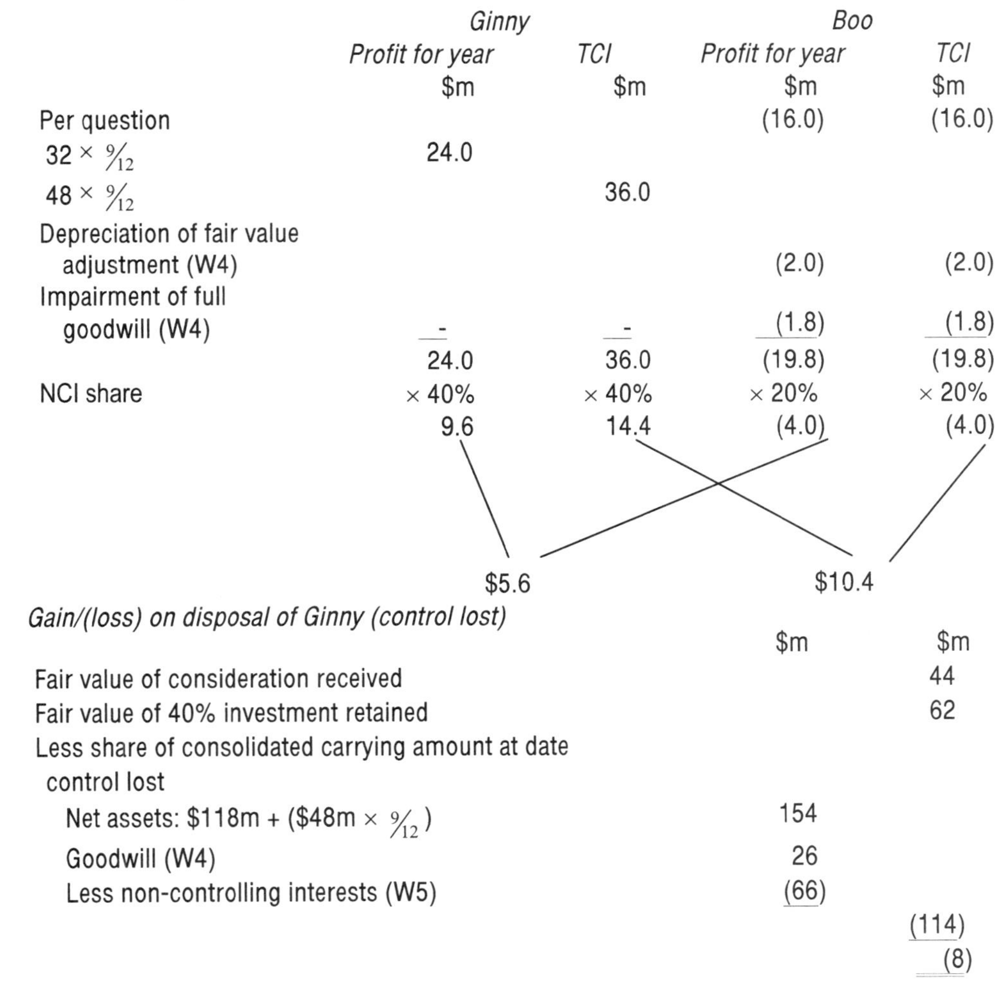

	Ginny		*Boo*	
	Profit for year	*TCI*	*Profit for year*	*TCI*
	$m	$m	$m	$m
Per question			(16.0)	(16.0)
32 × $\frac{9}{12}$	24.0			
48 × $\frac{9}{12}$		36.0		
Depreciation of fair value adjustment (W4)			(2.0)	(2.0)
Impairment of full goodwill (W4)	-	-	(1.8)	(1.8)
	24.0	36.0	(19.8)	(19.8)
NCI share	× 40%	× 40%	× 20%	× 20%
	9.6	14.4	(4.0)	(4.0)

$5.6 $10.4

3 *Gain/(loss) on disposal of Ginny (control lost)*

	$m	$m
Fair value of consideration received		44
Fair value of 40% investment retained		62
Less share of consolidated carrying amount at date control lost		
Net assets: $118m + ($48m × $\frac{9}{12}$)	154	
Goodwill (W4)	26	
Less non-controlling interests (W5)	(66)	
		(114)
		(8)

Note. The gain on disposal in the individual financial statements of Zippy would have been $44m – ($90m × 20%/60%) = $14m. This was included in Zippy's investment income and must be removed in arriving at consolidated investment income.

4 *Goodwill*

	Ginny	Boo
	$m	$m
Consideration transferred	90.0	60.0
Fair value of non-controlling interest	50.0	12.0
Fair value of net assets	(114.0)	(44.0)β
	26.0	28.0 (per qu.)
Effect of revaluation adjustment: $54m (per qu.) – $44m*	–	(10.0)
	–	18.0
Impairment loss: 10%	–	(1.8)
	26.0	16.2

***Note.** The final value of the identifiable net assets is $10m higher than as initially calculated, so goodwill is reduced by $10m. Additional depreciation should be charged to cost of sales of ($10m/5) = $2m. Note that the fair values were finalised within the initial accounting period (a maximum of twelve months from acquisition) so the adjustment is treated retrospectively Goodwill impairment of $1·8m is to be charged to other expenses.

5 *Non-controlling interests of Ginny(SOFP) at disposal*

	$m
Non-controlling interest at acquisition(W4)	50
NCI share of PARR to 31 March 20X6:	
($154m (W3) – $114m) × 40%	16
	66

6 *Investment property: ten-floor office block*

	Investment property	Owner occupied	Total
	$m	$m	$m
1 July 20X5: 90 × 8/10	72.0	18.0	90.0
90 × 2/10			
Depn. $18m/15 years	-	(1.2) (P/L)	(1.2)
	72.0	16.8	88.8
Fair value gain β	4.8 (P/L)	2.4 (OCI)	7.2
Fair value at 30 June 20X6: 96 × 8/10	76.8		
96 × 2/10		19.2	
			96.0

7 *Other investment property*

	$m
Fair value at 30 June 20X5	20
	(6) (P/L)
∴ Fair value loss β	
Fair value at 30 June 20X6	
	14

The provision of $3m should be reversed as there is no obligating event to carry out the repairs.

DEBIT	Provision	$3m	
CREDIT	Other expenses		$3m

8 *Defined benefit pension plan*

	$m
Net deficit at 30 June 20X5	14.0
Service costs for y/e 30 June 20X5	(10.0) (P/L)
Net interest on net defined benefit obligation: 14 × 10%	(1.4) (P/L)
Contributions to scheme	8.0
Remeasurement gains	4.0 (OCI)
Net obligation c/d 30 June 20X6	14.6

Service costs and interest will be charged to profit or loss for the year, service costs to administrative costs and interest to finance costs. Remeasurement gains will be credited to other comprehensive income for the year.

9 *Revenue recognition: Whizoo*

Manufacturing defects:

The $40 credit per unit is a revision to the transaction price for the first 6,000 units sold. Therefore there should be a reduction in revenue equal to (6,000 × $40) $0·24m for the first 6,000 units sold.

DEBIT	Revenue (6,000 × $40)	$0.24m	
CREDIT	Receivables		$0.24m

Further 7,000 units:

The negotiated price of $950 per unit is dependent on the purchase of the initial 10,000 units. Therefore it does not meet the conditions to be accounted for as a separate contract. Instead it is treated as a cancellation of the old contract together with the creation of a new contract. The revenue attributable to the further 7,000 units manufactured will therefore be calculated using a weighted average price as follows.

$$\frac{(4,000 \times \$1,000) + (5,000 \times \$950)}{(4,000 + 5,000)} = \$972 \text{ per item}$$

The additional revenue to be accrued for these 7,000 units is (7,000 × $972) = $6·8m.

DEBIT	Receivables (7,000 × $972)	$6.8m	
CREDIT	Revenue		$6.8m

No revenue can yet be included for the 2,000 units which have not been manufactured as at 30 June 20X6 as Zippy has not satisfied its performance obligation. The net increase to the revenue of Zippy should be ($6·8m – $0·24m) $6·6m.

(b) **Other comprehensive income and profit or loss**

Profit or loss includes all items of income and expense (including reclassification adjustments) except those items of income and expense which are recognised in other comprehensive income (OCI) as required or permitted by IFRS. However, there is a general lack of agreement about which items should be presented in profit or loss and in OCI. Currently under IFRS there is a rules – based approach, leaving it to each individual standard to define where each gain or loss should be presented. For example, with pension schemes the service cost component, including past service cost, must be immediately recognised in profit or loss whereas the remeasurement component is recognised as other comprehensive income, an item not to be reclassified to the profit or loss. (The directors are incorrect in believing that the remeasurement component may be immediately recognised in profit or loss or deferred using an applicable systematic method.) With no clear guiding principles of where gains and losses are reported, it is felt that anything controversial has been dumped into OCI. This would enable key ratios such as price/earnings to be free from distortion from less reliable gains and losses included within OCI.

There are several arguments for and against reclassification of gains and losses. If reclassification ceased, there would be no need to define profit or loss and presentation decisions could be left to each individual IFRS. It is argued that reclassification protects the integrity of profit or loss and provides users with relevant information. Errors within actuarial assumptions about life expectancy, wage inflation, service lives as well as differences between actual and expected returns are all included within the remeasurement component. It can be argued that there is no correlation between such items and the underlying performance of an entity. It could therefore be justified to classify the remeasurement component as an item which must not be recycled to profit or loss.

Arguments against recycling include that it adds unnecessary complexity to financial reporting and could lead to earnings management. Recycling could be easily misunderstood as essentially the same gain gets reported twice, once within equity and once within profit or loss. Additionally it is likely that there will be a mismatch on recycling as the gains or losses may be reported in a different period to when the underlying change in value of the asset or liability took place. The IASB is proposing that profit or loss should provide the primary source of information on the return of the entity. Other comprehensive income should be used only if it makes profit or loss more meaningful for the users.

Actuarial gains and losses can vary significantly from one year to the next. The immediate recognition may create volatility within the statement of financial position and other comprehensive income. It is, however, important that users are fully aware as to the extent of an entity's pension scheme obligations. This may not be evident if there is a deferral of the remeasurement component. It will not be possible to smooth gains and losses over the working lives of employees. It can be argued therefore that the immediate recognition leads to greater transparency of the financial statements.

(c) **Ethical implications of change of accounting policy**

IAS 8 *Accounting policies, changes in accounting estimates and errors* only permits a change in accounting policy if the change is: (i) required by an IFRS or (ii) results in the financial statements providing reliable and more relevant information about the effects of transactions, other events or conditions on the entity's financial position, financial performance or cash flows. A retrospective adjustment is required unless the change arises from a new accounting policy with transitional arrangements to account for the change. It is possible to depart from the requirements of IFRS but only in the extremely rare circumstances where compliance would be so misleading that it would conflict with the overall objectives of the financial statements. Practically this override is rarely, if ever, invoked.

IAS 19 *Employee benefits* requires all gains and losses on a defined benefit scheme to be recognised in profit or loss except for the remeasurement component which must be recognised in other comprehensive income. The directors' proposals cannot be justified on the grounds of fair presentation. The directors have an ethical responsibility to produce financial statements which are a true representation of the entity's performance and comply with all accounting standards.

There is a clear self-interest threat arising from the bonus scheme. The directors' change in policy appears to be motivated by an intention to overstate operating profit to maximise their bonus potential. The amendment to the pension scheme is a past service cost. This is likely to be fairly substantial and must be expensed to profit or loss. This would therefore be detrimental to the operating profits of Zippy and depress any potential bonus. Additionally, it appears that the directors wish to manipulate other aspects of the pension scheme such as the current service cost and, since the scheme is in deficit, the net finance cost. The directors are deliberately manipulating the presentation of these items by recording them in equity rather than in profit or loss. Such treatment is against the ACCA ethical principles of objectivity, integrity and professional behaviour. The directors should be reminded of their ethical responsibilities and must be dissuaded from implementing the proposed change in policy.

Question 2

Text reference. IAS 21 is covered in Chapter 16 of your Study Text, IAS 38 in Chapter 3 and IAS 24 in Chapter 11.

Top tips. Part (a) requires knowledge of the IAS 21 requirements relating to functional currency and their application to two scenarios, one clear cut and one less so. Part (b) required discussion and calculation of the amortisation and subsequent impairment of a trademark. IAS 38 is covered in your earlier studies, but the emphasis at P2 is on application. Part (c) is on related parties. You would be advised to jot down a plan or diagram before launching into your answer.

Easy marks. Part (a) is a 'gift' - the first part is textbook knowledge and the scenarios provide a lot of clues.

Examiner's comment. Examiner's comments were not available at the time of going to print.

Marking scheme

		Marks
(a)	1 mark per point up to maximum	9
(b)	1 mark per point up to maximum	7
(c)	1 mark per point up to maximum	7
Professional marks		2
		25

(a) **Foreign subsidiaries**

IAS 21 *The Effects of changes on foreign exchange rates* states that the functional currency is the currency of the primary economic environment in which the entity operates, which is normally the one in which it primarily generates and expends cash. An entity's management should consider the following factors (primary indicators) in determining its functional currency:

(i) The currency which mainly influences sales prices for goods and services

(ii) The currency of the country whose competitive forces and regulations mainly determine the sales prices of goods and services, and

(iii) The currency which mainly influences labour, material and other costs of providing goods and services

Further factors (secondary indicators), which may also provide evidence of an entity's functional currency, are the currency in which funds from financing activities are generated and in which receipts from operating activities are retained. Other factors include the autonomy of a foreign operation from the reporting entity, the level of transactions between the entities, whether the foreign operation generates sufficient cash flows to meet its debt obligations, and whether its cash flows directly affect those of the reporting entity.

Suntory

It appears that the dollar is the functional currency of Suntory. Suntory's sales prices are determined by legal requirements and the business environment in its own jurisdiction and the dollar is the currency in which the sales prices are denominated and settled. The operations are sourced locally in dollars. There is a small amount of trading in other currencies and Minor pays a dividend on a monthly basis in euros but the main currency of its operations is the dollar, which indicates that the dollar is the functional currency of the parent. Suntory need not consider the secondary factors.

Maior

The factors in the scenario seem to indicate the yen as being the functional currency of Maior. The sales prices for the subsidiary's golf equipment are determined by local legal and business conditions in yen. The yen is the currency in which those sales prices are denominated and settled. Some transactions are undertaken with China but these are relatively small. Although Maior sometimes imports and sells its parent's products, this is only a small part of its business activity. The yen is also used to pay the major operating costs. Thus without evidence to the contrary, the yen is the functional currency of Maior and Maior need not consider the secondary factors.

Minor

Minor imports golf clothing manufactured by Suntory and pays the parent in dollars. Suntory discounts the price paid by Minor for its products, which are sold in euros.

The prices are influenced both by the local legal and business conditions and the cost of the product purchased from Suntory. Also all price changes have to be approved by Suntory. Thus the exchange rate between the dollar and the euro will affect the pricing of the product. All other operating expenses are incurred locally and paid in euros. A dividend amounting to the net profit for the month is paid in euros to Suntory. The determination of the functional currency is not clear-cut.

The euro is the currency in which Minor's sales prices are set, denominated and settled. However, movements in the exchange rate between the euro and the dollar influence those selling prices. Minor's sales prices are also affected by the local legal and business conditions in Portugal. The costs of the products from Suntory are influenced by the dollar but all other costs of providing goods are in euros. As a result, the secondary factors should be considered.

Funds from financing activities are generated primarily in dollars and Minor keeps minimal cash reserves because any net profit is transferred to the parent in cash at the end of the month. Consequently, there is some support for the dollar as being the functional currency as Minor is not autonomous, transactions with the parent are a high proportion of the subsidiary's activities as Suntory is the subsidiary's only supplier and cash flows from the activities of Minor directly affect the cash flows of Suntory and are readily available for remittance to it. Thus it appears that the dollar is the functional currency of Minor.

(b) **Trademark**

IAS 38 *Intangible assets* states that the cost less residual value of an intangible asset with a finite useful life should be amortised on a systematic basis over that life, that the amortisation method should reflect the pattern of benefits and that it should be reviewed at least annually.

The amortisation method should be reviewed at least annually and, if the pattern of consumption of benefits has changed, the amortisation method should be changed prospectively as a change in estimate under IAS 8 *Accounting policies, changes in accounting estimates and errors.* Expected future reductions in sales could be indicative of a higher rate of consumption of the future economic benefits embodied in an asset. Hence, the trademark would be amortised over a 2·5-year period until May 20X8.

IAS 36 states that an entity should assess at the end of each reporting period whether there is any indication that an asset may be impaired. If any such indication exists, the entity should estimate the recoverable amount of the asset. Irrespective of whether there is any indication of impairment, an entity shall also test an intangible asset with an indefinite useful life or an intangible asset not yet available for use for impairment annually by comparing its carrying amount with its recoverable amount. This impairment test may be performed at any time during an annual period, provided it is performed at the same time every year. Thus, Suntory should test the trademark for impairment.

For the year ended 30 November 20X6

DEBIT Profit or loss (operating expenses) – amortisation of trademark	$840,000	
CREDIT Intangible asset (trademark) – accumulated amortisation		$840,000

To recognise the annual amortisation of the trademark during the period.

At 30 November 20X6

DEBIT Profit or loss (operating expenses) – impairment of trademark	$760,000	
CREDIT Intangible asset (finite life trademark) – impairment		$760,000

Workings

Cost of trademark $3m ÷ 10 years useful life = $300,000 amortisation per year. Therefore the carrying amount at 1 December 20X5 is ($3m cost less ($300,000 amortisation per year × 3 years since acquisition)) = $2·1m.

The useful life of the trademark is reduced to 2·5 years and therefore this amount has to be amortised over this period.

$2·1 m ÷ 2·5 years remaining useful life = $840,000 per year

Therefore the carrying amount at 30 November 20X6 is $3m cost less $900,000 less $840,000 = $1·26 million.

The recoverable amount is $500,000, so the impairment loss is $760,000.

(c) **Related parties**

IAS 24 *Related party disclosures* requires an entity's financial statements to contain the disclosures necessary to draw attention to the possibility that its financial position and profit or loss may have been affected by the existence of related parties and by transactions and outstanding balances with such parties.

A person or a close member of that person's family is related to a reporting entity if that person:

(i) Has control or joint control over the reporting entity,

(ii) Has significant influence over the reporting entity; or

(iii) Is a member of the key management personnel of the reporting entity or of a parent of the reporting entity

With regards to Suntory, the finance director is a related party, as he owns more than half of the voting power (60%). In the absence of evidence to the contrary, he controls Suntory and is a member of the key management personnel. The sales director is also a related party of Suntory as she is a member of the key management personnel and is a close member (spouse) of the family of the finance director. Their son is a related party of Suntory as he is a close member (son) of their family. The operations director is also a related party as he owns more than 20% of the voting power in Suntory. In the absence of evidence to the contrary, the operations director has significant influence over Suntory and is a member of the key management personnel.

An entity is related to a reporting entity if the entity is controlled or jointly controlled by a person identified as a related party. Hence, Baleel is a related party of Suntory. Baleel is controlled by related parties, the finance and sales directors, for the benefit of a close member of their family, ie their son.

In the absence of evidence to the contrary, the third owner of the shares is not a related party. The person is a passive investor who does not appear to exert significant influence over Suntory. The loan from the bank, which has been guaranteed by the finance director, will be disclosed as such in the financial statements. Disclosure of personal guarantees given by directors in respect of borrowings by the reporting entity should be disclosed in the notes to the financial statements.

Question 3

Text reference. Specialised industries are covered in general terms in Chapter 20 of your Study Text. IAS 32 and IFRS 9 are covered in Chapter 7. IFRS 5 is covered in Chapter 15. IAS 16 and IAS 40 are covered in Chapter 3 and IAS 12 in Chapter 6.

Top tips. In most specialised industry questions, the standards examined are not necessarily specialised, but the context may be unfamiliar. However, in this question, the reverse is true - real estate is an easy context, but the issues are not easy. Part (a) is tricky. It asks whether a bonus issue to be settled in the future should be classified as a financial liability or equity. It had to be classified as a financial liability as there was a contractual obligation to deliver cash as a result of a put option to sell the rights back to the company. An event after the reporting perios provided additional evidence of the valuation. Part (b) is more mainstream. The directors had not classified the assets of a subsidiary as held for sale, even though the IFRS 5 criteria were met, on the grounds that they did not have a binding agreement to sell. However, this is not required for a sale to be considered 'highly probable' under IFRS 5, and so the assets should have been classified as held for sale. Part (c) required consideration of three issues. First, a gain arising where a subsidiary which was purchased at less than the market value of its sole asset should not be treated as a bargain purchase because this treatment is only available for a business combination, and the substance of the transaction was the purchase of an asset rather than a business combination. Second, the company wishes to use the cost model, the asset should have been recorded at cost, even if this is less than market value, so the potential gain should not have been recorded in profit or loss or added to the cost of the asset. Third, the deferred tax liability arising on the difference from market value should not be capitalised as it is not linked to bringing the asset to the condition necessary for its operations,

Easy marks. There are no easy marks in this question. Marks are not as difficult to earn in Part (b), as opposed to Parts (a) or (c).

Examiner's comment. Examiner's comments were not available at the time of going to print.

Marking scheme

		Marks
(a)	1 mark per point up to maximum	8
(b)	1 mark per point up to maximum	9
(c)	1 mark per point up to maximum	6
Professional marks		2
		25

(a) **Obligation to purchase own equity instruments**

A financial liability for the present value of the maximum amount payable to shareholders should be recognised in the financial statements as of 31 August 20X6. At 31 August 20X6, the rights are equivalent to a written put option because they represent for Evolve a purchase obligation which gives shareholders the right to sell the entity's own equity instruments for a fixed price. The fundamental principle of IAS 32 *Financial instruments: presentation* is that a financial instrument should be classified as either a financial liability or an equity instrument according to the substance of the contract, not its legal form, and the definitions of financial liability and equity instrument. IAS 32 states that a contract which contains an entity's obligation to purchase its own equity instruments gives rise to a financial liability, which should be recognised at the present value of its redemption amount. IAS 32 also states that a contractual obligation for an entity to purchase its own equity instruments gives rise to a financial liability for the present value of the redemption amount even if the obligation is conditional on the counterparty exercising a right to redeem, as is the case with the scrip issue of Evolve.

Evolve had set up the conditions for the share capital increase in August 20X6 and, therefore, the contract gave rise to financial liabilities from that date and Evolve should have recognised a financial liability for the present value of the maximum amount payable to shareholders in its financial statements for the year ended 31 August 20X6. A non-adjusting event under IAS 10 *Events after the reporting period* is an event after the reporting period which is indicative of a condition which arose after the end of the reporting period. However, it could be argued that the transferring of the free allocation rights back to Evolve is in fact an adjusting event as it is an event after the reporting period which provides further evidence of conditions which existed at the end of the reporting period.

(b) **Classification as held for sale**

The non-current assets of Resource should have been presented as held for sale in the financial statements, in accordance with IFRS 5 *Non-current assets held for sale and discontinued operations*, as at 31 August 20X6. IFRS 5 states that the appropriate level of management must be committed to a plan to sell the asset for the sale to be probable. Evolve's acceptance of a binding offer in August 20X6 and the publication of this information indicated a high probability of sale. Despite the uncertainties surrounding the sale, the transaction remained highly probable at 31 August 20X6. IFRS 5 requires an entity to classify a non-current asset as held for sale if its carrying amount will be recovered principally through sale rather than through continuing use.

IFRS 5 does not require the existence of a binding sales agreement in order to classify a non-current asset as held for sale but only a high probability of its occurrence. The acceptance of an offer by Evolve indicates that the transaction met the criteria to be classified as held for sale at 31 August 20X6. The finalisation of the agreement on 20 September 20X6 only confirmed the situation existing at 31 August 20X6. Further, Evolve cannot apply IFRS 5 measurement criteria without classifying the item as held for sale in its statement of financial position particularly as a profit or impairment may arise when using such criteria. IFRS 5 also states that immediately before the initial classification of the asset as held for sale, the carrying amount of the asset should be measured in accordance with applicable IFRSs. This was already the case as regards the non-current assets of Resource.

Other criteria which indicate that the non-current assets should be shown as held for sale include the fact that a buyer for the non-current assets has been found, the sale occurred within 12 months of classification as held for sale, the asset was actively marketed for sale at a sales price which has been accepted, and despite the uncertainties at 31 August 20X6, events after the reporting period indicate that the contract was not significantly changed or withdrawn. The fact that the information regarding the uncertainties was not publicly disclosed is irrelevant.

Thus as the non-current assets met the criteria to be classified as held for sale, they should have been measured and presented as such in the financial statements. Assets classified as held for sale must be presented separately on the face of the statement of financial position.

(c) **Investment property**

IFRS 3 *Business combinations* must be applied when accounting for business combinations, but does not apply where the acquisition is not of a business. In this case, the acquisition was essentially that of an asset and therefore the measurement requirements of IFRS 3 would not apply.

IAS 40 *Investment property* states that the cost of an investment property comprises its purchase price and any directly attributable expenditure, such as professional fees for legal services. IAS 16 *Property, plant and equipment* states that the cost of an item of PPE comprises any cost directly attributable to bringing the asset to the condition necessary for it to be capable of operating in the manner intended by management. Hence if Evolve wishes to use the cost basis for accounting for the investment property, the potential gain should not have been recorded in profit or loss or added to the cost of the asset.

Evolve should have recognised the tax payment as an expense in the statement of profit or loss and other comprehensive income. Administrative and other general overhead costs are not costs of an item of PPE according to IAS 16. The specific fiscal treatment and the tax to be paid were not linked to bringing the asset to the condition necessary for its operations, as the asset would have been operational without the tax. As such, the tax is a cost linked to the activity of Evolve and should be accounted for as an expense in accordance with IAS 12 *Income taxes* and included in the profit or loss for the period, unless that tax arises from a transaction recognised outside profit or loss.

Question 4

Text reference. Materiality is covered in Chapter 1 of your Study Text in the context of the *Conceptual Framework*. Integrated reporting is covered in Chapter 18. Statements of cash flows, including the Exposure Draft, are covered in Chapter 17.

Top tips. This question deals with topical issues – materiality and problems with statements of cash flows. Part (b)(ii) is somewhat challenging, given that this was the first time IFRS 15 has been tested. The definition of materiality in Part (a)(i) is straightforward, but the consideration of how it could lead to a reduction in clarity and understandability needs more thought. Credit will be given for valid arguments, but do not be tempted to 'waffle'. Integrated reporting has been tested in a number of contexts, here in the context of materiality. You needed to consider how materiality is relevant to the objective of the International Integrated Reporting Framework. Part (a)(iii) required a discussion of current issues relating to statements of cash flows. While there were marks available for general issues, you also needed to know the details of the recent Exposure Draft, which was issued as part of the IASB's Disclosure Initiative. Part (b) was a numerical question based on this ED, requiring a draft note to the statement of cash flows including a reconciliation of changes. This was challenging as it required a level of detail greater than is normally expected. However, this was only 5 of the 25 marks, and you could make an attempt at it: a reconciliation is to opening and closing balances, so even if you don't know the specifics of the ED, you could put the opening balances in a table and the other balances in columns with the closing balances at the end.

Easy marks. The definition of materiality (Part (a)(i)) and the general points about issues with statements of cash flows (Part (a)(iii) are good ways to earn easy marks.

Examiner's comment. Examiner's comments were not available at the time of going to print.

Marking scheme

		Marks
(a)	(i) 1 mark per point up to maximum	7
	(ii) 1 mark per point up to maximum	4
	(iii) 1 mark per point up to maximum	7
	Professional marks	2
(b)	1 mark per point up to maximum	5
		25

(a) (i) **Definition of materiality and application of the concept**

Information is material if omitting it or misstating it could influence decisions which users make on the basis of financial information about a specific reporting entity. Materiality is an entity-specific aspect of relevance, based on the nature and/or magnitude of the items to which it relates in the context of the entity's financial report. It is therefore difficult to specify a uniform quantitative threshold for materiality or predetermine what could be material in a particular situation. Materiality should ensure that relevant information is not omitted or mis-stated and it should help filter out obscure information which is not useful to users of financial statements.

The *Conceptual Framework* describes materiality as an application of relevance by a particular entity. When an entity is assessing materiality, it is assessing whether the information is relevant to the readers of its own financial statements. Information relevant for one entity might not be as relevant for another entity. IAS 1 *Presentation of financial statements* says that an entity need not provide a specific disclosure required by an IFRS if the information is not material and that the application of IFRSs, with additional disclosure when necessary, is presumed to result in financial statements which achieve a fair presentation. In other words, material information must be disclosed irrespective of whether there is an explicit disclosure requirement.

Although preparers may understand the concept of materiality, they may be less certain about how it should be applied. Preparers may be reluctant to filter out information which is not relevant to users as auditors and regulators may challenge their reasons for the omissions. The way in which some IFRSs are drafted suggests that their specific requirements override the general statement in IAS 1 that an entity need not provide information which is not material. Standards are often complied with rigidly which leads to 'boiler plate' disclosures. Regulators are not keen to encourage the use of judgement but rather wish compliance with IFRS. If the concept of materiality was applied successfully, then immaterial information would be removed and the performance and the position of the entity would be more visible. Investors require better, more relevant, material information. The time and resources available in a reporting cycle may mean that many preparers are not capable or willing to make a materiality judgement. Regulators are often unwilling to apply a principle-based view, and are often quick to raise a query when a disclosure has been removed or not included.

Accounting policy disclosures often repeat information which was contained in IFRS and are not entity-specific. Information outside of financial statements cannot be policed and often key information is given in corporate presentations or outside the financial statements, which reinforces the perception that financial statements are a compliance document.

(ii) **Materiality and the International Integrated Reporting Framework**

Integrated reporting (IR) takes a broader view of business reporting, emphasising the need for entities to provide information to help investors assess the sustainability of their business model. IR is a process which results in communication, through the integrated report, about value creation over time. An integrated report is a concise communication about how an organisation's strategy, governance, performance and prospects lead to the creation of value over the short, medium and long term. The materiality definition for IR purposes would consider that material matters are those which are of such relevance and importance that they could substantively influence the assessments of the intended report users. In the case of IR, relevant matters are those which affect or have the

potential to affect the organisation's ability to create value over time. For financial reporting purposes, the nature or extent of an omission or misstatement in the organisation's financial statements determines relevance. Matters which are considered material for financial reporting purposes, or for other forms of reporting, may also be material for IR purposes if they are of such relevance and importance that they could change the assessments of providers of financial capital with regard to the organisation's ability to create value. Another feature of materiality for IR purposes is that the definition emphasises the involvement of senior management and those charged with governance in the materiality determination process in order for the organisation to determine how best to disclose its value creation development in a meaningful and transparent way.

(iii) **Current issues with IAS 7 *Statement of cash flows***

IAS 7 *Statement of cash flows* was first published in 1992 and has been barely changed since that date. However, there are issues with the current standard. For example, cash flows from the same transaction may be classified differently. A loan repayment would see the interest classified as operating or financing activities, whereas the principal will be classified as a financing activity. The operating activities in the cash flow statement can be presented in one of two ways: the direct method and the indirect method. The direct method is seldom used as it displays major classes of gross cash receipts and payments. Companies' systems often do not collect this type of data in an easily accessible form. The indirect method is more commonly used to present operating activities. The presentation of operating profit under the indirect method of the cash flow statement can start with either profit or loss before or after tax. A user's ability to make comparisons may be affected if entities present reconciliations with different starting points. There are concerns over the current classification of items in the statement of cash flows. For example, dividends and interest paid can be classified as either operating or financing activities. As a result, users have to make appropriate adjustments when comparing different entities, particularly when calculating free cash flow for valuation purposes. Additionally, when a user is assessing an entity's ability to service debt, interest paid would be reclassified from operating activities to financing activities.

Research expenditure is classified as cash from operating activities but is often considered to be a long-term investment. Some argue that such cash outflows should be included within investing activities, because they relate to items, which are intended to generate future income and cash flows. IAS 7 takes the view that, to be classified as an investing cash outflow, the expenditure must result in an asset being recognised in the statement of financial position.

Some items of property, plant and equipment are purchased from suppliers on similar credit terms to those for inventory and for amounts payable to other creditors. As a result, transactions for property, plant and equipment may be incorrectly included within changes in accounts payable for operating items. Consequently, unless payments for property, plant and equipment are separated from other payments related to operating activities, they can be allocated incorrectly to operating activities.

There are currently different views as to how to show lessee cash flows in the statement of cash flows. Some users would like the statement of cash flows to reflect lessee cash outflows in a way which is comparable to those of a financed purchase where the entity buys an asset and separately finances the purchase. Other users take the view that lease cash payments are similar in nature to capital expenditure and should be classified within investing activities in the statement of cash flows. Finally, there is concern about the current lack of comparability under IFRS because of the choice of treatment currently allowed. A lessee can classify interest payments within operating activities or within financing activities.

Partly as a result of the above practices, the IASB has published an Exposure Draft (ED), which proposes amendments to IAS 7. The main objective of the ED is to improve information about changes in an entity's liabilities which relate to financing activities and the availability of cash and cash equivalents including any restrictions on their use. The ED results from the IASB's Disclosure Initiative, which comprises several smaller projects to improve presentation and disclosure requirements in existing IFRSs. The proposed amendments would require an entity to provide a reconciliation of the opening and closing amounts in the statement of financial position for each liability for which cash flows are classified as financing activities. The proposed changes will require companies to reconcile the movement in debt from one period to another and together with the existing information from the statement of cash flows; this will facilitate net debt reconciliation.

Because many entities already voluntarily disclose a net debt reconciliation, the proposed changes should theoretically not impose any additional burden on issuers. The proposed amendments also require issuers to provide information to help users better understand any liquidity issues. The understanding of limitations on the use of liquid resource is important and some users would like additional disclosures to better understand the different types of debt financing by the entity. The changes should help users in making investment decisions.

(b) **Note showing components of financing activities under the ED**

Components of financing activities (excluding equity) $ million

Sanchera, a listed company, has prepared a statement of cash flows for the year ended 31 August 20X6. In financing activities, it has shown an increase in long-term borrowings to $140 million and an increase in the capital element of finance lease liabilities to $17 million.

		20X6			
			Non-cash changes		
	20X5	*Cash flow*	*Acquisition*	*New leases*	*Total*
Long-term borrowings	50	55	35		140
Lease liabilities	5	(3)	–	15	17
Long term debt	55	52	35	15	157

Sanchera showed interest paid on lease liabilities of $5 million in operating activities and this would remain there under the proposed exposure draft. Finally, Sanchera had an overdraft with the bank of $2 million and this would be shown in cash and cash equivalents and not in financing activities.

Mathematical tables

Present value table

Present value of 1 = $(1+r)^{-n}$ where r = discount rate, n = number of periods until payment.

This table shows the present value of £1 per annum, receivable or payable at the end of *n* years.

Periods	Discount rates (r)									
(n)	1%	2%	3%	4%	5%	6%	7%	8%	9%	10%
1	0.990	0.980	0.971	0.962	0.952	0.943	0.935	0.926	0.917	0.909
2	0.980	0.961	0.943	0.925	0.907	0.890	0.873	0.857	0.842	0.826
3	0.971	0.942	0.915	0.889	0.864	0.840	0.816	0.794	0.772	0.751
4	0.961	0.924	0.888	0.855	0.823	0.792	0.763	0.735	0.708	0.683
5	0.951	0.906	0.863	0.822	0.784	0.747	0.713	0.681	0.650	0.621
6	0.942	0.888	0.837	0.790	0.746	0.705	0.666	0.630	0.596	0.564
7	0.933	0.871	0.813	0.760	0.711	0.665	0.623	0.583	0.547	0.513
8	0.923	0.853	0.789	0.731	0.677	0.627	0.582	0.540	0.502	0.467
9	0.914	0.837	0.766	0.703	0.645	0.592	0.544	0.500	0.460	0.424
10	0.905	0.820	0.744	0.676	0.614	0.558	0.508	0.463	0.422	0.386
11	0.896	0.804	0.722	0.650	0.585	0.527	0.475	0.429	0.388	0.350
12	0.887	0.788	0.701	0.625	0.557	0.497	0.444	0.397	0.356	0.319
13	0.879	0.773	0.681	0.601	0.530	0.469	0.415	0.368	0.326	0.290
14	0.870	0.758	0.661	0.577	0.505	0.442	0.388	0.340	0.299	0.263
15	0.861	0.743	0.642	0.555	0.481	0.417	0.362	0.315	0.275	0.239
16	0.853	0.728	0.623	0.534	0.458	0.394	0.339	0.292	0.252	0.218
17	0.844	0.714	0.605	0.513	0.436	0.371	0.317	0.270	0.231	0.198
18	0.836	0.700	0.587	0.494	0.416	0.350	0.296	0.250	0.212	0.180
19	0.828	0.686	0.570	0.475	0.396	0.331	0.277	0.232	0.194	0.164
20	0.820	0.673	0.554	0.456	0.377	0.312	0.258	0.215	0.178	0.149

Periods	Discount rates (r)									
(n)	11%	12%	13%	14%	15%	16%	17%	18%	19%	20%
1	0.901	0.893	0.885	0.877	0.870	0.862	0.855	0.847	0.840	0.833
2	0.812	0.797	0.783	0.769	0.756	0.743	0.731	0.718	0.706	0.694
3	0.731	0.712	0.693	0.675	0.658	0.641	0.624	0.609	0.593	0.579
4	0.659	0.636	0.613	0.592	0.572	0.552	0.534	0.516	0.499	0.482
5	0.593	0.567	0.543	0.519	0.497	0.476	0.456	0.437	0.419	0.402
6	0.535	0.507	0.480	0.456	0.432	0.410	0.390	0.370	0.352	0.335
7	0.482	0.452	0.425	0.400	0.376	0.354	0.333	0.314	0.296	0.279
8	0.434	0.404	0.376	0.351	0.327	0.305	0.285	0.266	0.249	0.233
9	0.391	0.361	0.333	0.308	0.284	0.263	0.243	0.225	0.209	0.194
10	0.352	0.322	0.295	0.270	0.247	0.227	0.208	0.191	0.176	0.162
11	0.317	0.287	0.261	0.237	0.215	0.195	0.178	0.162	0.148	0.135
12	0.286	0.257	0.231	0.208	0.187	0.168	0.152	0.137	0.124	0.112
13	0.258	0.229	0.204	0.182	0.163	0.145	0.130	0.116	0.104	0.093
14	0.232	0.205	0.181	0.160	0.141	0.125	0.111	0.099	0.088	0.078
15	0.209	0.183	0.160	0.140	0.123	0.108	0.095	0.084	0.074	0.065
16	0.188	0.163	0.141	0.123	0.107	0.093	0.081	0.071	0.062	0.054
17	0.170	0.146	0.125	0.108	0.093	0.080	0.069	0.060	0.052	0.045
18	0.153	0.130	0.111	0.095	0.081	0.069	0.059	0.051	0.044	0.038
19	0.138	0.116	0.098	0.083	0.070	0.060	0.051	0.043	0.037	0.031
20	0.124	0.104	0.087	0.073	0.061	0.051	0.043	0.037	0.031	0.026

Cumulative present value table

This table shows the present value of £1 per annum, receivable or payable at the end of each year for *n* years.

Periods					Discount rates (r)					
(n)	1%	2%	3%	4%	5%	6%	7%	8%	9%	10%
1	0.990	0.980	0.971	0.962	0.952	0.943	0.935	0.926	0.917	0.909
2	1.970	1.942	1.913	1.886	1.859	1.833	1.808	1.783	1.759	1.736
3	2.941	2.884	2.829	2.775	2.723	2.673	2.624	2.577	2.531	2.487
4	3.902	3.808	3.717	3.630	3.546	3.465	3.387	3.312	3.240	3.170
5	4.853	4.713	4.580	4.452	4.329	4.212	4.100	3.993	3.890	3.791
6	5.795	5.601	5.417	5.242	5.076	4.917	4.767	4.623	4.486	4.355
7	6.728	6.472	6.230	6.002	5.786	5.582	5.389	5.206	5.033	4.868
8	7.652	7.325	7.020	6.733	6.463	6.210	5.971	5.747	5.535	5.335
9	8.566	8.162	7.786	7.435	7.108	6.802	6.515	6.247	5.995	5.759
10	9.471	8.983	8.530	8.111	7.722	7.360	7.024	6.710	6.418	6.145
11	10.37	9.787	9.253	8.760	8.306	7.887	7.499	7.139	6.805	6.495
12	11.26	10.58	9.954	9.385	8.863	8.384	7.943	7.536	7.161	6.814
13	12.13	11.35	10.63	9.986	9.394	8.853	8.358	7.904	7.487	7.103
14	13.00	12.11	11.30	10.56	9.899	9.295	8.745	8.244	7.786	7.367
15	13.87	12.85	11.94	11.12	10.38	9.712	9.108	8.559	8.061	7.606
16	14.718	13.578	12.561	11.652	10.838	10.106	9.447	8.851	8.313	7.824
17	15.562	14.292	13.166	12.166	11.274	10.477	9.763	9.122	8.544	8.022
18	16.398	14.992	13.754	12.659	11.690	10.828	10.059	9.372	8.756	8.201
19	17.226	15.678	14.324	13.134	12.085	11.158	10.336	9.604	8.950	8.365
20	18.046	16.351	14.877	13.590	12.462	11.470	10.594	9.818	9.129	8.514

Periods					Discount rates (r)					
(n)	11%	12%	13%	14%	15%	16%	17%	18%	19%	20%
1	0.901	0.893	0.885	0.877	0.870	0.862	0.855	0.847	0.840	0.833
2	1.713	1.690	1.668	1.647	1.626	1.605	1.585	1.566	1.547	1.528
3	2.444	2.402	2.361	2.322	2.283	2.246	2.210	2.174	2.140	2.106
4	3.102	3.037	2.974	2.914	2.855	2.798	2.743	2.690	2.639	2.589
5	3.696	3.605	3.517	3.433	3.352	3.274	3.199	3.127	3.058	2.991
6	4.231	4.111	3.998	3.889	3.784	3.685	3.589	3.498	3.410	3.326
7	4.712	4.564	4.423	4.288	4.160	4.039	3.922	3.812	3.706	3.605
8	5.146	4.968	4.799	4.639	4.487	4.344	4.207	4.078	3.954	3.837
9	5.537	5.328	5.132	4.946	4.772	4.607	4.451	4.303	4.163	4.031
10	5.889	5.650	5.426	5.216	5.019	4.833	4.659	4.494	4.339	4.192
11	6.207	5.938	5.687	5.453	5.234	5.029	4.836	4.656	4.486	4.327
12	6.492	6.194	5.918	5.660	5.421	5.197	4.988	4.793	4.611	4.439
13	6.750	6.424	6.122	5.842	5.583	5.342	5.118	4.910	4.715	4.533
14	6.982	6.628	6.302	6.002	5.724	5.468	5.229	5.008	4.802	4.611
15	7.191	6.811	6.462	6.142	5.847	5.575	5.324	5.092	4.876	4.675
16	7.379	6.974	6.604	6.265	5.954	5.668	5.405	5.162	4.938	4.730
17	7.549	7.120	6.729	6.373	6.047	5.749	5.475	5.222	4.990	4.775
18	7.702	7.250	6.840	6.467	6.128	5.818	5.534	5.273	5.033	4.812
19	7.839	7.366	6.938	6.550	6.198	5.877	5.584	5.316	5.070	4.843
20	7.963	7.469	7.025	6.623	6.259	5.929	5.628	5.353	5.101	4.870

Notes

Review Form – Paper P2 Corporate Reporting (International and United Kingdom) (02/17)

Name: ______________________ **Address:** ______________________

____

____

How have you used this Kit?
(Tick one box only)

☐ Home study (book only)

☐ On a course: college ______________________

☐ With 'correspondence' package

☐ Other ______________________

Why did you decide to purchase this Kit?
(Tick one box only)

☐ Have used the complementary Study text

☐ Have used other BPP products in the past

☐ Recommendation by friend/colleague

☐ Recommendation by a lecturer at college

☐ Saw advertising

☐ Other ______________________

During the past six months do you recall seeing/receiving any of the following?
(Tick as many boxes as are relevant)

☐ Our advertisement in *Student Accountant*

☐ Our advertisement in *Pass*

☐ Our advertisement in *PQ*

☐ Our brochure with a letter through the post

☐ Our website www.bpp.com

Which (if any) aspects of our advertising do you find useful?
(Tick as many boxes as are relevant)

☐ Prices and publication dates of new editions

☐ Information on product content

☐ Facility to order books off-the-page

☐ None of the above

Which BPP products have you used?

Text	☐	*Passcards*	☐	*Home Study Package*	☐
Kit	☑	*i-Pass*	☐		

Your ratings, comments and suggestions would be appreciated on the following areas.

	Very useful	*Useful*	*Not useful*
Passing P2	☐	☐	☐
Questions	☐	☐	☐
Top Tips etc in answers	☐	☐	☐
Content and structure of answers	☐	☐	☐
Mock exam answers	☐	☐	☐

Overall opinion of this Kit *Excellent* ☐ *Good* ☐ *Adequate* ☐ *Poor* ☐

Do you intend to continue using BPP products? *Yes* ☐ *No* ☐

The BPP author of this edition can be e-mailed at: accaqueries@bpp.com

Please return this form to: Head of ACCA & FIA Programmes, BPP Learning Media Ltd, FREEPOST, London, W12 8AA

Review Form (continued)

TELL US WHAT YOU THINK

Please note any further comments and suggestions/errors below.